Lecture Notes in Computer Science 7899

Commenced Publication in 1973
Founding and Former Series Editors:
Gerhard Goos, Juris Hartmanis, and Jan van Leeuwen

T0223914

Sandra Carberry   Stephan Weibelzahl
Alessandro Micarelli   Giovanni Semeraro (Eds.)

User Modeling, Adaptation and Personalization

21th International Conference, UMAP 2013
Rome, Italy, June 10-14, 2013
Proceedings

 Springer

Volume Editors

Sandra Carberry
University of Delaware
Newark, DE 19716, USA
E-mail: carberry@cis.udel.edu

Stephan Weibelzahl
National College of Ireland
Dublin 1, Ireland
E-mail: sweibelzahl@ncirl.ie

Alessandro Micarelli
Roma Tre University
00146 Rome, Italy
E-mail: micarelli@dia.uniroma3.it

Giovanni Semeraro
University of Bari Aldo Moro
70126 Bari, Italy
E-mail: giovanni.semeraro@uniba.it

ISSN 0302-9743   e-ISSN 1611-3349
ISBN 978-3-642-38843-9   e-ISBN 978-3-642-38844-6
DOI 10.1007/978-3-642-38844-6
Springer Heidelberg Dordrecht London New York

Library of Congress Control Number: 2013939440

CR Subject Classification (1998): H.5, H.3, I.2, H.4, K.4, K.3

LNCS Sublibrary: SL 3 – Information Systems and Application,
incl. Internet/Web and HCI

Typesetting: Camera-ready by author, data conversion by Scientific Publishing Services, Chennai, India

Printed on acid-free paper

Springer is part of Springer Science+Business Media (www.springer.com)

Preface

The 21st International Conference on User Modeling, Adaptation and Personalization (UMAP 2013) was held at Roma Tre University in Rome, Italy, during June 10–14, 2013. The General Chairs were Alessandro Micarelli from the Roma Tre University and Giovanni Semeraro from University of Bari Aldo Moro, Italy. UMAP is the successor to the biennial User Modeling and Adaptive Hypermedia conferences that were merged in 2009 and is organized under the auspices of User Modeling Inc.

The Research Track solicited papers presenting substantive new research results on user modeling, adaptation, and/or personalization. The Research Track Program Chairs were Sandra Carberry from the University of Delaware, USA, and Stephan Weibelzahl from the National College of Ireland. The international Program Committee consisted of 56 leading members of the user modeling and adaptive hypermedia communities as well as highly promising younger researchers. They were assisted by 24 additional reviewers. A separate Industry Track solicited innovative commercial implementations of UMAP technologies and experience in applying recent research advances in practice. The Industry Track Program Chairs were Alejandro Jaimes from Yahoo! Research, Spain, and Michael Pazzani from the University of California Riverside, USA. They were assisted by a Program Committee of leading industrial researchers. The conference solicited Long Research Papers and Industrial Track Papers of up to 11 pages of content. In addition, the conference solicited Short Research Papers of up to six pages in content, whose merit was assessed more in terms of originality and importance than maturity and technical validation. Both long and short papers were allowed unlimited extra pages for references. Papers in the Research and Industry Tracks were reviewed by three reviewers; reviewing was stringent and the overall acceptance rate was 30%.

The Main Technical Program of research and industrial track papers included sessions on a variety of established as well as emerging topics in user modeling, adaptation, and personalization. Among these were sessions on recommender systems, student modeling, social media and teams, human cognition, personality, privacy, Web curation and user profiles, travel and mobile applications, and systems for elderly and disabled individuals. In addition, three distinguished researchers gave plenary invited talks on allied topics: Andrei Broder who is a Distinguished Scientist at Google, Geert-Jan Houben who is Professor of Web Information Systems in the Software Technology Department at Delft University of Technology, and Lillian Lee who is Professor of Computer Science at Cornell University.

The conference also included a Doctoral Consortium, a forum for PhD students to present their ongoing research work and obtain feedback and advice from a Doctoral Consortium Committee of 17 leading UMAP researchers. The

Doctoral Consortium was chaired by Stephanie Elzer Schwartz from Millersville University, USA, and Marco de Gemmis from the University of Bari Aldo Moro, Italy. This track received 16 submissions of which 12 were accepted. The Poster and Demo Session of the conference was chaired by Olga C. Santos, UNED, Spain, and Eelco Herder, L3S Research Center, Germany. There were 27 submissions reviewed by a Program Committee of 39 researchers, and 10 submissions were accepted for the conference. The UMAP 2013 program also included the following workshops and tutorials that were selected by the Chairs, Shlomo Berkovsky from NICTA, Australia, and Pasquale Lops from the University of Bari Aldo Moro, Italy:

Tutorials

- Context-Aware User Modeling for Recommendation by Bamshad Mobasher
- Design and Evaluation of Recommender Systems — Bridging the Gap between Algorithms and User Experience by Paolo Cremonesi, Franca Garzotto, and Pearl Pu
- User Community Discovery: The Transition from Passive Site Visitors to Active Content Contributors by Georgios Paliouras

Workshops

- Emotions and Personality in Personalized Services by Marko Tkalčič, Nadja De Carolis, Marco de Gemmis, Ante Odić, and Andrej Košir
- Group Recommender Systems: Concepts, Technology, Evaluation by Tom Gross, Judith Masthoff, and Christoph Beckmann
- LifeLong User Modelling by Frank Hopfgartner, Till Plumbaum, Judy Kay, and Bob Kummerfeld
- Personalization Approaches in Learning Environments by Milos Kravcik, Olga C. Santos, Jesús G. Boticario, and Diana Pérez-Marín
- Personal Access to Cultural Heritage by Liliana Ardissono, Lora Aroyo, Luciana Bordoni, Tsvi Kuflik, and Judy Kay
- Personalization in eGovernment Services and Applications by Nikos Loutas, Fedelucio Narducci, Matteo Palmonari, and Cécile Paris
- Trust, Reputation and User Modeling by Surya Nepal, Julita Vassileva, Cécile Paris, and Jie Zhang
- User-Adaptive Visualization by Cristina Conati, Ben Steichen, Melanie Tory, and Paolo Buono
- Computational Models of Natural Argument by Nancy Green, Floriana Grasso, and Chris Reed

In addition to the contributors mentioned above, we would also like to thank Iván Cantador from the Universidad Autónoma de Madrid, Spain, who served as Publicity Chair, Fabio Gasparetti and Giuseppe Sansonetti from Roma Tre University, Italy, who served as Local Arrangements Chairs, Carla Limongelli from Roma Tre University, Italy, who organized the student volunteers, and Giuseppina Meniconi of Consulta Umbria, who provided secretarial support.

We also gratefully acknowledge our sponsors who helped us with funding and organizational expertise: User Modeling Inc., U.S. National Science Foundation, Microsoft Research, IPSE: Innovation Projects and Studies for Europe, Roma Tre University, the University of Bari Aldo Moro, the Italian Association for Artificial Intelligence, the Chen Family Foundation, and Springer. Finally, we want to acknowledge the use of EasyChair for the management of the review process and the preparation of the proceedings.

April 2013   Sandra Carberry
                                                         Stephan Weibelzahl
                                                        Alessandro Micarelli
                                                         Giovanni Semeraro

Organization

UMAP 2013 was organized by Roma Tre University, Italy, and University of Bari Aldo Moro, Italy, under the auspices of User Modeling Inc. The conference took place during June 10–14, 2013, in Rome, Italy.

Organizing Committee

General Co-chairs
Alessandro Micarelli   Roma Tre University, Italy
Giovanni Semeraro   University of Bari Aldo Moro, Italy

Program Co-chairs
Sandra Carberry   University of Delaware, USA
Stephan Weibelzahl   National College of Ireland

Industry Track Co-chairs
Alejandro Jaimes   Yahoo! Research, Spain
Michael Pazzani   University of California Riverside, California, USA

Workshop and Tutorial Co-chairs
Shlomo Berkovsky   NICTA, Australia
Pasquale Lops   University of Bari Aldo Moro, Italy

Doctoral Consortium Co-chairs
Stephanie Elzer Schwartz   Millersville University, USA
Marco de Gemmis   University of Bari Aldo Moro, Italy

Demo and Poster Co-chairs
Olga C. Santos   UNED, Spain
Eelco Herder   L3S Research Center, Germany

Publicity Chair
Iván Cantador   Universidad Autónoma de Madrid, Spain

Local Arrangements Co-chairs
Fabio Gasparetti   Roma Tre University, Italy
Giuseppe Sansonetti   Roma Tre University, Italy

Student Volunteers

Carla Limongelli   Roma Tre University, Italy

Research Track Program Committee

Fabian Abel	TU Delft, The Netherlands
Kenro Aihara	National Institute of Informatics, Japan
David Albrecht	Monash University, Australia
Liliana Ardissono	University of Turin, Italy
Lora Aroyo	VU University Amsterdam, The Netherlands
Mathias Bauer	mineway GmbH, Germany
Shlomo Berkovsky	NICTA, Australia
Peter Brusilovsky	University of Pittsburgh, USA
Susan Bull	University of Birmingham, UK
Richard Burns	West Chester University, USA
Sandra Carberry	University of Delaware, USA
Rosa M. Carro	Universidad Autónoma de Madrid, Spain
Federica Cena	University of Turin, Italy
Mihaela Cocea	University of Portsmouth, UK
Robin Cohen	University of Waterloo, Canada
Cristina Conati	University of British Columbia, Canada
Albert Corbett	Carnegie Mellon University, USA
Alexandra Cristea	University of Warwick, UK
Paul De Bra	Eindhoven University of Technology, The Netherlands
Marco de Gemmis	University of Bari Aldo Moro, Italy
Michel Desmarais	Ecole Polytechnique de Montreal, Canada
Vania Dimitrova	University of Leeds, UK
Benedict Du Boulay	University of Sussex, UK
Cristina Gena	University of Turin, Italy
Bradley Goodman	The MITRE Corporation, USA
Eduardo Guzmán	Universidad de Málaga, Spain
Melanie Hartmann	AGT Group GmbH, Germany
Nicola Henze	University of Hannover, Germany
Eelco Herder	L3S Research Center, Germany
Geert-Jan Houben	Delft University of Technology, The Netherlands
Anthony Jameson	DFKI, Germany
Dietmar Jannach	TU Dortmund, Germany
W. Lewis Johnson	Alelo Inc., USA
Judy Kay	University of Sydney, Australia
Alfred Kobsa	University of California, Irvine, USA
Tsvi Kuflik	The University of Haifa, Israel
James Lester	North Carolina State University, USA
Tobias Ley	Tallinn University, Estonia

Judith Masthoff	University of Aberdeen, UK
Gordon McCalla	University of Saskatchewan, Canada
Tanja Mitrovic	University of Canterbury, New Zealand
Riichiro Mizoguchi	University of Osaka, Japan
Georgios Paliouras	NCSR Demokritos, Greece
Alexandros Paramythis	CYBERhouse, Austria
Cécile Paris	CSIRO, Australia
Mykola Pechenizkiy	Eindhoven University of Technology, The Netherlands
Francesco Ricci	Free University of Bozen-Bolzano, Italy
Cristobal Romero Morales	University of Cordoba, Spain
Ryan S.J.D. Baker	Columbia University Teachers College, USA
Olga C. Santos	UNED, Spain
Barry Smyth	University College Dublin, Ireland
Carlo Tasso	University of Udine, Italy
Nava Tintarev	University of Aberdeen, UK
Julita Vassileva	University of Saskatchewan, Canada
Yang Wang	Syracuse University, USA
Gerhard Weber	University of Education Freiburg, Germany
Stephan Weibelzahl	National College of Ireland, Ireland
Kalina Yacef	University of Sydney, Australia
Ingrid Zukerman	Monash University, Australia

Industry Track Program Committee

Kamal Ali	Consumer Internet Start Up, USA
Daniel Billsus	eBay, USA
Robin Burke	DePaul University, USA
Pradheep Elango	Facebook, USA
Alejandro Jaimes	Yahoo! Research, Spain
Michael Pazzani	University of California Riverside, USA
Marco Pennacchiotti	eBay, USA

Poster and Demo Program Committee

Kenro Aihara	National Institute of Informatics, Japan
David Albrecht	Monash University, Australia
Liliana Ardissono	University of Turin, Italy
Mathias Bauer	mineway GmbH, German
Shlomo Berkovsky	NICTA, Australia
Richard Burns	West Chester University, USA
Federica Cena	University of Turin, Italy
David Chin	University of Hawaii, USA
Mihaela Cocea	University of Portsmouth, UK
Alexandra Cristea	University of Warwick, UK

Paul De Bra	Eindhoven University of Technology, The Netherlands
Marco de Gemmis	University of Bari Aldo Moro, Italy
Michel Desmarais	Ecole Polytechnique de Montreal, Canada
Vania Dimitrova	University of Leeds, UK
Peter Dolog	Aalborg University, Denmark
Benedict Du Boulay	University of Sussex, UK
Cristina Gena	University of Turin, Italy
Bradley Goodman	The MITRE Corporation, USA
Floriana Grasso	University of Liverpool, UK
Eduardo Guzmán	Universidad de Málaga, Spain
Neil Heffernan	Worcester Polytechnic Institute, USA
Nicola Henze	University of Hannover, Germany
Eelco Herder	L3S Research Center, Germany
Geert-Jan Houben	Delft University of Technology, The Netherlands
Dietmar Jannach	TU Dortmund, Germany
W. Lewis Johnson	Alelo Inc., USA
Judy Kay	University of Sydney, Australia
Tsvi Kuflik	The University of Haifa, Israel
Mark Maybury	The MITRE Corporation, USA
Gordon McCalla	University of Saskatchewan, Canada
Lorraine Mcginty	University College Dublin, Ireland
Riichiro Mizoguchi	University of Osaka, Japan
Georgios Paliouras	NCSR Demokritos, Greece
Cécile Paris	CSIRO, Australia
Olga C. Santos	UNED, Spain
Stephanie Elzer Schwartz	Millersville University, USA
Carlo Tasso	University of Udine, Italy
Nava Tintarev	University of Aberdeen, UK
Michael Yudelson	Carnegie Mellon University, USA

Doctoral Consortium Program Committee

Liliana Ardissono	University of Turin, Italy
Linas Baltrunas	Telefonica Research, Spain
Maria Bielikova	Slovak University of Technology, Slovakia
Federica Cena	University of Turin, Italy
Li Chen	Hong Kong Baptist University, Hong Kong
Paolo Cremonesi	Polytechnic University of Milan, Italy
Berardina De Carolis	University of Bari Aldo Moro, Italy
Vania Dimitrova	University of Leeds, UK
Fabio Gasparetti	Roma Tre University, Italy
Cristina Gena	University of Turin, Italy

Tsvi Kuflik   University of Haifa, Israel
Kathy McCoy   University of Delaware, USA
Francesco Ricci   Free University of Bozen-Bolzano, Italy
Melike Sah   Trinity College Dublin, Ireland
Marko Tkalcic   University of Ljubljana, Slovenia
Jie Zhang   Nanyang Technological University, Singapore
Ingrid Zukerman   Monash University, Australia

Additional Reviewers

Oluwabunmi Adewoyin   University of Saskatchewan, Canada
Geoffray Bonnin   TU Dortmund, Germany
Jeroen De Knijf   Eindhoven University of Technology,
                                     The Netherlands
Ronald Denaux   University of Leeds, UK
Dimoklis Despotakis   University of Leeds, UK
Fatih Gedikli   TU Dortmund, Germany
Johnson Iyilade   University of Saskatchewan, Canada
Samad Kardan   University of British Columbia, Canada
Julia Kiseleva   Eindhoven University of Technology,
                                     The Netherlands
Styliani Kleanthous Loizou   University of Cyprus, Cyprus
Anastasia Krithara   NCSR Demokritos, Greece
Pasquale Lops   University of Bari Aldo Moro, Italy
Bruce McLaren   Carnegie Mellon University, USA
Masud Moshtaghi   Monash University, Australia
Cataldo Musto   University of Bari Aldo Moro, Italy
Fedelucio Narducci   University of Milano Bicocca, Italy
Rita Orji   University of Saskatchewan, Canada
Alvaro Ortigosa   Universidad Autónoma de Madrid, Spain
Francesco Osborne   University of Turin, Italy
Dimitrios Pierrakos   NCSR Demokritos, Greece
Shaghayegh Sahebi   University of Pittsburgh, USA
Yanir Seroussi   Monash University, Australia
Ben Steichen   University of British Columbia, Canada
Dimitrios Vogiatzis   NCSR Demokritos, Greece

Link, Like, Follow, Friend: The Social Element in User Modeling and Adaptation

Geert-Jan Houben

Delft University of Technology (TU Delft)
Web Information Systems
PO Box 5031, 2600 GA Delft, The Netherlands
g.j.p.m.houben@tudelft.nl

Abstract. The social web is having a clear impact in our field of user modeling and adaptation. 'Links' and 'Likes' as well as 'Followers' and 'Friends' are part of a large source of data that is generated by users themselves, often for different purposes, and that provides an unprecedented potential for systems to understand their users and to adapt based on that understanding. As we can see from researchers and projects in a number of relevant fields, data on various manifestations of what users do socially on the web brings new opportunities. Exciting ideas are generated and first explorations show promising results. In this talk we take a look back at recent proposals and studies that consider the social web. We determine interesting patterns and we aim to understand the impact on methods and techniques for user modeling and adaptation. At the same time, the social web brings even more challenges. We look forward by identifying challenges that can drive our research. From technical challenges to explore the different social web sources to social challenges to understand how users behave when this potential is unlocked.

Language Adaptation

Lillian Lee

Department of Computer Science, Cornell University
llee@cs.cornell.edu

Abstract. As we all know, more and more of life is now manifested online, and many of the digital traces that are left by human activity are increasingly recorded in natural-language format. This availability offers us the opportunity to glean user-modeling information from individual users' linguistic behaviors. This talk will discuss the particular phenomenon of individual language adaptation, both in the short term and in the longer term. We'll look at connections between how people adapt their language to particular conversational partners or groups, on the one hand, and on the other hand, those people's relative power relationships, quality of relationship with the conversational partner, and propensity to remain a part of the group.

Audience Selection in Computational Advertising*

Andrei Broder

Google Inc., 1600 Amphitheatre Parkway, Mountain View, CA 94043, USA
broder@acm.org

Abstract. Online interaction is becoming increasingly individualized both via *explicit means* such as customizations, options, add-ons, skins, apps, etc., and via *implicit means*, that is, large scale analyses of user behavior (individually and in aggregate) that allow automated, user-specific content and experiences such as individualized top news selection based on inferred interests, personal "radio stations" that capture idiosyncratic tastes from past choices, individually recommended purchases via collaborative filtering, and so on.

Not surprisingly, since online content and services are often ad-funded, online advertising is becoming increasingly user-specific as well, supported by the emerging discipline of *Computational Advertising* whose main goal is to find the "best match" between a given user in a given context and a suitable ad. There is a wide variety of users and contexts and the number of potential ads might be in the billions. Thus, depending on the definition of "best match" this problem leads to a variety of massive optimization and search problems, with complicated constraints.

The focus of this talk is *audience selection*, a form of advertising whereby advertisers specify the features of their desired audience, either explicitly, by specifying characteristics such as demographics, location, and context, or implicitly by providing examples of their ideal audience. A particular form of audience selection is interest-based advertising where the desired audience is characterized by its manifested interests. We will discuss how audience selection fits the optimization framework above, present some of the technical mechanisms for selection, and briefly survey some issues surrounding advertising and user privacy. We will conclude with some speculations about the future of online advertising and pertinent areas of scientific research.

---

* This talk presents the personal opinions of the author and does not necessarily reflect the views of Google Inc. or any other entity.

Table of Contents

Full Research Papers

Short Research Papers

Industry Papers

Posters and Demo Papers

Doctoral Consortium

Opinion-Driven Matrix Factorization
for Rating Prediction

Štefan Pero and Tomáš Horváth

Institute of Computer Science,
Pavol Jozef Šafárik University, Košice, Slovakia
stefan.pero@student.upjs.sk, tomas.horvath@upjs.sk

Abstract. Rating prediction is a well-known recommendation task aiming to predict a user's rating for those items which were not rated yet by her. Predictions are computed from users' explicit feedback, i.e. their ratings provided on some items in the past. Another type of feedback are user reviews provided on items which implicitly express users' opinions on items. Recent studies indicate that opinions inferred from users' reviews on items are strong predictors of user's implicit feedback or even ratings and thus, should be utilized in computation. As far as we know, all the recent works on recommendation techniques utilizing opinions inferred from users' reviews are either focused on the item recommendation task or use only the opinion information, completely leaving users' ratings out of consideration. The approach proposed in this paper is filling this gap, providing a simple, personalized and scalable rating prediction framework utilizing both ratings provided by users and opinions inferred from their reviews. Experimental results provided on a dataset containing user ratings and reviews from the real-world Amazon Product Review Data show the effectiveness of the proposed framework.

Keywords: rating prediction, opinion mining, recommendation, personalization.

1 Introduction

Rating prediction is a well-known recommendation task [20] aiming to predict a user's ratings for those items which were not rated yet by the user. Very precise recommendations can be computed with matrix factorization techniques [11] by considering only the sparse user-item-rating relation on the input [17].

Rating is a coarse evaluation of user's opinion on items. Rating scales are often quite roughly grained (usually from 1 to 5 stars), forcing the user to choose either a lower or a higher rating in a case when her real attitude lies in between these two values. Moreover, user can also make a slip during the rating process.

Let's consider the following real-world examples from the data used in our experiments (described later in the section 6) of user ratings and reviews provided on items in the table 1: In the first row of this table, the attitude of user $u1$ on item $i2$ expressed in her review seems to fall between neutral and good (let's say

S. Carberry et al. (Eds.): UMAP 2013, LNCS 7899, pp. 1–13, 2013.

3.5 stars) but she had to choose either the neutral (3 stars) or the good (4 stars) rating. Probably, she has chosen the rating 4 because of her positive bias, i.e. a systematic tendency of her to give better ratings. In the next row of the table, however, the rating is probably a slip since the opinion of the same user on the item $i3$ expressed in her review is clearly good or excellent (4 or 5 stars) despite her poor (2 stars) rating given for that item. Moreover, while she rated the item $i2$ "above" her opinion expressed in the corresponding review, in the case of the item $i3$, the situation is the opposite.

Table 1. User ratings and reviews on items with the opinion (sentiment) scores computed from the reviews according to the algorithm presented in the section 4

User	Item	Rating	Review	Opinion score
u1	i2	4	"This CD is okay. Not a bad album at all. It just has to grow on you."	3
u1	i3	2	"This is a must have for a music DVD collection. So many great singers!"	4
u2	i1	5	"A good read. Not a bad beginner's guide. Some technology is a little dated, but useful."	4
u2	i4	5	"Interesting. A good overview, but Rumbelow's book is better researched and more comprehensive."	4
u3	i1	4	"Excellent. This book is an excellent novel. Excellent plot and characters. And riveting."	4
u3	i3	2	"Bad Vocals. Claude Williams is a good player, but this album is marred by some lousy vocal tracks."	3
u4	i3	1	"I didn't like this book and I couldn't get into it. The only thing I liked was the stripper with a Thumper tattoo. That was cute."	2
u4	i4	4	"Nice Good illustrations, tight bios of the buildings, not very gripping. For Main Line fans."	4

Biased matrix factorization techniques [11] computing the predictions from users' past ratings seem to be an adequate solution to the above mentioned issue of users' biases. However, real data shows that there is a variance in user's bias, i.e. a single user underrate some items while overrate some other items compared to her opinion expressed in her reviews (see the histograms of the differences between ratings and opinions in Figure 2).

[24,25] and also [6,13,18] claim that using only opinions (expressed in users' reviews) instead of ratings leads to better recommendation. Only [6,13] and [18] from these works are focused on the rating prediction problem. These works suggest that users' reviews are valuable sources of their opinions on items, often more accurate than their ratings and thus, do not consider rating information when learning the prediction model.

On the other hand, reviews are also biased by many factors such as the vocabulary of a user, sentences in a review not related to items or not expressing opinions, etc. In these cases, ratings can be used to infer some user-specific knowledge about reviews. Recommendation techniques utilizing both ratings and opinions were developed [1,12,10,22,4], however all of them are focused on the item recommendation task. Moreover, except [22], the mentioned approaches are either non-personalized, non-scalable or need more implementation effort.

In this paper, we focus on filling the above mentioned gaps by combining ideas from [13,18] (only opinions used) and [11] (only ratings used). The contributions of this paper are the following:

- Introducing a personalized, scalable and easy-to-implement framework for rating prediction utilizing opinions (sentiments) inferred from user reviews (section 4).
- An overview and analysis of the state-of-the-art recommendation techniques which utilize information derived from user reviews (section 5).
- Analysis of the relation between user ratings and derived opinions on a real-world Amazon Product Review Data (section 6).
- Experimental comparison of the proposed framework with some of the related approaches on the mentioned rel-world Amazon Data (section 7).

2 Matrix Factorization for Rating Prediction

Let $\mathcal{U}$ and $\mathcal{I}$ be the set of users and items, respectively, and $\mathcal{V} \subset \mathbb{R}$ be the set of values users can assign to items. A mapping $r : \mathcal{U} \times \mathcal{I} \to \mathcal{V}$ which defines a value r_{ui} assigned to an item i by the user u is called rating and is explicitly defined by a set of recorded past user-item feedbacks[1]

$$R = \{(u, i, r_{ui}) \mid u \in \mathcal{U}, \, i \in \mathcal{I}, \, r_{ui} \in \mathcal{V}\}$$

We usually split R into $R^{train}, R^{test} \subset R$ simulating users' past and future ratings, respectively, such that $R^{train} \cap R^{test} = \emptyset$.

The goal of rating prediction is, given R^{train}, to find a mapping $\hat{r} : \mathcal{U} \times \mathcal{I} \to \mathbb{R}$ such that

$$error(r, \hat{r}) = \sum_{(u,i,r_{ui}) \in R^{test}} (r_{ui} - \hat{r}_{ui})^2 \tag{1}$$

is minimal, where $\hat{r}_{ui}$ is the predicted rating given to the item i by the user u.

Biased matrix factorization [11] is a state-of-the-art approach to rating prediction, where R is viewed as a sparse matrix of type $\mathcal{V}^{|\mathcal{U}| \times |\mathcal{I}|}$ with r_{ui} being the values of its non-empty cells belonging either to R^{train} or R^{test} (similarly as mentioned above). The goal is to approximate a matrix R by the product of two smaller matrices $W \in \mathbb{R}^{|\mathcal{U}| \times k}$ and $H \in \mathbb{R}^{|\mathcal{I}| \times k}$ (where k is the number of factors), i.e. $R \approx WH^T$, and find vectors $b' \in \mathbb{R}^{|\mathcal{U}|}$, $b'' \in \mathbb{R}^{|\mathcal{I}|}$ as well as a constant μ such that[2]

$$\sum_{r_{ui} \in R^{test}} (r_{ui} - \mu - b'_u - b''_i - w_u h_i^T)^2 \tag{2}$$

is minimal. The predicted rating $\hat{r}_{ui}$, given W, H, b', b'' and μ is defined as

$$\hat{r}_{ui} = \mu + b'_u + b''_i + \sum_k w_{u_k} h_{i_k} \tag{3}$$

---

[1] Represented in the first three columns in the table 1.

[2] w_u (h_i) refers to the u-th (i-th) row of the matrix W (H), and, b'_u (b''_i) refers to the u-th (i-th) element of the vector b' (b'').

where μ refers to overall average rating and b', b'' are the vectors of users' and items' biases, respectively, indicating how ratings of users or items deviate from μ (capturing systematic tendencies for some users to give higher ratings than others, and for some items to receive higher ratings than others).

The most popular factorization technique used in the recommender systems community, exploits stochastic gradient descent optimization [11] to find the parameters W and H by minimizing the following objective function

$$\sum_{r_{ui} \in R^{train}} (r_{ui} - \hat{r}_{ui})^2 + \lambda(\|W\|^2 + \|H\|^2 + b'^2 + b''^2) \tag{4}$$

where $\hat{r}_{ui}$ is defined as in the equation 3 and λ is a regularization term to prevent the so-called over-fitting (i.e. when a model performs very well on the training data but poorly on the test data).

3   Opinion Mining

Opinion words are words that people use to express their positive or negative attitude to products or specific features of products. There are several techniques in the literature on opinion mining and sentiment analysis (see [15], for more details) from which we choose the most simple one:

Let the review, or comment, $c_{ui} = (w_1, \ldots, w_n)$ of the user u on the item i be represented as a sequence of words. Each word in c_{ui} is either an opinion word or not. Opinion words are words that are primarily used to express subjective opinions. Clearly, this is related to the existing work on distinguishing sentences (subsequences of c_{ui}) used to express subjective opinions from sentences used to objectively describe some information [8]. We use adjectives and phrases as opinion words collected in the Sentiment (Opinion) Lexicon [15] containing a list of about 6800 English words expressing positive or negative sentiments. We will denote the sentiment lexicon as $\mathcal{S} = \mathcal{S}^+ \cup \mathcal{S}^-$ with $\mathcal{S}^+$ and $\mathcal{S}^-$ denoting its subsets of positive and negative sentiment words, respectively.

For each word $w_j \in c_{ui}$ we identify its semantic orientation $s(w_j)$ as

$$s(w_j) = \begin{cases} +1, \text{if} & w_j \in \mathcal{S}^+ \\ -1, \text{if} & w_j \in \mathcal{S}^- \\ 0, \text{if} & w_j \notin \mathcal{S} \end{cases} \tag{5}$$

The overall orientation $o_{ui} \in [-1, +1]$ of the review c_{ui}, what we call the opinion or the sentiment of the review, is computed as

$$o_{ui} = \frac{\sum_{w_j \in c_{ui}} s(w_j)}{|\{w_j \in c_{ui} | w_j \in \mathcal{S}\}|} \tag{6}$$

There are plenty of other opinion mining and sentiment analysis techniques (see [16] for more details) as well as matrix factorization techniques (a unified view of which is introduced in [21]), which could be used in our framework.

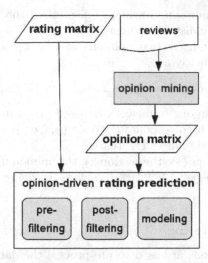

Fig. 1. The proposed framework

4 The Proposed Framework

Our framework is illustrated in Figure 1. Users' ratings (the rating matrix) and textual reviews on items are required on the input. The process consists of two steps, in general: First, an opinion matrix is created from the reviews by post-processing (discretizing) the result of the used opinion mining technique. In the second phase, a matrix factorization technique for rating prediction is employed utilizing this opinion matrix.

Similarly to the three paradigms of utilizing context in recommender systems [2], we distinguish three different approaches in the second step of our framework depending on which stages of the rating prediction process is the opinion matrix implied in. These are i) opinion pre-filtering, ii) opinion post-filtering and iii) opinion modeling. In all of these three approaches, we use the above presented biased matrix factorization.

However, even if we employ the three paradigms of context-aware recommendation, it is important to note that we do not perceive opinions as context here, but rather as regularizers of the prediction model.

4.1 The Opinion Matrix

As mentioned above in the section 3, the overall opinion expressed in the review of the user u on the item i is represented by a number $o_{ui} \in [-1, 1]$, in general, which expresses the polarity of her review on the given item with -1 and 1 being the most negative or positive, respectively. Ratings also expresses the polarity of the user's attitude to an item, with $min\,\mathcal{V}$ and $max\,\mathcal{V}$ being the most negative or positive, respectively. Since $\mathcal{V}$ usually consists of integers, discretizing the $[-1, 1]$ interval to $|\mathcal{V}|$ distinct values results in the same set of values for both opinions

o_{ui} and ratings r_{ui}. In our experiments we discretized the interval $[-1, 1]$ to $|\mathcal{V}|$ distinct values in an equidistant manner.

Similarly to ratings, discretized opinions can be viewed as a mapping $o :$ $\mathcal{U} \times \mathcal{I} \to \mathcal{V}$ defined explicitly as[3]

$$O = \{(u, i, o_{ui}) \mid u \in \mathcal{U}, \ i \in \mathcal{I}, \ o_{ui} \in \mathcal{V}, \ (u, i, r_{ui}) \in R\}$$

There is one assumption our framework is based on, namely that for all triple $(u, i, r_{ui}) \in R$ there is a corresponding triple $(u, i, o_{ui}) \in O$, i.e. users should provide both ratings and reviews for items.

As in the case of ratings (see the section 2), the opinion matrix O is considered as a sparse matrix of the type $\mathcal{V}^{|\mathcal{U}| \times |\mathcal{I}|}$, too, with o_{ui} being the values of its non-empty cells.

4.2   Opinion Pre-filtering

In this approach, opinions are used to pre-process the data for the recommendation technique being used.

The input relation matrix $\overline{R}^{train} \in \mathbb{R}^{|\mathcal{U}| \times |\mathcal{I}|}$ is created from the relations (matrices) R^{train} and O as

$$\overline{R}^{train} = \{\overline{r}_{ui} | \overline{r}_{ui} = \alpha r_{ui} + (1 - \alpha)o_{ui}, \ r_{ui} \in R^{train}, \ o_{ui} \in O\}$$

where $\alpha \in (0, 1)$. Thus, we modify the ratings in the train set such that they are closer to the opinions. This pre-processing step only affects the ratings in the training set, the ratings in the test set remain untouched.

Next, we factorize $\overline{R}^{train}$ to matrices $\overline{W} \in \mathbb{R}^{|\mathcal{U}| \times k}$ and $\overline{H} \in \mathbb{R}^{|\mathcal{I}| \times k}$ in a usual way as described in the section 2. The predicted rating $\hat{r}_{ui}$ of the user u for the item i is then defined according to the equation 3 as

$$\hat{r}_{ui} = \mu + b'_u + b''_i + \sum_k \overline{w}_{u_k} \overline{h}_{i_k} \tag{7}$$

4.3   Opinion Post-filtering

In this approach, we deal with two matrices R^{train} and the corresponding matrix O^{train} defined as

$$O^{train} = \{o_{ui} \in O | r_{ui} \in R^{train}\}$$

i.e. we keep only those cells from O which correspond to the cells of the train part of the rating matrix.

Then, R^{train} is factorized to matrices $W \in \mathbb{R}^{|\mathcal{U}| \times k}$ and $H \in \mathbb{R}^{|\mathcal{I}| \times k}$, while O^{train} is factorized to matrices $P \in \mathbb{R}^{|\mathcal{U}| \times l}$ and $Q \in \mathbb{R}^{|\mathcal{I}| \times l}$. In this way, we get two "interim" prediction models: $\hat{r}'_{ui}$ for the ratings, defined exactly as $\hat{r}_{ui}$ in the equation 3, and

$$\hat{o}'_{ui} = \mu^o + b'^o_u + b''^o_i \sum_l p_{u_l} q_{i_l} \tag{8}$$

---

[3] Represented in the first, second and last columns in the table 1.

for the opinions, where $\mu^o, b_u'^o, b_i''^o$ refer to overall sentiment (opinion) averages, and user and item sentiment (opinion) biases, respectively.

The predicted (post-filtered) rating $\hat{r}_{ui}$ of the user u for the item i is a linear combination of $\hat{r}'$ and $\hat{o}'$

$$\hat{r}_{ui} = \alpha\,\hat{r}'_{ui} + (1 - \alpha)\,\hat{o}'_{ui} \tag{9}$$

where $\alpha \in (0, 1)$.

4.4 Opinion Modeling

In the two previous approaches we used opinions explicitly in the pre- or the post-processing steps. Here, opinions are used implicitly in the factorization (or modeling) phase by changing the objective function (equation 4) to

$$\sum_{r_{ui} \in R^{train}} \alpha(r_{ui} - \hat{r}_{ui})^2 + \lambda(\|W\|^2 + \|H\|^2 + b'^2 + b''^2) \tag{10}$$

where

$$\alpha = \begin{cases} \delta \in (0,1), & \text{if } r_{ui} < \hat{r}_{ui} \le o_{ui} \\ & \text{or } o_{ui} \le \hat{r}_{ui} < r_{ui} \\ 1, & \text{otherwise} \end{cases} \tag{11}$$

i.e. we just simply factorize R^{train} in a usual way (see section 2) but giving less weight to the prediction error if the predicted value $\hat{r}_{ui}$ lies between the rating r_{ui} and the opinion o_{ui} or it is equal to the opinion value.

5 Related Work

The earliest work [1] using consumer product reviews for recommendation is based on computing the qualities of the features of products from aggregating reviewers' opinions on these features weighted by the level of reviewers' expertise. User queries of the form "I would like to know if Sony W70 is a good camera, specifically its interface and battery consumption" are required at the input of the presented recommender system. A similar system is presented in [12]. Since both systems aggregate all opinions on a single item or on its features to one score, *neither provides personalized recommendations*.

The research hypothesis investigated in [6,13] and also in [18] is that sentiments of reviews are better indicators of users' attitude to items than coarse star ratings, and thus, *these works use only the reviews (leaving ratings out of consideration)*. All these approaches consist of two main steps, the first of which is to infer for each review a numerical rating (an opinion) representing the sentiment level of the given review. The main difference from our approach lies in the second step, i.e. how the recommendations are made. In [6], domain and opinion specific meta-data are identified from reviews, and the final rating for a given item is predicted as an average rating of reviews sharing the same meta-data. In contrast to [6], a personalized recommendation approach is chosen in [13] and [18], where nearest-neighbor based collaborative filtering algorithms feeded by inferred opinions (sentiment scores) are used for recommendations.

A hybrid of content-based (CBF) and collaborative-filtering (CF) framework is presented in [10] where each item is represented as a vector consisting of the key aspects (relevant terms derived from user reviews and item descriptions) of items based on their importance values and sentiment scores. Such movie vectors (i.e. importance values and sentiment scores) are constructed for each user separately from the ratings and reviews of similar users to the given user. A binary ("recommendable" vs. "unrecommendable" item) classification model is learned from the derived aspect vectors for each user separately using classification techniques, which is then *used for item recommendation*.

The works introduced in [22,24,25] also *deal with item recommendation*. In [24], a nearest-Neighbor based collaborative filtering (CF) technique is used to recommend top-N items from a so-called virtual user rating matrix created from user reviews by sentiment classification. This matrix contains only binary values, i.e. a user likes or dislikes an item, regarding to the sentiment of her reviews on a given item. The presented framework is further augmented in [25] by considering also the keywords liked/disliked/unknown by the user. In a simple approach presented in [22], personalized recommendations (computed by a similarity-based CF technique) are further filtered according to the sentiments of experts' reviews on items. Thus, users are provided only with top-N items having positive reviews from experts.

A latent variable model for *content-based filtering* is introduced in [4], providing a supervised learning model for extraction of product features from reviews. The model can be trained on some available public datasets and then used to extract sentiments for reviews for which the rating is not provided. The presented model is implemented in the Opinion Space platform [3].

Similarly to our approach, the framework proposed in [19] assumes users to provide both ratings and reviews for items. However, *instead of a sentiment (opinion) score, a so-called "helpfulness" score of a review is considered*, derived from the feedbacks of other users provided on the given review (i.e. a ratio of users which found the given review helpful to all the users which have provided some feedback for the given review). Following the idea that a helpfulness score of a review indicates the quality of the corresponding rating, ratings are weighted by these helpfulness scores in the used factorization model.

The majority of the related work is focused on item recommendation. Works related to rating prediction are either non-scalable [6] or utilize only the opinions leaving ratings out of consideration [13,18], eventually, do not consider user sentiments (opinions) derived from reviews.

6 Data

We used the originally labeled Amazon Product Review Data[4] [9] in our experiments, which contains user-item-rating-review quadruples on movies, music or books. The rating scale is $\mathcal{V} = \{1, 2, 3, 4, 5\}$. We denote this dataset *original-data*. Since this dataset is very sparse (see the table 2) we created a smaller, much dense sample from it in the following way: We filtered out contributions from users who have provided fewer than 50 and more than 500 reviews. The resulting dataset is denoted as *sampled-data*. The main characteristics of these two datasets are shown in the table 2.

Table 2. Characteristics of datasets used in our experiments

dataset	#users	#items	#ratings = #reviews	sparsity (%)
original-data	2146275	1231018	5838898	0.000220994
sampled-data	4654	287666	606294	0.0452865

The histograms of differences between ratings and sentiment (opinion) scores inferred from reviews, for both datasets used are shown in Figure 2. Assuming that these differences are normally distributed we computed their mean and standard deviation: the mean is 0.44 and the standard deviation is 1.24 in case of original-data. In case of sampled-data, the mean of difference between ratings and opinions is 0.6 and the standard deviation is 1.53. This indicates that in general, users' ratings are a bit optimistic compared to their sentiments expressed in their reviews.

7 Experiments

We implemented the opinion mining technique described in the section 3 on our own. For biased matrix factorization, the algorithm from the MyMediaLite Recommender System Library [5] was used and modified if it was necessary, e.g. in case of the opinion-modeling approach (equation 10). For the computation, we used a computing cluster with 7 computing nodes with 24GB of RAM, each of which has 16 cores.

7.1 Baselines

The first baseline we used is the biased matrix factorization (*BiasedMF*) considering only the rating information [11], where the predicted ratings $\hat{r}_{ui}$ are computed according to the equation 3. Motivated by the two related works [13] and [18], we considered only the inferred opinions for learning $\hat{r}$ in our second baseline (*OpinionMF*). Here[5] we first factorized the opinion matrix and predict ratings as $\hat{r}_{ui} = \hat{o}'_{ui}$, computed according to the equation 8.

---

[4] Bing Liu, http://liu.cs.uic.edu/download/data/
[5] Note, that it is the same as setting $\alpha = 0$ in case of our pre-filtering approach.

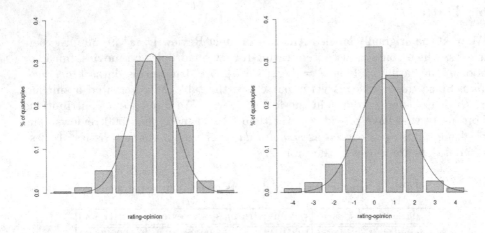

Fig. 2. The histogram of the ratios of user-item-rating-sentiment quadruples w.r.t. the differences in ratings and the computed sentiment (opinion) scores. On the left, histogram for sampled-data. On the right, histogram for original-data.

7.2   Hyper-parameters and Cross-Validation

We have used 5-fold cross-validation for testing the proposed framework as follows: In each of the 5 iterations, one fold was used for testing. From the remaining four folds, three were used for tuning the hyper-parameters of the model validated on the remaining fold. Hyper-parameters (number of factors, number of iterations, learn rate and regularization term) were tuned using grid search. The final model was trained with the best found hyper-parameter combination using all the remaining four folds. We set the value of the parameter α to 0.5.

7.3   Results

In the table 3, the average of the RMSE over the 5 folds is presented (for sampled-data as well as original-data) for the two baselines (denoted as *BiasedMF* and *OpinionMF*) and the proposed three approaches in our framework (denoted as *Pre*, *Post* and *Modeling*).

Table 3. RMSE averaged over the 5 folds

Dataset	BiasedMF	OpinionMF	Pre	Post	Modeling
sampled-data	0.9709	0.9486	0.9409	0.9060	0.9611
original-data	0.9712	0.9415	0.9542	0.9088	0.9645

The results on original-data are very similar to the results on sampled-data, even if the sparsity of these two datasets are considerably different.

The results of *BiasedMF* are significantly worse than the results of all the other approaches. Clearly, *Post* is the winner which provides significantly better results comparing to all other approaches the reason of what, in our opinion, could be that it behaves as a kind of an ensemble technique of two factorization models which tends to outperform single models [23]. *Pre* is significantly better than *BiasedMF* and *Modeling*, while *Modeling* is only significantly better than *BiasedMF*. Student's t-test was used to test statistical significance: except the case of *Modeling* vs. *BiasedMF* where the confidence level is 97%, all the other differences are significant with confidence level 99%.

The results also experimentally justified (with confidence level 97%) the ideas presented in [13] and [18], namely, that pure reviews tend to be better predictors than coarse ratings.

8 Conclusions

A generic matrix factorization framework for rating prediction utilizing user reviews was introduced in this paper. The proposed framework, based on biased matrix factorization, is a scalable, personalized and easy to implement recommendation framework. A simple opinion mining technique was used to derive users' sentiment on items. There is one assumption to the presented work, namely, that users provide both ratings and reviews for items.

We also provided a thorough review of the related state-of-the-art techniques providing with their main characteristics. The main idea of these works is that opinions expressed in users' reviews are good predictors of the ratings, and some works claim that opinions are even better predictors of ratings than are the ratings themselves. In this work, we deal with a combined usage of ratings and inferred sentiment (opinion) scores for rating prediction.

There are still some remaining issues to investigate regarding the proposed framework, e.g. how to deal with the cold-start problem, missing reviews, language biases present in reviews, and, how and in what extend does the proposed framework depend on the choice of the opinion mining algorithm. Following the ideas presented in [7] and [14], parallelization of our framework or its augmentation to include additional information (e.g. meta-data of users and items or additional relations between users), respectively, should be straightforward.

During the analysis of real-world data in our experiments, we have found out that there is a certain relationship between users' ratings on items and opinions expressed in their reviews on items. Since this paper was focused on rating prediction utilizing opinions, we would like to investigate this relationship between ratings and reviews from a user-modeling perspective in our future work.

Even if there are some remaining issues to investigate, experimental results show that the proposed framework is promising and worth of further research.

Acknowledgements. This work was partially supported by the research grants *VEGA 1/0832/12* and *VVGS-PF-2012-22*. We would like to thank to anonymous reviewers for their helpful and motivating comments and suggestions.

References

1. Aciar, S., Zhang, D., Simoff, S., Debenham, J.: Informed Recommender: Basing Recommendations on Consumer Product Reviews. IEEE Intelligent Systems 22, 3 (2007)
2. Adamovicius, G., Tuzhilin, A.: Context-Aware Recommender Systems. In: Ricci, F., et al. (eds.) Recommender Systems Handbook. Springer (2011) ISBN 978-0-387-85819-7
3. Faridani, S., Bitton, E., Ryokai, K., Goldberg, K.: Opinion space: a scalable tool for browsing online comments. In: Proceedings of the 28th International Conference on Human Factors in Computing Systems. ACM, New York (2010)
4. Faridani, S.: Using canonical correlation analysis for generalized sentiment analysis, product recommendation and search. In: Proceedings of the 5th ACM Conference on Recommender Systems. ACM, New York (2011)
5. Gantner, Z., Rendle, S., Freudenthaler, C., Schmidt-Thieme, L.: MyMediaLite: A Free Recommender System Library. In: Proceedings of the 5th ACM International Conference on Recommender Systems, Chicago, USA (2011)
6. Ganu, G., Elhadad, N., Marian, A.: Beyond the Stars: Improving Rating Predictions using Review Text Content. In: 12th International Workshop on the Web and Databases, Providence, Rhode Island, USA (2009)
7. Gemulla, R., Nijkamp, E., Haas, P.J., Sismanis, Y.: Large-scale matrix factorization with distributed stochastic gradient descent. In: Proceedings of the 17th ACM SIGKDD International Conference on Knowledge Discovery and Data Mining. ACM, New York (2011)
8. Hu, M., Liu, B.: Mining and Summarizing Customer Reviews. In: Proceedings of the ACM SIGKDD International Conference on Knowledge Discovery & Data Mining, Seattle, Washington, USA (2004)
9. Jindal, N., Liu, B.: Opinion Spam and Analysis. In: Proceedings of First ACM International Conference on Web Search and Data Mining (WSDM-2008), Stanford University, Stanford, California, USA (2008)
10. Ko, M., Kim, H.W., Yi, M.Y., Song, J., Liu, Y.: Movie Commenter: Aspect-based collaborative filtering by utilizing user comments. In: 7th International Conference on Collaborative Computing, Orlando, FL, USA (2011)
11. Koren, Y., Bell, R., Volinsky, C.: Matrix Factorization Techniques for Recommender Systems. Computer 42(8) (2009)
12. Kuroiwa, T., Bhalla, S.: Aizu-BUS: need-based book recommendation using web reviews and web services. In: Bhalla, S. (ed.) DNIS 2007. LNCS, vol. 4777, pp. 297–308. Springer, Heidelberg (2007)
13. Leung, C.W.K., Chan, S.C.F., Chung, F.: Integrating collaborative filtering and sentiment analysis: A rating inference approach. In: Proceedings of the ECAI 2006 Workshop on Recommender Systems (2006)
14. Lippert, C., Weber, S.H., Huang, Y., Tresp, V., Schubert, M., Kriegel, H.-P.: Relation Prediction in Multi-Relational Domains using Matrix Factorization. In: NIPS Workshop on Structured Input Structure Output (2008)
15. Liu, B.: Sentiment Analysis and Subjectivity. In: Handbook of Natural Language Processing, 2nd edn. (2010)
16. Pang, B., Lee, L.: Opinion mining and sentiment analysis. Foundations and Trends in Information Retrieval 2(1-2) (2008)
17. Pilászy, I., Tikk, D.: Recommending new movies: even a few ratings are more valuable than metadata. In: Proceedings of the Third ACM Conference on Recommender Systems. ACM, New York (2009)

18. Poirier, D., Fessant, F., Tellier, I.: Reducing the Cold-Start Problem in Content Recommendation through Opinion Classification. In: Proceedings of the 2010 IEEE/WIC/ACM International Conference on Web Intelligence and Intelligent Agent Technology. IEEE Computer Society, Washington, DC (2010)
19. Raghavan, S., Gunasekar, S., Ghosh, J.: Review quality aware collaborative filtering. In: Proceedings of the Sixth ACM Conference on Recommender Systems (RecSys 2012). ACM, New York (2012)
20. Ricci, F., Rokach, L., Shapira, B., Kantor, P.B.: Recommender Systems Handbook. Springer (2011)
21. Singh, A.P., Gordon, G.J.: A Unified View of Matrix Factorization Models. In: Daelemans, W., Goethals, B., Morik, K. (eds.) ECML PKDD 2008, Part II. LNCS (LNAI), vol. 5212, pp. 358–373. Springer, Heidelberg (2008)
22. Singh, V.K., Mukherjee, M., Mehta, G.K.: Combining collaborative filtering and sentiment classification for improved movie recommendations. In: Sombattheera, C., Agarwal, A., Udgata, S.K., Lavangnananda, K. (eds.) MIWAI 2011. LNCS, vol. 7080, pp. 38–50. Springer, Heidelberg (2011)
23. Wu, M.: Collaborative filtering via ensembles of matrix factorizations. In: KDD Cup and Workshop at the 13th ACM SIGKDD International Conference on Knowledge Discovery and Data Mining, San Jose, CA, USA (2007)
24. Zhang, W., Ding, G., Chen, L., Li, C.: Augmenting Chinese Online Video Recommendations by Using Virtual Ratings Predicted by Review Sentiment Classification. In: Proceedings of the 2010 IEEE ICDM Workshops. IEEE Computer Society, Washington, DC (2010)
25. Zhang, W., Ding, G., Chen, L., Li, C.: Augmenting Online Video Recommendations by Fusing Review Sentiment Classification. In: Proceedings of the 2nd ACM RecSys 2010 Workshop on Recommender Systems and the Social Web. ACM (2010)

Interaction Based Content Recommendation in Online Communities

Surya Nepal, Cécile Paris, Payam Aghaei Pour, Jill Freyne, and Sanat Kumar Bista

CSIRO ICT Centre
Marsfield, NSW, Australia
{firstname.lastname}@csiro.au

Abstract. Content recommender systems have become an invaluable tools in online communities where a huge volume of content items are generated for users to consume, making it difficult for users to find interesting content. Many recommender systems leverage articulated social networks or profile information (e.g, user background, interest, etc.) for content recommendation. These recommenders largely ignore the implied networks defined through user interactions. Yet these play an important role in formulating users' common interests. We propose an interaction based content recommender which leverages implicit user interactions to determine the relationship trust or strength, generating a richer, more informed implied network. An offline analysis on a 5000 person, 12 week dataset from an online community shows that our approach outperforms algorithms which focus on articulated networks that do not consider relationship trust or strength.

1 Introduction

Social Networks (SNs) have gained remarkable popularity and are fast becoming locations where content is shared and found. Facebook alone reports more than 800 million active users, with an average user connected to 80 communities and events, having 130 friends, and using the system for about one hour a day [5]. SNs aim to foster user interaction and a sense of community, allowing their users to establish and maintain relationships, share information, and express opinions. When SNs get large, issues of information overload and content discovery arise. These are typically addressed through newsfeeds, notifications and updates. User modelling techniques have been applied to these mechanisms, resulting in personalised notifications and news feeds to support users in finding interesting content [2, 6, 16].

Popular approaches for recommendations in SNs leverage the underlying social graph to identify people and content and have seen great success in friendship based networks [4, 7]. These approaches, however, often rely on articulated networks (also refer to as *explicit* networks) and highly interconnected graphs; features not found in some emerging SNs, where explicit friending or following is less common, e.g., SNs for health or the environment. There, implied networks (also refer to as *implicit* networks) built through interactions are more commonplace.

To address these issues, we propose a *social behavior based recommendation system*. It exploits users' interactions, using both articulated and implied relationships.

S. Carberry et al. (Eds.): UMAP 2013, LNCS 7899, pp. 14–24, 2013.

It employs a trust model reflecting the level of interaction between people. We developed four relevance algorithms and their variations and evaluate them on a real world data set [3]. The algorithms exploit the reputation of a node (a global value in the network), the tie strength between two nodes (a value local to nodes), or a combination of the two to determine the relevance of an item to an individual. The results show that the implied network approach outperforms both baseline algorithms and algorithms based on the articulated network for classification accuracy, precision, recall and coverage.

The paper is organised as follows. Section 2 presents related work. Section 3 details our approach, followed by its evaluation in Section 4. We conclude with a summary of findings and future work in Section 5.

2   Related Work

Recommender systems are used for both discovery and filtering in SN applications, to assist users in locating interesting people, content and activities and to prioritise information for consumption. A variety of implicit and explicit data sources inform various models. Explicit indicators typically take the form of user profiles, articulated friend networks, or group memberships. Recommenders often exploit explicit friendships or linkages to generate recommendation lists, e.g., the FOAF (Friend-Of-A-Friend) algorithm [4, 10] and EdgeRank Algorithm [23]. Profile content can be used to identify articles and other content deemed to be relevant [13]. Implicit interest indicators have become more common for recommenders in SNs for several reasons. Firstly, typical SNs represent relationships in a binary manner, friend or stranger, but research has shown that many types of relationship exist, and factors such as closeness and trust can better represent these relationships and facilitate better recommendations [2, 6, 8]. Secondly, in large and fast paced networks, where (a) content freshness is paramount, (b) content text limited and (c) explicit information difficult to obtain, relying on explicit information is not always practical.

Implicit interactions were first used to represent online relationships by a numerical value by Gilbert and Karaholios [2]. Paek et al. [16] used classifiers to identify the most predictive features of relationship strength and applied this model to tailor news feeds. Freyne et al. [6] and Berkovsky et al. [2] include relationship strengths with various content types to rank news feeds according to their type and their creator. Kleanthous and Dimitrova [20] have developed a community model using implicit relationships to monitor real time data in the community. This provides a valuable accelerated feedback for the community providers to inject new content addressing the issue of sustainability. Similarly, Paliouras [21] has used implicit information in the social web to achieve community-driven personalisation.

The structure of a SN affects the level of trust that exists. High density (i.e., high member inter-connectedness) can yield a high level of trust [16]. There are two types of trust: explicit and implicit. Models exploiting the explicit SN structure are usually based on the concepts of "Web of trust" or FOAF [9, 11, 14, 18, 19]. They capture only one aspect of trust computation: how members are related to each other and how trust flows through the network. They fail to capture the actual interactions between members. Implicit behaviours represented by volume, frequency and the nature of the interactions are also important indicators of trust in SNs, and some models exploit them [1, 12, 22]. Hybrid trust models, such as our STrust [15] model used in this paper, use both interactions and SN structure to compute social trust [17].

3   Social Behaviour Model and Recommendation Algorithms

We propose a content recommender system for SNs that exploits an implicit network to identify relevant content. In general, for a target member, the recommender system identifies and ranks a set of content items that members in their network have interacted with, as shown in Fig, 1 (a). Several variables contribute to the content items relevance score: (1) the network, (2) the member-to-member trust, (3) the member-to-content trust and (4) the member-to-community trust. We now describe the options considered for (1-4).

3.1   Implicit and Explicit Networks

Traditional SN representations reflect articulated friendships, binary in nature and containing linkages only between existing "friends" (network containing *explicit trust only* in Fig. 1 (a)). We refer to these networks as **social graphs**. We believe that exploiting member behaviour and observed interactions in a SN will provide better evidence for recommenders. We suggest that, if two members interact (passively, e.g., a member reading the other member's posts, or actively, e.g., a member rating the other member), this interaction should be reflected in the community graph. Example of passive interactions include reading someone's post, viewing content, etc. Active interactions include sending invitation, commenting on posts and performing certain activities together. We refer to the networks implied by all interactions as **behaviour graphs** (the *whole network* in Fig. 1 (a)).

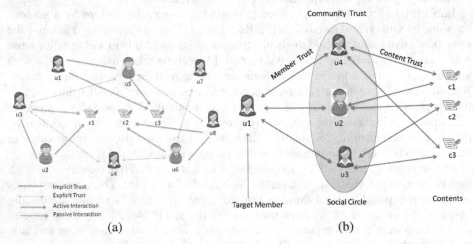

(a)   (b)

Fig. 1. The Different Variables Contributing to Content Score

3.2   Member Trust

Online relationships are as complex as real world ones, and yet many social networks represent the linkages between people in a binary manner. We believe that the actions of a user towards another user can inform the level of trust (or relationship strength) between two people. We developed *STrust*, a model that examines all interactions between two users (viewing, commenting, rating, friending, etc.) to determine the member-to-member relationship, or member trust score [15].

Member trust is determined by two weighted factors: popularity trust (*PopTrust*) and engagement trust (*EngTrust*), as given below.

$$\text{PopTrust}(u_1, u_2) = \frac{\text{\# positive trusting interactions towards } u_1 \text{ by } u_2 + 1}{\text{\# all trusting interactions towards } u_1 \text{ by } u_2 + 2} \tag{1}$$

$$\text{EngTrust}(u_1, u_2) = \frac{\text{\# positive trusted interactions by } u_1 \text{ towards } u_2 + 1}{\text{\# all trusted interactions by } u_1 \text{ towards } u_2 + 2} \tag{2}$$

$$\text{SocialTrust}(u_1, u_2) = \alpha. \text{PopTrust}(u_1, u_2) + (1 - \alpha). \text{EngTrust}(u_1, u_2) \tag{3}$$

where α represents the value of a weight in the range of 0 to 1, and u_1 represents a member in the community[1]. In brief, the popularity trust of a member measures how trusting other community members   (including those outside the member's social circle) are towards them (positive ratings or comments received), and the engagement trust refers to how trusting the member is towards others (providing positive ratings or comments to posts of other member). It is important to note that the equations (1) to (3) do not compute a mutual trust. They provide trusting values from u_1 to u_2 which could be different to those of u_2 to u_1.

3.3   Content Trust

When considering whether an item, with which someone in the target member's social circle (the "connection") had interacted, is likely to be interesting to the target member, we consider the interactions between the connection and the content item. Specifically, a variation of *EngTrust* detailed in Equation 2 is used as follows.

$$\text{EngTrust}(u_2, c_2) = \frac{\text{\# positive trusted interactions by } u_2 \text{ towards } c_2 + 1}{\text{\# all trusted interactions by } u_2 \text{ towards } c_2 + 2} \tag{4}$$

Note that u_2 is a member of a social circle of user u_1. Only content items which achieve an above average score for u_1 are considered.

3.4   Community Trust

A final trust score reflects a member's relationship with the community as a whole. We consider the inclusion of this score as it represents on a community level the trust

---

[1] We add 2 in the denominator and 1 in the numerator to avoid the divide-by-zero condition.

observed to and from a connection in a network. Once again, variations of equations 1-3 are used to determine community trust as follows:

$$PopTrust(u_2) = \frac{\text{\# positive trusting interactions towards } u_2 + 1}{\text{\# all trusting interactions towards } u_2 + 2} \tag{5}$$

$$EngTrust(u_2) = \frac{\text{\# positive trusted interactions by } u_2 + 1}{\text{\# all trusted interactions by } u_2 + 2} \tag{6}$$

$$SocialTrust(u_2) = \alpha. PopTrust(u_2) + (1 - \alpha). EngTrust(u_2) \tag{7}$$

3.5   Recommender Algorithms

We aim to understand how various implicit information between people, content and as a community can be combined to inform a content recommender for SNs. The first step in the recommender process is the identification of candidate recommendation items. This is achieved by considering all the content with which a target member's connections have interacted. We consider four different algorithms: two baseline algorithms and two network algorithms. The baseline algorithms calculate the content trust only: *"Most Popular"* chooses the content with highest content trust (i.e., the most viewed item), whereas *"Most Rated"* uses the content with the highest positive ratings. Two network algorithms include: *social graph* (candidates are all content items interacted with by friends, denoted SG_xxx) and *social behaviour* (candidates are all content items interacted by those with whom the target member interacts, denoted SB_xxx). The second step is the calculation of a relevance score for each candidate. We have four ways to calculate a relevance score for each network algorithm, i.e., four ranking methods. The simplest combines the user trust score with the content trust score of the member who has interacted with the item:

$$Rel(u_1, c_2) = Member\_Trust(u_1, u_2) * Eng(u_2, c_2) \tag{8}$$

where *Member_Trust* =1 for algorithms denoted by SG, or computed with equation 2 defined earlier for algorithms denoted by SB. Two ranking methods use this definition of relevance: SG_Eng and SB_Eng. A more complex ranking algorithm considers the community trust of the connection, the member trust and the content trust, as in:

$$Rel(u_1, c_2) = User\_Trust(u_1, u_2) * Eng(u_2, c_2) * Community\_Trust(u_2, c_2) \tag{9}$$

User_Trust is defined as in (8). We used three variations for *Community_Trust*: PopTrust, EngTrust and SocialTrust, given by equations 5, 6 and 7. α in all cases = 0.5.The resulting six ranking algorithms are denoted by SG_Eng_Pop, SG_Eng_Eng, SG_Eng_Social and SB_Eng_Pop, SB_Eng_Eng, SB_Eng_Social. Each of the four recommendation algorithms and six ranking methods returns a list of recommended items, ranked according to descending relevance scores.

4   Evaluation

We evaluated the performance of our algorithms and ranking methods through an offline analysis on an existing dataset gathered through an Australian online weight loss portal. The portal constitutes a stranger based SN. We carried out simulated analyses, judging performance in terms of accuracy, coverage and ranking.

The purpose of the recommender system is to identify unseen, relevant forum posts to recommend to network members. The aim of our analysis is twofold: (1) ascertain the applicability of social behavior and social graph based algorithms to identify relevant posts; and (2) investigate the success of various ranking methods to order candidate content items. We used the browsing logs of the portal as ground truth.

4.1   Data Set and Methodology

The data was gathered as part of a 5000 person, 12 week study into the role of social technologies in online dieting, using the CSIRO TWD Portal [3]. The portal had three key functional areas: *Social Networking platform, Diet Information* and *Diet Tools*. Each community member is represented by a profile page (an image, some personal information, food-related attributes, exercise and interests), a gallery, a friends list, a wall (message board) and a personal blog. Only friends could read or write on a person's wall. The portal contained a discussion forum where participants could post articles, questions and comments for the community and the support team. During the trial, the forum attracted 595 posts and 3129 comments. 1242 participants contributed to the forum, and 1193 viewed at least one piece of forum content.

We evaluated the two approaches (implicit and explicit) to determine the network structure, denoted by SB and SG in the algorithm names. For each approach, we tested the four ranking methods described earlier. We extracted from our data set 9577 occurrences where a user was viewing a post for the first time. Each occurrence is represented as a tuple: $Content\ Viewed\ Record = < u, c, t >$, where u is the user, c the content item and t a time-stamp. Given the interactions that occurred up until *time t*, each recommender algorithm was tasked to produce a ranked list of candidates (unseen posts) for the user. The target post is generated from the content viewed record using temporal filter. The algorithms were judged on their ability to generate recommendation lists (coverage), the inclusion of viewed content (from browsed record) in their list (precision, recall) and its position within the list (rank).

4.2   Results

We first examine the impact of four different ranking methods on the social graph and social behavior based recommenders to identify the best performing algorithm in each case. We then compare the approaches and the baselines in more details.

Ranking Methods. Fig. 2 (a,b) shows the recall and precision results for the ranking methods on the social graph based algorithms for N = 1 to 10, where N represents the top N contents from the recommendation list. We see performance gains in both precision and recall when Eq. 9, the relevance equation that exploits the viewers' standing in the community (Community Trust), is used. We note that there is no clear leader within the three algorithms employing this value. This is also reflected in the rank of the target item in the recommendation lists (found in the top 10 recommendations) - see Fig. 3 (a).

Fig. 2 (c,d) shows the recall and precision results for the social behaviour algorithms that exploit both the explicit and implicit networks. We note that, here, there is no notable difference between algorithms using the simple (Eq. 8) or the more complex (Eq. 9) relevance equations. Again, this is reflected in Fig. 3 (b) which shows the rank position of the target content. We observe that a user trust score has a monotonic relation to the recommendation list due to its higher value. We can further study the impact of the community trust by normalising the user trust score and community trust score. As it is presented here, personalised relationship information to the equation has a much higher weight in comparison to community relationship information.

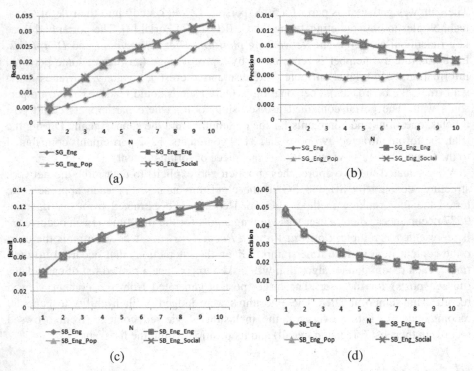

Fig. 2. Accuracy Results (a) Recall: SG alg., (b) Precision: SG alg., (c) Recall: SB alg., (d) Precision: SB alg

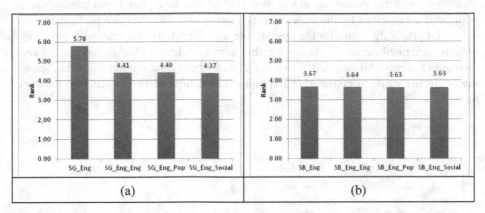

Fig. 3. Rank of target content item in recommendation list (a) social graph algorithms, (b) social behaviour algorithms

Implicit versus Explicit Network Modeling. We move to compare the two approaches to network construction, the social graph approach which uses only explicit friendships to link nodes in the network, and the social behaviour approach which uses implicit and explicit interactions to link nodes and weights these linkages to construct the network. We compare these to each other and to two baseline algorithms, *Most Popular* and *Most Rated*. The coverage (the algorithms' ability to generate a recommendation list) and hit rate (the inclusion of the target content item in this list) of each algorithm is shown in Table 1. We note the complete coverage by the baseline algorithms which, using generic measures, can always make a recommendation. We see that the social graph algorithm, which relies on articulated friendships, can only make recommendations for less than half of the identified browsing tuples. In contrast, by exploiting all users' interactions, the social behaviour algorithm can generate recommendations for 87% of tuples, showing a clear motivation for including implicit interactions to create networks when friendship levels are low.

Table 1. Coverage and Hit Rate

Algorithm	Coverage	HitRate	Relative HitRate (Coverage/HitRate)
Most popular	100%	93.53%	-
Most rated	100%	14.97%	-
Social graph	46.87%	11.56%	24.66%
Social behaviour	87.02%	30.97%	35.57%

The Hit Rate of an algorithm details the percentage of recommendation lists that contain the target content item when no size limit is placed on the list. That is, the algorithm's ability to classify an item as relevant to the user or not. The Relative Hit Rate takes into consideration whether a list was generated, and whether it contained the content item. We see a high hit rate for *Most Popular*, which is not surprising as all items previously viewed would appear as candidates for recommendation by this algorithm (note that the hit rate is less than 100% because an item is not considered as popular if it is viewed by the target member only). We note the poor performance of the social graph algorithm for the raw hit rate and the relative hit rate, with only 24% of lists generated correctly classifying the item as relevant. We observe a relative increase in relative hit rate of 35% when the social behaviour approach is used, showing again the value in considering implicit relationships when constructing network models.

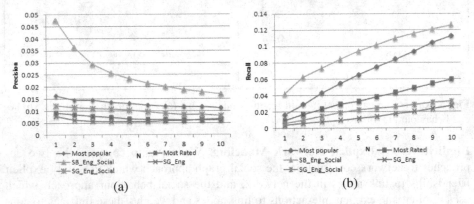

(a)   (b)

Fig. 4. Precision and Recall: SG and SB alg. and baselines

The ability to identify relevant candidate items is only part of the story. The real proof of an algorithm's applicability is in its positioning of items in the result list. We note that there are many potentially relevant items of content for any member at any time. Our analysis looks for a single piece of content, which, through the member's own motivation, they opted to view at a given moment. Fig. 4 (a) and (b) show precision and recall comparisons between the social graph and social behaviour algorithms and the two baselines. For clarity reasons, we include only one social behaviour algorithm (*SB_Eng_Social*), as all ranking methods performed comparatively. We show two ranking methods from the social graph algorithm (*SG_Eng_Social* (best performing) and *SG_Eng* (worst performing)). We see that the social behaviour based algorithm (*SB_Eng_Social*) outperforms all others for low values of N, achieving triple the precision of the next best algorithm and double the value for recall. Interestingly, the next best algorithm in terms of precision and recall is *Most Popular*. Also of note is the poor performance of the *SG_Eng* algorithm, which ranks content items according to their engagement with a person's friends. This finding is confirmed by the average rank position of the target items in the baseline recommendation lists. *Most Popular* returned items at position 4.9 on average, and *Most Rated* at 5.02; both are higher than the 5.78 of the *SG_Eng* algorithm. Whether an item ranked at 5 or above is of any importance to members is a separate research question that needs further investigation.

5   Conclusions

We presented and evaluated two approaches for identifying relevant content in a SN, exploiting differing representations of the trust network, and four relevance ranking methods. Our analysis showed that, in networks with low levels of friending, recommenders that consider only articulated friendships result in low levels of success in terms of their ability to generate recommendations and the accuracy of the items recommended. We see greater levels of coverage and hit rates and higher precision and recall with implied networks, meaning that looking beyond articulated friendships increases a member's chance of receiving useful recommendations. Our analysis of ranking methods indicated that the use of a community trust is useful with a social graph algorithm, but this parameter does not impact on the performance of social behaviour based algorithms. We will investigate this further in future work.

References

1. Adali, S., Escriva, R., Goldberg, M.K., Hayvanovych, M., Magdon-Ismail, M., Szymanski, B.K., Wallace, W.A., Williams, G.: Measuring behavioral trust in social networks. In: 2010 IEEE International Conference on Intelligence and Security Informatics (ISI), pp. 150–152 (2010)
2. Berkovsky, S., Freyne, J., Smith, G.: Personalized network updates: increasing social interactions and contributions in social networks. In: Masthoff, J., Mobasher, B., Desmarais, M.C., Nkambou, R. (eds.) UMAP 2012. LNCS, vol. 7379, pp. 1–13. Springer, Heidelberg (2012)
3. Brindal, E., Freyne, J., Saunders, I., Berkovsky, S., Noakes, M.: Weight tracking is predictive of weight loss for overweight/obese participants in a purely web-based intervention. J. Med. Internet Res (to appear, 2013)
4. Chen, J., Geyer, W., Dugan, C., Muller, M., Guy, I.: Make new friends, but keep the old: recommending people on social networking sites. In: Proceedings of the SIGCHI Conference on Human Factors in Computing Systems, Boston, MA, USA, pp. 201–210. ACM (2009)
5. Facebook Statistics, http://www.facebook.com/press/info.php?statistics (accessed December 2011)
6. Freyne, J., Berkovsky, S., Daly, E.M., Geyer, W.: Social networking feeds: recommending items of interest. In: Proceedings of the Fourth ACM Conference on Recommender Systems, Barcelona, Spain, pp. 277–280. ACM (2010)
7. Freyne, J., Jacovi, M., Guy, I., Geyer, W.: Increasing engagement through early recommender intervention. In: Proceedings of the Third ACM Conference on Recommender Systems, New York, USA, pp. 85–92. ACM (2009)
8. Gilbert, E., Karahalios, K.: Predicting tie strength with social media. In: Proceedings of the SIGCHI Conference on Human Factors in Computing Systems, Boston, MA, USA, pp. 211–220. ACM (2009)
9. Golbeck, J.: Trust on the world wide web: a survey. Foundations and Trends in Web Science 1, 131–197 (2006)

10. Guy, I., Ur, S., Ronen, I., Perer, A., Jacovi, M.: Do you want to know?: recommending strangers in the enterprise. In: Proceedings of the ACM 2011 Conference on Computer Supported Cooperative Work, Hangzhou, China, pp. 285–294. ACM (2011)
11. Kim, Y.A.: Building a web of trust without explicit trust ratings. In: 2008 IEEE 24th International Conference on Data Engineering Workshop, pp. 531–536 (2008)
12. Liu, H., Lim, E.-P., Lauw, H.W., Le, M.-T., Sun, A., Srivastava, J., Kim, Y.A.: Predicting trusts among users of online communities: an epinions case study. In: Proceedings of the 9th ACM Conference on Electronic Commerce, EC 2008, pp. 310–319. ACM, New York (2008)
13. Liu, H., Maes, P.: Interestmap: Harvesting social network profiles for recommendations. In: Beyond Personalization-IUI (2005)
14. Maheswaran, M., Tang, H.C., Ghunaim, A.: Towards a gravity-based trust model for social networking systems. In: Proceedings of the International Conference on Distributed Computing Systems Workshops, p. 24. IEEE Computer Society, Los Alamitos (2007)
15. Nepal, S., Sherchan, W., Paris, C.: STrust: a trust model for Social Networks. In: IEEE 10th International Conference on Trust, Security and Privacy in Computing and Communications (TrustCom), pp. 841–846 (2011)
16. Paek, T., Gamon, M., Counts, S., Chickering, D.M., Dhesi, A.: Predicting the Importance of Newsfeed Posts and Social Network Friends (2010)
17. Trifunovic, S., Legendre, F., Anastasiades, C.: Social trust in opportunistic networks. In: Proceeding of 2010 INFOCOM IEEE Conference on Computer Communications Workshops, pp. 1–6. IEEE (2010)
18. WeiHang, C., Singh, M.P.: Trust-based recommendation based on graph similarity. In: 13th AAMAS Workshop on Trust in Agent Societies (2010)
19. Zuo, Y., Hu, W.-C., O'Keefe, T.: Trust computing for social networking. In: Proceedings of the 2009 Sixth International Conference on Information Technology: New Generations, pp. 1534–1539. IEEE Computer Society, Washington, DC (2009)
20. Kleanthous, S., Dimitrova, V.: Analyzing Community Knowledge Sharing Behavior. In: De Bra, P., Kobsa, A., Chin, D. (eds.) UMAP 2010. LNCS, vol. 6075, pp. 231–242. Springer, Heidelberg (2010)
21. Paliouras, G.: Discovery of Web user communities and their role in personalization. User Model. User-Adapt. Interact. 22(1-2), 151–175 (2012)
22. Walter, F.E., Battiston, S., Schweitzer, F.: A model of a trust-based recommendation system on a social network. Autonomous Agents and Multi-Agent Systems 16(1), 57–74 (2008)
23. Kincaid, J.: EdgeRank: The secret sauce that makes Facebook's news feed tick (2010), http://techcrunch.com/2010/04/22/facebook-edgerank (retrieved from March 15, 2013)

What Recommenders Recommend – An Analysis of Accuracy, Popularity, and Sales Diversity Effects

Dietmar Jannach, Lukas Lerche, Fatih Gedikli, and Geoffray Bonnin

TU Dortmund, 44227 Dortmund, Germany
{firstname.lastname}@tu-dortmund.de

Abstract. In academic studies, the evaluation of recommender system (RS) algorithms is often limited to offline experimental designs based on historical data sets and metrics from the fields of Machine Learning or Information Retrieval. In real-world settings, however, other business-oriented metrics such as click-through-rates, customer retention or effects on the sales spectrum might be the true evaluation criteria for RS effectiveness. In this paper, we compare different RS algorithms with respect to their tendency of focusing on certain parts of the product spectrum. Our first analysis on different data sets shows that some algorithms – while able to generate highly accurate predictions – concentrate their top 10 recommendations on a very small fraction of the product catalog or have a strong bias to recommending only relatively popular items than others. We see our work as a further step toward multiple-metric offline evaluation and to help service providers make better-informed decisions when looking for a recommendation strategy that is in line with the overall goals of the recommendation service.

1 Introduction

A recent survey covering 330 papers published in the last five years showed that research in recommender systems (RS) is heavily dominated by offline experimental designs and comparative evaluations based on accuracy metrics [1]. Already some years ago, a too strong focus on accuracy as the only evaluation criterion was identified to be potentially problematic, e.g., in [2]. In recent years, aspects such as novelty, diversity, the popularity-bias of RS as well as potential trade-offs between different quality aspects obtained more attention in research, see, e.g., [3] or [4]. At the same time, laboratory studies and real-world online experiments indicated that higher predictive accuracy does not always correspond to the higher levels of user-perceived quality or to increased sales [5,6]. In fact, content-based approaches showed to work surprisingly well in these studies and recent others such as [7]. With respect to precision and recall – the most popular accuracy metrics according to [1] – recent work also showed that popularity-based methods can represent a comparably strong baseline ([4], [8]). However, as reported in [6], recommending only popular items does not lead to

S. Carberry et al. (Eds.): UMAP 2013, LNCS 7899, pp. 25–37, 2013.

the desired sales or persuasion effects. In addition, the recommendation of only popular items – or focusing in general on a small set of recommended items – will naturally lead to an undesired reinforcement of already popular items, thus leading to limited sales diversity and catalog coverage, see e.g., [9] or [10].

In this work we analyze different recommendation algorithms with respect to a number of measures and in particular also with respect to their characteristics in terms of "aggregate" diversity and the concentration on certain items in the sense of [3] and [11]. Our results show that while some algorithms are on a par or comparable with respect to their accuracy, they recommend items from quite different areas of the product spectrum. Furthermore, some highly accurate algorithms tend to focus on a tiny fraction of the item catalog. A simulated experiment finally indicates that some algorithms may lead to an undesired popularity boost of already popular items, which can be in contrast to the potential goal of an RS to promote long-tail items. Overall, we see our work as a further step towards RS evaluation methods that are more focused on their potential utility in multiple dimensions like the utility for the customer or service provider as described in [12]. In order to further support the openness and reproducibility of RS research results in the sense of [13], we make the source code of the evaluation framework used in our experiments available as open source[1].

2   A Multi-metric Experimental Evaluation

In this section, we will first describe our experimental setting which is a multiple-metric evaluation similar to [14]. We will shortly describe the various algorithms included in the measurements and characterize the particular data set for which we will report more details. Then, we present the results of our multiple-metric evaluation beginning with standard accuracy metrics such as the RMSE, Precision and Recall. In order to analyze the characteristics of individual algorithms in a more comprehensive and utility-oriented way, we then use further metrics which will be described in the corresponding sections. In particular, we are interested in the algorithms' capability of recommending long-tail items, their tendency of recommending only popular items as well as possibly resulting concentration effects.

2.1   Algorithms and Data Sets

Table 1 gives an overview of the algorithms which were evaluated in our study. We chose both popular baselines as well as different types of algorithms from recent research including a learning-to-rank method and a content-based technique, thus covering a broad range of RS approaches. For each data set and algorithm we empirically determined algorithm parameter values that led to high accuracy values. We did however not systematically optimize these values. The algorithms were tested on different data sets, see Section 3, but we will focus

---

[1] http://ls13-www.cs.uni-dortmund.de/homepage/recommender101

on the popular MovieLens data set here. We are aware that the data sets are quite small when compared to the Netflix Prize data set. However, we believe that most observed phenomena reported later on are more related to density and distribution characteristics of the data set than the plain number of available ratings. Furthermore, also in many real-world application scenarios and domains, we are often confronted with a limited number of ratings per user or items.

Table 1. Overview of the compared algorithms

Non-personalized baselines	
POPRANK	Popularity-based ranking.
ITEMAVGP	Prediction and ranking based on item average rating.
Simple weighting schemes	
WEIGHTEDAVG	Predicts the weighted combination of the active user's average and the target item's average rating. Weight factors for users and items are determined through error minimization.[2]
RF-REC	A similar weighting scheme that makes predictions based on rating frequencies [16].
Standard CF algorithms	
WEIGHTED SLOPEONE	Recommendation based on rating differences [17].
USER-kNN, ITEM-kNN	Nearest neighbor methods (nb. of neighbors $k = 100$, similarity threshold $= 0$, min. nb. of co-rated items $= 3$).
FUNK-SVD	A typical matrix factorization (MF) method (50 factors, 100 initialization rounds) [18].
KOREN-MF	Koren's factorized neighborhood model (Item-based approach, 50 factors, 100 initialization rounds, optimization parameters γ and λ were varied across data sets) [15].
Alternative item ranking approaches	
BPR	Bayesian Personalized Ranking [19], a method that learns to rank items based on implicit feedback. Default settings from the MyMediaLite implementation were used. (http://www.ismll.uni-hildesheim.de/mymedialite/)
CB-FILTERING	A content-based ranking method based on TF-IDF vectors. Items are ranked based on the cosine similarity with the user profile (average vector of all liked items).

Next, we will report the observations made using a data set which is based on a subset of the MovieLens10M data set. As we are interested also in the behavior of computationally-intensive neighborhood-based methods, we randomly sampled about 5,000 active users (at least ten ratings given) and about 1,000 popular items (at least 10 ratings received), ending up with about 400,000 ratings. For these 1,000 movies, we harvested content-descriptions from the IMDb Web site and call this data set MovieLens400k. We have repeated the measurements for a number of other data sets, leading mostly to results which are generally in line with the observations for MovieLens400k. Details will be given later in Section 3.

---

[2] This method is in some respect similar to the baseline predictor in [15].

2.2   Accuracy Results

The accuracy results obtained through a 4-fold cross-validation procedure with 75/25 splits are shown in Table 2. The first three columns – showing the root-mean-square error, as well as precision and recall within the top-10 recommendations – are not particularly surprising and generally in line with findings reported, e.g., for LensKit, in [13]. The differences among CF algorithms in terms of the RMSE are small and larger wins of the MF methods might only be visible for larger data sets, where automatically optimized parameter settings are required. With respect to precision, which was measured by counting only the elements for which a rating was available in the test set (denoted with *TS* in the table), all algorithms managed to place the few items rated with 5 stars at the top and thus outperformed the "most popular" baseline. Additional measurements of the NDCG and Area Under Curve metrics followed the trend of precision and recall. As another side observation, we noted that the unpersonalized ITEMAVGP strategy on many data sets including this one or Yahoo!Movies performed very well on the NDCG and ROCAUC and was often nearly on a par with neighborhood-based methods or SLOPEONE. We do not report further detailed results here due to space limitations.

Table 2. Accuracy metrics for the MovieLens400k data set

Algorithm	RMSE	Pre@10(TS)	Rec@10(TS)	Pre@10(All)	Rec@10(All)
FUNK-SVD	**0.847**	**0.416**	**0.788**	0.056	0.095
SLOPEONE	0.855	0.412	0.782	0.029	0.046
USER-kNN	0.856	0.413	0.783	0.035	0.064
KOREN-MF	0.861	0.408	0.777	0.028	0.052
RF-REC	0.862	0.408	0.777	0.039	0.072
ITEM-kNN	0.864	0.407	0.776	0.030	0.058
WEIGHTEDAVERAGE	0.893	0.407	0.776	0.030	0.058
ITEMAVGP	0.925	0.407	0.776	0.027	0.056
BPR	-	0.361	0.716	**0.109**	**0.249**
POPRANK	-	0.354	0.709	0.051	0.124
CB-FILTERING	-	0.346	0.700	0.021	0.036

However, when we used a different scheme to measure precision and recall by including all items in the test set (denoted with "All") the results are different. The outcome of this measuring scheme for precision and recall depends on the overall number of items in the test set, possibly leading to very small numbers for large catalogs. However, as our data set contains about 1,000 items, the measurement method is in some sense similar to the procedure used in [8] where 1,000 items with unknown ratings were placed in the test set. Now, as also reported in [8], the popularity-based baseline is hard to beat even for MF approaches. In our setting, POPRANK for example had a much better recall than FUNK-SVD and comparable precision, even though slight improvements for FUNK-SVD might be possible by further tweaking algorithm parameters. The comparably simple RF-REC scheme is also ranked higher in the comparison when a different method for measuring is chosen. Overall, however, the best-ranked method on these measures is the "learning-to-rank" approach BPR which outperforms the other techniques by far.

Therefore, as reported in the literature, the ranking of algorithms based on offline experimentation might not only follow different trends when using the RMSE and precision/recall as a metric but can also depend on the particular way a metric is determined. Furthermore, the question which algorithm is the most appropriate, depends on the recommendation scenario (e.g., "find all good items" etc. [20]) so that in one application scenario an algorithm with higher recall might be more favorable than a highly precise one.

As we will see next, the good performance of RF-REC and also BPR in the first measurement might be found in their tendency of focusing on popular items.

2.3   Popularity-Bias, Coverage, and Aggregate Diversity

The number of ratings per movie in the MovieLens400k data set as most RS research data sets resembles a typical "Long Tail" distribution. Beside the provision of accurate recommendations, the goal of an RS provider could be to sell more niche items from this long tail. We were therefore interested whether or not the RS algorithms shown in Table 1 behave differently with respect to their ability to recommend products from the whole product catalog. In particular, we measured how many items of the catalog actually ever appear in top-10 recommendation lists. Note that we use the term "(aggregate) diversity" to denote this special form of catalog coverage as done in [3] or [11]. In other works, the diversity of items in recommendation lists with respect to their content features was also identified to be an important factor that can influence the perceived value of a recommender system, see e.g., in [21]. Measuring the level of intra-list diversity was however not in the focus of our current study.

Catalog Coverage and Aggregate Diversity. As a first step of our analysis, we used the evaluation approach described in [11]: We grouped items in bins of 100 elements and sorted them in increasing order based on their actual frequency of appearing in top-10 recommendation lists. Figure 1 shows the first four bins containing the most frequently recommended items by a representative subset of the analyzed algorithms for illustration purposes[3].

We can observe that for many of the strategies, only a tiny fraction of the available items ever appears in top-10 lists. In particular, the RF-REC scheme and Koren's neighborhood MF scheme (merged in "Other" in Figure 1) focused on only about 40 different items[4]. On the other end the user-based kNN recommender had a range of 270 items, from which about 100 items (see bin 1 in Figure 1) are recommended with a chance of 97.68%. Both FUNK-SVD (860

---

[3] We show 4 out of 10 bins for the 963 items of the MovieLens400k data set. "Other" characterizes the seven remaining algorithms from Table 1, which all concentrate their recommendations on less than 90 items.

[4] In this measurement, all items unseen by a user were part of the test set. Various parameter variations of Koren's method did not lead to different algorithm behavior. One explanation could be a strong effect of the item-bias factor of the learned model.

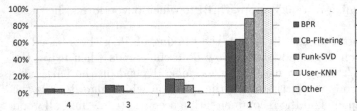

Fig. 1. Distribution of actual recommendations (= being in the top-10 of a recommendation list) for the first 400 most recommended items (grouped into 4 bins with 100 items each), as well as the Gini index for the MovieLens400k data set

items) and BPR (868) as well as content-based filtering (893) nearly cover the whole item space. The distribution of recommendations nevertheless still has the form of a long-tail, which is however far wider. The top 100 products for FUNK-SVD, BPR, and CB-FILTERING still accounted for 87.89%, 61.0% and 63.20% of the recommendations.

Figure 1 also shows the corresponding Gini index values for the concentration of the recommendations, see also [11]. Higher values of this index – whose values can be between 0 and 1 – indicate a stronger concentration on a small set of items. The results show that many RS algorithms have a very strong tendency to concentrate on a small product spectrum as indicated in Figure 1. Again, when ranking the algorithms according to the potential business goal of good catalog coverage and long-tail recommendations, a different order is advisable than when only considering accuracy.

Effects of Algorithm Parameters: Diversity and Accuracy. Given the strong difference between the two MF methods with respect to the Gini index, we hypothesized that the algorithm parameters will not only influence the accuracy but also the concentration index. Figure 2 shows the effect of varying the number of initial training rounds for the FUNK-SVD method.

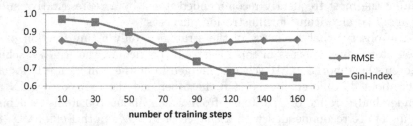

Fig. 2. RMSE and Gini index depending on number of training steps for FUNK-SVD

We can see that increasing the number of rounds has a positive impact on the RMSE and reaches the best values already after about 50 rounds (see also [13] who observed a flattening at about 100 rounds) and then remains stable or slightly increases again, which can be caused by an overfitting tendency. Since the number of training rounds strongly influences the computation time of the method, one might be tempted to set the value to about 50 rounds or even to much smaller values as comparably good RMSE values can be achieved relatively quickly. When considering the development of the Gini index, however, it becomes evident that a much higher number of iterations is required to avoid the possibly undesired algorithm behavior of concentrating on a very small fraction of the catalog. As shown in Figure 2 the curve begins to flatten out after about 120 iterations[5]. Therefore a tradeoff-decision between accuracy, diversity and efficiency might be required.

The KOREN-MF algorithm is likewise very dependent on its parametrization. For this particular data set we found a similar dependency for RMSE and Gini index with the step-size parameter γ. Other algorithms parameters however did not influence the two metrics considerably.

Popularity Bias of Algorithms. After having analyzed how many different items are actually being recommended, another question is whether some algorithms have a tendency to focus on popular items. To assess this algorithm property, we again created top-10 recommendations for each user using different algorithms and measured (I) the popularity of items based on the average item rating, (II) the average popularity of the recommended items in terms of the number of available ratings per item, (III) the distribution of recommendations when the items are organized in bins based on their popularity, again measured using the number of ratings.

Regarding measure (I) we could observe that the average item rating was around 4 for most algorithms. Exceptions were BPR (average = 3.4), CB-FILTERING (3.2) and POPRANK (3.6), which also recommended movies that were not liked by everyone (but have been seen and rated by many people). On measure (II), POP-RANK naturally is the "winner" and only recommends blockbusters to everyone (about 1.600 ratings per item). However, BPR is second on this list (940 ratings) while SLOPEONE (380) and CB-FILTERING (330) form the other end of the spectrum and recommend also long-tail items.

Figure 3 visualizes measure (III)[6], the distribution of recommended items when they are organized in 9 equally sized bins of increasing popularity (based on the number of ratings). We are aware that the figure has to be interpreted carefully as a higher value for some bins can be caused by a very small set of items which are recommended to everyone by some algorithm. Still, we see some general tendencies for the different algorithms, in particular that BPR very often picks items from the bin that contains the most popular items and that popularity of an item correlates strongly with the chance of being recommended. FUNK-SVD and CB-FILTERING have no strong popularity bias and USER-kNN seems to tend to the extremes of the scale; SLOPEONE, as expected due to its design, also recommends unpopular items.

---

[5] We also varied the number of latent features for FUNK-SVD but could not observe strongly varying results.

[6] We omit POPRANK whose recommendations are all in the "most popular"-bin.

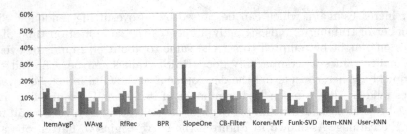

Fig. 3. Distribution of recommendations (= being in the top-10 of a recommendation list) for all items sorted by popularity (number of ratings) and grouped into 9 bins

Injecting a Stronger Popularity Bias. Our measurements so far as well as observations from the literature suggest that recommending popular items is a very simple strategy to achieve high precision and recall values, at least when all items in the test set are considered. Thus, when using such a measure, it might be quite easy to improve an algorithm's accuracy simply by introducing an artificial popularity bias. While such more biased recommendations might be of little value in practice (see also [8] or the real-world study presented in [6]), researchers might draw wrong conclusions about an algorithm's true value when only relying on precision/recall metrics.

To illustrate the effects of introducing an artificial popularity bias, we conducted an experiment in which we used the popular FUNK-SVD algorithm and filtered its recommendations in a way that we only retained items, which were rated by at least k users. For this measurement, we used the publicly available standard MovieLens100k data set.

Table 3. Effects of an artificial popularity bias for precision and recall strategies *All* (all items in the test set) and *TS* (only items with known ratings in the test set)

Algorithm	Pre@10(All)	Rec@10(All)	Pre@10(TS)	Rec@10(TS)
POPRANK	0.053	0.098	0.356	0.640
FUNKSVD	0.057	0.065	0.415	0.705
FUNKSVD, k=100	0.098	0.117	0.416	0.568
FUNKSVD, k=200	0.114	0.138	0.384	0.319
FUNKSVD, k=300	0.103	0.117	0.314	0.121

Table 3 shows that focusing on popular items can actually increase precision and recall values when a certain measurement method is used. The strategy chosen in the experiment is very simple and leads to poorer results when the threshold value is set too high. Other, more elaborate schemes could however help to even further improve the numbers. When compared with the common measurement method *Precision TS*, we can in contrast see that adding a stronger popularity bias leads to poorer results. Given this observation, the usage of the *Precision/Recall TS* measurement methods might be more appropriate for application domains where a too strong focus on popular items can be risky.

2.4 Popularity Reinforcement

Providers of recommendation services on e-commerce platforms are typically interested in the long-term effects of the service on user satisfaction or sales. Unfortunately, measuring such long-term effects is difficult even when it is possible to conduct A/B tests. One of the few works in that direction are the ones by [22] and [23], who observed that the online recommender systems guided customers to a different part of the product spectrum.

The opposite effect, namely that recommenders can even lead to decreased sales diversity and increase the popularity of already popular items was discussed, e.g., by [9]. In order to assess possible effects of different algorithms on the popularity distribution in an offline experimental design, we ran the following simulation on a 200k-rating subset of MovieLens400k[7] to simulate the popularity-enforcing effect of each algorithm over time.

First, we generated a top-10 recommendation list for each user with the algorithm under investigation. To simplify the simulation, we assumed that users only rate items appearing in the recommendation list. We therefore randomly pick one of the recommended items and create an artificial rating for it. This simulated rating is randomly taken according to the overall rating distribution in the data set[8]. Once such an artificial rating was created for each user, all these new ratings are added to the database. This procedure was repeated 50 times to simulate the evolution of the rating database. At each iteration we measured (I) the *concentration of the ratings in the data set* using the Gini index (Figure 4) with bins of 30 products and (II) the number of different products recommended to all users in that run.

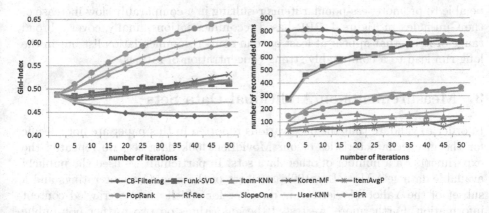

Fig. 4. Simulation results - Gini index

---

[7] We reduced the data set size because of the long running-times of the neighborhood-based schemes. The data set characteristics are similar to the larger data set.

[8] Selecting the rating based on the distribution of ratings of an individual item or user would have also been possible.

Figure 4 shows that the effects on the rating distributions strongly vary depending on the chosen algorithm. One class of algorithms – including of course POPRANK – leads to a stronger effect in the rating database and already popular items become even more popular and constantly appear in the recommendation lists of even more other users. Both RF-REC and BPR fall into this category. For another class of algorithms including the MF approaches and ITEM-kNN, the concentration index only slowly increases over time. KOREN-MF also belongs to this category, which indicates that the recommendation of popular items is only boosted slowly over time. Finally, USER-kNN and CB-FILTERING initially lead to a stronger diversification of the ratings which then remains stable or increases again.

While the effects are clearly amplified through our specific simulation strategy, we believe that the obtained results indicate that there are significant differences between algorithms, which should be taken into account when looking for an appropriate recommendation strategy.

Looking at measure (II) at the right hand side of Figure 4, the number of distinct items recommended in one iteration per algorithm vary across data sets. Given that there are about 1,000 items in the catalog, CB-FILTERING and BPR initially recommend nearly every item to at least one user. Over time, this number slightly decreases. FUNK-SVD and USER-kNN represent another category of algorithms which start with a comparably high number of recommended items and later on strongly diversify their recommendations[9]. All other algorithms initially recommended a small number of items and only slightly increase the recommendation spectrum over time.

Combining these results with the tendency of some algorithms to concentrate on a small item spectrum, we can observe that both RF-REC as well as KOREN-MF only recommend very few items (see Figure 4). KOREN-MF, however, seems to be able to promote less-popular items resulting in a comparably slow increase of the Gini index in Figure 4. BPR-based recommendations, finally, cover a broad range of items that appear at least once in some recommendation list but in the long run lead to a comparably strong concentration of ratings.

3   Measurements on Additional Data Sets

In order to validate that the observations reported in this paper are not specific for the given characteristics of our MovieLens400k data set, we repeated the experiments on a number of other data sets. In particular, we used the publicly available data sets MovieLens100k, a subset of the BookCrossing ratings and a subset of the Yahoo!Movies rating data set for which we also crawled content information. Furthermore, we tested the algorithms on two further non-public data sets from a telecommunication provider [6] and a data set obtained from the hotel booking platform HRS.com [24]. Except MovieLens100k, all other data sets have a considerably higher sparsity (0.002 to 0.011) than the relatively dense

---

[9] Note that this is not in contradiction with the observations for FUNKSVD reported in Figure 4, where we could see an increase of the rating concentration.

MovieLens400k data set (0.084). Regarding the available ratings MovieLens100k has at least 20 ratings per user and item, whereas for all other data sets we created rating subsets such that the minimum number of ratings was at least 10.

Overall, the general trends reported for the MovieLens400k data set can also be observed for the other data sets. As for RMSE and *Precision/Recall TS*, the matrix factorization (MF) approaches were in most cases only slightly better or on a par with classical kNN schemes, SLOPEONE or simple weighting schemes and their advantages might only become visible for larger data sets. With respect to *Precision/Recall All*, the MF methods however outperformed the traditional schemes also for the given small data sets. Considering the parametrization of the algorithms for the data sets, we observed that in particular the results of the KOREN-MF method vary strongly depending on the values of the algorithm parameters. These parameters must therefore be carefully tuned in practical settings. Finally, while the accuracy of kNN methods is most of the times comparably good, these techniques often suffer from a limited prediction coverage.

The general trend of a strong concentration on only a small set of items by RF-REC and the KOREN-MF method could also be observed for the other data sets. Similarly, the superior performance of BPR and also POPRANK with respect to *Precision/Recall All* and their trend to reinforce the popularity of already popular items was visible across the different data sets.

4   Conclusion

The current practice of evaluating RS based mainly on accuracy metrics is facing various (known) limitations as well as potential methodological problems such as not reported baselines and inconsistently used metrics. Due to these issues, the results of offline analyzes may remain inconclusive or even misleading and the correspondence of such measurements with real-world performance metrics can be unclear. Real-world evaluations and, to some extent, lab studies represent probably the best methods to evaluate systems. Still, we believe that more practically-relevant insights can be achieved also in offline experimental studies, when algorithms are evaluated along several dimensions and on different data sets. In particular, we believe that the analysis of potential trade-offs (e.g., between diversity and accuracy) as done in a growing number of recent papers should be put even more into the focus of future research.

In this paper, we have analyzed known algorithms with respect to the diversity, item popularity and accuracy of the recommendations. Our observations indicate that – depending on their parametrization and the usage scenario – different algorithms lead to different effects and that the choice of the "best" approach to be deployed in a live system should be guided by the consideration of these effects. With the provision of the software used in the experiments, we finally hope to contribute to the reproducibility of RS research.

References

1. Jannach, D., Zanker, M., Ge, M., Gröning, M.: Recommender systems in computer science and information systems - a landscape of research. In: Huemer, C., Lops, P. (eds.) EC-Web 2012. LNBIP, vol. 123, pp. 76–87. Springer, Heidelberg (2012)
2. McNee, S.M., Riedl, J., Konstan, J.A.: Being accurate is not enough: how accuracy metrics have hurt recommender systems. In: Proceedings of the 2006 Conference on Human Factors in Computing Systems (CHI 2006), pp. 1097–1101 (2006)
3. Adomavicius, G., Kwon, Y.: Improving aggregate recommendation diversity using ranking-based techniques. IEEE Transactions on Knowledge and Data Engineering 24(5), 896–911 (2012)
4. Steck, H.: Item popularity and recommendation accuracy. In: Proceedings of the 2011 ACM Conference on Recommender Systems, Chicago, Illinois, USA, pp. 125–132 (2011)
5. Cremonesi, P., Garzotto, F., Negro, S., Papadopoulos, A.V., Turrin, R.: Looking for "good" recommendations: A comparative evaluation of recommender systems. In: Campos, P., Graham, N., Jorge, J., Nunes, N., Palanque, P., Winckler, M. (eds.) INTERACT 2011, Part III. LNCS, vol. 6948, pp. 152–168. Springer, Heidelberg (2011)
6. Jannach, D., Hegelich, K.: A case study on the effectiveness of recommendations in the mobile internet. In: Proceedings of the 2009 ACM Conference on Recommender Systems, New York, pp. 41–50 (2009)
7. Kirshenbaum, E., Forman, G., Dugan, M.: A live comparison of methods for personalized article recommendation at Forbes.com. In: Flach, P.A., De Bie, T., Cristianini, N. (eds.) ECML PKDD 2012, Part II. LNCS, vol. 7524, pp. 51–66. Springer, Heidelberg (2012)
8. Cremonesi, P., Koren, Y., Turrin, R.: Algorithms on top-n recommendation tasks. In: Proceedings of the 2010 ACM Conference on Recommender Systems, Barcelona, pp. 39–46 (2010)
9. Fleder, D., Hosanagar, K.: Blockbuster culture's next rise or fall: The impact of recommender systems on sales diversity. Management Science 55(5), 205–208 (2009)
10. Prawesh, S., Padmanabhan, B.: The "top N" news recommender: count distortion and manipulation resistance. In: Proceedings of the 2011 ACM Conference on Recommender Systems, Chicago, USA, pp. 237–244 (2011)
11. Zhang, M.: Enhancing the diversity of collaborative filtering recommender systems. PhD Thesis. Univ. College Dublin (2010)
12. Said, A., Tikk, D., Shi, Y.: Recommender Systems Evaluation: A 3D Benchmark. In: ACM RecSys 2012 Workshop on Recommendation Utility Evaluation: Beyond RMSE, Dublin, Ireland, pp. 21–23 (2012)
13. Ekstrand, M.D., Ludwig, M., Konstan, J.A., Riedl, J.T.: Rethinking the recommender research ecosystem: reproducibility, openness, and LensKit. In: Proceedings of the 2011 ACM Conference on Recommender Systems, Chicago, Illinois, USA, pp. 133–140 (2011)
14. Meyer, F., Fessant, F., Clérot, F., Gaussier, E.: Toward a new protocol to evaluate recommender systems. In: ACM RecSys 2012 Workshop on Recommendation Utility Evaluation: Beyond RMSE, Dublin, Ireland, pp. 9–14 (2012)
15. Koren, Y.: Factorization meets the neighborhood: a multifaceted collaborative filtering model. In: Proceedings of the 14th ACM SIGKDD International Conference on Knowledge Discovery and Data Mining, Las Vegas, USA, pp. 426–434 (2008)

16. Gedikli, F., Bagdat, F., Ge, M., Jannach, D.: RF-REC: Fast and accurate computation of recommendations based on rating frequencies. In: 13th IEEE Conference on Commerce and Enterprise Computing, CEC 2011, Luxembourg, pp. 50–57 (2011)

17. Lemire, D., Maclachlan, A.: Slope one predictors for online rating-based collaborative filtering. In: SIAM Conference on Data Mining, Newport Beach, pp. 471–480 (2005)

18. (2006), http://sifter.org/~simon/journal/20061211.html (last accessed March 2013)

19. Rendle, S., Freudenthaler, C., Gantner, Z., Schmidt-Thieme, L.: BPR: Bayesian Personalized Ranking from Implicit Feedback. In: Proceedings of the Twenty-Fifth Conference on Uncertainty in Artificial Intelligence, Montreal, Canada, pp. 452–461 (2009)

20. Herlocker, J.L., Konstan, J.A., Terveen, L.G., Riedl, J.T.: Evaluating collaborative filtering recommender systems. ACM Transactions on Information Systems 22(1), 5–53 (2004)

21. Castagnos, S., Jones, N., Pu, P.: Eye-Tracking Product Recommenders' Usage. In: Proceedings of the 2010 ACM Conference on Recommender Systems, Barcelona, Spain, pp. 29–36 (2010)

22. Dias, M.B., Locher, D., Li, M., El-Deredy, W., Lisboa, P.J.: The value of personalised recommender systems to e-business: A case study. In: Proceedings of the 2008 ACM Conference on Recommender Systems, Lausanne, Switzerland, pp. 291–294 (2008)

23. Zanker, M., Bricman, M., Gordea, S., Jannach, D., Jessenitschnig, M.: Persuasive online-selling in quality & taste domains. In: Bauknecht, K., Pröll, B., Werthner, H. (eds.) EC-Web 2006. LNCS, vol. 4082, pp. 51–60. Springer, Heidelberg (2006)

24. Jannach, D., Karakaya, Z., Gedikli, F.: Accuracy improvements for multi-criteria recommender systems. In: Proceedings of the 13th ACM Conference on Electronic Commerce, EC 2012, Valencia, Spain, pp. 674–689 (2012)

A Framework for Trust-Based Multidisciplinary Team Recommendation

Lorenzo Bossi[1], Stefano Braghin[2], Anwitaman Datta[2], and Alberto Trombetta[1]

[1] DiSTA
University of Insubria Italy
{lorenzo.bossi,alberto.trombetta}@uninsubria.it
[2] School of Computer Engineering
Nanyang Technological University Singapore
{s.braghin,anwitaman}@ntu.edu.sg

Abstract. Often one needs to form teams in order to perform a complex collaborative task. Therefore, it is interesting and useful to assess how well constituents of a team have performed, and leverage this knowledge to guide future team formation. In this work we propose a model for assessing the reputation of participants in collaborative teams. The model takes into account several features such as the different skills that a participant has and the feedback of team participants on her/his previous works. We validate our model based on synthetic datasets extrapolated from real-life scenarios.

1 Introduction

With the advent of Web 2.0, social networking and crowd-sourcing technologies, there is an increasing trend of collaborative teamwork in online environments. This is naturally receiving an ever-growing academic attention as well [1,2,3]. Previous work (as we will see in Section 2) focuses on how to find an optimal solution for the allocation of users for accomplishing the given tasks, taking into consideration how well the users are mutually compatible. Compatibility among users may be extracted from external sources, like interaction graphs in online social networks. User skills are often determined by the system by *fiat* and in a static, immutable manner. More precisely, a set of users – each possessing some skills – and a set of tasks, that need certain skills to be accomplished are assumed a priori. Then, upon requiring that a certain set of tasks has to be performed (from now on, for simplicity we consider the case in which there is a single task to be performed), the "best" set of users having the required skills is provided, thus forming the best suited team for the said task.

In this work, we present a framework for team formation in which the assessment on how good a user is in a given skill is determined dynamically – depending on, among other things – the judgments or feedback ratings that the user had obtained when performing tasks requiring similar skills. Naturally, taking into account users' ratings lends itself to a system dealing with the reputations of the users themselves. That is, users – by giving (and receiving) ratings about the

S. Carberry et al. (Eds.): UMAP 2013, LNCS 7899, pp. 38–50, 2013.

work other users have done (and about the work they have done) – form a *web of trust* such that (i) two users are directly connected if one rated the work done by the other; (ii) the overall reputation of a user (with respect to a given skill) is computed as an aggregate value of the ratings (relative to such skill) given by other users; (iii) the perception of the reputation of user u from the point of view of another user v depends on the reputations and ratings of the users connecting (possibly by multiple hops over the web of trust) users u and v. An important aspect of the presented work is that we take into account how skills are related among them. In other words, we consider the skills to be similar (in varying degrees) and this contributes in determining who are the best team members that can cope with the task to be performed. The computation of reputation takes into account skills' similarities thanks to the "multi-dimensionality" of the web of trust, that takes into account users' ratings for every skill, along with information about skills' similarities. We next outline and discuss some relevant points concerning how reputation may be computed and used in assembling the best possible team for a given task.

Reputation in a Team Formation Setting. In real-world settings it is fairly common to have different reputations, depending on the different skills that are being evaluated. Furthermore, such reputations may be correlated, given that the corresponding skills are similar and can be different according to the reference group (see Section 3). We try to capture this natural phenomenon in our model. Once a team has been formed, team members may rate each other about the work done. We assume that every team member sees everything that has been done by every other team member. While performing such ratings, they add to the reputation system new information regarding the trust they have about particular skills of other users. In this fashion, the reputation of a user is determined not only on the basis as assessed by the team recommendation system (an *ex-ante* process which derives information by graph mining and information retrieval mechanisms [1,4,3,5]), but also on the ex-post judgment of one's peers.

In our approach, user reputation is computed locally, so – in principle – every user may compute a different reputation based on his/her previous personal experiences with other users (asymmetry). Informally, a user is encouraged to report truthful information about his/her previous team interactions because every user privately computes the reputation of other users. Hence, misreporting information has consequences only on his/her own reputation computation. In order to compute the reputation of a user from the point of view of another in the absence of direct trust information, the system infers it by searching for a trust path between the two users (trust transitivity). The paper is organized as follows: In Section 2 we present a review of the literature on team formation techniques. After that, we define the terminology adopted in this work and then we describe our motivating example in Section 3. The proposed model is formalized in Section 4, while in Section 5 we present an experimental validation of the model. Finally, in Section 6 we conclude with a brief discussion of possible future works.

2 Related Work

With the ease of finding digital footprints from online social networks and structured communities, harnessing it to form multidisciplinary teams has become an interesting subject of study.

A framework similar to ours is presented in [3], where the authors model a system to manage users, tasks and skills. The compatibilities among users are inferred from an underlying social network. The social network is represented as an undirected, edge-weighted graph, where the weights denote how well the corresponding users may collaborate. Thus, the problem is to find, given a task t, a subgraph of the social network such that every skill needed for accomplishing t is possessed by at least one node in the subgraph. It is shown that this problem is NP-Hard and accordingly, approximation algorithms that perform well in real-world datasets are given. However, similarities among enumerated skills are ignored in that approach. Likewise, past interactions among users in previously formed teams are overlooked.

In [1], a similar framework (tasks, skills, etc.) is taken into account but here the problem is how to optimally allocate the users' skills to cope with multiple, concurrent tasks. As in the previous work, the allocation of skills takes into account the social interactions among users, as recorded by a social network. The model presented in this work is utility-based. That is, given a set of concurrent tasks that require certain skills, the aim is to find a skill allocation that maximizes the probability of successfully completing the highest number of tasks. Thus, the problem is dual to what we study here. Furthermore, again the effect of interactions among users being involved in past teamwork is not taken into account.

The problem of how to define and compute trust in an online community is a well-known and thoroughly researched problem. It has been analyzed and modeled with very different approaches. One of them consists of computing transitive closure of trust in a single dimensional model using subjective logic [6]. Other approaches are probabilistic, like in [7] where authors propose a model to compute trust of generic provider agents; while in [2] authors develop a probabilistic multidimensional trust model focused on how trust can be propagated in a real-world scenario of a supply chain market. In [8] authors compute trust in a multidimensional network where agents can estimate the utility of a contract by computing the probability that each dimension of a contract can be fulfilled. They also propose a protocol to propagate rumors and compute trust in a totally distributed network.

A similar scenario, where a multidimensional network is used to automatically make recommendations to users, is described in [9]. In this work the authors use a multidimensional social network on a Flickr dataset to suggest potentially interesting users. They create a multidimensional graph where every node is a user and edges on a single dimension represent some kind of relation between users (i.e. both commented the same photo). Finally they aggregate information of all dimensions to create a list of *similar users* to suggest. User's feedback about suggestions is used to correct the weight used to aggregate the different dimensions.

A method to propagate social trust through friendship relations is presented in [10]. The purpose of this work is to compute the popularity of the users in the system. The authors show that their approach can be used to model the *friendship effects* in a social network (i.e. a person followed by a popular person is likely to have more follower).

Pizzato et al. describe, in various works [11,12,13], the people-to-people class of recommender systems using the case of online dating. They focus on the fact that this kind of recommender systems differ from the traditional items-to-people recommenders as they must satisfy both parties and they call this type of rec-ommenders *reciprocal*. They also notice that, in such kind of recommenders, the cost of a poor recommendation can be quite high because users are more afraid of continuous rejects from other people than wrong suggestions on purchasable items.

In [14] Masthoff discusses how a system can aggregate recommender informa-tion from individual users to make a recommendation for a group of users (i.e. suggest which movie to watch among certain friends).

For multidisciplinary team recommendation, coverage of the necessary skills as well as collective compatibility among the members of the team are essential, and this work looks at these issues that are typically studied in isolation in a holistic manner.

3   Motivating Example

The terms *trust* and *reputation* denote concepts involving several subjective features related to a wide range of human activities and behaviors. As such, framing them into a – more or less – formal definition is far from trivial. Many different approaches have been proposed [15]. For our purposes, we stick with the informal definition given by Jøsang [16], namely: *"Trust is the extent to which one party is willing to depend on the other party in a given situation with a feeling of relative security, even through negative consequences are possible"*. As we can see from this definition, trust is a subjective value, derived usually by direct experience. Generally speaking *reputation* quantifies a public opinion, and – for our purposes – we consider it as the aggregations of trust from different people.

In order to show how such concepts may be related to finding the right people for performing a given task, we consider the following scenario. Alice is a singer who wants find people able to compose songs (that is, their music and lyrics) and play them as well. Since Alice is no good in composing, she look for the help from Carl, a composer she knows. In doing so, she is depending on him and implicitly taking the associated risks of failure because she trusts him. Alice also looks for a guitarist, but she does not know anyone with such skill. Thus, she asks some of her friends for a recommendation, with the goal to find some good – that is, with a high reputation – guitarist. From the collected suggestions, Alice has to choose only one person. In doing this, Alice takes into account how much she trusts the friend that made the suggestion and how much such friend trusts as guitarist the suggested person. It is not sufficient Alice trusts her friend on a general ground, rather it is essential that Alice trusts him/her as an expert in rating musicians. It is thus very important that both reputation and trust are relative about a particular skill (as suggested in [17]). In real-world scenarios it is common for a person to have different reputations, which may show a degree of correlation among themselves.

That is, Alice does not trust any recommendation of her musician friends, but she trusts the recommendation of another friend of her, who is very knowledgeable in music trends. This may succeed because skills are not totally unrelated among each other. Thus, the knowledge of the reputation of someone with respect to a particular skill (rating music) can be used to infer the reputation about some other related skill (rating a guitarist).

Asking for a recommendation is thus based on a sort of transitive closure of trust. But, generally speaking, trust cannot be assumed to be a transitive relation [18] unless consider further constraints [16] are specified. In our approach, we explicit such constraints introducing a similarity function over a given set of skills. Skills are not considered as independent one from another, but we take into account the fact that if one possesses some given skill then it is highly probable that she/has some proficiency in another, related one. We use such skill similarity in order to build transitive trust relationships among users that do not have direct connections. As a consequence (as we will explain formally in Section 4) one of the more relevant features of our approach is that a user may have different reputations about a given skill, depending on which user is asking for it. In literature, such feature has been referred to as *asymmetry* of reputation and plays a fundamental role in guaranteeing the trustworthiness of users' ratings, as explained in [19]. The fact that the users' reputations are computed in an asymmetric way takes into account that one's reputation in a given skill s depends on – of course – on the expertise she/he has in skill s, but also on the expertise that other raters have in skills related to s.

Now Alice needs a drummer, too. None of her friends knows such a musician, and she looks for recommendations from friends of her friends. This way of proceeding can be iterated and if everyone in the sequence of recommendations is trustworthy, Alice accepts these recommendations by means of a *chain of trust*, that is a directed graph in which the node relative to person A is connected with an directed edge to the node relative to person B if A trusts B.

We present in an informal way how reputation is managed in our approach by explaining a possible way for Alice to decide over three candidates, as shown in Figure 1(a). The first one is considered untrustworthy by a trustworthy person (Dave) and Alice decides against this candidate; the second one is recommended by Eve and – since Alice does not consider Eve trustworthy – she decides against such candidate as well; Alice finally accepts the recommendation from Carl because refers to a trustworthy person recommended only by trustworthy persons. Furthermore, an important issue is how to deal with different – possibly discording – recommendations. This happens fairly often in real-world situations as well: people may choose to trust more the ratings coming from persons "closer" to them (that is, chains of trust involving the minimum number of persons); or they may opt for ratings from the persons with highest reputation (disregarding the "distance" from such persons) As we will explain in Section 4, we aim at finding a chain of trust that minimizes its length while maximizing the reputations of the recommenders included in it. Hence, in the example in Figure 1(b), if Alice asks for the reputation of Greg in playing guitar, she has two different paths. We remark the in the computation of the reputation, the similarity of the skills are taken into account by adding a weight on an edge connecting two persons (the higher the weight, the less similar the relative skills).

The shortest one (from Steve) has the first edge labeled with a skill very different from *playing guitar*, so its weight is very high. For this reason, the longer path weights less than the previous one and it is used to compute the reputation.

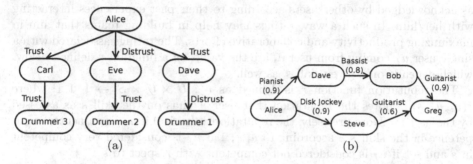

Fig. 1. Transitive closure of trust

4   The Model

We now introduce the model in which we define in a precise way the approach sketched so far. We assume a finite set $U = \{u_1, \ldots, u_n\}$ of users, that will be grouped in teams. We also assume a finite set $S = \{s_1, s_2, \ldots, s_k\}$ of skills which users are apt to perform. Skills may be related, and we introduce a *similarity* function $l : S \times S \to [0, 1]$ to take into account such relationships. We write $l(s, s')$ to denote the probability that given the presence of skill s it is likely that s' is present as well.

For example, over a set of music-related skills, one may assume that if a user is skilled in playing the acoustic guitar, she/he would more likely be able to play the electric guitar than to play the trumpet.

Furthermore, we assume that the similarity function l satisfies the following (rather intuitive) properties: (i) $\forall s \in S, l(s, s) = 1$, which means that every skill is similar to itself, and that (ii) $\forall s, s' \in S, l(s, s') = l(s', s)$, which means that a skill s is similar to another skill s' as much as s' is similar to s. We do not assume that l holds a transitivity-like or triangle inequality like property such that $\forall s, s', s'' \in S$, if $l(s, s') = x$ and $l(s', s'') = y$ then $l(s, s'') \simeq x$ or y

or $\leq x + y$. In fact, given the similarity values between s and s' and the one between s' and s'', nothing can be inferred on the existing relationship between s and s''. The exact definition of the similarity function depends of the problem instance.

In our model, both users and tasks are characterized by a set of skills. The user's skill set identifies her/his competences, while the skill set of a task denotes the competences required to accomplish it. Note that a user may participate in solving different, concurrent tasks – contributing with at least one of her/his skills – and a task may be accomplished by different teams of users having the required skills. As introduced in Section 1, the goal of this work is to find the best team to successfully accomplish a given task t characterized by a set of skills $S_t = \{s_1, \dots, s_m\}$. To do this, we take advantage of ratings assigned to each user from her/his past team co-members. Thus, the proposed model does not only leverage on skills' competence as declared by a user, but on such competencies as acknowledged by other users according to their past experiences interacting with her/him. In such a way, ratings may help in building teams that aim in maximizing productivity and collaborative efforts. The ratings associated with a single user u_f coming from user u_i are the values of a function r defined below, which depends on a given skill s, as well.

The reputation function r is defined as $r : U \times U \times S \rightarrow [-1, 1]$ where $r(u_i, u_f, s)$ denotes the reputation that user u_f has on the skill s as assessed by the user u_i. More precisely, the reputation value is 0 if u_f has a neutral competence in the skill s – according to u_i –, 1 if u_f is considered very competent in s and -1 if u_f is considered not competent with respect to s.

The reputation function r induces a directed, weighted, labeled, multigraph $\mathcal{G}$ over the set U of users: two users u_i and u_f are connected by a directed edge labeled with s and weighted with the value x if (and only if) the reputation function is such that $r(u_i, u_f, s) = x$. In general, when dealing with large online communities, we may assume that the graph $\mathcal{G}$ is not completely connected, which means that it is unlikely that all users directly know each other. Hence, we do not have all the possible reputations for all the possible users over all the existing skills. Moreover, we may assume that directly connected users have common interests, that is, they may possess similar skill sets [20].

Based on such assumptions, we propose an algorithm for computing the reputation on a skill s, between two users not necessarily directly connected in $\mathcal{G}$ by an edge labeled with skill s. This is achieved by searching the shortest path $SP(u_i, u_f)$ in $\mathcal{G}$ between u_i and u_f such that its edges satisfy the following condition: given a skill $s \in S$ and an edge $e \in E$, the weight of the edge e with respect to s, denoted by $w_s(e)$ is computed as:

$$w_s(e) = \frac{1}{l(s, s(e)) \cdot (2 + r(e))} \tag{1}$$

Informally, Formula 1 assigns higher weights to edges with skills not similar to the requested one (when they are totally different the similarity function is null, so the weight is infinite) and with low reputation. In this way, the algorithm yields a shortest path having edges with highest reputation labeled with skills more similar to the requested one. Furthermore, we require that $\forall e \in SP_s(u_i, u_f) r(e) \geq 0$, unless u_f is the starting point of edge e. We introduce such constraint because in a chain of trust one does not want rankings from untrusted sources. On the other hand, the last edge may be negative because, in such case, we are trusting a negative opinion expressed by a trusted source. We refer to such a path between two nodes as an *admissible path*.

Having defined what is an admissible path between two nodes in $\mathcal{G}$, we now proceed to describe how to compute the reputation between them with respect to a skill $s \in S$. We define an *extended* reputation function $r_s^* : U \times U \to [-1, 1]$ that takes as input a pair of users u_i, u_f and measures the reputation that u_i has of u_f about skill s. The computation of the extended reputation function is based on the reputation values defined, by different users, on the edges composing an admissible path between u_i and u_f and is the minimum value found on the admissible path of the reputation multiplied by the similarity between the skills. Thus, the extended reputation function acts as a basis for a chain of trust, introduced in Section 3, intended as a path between two users, usually composed by several edges with high reputation.

We have now the tools required to suggest a suitable team for a given task t. We propose two possible scenarios. At first we consider an ego-centric team formation, since the user asking for the task t wants to be a member of the team which will accomplish t. Then, we generalize the approach assuming a scenario in which a manager who commissions a team for a task will not be contributing personally. Given that a task t is defined over a set of skills $s_t = \{s_1, \ldots, s_n\}$, our objective is to find a set of users $T \subseteq U$ such that (i) all the skills required to accomplish the task are provided by the team members – which means that $s_t \subseteq \{\bigcup_{u \in T} s_u\}$ – (ii) each team member contributes to the fulfillment of the task with at least a skill – which means that $\forall u \in T, s_u \cap s_t \neq \varnothing$ –, (iii) the size of the team is the smallest possible, in the sense that there is a maximum of one member for each requested skill and (iv) the reputation of the team is maximized. Based on the function r^* previously described, we define the reputation of a team $T = \{u_1, u_2, \ldots, u_n\}$ as the average of the reputation of all its members, i.e., $r(T) = \frac{\sum_{u \in T} \sum_{v \in T \setminus \{u\}} r_{s_v}^*(u, v)}{|T|(|T|-1)}$.

In the first scenario, in which the user u who asked for the fulfillment of the task is also a member of the team, the algorithm first selects the "best" skill for the existing user. This is done choosing the skill with the highest reputation score according to the edges having u as end point. After this, the algorithm searches for the best user for each remaining skill. This is achieved exploring the shortest paths, rooted in u, searching for the best team member for each skill (see Algorithm 1).

The generalized version of the proposed algorithm, which is suitable for the second scenario where a third party u searches for a team in order to complete the required task according to the available reputations. The algorithm works for an egocentric team (see Algorithm 1) for every user at a fixed distance from u and returning the team with higher reputation, if it exists.

Data: a map *userskill* between skills and a list of users who possess that skill
Input: A task $t = \{s_1, \ldots, s_n\}$, an initial user $u \in U$, a searching depth limit d
Output: A team T or $\bot$ if such team can not be found within depth d
begin

$su = \texttt{select\_best\_skill}(s_u \cap s_t, u)$;
$userskill = \varnothing$;
for *each user u' distant at most d from u* **do**
  for *each skill s' of u'* **do**
    if $s' \in s_t$ **then**
      $userskill[s'].add(u')$;

if *userskill does not contain at least a user for each skill in $s_t \setminus s_u$* **then**
  Failed to find a suitable candidate for some task skill;
  return $\bot$;

for *every team T in userskill* **do**
  compute $r(T \cup u)$ and return the team with maximum reputation

Algorithm 1. Team selection given a user (egocentric team)

5 Evaluation

We now present the experimental results of the proposed approach. To the best of our knowledge there are no public datasets on team collaboration. Therefore, in order to evaluate the proposed approach, we generate a synthetic dataset.

5.1 Dataset Generation

The datasets used in the evaluation of the proposed algorithms have been generated in such a way that they respect the properties of real world social network graphs. Thus, to be comparable with real data. In particular, many studies show that complex networks vertex connectivity follows a power law distribution, mainly because new vertexes connect preferentially with already well connected ones [21,22]. Thus, to make a dataset suitable for our purposes, we create a graph of users where the edges – representing the past interactions between users – follow a power law distribution. To obtain such graph, we take advantage of a well known social graph generation algorithm from Eppstein [23] (see [24] for a more comprehensive discussion on graph generation algorithms). We tweak the algorithm so that the generated graphs resemble the Extended Epinions dataset [25] because, to the best of our knowledge, it is the real dataset most similar to what we need to evaluate our algorithms. We consider 10 skills to be sufficient to describe the competences of a significantly large community (as stated – for example – by U.S. National Research Council [26] in the case of Computer

Science). We classify the skills with a binary tree, and take as the similarity function their distance in such tree: if it is greater than the half of the longest path we consider the skills unrelated.

The assignment of the skills to users is made using different algorithms in order to simulate different degrees of cohesion in the community. The number of skills of a given user is a random number drawn with geometric distribution, since in this way there are few users with many skills, while a large number of users have only a few of them. Starting with a subset of users, we uniformly select a skill for each user in such subset. For each of such skills, we then randomly generate a set of related skills and we assign them to the neighbours of the users in the initial subset.

After that, we use a beta distribution, modeled according to real rating from Epinions dataset, to compute at random his reputation as seen from other users. We chose such distribution type for it better fits the Epinions data.

5.2   Experimental Results

To evaluate the algorithm, we performed several series of tests with the datasets generated according to the specifications previously described. For each dataset we identified the top user for each skill. That is, the user with the highest reputation for a given skill according to its incoming edges.

We simulate only the scenario in which a user wants to perform a task being one of the member of team (see Algorithm 1) because the scenario in which a user wants to commission a task to some other users is a generalized version of the first one, where the first algorithm acts as a sub-procedure for each possible team leader. We limit the search of suitable users to different distances $d \in \{4, 5, 6\}$ noting that, while increasing the search distance from 4 to 5 there is a non-negligible growth of the average reputation, for distances greater than 6 the reputation levels off.

We compare the reputation of the generated team with those of the team composed by the top users and the teams created substituting each user of the original team with the corresponding top user (excluding the user who requested the generation of the team). Figure 2 shows the team reputations using a cumulative distribution function.

We can observe that, on average, the teams generated by our algorithms have a better reputation score than the ones consisting only of top users and than the teams in which we substituted a member with a top user, especially when the user graph grows bigger, because it is more difficult to have a top user as neighbour of the selected team. We remind that the computed reputation takes into account indirect trust, therefore the computed value is greatly affected by the subjective trust that each user has in the others member of the team. Hence, according to the presented experimental results, we state that the proposed algorithm is a suitable way to identify cohesive teams that cope with the appointed tasks.

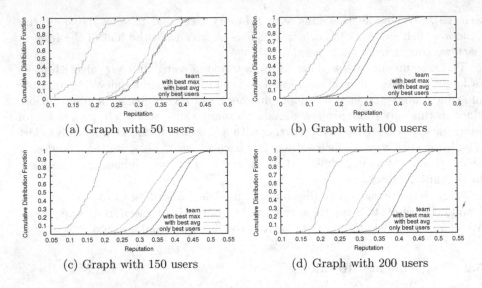

(a) Graph with 50 users   (b) Graph with 100 users

(c) Graph with 150 users   (d) Graph with 200 users

Fig. 2. The results for commissioned team in different graphs

6   Conclusions

In this paper we presented new reputation-based algorithms for team recommendation and formation. Such algorithms maximize the overall reputation between the team members. We empirically validate the algorithms on synthetic data. Such data have been generated in such a way that the obtained reputation graphs are similar to real-world social graphs. With similar we mean that the generated and real-world graphs present similar characteristics in terms of node connectivity, distribution of number of connections, and so forth.

Future Work. We are currently implementing the algorithms as module of a web-application for team recommendation [4]. The reason to do that is twofold. First of all to use the application to collect real-world team data that are required to further validate the proposed algorithms. Secondly, using crowdsourcing techniques, we will be able to extend the algorithms including a feedback mechanism. More precisely we are working on the possibility to extend the algorithms such that the result of one execution will update the social graph to provide, hopefully, better results upon subsequent executions. Eventually we are searching for some heuristic to limit the search space and speedup the team formation algorithms with the minimum loss of quality, because we are aware that the current approach becomes very slow when the graph increase in size.

Acknowledgements. S. Braghin and A. Datta's work was supported by A*Star TSRP grant number 102 158 0038. L. Bossi did part of the work during his internship at NTU Singapore.

References

1. Chhabra, M., Das, S., Szymanski, B.: Team formation in social networks. In: Proceedings of the 27th International Symposium on Computer and Information Sciences (2012)
2. Reece, S., Roberts, S., Rogers, A., Jennings, N.R.: A multi-dimensional trust model for heterogeneous contract observations. In: Proceedings of the 22nd National Conference on Artificial Intelligence, AAAI 2007, vol. 1, pp. 128–135. AAAI Press (2007)
3. Lappas, T., Liu, K., Terzi, E.: Finding a team of experts in social networks. In: Elder IV, J.F., Fogelman-Soulié, F., Flach, P.A., Zaki, M.J. (eds.) KDD, pp. 467–476. ACM (2009)
4. Braghin, S., Yong, J.T.T., Ventresque, A., Datta, A.: SWAT: Social Web Application for Team Recommendation. In: Proceedings of IEEE International Workshop on Scalable Computing for Big Data Analytics, SC-BDA (2012)
5. Kardan, A., Omidvar, A., Farahmandnia, F.: Expert finding on social network with link analysis approach. In: 2011 19th Iranian Conference on Electrical Engineering (ICEE), pp. 1–6 (May 2011)
6. Jøsang, A., Hayward, R., Pope, S.: Trust network analysis with subjective logic. In: Proceedings of the 29th Australasian Computer Science Conference, ACSC 2006, vol. 48, pp. 85–94. Australian Computer Society, Inc., Darlinghurst (2006)
7. Zheng, X., Wu, Z., Chen, H., Mao, Y.: Developing a composite trust model for multi-agent systems. In: Proceedings of the Fifth International Joint Conference on Autonomous Agents and Multiagent Systems. AAMAS 2006, pp. 1257–1259. ACM, New York (2006)
8. Reece, S., Rogers, A., Roberts, S., Jennings, N.R.: Rumours and reputation: evaluating multi-dimensional trust within a decentralised reputation system. In: Proceedings of the 6th International Joint Conference on Autonomous Agents and Multiagent Systems. AAMAS 2007, pp. 165:1–165:8. ACM, New York (2007)
9. Kazienko, P., Musiał, K., Kajdanowicz, T.: Multidimensional Social Network in the Social Recommender System. IEEE Transactions on Systems, Man, and Cybernetics - Part A: Systems and Humans 41(4), 746–759 (2011)
10. Nepal, S., Bista, S.K., Paris, C.: An association based approach to propagate social trust in social networks. In: UMAP Workshops (2012)
11. Pizzato, L., Rej, T., Akehurst, J., Koprinska, I., Yacef, K., Kay, J.: Recommending people to people: the nature of reciprocal recommenders with a case study in online dating. User Modeling and User-Adapted Interaction, 1–42 (2012)
12. Pizzato, L., Rej, T., Chung, T., Koprinska, I., Kay, J.: Recon: a reciprocal recommender for online dating. In: Proceedings of the Fourth ACM Conference on Recommender Systems, RecSys 2010, pp. 207–214. ACM, New York (2010)
13. Pizzato, L.A., Rej, T., Yacef, K., Koprinska, I., Kay, J.: Finding someone you will like and who won't reject you. In: Konstan, J.A., Conejo, R., Marzo, J.L., Oliver, N. (eds.) UMAP 2011. LNCS, vol. 6787, pp. 269–280. Springer, Heidelberg (2011)
14. Masthoff, J.: Group recommender systems: Combining individual models. In: Recommender Systems Handbook, pp. 677–702 (2011)
15. Grandison, T., Sloman, M.: A survey of trust in internet applications. Commun. Surveys Tuts. 3(4), 2–16 (2000)
16. Jøsang, A., Pope, S.: Semantic constraints for trust transitivity. In: Proceedings of the 2nd Asia-Pacific Conference on Conceptual Modelling, APCCM 2005, vol. 43, pp. 59–68. Australian Computer Society, Inc., Darlinghurst (2005)

17. Nepal, S., Sherchan, W., Paris, C.: Building trust communities using social trust. In: Ardissono, L., Kuflik, T. (eds.) UMAP Workshops 2011. LNCS, vol. 7138, pp. 243–255. Springer, Heidelberg (2012)
18. Christianson, B., Harbison, W.S.: Why isn't trust transitive? In: Crispo, B. (ed.) Security Protocols 1996. LNCS, vol. 1189, pp. 171–176. Springer, Heidelberg (1997)
19. Noam, N., Roughgarden, T., Tardos, E., Vazirani, V.V.: Algorithmic Game Theory, ch. 27. Cambridge University Press, Cambridge (2007)
20. Sarwar, B.M., Karypis, G., Konstan, J.A., Riedl, J.T.: Application of dimensionality reduction in recommender system – a case study. In: ACM Web KDD Workshop (2000)
21. Adamic, L.A., Huberman, B.A.: Power-Law Distribution of the World Wide Web. Science 287(5461), 2115 (2000)
22. Barabasi, A.L., Albert, R.: Emergence of scaling in random networks. Science 286(5439), 509–512 (1999)
23. Eppstein, D., Wang, J.: A steady state model for graph power laws. In: International Workshop on Web Dynamics (2002)
24. Chakrabarti, D., Faloutsos, C.: Graph mining: Laws, generators, and algorithms. ACM Comput. Surv. 38(1) (June 2006)
25. Massa, P., Avesani, P.: Trust-aware bootstrapping of recommender systems. In: Proceedings of ECAI 2006 Workshop on Recommender Systems, pp. 29–33 (2006)
26. On the Fundamentals of Computer Science: Challenges, N.R.C.U.C., Opportunities: Computer Science: Reflections on the Field, Reflections from the Field. National Academies Press (2004)

Semantic Aggregation and Zooming of User Viewpoints in Social Media Content

Dimoklis Despotakis, Vania Dimitrova, Lydia Lau, and Dhavalkumar Thakker

University of Leeds, School of Computing, Leeds, LS2 9JT, United Kingdom
{D.Despotakis,V.G.Dimitrova,L.M.S.Lau,D.Thakker}@leeds.ac.uk

Abstract. Social web provides rich content for gaining an understanding about the users which can empower adaptation. There is a current trend to extract user profiles from social media content using semantic augmentation and linking to domain ontologies. The paper shows a further step in this research strand, exploiting semantics to get a deeper understanding about the users by extracting the domain regions where the users focus, which are defined as viewpoints. The paper outlines a formal framework for extracting viewpoints from semantic tags associated with user comments. This enables zooming into the viewpoints at different aggregation layers, as well as comparing users on the basis of the areas where they focus. The framework is applied on YouTube content, illustrating an insight into emotions users refer to in their comments on job interview videos.

Keywords: Social media content, User model representation and extraction, Viewpoints, YouTube, Adaptive learning.

1   Introduction

The Social Web offers an abundance of user-generated content. It consists of uploaded resources and exchange of statements from readers and creators of these resources (e.g. in YouTube). For the user modelling community, this provides a rich source for extracting some knowledge-nuggets about the users. A better understanding of users will help improve subsequent adaptation and personalization. There is a recent trend in exploiting Semantic Web technologies for understanding user behaviour in social media [1, 2]. Semantics offers a great potential for modelling users by providing structure, facilitating organisation and aggregation of user contributions. This enables exploration of the large volume of user-generated content and the breath of opinions expressed by users providing opportunities to build on diversity [3] [4].

A common approach for user modelling from social media is to extract user characteristics based on concept/term lists linked to an ontology. This paper argues that semantics offers a greater potential for user modelling by providing an explicit structure to position a user model within the domain. This can allow discovering similarity, complementarity and overlap in user models to enrich the personalised experiences.

S. Carberry et al. (Eds.): UMAP 2013, LNCS 7899, pp. 51–63, 2013.

This paper proposes a framework for exploiting semantics to get a deeper understanding about the users by extracting the domain regions where the users focus. These focal areas are defined as viewpoints. The paper outlines a formal framework for extracting viewpoints from semantic tags associated with user comments. The framework is reported in (Section 3). The application of the framework is illustrated by a case study (section 4) on the detection of user viewpoints on social signals (emotion and body language) and the diversity of the viewpoints in a set of videos related to job interview.

2   Related Work

This work contributes to recent research on modelling users from Social Web, e.g. to interpret social web interactions [5] or address the cold-start problem in recommender systems [1]. Semantic Web technologies are being increasingly adopted as a powerful mechanism to make sense, aggregate and organise Social Web content by linking it with ontology concepts [2]. The extracted user profile is in the form of a set of concepts from one or several ontologies, which can enable inferring additional knowledge about the user [6]. We build on this base line and use semantic augmentation linking user comments to concepts in an ontology that presents the domain of interest. Our significant contribution to user modeling from Social Web is the further semantic analysis we conduct over the ontology concepts to aggregate them into regions that show where a user (or a group of users) is focusing on, representing this formally as viewpoints. Furthermore, we provide a zooming mechanism to analyse viewpoints at different granularity levels for concept aggregation.

The notion of user viewpoints is related to perspectives and opinions. The PerspectiveSpace presented in [7] builds upon a quantitative representation of beliefs about items, exemplified with a recommender system that exploits belief-based similarity of items (measuring user agreement and disagreement). Opinion mining research (c.f. [8, 9]) provides quantitative models where viewpoints are compared using polarity (positive to negative) or classified based on category assignment scales. Similarly, diversity of opinions in text is analysed in a quantitative way [10, 11]. User diversity is examined in [12] based on folksonomies derived from social annotations and conducting quantitative analysis of user tags. All these approaches lack qualitative analysis of content that can show user positions within the domain of interest, and can be used to explain the diversity in user generated content. The approach presented here provides such qualitative analysis, exploiting semantic aggregation and zooming.

Our qualitative modelling approach for deriving viewpoints is based on Formal Concept Analysis (FCA) [13] over an ontology concept space. FCA has been utilised for ontology navigation [14], for user profiling over document tags [15], and for deriving personal ontologies over document structuring with tags [16]. Uniquely, the FCA adaptation shown in this paper exploits an ontology that represents the domain, and defines parameters for extracting user viewpoints and related focus spaces.

3   User Viewpoints Modelling

We present here a framework for capturing, representing and analyzing user Viewpoint Semantics (ViewS) from Social media content.

Preliminaries. ViewS takes as an input user statements from a set of social media **digital objects** which include <u>user-generated textual content</u> related to a <u>specific topic</u> (e.g. user comments on YouTube videos related to job interview, a blog with user stories about travelling, or a collection of Tweets about a conference). The specific topic is linked to a **domain ontology** (or several ontologies); each ontology corresponds to some dimension about the topic which is of interest for further investigation (e.g. WordNet-Affect[1] can be used to analyse what emotions people mention when watching YouTube videos on job interviews, Geonames[2] can be used to analyse the locations people mention in travelling blogs, or the Conference Ontology[3] can be used to analyse what conference concepts are being discussed in tweets). We assume that the domain ontology is represented in RDF or OWL, which ensures that ViewS complies with existing standards and can exploit existing ontologies and available ontological tools. **Semantic augmentation** is conducted over the user-generated content, linking textual input to entities in the chosen domain ontologies. The output of semantic augmentation – a set of ontology entities - is used to analyse the focus of attention of the users, which is represented as viewpoints (as defined below).

Definition 1: User Viewpoint. Consider a set of users U ($|U| \geq 1$, where U can present an individual user or a group of users) who have made statements in a set of digital objects O ($|O| \geq 1$) related to the same domain, represented with an ontology Ω. After some semantic augmentation, the user statements are linked to a set of ontology entities C ($C \subseteq \Omega$). Using these notations, the viewpoint of user(s) U is defined as a tuple $V_U = \langle U, O, \Omega, C, F \rangle$, where F is the <u>viewpoint focus space</u> which is a layered overview onto the hierarchy graph of the ontology Ω (see Definition 5 below).

Following the above definition, *the key challenge for extracting viewpoints* is how to **extract the viewpoint focus space** F from the set of ontology entities C which is overlaid upon the ontology Ω. This requires a mechanism for deriving *sub-graphs* in Ω which show *regions of the domain* where the set of users U are focusing on, i.e. there is an *aggregation of ontology entities* from C in *close semantic proximity*. As a first step for extracting the viewpoint focus space we need an algorithm for calculating the semantic distance between two ontology entities.

Semantic Distance between Ontology Entities. To calculate the distance between two ontology entities, we exploit the subsumption (`rdfs:subClassOf`) and membership (`rdf:type`) relationships in Ω; the algorithm is presented in Fig. 1.

---

[1] http://wndomains.fbk.eu/wnaffect.html
[2] http://www.geonames.org/
[3] http://data.semanticweb.org/ns/swc/swc_2009-05-09.html

```
calculate_distance(c₁,c₂,Ω) // input is an ontology Ω and two ontology entities c₁ ∈ Ω and c₂ ∈ Ω
    if (c₁ isa c₂) or (c₂ isa c₁) or (c₁ equals c₂): // the two entities are the same or one of the entities is an instance of the other
        return 0; // the distance between an instance and its parent is assigned to 0
    else:
        p₁ = getPathToOWLThing(c₁,Ω,()) //get all paths from c₁ to the top concept in the ontology
        p₂ = getPathToOWLThing(c₂,Ω,()) //get all paths from c₂ to the top concept in the ontology

        P = (p₁ ∩ p₂)   //get the intersection of both sets of paths which provides an ordered set of common parents to the top

        if P(0) equals owl:Thing:   //get the first element from the ordered set of common parents and check if it is the top
            return ∞;// both entities are connected via the top concept, so belong to two different ontology branches, i.e. are too far
        else:
            return |(p₁ − P) ∪ (p₂ − P) ∪ P(0)|; //distance is the number of concepts in the path between the two entities
                                                  //going through their most specific common parent

getPathToOWLThing(c,Ω,p): // a recursive algorithm to get the path from an entity c to the top element in the ontology
    if c equals owl:Thing:
        return p ∪ c;
    else:
        p = p ∪ c
    return getPathToOWLThing(getParent(c|Ω),Ω,p); //get the super-class or type of c in Ω
```

Fig. 1. The algorithm to calculate semantic distance between two ontology entities. The algorithm calculates the shortest path between ontology entities based on the first common parent in the ontology hierarchy (subsumption and membership relationships).

Aggregation Mechanism. The semantic distance provides a crucial ingredient for deriving aggregated areas within the ontology space but is not sufficient to derive viewpoint focus space – we need an appropriate aggregation mechanism which utilises the computation of semantic distance. There are two crucial requirements for such a mechanism: (a) it has to allow *grouping* of entities into some abstract conceptual structures and (b) it has to deal with changing the *granularity* of the aggregation to allow analysis of viewpoints at coarse-grain or finer-grain over the domain.

To address the above requirements, we will define a qualitative framework for deriving the viewpoint focus space which adopts the Formal Concept Analysis (FCA)[13]. FCA provides a formally defined way to extract abstract conceptual structures from a collection of objects and their attributes. This adoption is based on the FCA main components, as follows:

— *formal context*, which assigns attributes to objects;
— *formal concepts*, which are the derived collections of objects and attributes through the knowledge context;
— *concept lattice*, which defines a conceptual knowledge structure with hierarchical relationships between the derived knowledge concepts.

The above points are defined below, utilising also the semantic distance algorithm.

Definition 2: Formal Context ≡ Viewpoint Context. The viewpoint context $\mathbb{V}$ is a triple $\mathbb{V} = \langle C_A, C_B, I \rangle$ where $C_A \equiv C_B \equiv C$ (i.e. the viewpoint's set of ontology entities is used as both objects and attributes for FCA; we preserve distinct annotations to follow the FCA definitions). I is read as: $c_1 \in C_A$ is related to $c_2 \in C_B$ iff $d(c_1, c_2) \leq \theta$, where $d(c_1, c_2)$ is the semantic distance, calculated with the algorithm presented in Fig 1., while θ is a threshold for assigning the binary function I based on the semantic distance d between objects and attributes in $\mathbb{V}$ (i.e. ontology entities)and is calculated with equation (1).

$$\theta = \frac{\sum_0^n w_i * d_i}{\sum_0^n w_i}, \theta : [1, \max_i d_i] \tag{1}$$

where d_i is an index distance value of all possible distances between annotated ontology entities in C and w_i is the frequency of it. θ is lower capped to 1.

Definition 3: Formal Concept $\equiv$ Viewpoint Element. Consider a viewpoint context $\mathbb{V} = \langle C_A, C_B, I \rangle$ and let $A \subseteq C_A$ and $B \subseteq C_B$. The pair (A, B) is called a viewpoint element $v = (A, B)$ iff $A = B'$ and $B = A'$: A' is the set of ontology entities related to all the ontology entities belonging to $B, i.e.$ $A' = \{c_B \in C_B | (c_A, c_B) \, \forall c_A \in A\}$, and B' is the set of ontology entities of which the related ontology entities belong to A, i.e. $B' = \{c_A \in C_A | (c_A, c_B) \, \forall c_B \in B\}$. A and B represent the extent and the intent of the viewpoint element. A forms a cluster of annotated ontology entities formed based on the application of I, i.e. these are ontology entities which are close given the semantic distance and the threshold. The set of viewpoint elements is denoted as $L(\mathbb{V})$.

Definition 4: Viewpoint Focus Element. Let $v = (A, B), v \in L(\mathbb{V})$ be a viewpoint element. The set of object entities A constitutes the boundary of a region in Ω. Using A, we define the viewpoint focus element $\mathbf{f(v)}$ as the ontology sub-graph representing the product of the aggregation of all possible paths between all elements of A over Ω.

Definition 5: Viewpoint Focus Space. The viewpoint focus space $\mathbf{F}$ is defined as the union of all the viewpoint focus elements extracted by the viewpoint elements in the viewpoint context: $F(V) = \cup f(v), \forall v \in L(\mathbb{V})$.

Definition 6: Concept Lattice $\equiv$ Viewpoint Lattice. Given a viewpoint context $\mathbb{V} = \langle C_A, C_B, I \rangle$, let $v_1 = (A_1, B_1)$ and $v_2 = (A_2, B_2)$, $v_1, v_2 \in L(\mathbb{V})$ two viewpoint elements. An <u>inheritance relation</u> is defined as $v_2 \leq v_1$ with v_2 be a sub-concept of v_1 (and vice versa, super-concept) according to the condition: $iff \, A_2 \subseteq A_1(iff \, B_1 \subseteq B_2)$. Then $\forall v \in L(\mathbb{V}), \mathfrak{B} \, (\mathbb{K}) = (L(\mathbb{V}), \leq)$ is a complete lattice, called viewpoint lattice, denoting viewpoint element relations.

The viewpoint lattice provides a structure to explore the viewpoint focus space. This structure is a composition of aggregates of ontology entities and enables semantic zooming into different granularity for aggregation. The lowest level of the lattice includes a list of ontology entities without any grouping. The highest level in the lattice gives the aggregated focus region which a user (or a group of users) has focused on. Going up in the lattice, we are exploring a more abstract space. Hence, following upward links in the lattice allows zooming into the viewpoint focus space, i.e. we get larger aggregates of ontology entities. In the following section, we will illustrate an exploration through the focus space of viewpoints derived from YouTube content.

Implementation[4]: ViewS-Microscope. The ViewS framework has been implemented in Java. The semantic augmentation utilises the Stanford Parser for text processing, as well as linguistic and semantic resources for semantic enrichment and tagging. This is presented in more detail in [17]. For ontology processing, we use the Jena Semantic Web framework[5] to retrieve the ontology(ies) structure, which is then transformed to a tree-graph representation with vertices ontology entities (concepts and instances) and edges the `rdfs:subClassOf` and `rdf:type` relationships. The formal mechanism presented in section 3 is implemented A visualisation software is implemented to illustrate the outputs of the formal framework presented in Section 3. This allows to load an ontology and semantically augmented corpus of user-generated content linked to this ontology. Using the ontology entities from the semantic tagging, the corresponding viewpoint context, elements, and lattice are constructed following the above definitions. Furthermore, two sets of ontology entities over the same ontology representing different users or groups of uses can be loaded and compared using their aggregated viewpoint focus spaces. The viewpoint point focus space is explored through the lattice by zooming into different granularity levels of aggregation. This resembles *microscope-like* exploration of viewpoints.

4   Examining YouTube Content with ViewS-Microscope

This section will illustrate the benefits of the formal mechanism for semantic aggregation and zooming presented above, by using the viewpoint visualization software ViewS-Microscope to explore the extracted viewpoints. An experimental study was conducted within one of the use cases of the EU ImREAL[6] project. ImREAL examines social signals in interpersonal communication to enrich simulated environments for learning. Job interview was selected as an interpersonal communication scenario where emotion is an important dimension.

YouTube provides a rich corpus of user interviews, where user comments can provide useful insight about emotions people associate with job interview situations. Querying the YouTube API, a corpus of 600 videos with 10,656 comments from 8,083 users was collected[7]. The YouTube API queries were constructed based on keywords elicited during a study for the evaluation of an activity modelling ontology – AMOn - including job interviews[8]. The videos were filtered based on the video metadata for video category (including "Education", "Non-profit and Activism", "People and Blogging" and "How-to and Style") and video tags (e.g. "job" and "interview"). For semantic augmentation of the textual comments WordNet-Affect was utilised to represent a taxonomy of emotions. The configuration also included selection of

---

[4] The views software is accessible at
      http://imash.leeds.ac.uk/services/ViewS
[5] *Jena Semantic Web framework* at: http://jena.apache.org/
[6] http://www.imreal-project.eu/
[7] The data and annotations are available at: http://imash.leeds.ac.uk/
      services/ViewS/Data/YouTubeDataAnnotated_JI.xml
[8] *ImREAL EU Project, deliverable D7.3*: http://www.imreal-project.eu/

WordNet lexical categories (e.g. noun.communication, verb.emotion) and SUMO concepts (e.g. Answering, SubjectiveAssessmentAttribute), relevant to interpersonal communication and social signals[9] for sense detection during the semantic enrichment process. ViewS was run to extract viewpoints, and ViewS-Microscope was utilised for exploring the focus spaces.

4.1   Semantic Aggregation and Zooming of Group Viewpoints

We will illustrate the application of ViewS over the complete set of comments, selecting age[10] as the characteristic for user grouping and comparison. Based on the indicated age in the YouTube profiles, the data sets (min:13 max:85 median: 26 mean: 20.09 sd: 9.63) was divided into six groups: [13-18], [19-21], [22-26], [27-36], [37-54] and [55-85] according to the normal distribution. Quantitative analysis over the tagged corpus showed that as age increased, concepts related to emotion were more frequently mentioned (Spearman's rho = 0.94, p = 0.034), and more distinct ontology entities were extracted (however no significant correlation was detected for this). Based on this, it could be assumed that older users mentioned a larger breadth of emotion entities[11]. However, quantitative analysis could not give an insight into the differences.

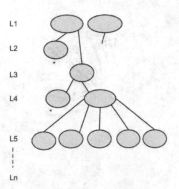

L1
L2
L3
L4
L5
Ln

Fig. 2. Partial structure of the viewpoint lattice in the study
* indicates partial view of a branch

To illustrate the benefit of ViewS for comparing user groups, we select the groups of the youngest and oldest users. With ViewS-Microscope we can examine user viewpoints at different granularity level. Ontology entities extracted from user statements are grouped in viewpoint focus elements (Definition 5), organised on a viewpoint lattice (Definition 6). ViewS-Microscope can zoom into different lattice layers enabling exploration of these elements based on the lattice hierarchy relationships (see Fig. 2). Each node in the example shows a viewpoint focus element.

The analysis starts with a viewpoint focus element in the first level (e.g. L1 in Fig. 2), which shows the smallest clusters of ontology entities. For both groups, the first level is made of two ontology entities anger and general emotion.

---

[9] The selection was performed by a social scientist expert in manual content annotation for activity modelling.

[10] The calculation are based only on those profiles for which age was provided and was smaller than 85 years old.

[11] This analysis aimed at gaining an insight of the data set possible trends, rather than concluding to decisions for stereotyping, for which deeper analysis and evaluation would be required in more domain.

After zooming into lower layer viewpoint elements linked to anger (e.g. L3 in Fig. 2), it is possible to see an expanded viewpoint focus space for both age groups (Fig. 3a and 3b). The difference between the groups is hardly noticeable.

(3.a) Younger group L2 viewpoint focus element derived from anger at L1: anger, anxiety, compassion, emotion, humility, sadness and shame, general-dislike

(3.b) Older group L2 viewpoint focus element derived from anger at L1: anger, anxiety, compassion, emotion, humility, ingratitude, sadness and shame, general-dislike

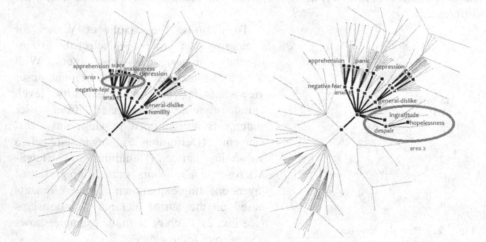

(3.c) Younger group, L5 viewpoint focus element (derived from anger at L1)

(3.d.) Older group, L5 viewpoint focus element (derived from anger at L1)

Fig. 3. Zooming into the viewpoints of both groups with ViewS-Microscope starting from layer 1 viewpoint focus element - anger. Each dot indicates an entity from the ontology. Each highlighted/darken dot indicates an entity from the viewpoint by the particular group.

However, when zooming further into L5 (which gives more inclusive level of aggregation with larger semantic distances between ontology elements), it is possible to see more clearly some difference and similarity between the groups. For example, in Figure 3c, for the younger group, the area around three particular concepts - negative-fear, anxiety and sadness (marked as area 1) is dense which indicates greater focus of this group around these three concepts. With a similar zooming (e.g. same level and viewpoint element) on the older group, a proportion of the concept space (e.g. marked as area 2) is only seen in this group (concepts: ingratitude, despair and hopelessness).

In a similar way, the focus space of positive emotions mentioned by each group is examined (Fig. 4). At L5, a slight diversity in the viewpoint focus elements is detected - compared to the older group, the younger group has more breadth in concepts related to general positive emotions.

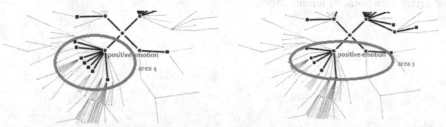

(a) Younger group, L5 viewpoint focus element in the positive emotion branch   (b) Younger group, L5 viewpoint focus element in the positive emotion branch

Fig. 4. Zooming into the YouTube comments from both groups in the ViewS Microscope for the ontology branch on positive emotions

While the quantitative comparison indicates differences between the two user groups, it does not give an insight into what these differences are with respect to the domain. The comparison with ViewS-Microscope gives deeper insight into the areas of focus for these groups over WordNet-Affect, showing their differences. Zooming into different aggregation points facilitates exploration of the underlying reason.

4.2   Semantic Aggregation for Individual User's Viewpoint Focus

The previous section illustrated the use of ViewS-Microscope for examining viewpoints of different groups which, by its nature, generally has higher number of statements and denser ontology entities. In this section, we will use ViewS-Microscope to examine viewpoints of individuals where sparse ontology entities are a norm.

For this analysis, we selected four YouTube videos used within an exploratory search environment (called I-CAW[18]) developed as part of the ImREAL project. I-CAW is a semantic data browser that aggregates digital traces, such as social media comments or personal stories, on a specific topic (e.g. Job Interview) for informal learning. The selected four YouTube videos resemble real job interview situations.

ViewS-Microscope allows exploration of an individual user's viewpoint, based on the semantic tags by that user – to illustrate this, we have chosen a female aged 22 from US. Her viewpoint focus element at L1 is plotted in Fig. 5a. The conceptual space is quite sparse and is around the ontology entity "anxiety". Fig. 5b shows the closest group to this user (i.e. female users, aged 22-26, from the US). The group has mentioned a broader range of emotion concepts. It is also possible to see additional (complimentary and contrasting) ontology entities within the group viewpoint focus.

Plotting the viewpoint of all female users (Fig. 5d) without restricting location, similar comparisons can be made. For example, overall the US female in dataset under study is utilising fewer types of positive and negative emotions, both depth and breadth-wise, than the females all over the world combined. In a similar ways, we can make comparison between two genders. In the used dataset, male users have mentioned more emotion concepts (both depth and breadth-wise). More importantly, males have named several concepts under the neutral emotion branch that are missing in the group viewpoint of female users.

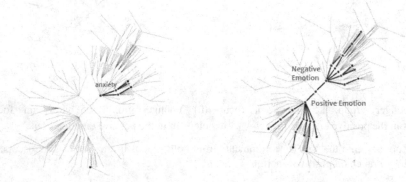

(a) Viewpoint focus element L1 of a user – female, age 22, US

(b) Viewpoint focus element L1 for a group of users – female, age 22-26, US

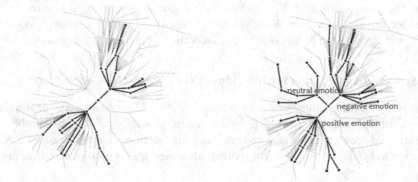

(c) Viewpoint focus element L1 for a group of users – females, age 22-26 any location

(d) Viewpoint focus element L1 for a group of users – males, age 22-26, any location

Fig. 5. Semantic aggregation for an individual user's viewpoint focus – applied over a subset of four YouTube videos showing job interview examples

5   Discussion and Conclusions

This paper presented a framework for capturing, representing and analysing user viewpoints from social media content. Central to this framework is the performing of qualitative analysis by exploiting semantics to get a deeper understanding about users.

This contributes to user modelling research by providing a richer representation of the user, extracted from social media content - viewpoints can be seen as a qualitative representation of user models (groups or individuals). Crucially, our approach allows semantic aggregation and zooming into different granularity levels of the semantic space which can empower user adaptation. We will illustrate this within a user-adaptive learning domain, considering the application context of ImREAL.

Augmented User Modelling. Augmented user modelling is about getting insights about users from social web to improve adaptation in traditional systems. People nowadays are leaving digital traces in terms of blogs, tweets, comments etc. on the Social Web, providing a *sensor* of user activities and experiences, which can be a valuable source for personalisation.   An application that can benefit from augmented user modelling is a user-adaptive simulated environment for learning which adapts the content to user profiles. One of the known challenges for such adaptation is the *cold start* problem. Using ViewS, it is possible to create group profiles from social content by aggregating and representing various group viewpoints and focus spaces. Using ViewS viewpoints of groups (e.g. based on age) based on collective statements made on digital objects representing some activity (e.g. an activity in the simulator) can be derived.   A new user of the simulated environment can be assumed to get *similar viewpoints* to a user group with the close demographics, i.e. the group viewpoints can be used in a stereotype-like way. If we a viewpoint of the user (e.g. she has made a comment and it is linked to domain concepts) ViewS can help with mapping of the individual user's viewpoint with the group viewpoint and finding complementary and similarity with viewpoint elements (and subsequent statements). This can be utilised to perform adaptation and broaden the user's perspective over the domain space.

Adaptation Authoring. User-adaptive learning applications generally have a design phase where instructional designers plan scenarios, exploration paths and content to offer to users. Zooming through the viewpoint lattice over the focus space allows: (a) Path selection: the path scenario can be built over the viewpoint lattice given current situations represented by viewpoint and going from specific to more generic spaces, i.e. exploring broader aspects. As demonstrated in Section 4.1, a current situation can include a small number of entities and progressively, by following upward links, can expand the knowledge space based on the viewpoints structure. (b) Content presentation: different granularity aggregates of focus can be presented to users, e.g. of different expertise and awareness, and at a different progress stage. As demonstrated in Section 4.2, it is possible to analyse viewpoint focus of younger group and discover areas they concentrate on, areas they miss (for example, a particular category of emotion missed by this group). The instruction designer might decide to include a scenario and training content that include domain areas this group may be missing.

Future Work. The implementation of the framework is dependent on three main parameters: (a) the definition of θ which can vary the viewpoint lattice and focus space composition, (b) the ontology structure represented by ontology features, e.g. density and expressivity, (c) definitions of lists of abstract concepts for partitioning the ontology, e.g. the concept emotion could be considered as abstract (the same as the top concept), and excluded from semantic distance paths. This will allow clustering at a lower level by separating positive and negative branches. We are implementing automatic functionalities to parse and query the viewpoint focus space based on the extracted lattice structure, and plan to examine the effect of different parameters.

Acknowledgments. The research leading to these results has received funding from the European Union Seventh Framework Programme (FP7/2007-2013) under grant agreement no ICT 257831 (ImREAL project).

References

1. Abel, F., Herder, E., Houben, G.-J., Henze, N., Krause, D.: Cross-system user modeling and personalization on the Social Web. User Modeling and User-Adapted Interaction, 1–41 (2012)
2. Bontcheva, K., Rout, D.: Making Sense of Social Media Streams through Semantics: a Survey. Semantic Web Journal (to appear)
3. Resnick, P.: Keynote: Personalised Filters Yes; Bubbles No. In: 19th International Conference on User Modeling, Adaptation, and Personalization, UMAP (2011)
4. ACM, http://acmrecsys.wordpress.com/2011/10/25/panel-on-the-filter-bubble/
5. Gao, Q., Abel, F., Houben, G.-J., Yu, Y.: A Comparative Study of Users' Microblogging Behavior on Sina Weibo and Twitter. In: Masthoff, J., Mobasher, B., Desmarais, M.C., Nkambou, R. (eds.) UMAP 2012. LNCS, vol. 7379, pp. 88–101. Springer, Heidelberg (2012)
6. Carmagnola, F., Cena, F., Console, L., Cortassa, O., Gena, C., Goy, A., Torre, I., Toso, A., Vernero, F.: Tag-based user modeling for social multi-device adaptive guides. User Modeling and User-Adapted Interaction 18, 497–538 (2008)
7. Alonso, J.B., Havasi, C., Lieberman, H.: PerspectiveSpace: Opinion Modeling with Dimensionality Reduction. In: Houben, G.-J., McCalla, G., Pianesi, F., Zancanaro, M. (eds.) UMAP 2009. LNCS, vol. 5535, pp. 162–172. Springer, Heidelberg (2009)
8. Paul, M.J., Zhai, C., Girju, R.: Summarizing contrastive viewpoints in opinionated text. In: Proceedings of the 2010 Conference on Empirical Methods in Natural Language Processing, pp. 66–76. Association for Computational Linguistics, Cambridge (2010)
9. Fang, Y., Si, L., Somasundaram, N., Yu, Z.: Mining contrastive opinions on political texts using cross-perspective topic model. In: Proceedings of the Fifth ACM International Conference on Web Search and Data Mining, pp. 63–72. ACM, Seattle (2012)
10. Bizău, A., Rusu, D., Mladenic, D.: Expressing Opinion Diversity. In: First International Workshop on Knowledge Diversity on the Web (DiversiWeb 2011), 20th World Wide Web Conference (WWW 2011), Hyderabad, India (2011)
11. Pochampally, R., Karlapalem, K.: Mining Diverse Views from Related Articles. In: First International Workshop on Knowledge Diversity on the Web (DiversiWeb 2011), 20th World Wide Web Conference (WWW 2011), Hyderabad, India (2011)
12. Kang, J.-H., Lerman, K.: Leveraging User Diversity to Harvest Knowledge on the Social Web. In: The Third IEEE International Conference on Social Computing (SocialCom 2011), Boston, USA (2011)

13. Wille, R.: Formal Concept Analysis as Mathematical Theory of Concepts and Concept Hierarchies. In: Ganter, B., Stumme, G., Wille, R. (eds.) Formal Concept Analysis. LNCS (LNAI), vol. 3626, pp. 1–33. Springer, Heidelberg (2005)
14. Cimiano, P., Hotho, A., Stumme, G., Tane, J.: Conceptual Knowledge Processing with Formal Concept Analysis and Ontologies. In: Eklund, P. (ed.) ICFCA 2004. LNCS (LNAI), vol. 2961, pp. 189–207. Springer, Heidelberg (2004)
15. Yun, Z., Boqin, F.: Tag-based user modeling using formal concept analysis. In: 8th IEEE International Conference on Computer and Information Technology (CIT), pp. 485–490 (2008)
16. Kim, S., Hall, W., Keane, A.: Using Document Structures for Personal Ontologies and User Modeling. In: Bauer, M., Gmytrasiewicz, P.J., Vassileva, J. (eds.) UM 2001. LNCS (LNAI), vol. 2109, pp. 240–242. Springer, Heidelberg (2001)
17. Despotakis, D., Thakker, D., Dimitrova, V., Lau, L.: Diversity of user viewpoints on social signals: a study with YouTube content. In: International Workshop on Augmented User Modeling (AUM) in UMAP, Montreal, Canada (2012)
18. Thakker, D., Despotakis, D., Dimitrova, V., Lau, L., Brna, P.: Taming digital traces for informal learning: a semantic-driven approach. In: Ravenscroft, A., Lindstaedt, S., Kloos, C.D., Hernández-Leo, D. (eds.) EC-TEL 2012. LNCS, vol. 7563, pp. 348–362. Springer, Heidelberg (2012)

Learning Likely Locations

John Krumm, Rich Caruana, and Scott Counts

Microsoft Research
Microsoft Corporation
One Microsoft Way
Redmond, WA 98052
USA
{jckrumm,rcaruana,counts}@microsoft.com

Abstract. We show that people's travel destinations are predictable based on simple features of their home and destination. Using geotagged Twitter data from over 200,000 people in the U.S., with a median of 10 visits per user, we use machine learning to classify whether or not a person will visit a given location. We find that travel distance is the most important predictive feature. Ignoring distance, using only demographic features pertaining to race, age, income, land area, and household density, we can predict travel destinations with 84% accuracy. We present a careful analysis of the power of individual and grouped demographic features to show which ones have the most predictive impact for where people go.

Keywords: Human mobility, location prediction, Twitter.

1 Introduction

We are interested in how we can predict whether or not a person will travel to a given destination away from their home. Such predictions could be used to better understand a person's Web search intentions when they enter an ambiguous place name, and it could be used to target advertising for potential travel destinations. We are also interested in what features of a person's home and candidate destination are important for making accurate predictions. In this paper we examine the predictive power of travel distance, demographics, and spatial features of the home and candidate destinations.

Our training and test data come from geotagged Twitter posts ("tweets") in the U.S. With the introduction of cell phones and mobile social networking sites, researchers have enjoyed a plethora of location data with which to explore human mobility. For example, MIT's Reality Mining dataset offers cell tower data from 100 people over the course of 9 months [1], and has been used for a variety of mobility studies, such as discovering frequent travel patterns [2]. Using data from 100,000 mobile phone users, Gonzalez *et al.* found that people follow simple, predictable patterns and return to just a few locations frequently [3]. In their study of bank note travel, Brockman *et al.* showed that human travel distances decay as a power law [4].

S. Carberry et al. (Eds.): UMAP 2013, LNCS 7899, pp. 64–76, 2013.

Isaacman *et al.* develop a way to generate synthetic cell phone records and show they can accurately model mobility inside urban areas [5].

Besides cell phones and bank notes, human mobility data exists on many different social networking sites, including Twitter. Certain Twitter client applications let users attach a latitude/longitude to their tweets, and these time-stamped locations give a sparsely sampled record of the users' travels. Cheng *et al.* present an interesting analysis of over 22 million geotagged tweets from over 225,000 users [6]. They examine the variation in the number geotagged tweets over time, confirm the power law distribution of displacements, and show that residents of different cities have different radii of travel. They also show that the radius of travel generally goes up with increasing income and population density of a person's home region.

As with the work above, we are interested in the interplay between travel propensity, distance, and demographics. However, unlike previous work, we attempt to learn about the attractiveness of a candidate destination, not just how far people will travel. Specifically, we want to compute whether or not a person from a given region will travel to another region, based on the distance between them and the demographic and spatial features of both. This is an important next step in analyzing human mobility, because it begins to answers questions about why people travel, which goes beyond numerical statistics about their behavior. Like Cheng *et al.*, we also use geotagged Twitter data, and we also begin by estimating each user's home location, both of which we describe in the next section.

2 Twitter Data and Home Locations

We gathered geotagged Twitter data for a period of several weeks in mid-2012. Each geotagged tweet comes with a user name, UTC time stamp, and a latitude/longitude giving the user's reported location. After the processing described below, we used data from 213,210 different Twitter users, each with at least one geotagged tweet away from their home.

For each user, we needed an estimate of their home location in order to look up the demographic and spatial features of their home region for later input to our machine learning algorithm. There are many methods for estimating home locations. For instance, Cheng *et al.* uses a recursive search grid to find the mode of the distribution of latitude/longitude locations [6]. Krumm presents four simple home-finding algorithms [7]. The best performing algorithm looked at the latitude/longitude measured nearest to, but not after, 3 a.m. each day and then computed the median latitude and longitude from these points over all days as the home location.

A more principled approach to estimating home location starts by considering when people are normally home. For the U.S., this is available from the American Time Use Survey (ATUS, http://www.bls.gov/tus/). The ATUS is an annual survey sponsored by the U.S. Bureau of Labor Statistics and administered by the U.S. Census Bureau. The survey uses telephone interviews to collect data on how, where, and with whom people spend their time. The raw data is freely available for downloading. We used ATUS data from 2006-2008 inclusive, which consists of survey results from

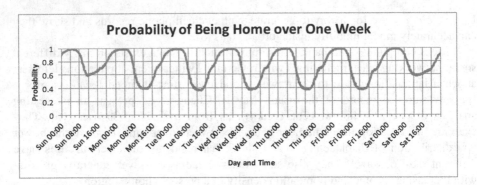

Fig. 1. Probability of being home. The probability of being home varies according to the time of day and the day of the week. The data used to derive this function comes from the American Time Use Survey (http://www.bls.gov/tus/). We used this to help estimate a person's home location from time-stamped latitude/longitude values.

almost 38,000 people. From this, we derived the time-varying probability of a person being at home, averaged into 10-minute bins over a period of one week, shown in **Fig. 1**. This plot shows that the probability of being home peaks at almost 1.0 around 1:30 a.m. on most days and drops to slightly less than 0.4 around noon on most days. The probabilities of being home during the day on weekends are less than for weekdays.

Given a set of time-stamped latitude/longitude values, we would expect the locations occurring at times of larger home probability would be more indicative of a person's home than those occurring at times of lower home probability. We formalize this by taking a weighted median of each Twitter user's latitude/longitude values, where the weights come from the home probabilities in **Fig. 1**. That is, given a time-stamped latitude/longitude, we look up the probability of being home at that time from the data in **Fig. 1**. This probability serves as the weight on both latitude and longitude, and we compute the weighted median of latitude and longitude separately to find the estimate of the home location. We use a median to avoid problems with outliers. Note that Twitter's time stamps are in coordinated universal time (UTC), and ATUS time stamps are in local time. Therefore, we used the latitude/longitude of each geotagged tweet to first convert its time stamp to local time before looking up its corresponding probability of being a home location.

We expect that the user's home location has an effect on where the user will travel. In the next section, we describe the demographic and spatial features we used as input to our predictor.

3   Spatial and Demographic Features of Visits

For each user in our database, we have their home location, as computed in the previous section, and the locations to which they've traveled, from their geotagged tweets. Our goal is to predict, for a candidate destination, whether or not a person would likely travel there. We make this prediction based on features of the person's home location and the candidate destination. Each geotagged tweet that is not at the person's home serves as a positive example of a visit. This section describes the features we used to characterize these visits for machine learning.

Other research has shown that human travel is governed by distance, with spatial displacements following certain simple distributions [3, 4]. Therefore, one of the features we use is the great circle distance between the user's home and destination. As we will see, this feature is the most powerful predictor of whether or not a user will visit a candidate destination.

The remainder of our features are demographic and spatial features in the regions of the home and destination. We take these from the 2010 American Community Survey (ACS) (http://www.census.gov/acs/www/), which is an ongoing, statistical survey from the U.S. Census Bureau. In contrast to the regular U.S. Census, the ACS is based on a subsample of the U.S. population. Our data gives aggregate demographic and spatial features for each block group in the U.S. A block group is defined by the U.S. Census, and is designed to contain 600 to 3000 people, with an ideal size of 1500 people. Our database contains 217,739 block groups for the U.S. For each block group, we have the fraction that is land (as opposed to water), number of households, median household size, median household income, and fractions of different races and ages. We use these block groups to discretize the map, computing visit probabilities for each distinct pair.

A visit is defined by a move from a user's home block group to a different block group. Approximately 1/3 the features describing a visit come from 20 demographic and spatial features of the block group containing the user's computed home location. For example, one of these features is the median income of the households in the user's home block group. Other features give the fraction of people of different races and age ranges. We use these home features to account for the possibility that characteristics of a user's home will affect their travel choices. Any tweet occurring outside the user's home block group is considered a visit, and another 1/3 of the visit's features come from the same 20 demographic and spatial features of the destination block group as we use for the home block group, e.g. the median income of the destination block group. The destination features account for the possibility that characteristics of the destination will affect the user's travel choices. Thus for each visit we have demographic and spatial features pertaining to the user's home and destination block groups. The last 1/3 of the features come from the differences between the 20 corresponding home and destination features, specifically the value of the destination feature subtracted from the corresponding home feature. For median income, this would be the amount that the home block group's median income exceeds the destination block group's median income. We include these features to account for the possibility that signed differences in features may affect a user's travel choices. For instance, it may be that people tend to visit places with incomes similar to their own.

Thus there are 60 demographic and spatial features for each visit: 20 for the home block group, 20 for the destination block group, and 20 for the differences between the home and destination block groups. In addition to these features, we add one more that gives the great circle distance between the computed home location and the geotagged latitutde/longitude of the destination.

All 61 features are detailed in Table 1. There are many more possible features to compute, such as types and density of businesses, fractions of owned and rented homes, and local attractions. We leave this for future work.

To qualify as a visit, a geotagged tweet must occur in a block group other than the user's home block group. Because of this, we ignore many geotagged tweets in the user's home block group. With this definition of a visit, we have 213,210 users in our study who have made at least one visit. The total number of visits was 3,278,230, with a mean 15.4 per user, and a median 10 per user. The minimum per user was 1, and maximum 21,763.

From our database of geotagged tweets we get positive examples of visits. To learn a classifier, we need negative examples as well. We generate synthetic negative examples for each user by randomly picking block groups that the user was not observed to visit in our data. For balance, we generate the same number of negative examples as we have positive examples for each user. To compute distance to a negative block group, we use the block group's centroid.

4   Classifying Candidate Destinations

Our goal is to create a classifier whose input is a vector of the 61 scalar features described in the previous section and whose output is a probability representing the likelihood that a person in the home block group would visit the destination block group. For training and testing, we have ground truth Twitter data with approximately 3.2 million visits and an equal number of synthetically generated negative examples.

Table 1. These are the groups, names, and descriptions of the 61 features we used for classifying candidate visits. The check marks indicate those features computed for the user's home and destination locations as well as the difference in value between the home and destination locations.

Feature Group	Feature Name	Description	Home	Dest.	Diff.
Distance	Distance	Distance between home and destination			✓
Income	Median income	Median income in U.S. dollars	✓	✓	✓
Race	Non-Hispanic White	Fraction non-Hispanic whites	✓	✓	✓
	Non-Hispanic Black	Fraction non-Hispanic blacks	✓	✓	✓
	Non-Hispanic Indian	Fraction non-Hispanic Indians	✓	✓	✓
	Non-Hispanic Asian	Fraction non-Hispanic Asians	✓	✓	✓
	Non-Hispanic Islander	Fraction non-Hispanic islanders	✓	✓	✓
	Non-Hispanic Other	Fraction non-Hispanic other than above	✓	✓	✓
	Non-Hispanic Two	Fraction non-Hispanic two or more races	✓	✓	✓
	Hispanic	Fraction Hispanic	✓	✓	✓
Age	Under 10	Fraction under 10 years old	✓	✓	✓
	10-19	Fraction 10-19 years old	✓	✓	✓
	20-29	Fraction 20-29 years old	✓	✓	✓
	30-39	Fraction 30-39 years old	✓	✓	✓
	40-49	Fraction 40-49 years old	✓	✓	✓
	50-59	Fraction 50-59 years old	✓	✓	✓
	60-69	Fraction 60-69 years old	✓	✓	✓
	Over 69	Fraction over 69 years old	✓	✓	✓
Household Size	Mean household size	Mean number of persons in household	✓	✓	✓
Household Density	Houshold Density	Households per unit land area	✓	✓	✓
Land Fraction	Land Fraction	Fraction of land area (as opposed to water)	✓	✓	✓

Our classifier is a boosted decision tree. Boosting [8] is a meta-learning procedure that can be applied to different supervised learning methods such as decision trees, neural nets, and SVMs. In this paper we apply boosting to decision trees. In the 1st round of boosting, a decision tree is trained on the data set with equal importance given to all training examples. This tree is added to the model, and the prediction errors it makes on the training set are recorded. In the 2nd round a 2nd tree is trained on the training set which gives more emphasis to the errors made by the 1st model. The predictions of this 2nd tree are added to the predictions of the 1st tree. The combined predictions of the two trees usually are more accurate than the predictions of either tree alone. This process of adding trees to the prediction model, with each new tree being trained to correct the errors made by the previous trees, is repeated until the model contains a fixed number of trees, or until accuracy stops improving as more trees are added to the model. For the boosted models in this paper, we use 100 iterations of boosting and observed that accuracy improved by less than 2 percentage points after adding more trees up to 1000. In practice, boosted decision trees yield high accuracy models on many problems and for many different metrics [9].

One advantage of models based on decision trees is that decision tree models are not sensitive to the particular range or *shape* of a feature distribution. Features such as distance, household income, and household density are not naturally expressed with similar ranges of numbers and are far from uniformly distributed. For example it is common in machine learning to transform features such as household income by normalizing or taking the log of the value, or by computing a fraction into the cumulative household income distribution, to linearize these non-uniform features in order to make them more suitable for models such as linear regression, neural nets, or SVMs with linear or non-linear kernels. Decision trees, however, because they are based on threshold cuts on feature values, are not sensitive to the ranges nor shapes of feature distributions and are unaffected by monotonic feature transformations. Thus there is no need to find suitable transformations for features such as income or distance prior to training the model. This makes applying decision trees to data sets with non-uniform features easier. It also makes it easier to interpret the results of experiments that measure the importance of features, because they are not biased by the feature distribution. We explore the predictive power of various features in the next section.

5   Results and Discussion

In this section we discuss classification accuracy and look for which features work best to find likely travel destinations.

Using two-fold cross validation, our average overall classification accuracy was 0.95. This means that our classifier correctly classified 95% of the test visits. Since our classifier produces a probability, we can set a classification threshold to trade off false positives (classifying a visit as positive when it is not) and false negatives (classifying a visit as negative when it is not). This tradeoff is embodied in the ROC curves shown in Fig. 2. The ideal operating point is the upper left, which has all true positives and no false positives. Using all 61 features comes close to this point. Using distance alone works well, too, followed by using all the features but distance. Section 5.2 examines more closely the predictive power of certain features.

We were careful not to split users' data in our cross validation runs. If we made an arbitrary 50/50 split for two-fold cross validation, it may be that the data from some users would be split between testing and training, which may give an artificial accuracy boost. Instead, we made sure that the users in the testing and training datasets were non-overlapping.

5.1   Example Maps

Fig. 3 shows results of our classification algorithm. The first map shows places likely visited by someone living in Redondo Beach, California, whose location is shown as a large disk. The smaller disks show the centers of all the block groups that were classified as a destination by someone living in Redondo Beach. There is a dense cluster in the lower 2/3 of California, and another strong cluster along the coast in the northeast U.S. The second map shows likely destinations of someone living in Manhattan, NY. Here we see results clustered around the home location, and also up and down both coasts. The third map shows destinations for someone whose home is in the small town of Milburn, Nebraska (population 55). Unlike the previous two maps, many of Milburn's likely destinations are in the so-called flyover states in the middle of the country. For all three home locations, popular destinations are southern California, Florida, and the area around New York City and Washington, D.C.

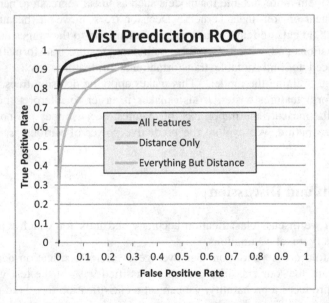

Fig. 2. Receiver operating characteristic curve for visit classifier. Using all features works best, followed by distance only, and then all features but distance.

The analysis above looks at the probability of all destinations given a certain home location. We can also reverse the condition and look at the probability of all home locations given a certain destination. For the given destination, this shows which locations contain people who would want to travel there. Fig. 4 shows some samples. The first map suggests that people in every part of the U.S. would find it attractive to visit Redondo Beach. In fact, the classification results give a high probability of visiting Redondo Beach from *every* block group in the U.S., with the lowest probability being 0.93. The second map shows that Minneapolis, Minnesota has regional appeal to the neighboring states. The third map in Fig. 4 suggests that tiny Milburn, Nebraska appeals to mostly people from the same state. An analysis like this could be useful for targeting travel-related ads to those most likely to respond positively.

Home in Redondo Beach, Home in Manhattan, New Home in Milburn, Nebraska
California   York   (population 55)

Fig. 3. Destination predictions for three different home locations. The home locations are shown as large disks, and the visited locations are shown as smaller disks, with darker ones more probable. Depending on the home location, the predicted destinations change significantly, with a cluster around the home location.

One of the reasons we chose Milburn, Nebraska as an example is that we have only four tweets from its block group, all from two users who appear to have uniformly covered most of the U.S. with geotagged tweets. There is only one user whose home was placed in Milburn's block group. While this is not nearly enough raw data to make predictions about Milburn's travel likelihoods, we can still make a reasonable prediction for this home region. Our features group Milburn with other regions of similar demographic and spatial features, meaning we can overcome the paucity of available data. This is one of the advantages of abstracting away the raw latitude/longitude locations in favor of descriptive features. The abstraction also helps us understand which features affect people's travel choices, which we explore next.

5.2 Feature Subsets

While it is gratifying to know we can classify accurately, it is more interesting to know which features lead to this level of accuracy. This is the core of our contribution, because it begins to answer, for the first time, how a person might choose their travel destinations. This is the natural next investigative step to take after much past research on the numerical statistics of human mobility.

Redondo Beach has strong, wide appeal | Minneapolis, Minnesota has regional appeal | Milburn has more limited appeal

Fig. 4. Classifying which home locations find a given destination attractive. The destination locations are shown as large disks, and the home locations are shown as smaller disks, with darker ones more probable.

Table 2. Classification accuracy of individual features. Distance is the best single feature.

Feature	Classification Accuracy	Feature	Classification Accuracy
Distance	0.91	Age 50-59 Fraction (home - destination)	0.57
Race Not Hispanic Asian Fraction (destination)	0.67	Land Area Fraction (destination)	0.56
Age 20-29 Fraction (destination)	0.64	Age Under 10 Fraction (home - destination)	0.56
Race Not Hispanic White Fraction (home - destination)	0.64	Age 30-39 Fraction (home - destination)	0.56
Race Not Hispanic White Fraction (destination)	0.63	Race Not Hispanic Islander Fraction (home - destination)	0.55
Age 30-39 Fraction (destination)	0.62	Race Not Hispanic Indian Fraction (home - destination)	0.54
Age 10-19 Fraction (destination)	0.62	Age 40-49 Fraction (home - destination)	0.53
Household Density (destination)	0.62	Median Income (home - destination)	0.53
Race Hispanic Fraction (destination)	0.62	Mean Household Size (home - destination)	0.53
Race Not Hispanic Two or More Fraction (destination)	0.61	Race Not Hispanic Indian Fraction (destination)	0.52
Race Not Hispanic Other Fraction (destination)	0.61	Race Not Hispanic Other Fraction (home)	0.50
Race Not Hispanic Asian Fraction (home - destination)	0.61	Race Not Hispanic Islander Fraction (home)	0.50
Age Under 10 Fraction (destination)	0.60	Race Not Hispanic Indian Fraction (home)	0.50
Age 60-69 Fraction (destination)	0.60	Race Not Hispanic Two or More Fraction (home)	0.50
Race Hispanic Fraction (home - destination)	0.60	Race Not Hispanic Asian Fraction (home)	0.50
Race Not Hispanic Black Fraction (destination)	0.60	Age 40-49 Fraction (home)	0.50
Age 50-59 Fraction (destination)	0.60	Land Area Fraction (home)	0.50
Race Not Hispanic Black Fraction (home - destination)	0.59	Age 50-59 Fraction (home)	0.50
Race Not Hispanic Two or More Fraction (home - destination)	0.59	Age 60-69 Fraction (home)	0.50
Age 20-29 Fraction (home - destination)	0.59	Age Over 69 Fraction (home)	0.50
Race Not Hispanic Islander Fraction (destination)	0.58	Race Hispanic Fraction (home)	0.50
Age 60-69 Fraction (home - destination)	0.57	Age 20-29 Fraction (home)	0.50
Household Density (home - destination)	0.57	Age 30-39 Fraction (home)	0.50
Age Over 69 Fraction (home - destination)	0.57	Race Not Hispanic Black Fraction (home)	0.50
Race Not Hispanic Other Fraction (home - destination)	0.57	Age Under 10 Fraction (home)	0.50
Mean Household Size (destination)	0.57	Race Not Hispanic White Fraction (home)	0.50
Median Income (destination)	0.57	Age 10-19 Fraction (home)	0.50
Land Area Fraction (home - destination)	0.57	Mean Household Size (home)	0.50
Age 10-19 Fraction (home - destination)	0.57	Household Density (home)	0.50
Age 40-49 Fraction (destination)	0.57	Median Income (home)	0.50

We can easily assess the classification power of single features by rerunning our learning and test procedure on each feature individually. For instance, we can compute the classification accuracy using distance alone, median home income alone, *etc.* The results of this experiment are show in Table 2. This shows that distance is the best individual feature in terms of classification accuracy. The 19 worst features give classification accuracies of 0.5, which means they are no better than random guessing for this two-class problem. The second best feature is "Race Not Hispanic Asian Fraction (destination)", which implies that the fraction of Asians at the destination is a relatively important feature, although it only achieves a classification accuracy of 0.67 when used alone.

If a feature works well by itself, then it will continue to work well in combination with others. The opposite is not true: if a feature does not work well by itself, it can still be effective in combination with others. Thus we next examine groups of features.

Table 3. Classification accuracy of selected groups of features. Omitting distance still gives good accuracy. Race is somewhat high, while features around the home are not important when used alone in a group.

Feature Group	Classification Accuracy
All Features	0.95
Distance	0.91
All But Distance	0.84
Race	0.81
Destination (All Features)	0.79
Home - Destination (All Features)	0.79
Race at Destination	0.74
Age	0.73
Race (Home - Destination)	0.73
Age at Destination	0.71
Age (Home - Destination)	0.67
Household Density	0.65
Income	0.60
Land Fraction	0.59
Household Size	0.59
Race at Home	0.49
Age at Home	0.49
Home (All Features)	0.49

This analysis of individual features suggests that some groups of features may be more powerful than others. For instance, in Table 2, we see that destination features are generally ranked above home features. Also, after the distance feature, we see a mix of race and age features until "Mean Household Size (destination)" at number 27.

We can assess groups of features in the same way, by training and testing our classifier on certain subsets of features. Table 3 shows the results of this experiment for some manually chosen feature subsets. The constituent features in most of the groups are obvious by the group names. Note that the Race feature group contains all the race fraction features, and the Age feature group contains all the age range features. Only "All Features" and "Distance" have the distance feature. Other groups include those features computed from the home and destination block groups as well as the differences between features in these block groups.

We see that using all features gives an accuracy of 0.95, followed closely by distance alone at 0.91. Combined with our analysis of individual features above, this shows that distance is the dominant feature determining travel. Equally interesting, however, is the relatively high accuracy of the all-but-distance group at 0.84. This shows that demographic and spatial features are important considerations in picking a travel destination. While the distance feature alone works well, it is helped by non-distance features, boosting accuracy from 0.91 to 0.95. We also see that race is an important consideration, with a classification accuracy of 0.81. While this seems a somewhat uncomfortable conclusion, it may well be that race is not an explicit consideration when choosing a destination, but serves as a proxy for visiting relatives or cultural events. We note that "Race at Destination" ranks significantly higher than "Race at Home". Home features generally rank lower than those involving the destination, with "Home (All Features)" (all features around home) doing no better than random guessing. Apparently, the destination is a more important consideration than the person's home when choosing where to go.

While the analysis above shows which features are important in predicting destinations, it does not show *how* the features affect a destination's likelihood. For instance, we have shown that distance is an important predictive feature, but we don't yet know if smaller distances increase or decrease the likelihood of a visit. For individual features, we can answer this question by looking at the distributions of the feature's values for both positive and negative examples. As we expect, for the distance feature, the mean distance of the positive examples is less than the mean distance for the negative examples, and this difference in means is statistically significant. This means that nearby destinations are more attractive than distant ones. We did this test on all 61 individual features, and the results are shown in Table 4. For each feature, we computed the means of the positive and negative examples. We used a two-sample t-test to accept or reject the hypothesis that the means were equal. In Table 4, an arrow indicates that the difference in means for a feature was statistically significant at the $\alpha=0.05$ level. If the arrow points up, then the mean of the positives was greater than the mean of the negatives. For instance, the up arrow for "Median income" at the destination means that the median income at positive sample destinations was higher than that at negative samples. Apparently higher median income makes a destination more attractive. We can also look at the difference (home − visit) of "Median Income", which has a down arrow. This feature looks at the difference in median income between the home and destination, and the down arrow

Table 4. Individual features' effects on visit likelihood. An up arrow indicates that the mean of the feature is higher for visits than it is for non-visits. A down arrow indicates that the mean feature value is lower for visits. An × indicates that the difference in means was not statistically significant. None of the purely "home" features showed a significant difference in the means.

Feature Group	Feature Name	Description	Home	Dest.	Diff.
Distance	Distance	Distance between home and destination	N/A	N/A	↓
Income	Median income	Median income in U.S. dollars	✗	↑	↓
Race	Non-Hispanic White	Fraction non-Hispanic whites	✗	↓	↑
	Non-Hispanic Black	Fraction non-Hispanic blacks	✗	↑	↓
	Non-Hispanic Indian	Fraction non-Hispanic Indians	✗	↓	↑
	Non-Hispanic Asian	Fraction non-Hispanic Asians	✗	↑	↓
	Non-Hispanic Islander	Fraction non-Hispanic islanders	✗	↑	↓
	Non-Hispanic Other	Fraction non-Hispanic other than above	✗	↑	↓
	Non-Hispanic Two	Fraction non-Hispanic two or more races	✗	↑	↓
	Hispanic	Fraction Hispanic	✗	↑	↓
Age	Under 10	Fraction under 10 years old	✗	↓	↑
	10-19	Fraction 10-19 years old	✗	↓	↑
	20-29	Fraction 20-29 years old	✗	↑	↓
	30-39	Fraction 30-39 years old	✗	↑	↓
	40-49	Fraction 40-49 years old	✗	↓	↑
	50-59	Fraction 50-59 years old	✗	↓	↑
	60-69	Fraction 60-69 years old	✗	↓	↑
	Over 69	Fraction over 69 years old	✗	↓	↑
Household Size	Mean household size	Mean number of persons in household	✗	↑	↓
Household Density	Houshold Density	Households per unit land area	✗	↑	↓
Land Fraction	Land Fraction	Fraction of land area (as opposed to water)	✗	↓	↑

implies that a smaller difference makes the visit more likely. An interesting pattern in Table 4 is that all the purely "home" features are not statistically significant, implying that they have little effect on the choice of a destination. This supports a similar conclusion we made after looking at the predictive power of the whole group of purely "home" features in Table 3. We also note that a higher proportion of people in the age range 20-39 increases the attractiveness of a destination, while people in other age ranges tends to decrease its attractiveness. To the best of our knowledge, this is the first systematic examination of how various features affect the likelihood of a visit.

6   Conclusions

We have shown that we can accurately predict which places a person will visit based on the travel distance, demographics, and spatial features of the person's home and destination. Our experiments were based on over 3.2 million visits made by over 200,000 Twitter users. These experiments are some of the first to attempt to understand how people pick destinations, going beyond just statistics about their travel. We found that we could predict destinations down to the Census block level with 95% accuracy, or 84% accuracy if we ignore travel distance. We found that distance is the dominant feature in predicting where someone will go, but that non-distance features still perform well, and they help in combination with distance. In examining groups of features, we found that features around the home are in general less powerful predictors than features around the destination. We also showed how the relative values of features affect the likelihood of a visit.

We see our work as one of the first steps toward automatically understanding how people pick travel destinations. Future work should examine the role of other features, like businesses, attractions, weather, and seasons, which we feel will be important.

Acknowledgments. Thank you to the TLC team at Microsoft Research for providing their machine learning package and to Ed Katibah of SQL Server for spatial data.

References

1. Eagle, N., Pentland, A.: Reality mining: sensing complex social systems. Personal and Ubiquitous Computing 10(4), 255–268 (2006)
2. Bayir, M.A., Demirbas, M., Eagle, N.: Discovering SpatioTemporal Mobility Profiles of Cellphone Users. In: 10th IEEE International Symposium on a World of Wireless Mobile and Multimedia Networks (WoWMoM 2009), Kos, Greece, pp. 1–9 (2009)
3. González, M.C., Hidalgo, C.A., Barabási, A.-L.: Understanding individual human mobility patterns. Nature (453), 779–782 (2008)
4. Brockmann, D., Hufnagel, L., Geisel, T.: The scaling laws of human travel. Nature 439, 462–465 (2006)
5. Isaacman, S., et al.: Human Mobility Modeling at Metropolitan Scales. In: Tenth Annual International Conference on Mobile Systems, Applications, and Services (MobiSys 2012), Low Wood Bay, Lake District, UK (2012)

6. Cheng, Z., et al.: Exploring Millions of Footprints in Location Sharing Services. In: 5th International AAAI Conference on Weblogs and Social Media (ICWSM), Barcelona, Spain (2011)
7. Krumm, J.: Inference Attacks on Location Tracks. In: LaMarca, A., Langheinrich, M., Truong, K.N. (eds.) Pervasive 2007. LNCS, vol. 4480, pp. 127–143. Springer, Heidelberg (2007)
8. Friedman, J.H.: Greedy Function Approximation: A Gradient Boosting Machine. The Annals of Statistics 29(5), 1189–1232 (2001)
9. Caruana, R., Niculescu-Mizil, A.: An Empirical Comparison of Supervised Learning Algorithms. In: 23rd International Conference on Machine Learning (ICML 2006), pp. 161–168 (2006)

Scrutable User Models and Personalised Item Recommendation in Mobile Lifestyle Applications

Rainer Wasinger[1], James Wallbank[1], Luiz Pizzato[1], Judy Kay[1], Bob Kummerfeld[1], Matthias Böhmer[2], and Antonio Krüger[2]

[1] School of Information Technologies, The University of Sydney, 2006, Australia
[2] DFKI GmbH, Saarbrücken, 66123, Germany
{rainer.wasinger,james.wallbank,luiz.pizzato,judy.kay,
bob.kummerfeld}@sydney.edu.au, {matthias.boehmer,krueger}@dfki.de

Abstract. This paper presents our work on supporting scrutable user models for use in mobile applications that provide personalised item recommendations. In particular, we describe a mobile lifestyle application in the fine-dining domain, designed to recommend meals at a particular restaurant based on a person's user model. The contributions of this work are three-fold. First is the mobile application and its personalisation engine for item recommendation using a content and critique-based hybrid recommender. Second, we illustrate the control and scrutability that a user has in configuring their user model and browsing a content list. Thirdly, this is validated in a user experiment that illustrates how new digital features may revolutionise the way that paper-based systems (like restaurant menus) currently work. Although this work is based on restaurant menu recommendations, its approach to scrutability and mobile client-side personalisation carry across to a broad class of commercial applications.

Keywords: Mobile personalisation, user modelling, scrutability, and recommender technology.

1 Introduction

Mobile computing devices and other pervasive hardware have become powerful and affordable enough to enable ubiquitous computing environments to become a part of everyday life. There is a great potential for the use of mobile devices in retail and hospitality domains, and these domains are only just beginning to experiment with the use of pervasive computing.

Greater interaction between consumers, services, and products introduces new areas of exploration for user control and understanding of what is actually happening in these environments. A key way to tackle this is to make scrutable pervasive personalised systems. That is, we explore how a recommendation system can explain to a user why it made the personalised choices that it did.

S. Carberry et al. (Eds.): UMAP 2013, LNCS 7899, pp. 77–88, 2013.

Similarly, user control can be achieved when a user gives feedback within the scrutable interface to refine the recommendation process.

Building upon our previous work [14,9], this research aims to explore, via an implemented mobile application, the use of client-side and user-owned user models and increased levels of user scrutability, and to provide a practical approach to mobile personalisation using customised recommendation logic. This work is significant because it presents an implemented solution that addresses a range of mobile personalisation and user modelling concerns highlighted as important in the literature, such as ownership, accessibility, scrutability, and user control [15,3,7]. From the user's perspective, this work provides a personalised recommender where the user has complete control over the management and use of their personal data and where this personal information remains on their own mobile device.

2   Related Work

Traditional paper-based menus have not changed very much over time. They typically list dishes, often grouped by type or course; ingredients; prices; and sometimes pictures. However, the ongoing transition from printed to digital menus has introduced new options, including new rich multimedia content, detailed information (e.g. nutrition), and personalisation [9].

In contrast, in the area of recipe and food recommendation, much work has already been done (e.g. [4,1,5,11]). Although much of this work could theoretically be integrated into mobile lifestyle applications like digital restaurant menus, it is unclear with the many options available which would actually succeed and be accepted by users as an alternative to paper-based methods.

Some vendors have deployed digital restaurant menus using different form factors, such as the E-Table (http://www.e-table-interactive.com) and the eMenu (http://www.emenu-international.com). Both systems have features such as direct ordering (i.e. without calling a waiter) and visualizing dishes. Neither, however, supports client-side user-modelling, mobile personalisation, and scrutability.

Outlined in [15,8], modern adaptive systems that incorporate user-modelling components need to satisfy not just a number of functional requirements but also end-user requirements such as the accessibility, location, ownership, scrutability, user control, and reuse of user model content. Although there has been research conducted into user-modelling (see [8] for a state-of-the-art survey), recommender strategies [12], and even scrutability [7,2,13], there is a gap between research with these individual themes and the practical application of these themes in working prototypes that have been evaluated by end-users.

3   Menu Mentor - A Digital Restaurant Menu System

Menu Mentor is a mobile application that provides its users with digital restaurant menus. It is capable of recommending meals for a particular restaurant to a user on their mobile device, using food-related information about that user (i.e. dislikes, allergies and food constraints associated with user goals in terms of healthy eating). The application essentially allows for a completely new customer experience that is built upon a digital experience rather than the traditional paper-based experience as is currently commonplace in restaurants.

When in the 'standard' mode, the customer is presented with a physical restaurant menu in a digital form appropriate to the mobile device (e.g. smartphone and/or tablet). In addition to regular restaurant menu features, the customer is provided with new functionalities, such as the logging of meal nutritional information into a user model. In the 'personalised' mode, Menu Mentor presents a ranked list of meal recommendations and makes it easy to determine why a meal was or was not recommended. Upon visiting another restaurant, the customer's previous meal feedback is used to inform new recommendations.

3.1   Scenario Walkthrough

Jane Smith is a customer at the Shelly's Farm and Sea Gourmet restaurant. Jane has used Menu Mentor before and has previously provided information on her likes, dislikes, and allergies. These are now stored in her client-side PersonisJ user model [6]. Her user model also contains individual meal ratings, and the weightings for specific ingredients, based on Jane's previous ratings of other restaurant meals.

The digital version of the restaurant's menu contains a comprehensive list of items available at the venue. The descriptions include both information that is standard in physical restaurant menus as well as new information that is more suited to a digital menu and that is not typically found in a physical restaurant menu, such as estimated waiting time, chef's comments, nutritional information, detailed ingredient listings, meal history, and drink suggestions.

In this scenario, the Menu Mentor application installed on Jane's mobile device receives the menu model from the restaurant and displays Shelly's Farm and Sea Gourmet restaurant as being nearby (Figure 1A). On selection of the restaurant, the restaurant menu is passed along with Jane's user model to a personalisation engine. This process returns a total personalised score for each meal as well as information about what likes, dislikes, allergies, and ingredients correspond to each meal.

Jane is then presented with the navigation page of the menu application. She wants a three course meal, but would like recommendations for the main meals. Jane navigates to the main meals section (Figure 1B) and switches the application into the personalised mode. She sees the following ranked items: 1.Grilled Seafood Platter for Two, 2.Lobster Mornay, 3.Spaghetti Marinara, 4.Surf and Turf, etc. (Figure 1C).

Jane likes all of the recommended meals but is confused that 'Surf and Turf' is not suggested first. She drills down into the meal's details and sees the positives and negatives that contributed to the meal's personalised score (Figure 2, left): positive is that she likes beef and garlic; negative is that she dislikes onion. Jane

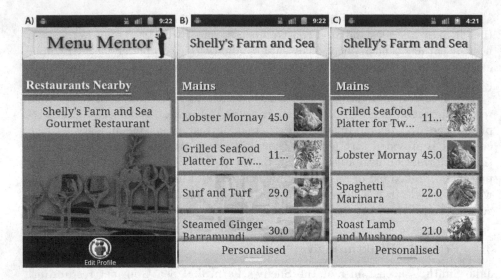

Fig. 1. Menu Mentor lists nearby restaurants (A), a non-personalised menu (B), and a personalised menu with recipes in green and red indicating their recommendation score (C)

realises that, even though this meal has a positive overall score, meals ranked higher had no dislikes, and hence were deemed preferable for her.

At this point in the example, if Jane still thinks the Surf and Turf is not being recommended to her properly she can take one or more of the following actions: remove her dislike of onion from her profile; add prawns and green beans as likes to her profile; or give a high star rating for the meal. However, Jane did not know this meal contained onion and is no longer confused about its rank in the recommendations. With this new knowledge, she calls the waiter and orders the Lobster Mornay.

3.2   Architecture and Implementation

As shown in Figure 3, the Menu Mentor application architecture consists of two main components: the restaurant data repository, which is stored on a publicly-accessible server, and the mobile application, which has been built for the Android platform. A novel aspect of this work is that it illustrates how client-side user-models - i.e. those that are owned and controlled by users themselves - can be integrated into larger public systems. In particular, Figure 3 illustrates how the server provides only the restaurant menu data to the mobile application, with all personalisation taking place on the device itself.

Restaurant Data Repository and Client-Side User Modelling. The restaurant data repository (Figure 3, left) holds the menus of all participating

Fig. 2. Scrutable meal feedback for the 'Surf and Turf' main meal, displayed as a scrollable list that has (for illustration purposes) been split into three columns

restaurants. The Venue Menu Schema (VMS) provides a standard XML format for venue menus and was developed specifically for this application, based on the recipe markup language RecipeML. Each restaurant's menu is paired with the GPS coordinates of the restaurant so that customers can be provided with digital menu information for venues that are near to their physical location.

The Menu Mentor application makes use of the PersonisJ mobile client-side user-modelling framework [6]. This runs on Android devices and provides its users with the ability to securely store and share user information between applications on the mobile device as well as to synchronise such information with a user's cloud-based user model (Figure 3, right). An important feature of the implementation is that it provides a white-list functionality that requires users to specifically allow access to their user model for each application that requests such access. Without this feature, there would be a fundamental lack of user control. Among the data stored in the PersonisJ model are the user's likes, dislikes, and allergies. In addition, the user can also provide meal ratings and ingredient weightings, all recorded as a value from 0 to 5.

Control and Scrutability. As argued in [15,7], user model scrutability should be an important part of all personalised mobile applications. By increasing a user's understanding of how their user model and feedback contributes to the resulting menu item rankings, the application helps the user feel in control of their recommendations, thereby enhancing their experience of the system.

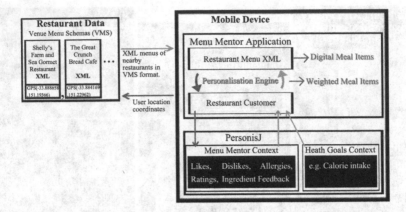

Fig. 3. The Menu Mentor system architecture, showing the server-side restaurant data on the left, and the mobile device application (including user model) on the right

In the Menu Mentor prototype, scrutability is provided at the menu item level along with the other meal details. The feedback is only shown when in the "personalised" mode, and it is organised under the "Personalised Score" heading (Figure 2). The user sees a total score, which is either green or red depending on whether the score is positive or negative. Underneath the total, is an itemised list showing the scores that contribute to the total personalised score. This list contains the user's meal rating, matched likes, dislikes and allergies, as well as individual ingredient feedback. These itemised scores are similarly coloured green or red to indicate positive or negative score contributions. By viewing this, a user is able to tell which specific ingredients or categories in a particular meal affect that meal's personalised score. This information can be used to either confirm the user's own assumptions, or alternatively, to prompt the user to adjust their personal information and meal rating.

Mobile Client-Side Personalisation. Mobile client-side personalisation is a key focus of this work, and refers to the implemented mobile personalisation engine as well as the adopted menu item recommender strategy. Notably, the recommender strategy combines content and critique-based meal recommendations with scrutability and user feedback. Additionally, mobile personalisation encapsulates the use of digital menu features to enhance pervasive client-side mobile personalisation on both the Menu Mentor application and other applications with access to the mobile owner's user model. In the domain of healthy eating, such features include the ability to save the nutrition of a meal to the phone's user model and the defining of health goals in this model to drive personalised meal recommendations.

The Menu Mentor system uses a content and critique-based hybrid recommender strategy [12]. This differs from previous work by exploiting multiple sources of user input such as the user's likes, dislikes, allergies, meal ratings, and long-term ingredient feedback. These weightings are then used to display menu items sorted in descending order, with the highest score being the most recommended. All of these sources are loaded from and added to the smartphone owner's user model. The simple act of enabling users to enter their main ingredient or category likes, dislikes, and allergies, is shown in the study to provide a sense of personalised user control over a restaurant menu.

We explain the recommendation approach in detail because the design was influenced by the goal of scrutability. Weightings in the recommendation algorithm were heuristically derived such that allergies were weighted more heavily than a user's star rating for meals, their specified ingredient likes and dislikes, and their feedback on individual ingredients. In this implementation, a positive weight of twenty was given to user likes and a negative weight of twenty was given to user dislikes. This was deemed appropriate as it provided enough power for likes and dislikes to distinguish clearly between preferred meals. Allergies, in comparison, were given a negative weighting of five hundred to guarantee that they would not be recommended regardless of other feedback for that meal. Assigning a score for such meals meant that they were still provided as part of the recommendation list.

Allowing users to dynamically correct recommendations has been shown to be very influential on the user perception of recommendation reliability [5]. This prototype system allows the user to critique presented items via meal star ratings (Figure 2, left). Each unique meal star rating is recorded to the local user model and has a direct positive effect on the meal's personalised score, with high star ratings having a larger score weighting than low star ratings. In our implementation, the maximum contribution of the meal rating is one hundred. This was chosen because it meant that a user's own personal rating was very influential and could override meal recommendations in the case of user disagreement with a particular meal's personalisation.

Additionally, the meal rating value affects the personalised weighting score of each ingredient or category in the rated meal. Ingredients and categories that have no prior weighting are simply assigned the meal rating as their weight. Ingredients and categories with existing weights from other meal ratings have their weights recalculated, taking the average of all ratings of meals with that ingredient or category. These updated ingredient weightings are then normalised and contribute a percentage of the statically defined "maximum ingredient feedback" to the meal's total personalised score. The maximum feedback contribution for this prototype was chosen to be twenty so that the feedback results contributed to the ranking of meal recommendations without overriding the more direct influences of user likes, dislikes, allergies, and ratings.

The ingredient and category feedback is particularly valuable over time as the system will accumulate detailed information regarding what types of meals a user prefers based on what is contained in a meal. This means that the accuracy of recommendations will improve as the system is used more. A positive consequence is that this growing preference source is available to a user in their lifelong user model, stored on their own mobile device and accessible also (if desired) by other applications.

4   User Study into Digital Restaurant Menus

This study was designed to obtain qualitative and quantitative feedback regarding the implemented system with specific questions aimed at exploring the key themes of this work, i.e. mobile client-side personalisation, scrutability, user control, and ease-of-use.

A primary goal was to assess the perceived usefulness of the implemented system and whether the system successfully supports important scrutability features such as being able to view one's user model and understand the reasons for recommendations.

Another goal of the study was to implement and evaluate new innovative features that are not normally present in a physical restaurant menu. These include both the refinement of current functionality and completely new functionality, including detailed nutritional information, health advice, historical information (e.g. when and why the chef added an item to the menu), nutritional comparisons between items, and average preparation times.

4.1   Study Design

The usability methods used were direct observation (i.e. the 'simplified thinking aloud' technique [10]) and questionnaire (both pre- and post-experiment questionnaires). Data collected during the experiment included both quantitative data - in the form of Likert-scale responses - and qualitative data about the participants' reactions and feelings about the system.

An informal pre-study was also first conducted to set benchmarks for user experience and to shape the initial system designs, and to identify and resolve any major system usability flaws. This allowed participants in the ensuing think-aloud study (N=8) to focus on the important system themes and functionalities without undue distraction.

For the purpose of this user study, a fictional restaurant menu named 'Shelly's Farm and Sea' was constructed. This menu was populated using publicly available recipes and nutritional information, and it included details such as the full list of ingredients, cooking methods, cooking times, and nutritional information.

Participant Demographics. The think-aloud was conducted in a laboratory setting with 8 English-speaking participants (5 male, 3 female; average age=27). All were familiar with computers and all identified themselves as smartphone users, with participants on average rating their skill with using smartphones as advanced. Four participants mentioned that they had used a meal or recipe recommender application previously (e.g. Urban Spoon, www.urbanspoon.com), and the majority of participants reported visiting restaurants on a frequent basis (weekly=5, fortnightly=1, monthly=2).

Experiment Procedure. After completing a background questionnaire, participants were asked to familiarise themselves with the Menu Mentor mobile application through a small number of introductory tasks. Once comfortable with the application and the Android device (in this case a smartphone), participants were instructed to complete two sets of tasks focused on 'digital menu functionalities' and 'mobile client-side personalisation'. Participants were encouraged to voice any thoughts about the system during the experiment, and while the participant was working through the think-aloud tasks, the experimenter took handwritten notes recording user reactions to the system. At the end of the experiment participants completed a post-experiment questionnaire consisting of 18 questions. The whole experiment typically took participants between 45-60 minutes to complete.

4.2   Results

Digital Menu Functionalities. The digital menu think-aloud task had fifteen components and demonstrated an array of digital menu functionalities implemented in the Menu Mentor application. Each task corresponded to one feature and allowed the participant to state their thoughts about that feature. These tasks were designed to provide qualitative feedback on the transformation of a physical restaurant menu to a digital restaurant menu. More specifically, these tasks aimed to identify which features a participant liked, disliked, what they thought could be improved, and what other innovations they would expect to see from such a system. Following the think-aloud, participants were asked to rate a list of functionalities in the post-experiment questionnaire, the majority of which were seen by the participant during the practical think-aloud component of the experiment. The rating scale used in the questionnaire was: 'not useful', 'slightly useful', 'useful' and 'very useful' (Figure 4).

The quantitative results from the questionnaire show that participants find having meals recommended based on personal information and the listing of a meal's ingredients to be highly useful; this is functionality that paper-based menus can rarely provide due to paper-based limitations such as space constraints and the costs involved in maintaining and updating such menus. Only slightly behind were the functionalities of saving the nutritional information of a meal and seeing chef meal suggestions and specials. On average, no functionalities were rated less than slightly useful, however four functionalities did fall into this category (see Figure 4). By analysing participant feedback from the think-aloud experiment notes, it can be seen that these features are viewed by a few participants as unwanted distractions, and by the majority, as nice-to-have but unnecessary.

Mobile Client-Side Personalisation. The personalisation task had twelve individual components and delved into the personalisation of the Menu Mentor application. Specific focus was given to the participant's sense of control over the meal recommendation process and whether this personalisation was intuitive to use. Additionally, focus was given to determining if the given scrutable feedback on meal recommendations was understandable and how this could be improved.

All participants liked that the application allowed personalisation on any submenu level; this allowed a user to go into the entrees menu and be recommended

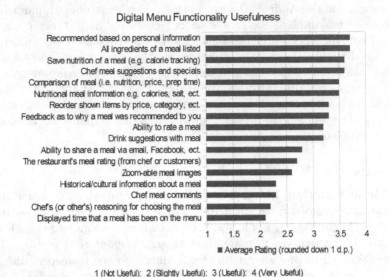

Digital Menu Functionality Usefulness

1 (Not Useful): 2 (Slightly Useful): 3 (Useful): 4 (Very Useful)

Fig. 4. Average participant usefulness ratings of digital menu functionalities

an entree, or to go into the 'All' menu and be recommended meals from all of
the restaurant's meal items. Encouragingly, some participants liked the personalisation feature because they wanted their options to be narrowed down. One
participant commented that "filtering is good. More things should have filtering
in the world." The use of green and red colours for positive and negative recommendations was understood by all participants, however a few participants were
not completely able to understand that the plain coloured meals represented
items that were neither positively nor negatively ranked.

Participants were presented with the personalised score of one of the recommended meals in order to determine if they understood why it had been recommended to them. Participants indicated a strong preference for symbolic feedback
rather than the numeric information provided by the system in its current form
(see Figure 2). Even though participants found the numerical information confus-
ing, they were easily able to identify why a meal was recommended or not recommended based on the listed likes, dislikes, and allergies. As a result, participants
also found it easy to identify why one meal was deemed more preferable for them
than another.

All eight participants answered 'yes' when asked whether they would use the
personalisation feature implemented in the Menu Mentor application, and on
average, participants agreed that they were able to understand why a meal had
been recommended to them in the personalised mode. After learning how the
system worked through the set tasks, the majority of participants either agreed
or strongly agreed that they would feel comfortable using a digital personalised
restaurant menu as a substitute for a paper-based menu.

Summary and Discussion. This study has shown that a personalised digital restaurant menu, when used in combination with a mobile device, can be a much more useful meal browsing tool than a physical restaurant menu. Five participants "strongly agreed" and three "agreed" that the Menu Mentor system was more useful than a standard restaurant menu. Six of the eight participants indicated that they would prefer to use a personalised restaurant menu as opposed to a menu that was simply digital. Additionally, seven of the eight participants said they would prefer a digital menu that had new innovative features not present in a physical menu, rather than a system that merely replicated a standard restaurant menu.

On average, participants agreed that the implemented system enhanced personal control over a restaurant menu and that an average restaurant customer would benefit from using such a personalised menu. When asked whether they could see this type of mobile application as useful in other domains like a clothes shop, the majority of participants responded "Yes". However, when asked to explain this response, participants indicated that their response was conditional, acknowledging that certain domains would not be appropriate for such a system or would be very difficult to personalise.

5 Conclusions

In this paper, we have presented a mobile lifestyle application in the fine-dining domain, supporting scrutable user models and mobile client-side personalisation. We have outlined its personalisation engine and content and critique-based hybrid recommender strategy. We have provided a scenario walkthrough illustrating the level of control and scrutability that a user has in configuring their user model in applications like this one, and we have presented results from a user experiment demonstrating how new digital features are likely to extend and ultimately replace traditional paper-based systems (in this case for restaurant menus), and in which we highlight user acceptance of the scrutability features and recommendation processes of the system, in which menu recommendations are justified and explained in detail by the system. This paper furthermore provides - by way of a working prototype - validation on how client-side user models and client-side personalisation can be incorporated into mobile applications.

Acknowledgment. This work is partially funded by the Smart Services CRC, as part of the Multi-channel Content Delivery and Mobile Personalisation Project.

References

1. Berkovsky, S., Freyne, J.: Group-based Recipe Recommendations: Analysis of Data Aggregation Strategies. In: Proceedings of RecSys, pp. 111–118. ACM, New York (2010)
2. Czarkowski, M., Kay, J., Potts, S.: Scrutability as a Core Interface Element. In: Proceedings of Artificial Intelligence in Education, pp. 783–785. IOS Press, Amsterdam (2005)

3. Fink, J., Kobsa, A.: A Review and Analysis of Commercial User Modeling Servers for Personalization on the World Wide Web. UMUAI 10, 209–249 (2000)
4. Freyne, J., Berkovsky, S.: Recommending food: Reasoning on recipes and ingredients. In: De Bra, P., Kobsa, A., Chin, D. (eds.) UMAP 2010. LNCS, vol. 6075, pp. 381–386. Springer, Heidelberg (2010)
5. Geleijnse, G., Nachtigall, P., Kaam, P., Wijgergangs, L.: A Personalized Recipe Advice System to Promote Healthful Choices. In: Proceedings of the 16th International Conference on Intelligent User Interfaces (IUI), pp. 437–438. ACM (2011)
6. Gerber, S., Fry, M., Kay, J., Kummerfeld, B., Pink, G., Wasinger, R.: PersonisJ: Mobile, Client-Side User Modelling. In: De Bra, P., Kobsa, A., Chin, D. (eds.) UMAP 2010. LNCS, vol. 6075, pp. 111–122. Springer, Heidelberg (2010)
7. Kay, J.: Lifelong Learner Modeling for Lifelong Personalized Pervasive Learning. IEEE Transactions on Learning Technologies 1(4), 215–228 (2008)
8. Kobsa, A.: Generic User Modeling Systems. In: Brusilovsky, P., Kobsa, A., Nejdl, W. (eds.) Adaptive Web 2007. LNCS, vol. 4321, pp. 136–154. Springer, Heidelberg (2007)
9. Lessel, P., Böhmer, M., Kröner, A., Krüger, A.: User Requirements and Design Guidelines for Digital Restaurant Menus. In: Proceedings of the 7th Nordic Conference on Human-Computer Interaction (NordiCHI): Making Sense Through Design, pp. 524–533. ACM (2012)
10. Nielsen, J.: Guerrilla HCI: Using Discount Usability Engineering to Penetrate the Intimidation Barrier. In: Cost-Justifying Usability, pp. 245–272. Academic Press, Inc. (1994)
11. van Pinxteren, Y., Geleijnse, G., Kamsteeg, P.: Deriving a Recipe Similarity Measure for Recommending Healthful Meals. In: Proceedings of the 16th International Conference on Intelligent User Interfaces (IUI), pp. 105–114. ACM, New York (2011)
12. Ricci, F.: Mobile Recommender Systems. In: Information Technology and Tourism, vol. 12, pp. 205–231. Cognizant Communication Corporation (2011)
13. Wahlster, W., Kröner, A., Heckmann, D.: SharedLife: Towards Selective Sharing of Augmented Personal Memories. In: Stock, O., Schaerf, M. (eds.) Aiello Festschrift, LNCS (LNAI), vol. 4155, pp. 327–342. Springer, Heidelberg (2006)
14. Wallbank, J.: Enhancing Restaurant Menus Through Personalised Meal Recommendations. Master's thesis, School of Information Technologies, The University of Sydney (2011)
15. Wasinger, R., Fry, M., Kay, J., Kummerfeld, B.: User Modelling Ecosystems: A User-centred Approach. In: Masthoff, J., Mobasher, B., Desmarais, M.C., Nkambou, R. (eds.) UMAP 2012. LNCS, vol. 7379, pp. 334–339. Springer, Heidelberg (2012)

Days of Our Lives: Assessing Day
Similarity from Location Traces

James Biagioni[1] and John Krumm[2]

[1] Department of Computer Science, University of Illinois at Chicago, Chicago, IL, USA
jbiagi1@uic.edu
[2] Microsoft Research, Microsoft Corporation, Redmond, WA, USA
jckrumm@microsoft.com

Abstract. We develop and test algorithms for assessing the similarity of a person's days based on location traces recorded from GPS. An accurate similarity measure could be used to find anomalous behavior, to cluster similar days, and to predict future travel. We gathered an average of 46 days of GPS traces from 30 volunteer subjects. Each subject was shown random pairs of days and asked to assess their similarity. We tested eight different similarity algorithms in an effort to accurately reproduce our subjects' assessments, and our statistical tests found two algorithms that performed better than the rest. We also successfully applied one of our similarity algorithms to clustering days using location traces.

Keywords: location traces, similarity, anomaly detection, clustering.

1   Introduction

Both consumers and corporations recognize the value of location traces for understanding daily habits and anticipating occasional needs, and the proliferation of GPS-equipped smart phones is making them ever easier to collect. These traces can help in understanding our daily activities; in particular, we can use location traces to find anomalous days and to cluster similar days, leading to a better understanding of our daily routines. Both of these tasks require a way to compare days to one another.

This paper develops and tests algorithms to measure the similarity of days represented by location traces, tested against similarity assessments from real users. With a reliable way to measure similarity we can find days that stand out from the rest as anomalies, which may indicate confusion (an important phenomenon to detect among populations of users with cognitive impairments [3]) or a change of habits. We can also make sensible clusters of days that belong together to assess variety and make predictions about how a day will evolve, providing useful basic knowledge for future adaptive systems to leverage. We believe this is the first effort aimed at measuring the similarity of days using location traces in a way that reflects human assessments.

A variety of sensors could be used to characterize a day, such as activity measured on a person's mobile phone, desktop computer, vehicle, social networking sites, biometric sensors, *etc*. Our work is aimed at location traces, usually measured with GPS. One advantage of this is that location is a constantly existent state (if not always

S. Carberry et al. (Eds.): UMAP 2013, LNCS 7899, pp. 89–101, 2013.
© Springer-Verlag Berlin Heidelberg 2013

measurable) as opposed to event-based activities, such as texting events, that only happen occasionally. Location is also dynamic for most people and easy to measure outdoors with GPS. These characteristics make location a convenient variable to use for measuring the similarity between a person's days.

The GIS community has looked extensively at location trace similarity, *e.g.* [1], but these efforts are aimed primarily at machine processing. We are interested in matching human assessments of similarity, which appears more commonly in research for anomaly detection. In [2], Ma detects anomalies from GPS traces by first representing a normal trace as a sequence of rectangles on the ground. An anomaly is declared if a new trace's rectangles are sufficiently different from those of the normal trace. Here the similarity measure is explicit in that it depends on a quantity measuring the geographic difference between the normal trip and the query trip. It also ignores time. In [3], Patterson *et al.* detect anomalous behavior based on GPS tracking. They train a dynamic, probabilistic model from a person's historical GPS traces. If the uncertainty of the trained model exceeds the uncertainty of a general prior model of human motion, then the system declares an anomaly. This is an example of an implicit similarity measure. Both [2] and [3] are aimed at detecting anomalies in the lives of the cognitively impaired. The system of Giroux *et al.* [4] has the same goal, only they use sensors in a home to detect anomalies in predefined daily routines, like making coffee. An anomaly is declared if the normal sequence of events is violated or if the timing of the sequence is sufficiently different from normal. Researchers have also detected anomalies in video, such as Xian and Gong [5], whose system automatically builds models of normality from training video.

All of these techniques depend on learning a model of normal behavior from observation, which means they must be trained anew for new subjects. One of our goals is to find a single similarity measure that works well for multiple people, without requiring any training. In addition, previous techniques detect dissimilar behavior based on an algorithm or threshold designed by the researcher. Instead, another of our goals is to find a similarity measure that approximates what a human subject would say about their own data. Achieving these goals will allow us to provide future adaptive systems with a way to accurately reproduce human assessments of day similarity that works well for the general population, and requires no training time; perhaps helping to mitigate the cold-start problem in relevant applications. Toward this end, we gathered GPS data from 30 volunteer subjects and then asked them to assess the similarity of their own days. Armed with this ground truth data, we tested various similarity measures and were able to find two that reproduced the assessments from our subjects quite well. We begin by describing how we gathered the data for our experiment.

2   GPS Data and Preprocessing

In order to perform our experiments for assessing day similarity based on location traces, we gathered GPS data from the vehicles of volunteers. This section describes our data logging and preprocessing for the experiment described in Section 3.

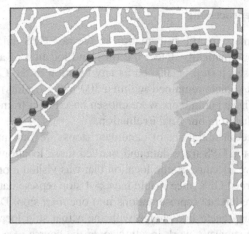

Fig. 1. A short sequence of GPS points sampled at an interval of 10 seconds

2.1   GPS Data from Volunteers

We logged GPS data from 30 volunteers (8 female). Each volunteer borrowed a RoyalTek RBT-2300 GPS logger and placed it in their main vehicle, powered by the cigarette lighter. All our subjects were employees of Microsoft Corporation in Redmond, WA, USA, and most were compensated with a US$ 30 cafeteria spending card. A few subjects agreed to participate without any compensation. Our goal was to collect at least six weeks of data from each subject. In the end we obtained GPS data for an average of 46 days from each subject, varying from 20 to 60 days, where the majority of the recorded drives consisted of simple weekday home/work commute trips and weekend drives in the local community; a dataset we believe generalizes well to the larger population of people with regular work routines. Each subject was in possession of the GPS logger for at least six weeks, but some did not drive every day. In order to reach 30 subjects, we started logging with 39 subjects, but later found that 9 did not provide suitable data due to mysterious stoppages in logging, a late refusal to log, frequent sharing of their vehicle (which violated our survey criteria), and two unexpected departures. We also ignored two subjects who had only 14 and 18 days of logging.

The loggers were set to record a time-stamped coordinate pair (latitude, longitude) every 10 seconds. Fig. 1 shows a short sequence of GPS points from one of our subjects with 10-second sampling. Since we ran our loggers without their rechargeable batteries, they logged only when the vehicle's cigarette lighter was powered. For some vehicles, this happens only when the vehicle is turned on, and for others the cigarette lighter is powered continuously. In our preprocessing, detailed below, we filled in gaps corresponding to these and other limitations of the recorded GPS stream.

2.2   GPS Data Preprocessing

In order to attach some semantic information to the raw GPS data, our first preprocessing step was to automatically detect the time and location of all *stops* in the raw
traces. For our purposes, a stop is defined as any location in the GPS data where we
detect that the subject/vehicle remained within a 300-meter (radius) circular region for
5 minutes or more. These parameters were chosen based on a training dataset, whose
subjects were not included in our final evaluation.

In order to produce an initial set of candidate stops, we first made a linear time-
ordered pass through the GPS trace data and marked those locations that met our stop
criterion, defined above. Because a stop location that was visited more than once during
the course of the recorded GPS trace would have > 1 stop representation in our data, we
then collapsed those redundant representations into one *final* stop. Doing so allowed us
to associate a set of aggregate knowledge with the actual stop location. For example,
consider the case of a subject's work location; over the course of a typical work-week
their trace data will initially represent "work" with five separate stop representations
(one for each day). By collapsing these five representations into one, we obtain one stop
location that represents the aggregate knowledge of the original five (*i.e.*, days of the
week the location was visited, times the subject arrived/departed, etc.), which is significantly more useful than five disparate time/location observations. In order to collapse
the stops, we applied agglomerative clustering [6] to the candidate stops using the same
300-meter distance threshold (as above) as the criterion for merging.

Once we determined the final set of stops, we then leveraged the aggregate information contained therein to apply semantic labels to certain stops. Specifically, we
used data from the American Time Use Survey (ATUS) [7] to classify the most-likely
pair of stops as either *Home* or *Work* locations. Since our final stops contained knowledge of the days and times of arrival/departure, length of stay, and frequency of visits, we built and trained a classifier to perform probabilistic Home/Work labeling
based entirely on these criteria. Since Home/Work stops occur very frequently in
many subjects' GPS datasets, it was important to be able to distinguish them for our
subjects' later assessment of their data. Specifically, having these labels helped our
subjects orient themselves quickly and easily to the type of days they were observing
(*e.g.*, weekday/weekend), and distinguish between regular and anomalous days more
easily.

Finally, as one last preprocessing step, we created a *symbolized stop representation*
of each day of data from the raw GPS traces (where a *day* is defined from 4:00am –
3:59am). Specifically, for each location in the raw GPS data, we replaced its coordinate pair with its associated *Stop ID* (a unique identifier associated with each stop),
and interpolated in time for those vehicles that logged only when they were turned on.
If a given coordinate pair was not associated with (*i.e.*, located at) a stop location, it
was replaced with a *From Stop ID-To Stop ID* pair, denoting travel between stops.
Simplifying the raw trace data into a series of symbols denoting time spent at (and
traveling between) stops not only provides us with a more compact representation of
the trace data, but also a more abstract representation for use with evaluation algorithms that aren't geographically-aware (see Section 4).

3   Human Assessment of Day Similarity

Our goal is to find an algorithm that can assess the similarity of days in a way that matches human assessment. Toward this end, we asked each of our subjects to make similarity assessments of their own location data. Guided by one of the authors, each of our 30 subjects was invited to run a custom program that displayed, and asked them to make similarity assessments on their own recently recorded data. The program started by displaying a calendar indicating the days for which we had GPS data available for the subject. For a selected day, the program showed that day's location traces in three different ways:

1. **Map** - An interactive map, shown in Fig. 2(a), displayed the stops we found (as described in Section 2.2), each with its unique ID number. It also showed the GPS traces between the stops. This visualization emphasized the spatial layout of the day's trips and stops.
2. **Graph** – An interactive graph, as in Fig. 2(b), showed the subject's stops as nodes and their trips as straight edges. Thicker edges indicated more trips between their connected stops. The *Home* and *Work* stops were labeled if we found them, otherwise stops were labeled with only their unique ID number that matched the numbers on the map. Clicking on a node or edge in the graph highlighted the corresponding stop or GPS trace on the map, making for convenient exploration. This visualization emphasized the number of stops and the transitions between them.
3. **Timeline** - A timeline, as in Fig. 3, displayed each stop in a different color block, laid out along a horizontal timeline. The time periods denoting trips between stops were colored black. This gave a temporal view of the day that was lacking in the other two visualizations.

After starting the program, we asked each of our subjects to familiarize themselves with the visualizations by picking a day and briefly describing it to us using the visualizations.

(a) An interactive map for viewing a day's GPS data

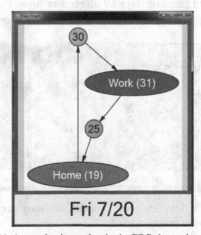

(b) A graph view of a day's GPS data, showing stops and the trips between them

Fig. 2. Two visualizations of a day for our subjects

The main part of our user study came next: each subject was asked to assess the relative similarity of pairs of pairs of their days. That is, each subject was shown four randomly selected days simultaneously, using the visualizations described above, and as shown in Fig. 4. We then asked the subject to indicate which of the two pairs was most similar. For instance, if the two pairs of days were A & B and C & D, we asked the subject to indicate if A & B were more similar to each other than C & D, or vice-versa. We chose this simple assessment after first piloting a different survey that asked subjects to give a numerical similarity rating to a pair of days. This proved too difficult, so we reverted to this simpler question about the relative similarity of pairs of days. The example shown in Fig. 4 is a good representation of the complexity of the typical comparison problem presented to our subjects; with an average of 5 stops per day, the left-most pair of days represents a simpler case, and the right-most pair a more complex case. Each subject rated 30 pairs of pairs, which took approximately 30 minutes in total for each subject.

With these partial rankings, we next experimented with several different algorithms for assessing day similarity that we hoped would accurately reproduce the assessments of our subjects.

4   Algorithms for Assessing Day Similarity

To find an algorithm that computes a numerical similarity (or "distance" score) between pairs of days that matches the similarity rankings of our subjects, we implemented and evaluated four trajectory similarity algorithms in both *standard* and *modified* forms. The *standard* form of each algorithm is that given by its original definition, described in the following sub-sections. The *modified* form of each algorithm consisted of its original definition being adapted to use Dynamic Time Warping (DTW) [8], a technique which allows us to relax the assumption that activities between pairs of days be aligned in time. For example, consider two days A and B consisting of the same simple "Home → Work → Home" activity pattern. On Day A, the

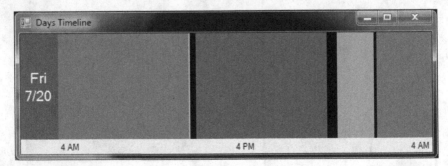

Fig. 3. Timeline view of a day, showing stops as blocks of color and trips between stops as narrower bands of black

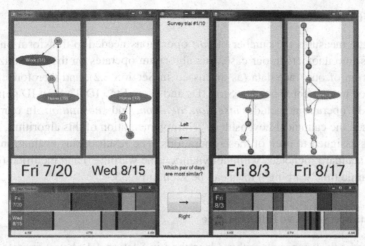

Fig. 4. The main part of our user study, where we asked subjects to indicate which pair of days was most similar to each other

subject leaves home at 8:30am, arrives at work at 9am, departs work at 6pm, and returns home at 6:30pm. On Day B, the subject leaves home at 8am, arrives at work at 8:30am, departs work at 5:30pm, and returns home at 6pm. Since days A and B both consist of a 9-hour work-day with a 30-minute commute from/to home, subjectively speaking they are virtually identical. However, because of the 30-minute time-shift between them, they will necessarily incur a penalty from any objective similarity measure. Therefore, our motivation behind evaluating a DTW-modified version of each algorithm was to establish whether our subjects ignore these shifts in time, and if so, to more accurately capture and reproduce the subjective nature of their evaluations.

Formally speaking, in the *modified* implementation of each algorithm we measured the DTW-distance (*DTW*) by bootstrapping the corresponding *distance* function defined by each algorithm. The DTW-distance between days A and B is computed as follows, where $A = \langle a_1, a_2, ..., a_n \rangle$, Head(A) $= a_1$, Tail(A) $= \langle a_2, ..., a_n \rangle$, and each a_i corresponds to either a Stop ID or coordinate pair depending on the algorithm being modified (and, similarly for B):

$$DTW(A, B) = \begin{cases} 0, if\ length(A) = 0\ and\ length(B) = 0 \\ \infty, if\ length(A) = 0\ or\ length(B) = 0 \\ distance\big(Head(A), Head(B)\big) + min \begin{cases} DTW\big(A, Tail(B)\big) \\ DTW\big(Tail(A), B\big) \\ DTW\big(Tail(A), Tail(B)\big) \end{cases} \end{cases}$$

In effect, dynamic time warping warps the time axes of the two sequences so they match optimally. Below we describe the four standard trajectory similarity algorithms.

4.1   Edit Distance

Edit distance measures the number of *edit* operations needed to transform one string of symbols into another. In our case, this algorithm operates on the symbolized stop representation of our trace data (as discussed in Section 2.2), and therefore the *symbols* referred to here correspond to Stop IDs and From Stop ID-To Stop ID pairs.

Valid edit operations include: *insertion*, *deletion*, and *substitution*. In our evaluation, we used the canonical Levenshtein [9] implementation of this algorithm, where a unit cost is assigned to each of these operations. The result of this evaluation metric, in both its standard (denoted "without dynamic time warping") and modified (denoted "with dynamic time warping") form can be seen in Fig. 5.

4.2   Distance Sensitive Edit Distance

The standard edit distance algorithm (described in Section 4.1 above) operates entirely on the symbolized stop representation of a given day, without taking into consideration the stops' geographic locations. In order to account for the geographic location of stops we modified the standard Levenshtein algorithm [9] to use great-circle distance, measured using the Haversine formula [10], as its cost function for each of the edit operations. This means, for example, that the cost of performing the *substitution* operation for two Stops #60 and #157 is no longer 1, but rather the distance in meters between Stops #60 and #157 according to their coordinate locations. The results of this evaluation metric can be seen in Fig. 5.

4.3   Stop Type Distance

The symbolized stop representation of a subject's days requires an exact correspondence between IDs to be considered a match. Because this definition can be overly restrictive, we generalized the representation of each stop by classifying its location *type*. In order to perform this classification, we provided the coordinates of each stop to Bing Local Search, which returned a list of categorized businesses and their distances from our stop within a radius of 250 meters. Example business types include "Restaurant," "Grocery & Food Stores" and "Banks & Credit Unions," among many others. Using this data we then built a location-type probability distribution for each stop, based on the proportion of returned business types and weighted by their distance from the original stop location.

Replacing each Stop ID with its corresponding location-type probability distribution, we then computed the distance between days as the sum of the KL-divergence [11] scores between their probability distributions. The results of this evaluation metric can be seen in Fig. 5.

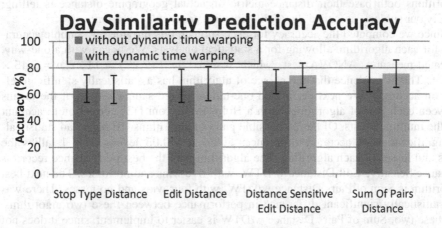

Fig. 5. Accuracy results for our eight similarity algorithms. Error bars show +/- 1 standard deviation over all 30 test subjects.

4.4 Sum of Pairs Distance

This metric [12] computes the distance between days based on their raw location traces, rather than the symbolized stop representations used above. As a result, this metric does not take into account any of the related semantic information.

Sum of pairs distance measures the sum of the great-circle distance between every pair of trace locations (coordinate pairs). Since this metric requires that the traces for days A and B be of equal length, we first perform simple linear interpolation and then compute their distance. The results of this evaluation metric can be seen in Fig. 5.

5   Results

We evaluated our similarity algorithms both on the task of matching our subjects' similarity assessments and on a clustering task.

5.1   Matching Subjects' Similarity Assessments

We ran our eight similarity algorithms on the data from our 30 subjects. Recall that each subject was shown 30 sets of 4 days each. Each set of four days was split into two pairs, and the subject chose which pair was most similar. We gave these same sets of days to our similarity algorithms and recorded their assessment of which days were most similar. The accuracy results we report show the proportion of human decisions our algorithms were able to correctly reproduce.

The accuracy results are shown in Fig. 5. Ignoring statistical significance, the best performing algorithm was Sum of Pairs Distance with Dynamic Time Warping (w/DTW), with a mean accuracy of 75.5% (SD=10.4%). This algorithm looks at the great circle distance between points in the two location traces, with local adjustments for time shifts. In second place was Distance Sensitive Edit Distance w/DTW with an overall mean accuracy of 74.2% (SD=9.3%). The fact that our two best-performing algorithms both base their distance metric on actual geographic distance is telling; clearly our subjects associate *day similarity* with *geographic proximity*.

Since we computed the accuracy for each subject, this provided 30 sample accuracies for each algorithm, allowing for a statistical analysis. We began with a one-way, repeated-measures ANOVA test, which resulted in $F(7,29) = 11.22, p = 5.45 \times 10^{-12}$. This is evidence that the choice of algorithm has a statistically significant effect on accuracy. We next performed one-tailed, paired-sample t-tests of the means between each pair of algorithms, with a Holm-Bonferroni [13] correction to account for the multiple t-tests. Of the 28 possible pairs of algorithms, 16 pairs had statistically significant mean accuracy differences at the $\alpha = 0.05$ level. Table 1 tallies the wins and losses of each algorithm. The algorithm with the best performance record is Distance Sensitive Edit Distance w/DTW, with five wins and no losses. The next best algorithm is Sum of Pairs Distance w/DTW, with four wins and no losses. There was no statistically significant difference in performance between these two algorithms. Of these two, Sum of Pairs Distance w/DTW is easier to implement, since it does not require the identification of stops in the location traces. While the two best-performing algorithms both used DTW, it produced a statistically significant performance improvement for only the Distance Sensitive Edit Distance algorithm, over its non-DTW counterpart.

Overall, for accuracy and ease of implementation, we are inclined to recommend Sum of Pairs Distance w/DTW as the best algorithm we tested for assessing the similarity of days.

5.2 Application to Clustering

One application of our similarity measure is clustering, where we can find groups of similar days. We tested this by having our 30 subjects assess clusterings of their own days. We clustered days with a spectral clustering algorithm (eigenvectors of random walk Laplacian, with k-means [14]). We computed clusters using the Edit Distance w/o DTW algorithm as our distance metric. Edit Distance w/o DTW had a mean accuracy of 66.2% (SD=12.5%), slightly lower than the best accuracy of 75.5% for Sum of Pairs Distance w/DTW. We used Edit Distance w/o DTW for our survey, because at the time we conducted our study we hadn't yet been able to test for the best performing algorithm.

Table 1. Number of statistically significant wins and losses for our similarity algorithms

Algorithm	Wins	Losses
Edit Distance w/o DTW	0	3
Edit Distance w/DTW	0	1
Distance Sensitive Edit Distance w/o DTW	2	2
Distance Sensitive Edit Distance w/DTW	5	0
Stops Categories Distance w/o DTW	0	4
Stops Categories Distance w/DTW	0	4
Sum of Pairs Distance w/o DTW	3	0
Sum of Pairs Distance w/DTW	4	0

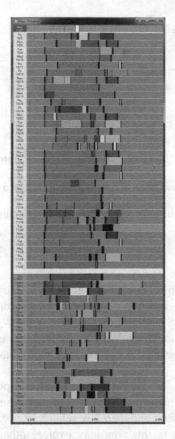

Fig. 6. These are three clusters shown on a timeline. Each row is one day. The single day in the top cluster is an outlier. The main central cluster shows 32 work days, and the bottom cluster shows 19 non-work days.

For the clustering portion of the survey, we asked each subject to increment through the number of clusters, k, starting at two. For each k, the program displayed the clustered days in groups using the same visualizations described in Section 3. An example of a timeline showing three clusters is depicted in Fig. 6, where the day-groupings are indicated by the colored labels on the left-hand side of each row.

Each subject was asked to pick the best k and then to rate the clustering on a Likert scale by indicating their level of agreement with the statement, "My days have been accurately separated into sensible groups." The results of this question are shown in Fig. 7, where we see that 20 out of 30 subjects answered either "Agree" or "Strongly agree", indicating that the clustering was generally successful. This, in turn, further supports the assertion that our Edit Distance w/o DTW similarity algorithm comes close to matching human similarity assessments. We would expect Sum of Pairs Distance w/DTW to work even better, since it was the most accurate algorithm based on our analysis in Section 5.1.

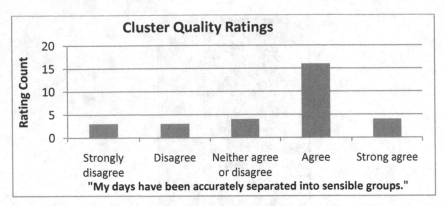

Fig. 7. Most of our subjects were happy with the clustering results

6   Conclusions

Based on a survey of 30 subjects, we assessed the accuracy of 8 different similarity algorithms on their location traces. We found that two algorithms, Sum of Pairs Distance w/DTW and Distance Sensitive Edit Distance w/DTW, worked best at matching human assessments of day similarity. We also showed that one of our similarity algorithms worked well for clustering days of location traces, based on an evaluation from our subjects.

In addition to clustering, these similarity algorithms can potentially be used to find anomalies and help predict behavior. None of our algorithms depend on training, so they are generic across all users, and therefore relatively easy to use.

We envision future work in this area may explore other similarity algorithms as well as experiments to detect anomalies. We would expect anomaly detection to work well because of the good performance shown here by our algorithms at matching human assessments of the similarity of days.

References

1. Deng, K., et al.: Trajectory Indexing and Retrieval. In: Zheng, Y., Zhou, X. (eds.) Computing with Spatial Trajectories, Springer, New York (2011)
2. Ma, T.-S.: Real-Time Anomaly Detection for Traveling Individuals. In: Eleventh International ACM SIGACCESS Conference on Computers and Accessibility (ASSETS 2009), Pittsburgh, PA USA, pp. 273–274 (2009)
3. Patterson, D.J., et al.: Opportunity Knocks: a System to Provide Cognitive Assistance with Transportation Services. In: Mynatt, E.D., Siio, I. (eds.) UbiComp 2004. LNCS, vol. 3205, pp. 433–450. Springer, Heidelberg (2004)
4. Giroux, S., et al.: Pervasive Behavior Tracking for Cognitive Assistance. In: 1st International Conference on PErvasive Technologies Related to Assistive Environments (PETRA 2008). ACM (2008)
5. Xiang, T., Gong, S.: Video Behavior Profiling for Anomaly Detection. IEEE Transactions on Pattern Analysis and Machine Intelligence 30(5), 893–908 (2008)

6. Hastie, T., Tibshirani, R., Friedman, J.: The Elements of Statistical Learning, pp. 520–528. Springer, New York (2009)
7. United States Bureau of Labor Statistics. American Time Use Survey (ATUS), http://www.bls.gov/tus/
8. Yi, B.-K., Jagadish, H.V., Faloutsos, C.: Efficient Retrieval of Similar Time Sequences Under Time Warping. In: 14th International Conference on Data Engineering, Orlando, Florida USA, pp. 201–208 (1998)
9. Levenshtein, V.: Binary Codes Capable of Correcting Deletions, Insertions and Reversals. Soviet Physics Doklady 10(8), 707–710 (1966)
10. Sinnott, R.W.: Virtues of the Haversine. Sky and Telescope 68(2), 159 (1984)
11. Kullback, S.: Information Theory and Statistics. Dover, Mineola (1968)
12. Agrawal, R., Faloutsos, C., Swami, A.: Efficient Similarity Search in Sequence Databases. In: Lomet, D.B. (ed.) FODO 1993. LNCS, vol. 730, pp. 69–84. Springer, Heidelberg (1993)
13. Holm, S.: A Simple Sequentially Rejective Multiple Test Procedure. Scandinavian Journal of Statistics 6(2), 65–70 (1979)
14. von Luxburg, U.: A Tutorial on Spectral Clustering. Statistics and Computing 17(4), 395–416 (2007)

Studying the Effect of Human Cognition
on User Authentication Tasks

Marios Belk[1], Panagiotis Germanakos[1,2], Christos Fidas[1], and George Samaras[1]

[1] Department of Computer Science, University of Cyprus, CY-1678 Nicosia, Cyprus
[2] SAP AG, Dietmar-Hopp-Allee 16, 69190 Walldorf, Germany
{belk,pgerman,christos.fidas,cssamara}@cs.ucy.ac.cy

Abstract. This paper studies the effect of individual differences in human cognition on user performance in authentication tasks. In particular, a text-based password and a recognition-based graphical authentication mechanism were deployed in the frame of an ecological valid experimental design, to investigate the effect of individuals' different cognitive processing abilities toward efficiency and effectiveness of user authentication tasks. A total of 107 users participated in the reported study during a three-month period between September and November 2012. The results of this recent study can be interpreted under the light of human information processing as they demonstrate a main effect of users' cognitive processing abilities on both efficiency and effectiveness related to authentication mechanisms. The main findings can be considered valuable for future deployment of adaptive security mechanisms since it has been initially shown that specific cognitive characteristics of users could be a determinant factor for the adaptation of security mechanisms.

Keywords: Individual Differences, Cognitive Processing Characteristics, User Authentication, Efficiency, Effectiveness, User Study.

1   Introduction

Over the last decade, the World Wide Web has ingrained itself into everyday life and has contributed to the exponential increase of internet usage since the late 1990s. Its fundamental concept as a medium for collaboration and sharing of information has generated extensive enthusiasm driving many of the world's markets. Within this realm, there is an increasing demand to provide usable and secure interactions to users in various application domains like e-government, e-health, e-learning, e-banking, etc. One of the most important security concerns of Web application providers is to protect their systems from unauthorized access, primarily through user authentication. User authentication over the Internet is primarily achieved with the use of text-based passwords and some suggest that passwords will remain the main means of authentication for the following years [1]. It is estimated that more than 80% of US and UK companies apply some form of text-based password authentication; in many cases it is their solely method for user authentication [2].

Password mechanisms have two main requirements; they need to meet high security standards for keeping malicious users from accessing system accounts, and they

S. Carberry et al. (Eds.): UMAP 2013, LNCS 7899, pp. 102–113, 2013.
© Springer-Verlag Berlin Heidelberg 2013

need to meet usability standards and provide effective and efficient user interactions. Both are important, and every authentication mechanism is a balancing act between the two [3, 4]. For example, as the password strength increases, its memorability, and thus usability decreases, and vice versa.

The security and usability shortcomings of passwords are many and well-known. For example, passwords are vulnerable to guessing, brute-forcing, and more recently to phishing and keystroke logging, and are typically difficult to remember [5, 1]. The latter is further strengthened with the increasing computational power of today's information systems, by demanding the usage of complex and hard-to-guess passwords. In this context, research on graphical authentication mechanisms has received significant attention lately (see [6] for a recent review) with the aim to improve user memorability, and at the same time decrease guessing attacks by malicious software and users. In graphical authentication mechanisms, human memory is leveraged for visual information in hope of a reduced memory burden that will facilitate the selection and use of more secure authentication keys [6]. Graphical authentication mechanisms principally require from a user to enter an authentication key represented by images in a specific sequence. Examples include among others Draw-a-Secret [7] which is one of the first graphical authentication mechanisms proposed, that requires users to draw their authentication key on a two dimensional grid, Pass-Go [8], where users draw their authentication key using grid intersection points, Gaze-based authentication [9] that supports users in selecting secure gaze-based graphical authentication keys, Passfaces [10] that requires from the user to create an authentication key by selecting and memorizing specific images that illustrate human faces, and then recognize the images among decoys to authenticate, and similarly to Passfaces, ImagePass [11] that utilizes single-object images as the authentication key, instead of human faces, since their study suggested that single-object images are more memorable than abstract images and images that illustrate human faces.

A variety of studies have been reported that underpin the necessity for increasing usability in user authentication mechanisms. An early study in [12], which investigated password memorability of users, underpinned the necessity of usable passwords since results from the study indicated that choosing secure passwords that are memorable has been proven to be a difficult task for many users. Furthermore, a large-scale study of half a million users, which investigated the usage habits of user authentication, supports the need of memorable and secure authentication keys [13]. A more recent study in [14] that investigated the impact of authentication policies on users' productivity and experience, suggested that security policies should be driven by the users' needs helping them to set stronger authentication keys instead of focusing on maximizing their strength.

In this context, ineffective practice of usability in user authentication, does not naturally embed the users' characteristics in the design process, and usually adopts a "one-size-fits-all" approach when concerning user authentication designs ignoring the fact that different users have different characteristics and develop different structural and functional mental models, and thus need individual scaffolding. In this respect, supporting usability of user authentication mechanisms with user-adaptive technologies [15] is based on the promise that understanding and modeling human behavior in terms of structural and functional user requirements related to such security tasks can provide an alternative to the "one-size-fits-all" approach with the aim to improve the system's usability and provide a positive user experience.

Consequently, a first step toward designing an adaptive user authentication mechanism is to identify which individual characteristics (e.g., knowledge, previous experience, lingual characteristics, cognitive characteristics, etc.) are considered important for adapting such mechanisms. Bearing in mind that human computer interactions with regard to authentication mechanisms are in principal cognitive tasks that embrace to recall and/or recognize, process and store information, we suggest that these interactions should be analyzed in more detail under the light of human information processing. In this respect, the purpose of this paper is to investigate whether there is a main effect of specific individual characteristics targeting on cognitive processing abilities (i.e., speed of processing, controlled attention and working memory capacity), toward efficiency and effectiveness of two different types of authentication mechanisms; text-based password and graphical authentication mechanisms.

Such an endeavor is considered valuable for the design and the deployment of more usable computer human interaction processes with the aim to offer adaptive and personalized user authentication mechanisms aiming to assist users to accomplish efficiently and effectively comprehensive and usable authentication tasks. For example, an adaptive authentication mechanism could provide to users a personalized type of authentication mechanism (text-based or graphical) according to their cognitive processing abilities with the aim to improve the efficiency and effectiveness of the authentication task, and minimize users' cognitive load and erroneous interactions.

The paper is structured as follows: next we present the underlying theory of this work. Furthermore, we describe the context of an empirical study, sampling and procedure. Thereafter, we analyze and discuss our findings. Finally, we summarize our paper and outline the implications of the reported research.

2   Individual Differences in Human Cognition

Human interaction with authentication mechanisms is principally an information processing task consisting of several processing stages [16]. These include perceptual processing of the initial stimulus of the authentication mechanism, cognitive processing to give meaning to this information and further retrieve the memorized authentication key from long-term memory into the working memory system for processing, and finally carrying out the action, which is, the user provides the retrieved authentication key to the authentication form for accessing the system.

Various theories of individual differences in human cognition have been developed with the aim to describe and explain how and why individuals differ in cognitive abilities [17, 18]. In this respect, various researchers attempted to explain the functioning of the human mind in terms of more basic processes, such as *speed of processing, controlled attention* and *working memory capacity* [19]. *Speed of processing* refers to the maximum speed at which a given mental act may be efficiently executed. In order to elicit speed of processing of individuals, the response time for recognizing a simple stimulus is measured, such as, reading single words or identifying a geometrical figure. In this context, speed of processing indicates the time needed by the human mind to record and give meaning to information; individuals recognizing stimuli faster, are considered more efficient in processing [20, 21].

Controlled attention refers to cognitive processes that can identify and concentrate on goal-relevant information. A classic measure of cognitive control is the Stroop task which requires individuals to name the color in which a word has been printed, while ignoring the word itself [22]. Conflict arises when the color of the word and the word itself are incongruent, e.g., the word "blue" is printed in red color. Individuals must override the dominant aspect of the stimuli (the tendency to read a word) with the processing of their weaker but goal-relevant aspect (the recognition of ink color). In this respect, the difference between the two kinds of measures is taken as an index of inhibition, which is the basic component of controlled attention [20, 22]. People being faster indicating the color of the word tend to have more efficient controlled attention.

Working memory capacity is defined as the maximum amount of information that the mind can efficiently activate during information processing. The conception of working memory grew out of the literature on short-term memory [23, 24] as an empirical model of cognitive functions used for temporarily storing and manipulating information. Enhanced working memory increases the connections and associations that can be built either between the items of the newly encountered information or between this information and information already stored in the long-term memory.

Various research works argue that the aforementioned cognitive processes have an effect on comprehension, learning and problem solving [25, 26]. They are mainly used in mental tasks, such as arithmetic tasks; remembering a number in a multiplication problem and adding that number later on, or creating a new password and using that password later for authentication.

To this end, given that the aforementioned cognitive factors have a main effect in problem solving and other tasks (e.g., individuals with increased working memory capacity accomplish tasks more efficiently), we suggest that such characteristics should be utilized as part of an adaptive interactive system specialized in personalizing user authentication tasks to the cognitive processing abilities of each user. In this respect we further describe the results and findings of a user study that aimed to investigate whether there is a main effect of users' cognitive processing abilities, targeting on speed of processing, controlled attention and working memory capacity, on the efficiency and effectiveness of different types of authentication mechanisms.

3   Method of Study

3.1   Procedure

A Web-based environment was deployed within the frame of various university courses. Students were required to provide their demographic information during the enrolment process (i.e., email, age, gender, and department) and create their authentication key that would be used throughout the semester for accessing the courses' material (i.e., course slides, homework) and for viewing their grades. A text-based password and a recognition-based graphical authentication mechanism were utilized as the authentication scheme of the Web-site. The type of authentication mechanism (i.e., text-based password or graphical) was randomly provided during the enrolment process. At the end of the process the sample consisted of 50% of the students having enrolled with a text-based password and 50% of the students having enrolled with a graphical authentication mechanism. In both types of authentication mechanisms, the key created was chosen freely by the user.

The text-based password mechanism (Figure 1) involved alphanumeric and special keyboard characters. A minimum of eight characters including numbers, a mixture of lower- and upper-case letters, and special characters were required to be entered by the users.

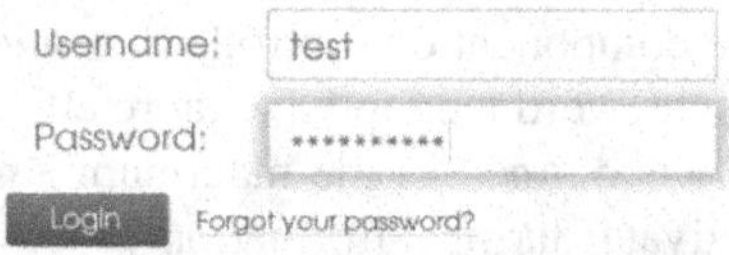

Username: test

Password: ••••••••••

Login   Forgot your password?

Fig. 1. A text-based password mechanism used during the study

A graphical authentication mechanism (Figure 2) that involved single-object images was developed based on the recognition-based, graphical authentication mechanism proposed in [11]. During the authentication key creation, users had to select between eight to twelve images, in a specific sequence out of a random subset of thirty images that were retrieved from a large image database. After the graphical authentication key was created, a fixed image set of sixteen images, containing the user-selected authentication images and system-selected decoy images were permanently attached to the username in order to increase security, since if the decoy images were to change every authentication session, the authentication key could be easily revealed by eliminating the non-repeated images through subsequent sessions [11]. During authentication a 4 x 4 grid containing the user-selected and system-selected decoy images were presented. Thereafter, users had to select their images in the specific sequence, as entered in the enrolment process in order to get permission for accessing the system.

Both client-side and server-side scripts were developed to monitor the users' behavior during interaction with the authentication mechanisms. In particular, the total time (efficiency) and total number of attempts (effectiveness) required for successfully authenticating were monitored on the client-side utilizing a browser-based logging facility that started recording time as soon the users provided their username, until they successfully completed the authentication process.

Controlled laboratory sessions were also conducted throughout the period of the study to elicit the users' cognitive factors (speed of processing, controlled attention and working memory capacity) through a series of psychometric tests [24, 26]. With the aim to apply the psychometric tests in a scientific right manner, we conducted several sessions with a maximum of 5 participants by following the protocol suggested by the inventors of the psychometric tests. The psychometric tests utilized in the study are described next.

Username: test

Login   Reset   Forgot your authentication key?

Fig. 2. A graphical authentication mechanism used during the study

Users' Speed of Processing Elicitation Test. A Stroop-like task was devised to measure simple choice reaction time to address speed of processing. Participants were instructed to read a number of words denoting a color written in the same or different ink color (e.g., the word "red" written in red ink color). A total of eighteen words were illustrated to the participant illustrating the words "red", "green" or "blue" either written in red, green or blue ink color. The participants were instructed to press the R keyboard key for the word "red", the G key for the word "green" and the B key for the word "blue". The reaction times between eighteen stimuli and responses onset were recorded and their mean and median were automatically calculated. A filter set at 5000 ms was used to exclude unreasonably slow responses, and wrong responses were also automatically excluded (as suggested in [26]).

Users' Controlled Attention Elicitation Test. Similar to the speed of processing elicitation test, a Stroop-like task was devised, but instead of denoting the word itself, participants were asked to recognize the ink color of words denoting a color different than the ink (e.g., the word "green" written in blue ink). A total of eighteen words were illustrated to the participants illustrating the words "red", "green" or "blue" either written in red, green or blue ink color. The participants were instructed to press the R keyboard key for the word written in red ink color, the G key for the word written in green ink color and the B key for the word written in blue ink color. The reaction times between eighteen stimuli and responses onset were recorded and their mean and median were automatically calculated. A filter set at 5000 ms was used to exclude unreasonably slow responses, and wrong responses were also automatically excluded (as suggested in [26]).

Users' Working Memory Capacity Elicitation Test. A visual test was utilized to indicate a user's working memory capacity based on [24]. The test illustrated a geometric figure on the screen and the participant was required to memorize the figure. Thereafter, the figure disappeared and five similar figures were illustrated on the screen, numbered from one to five. The participant was required to provide the number (utilizing the keyboard) of the corresponding figure that was the same as the initial figure. The test consisted of twenty one figures (seven levels of three trials each). As the participant correctly identified the figures of each trial, the test provided more complex figures as the levels increased indicating an enhanced working memory capacity.

3.2 Participants

The study was conducted between September and November 2012 with a total of 107 participants (52 male, 55 female, age 17-26, mean 22). Participants were undergraduate students of Computer Science, Electrical Engineering, Psychology and Social Science departments. A total of 2067 authentication sessions have been recorded during the three-month period.

3.3 Hypothesis

The following hypothesis was formulated for the purpose of our research:

H_1. There is significant difference with regard to time (efficiency) and total number of attempts (effectiveness) needed to authenticate through a text-based password mechanism or a recognition-based, graphical authentication mechanism among users with different cognitive processing abilities.

3.4 Analysis of Results

For our analysis, we separated participants into different categories based on their cognitive processing abilities (limited, enhanced) of each cognitive factor (speed of processing, controlled attention, working memory capacity), which are summarized in Table 1.

Table 1. User Groups based on Cognitive Processing Abilities

	Speed of Processing		Controlled Attention		Working Memory Capacity	
	Total	%	Total	%	Total	%
Enhanced	73	68.2	51	47.7	69	64.5
Limited	34	31.8	56	52.3	38	35.5
Total	107	100	107	100	107	100

User Authentication Efficiency. A one-way analysis of variance (ANOVA) was conducted to examine main effects of authentication type (text-based password vs. graphical) on the time needed to successfully authenticate. Results revealed that users in general performed significantly faster in the text-based password mechanism compared to the graphical ($F(1,1134)=192.618$, $p<0.001$). Furthermore, a series of two by two factorial analyses of variance were conducted aiming to examine main effects of users' cognitive processing differences (i.e., limited, enhanced) and user authentication type on the time needed to accomplish the authentication task. Figure 3 illustrates the means of performance per cognitive factor group in regard with the speed of processing (SP), controlled attention (CA) and working memory capacity (WMC) dimension, and user authentication type (text-based password and graphical).

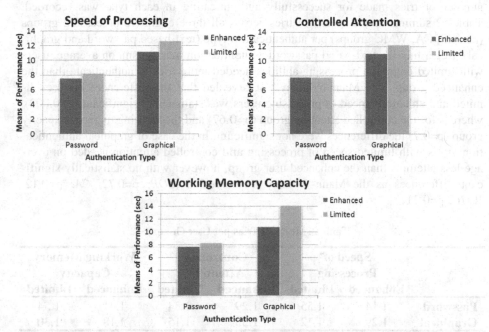

Fig. 3. Means of Performance for Speed of Processing (top left), Controlled Attention (top right) and Working Memory Capacity (bottom) User Groups

The main observation based on all three graphs is that users with enhanced cognitive processing abilities performed significantly faster in the graphical authentication mechanism than users with limited cognitive processing abilities (*SOP Group*: $F(1,496)=8.981$, $p=0.003$; *CA Group*: $F(1,496)=7.269$, $p=0.007$; *WMC Group*: $F(1,496)=45.199$, $p<0.001$). On the other hand, no significant differences in text-based password performances between the two user groups (limited vs. enhanced) were observed. An interpretation of this result might be based on the fact that all users were more familiar and experienced interacting with text-based passwords, hence no significant differences were observed between the limited and enhanced user groups across all three cognitive factors. However, since the familiarity factor did not affect the graphical authentication mechanism, we have observed that the users' enhanced ability of processing information has positively affected their performance compared to users with limited cognitive processing abilities.

Furthermore, a between authentication type comparison revealed that users with enhanced working memory capacity did not perform significantly different between the text-based password and the graphical authentication mechanism. Given the fact that pictures are visually and aesthetically richer than plain text, from a user-adaptation point of view, this result suggests providing graphical authentication mechanisms to users with enhanced working memory capacity with the aim to provide a positive user experience during user authentication [11].

User Authentication Effectiveness. For each user authentication session the total number of tries made for successfully authenticating in each type was recorded. Tables 2 summarize the means of tries across all three cognitive processing groups (i.e., SP, CA, WMC groups) per authentication type (text-based password and graphical). Regarding the text-based password authentication mechanism, on average, users with limited cognitive processing abilities needed more tries to authenticate than the enhanced group. The Mann-Whitney test revealed that the differences between limited and enhanced speed of processing users was statistically significant (p=0.002), whereas for the controlled attention group (p=0.67) and the working memory capacity group (p=0.7) the differences were not significant. In the case of graphical authentication, users with limited speed of processing and controlled attention needed on average less attempts than the enhanced user group, however with no statistically significant differences as the Mann-Whitney test revealed (*SOP:* p=0.72; *CA:* p=0.12; *WMC:* p=0.21).

Table 2. Means of Tries per User Group

	Speed of Processing		Controlled Attention		Working Memory Capacity	
	Enhanced	Limited	Enhanced	Limited	Enhanced	Limited
Password	1.14	1.55	1.29	1.34	1.31	1.54
Graphical	1.29	1.12	1.33	1.15	1.18	1.30

A between authentication type comparison, revealed that as our sample increased there was a growing tendency of users with limited cognitive processing abilities, toward solving graphical authentication mechanisms more effective than text-based passwords. The Mann-Whitney test revealed that users with limited speed of processing and limited working memory capacity needed less attempts in graphical authentication than text-based password authentication, with statistical significant differences (*SOP:* p=0.006; *WMC:* p=0.047). Taking into consideration that a graphical authentication mechanism is from a memory recall point of view a less demanding cognitive task than a password (recall through recognition vs. recall of information), an interpretation of this result can be based on the fact that graphical authentication mechanisms leverage human memory for visual information [6] and thus users with decreased speed of processing and working memory capacity needed less attempts in graphical authentication than in text-based passwords since the images illustrated helped them recognize and recall their authentication key.

4   Conclusions

The overarching aim of this work was to increase our understanding and knowledge on supporting usable security interaction design through user modeling, and adaptivity in user interface designs aiming to assist users to accomplish efficiently and effectively comprehensive and usable authentication tasks. In this respect, a three-month ecological valid user study was designed which entailed credible psychometric-based tests for eliciting the users' cognitive processing abilities (speed of processing, controlled attention, working memory capacity) and two types of user authentication mechanisms (text-based password and graphical), with the aim to investigate whether individuals with different cognitive processing abilities perform different in terms of efficiency and effectiveness in user authentication tasks.

Initial results demonstrate a main effect of cognitive processing abilities in both efficiency and effectiveness of user authentication mechanisms. In particular, results revealed that users with enhanced cognitive processing abilities performed significantly faster than users with limited cognitive processing abilities in graphical authentication. Regarding text-based password mechanisms, both user types with enhanced and limited cognitive processing abilities performed similarly with no significant differences. A possible interpretation of this result can be based on the familiarity factor of text-password mechanisms, thus, no significant differences were observed between the limited and enhanced user groups. However, since the users were not familiar with the graphical authentication mechanism, results indicated that the enhanced information processing abilities and temporary storage capacity of users have positively affected their performance compared to users with limited cognitive processing abilities. Another important result revealed that users with limited cognitive processing abilities needed significantly less attempts in graphical authentication than text-based password authentication suggesting that graphical authentication keys are easier to be retained in memory for this user group. These findings could be interpreted under the light of the picture superiority effect which suggests that pictures are better recognized and recalled by the human brain than textual information [27, 28]. Accordingly, various studies explain that pictures are more perceptually rich than words which lend them an advantage in memory recall (i.e., recall through recognition), and thus support the fact that users with decreased working memory capacity were more effective in graphical authentication mechanisms than in text-based password mechanisms. On the other hand, given that pictures are more perceptually rich than words, and thus are more demanding from a processing point of view, users with enhanced cognitive processing abilities were significantly faster in graphical authentication mechanisms than users with limited cognitive processing abilities.

From a user-adaptation point of view, such findings suggest that individual differences in human cognition are important to take into account in the personalization process of an adaptive interactive system. For instance, given that users with enhanced working memory capacity needed less tries in graphical authentication, and did not perform significantly different in either authentication type, such a result suggests providing a user with increased working memory capacity with a graphical authentication mechanism. In this respect, adapting the authentication task based on users' cognitive processing abilities could improve authentication task efficiency and effectiveness, and minimize users' cognitive loads and erroneous interactions. A practical implication of this work could be to explicitly elicit the users' cognitive processing abilities and accordingly suggest the "best-fit" authentication mechanism. A more sophisticated architecture could in addition, implicitly recommend the "best-fit" authentication mechanism based on historical usage data of the user in regard with efficiency and effectiveness of authentication tasks.

The limitations of the reported study are related to the fact that participants were only university students with an age between 17 to 26 years. In addition, carrying out a single assessment of users' cognitive factors might not fully justify the users' classification into specific cognitive-based groups since individuals might be influenced by other circumstances over time such as emotions, urgency, etc. In this respect, further studies need to be conducted in order to reach more concrete conclusions about the effect of individuals' cognitive processing abilities on their performance in authentication tasks. Furthermore, there has been an effort to increase ecological and internal validity of the research since the user authentication tasks were integrated in a real Web-based system and the participants were involved at their own physical environments without the intervention of any experimental equipment or person.

Given that future studies will contribute to the external validity of the reported research, we suggest that providing personalized user authentication mechanisms, adapted to users' individual characteristics could improve the overall user experience with regard to authentication tasks.

Acknowledgements. The work is co-funded by the PersonaWeb project under the Cyprus Research Promotion Foundation (ΤΠΕ/ΠΛΗΡΟ/0311(BIE)/10), and the EU projects Co-LIVING (60-61700-98-009) and SocialRobot (285870).

References

1. Herley, C., van Oorschot, P.: A Research Agenda Acknowledging the Persistence of Passwords. Security and Privacy 10(1), 28–36 (2012)
2. Zhang, J., Luo, X., Akkaladevi, S., Ziegelmayer, J.: Improving Multiple-password Recall: An Empirical Study. Information Security 18(2), 165–176 (2009)
3. Schneier, B.: The Secret Question Is: Why do IT Systems use Insecure Passwords? The Guardian, UK (2009)
4. Cranor, F., Garfinkel, S.: Security and Usability: Designing Secure Systems That People Can Use. O'Reilly & Associates, Sebastopol (2005)
5. Jakobsson, M., Myers, S.: Phishing and Countermeasures: Understanding the Increasing Problem of Electronic Identity Theft. Wiley-Interscience (2006)
6. Biddle, R., Chiasson, S., van Oorschot, P.: Graphical Passwords: Learning from the First Twelve Years. ACM Computing Surveys 44(4), Article 19 (2012)
7. Jermyn, I., Mayer, A., Monrose, F., Reiter, M., Rubin, A.: The Design and Analysis of Graphical Passwords. In: USENIX International Security Symposium, p. 1. USENIX Association, Berkley (1999)
8. Tao, H., Adams, C.: Pass-Go: A Proposal to Improve the Usability of Graphical Passwords. Network Security 7(2), 273–292 (2008)

9. Bulling, A., Alt, F., Schmidt, A.: Increasing the Security of Gaze-based Cued-recall Graphical Passwords using Saliency Masks. In: ACM SIGCHI International Conference on Human Factors in Computing Systems, pp. 3011–3020. ACM Press, New York (2012)
10. Passfaces Corporation, The science behind Passfaces, http://passfaces.com/enterprise/resources/whitepapers.htm
11. Mihajlov, M., Jerman-Blazic, B.: On Designing Usable and Secure Recognition-based Graphical Authentication Mechanisms. Interacting with Computers 23(6), 582–593 (2011)
12. Adams, A., Sasse, A.: Users are not the Enemy: Why Users Compromise Security Mechanisms and How to Take Remedial Measures. Communications of the ACM 42(12), 40–46 (1999)
13. Florencio, D., Herley, C.A.: Large-scale Study of Web Password Habits. In: ACM International Conference on World Wide Web, pp. 657–666. ACM Press, New York (2007)
14. Inglesant, P., Sasse, A.: The True Cost of Unusable Password Policies: Password use in the Wild. In: ACM SIGCHI International Conference on Human Factors in Computing Systems, pp. 383–392. ACM Press, New York (2010)
15. Brusilovsky, P., Kobsa, A., Nejdl, W. (eds.): Adaptive Web 2007. LNCS, vol. 4321. Springer, Heidelberg (2007)
16. Card, S.K., Moran, T.P., Newell, A.: The Model Human Processor: An Engineering Model of Human Performance. In: Boff, K.R., Kaufman, L., Thomas, J.P. (eds.) Handbook of Perception and Human Performance. Cognitive Processes and Performance, vol. 2, pp. 1–35 (1986)
17. Demetriou, A., Spanoudis, G., Shayer, S., Mouyi, A., Kazi, S., Platsidou, M.: Cycles in Speed-Working Memory-G Relations: Towards a Developmental-Differential Theory of the Mind. Intelligence 41, 34–50 (2013)
18. Hunt, E.B.: Human Intelligence. Cambridge University Press, New York (2011)
19. Demetriou, A., Spanoudis, G., Mouyi, A.: Educating the Developing Mind: Towards an Overarching Paradigm. Educational Psychology Review 23(4), 601–663 (2011)
20. MacLeod, C.M.: Half a Century of Research on the Stroop Effect: An Integrative review. Psychological Bulletin 109, 163–203 (1991)
21. Posner, M.I., Raicle, M.E.: Images of Mind. Scientific American Library, New York (1997)
22. Stroop, J.R.: Studies of Interference in Serial Verbal Reactions. Experimental Psychology 18, 643–662 (1935)
23. Baddeley, A.: Working Memory: Theories, Models, and Controversies. Annual Review of Psychology 63, 1–29 (2012)
24. Baddeley, A.: Working Memory. Science 255(5044), 556–559 (1992)
25. Shipstead, Z., Broadway, J.: Individual Differences in Working Memory Capacity and the Stroop Effect: Do High Spans Block the Words? Learning and Individual Differences (in press)
26. Demetriou, A., Christou, C., Spanoudis, G., Platsidou, M.: The Development of Mental Processing: Efficiency, Working Memory and Thinking. Monographs of the Society for Research in Child Development 67(1) (2002)
27. Anderson, J.R.: Cognitive Psychology and its Implications, 7th edn. Worth Publishers, New York (2009)
28. Ally, B.A., Budson, A.E.: The Worth of Pictures: Using High Density Event Related Potentials to Understand the Memorial Power of Pictures and the Dynamics of Recognition Memory. NeuroImage 35, 378–395 (2007)

Modeling a Graph Viewer's Effort in Recognizing Messages Conveyed by Grouped Bar Charts

Richard Burns[1], Sandra Carberry[2], and Stephanie Elzer Schwartz[3]

[1] Dept. of Computer Science, West Chester University, West Chester, PA 19383 USA
rburns@wcupa.edu
[2] Dept. of Computer Science, University of Delaware, Newark, DE 19716 USA
carberry@cis.udel.edu
[3] Dept. of Computer Science, Millersville University, Millserville, PA 17551 USA
stephanie.schwartz@millersville.edu

Abstract. Information graphics (bar charts, line graphs, etc.) in popular media generally have a high-level message that they are intended to convey. These messages are seldom repeated in the document's text yet contribute to understanding the overall document. The relative perceptual effort required to recognize a particular message is a communicative signal that serves as a clue about whether that message is the one intended by the graph designer. This paper presents a model of relative effort by a viewer for recognizing different messages from grouped bar charts. The model is implemented within the ACT-R cognitive framework and has been validated by human subjects experiments. We also present a statistical analysis of the contribution of effort in recognizing the intended message of a grouped bar chart.

1 Introduction

Information graphics are non-pictorial visual devices, such as simple bar charts, line graphs, pie charts, and grouped bar charts. They are incorporated into a multimodal document in order to achieve one or more communicative goals [12,11]. In the case of scientific documents, the communicative goal might be to present data or to help the reader visualize information. However, when information graphics appear in popular media such as periodicals (*USA Today, Wall Street Journal*) and magazines (*The Economist, Time*), they generally have a high-level message that they are intended to convey. For example, consider the graphics in Figures 1 and 2 which ostensibly convey that *"Women are more likely than men to delay medical treatment"* and that *"food prices are lower in Iraq than in the United States"*. Although the caption in Figure 1 explicitly states the graphic's message, the caption in Figure 2 does not help recognize the message of that graphic. A study by Carberry et al. [5] found that a graphic's message is often not contained in the graphic's caption or in the article accompanying the graphic. Yet the graphic's message is integral to understanding the full content of a multimodal document.

We are developing systems for recognizing the intended message of an information graphic in popular media. Our work has several applications. The first

S. Carberry et al. (Eds.): UMAP 2013, LNCS 7899, pp. 114–126, 2013.
© Springer-Verlag Berlin Heidelberg 2013

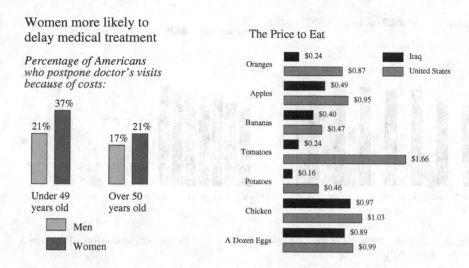

Fig. 1. "Snapshot" graphic from *USA Today*, June 16, 2003

Fig. 2. Graphic from *USA Today*, "Markets' prices shelve thrill of new selections", March 10, 2005

is a system that provides alternative access to information graphics for sight-impaired individuals by conveying their high-level content to the user via speech [8]. The second is the retrieval of information graphics from a digital library where the graphic's message is used to capture its high-level content [5]. The third application is the summarization of multimodal documents that takes into account their information graphics rather than ignoring them or merely considering only their captions [21].

Previous work has focused on message recognition for simple bar charts [9] and line graphs [22]. Grouped bar charts are another type of information graphic. Although grouped bar charts and simple bar charts both display bars that depict quantifiable relationships among the values of entities, grouped bar charts also contain a *grouping* dimension. For example, Figures 1, 2, and 5 respectively contain two groups of two bars each, seven groups of two bars each, and three groups of four bars each. Consequently, grouped bar charts convey a much wider variety of messages than simple bar charts or line graphs, and thus the recognition of their messages is much more complex.

The overall objective of our research is a system for recognizing the high-level messages conveyed by a grouped bar chart [4]. An important component of the system is a model that estimates the relative effort that a graph viewer would have to expend in order to recognize a particular message for a given grouped bar chart. Consider the graphic in Figure 4 which depicts the same data as is displayed in Figure 3. Although the graphic in Figure 3 facilitates an easy comparison of Internet usage between the United States and China for each year from 2002 to 2008, such a comparison is more difficult in Figure 4 due to the different organization. Thus while the primary message conveyed by the graphic

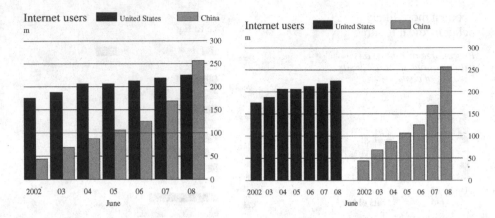

Fig. 3. Graphic from *The Economist Daily Chart*, July 31, 2008

Fig. 4. A different organization of Figure 3

in Figure 4 is the rising trend in Internet usage in both countries[1], the primary message of the graphic in Figure 3 is that the gap in Internet usage between the two countries has decreased and in fact reversed (with China now having higher usage than the United States). This correlates with an observation by Larkin and Simon [13] that graphics that are informationally equivalent (that is, they convey the same data) are not necessarily computationally equivalent (it can be more difficult to extract certain information from one graphic than from the other). The AutoBrief project [11] hypothesized that graph designers construct graphics that enable the easy performance of tasks that are needed to recognize the graphic's communicative goal. Thus we view the relative effort needed to recognize a particular message from a graphic as evidence of whether that was the message intended by the graph designer — that is, the more effort required to recognize a particular message relative to other messages, the less likely that was the message that the graph designer intended to convey.

This paper presents our model of the relative effort that is required for a viewer to recognize messages from grouped bar charts and its effect on our overall system. Our model is implemented in the ACT-R cognitive framework [2] and is based on research in the area of graph comprehension as well as our own motivating eye-tracking experiments. Validation experiments quantitatively and qualitatively support our model.

Section 2 of this paper discusses related work. Section 3 of the paper describes the types of messages that grouped bar chart information graphics convey in popular media. Section 4 then presents our model that estimates the relative effort required for a user to recognize a particular message given a graphic. It presents the cognitive research underlying the model, describes its implementation, and presents the results of an experiment validating the model. Section 5

---

[1] And perhaps that it is rising faster in China.

very briefly describes how the model, along with other communicative signals, is incorporated into a Bayesian message recognition system.

2   Related Work

Elzer [9] and Wu [22] have implemented intended message recognition systems for simple bar charts and line graphs, respectively. Their systems are similar to our grouped bar chart system in that they also use Bayesian networks to probabilistically capture the relationships between high-level intended messages and communicative signals. However, grouped bar charts are more complex than simple bar charts and they convey a much richer set of messages. The system for simple bar charts modeled relative effort [10], but it followed the GOMS paradigm [6] in which perceptual tasks were decomposed into primitive tasks whose effort estimates were summed. However, grouped bar charts require more complex reasoning that also takes into account peripheral vision, high-level visual patterns, the re-encoding of graph objects, and other aspects of perceptual processing that were not considered in the effort model for simple bar charts. Consequently, our effort model for grouped bar charts is implemented within the ACT-R cognitive modeling framework [2] which facilitates such complex reasoning.

3   Messages Conveyed in Grouped Bar Charts

We collected 330 grouped bar charts from a variety of popular media sources and assembled them into a corpus that is available online.[2] In analyzing the corpus, we identified 25 different *message categories* that capture the kinds of messages conveyed by grouped bar charts [4]. Parameters in the message categories become instantiated to fully capture the intended *messages*. Each graph in the collected corpus was examined by a team of annotators who identified the graphic's high-level *primary* message and *secondary* message[3], based on our generalization of message categories, terminology, and parameters.[4] Consensus-based annotation [3] was performed to resolve cases of disagreement to enable the inclusion of difficult examples where the message was not obvious and there was not complete agreement amongst the annotators [14]. The final consensus for the intended messages in the corpus is also published online.[5] In this section, we briefly present some of the most commonly occurring message categories.[6]

Trend Messages. Trend messages convey a general trend that is either rising, falling, or steady. The trend exists over a set of ordinal data points. Trend messages can be within-groups in which case each group of bars comprises a graph

---

[2] Accessible at: http://www.cis.udel.edu/~burns/corpus
[3] A second intended message that is not as apparent.
[4] The full terminology is presented in [4].
[5] Available at: http://www.cis.udel.edu/~burns/corpus/view-consensus.php
[6] Space limitations preclude the description of all identified message categories.

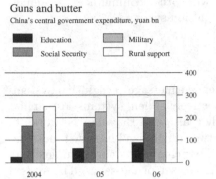

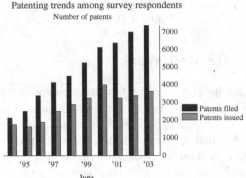

Fig. 5. Graphic from *The Economist*, "Planning the new socialist countryside", March 9, 2006

Fig. 6. Graphic from *Technology Review*, "A Mixed Bag of U.S. Institutions", July 2005

group entity or across-groups in which case the ith bar from each group forms a graph series entity. For example, the grouped bar chart in Figure 5 ostensibly conveys the primary message that *"China increased spending on education, social security, military, and rural support from 2004 to 2006"*; it is an *across-groups* message since the ith bar from each of the three groups comprises the ith trend. We generalize this and similar messages into the *Rising-Trend* message category.

Relationship Messages. Relationship messages capture the consistency of relative values for a set of graphed entities, or the inconsistency of one set of relative values with respect to the other sets. For example, the graphic in Figure 7 ostensibly conveys the message that *"the increased funding to the area of Life Sciences is in contrast to the steady or decreased funding to the other areas"*. This messages contrasts *Life Sciences* with the other entities, and the comparison with respect to research funding is within-groups. We identify it as an *Entity-Relationship-Contrast* message category. Messages that convey the *identical* relative ordering of values of a set of graphed entities (that is, there is no contrasting entity) are generalized into the *Same-Relationship-All* message category. The *Opposite-Relationship* message category captures messages that convey two entities with a different relative ordering of bar values.

Gap Messages. The gap message category captures high-level messages involving either one *gap*, or a trend in the size of multiple *gaps*, where a *gap* is the approximate absolute difference between two values within the same entity. Gap messages can refer to gaps within-groups or to gaps across-groups. There are several interesting types of gap messages that occur in grouped bar charts.

Figure 6 displays a graphic whose message falls into the *Gap-Increasing* message category, where the graph is intended to convey that the trending of the gaps (gaps within-groups) is increasing. Ostensibly, the graph conveys that the *"gap between the number of patents filed and issued increased over the period from 1994 to 2003"*.

The *Gap-Crossover* message category captures messages conveying that the trending of one entity surpasses the trending of another entity. For example, the grouped bar chart in Figure 3 conveys that *"the gap between the number of Internet users in the US and China has steadily decreased until now China has more Internet users than the US"*.

Comparison Messages. Some grouped bar chart messages compare either the gap of a single entity to the gaps of the other entities, or the entire single entity itself to all of the other entities. These message categories are called *Gap-Comparison* and *Entity-Comparison*, respectively.

Consider the grouped bar chart in Figure 8. Its *primary* intended message is *"that the percentage of pirated software is greater in China than in the World"*. However, to a much lesser degree, the graphic *secondarily* conveys *"that the decrease in piracy between 1994 and 2002 is less in China than in the World"*. The former message captures the comparison of the *size* of piracy in China with the other entity (the World) and is an *Entity-Comparison* message, whereas the latter represents a comparison of the *gap* between piracy in 1994 and 2002 for China with the other entity (the World) and is a *Gap-Comparison* message.

4   Effort

From a given graphic, one can extract a number of different messages, such as a trend within groups, a relationship across groups, a comparison of gaps among group entities, etc. Green et al. [11] hypothesizes that the design of a graph should facilitate as much as possible the tasks that the graph viewer will need to perform in order to understand the graphic's intended message. Thus, because our motivation is an overall intention recognition system that can hypothesize the messages that are most likely to be the ones intended by the graph designer, the ability to model which messages in a graphic are relatively easy to recognize in comparison

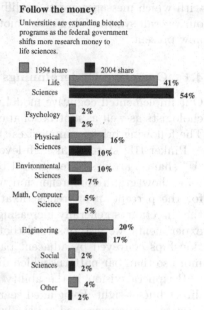

Fig. 7. Graphic from *USA Today*, "Universities gird for battle for biosciences supremacy", June 24, 2005

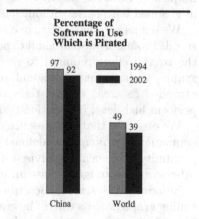

Fig. 8. Graphic from *NewsWeek*, "Microsoft Cozies Up to China", June 28, 2004

with which messages are more difficult to recognize, may be a useful factor for our overall system. This is the motivation for our *relative effort model* that we now present.

4.1 Cognitive Underpinnings

Our implemented cognitive model was motivated by research by cognitive psychologists as well as motivational eye-tracking experiments that we performed. The following briefly summarizes these principles and observations.

Pinker [15] states that high-level visual patterns, such as straight lines and "U" shapes, are easily recognized by the human visual system. Shah et al. [17] notes how graph comprehension utilizes *bottom-up* visual pattern recognition for the perception of trends (fixating on adjacent bars to determine whether the direction is generally increasing, decreasing or steady). In our motivational experiments, we also observed that subjects were able to quickly identify relationships conveyed by adjacent bars whose values represented a straight line, more so than bar patterns which did not capture a familiar perceptual pattern.

Peripheral vision is the ability to visually process objects that are not in direct line-of-sight. For guided search tasks, Anderson [1] showed how multiple objects can be processed in parallel through the use of peripheral vision. In our motivational eye-tracking experiments, we also observed how subjects processed entities in a graph by using peripheral vision — that is, all of the entities in a graph were processed without fixating on each individual entity. For example, we frequently observed instances in which subjects could correctly identify trends in grouped bar charts without looking at every bar.

We define an *exception* as one or more bars that do not conform to an overall trend. From our motivational experiments, we found that exceptions do impact the overall effort required to recognize a trend. When presented with noisier graphs with a greater amount of "trend exceptions", subjects frequently re-attended to areas around the exception location, and overall, took longer to perform high-level recognition tasks on the graphic.

We observed that the presence of *visual clutter* and violations of the *proximity compatibility principle* (as defined by Wickens and Carswell [20], that perceptual proximity of elements is advised if the elements are part of the same task and is otherwise discouraged) cause an increase in processing time for subjects.

Simkin and Hastie [18] describe *superimposition* as an elementary spatial reasoning graph process where the graph viewer spatially moves objects in the graph around to ease comparison with other graph objects. Trickett and Trafton [19] additionally hypothesize that superimposition is used for the mental averaging within a group for performing the task of comparing the heights of groups in grouped bar charts.

4.2 ACT-R Model of Effort

We implemented our model of effort in the ACT-R cognitive modeling framework [2] with the EMMA add-on [16]. Models implemented in ACT-R are intended to reflect the ACT-R theory of human cognition. Model accuracy is usually demonstrated by comparing the model on some task to that of a human performing the same task. However, it is important to emphasize that our goal is <u>not</u> to construct a cognitive model that simulates how humans comprehend graphs, but rather to create a model that estimates the *relative* difficulty for a user to recognize one message vs. another in the same graphic.

ACT-R models how the cognitive system *uses* visual attention, but it is unable to automatically recognize that the data points representing the tops of bars can be encoded to form a visual pattern, unless that relationship is explicitly declared. Therefore to implement pattern recognition, a small preprocessing script was also implemented. High-level patterns that the script identifies are then declared in model to simulate *top-down* encoding (recognizing the direction of a trend with only a few fixations because the bars generally form a straight line, or quickly recognizing that several groups of bars each form a common visual pattern such as a "U" shape and thus convey similar relationships).

We implemented 12 different cognitive submodels in our overall model of relative effort for grouped bar charts. Some submodels estimate the relative effort for multiple messages categories. For example, the same cognitive submodel can process both *Rising-Trends* and *Falling-Trends* that exist *across-groups*. The following presents the significant parts of the submodels that estimate the relative difficulty for a user to recognize the message categories presented in Section 3.[7]

Trends (Within-Groups) Model. This model estimates the relative perceptual effort required for the recognition of trends *within-groups*. The model attends to and encodes each group until all groups have been processed. The total processing time for the model is dependent on the cost of encoding each group as well as the number of groups in the graph. The increase in cost as a result of additional groups was significant in the motivational eye-tracking experiments.

High-level visual patterns may exist in a group and are identified through the preprocessing. Exceptions are also possible. As expected, because of high-level visual pattern recognition ability and peripheral vision, the motivational eye-tracking experiments also showed that the number of bars per group did not significantly affect recognition time. The model ultimately encodes each group top-down or bottom-up into a trend representation when a trend exists.

Relationship (Within-Groups) Model. The *Relationship* model is very similar to the *Trend* model. Each group is encoded until all of the group entities are processed. Entities with contrasting relationships are re-encoded. Any visual patterns are identified in preprocessing.

Gap Trend (Gaps Within-Groups) Model. The design of this model follows observations from the motivational eye-tracking data that high-level visual patterns are utilized in the recognition of the *Gap-Increasing (gaps within-groups)* messages and that additional fixations tend to occur around the "*crossover*

---

[7] Space precludes us from describing all of the submodels in our system.

point" in a *Gap-Crossover (gaps within-groups)* message.[8] The model repeatedly alternatives between attending to each series, to simulate the encoding of gaps between adjacent groups. In addition, high-level visual patterns across groups are processed by the model which allows some bar entities to be encoded without an explicit attention and ultimately speeds up the overall processing time. Crossover points are identified by the model as instances of visual clutter that induce additional attentions.

Entity-Comparison (Group Entity Instantiation) Model. Unlike the previous models, this model also requires an instantiated parameter: a specific group entity to compare with the other groups. Thus, the model's estimate of effort is dependent on the instantiation.

The *Entity-Comparison* message category sometimes captures a message of *rank*, such as *"the instantiated entity is the 2nd tallest group"*. The model processes the graphic by beginning with an instantiated entity and repeatedly finding the next tallest entity in the grouped bar chart until no more exist. Thus, the model attends to a subset of entities in the graphic and compares the instantiated entity with all of the entities in that subset. Because it is easier to recognize the rank of an entity in a grouped bar chart if the entities are sorted by bar height, preprocessing in the model determines if the entities in the grouped bar chart are sorted by bar height. If they are, the model will recognize the rank of the instantiated entity more quickly by following in a straight path all of the entities that are taller than it.

Gap-Comparison (Gaps Within-Groups Instantiation) Model. This model requires an instantiation of a gap that exists within a group entity. Intuitively, the recognition of the size of a gap is dependent on its similarity to the size of the gaps in the other group entities; thus, it is important which entity is instantiated. The model first encodes the gap of the instantiated entity. Then the model encodes all of the other gaps in the grouped bar chart while re-attending to any whose gap size is approximately similar to that of the instantiated entity.

4.3   Validation Experiment

Design. We validated our model by comparing the relative effort estimates for a given set of grouped bar charts against the relative effort required by human subjects performing the same tasks on the same set of graphics.[9] 46 human subjects participated in the experiment, each performing graph tasks on 48 grouped bar charts. Each subject was initially presented with learning and practice slides that explained the types of tasks that they would be asked to perform. Then the appropriate task was prompted to the subjects before each graph in the actual experiment. As an example, a prompt for the *Trend* graph task was: *"In the following graph, is each country's revenue generally increasing? are all revenues*

---

[8] In Figure 3, the "crossover point" is between the *07* and *08* groups.
[9] Graphs and subjects were different than in the motivational experiments.

increasing except for one country? except for 2 or more countries? or do all of the revenues first increase and then decrease?"

Quantitative Results. For each grouped bar chart, the average mean timing for a subject to perform the prompt task was calculated.[10] These means were ranked to produce an ordered set. The times estimated by the model for the same set of grouped bar charts and graph tasks were also ranked.

The Spearman rank-order correlation measures the relation between two sets of rank-ordered data. Values approaching 1.0 indicate a strong correlation between the ranking of two sets. The overall Spearman correlation for the ranking of all 48 tasks and graphics is $\rho = .725$, $p < .001$. This strong correlation suggests that the models capture the relative effort for recognizing different messages from a graphic and thus should serve as a useful piece of evidence in our overall intention recognition system (Section 5).

Qualitative Results. Additionally, the subject data from the validation experiment was qualitatively consistent with many of the intuitions that were incorporated into the design of the models. For example:

- subjects recognized trends within-groups with less effort when there were fewer groups and more visual patterns
- additional bars per group increased the effort for within-group relationship comparisons
- relationship comparisons within-groups were generally less effortful than across-groups
- additional groups in a graph increased the effort required for recognizing the group with the largest gap unless that largest gap was extremely salient
- a group was more easily identified in entity comparisons when its bar entities were each taller than the bars comprising the other groups
- subjects recognized gap trends where the gap was within groups much easier than when the graph was designed with the gaps across groups

5   Role of Effort in Message Recognition

Our overall system that automatically recognizes the intended message of a graphic is implemented as a Bayesian network graphical model [4]. Given a grouped bar chart, a computer vision system [7] first processes the graphic and extracts its features: the positioning of bars, their bar heights, etc. These features are passed to the effort models and Bayesian network.

Various pieces of *communicative evidence* are input into the overall system so that the Bayesian network can hypothesize the most likely intended message of a graph. One major piece of evidence is the relative effort required to recognize a message. For each possible message that might be recognized from a graphic, effort is discretized into three categories: *Easy*, *Medium*, and *Hard*, capturing how relatively easy or difficult it would be for a viewer to recognize that message from

---

[10] Incorrect responses by subjects were omitted.

Table 1. Impact of Evidence in the Bayesian System

Included Evidence in Overall System	Accuracy	McNemar's Test
Baseline: None	98 / 330 (29.7%)	$\chi^2 = 15.803, p < .0001$
Effort Only	153 / 330 (46.4%)	

the graphic. Many other types of communicative evidence are also incorporated into the system, such as if a group entity is much taller than the others. Using leave-one-out cross-validation, the overall system accuracy for recognizing the primary intended message of a grouped bar chart is 65.6%, which far exceeds a baseline accuracy of 18.8% that results from selecting the most commonly occurring possible message.

It is interesting to consider the impact of effort on our Bayesian recognition system. As noted earlier, it is common for grouped bar charts to have both a primary and a secondary message. Our annotators also annotated our corpus for secondary messages and found that 177 of 330 grouped bar charts had *strong* secondary messages. These secondary messages were only identified by the annotators when they were quickly apparent and recognizable with minimal effort.

We hypothesize that effort is an important factor for the recognition of messages. Communicative signals other than effort (coloring, salience by height or position, salience by mention in a caption, etc.) contribute to the recognition of a graphic's primary message, and the absence of one kind of communicative signal can be compensated for by the presence of other communicative signals. On the other hand, these other communicative signals may detract from the recognition of a secondary message that relies mostly on being readily apparent. Thus to see if our effort model has a positive impact on our recognition of messages, we ran an experiment that considers both a graph's primary and secondary message (if any). We first ran our Bayesian system without any evidence nodes to establish a baseline, and then ran the system once again with only effort as evidence. When no evidence was considered (only the a priori probabilities of messages are present), the system's baseline for correctly predicting either the primary or secondary message of a graphic within the top two messages that it hypothesizes is 29.7%. When we add only effort evidence into the system, this performance improves to 46.4% — demonstrating that the learned probabilistic relationships between intended messages and relative effort is a beneficial evidence source for the overall system. These results are shown in Table 1 along with a statistical significance measurement as calculated by McNemar's test, which is used on nominal, matched-pair data to show the statistical significance of change.

6   Conclusion

Prior work has modeled the relative difficulty for a user to recognize primary messages in simple bar charts. However, grouped bar charts convey a far richer set of messages—including secondary messages—that require a richer model of relative effort. This paper has presented our model of relative effort for grouped bar charts, including the cognitive underpinnings of the model and its validation. It also briefly explored the benefit of a model of relative effort as an evidence source in our overall intention recognition system that aims to automatically identify both primary and secondary messages in grouped bar charts.

References

1. Anderson, J.R., Lebiere, C.: The Atomic Components of Thought. Lawrence Erlbaum Associates, Mahwah (1998)
2. Anderson, J.R., Matessa, M., Lebiere, C.: Act-r: A theory of higher level cognition and its relation to visual attenion. Human-Computer Interaction 12, 439–462 (1997)
3. Ang, J., Dhillon, R., Krupski, A., Shriberg, E., Stolcke, A.: Prosody-based automatic detection of annoyance and frustration in human-computer dialog. In: Proceedings of the International Conference on Spoken Language Processing, pp. 2037–2040 (2002)
4. Burns, R.: Automated Intention Recognition of Grouped Bar Charts in Multimodal Documents. Ph.D. thesis, University of Delaware (2012)
5. Carberry, S., Elzer, S., Demir, S.: Information graphics: An untapped resource of digital libraries. In: Proceedings of 9th International ACM SigIR Conference on Research and Development on Information Retrieval, pp. 581–588. ACM, New York (2006)
6. Card, S., Moran, T.P., Newell, A.: The Psychology of Human-Computer Interaction. Lawrence Erlbaum Associates, Hillsdale (1983)
7. Chester, D., Elzer, S.: Getting computers to see information graphics so users do not have to. In: Hacid, M.-S., Murray, N.V., Raś, Z.W., Tsumoto, S. (eds.) ISMIS 2005. LNCS (LNAI), vol. 3488, pp. 660–668. Springer, Heidelberg (2005)
8. Demir, S., Oliver, D., Schwartz, E., Elzer, S., Carberry, S., McCoy, K.F.: Interactive sight into information graphics. In: Proceedings of the 2010 International Cross Disciplinary Conference on Web Accessibility (W4A), pp. 16:1–16:10. ACM, New York (2010)
9. Elzer, S., Carberry, S., Zukerman, I.: The automated understanding of simple bar charts. Artificial Intelligence 175(2), 526–555 (2011)
10. Elzer, S., Green, N., Carberry, S., Hoffman, J.: A model of perceptual task effort for bar charts and its role in recognizing intention. International Journal on User Modeling and User-Adapted Interaction 16, 1–30 (2006)
11. Green, N.L., Carenini, G., Kerpedjiev, S., Mattis, J., Moore, J.D., Roth, S.F.: Autobrief: an experimental system for the automatic generation of briefings in integrated text and information graphics. International Journal of Human-Computer Studies 61(1), 32–70 (2004)
12. Iverson, G., Gergen, M.: Statistics: The Conceptual Approach. Springer, New York (1997)
13. Larkin, J.H., Simon, H.A.: Why a diagram is (sometimes) worth a thousand words. Cognitive Science 11, 65–99 (1987)
14. Litman, D.J., Forbes-Riley, K.: Predicting student emotions in computer-human tutoring dialogues. In: Proceedings of the 42nd Annual Meeting on Association for Computational Linguistics, pp. 352–359. Association for Computational Linguistics, Morristown (2004)

15. Pinker, S.: A theory of graph comprehension. No. 15 in Occasional Papers, Center for Cognitive Science, Massachusetts Institute of Technology, Cambridge, MA (1981)
16. Salvucci, D.D.: An integrated model of eye movements and visual encoding. Cognitive Systems Research 1, 201–220 (2001)
17. Shah, P., Mayer, R.E., Hegarty, M.: Graphs as aids to knowledge construction: Signaling techniques for guiding the process of graph comprehension. Educational Psychology 91, 690–702 (1999)
18. Simkin, D., Hastie, R.: An information-processing analysis of graph perception. American Statistical Association 82, 454–465 (1987)
19. Trickett, S.B., Trafton, J.G.: Toward a comprehensive model of graph comprehension: Making the case for spatial cognition. In: Barker-Plummer, D., Cox, R., Swoboda, N. (eds.) Diagrams 2006. LNCS (LNAI), vol. 4045, pp. 286–300. Springer, Heidelberg (2006)
20. Wickens, C.D., Carswell, C.M.: The proximity compatibility principle: Its psychological foundation and relevance to display design. Human Factors 37, 473–494 (1995)
21. Wu, P., Carberry, S.: Toward extractive summarization of multimodal documents. In: Proceedings of the Workshop on Text Summarization at the Canadian Conference on Artificial Intelligence, pp. 53–61 (2011)
22. Wu, P., Carberry, S., Elzer, S., Chester, D.: Recognizing the intended message of line graphs. In: Goel, A.K., Jamnik, M., Narayanan, N.H. (eds.) Diagrams 2010. LNCS (LNAI), vol. 6170, pp. 220–234. Springer, Heidelberg (2010)

Evaluation of Attention Levels in a Tetris Game Using a Brain Computer Interface

Georgios Patsis[1,2], Hichem Sahli[1], Werner Verhelst[1,2], and Olga De Troyer[3]

[1] Dept. of Electronics and Informatics (ETRO), Vrije Universiteit Brussel (VUB),
Pleinlaan 2, 1050 Brussels, Belgium
[2] iMinds, Gaston Crommenlaan 8, 9050 Ghent, Belgium
{gpatsis,hsahli,wverhels}@etro.vub.ac.be
[3] Web & Information Systems Engineering (WISE) Laboratory,
Vrije Universiteit Brussel (VUB), Pleinlaan 2, 1050 Brussels, Belgium
Olga.DeTroyer@vub.ac.be

Abstract. This paper investigates the possibility of using information from brain signals, obtained through a light and inexpensive Brain Computer Interface (BCI), in order to dynamically adjust the difficulty of an educational video game and adapt the level of challenge to players' abilities. In this experiment, attention levels of Tetris players – measured with the BCI – have been evaluated as a function of game difficulty. Processing of the data revealed that both in intra- and inter- player analysis, an increase in game difficulty was followed by an increase in attention. These results come in accordance with similar experiments performed with a 19 sensor EEG cap, as opposed to the single-dry-sensor BCI used here. These findings give new possibilities in the development of educational games that adapt to the mental state of player/learner.

Keywords: brain signal, brain computer interface, attention levels, Tetris, dynamically adjust game difficulty.

1 Introduction

The use of educational video games (edu-games) is a way to increase motivation in the learning process, but the risk that learners get bored still exists. Therefore, understanding the learner's cognitive state is important when using edu-games, and enabling the edu-game to dynamically respond to the learner's behavior and mental state through adaptive actions could be beneficial. In this paper we are investigating if we can monitor player's behavior and mental state using a simple Brain Computer Interface (BCI). More precisely we are testing if changes in game difficulty are followed by changes in the brainwaves. The work presented here is part of an interdisciplinary research project on adaptive educational games. Among other issues, we are investigating ways of controlling game difficulty by getting direct input of the mental state of the player with physiological sensors. In this first experiment we are using an EEG sensor. Over the last few years a number of new light and inexpensive devices, so-called Brain Computer Interfaces (BCI), have appeared in the market. A BCI is a

S. Carberry et al. (Eds.): UMAP 2013, LNCS 7899, pp. 127–138, 2013.
© Springer-Verlag Berlin Heidelberg 2013

device that can capture brain waves (very low electrical signals produced by the brain). These new technologies have made it possible to measure at low cost and in a less intrusive way basic brain activity. Until then, brain activity could be measured only with dedicated equipment using an EEG cap (Electroencephalography), which is of course much more reliable but not usable outside a lab or medical environment. In order to test the usefulness of the device in the context of our work, we have performed some preliminary tests and studies. After doing a market research we decided to use the MindWave BCI from NeuroSky (www.neurosky.com), which is specially designed for and targets the gaming market. It is a low cost wireless device, highly user friendly, with a single dry-sensor positioned on the forehead (FP1). Except the raw brain signal, this device also provides levels of attention in the scale of 0 to 100. NeuroSky does not provide a description of the algorithms used to calculate attention levels since they are protected as trade secret. For our experiments we didn't use the raw EEG signal applying processing algorithms, but the readings of attention straight from the device. Our intention is to test the usefulness of new BCI technologies based on work that has already been done. The specific device is a product of university research carried out together with physiologists. Several research groups have already carried out studies using the device [1], [2], [3], [4] and [5]. To our knowledge, this is the first time that a BCI is used in experiments evaluating attention levels of users playing Tetris or any other game in different difficulties. Results reported so far using the MindWave BCI was mainly focused on assessing attention levels during mental tasks. We performed an experiment based on a gaming protocol introduced by G. Channel et al. [6] in order to investigate if changes in game difficulty are followed by changes in brain activity. In their experiments, they used a number of physiological sensors capturing signals like galvanic skin response, blood volume pulse, heart rate, chest cavity expansion, and skin temperature. In 14 of 20 participants an EEG cap (19 electrodes) was used for capturing brain waves. The authors of [6] investigated the use of emotion assessment from physiological signals to adapt the difficulty of a Tetris game. They found that playing the game in different difficulty levels gave rise to different emotions. In easy difficulty players were bored, in medium they were in an engagement mode and in hard levels they felt anxiety. Moreover they found that engagement of a player in the game is decreasing if the level of difficulty does not change. Except the statistical analysis to determine the emotional states of players in different levels, classification has been also performed in order to investigate the possibility of recognizing these states from the physiological signals. For our experiment we used only the BCI which has a single dry sensor placed on the forehead (position FP1) and can capture EEG signal from the brain. In the experiments described in [6], the Tetris game was used. As our goal was to investigate if the BCI could provide information in the same line as the results reported in [6], we also used Tetris since it is easy to control the difficulty by changing the speed of the falling blocks. In the regular Tetris game the speed of the falling blocks is gradually increased as the player is making more lines. We adapted the code of an open source version so we could control the speed of the falling blocks and keep it constant through a gameplay. Speed could be changed in 25 steps (levels).

2   Data Capture

The experiment was conducted in the recording room of AV Lab, the audiovisual laboratory of the Department of Electronics and Informatics (ETRO) of our university [7]. Except the BCI we also used 2 cameras: one USB camera attached on the PC monitor (video chat position) recording the front view of the face of each player and a camcorder recording the game from a second monitor that was reproducing game player's view. Signals from the 2 video cameras and the BCI were in synch using timestamps. More specifically, the software used to capture the video of the USB camera (www.webcamxp.com) is naming the produced file with the timestamp of the PC used. Also, the BCI comes with a SDK where in the resulting text file with all the data, a time stamp is introduced when capture started. Both the USB camera and the BCI are installed in the same PC, so timestamps refer to the same clock. In order to synchronize the camcorder with the USB camera, we used the classic hand clapping, so we can align video's using the high peak produced by the clapping in the sound clip of both signals. With timestamps introduced by the local clock of the PC, we manage to have a synch down to one second, which is the time resolution of the BCI for levels of attention. The information from the videos was used for segmentation and in order to extract other useful information that could help in the analysis.

3   Experiments

We have conducted the experiment, letting 14 post-graduate students of our university (7 male and 7 female) to play 6 Tetris games in 3 difficulty levels: 2 easy, 2 medium and 2 hard games in an arbitrary order, according to the gaming protocol introduced in [6]. All players had to play each game for a 5 minute period. In case where a player would lose the game before the 5 minute period he/she had to stop. In a very few cases, some players wanted to continue beyond the 5 minute limit. We let them do so. Between the games, players had to rest for 5 minutes and fill in a self-evaluation form giving scores for their valence/arousal (according to the SAM system [9]) and their perceived game difficulty (easy, medium, or hard). We used the five scale visual representation for valance and arousal levels of the SAM system, explaining to players how to give their scores for each dimension. For valance, they had to give a score between lowest (one), feeling very unhappy with their performance, and highest (five), feeling very happy with their performance. For arousal, they had to give a score between one, felling very bored and five feeling very excited. As already indicated, in Tetris, game difficulty can be controlled by the speed of the falling blocks. We used an open source implementation of the game found on Sourceforge (sourceforge.net/projects/tetrominusrex/), where we adjusted the code so that speed and therefore the difficulty could be constant.

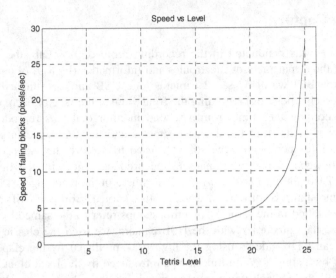

Fig. 1. Speed of falling blocks as a function of Tetris level

We adjusted the Tetris game in order to have a total of 25 levels. The higher the level, the higher the speed of the falling blocks. In order to find the relation between Tetris level and the speed of the falling blocks, we measured the speed of the falling blocks (in pixels per second). We found that speed is increasing exponentially with the level (Fig 1).

We first let players practice for 15 minutes in a level that was comfortable for them: a level that is not too easy but not too hard. It is the level that players can feel satisfaction and engagement playing focused for long time. According to [6] this is the level where the skills of a player meet game difficulty and it is defined by the flow theory proposed by Mihaly *Csikszentmihalyi* [8]. Flow is the mental state where a person in an activity is fully immersed in a feeling of energized focus and full involvement. In order to identify this level (medium game difficulty) for each player we let them play for a short period starting from level 15 and increasing the level until they felt they were in a state that it was not too easy but also not too difficult to play the game. We call this level the starting level and it gives an indication of player's skill in Tetris. For all players this state was between Tetris levels 15 and 22 (Table 1). For easy and hard games we used Tetris levels 1 to 5[1], respectively 22 to 24 as shown in Table 1.

Players were asked to evaluate the (perceived) difficulty of each 5-minute game (easy, medium or hard). In our analysis, we used these data of player's self-evaluation (for game difficulty) as ground truth. By analyzing the videos from the 2 cameras for each player we extracted the start and end time for each game and use them for the analysis of the corresponding attention data segments. In total we end up with 84 instances of games (14 players x 6 games).

---

[1] We only considered levels 1-5 because the increase in speed between levels 5 and 15 is very small (see Fig 1).

Table 1. Tetris levels used for each of the 3 game difficulties

Game Difficulty	Tetris Level
Easy	1 - 5
Medium	15 - 22
Hard	22 - 24

4   Affective State Assessment

We first analyze the results obtained for Valence/Arousal for all 84 instances. We wanted to have a global view of player's emotional state in the 3 different game difficulties so we can use this as the ground truth for further analysis of attention levels. For our analysis we have split the valence/arousal plane in 4 quadrants, each one representing a different emotion according to the mapping introduced by Russel [9]. We used the 4 basic emotions found in a gaming experience (Fig 2). When game difficulty is easy, players are getting bored but when it is (too) hard they get stressed. Between these two states there is a flow zone, where skills of the player meet game difficulty, players are engaged and can enjoy playing the game showing positive emotions like joy or excitement.

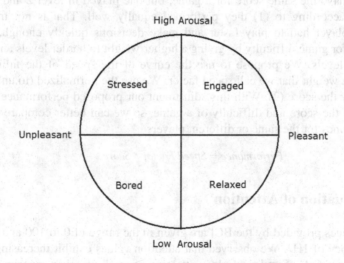

Fig. 2. Valence/Arousal space used in our experiments

In Table 2 we give the results of player's self-evaluation for all 84 instances. We observe that when players evaluate game difficulty as easy in 65.51% of the instances they felt bored. When they had evaluated difficulty as normal, in 57.14% of instances they felt engaged and in case of hard difficulty in 55.55% of instances they were stressed.

Table 2. Percentage of instances for each emotion according the player's self-evaluation

Game Difficulty Player	Engaged	Relaxed	Bored	Stressed
Easy	17.24	13.79	65.51	3.44
Normal	57.14	0	24.42	21.42
Hard	40.74	0	3.70	55.55

5   Performance Metric

A possible measurement of player's performance in a Tetris game is the total score (total number of lines). We could use this performance metric to compare the overall performance of the 6 games among players. If we want to compare player's (same or different) performance in individual games we could use the score, where A is a constant:

$$Performance = A * Score \tag{1}$$

The problem by using this performance metric is that it doesn't take into account the difficulty level, which is a function of the speed of the falling blocks. If for example two players have the same score for a game, but one played in level 2 and the other in level 22 according to (1) they performed equally well. That is not true, since the second player had to play faster and make decisions quickly enough. We can compensate for game difficulty by giving a higher weight to harder levels and a lower one to easy levels. We propose to use the curve of the speed of the falling block (Fig 2) as the weight that we call speed factor. We use the normalized (to unity) curve multiplied by the score (2). With this adjustment our proposed performance metric is a function of the score and difficulty of a game, so we can better compare results of individual games for the same or different players.

$$Performance = Speed\ Factor * Score \tag{2}$$

6   Evaluation of Attention

Attention values provided by the BCI are given in the range of 0 to 100 and at a sampling frequency of 1Hz. We observed that attention values exhibit increasing (A+) or decreasing trends (A-).Similar trends in attention were observed in experiments using the specific BCI with archers in shooting process [10]. In their analysis, attention trends were linked with archer's skills. For this reason we will also investigate the role of these trends and find if there is a relation between attention trends and players.

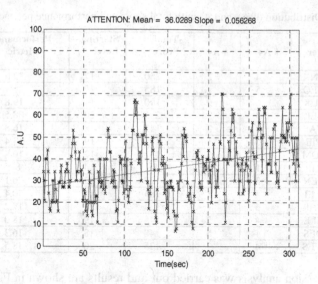

Fig. 3. Attention values for a game with a positive trend (A+)

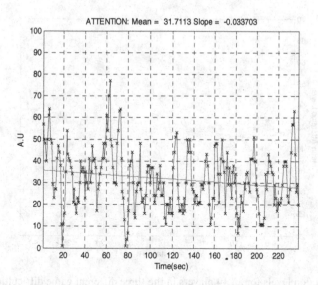

Fig. 4. Attention values for a game with a negative trend (A-)

In Table 3 we give the distribution of A+ and A- for all 14 players together with total score and performance metric for comparison. For each player we calculated the mean value of attention per game and difficulty, as it was evaluated by them.

Table 3. Distribution of A+ and A- with total score and performance per each player

Player	# A+	# A-	Total Score	Starting Level	Performance Metric
ANK	4	2	250	17	32.6
GEO	5	1	185	20	26.4
LUK	6	0	190	17	19.8
SEL	3	3	235	20	38.5
VAS	4	2	142	18	16.8
PIE	5	1	115	19	13.4
TOM	3	3	131	12	10.8
TIF	1	5	88	14	8.3
PEN	3	3	127	22	20.1
YEI	5	1	184	17	20.4
CHR	5	1	124	21	17.2
ELE	4	2	145	19	18.0
DES	1	5	148	18	16.3
WES	4	2	125	20	18.5

Linear regression analysis was carried out and results are shown in Fig 5. This intra- player analysis indicates that attention levels are increasing with game difficulty.

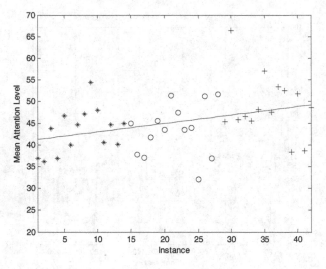

Fig. 5. Mean attention levels for all 14 players in the three different game difficulties (* Easy, o Medium, + Hard)

Following an inter-player approach, we found that out of all 84 instances (14 players x 6 games), 53 instances (63%) showed a positive trend in attention (A+) and the rest 31 (37%) a negative one (A-). For every instance we obtained an attention value averaging over values provided by the BCI. We then calculate mean values of attention, arousal and performance for each difficulty level. In Table 4 we give these results for all instances and for A+ and A- instances separately. We made this distinction in order to examine the effect of attention trends in our results.

Table 4. Attention and Performance as a function of game difficulty

	Number of Instances	p-value (ANOVA)	Mean Attention	Mean Arousal	Mean Performance
All instances (84)					
Easy	29		43.43	3.96	1.57
Medium	28	0.0073	42.70	5.85	5.17
Hard	27		48.66	6.85	3.22
A+ instances (53)					
Easy	17		41.24	3.70	1.51
Medium	21	0.0002	43.06	5.85	5.14
Hard	15		51.87	7.13	2.55
A- instances (31)					
Easy	12		46.54	4.33	1.67
Medium	7	0.3699	41.63	5.85	5.26
Hard	12		44.64	6.50	4.07

An ANOVA test was carried out on attention values to test for differences in the three conditions (easy, medium and hard difficulty) indicating the significance of results. By analyzing data from the SAM based self-evaluation we found that in the majority of instances players felt bored when playing in easy levels, engaged when played in medium level and stressed when the level of Tetris was hard (Table 2). Also, according to Table 4, players had their best performance (on average) when playing in medium game difficulty, where player's skills meet game's difficulty. These results are in alignment with the flow theory [6] and give us an indication that players were more likely to be in the flow zone when playing in medium game difficulty. From Table 4, we also observe that the mean arousal level, calculated from player's self-evaluation, is increasing with game difficulty, but performance is increasing up to a point and when levels of arousal are too high is decreasing. This experimentally observed fact comes in accordance with the Yerkes-Dobson law, describing the relation between arousal and performance [11]. By analyzing attention trends we found out that 2/3 of game instances exhibited a positive trend in attention (A+) and the remaining 1/3 a negative one (A-). By comparing results of Table 3, we conclude that attention trends are not related to players or their performance: all 14 players (except one) exhibit a positive and negative attention trend and their performance is not linked with the number of games with A+ or A- trend. We investigated whether there was a relation between attention trends, skills and performance. We found low values of correlation coefficient between A+ and starting level (0.29), A+ and total score (0.28), A+ and performance metric (0.21).

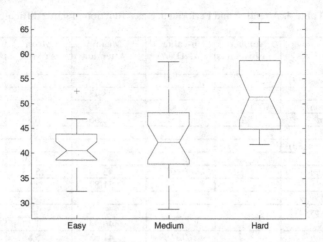

Fig. 6. Boxplot of A+ for the different game difficulties

Another important finding from Table 4 is that 21 out of 28 (percentage 75%) instances referred to medium difficulty, are related to positive trend in attention and only 7 out of 28 (percentage 25%) of medium difficulty are related to a negative trend. We can conclude that when a player is in the flow zone, it is more likely that attention will exhibit a positive trend. Based on the results of Table 4, we have built a model for attention using only instances of attention with a positive trend. In this model, attention is increasing with game difficulty (Fig 6). In [6], G. Chanel et al. observed a similar behavior in the feature EEG_W (Fig 4 in [6]), which is known to be related with cognitive processes like workload, engagement, attention, and fatigue [12]. We noticed that attention instances with a negative trend showed a high p-value (0.3699) in the ANOVA results (Table 4). This is a strong indication that these instances are not really part of a pattern, but just chance and are possibly related with loss of interest for the game, something we have to investigate in the future. These instances do not contribute to the model: they work counter-wise. If we make the hypothesis that attention measurements of the BCI are related to a similar feature like EEG_W for brain activity, our results come in alignment with results in [6]. We then calculate the mean of mean values of A+ in each game difficulty. The observed similarities between the increase in the speed of falling blocks (Fig 1) and the mean of means attention (Fig 6), suggests that a non-linear increase in game difficulty results in a non-linear increase in attention.

7   Conclusions

We tested the usefulness of a commercially available BCI dedicated for gaming in measuring levels of attention. Based on a gaming protocol for Tetris introduced by G. Channel et al. we performed an experiment with 14 participants. Players felt bored when game difficulty was easy, engaged when game level was medium and stressed when it was hard. Similar results were reported by G. Channel et al. [6]. By analyzing data obtained from self-evaluation questionnaires given to participants playing Tetris with the same gaming protocol, they found out that the three different gaming conditions (levels of difficulty) gave rise to three different emotional states: boredom for the easy conditions, engagement for the normal and anxiety for the hard condition. We proposed a performance measure for Tetris that takes into account the non-linear increase in the speed of the falling blocks and according to flow theory of Csikszentmihalyi and the Yerkes-Dobson law results are consistent. Based on a statistical analysis of the obtained data, we introduced a model for attention where a non-linear increase in game difficulty is followed by a non-linear increase in attention. The proposed model for attention comes in accordance with similar results obtained by G. Channel et al. [6] using the same gaming protocol with Tetris and a full EEG cap to capture signals from the brain. As feature they used EEG_W (ratio of energies for alpha, beta and theta brain waves) which is related to attention and workload. By letting players playing the Tetris game in different difficulties (low, normal and hard) they also found that the EEG_W values were increasing on average with game difficulty. For their experiments they also used 14 participants.

8   Limitations and Future Work

As results of this preliminary study using the BCI were encouraging, we will repeat the experiment using a bigger sample of players and higher number of Tetris games per player, in order to have a stronger proof that the model for attention proposed here stands also for each player. With more data it would be possible to build a classifier that can distinguish between states of low, medium and high attention. Based on flow theory the model for attention can be further tested by incorporating (in the game) the dynamic adjustment of difficulty and by evaluating the effect in players' performance and engagement.

Acknowledgments. The results presented here are part of ongoing work in the context of the interdisciplinary research project CAdE (Towards Cognitive Adaptive Edu-Games) sponsored by the Vrije Universiteit Brussel (Belgium).

References

1. Luo, A., Sullivan, T.J.: A user-friendly SSVEP-based brain–computer interface using a time-domain classifier. J. Neural Eng. 7 (2010)
2. Yasui, Y.: A brainwave signal measurement and data processing technique for daily life applications. J. Physiol. Anthropol. 28(3), 145–150 (2009)
3. Rebolledo-Mendez, G., Dunwell, I., Martínez-Mirón, E.A., Vargas-Cerdán, M.D., de Freitas, S., Liarokapis, F., García-Gaona, A.R.: Assessing NeuroSky's usability to detect attention levels in an assessment exercise. In: Jacko, J.A. (ed.) HCI International 2009, Part I. LNCS, vol. 5610, pp. 149–158. Springer, Heidelberg (2009)

4. Crowley, K., Sliney, A., Pitt, I., Murphy, D.: Evaluating a Brain-Computer Interface to Categorize Human Emotional Response. In: 10th IEEE International Conference on Advanced Learning Technologies, pp. 276–278 (2010)
5. Haapalainen, E., Kim, S., Forlizzi, J.F., Dey, A.K.: Psycho-physiological measures for assessing cognitive load. In: Proceedings of the 12th ACM International Conference on Ubiquitous Computing, NY, USA, pp. 301–310 (2010)
6. Chanel, G., Rebetez, C., Bétrancourt, M., Pun, T.: Emotion Assessment From Physiological Signals for Adaptation of Game Difficulty. IEEE Trans. on Sysytems, Man, and Cybernetics—Part A: Systems and Humans 41(6) (November 2011)
7. AV Lab, Audio-visual lab of ETRO, VUB,
   http://www.etro.vub.ac.be/Research/Nosey_Elephant_Studios/
8. Csikszentmihalyi, M.: Flow: The Psychology of Optimal Experience. Harper and Row, New York (1990)
9. Russell, J.A.: A Circumplex Model of Affect. Journal of Personality and Social Psychology 39(6), 1161–1178 (1980)
10. Lee, K.: Evaluation of Attention and Relaxation Levels of Archers in Shooting Process using Brain Wave Signal Analysis Algorithms. 감성과학 12(3), 341–350 (2009)
11. Yerkes, R.M., Dodson, J.D.: The relation of strength of stimulus to rapidity of habit-formation. Journal of Comparative Neurology and Psychology 18, 459–482 (1908)
12. Berka, C., Levendowski, D.J., Cvetinovic, M.M., Petrovic, M.M., Davis, G., Lumicao, M.N., Zivkovic, V.T., Popovic, M.V., Olmstead, R.: Real-time analysis of EEG indexes of alertness, cognition, and memory acquired with a wireless EEG headset. Int. J. Human-Comput. Interact. 17(2), 151–170 (2004)

Monitoring Personal Safety by Unobtrusively Detecting Unusual Periods of Inactivity

Masud Moshtaghi[1], Ingrid Zukerman[1], David Albrecht[1],
and R. Andrew Russell[2]

[1] Faculty of Information Technology
[2] Faculty of Engineering
Monash University, Clayton, Victoria 3800
{firstname.lastname,Andy.Russell}@monash.edu

Abstract. Due to the ageing of the world population, a growing number of elderly people remain in their homes, requiring different levels of care. Our formative user studies show that the main concern of elderly people and their families is "fall detection and safe movement in the house", while eschewing intrusive monitoring devices. This paper introduces a statistical model based on non-intrusive sensor observations that posits whether a person is *not* safe by identifying unusually long periods of inactivity within different regions in the home. Evaluation on two real-life datasets shows that our system outperforms a state-of-the-art system.

Keywords: Older adults, sensors, inactivity detection, statistical model.

1 Introduction

The world is facing an ageing population, with a significant increase predicted in the next 20 years [1]. Economic imperatives, coupled with the desire of elderly people to maintain their independence, underscore the need for solutions that support older adults in their homes. This has motivated a plethora of research projects that study computer-based *in-home monitoring systems* (*IHMSs*), e.g., [2–4]. However, most of these projects focus on technical considerations, often overlooking the needs and preferences of the target population. This is problematic, since the adoption of a system relies on user acceptance [5].

In this paper, we describe an IHMS built as part of the *MIA* project (*Monitoring, Interacting and Assisting*). The IHMS's design is based on the results of a formative user study which elicited the requirements and concerns of elderly Australians with vision impairment and their carers regarding IHMSs [6]. According to this study, the main reason for installing an IHMS is *fall detection and safe movement in the home*; non-intrusiveness is a recurring concern (participants objected to intrusive devices, such as video cameras and wearables); and affordability, ease of use, integrity and reliability were important requirements.

Our IHMS addresses safety in the home, and is built with components sourced mainly from the burglar-alarm industry, which fulfill the above requirements (e.g., passive infrared (PIR) motion sensors and reed sensors) [6]. The IHMS

S. Carberry et al. (Eds.): UMAP 2013, LNCS 7899, pp. 139–151, 2013.
© Springer-Verlag Berlin Heidelberg 2013

uses an adaptive algorithm for detecting abnormally long periods of inactivity, which is the focus of this paper. Adaptivity is spatial and temporal, taking into account respectively how the region in the house and the progression of time affect user behaviour. Our algorithm outperforms a state-of-the-art system [7, 8] in terms of number of false alerts and timeliness of potential true alerts.

The next section summarizes related work. In Sections 3 and 4, we describe the design of our sensor network and our statistical model respectively. Section 5 presents the results of our evaluation, and Section 6 offers concluding remarks.

2   Related Work

Our user study showed that fall detection and safety are the main priorities of older adults and their caregivers [6]. Fall detection has been performed using wearables [9] and camera-based stationary systems [10]. However, as mentioned above, our target population objects to both of these approaches. The system closest to ours is the stationary, adaptive system developed by Cuddihy, Weisenberg et al. [7, 8], which we use as a baseline in our evaluation (Section 5). This system employs non-intrusive PIR motion sensors and reed sensors to detect long periods of inactivity in the residence of older adults. Their algorithm inspects information obtained from sensors at half-hourly intervals over 24 hours (i.e., 48 sensor readings per day), and uses percentile information to compute a threshold for acceptable elapsed inactivity for these 48 daily intervals. An alert is issued if the resident has been inactive for longer than this threshold.

The main disadvantage of Cuddihy, Weisenberg et al.'s system is that its 48 daily sensor readings are insufficient for taking into account the area of the house where activity was last observed, potentially causing a failure to issue a necessary alert. For example, if no activity has been detected in the bedroom for several hours at night, there should be no cause for alarm, but if no activity has been observed for as little as 15 minutes after triggering a sensor in a hallway (even in the middle of the night), then there is cause for concern.

3   Design of the *MIA* Sensor Network

Following the findings in [6], we equipped the house of a volunteer older adult with the following types of inexpensive and non-intrusive sensors. The data stream from the sensors was logged in a base station as a time-stamped sequence of *violated/normal* signals, which constitutes the *GT2* dataset used in our evaluation (Section 5).

- PIR motion sensors detect movement in their coverage area. When movement is detected, the sensor sends a violated signal, and when movement is no longer observed, it sends a normal signal.
- Reed sensors, which are attached to doors (e.g., fridge door) and drawers, send a violated signal upon opening, and a normal signal upon closing.

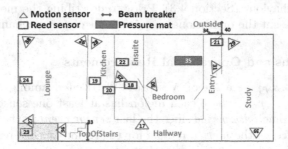

Fig. 1. Layout of *GT2* house with sensors and regions

- Beam breakers, which are placed at entry/exit points, send a signal when the infrared beam between the emitter and the receiver of the device is broken.
- A pressure mat, which is positioned under the mattress, consists of a set of pressure switches. It sends a violated signal when at least one switch makes contact due to a person sitting or lying down on the mattress, and a normal signal when all the switches disconnect.

The findings in [6] indicate that in addition to low per-sensor cost, it is desirable to install the fewest sensors that produce reliable alerts. To make a good initial selection of sensors, it is helpful to ascertain the types of activities performed in different areas of the house, e.g., if the resident often sits quietly in the lounge room, additional motion sensors are appropriate. An advantage of our region-based approach is that it enables us to identify areas that produce false alerts due to insufficient data, and hence are under-sensored. For example, initially our system had only 15 PIR and reed sensors, but after observing its performance, we installed another 7 sensors: 3 beam breakers, 3 PIR sensors and 1 pressure mat (Fig. 1). Four of these sensors were added to entry/exit points to improve our ability to detect when the resident has left the house;[1] the other sensors were added in areas where people make small movements, such as typing or pressing the TV remote control (Lounge, Study and Bedroom). The results reported in this paper were obtained with the full set of 22 sensors (Section 5).

4   Statistical Model for Inactivity Detection

Our inactivity detection mechanism has two main stages: (1) building a model of *normal* inactivity periods from sensor observations; and (2) detecting *abnormally long* periods of inactivity on the basis of this model (Section 4.4). The model of normal inactivity is in turn constructed in two stages: *initialization*, where we learn a start-up model for the detection of normal inactivity periods from sensor readings (Section 4.2); and *adaptation*, where the model gradually adapts

---

[1] This is a crucial problem, as inability to distinguish between an empty house and an unusual amount of inactivity yields false alerts, which reduce system acceptance [11].

to changes in behaviour (Section 4.3). Prior to describing the model, we define concepts and present the operational requirements of our mechanism.

4.1 Definitions and Operational Requirements

Let $S = \{s_1, \ldots, s_N\}$ be a set of N sensors distributed among L regions in a house, $R = \{r_1, \ldots, r_L\}$, where each region has at least one sensor. An alert is issued when the *inactivity period* since the last *sensor event* in the most recently visited region exceeds the *alert threshold* for the region at the current time.

For reed sensors, beam breakers and the pressure mat, a **sensor event** is a violated/normal signal indicating opening/closing of a door or drawer, passing through a threshold, or lying-down/getting-up respectively. Any signal from these sensors indicates 'signs of life' (e.g., opening a door and closing it much later), and counts both as the start and the end of a sensor event. For PIR motion sensors, a **sensor event** starts with a violated signal indicating that movement has been detected, and ends with a normal signal from the same sensor (which indicates that motion has ceased) or the start of a sensor event in another region (which can happen due to transmission delays from the originating sensor).

An **inactivity period** t_{ij} in region r_i at hour h_j is the time elapsed since the end of a sensor event in r_i and the start of the next sensor event (in any region) or the end of the hour. An inactivity period that spans an hour boundary, e.g., starts at 3:50 and ends at 4:10, is ascribed to both hours, e.g., 10 minutes between 3-4 and the entire 20 minutes between 4-5.

An **alert threshold** τ_{ij} for region r_i and hour h_j is a time span such that an inactivity period $t_{ij} > \tau_{ij}$ is deemed unusually long, i.e., it causes an alert.

Ideally, an IHMS minimizes the number of false alerts, while issuing true alerts with the least delay. Intuitively, higher alert thresholds reduce the number of false alerts, while lower thresholds reduce the delay of real alerts. We aim to generate alert thresholds that are *appropriate* for each region in the home and time of the day. For instance, a low threshold in the bedroom during the night may trigger a false alert, which would disturb the resident, while a similar threshold in another region or time of the day would be appropriate.

4.2 Model Initialization

We model the distribution of the normal inactivity periods for each region of the house and hour of the day, and then calculate an upper bound for the distribution. In [12], we showed that the exponential distribution, which is widely used to model the time between two events, is not suitable for our data. This is because the distributions of inactivity periods have a much longer tail than the exponential distribution.

According to [13], long-tailed distributions can be approximated arbitrarily closely by a mixture of exponential distributions. To calculate an upper bound for the distribution of inactivity periods, we focus on the largest values in the tail of the distribution, and employ a similar approach to that described in [14]. This approach uses a *Coefficient of Variation* (CV), defined as σ/μ (the ratio of the standard deviation to the mean, which is 1 for an exponential distribution), to identify the last exponential distribution of the tail. The identification is performed by accumulating periods of inactivity from the largest sample to the smallest until the CV estimated from the $\hat{\mu}$ and $\hat{\sigma}$ of these periods exceeds or equals 1. More formally, given a sequence of inactivity periods $T = \{t_{ij1} \leq t_{ij2} \leq \ldots \leq t_{ijl}\}$ for region r_i and hour h_j, we consider $c_{ijk} = \{t_{ijk}, t_{ij,k+1}, \ldots, t_{ijl}\}$ the tail of the distribution, where $cut\text{-}point$ k is the highest index for which $CV(c_{ij,k+1}) < 1$ and $CV(c_{ijk}) \geq 1$. We denote the number of samples in c_{ijk} by $n_{t,ij} = l - k + 1$.

If there are enough data points for reliable estimation, we apply a robust estimator of the sample mean that handles outliers (Eqn. 1) to estimate β_{ij}, the mean of the exponential distribution that fits c_{ijk}.

$$\hat{\beta}_{ij} = \frac{1}{\ln 2} \text{med}(t_{ijk}, t_{ij,k+1}, \ldots, t_{ijl}). \tag{1}$$

To check whether we have enough data points, we use $\left((Z_{\gamma/2})\sigma/E\right)^2$, which calculates the minimum number of data points required for an estimation within a margin of error E [15], where $Z_{\gamma/2}$ is the value that yields $1 - \gamma/2$ for the cumulative normal distribution. Setting E to $\mu/2$ and choosing a 95% confidence interval (for which $Z_{\gamma/2} \approx 2$) yields roughly 16 data points. If $n_{t,ij} < 16$ in a region-hour pair, we do not fit an exponential distribution to the data, and estimate a threshold by interpolation during an adjustment phase (Section 4.4).

4.3   Model Adaptation

In order to determine whether the models learned so far are likely to benefit from adaptation, we compared the distribution of inactivity periods for each region-hour pair across different weeks using a two-sample Kolmogorov-Smirnov test [16] (weekly data distributions were compared, as a week is a unit of time where people often repeat patterns of behaviour). The tests showed that in most cases these data distributions change with time.

To accommodate these changes, we implemented an adaptation regime based on the idea of gracefully forgetting data from the past [17, 18]. This was done by introducing a *forgetting factor* $0 < \lambda < 1$, where the inactivity periods from A *adaptation steps* ago are weighted by λ^A (λ is set as described in Section 5). The cut-point c_{ijk} of the tail of the distribution is calculated using CV, which in the adaptive model is computed from the *weighted* mean $\hat{\mu}_{ijw}$ and standard deviation $\hat{\sigma}_{ijw}$ of the exponential distribution. Given a sequence of inactivity periods $T = \{t_{ijk}, \ldots, t_{ijl}\}$ for region r_i and hour h_j, weighted by $W = \{w_{ijk}, \ldots, w_{ijl}\}$ (where $w_{ijk} \in \{\lambda^A, 1\}$, several w_{ijk} may have the same value, and λ is the same for all regions), $\hat{\mu}_{ijw}$ and $\hat{\sigma}_{ijw}$ are calculated as follows [19].

$$\hat{\mu}_{ijw} = \frac{\sum_{a=k}^{l} w_{ija} t_{ija}}{\sum_{a=k}^{l} w_{ija}} \tag{2}$$

$$\hat{\sigma}_{ijw}^2 = \frac{n_{t,ij} + 1}{n_{t,ij}} \cdot \frac{\sum_{a=k}^{l} w_{ija}(t_{ija} - \hat{\mu}_{ijw})^2}{\sum_{a=k}^{l} w_{ija}}.$$

We estimate the parameter β_{ij} of the exponential distribution that fits the 'adapted' tail by calculating the *weighted median* of the data – a value such that the total weight of the samples above and below this value is approximately equal to half the total weight of all samples.

4.4 Detecting Abnormally Long Periods of Inactivity

To detect abnormally long periods of inactivity, we (1) calculate an alert threshold τ_{ij} for each region r_i and hour h_j from the distributions obtained above, (2) adjust the thresholds, and (3) derive and adjust an *alert line* for each region. This is a line that connects the thresholds estimated for a region throughout the day, indicating how long a resident would have to be inactive at each point in time to warrant an alert.

Alert Threshold Calculation. To set an alert threshold for a region-hour pair, we determine how much variation one can expect from the mean of the tail-distribution fitted by the above processes. That is, the threshold must be such that we can be confident that no inactivity period from the distribution exceeds this threshold. Schultze and Pawlitschko [20] suggest the threshold τ_{ij} in Eqn. 3 to identify outliers in exponentially distributed data.

$$\tau_{ij} = \hat{\beta}_{ij} \cdot g(n_{t,ij}, \alpha) \,, \tag{3}$$

where α marks the α-*outlier region* of the distribution, such that the probability of seeing a value from the distribution is less than α (α is a configurable parameter, Section 5); and $g(n_{t,ij}, \alpha)$ is a multiplier that defines the width of the no-alert region (g does not have a closed form, hence it is computed by simulation as described in [21]).

Threshold Adjustment. As mentioned above, there may be situations where thresholds cannot be estimated due to insufficient data points (*missing* thresholds). In addition, the above processes may produce *low* thresholds of only a few minutes in high-traffic regions, such as hallways, which are too short for issuing an alert. These problems are addressed as follows.

Missing thresholds are estimated by a weighted average of the nearest valid thresholds, where the weight for a 'neighbouring' threshold depends on the time difference between the hour with the threshold and the hour without a threshold (longer time differences imply a weaker relation). For example, if we cannot calculate a threshold for region r_i at 3 am, and the nearest valid thresholds for region r_i are τ_{i1} at 1 am and τ_{i7} at 7 am, the 3 am threshold for region r_i will be $(1 - \frac{|1-3|}{7-1}) \cdot \tau_{i1} + (1 - \frac{|7-3|}{7-1}) \cdot \tau_{i7}$.

Low thresholds are replaced by a *minimum threshold MT* below which an alert cannot be raised (currently $MT = 15$ minutes for all regions). This is a configurable system parameter.

Table 1. Dataset details

Dataset	# of Residents	Gender & Age	House size	Trial length	# of sensors	Pres. mat /Beam br.
GT2	2 (1 goes to work)	male mid 50s	9 regions	11 weeks	22	4
Aruba	1	elderly female	13 regions	18 weeks	35	0

Alert Line Derivation and Adjustment. An alert line for a region is derived by connecting the thresholds for that region throughout a 24 hour period. An alert line may have *inconsistent* thresholds, which depict sharp changes in behaviour that are unrealistic. It may also have *unreachable* thresholds, which cannot be physically reached. For example, if the threshold for the bedroom at 3 pm is 4 hours, and at 2 pm it is 1 hour, it is impossible to reach 4 hours of inactivity at 3 pm without first triggering an alert at 2 pm. To address these problems, we make the following adjustments.

Inconsistent thresholds are corrected by means of a simple moving average low pass filter to smooth the alert line.

Unreachable thresholds are decreased to their maximum useful value, which in the above example is 2 hours at 3 pm.

5 Evaluation

Our model does not flag 'negative' events (inactivity periods under the thresholds). Rather, it will eventually flag 'positive' events (alerts, which in our trials are all false) for excessive periods of inactivity. Thus, our performance criteria are: the number of false alerts, and the potential for generating timely true alerts.

In our experiments, we compared the performance of our adaptive model on two datasets (Section 5.1) with that of the baseline from [7, 8] and with a static version of our model. The adaptive model was recalculated at weekly intervals after the initialization period, and the performance of the model was evaluated during the next week.

We now describe the datasets used in our evaluation, followed by our experimental set-up and results.

5.1 Datasets

In addition to our own dataset *GT2*, our model was tested with the *Aruba* dataset from the Washington State University *CASAS* smart-home project, which was obtained using PIR motion sensors and reed sensors [4] (http://ailab.wsu.edu/casas/datasets/). Fig. 1 shows the layout of the *GT2* house (the layout of the *Aruba* house has been omitted owing to space limitations); the details of the datasets appear in Table 1. It is worth noting that in the two datasets there are no situations where an alert should be issued, hence any alert is a false alert.

In our experiments, we use only data from periods when the resident is at home. At present, we determine that the resident has left the house by running a pre-processing step that applies the following heuristics.[2]

GT2:   from the time one of sensors {23, 36, 40} in Fig. 1 was triggered, until an event from a different sensor was observed.

Aruba: one hour has elapsed without sign of activity after triggering a sensor in an entry/exit region, and the next activity is also in such a region.

5.2   Experimental Setup

Settings of the Model. We considered two settings of our model: (a) *Entire house*, where the whole house is viewed as one region; and (b) *Region based*, where we build a model for each region of the house. The entire-house setting enables us to directly compare our approach with the baseline approach, which cannot be readily adapted to regions (Section 2).

Parameters of the Model and the Adaptation. In both settings, we used $\alpha = 0.01$ for our model, and the comparable value $MP = 90\%$ for the Maximum Percentile (*MP*) parameter of the baseline. The other baseline parameters were set to the values suggested in [7]. For the adaptation stage, we determined the size of the initialization dataset and the value of the forgetting factor λ. It is worth noting that the baseline system uses a sliding window of size equal to the initialization step, rather than a forgetting factor.

Initialization. Intuitively, the more data we collect for our initial models, the better the basis for adaptation. At the same time, data must be collected for a relatively short period of time for a system to be useful. Since the *GT2* dataset has 11 weeks of data in total (Table 1), we selected 6 weeks for initialization, which leaves 5 weeks for adaptation/testing for *GT2* and 12 weeks for *Aruba*. We then examined the effect of this decision by plotting the average number of weekly false alerts against the number of weeks in the initialization data under the entire-house setting, starting from week 2, with adaptation being performed in the remaining weeks (Figure 2(a)). For example, after initializing the adaptive model for 3 weeks on *GT2*, there were about 3 weekly alerts on average for the 8 adaptation weeks. Note that the performance of our model on *GT2* kept improving for up to 8 weeks of initialization, while there was no clear trend for *Aruba* until week 13, after which there were no false alerts.

Value of λ. The exponential forgetting employed in our adaptive model is widely used in the estimation literature [18], and the suggested value for λ is $[0.9, 1)$. We selected $\lambda = 0.9$ to be able to observe the effect of adaptation in our experiments. We also plotted the average number of weekly alerts obtained by our model for different values of λ in the $[0.8, 0.98]$ range under the entire-house setting (Figure 2(b)). As seen in Figure 2(b), the value of λ we selected

---

[2] The heuristics differ because we can control the sensor positions in the *GT2* dataset. In the future, we will develop more refined models to infer departures from the house.

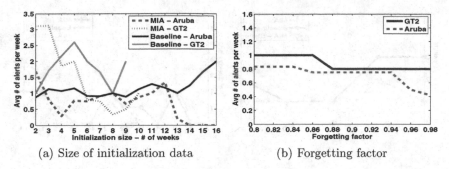

(a) Size of initialization data   (b) Forgetting factor

Fig. 2. Effect of the size of the initialization data and the forgetting factor on the average number of weekly alerts under the entire-house setting

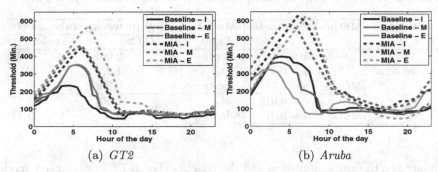

(a) *GT2*   (b) *Aruba*

Fig. 3. Alert lines for the entire-house setting during a 24 hour period for the Initial, Middle and End stages of the adaptation process: *MIA*-adaptive versus baseline

is adequate for the *GT2* dataset, but a higher value would have yielded better results for *Aruba*.

5.3   Results

Entire-house Setting. Fig. 3 displays the estimated alert thresholds during a 24 hour period for both datasets at different stages of the experiment: Initial (after 6 weeks), Middle (9 weeks for *GT2* and 12 for *Aruba*) and End (11 weeks for *GT2* and 18 for *Aruba*). Both *MIA* and the baseline yield higher thresholds at night than during the day. However, *MIA*'s nighttime thresholds increase to an excessive 9 hours for *GT2* and 10 hours for *Aruba* at the end of the experiment, while the baseline's thresholds increase to 6 hours for *GT2* and decrease to about 5.5 hours for *Aruba*. It is worth noting that although high nighttime thresholds are convenient, they highlight the main shortcoming of the entire-house setting: it can take hours to discover an incident that occurs at night (e.g., falling after leaving the bed).

Fig. 4 shows the number of false alerts triggered by our adaptive approach for each week of the adaptation process (5 weeks for *GT2* and 12 weeks for *Aruba*),

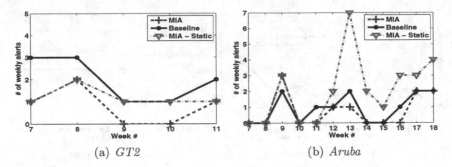

(a) *GT2*   (b) *Aruba*

Fig. 4. False alerts for the entire-house setting for each week of the adaptation process: *MIA*-adaptive, *MIA*-static and baseline

Table 2. Average number of weekly false alerts for the *GT2* and *Aruba* datasets

Setting	Method	Parameter	Model Type	Ave. # of weekly false alerts	
				GT2	*Aruba*
Entire house	Baseline	$MP = 90\%$	Adaptive	2.00	0.92
	MIA	$\alpha = 0.01$	Static	1.20	2.08
	MIA	$\alpha = 0.01$	Adaptive	0.80	0.75
Region-based	*MIA*	$\alpha = 0.01$	Static	10.60	8.67
	MIA	$\alpha = 0.01$	Adaptive	9.00	7.17

compared to the static approach and the baseline. For *GT2*, our adaptive model outperforms or performs as well as our static model and the baseline for the entire adaptation period; and for *Aruba*, this happens from week 10 onwards.

The top three rows of Table 2 show the average number of weekly false alerts generated by the baseline, our static model and our adaptive model for the *GT2* and *Aruba* datasets under the entire-house setting. On average, our adaptive model generates less weekly false alerts than the baseline for both *GT2* and *Aruba*. In addition, our adaptive model outperforms our static model for both datasets, while the static model outperforms the baseline only for *GT2*.

Region-Based Setting. Fig. 5 shows the average alert lines obtained by *MIA* for sample regions of the *GT2* and *Aruba* houses, compared to the baseline alert lines, with the 'error bars' indicating variation due to adaptation. In both houses, only the bedroom region has high thresholds, which appropriately happens during the night, peaking at about 8.3 hours at 6 am in the *GT2* house (Fig. 5(a)), and at an excessive 11 hours in the *Aruba* house (Fig. 5(b)). This high threshold may be partly explained by the *Aruba* house not having a bed pressure mat.

As seen in Fig. 5, the region-based thresholds are lower than the baseline thresholds for most regions and during most hours of the day. Further, 4 of the 9 regions in the *GT2* house, and 7 of the 13 regions in the *Aruba* house have alert lines under $MT = 15$ minutes. However, these are not the regions that produce most of the false alerts. In fact, most of the alerts come from regions that were

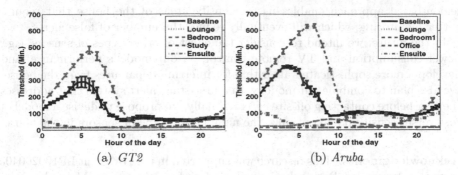

(a) *GT2*　　　　　　　　　　　　　　(b) *Aruba*

Fig. 5. Alert lines with error bars for sample regions during a 24 hour period

identified as problematic in Section 3: 47% of the alerts for the *GT2* dataset come
from the two exit points, Outside and TopOfStairs (Fig. 1), with the Study and
Lounge regions producing an additional 40% of the alerts. A similar result was
obtained for the *Aruba* dataset: 36% of the alerts originate in the entry/exit
point GarageDoor, 41% in the Lounge, and 11% in Bedroom1. Although we
added sensors to the problematic regions in the *GT2* house (Section 3), our
results confirm that we need additional sensors or different types of sensors in
regions were residents make small movements, and more sophisticated models
to identify departures from the house.

As seen in Table 2, the number of false alerts for the region-based setting is
substantially higher than for the entire-house setting for both the static and the
adaptive model. This may be partly attributed to the fact that the region-based
setting requires more data to build its models than the entire-house setting (it
needs to estimate 9 times more parameters for *GT2* and 13 times more parameters for *Aruba*). In addition, as for the entire-house setting, our adaptive model
outperforms our static model for both datasets.

6   Conclusions and Future Work

We have proposed an adaptive method which employs time and location information to detect unusually long periods of inactivity of older adults in their
homes. On average, our adaptive model produces less weekly false alerts than our
static model for the *GT2* and the *Aruba* datasets under both the entire-house
setting and the region-based setting. Further, under the entire-house setting,
our adaptive model produces less weekly false alerts than the state-of-the-art
approach described in [7, 8] for both datasets. The region-based setting generates more false alerts than the entire-house setting, arguably because it requires
more data. However, its region-appropriate thresholds support the timely detection of emergencies, which would be significantly delayed under the entire-house
setting. In fact, the region-based approach yields lower thresholds than the baseline in all the high-traffic areas of the house for both datasets. Additionally, the

region-based approach enables us to identify areas of the house that require better monitoring, which will eventually reduce the number of false alerts.

In the future, we intend to consider the effect of other types of sensors, e.g., power consumption and TV remote control, on our model's performance, and develop a more sophisticated algorithm for inferring departures from the house. We also plan to combine our model with a first-stage alert system that addresses the user before contacting off-site carers. Finally, we propose to devise a model of cost versus sensitivity to optimize the number and type of sensors in the house.

Acknowledgments. This research was supported in part by grant LP100200405 from the Australian Research Council, and endowments from Meticube, Portugal, VicHealth and the Helen McPherson Smith Trust. The authors thank M. Larizza and G. Rees for their insights in the initial stages of this study.

References

1. Pollack, M.E.: Intelligent technology for an aging population: The use of AI to assist elders with cognitive impairment. AI Magazine 26(2), 9–24 (2005)
2. Mynatt, E., Rogers, W.: Developing technology to support the functional independence of older adults. Ageing International 27, 24–41 (2001)
3. Kasteren, T.L., Englebienne, G., Kröse, B.J.: An activity monitoring system for elderly care using generative and discriminative models. Personal Ubiquitous Computing 14(6), 489–498 (2010)
4. Cook, D.: Learning setting-generalized activity models for smart spaces. IEEE Intelligent Systems 27(1), 32–38 (2012)
5. Courtney, K., Demiris, G., Rantz, M.: Needing smart home technologies: The perspective of older adults in continuing care retirement communities. Informatics in Primary Care 16(3), 195–201 (2008)
6. Larizza, M., Zukerman, I., Bohnert, F., Russell, R.A., Busija, L., Albrecht, D.W., Rees, G.: Studies to determine user requirements regarding in-home monitoring systems. In: Masthoff, J., Mobasher, B., Desmarais, M.C., Nkambou, R. (eds.) UMAP 2012. LNCS, vol. 7379, pp. 139–150. Springer, Heidelberg (2012)
7. Cuddihy, P., Weisenberg, J., Graichen, C., Ganesh, M.: Algorithm to automatically detect abnormally long periods of inactivity in a home. In: HealthNet 2007 – Proceedings of the 1st ACM International Workshop on Systems and Networking Support for Healthcare and Assisted Living Environments, San Juan, Puerto Rico, pp. 89–94 (2007)
8. Weisenberg, J., Cuddihy, P., Rajiv, V.: Augmenting motion sensing to improve detection of periods of unusual inactivity. In: HealthNet 2008 – Proceedings of the 2nd ACM International Workshop on Systems and Networking Support for Healthcare and Assisted Living Environments, Breckenridge, Colorado, pp. 2:1–2:6 (2008)
9. Yu, X.: Approaches and principles of fall detection for elderly and patient. In: IEEE HealthCom 2008 – Proceedings of the International Conference on e-Health Networking, Applications and Services, Singapore, pp. 42–47 (2008)
10. Nait-Charif, H., McKenna, S.: Activity summarisation and fall detection in a supportive home environment. In: ICPR 2004 – Proceedings of the 17th International Conference on Pattern Recognition, Cambridge, England, vol. 4, pp. 323–326 (2004)

11. Haigh, K., Kiff, L., Myers, J., Guralnik, V., Geib, C., Phelps, J., Wagner, T.: The independent lifestyle assistant (I.L.S.A.): AI lessons learned. In: IAAI 2004 – Proceedings of the 16th Conference on Innovative Applications of Artificial Intelligence, San Jose, California, pp. 25–29 (2004)
12. Moshtaghi, M., Zukerman, I., Russell, R.A., Albrecht, D.: Towards detecting inactivity using an in-home monitoring system. In: IEEE Conference on Industrial Electronics and Applications, Melbourne, Australia (2013)
13. Feldmann, A., Whitt, W.: Fitting mixtures of exponentials to long-tail distributions to analyze network performance models. Performance Evaluation, 245–279 (1998)
14. Riska, A., Diev, V., Smirni, E.: Efficient fitting of long-tailed data sets into hyperexponential distributions. In: GLOBECOM 2002 – Proceedings of the IEEE Global Telecommunications Conference, Taipei, Taiwan, vol. 3, pp. 2513–2517 (2002)
15. Moore, D., McCabe, G., Craig, B.: Introduction to the Practice of Statistics. Macmillan Higher Education (2009)
16. Massey, F.: The Kolmogorov-Smirnov test for goodness of fit. Journal of the American Statistical Association 46(253), 68–78 (1951)
17. Davison, B., Hirsh, H.: Predicting sequences of user actions. In: Notes of the AAAI/ICML 1998 Workshop on Predicting the Future: AI Approaches to Time-Series Analysis, Madison, Wisconsin (1998)
18. Ljung, L.: System Identification: Theory for the User, 2nd edn. Prentice Hall (1999)
19. Deaton, A.: The Analysis of Household Surveys: A Microeconomic Approach to Development Policy. World Bank Publications (1997)
20. Schultze, V., Pawlitschko, J.: The identification of outliers in exponential samples. Statistica Neerlandica 56(1), 41–57 (2002)
21. Davies, L., Gather, U.: The identification of multiple outliers. Journal of the American Statistical Association 88(423), 782–792 (1993)

Recommendation with Differential Context Weighting

Yong Zheng, Robin Burke, and Bamshad Mobasher

Center for Web Intelligence, School of Computing, DePaul University
243 South Wabash Ave, Chicago, Illinois 60604
{yzheng8,rburke,mobasher}@cs.depaul.edu

Abstract. Context-aware recommender systems (CARS) adapt their recommendations to users' specific situations. In many recommender systems, particularly those based on collaborative filtering, the contextual constraints may lead to sparsity: fewer matches between the current user context and previous situations. Our earlier work proposed an approach called *differential context relaxation* (DCR), in which different subsets of contextual features were applied in different components of a recommendation algorithm. In this paper, we expand on our previous work on DCR, proposing a more general approach – *differential context weighting* (DCW), in which contextual features are weighted. We compare DCR and DCW on two real-world datasets, and DCW demonstrates improved accuracy over DCR with comparable coverage. We also show that particle swarm optimization (PSO) can be used to efficiently determine the weights for DCW.

Keywords: recommender systems, collaborative filtering, context, context-aware recommendation.

1   Introduction

Researchers in the domain of recommender systems started to realize that it is useful to take contexts into account when making recommendations. Context-aware recommender systems (CARS) have shown improved accuracy in many recommendation tasks, such as travel accommodation [22,14,29], food menus [24,30], movie recommendation [3,13], music recommendation [25,20], and mobile applications [28,7].

The fundamental assumption of CARS is that a rating for an item is a function not just of the user and item but also of the context in which the item is evaluated or used. This suggests that ratings for context c_1 may be of limited value when predicting for context c_2. However, if we partition all of our ratings by their contexts, the purpose of collaborative recommendation is defeated – no two individuals are ever in exactly the same situation and so prior ratings cannot be used to extrapolate future preferences.

Applying contexts in recommendation is therefore a matter of separating those aspects of the context that are relevant to the recommendation from those that are not. In the movie example, "companion" is clearly an important contextual variable, but "time of day" perhaps is not. Selecting contextual variables is clearly a blunt instrument. Although additional contextual information fine-tunes the recommendation process, every variable included also fragments the data, with the result that most researchers tend to stick with a single contextual variable unless their data is particularly dense.

S. Carberry et al. (Eds.): UMAP 2013, LNCS 7899, pp. 152–164, 2013.

Therefore, how to select contextual variables, and how to use and apply selected contexts in recommendation algorithms are really serious problems, especially when contextual information is not dense in the data. In our previous research, we sought to escape from the dilemma of contextual variable selection through *differential context relaxation* (DCR) [29,30]. DCR divides the recommendation algorithm into components and allows each part to treat context differently – this is the "differential" part. Rather than choose a priori among the possible contextual variables, we use an optimization approach to select the best set of variables for each component. Because we think of the contextual variables as constraints on the operation of the components, we consider this a matter of finding the optimal relaxation of the context.

Although DCR does allow a recommender to take context into account and is an improvement on global context selection, we found that in some cases, it did increase sparsity more than was desirable. In this paper, we show that the DCR approach can be extended to an algorithm – differential context weighting (DCW) in which the contribution of each contextual variable is weighted. Below, we introduce DCR and DCW and demonstrate the relative benefits of DCW in two real-world datasets.

Optimization is an important part of this research. The DCR algorithm requires an optimal set of contextual variables for each component; DCW requires an optimal set of weights for each contextual variables for each component. We show that particle swarm optimization can be used to solve this non-linear optimization problem for our sample datasets.

2 Related Work

Traditional recommendation problem can be modeled as a two-dimensional (2D) prediction – R: *Users* × *Items* → *Ratings*, where the recommender system's task is to predict that user's rating for that item. Context-aware recommender systems try to additionally incorporate contexts to estimate user preferences, which turns the prediction into a "*multidimensional*" rating function – R: *Users* × *Items* × *Contexts* → *Ratings* [2].

Adomavicius, *et al.* [2] introduce a two-part classification of contextual information. Their taxonomy is based on two considerations: what a recommender system knows about a contextual factor and how the contextual factor changes over time. System knowledge can be subdivided into *fully observable*, *partially observable* and *unobservable*. The temporal aspect of a factor can be categorized as *static* or *dynamic*. This analysis yields six possible classes for contextual factors, which characterizes possible contextual situations in the applications of CARS. In this paper, we are concerned with *static* and *fully observable* factors – we have a set of known potential contextual variables at hand which remain stable over time.

The problem of sparse contexts is a well-known one in CARS research. Users may rate items in different contexts, but it is not guaranteed that we can find dense contextual ratings under the same contexts, i.e. there may be very few users who have rated the items in the same contexts. The solutions for this problem can be categorized into two branches: *context selection* and *context relaxation*.

Context selection identifies the most influential contextual variables and then applies them into recommendation algorithms. There are several different means of discovering influential contextual variables [6,27,15]. Odic *et al.* [5] summarized and categorized those approaches into the relevancy assessment from the user survey and the relevancy detection with statistical testing. However, each of these techniques has its drawbacks. Survey assessment requires a lot of user effort. Statistical testing are not reliable unless the data set is dense – items have been rated multiple times in different contexts.

The notion of context relaxation was first applied by De Pessemier *et al.* [9] in 2010. The researcher sought to alleviate sparisty by removing one of the contextual variables in a set of contextual features. We propose the different context relaxation model in our previous work [29,30]. DCR allows the context relaxation to be realized by looking at arbitrary subsets of the contextual variables instead of a single feature. More significantly, DCR applies this relaxation approach to multiple components of the recommendation algorithm using different relaxations for different components. In this paper, we propose DCW which weights contexts other than context selections or relaxations, and context weighting can be considered as a novel approach as another solution for the problem of context sparsity. To our best knowledge, contexts were not weighted in existing research on CARS.

Context-aware recommendation algorithms fall into three categories: contextual pre-filtering, contextual post-filtering and contextual modeling [4] based on how and where context is applied in the recommendation process. As indicated by our previous work [29], DCR can be considered a hybrid context-aware modeling approach because contexts are applied in not only the neighborhood filtering process, but also the recommendation process; and DCW is similar. Our approach is unique in that contextual constraints are applied differentially across the algorithm components, rather than being fixed for the entire algorithm.

3   Differential Context Relaxation

As discussed above, the idea of DCR is that we treat a recommendation algorithm as a collection of functional components and apply context relaxation differently in each component. Furthermore, we treat the context as a set of constraints that the input to the component must satisfy. Those constraints can be relaxed to manage the balance between coverage and accuracy in recommendation.

For example, in movie recommendation as the example shown in Table 1, we might know where the user watched a film (in a theater vs at home), companion (solo, family, girlfriend, etc), and what day of the week. If we want to predict whether U1 will like the movie *Titanic* at home (Location) with his sister (Companion) on a weekday (Time), we could use only peers who had rated the movie under exactly the same circumstances. This would amount to filtering the input to the neighborhood formation component using the context C. We might find that this produces too much sparsity – maybe there are no neighbors that meet this constraint – as shown in Table 1, no users rated *Titanic* in such contexts. It may be possible to form neighborhoods with a relaxed version of C, perhaps by dropping one of the variables to make the constraint less restrictive, e.g. relaxed contexts as {*weekday, sister*} or {*weekday, home*}. Or, there would be more matched ratings if we just consider one dimension, e.g. {*weekday*}.

We take as our starting point the well-known Resnick's algorithm for kNN user-based collaborative filtering (uCF)recommendation as shown in Equation 1, where a is

Table 1. Example: users' contextual ratings for movie *Titanic*

User	Time	Location	Companion	Rating
U1	Weekend	Home	Girlfriend	4
U2	Weekday	Home	Girlfriend	5
U3	Weekday	Theater	Sister	4
U1	Weekday	Home	Sister	?

a user, i is an item, and N_a is a neighborhood of k users similar to a. The algorithm calculates $P_{a,i}$, which is the predicted rating that user a is expected to assign to item i.

$$P_{a,i} = \bar{r}_a + \frac{\sum\limits_{u \in N_a} (r_{u,i} - \bar{r}_u) \times sim(a,u)}{\sum\limits_{u \in N_a} sim(a,u)} \tag{1}$$

To introduce DCR, let us define a context c as a vector of values $\langle f_1, f_2, .., f_n \rangle$, one for each contextual variable known to a recommendation application. Let s be a binary vector $\langle s_1, s_2, ..., s_n \rangle$. The projection function $\pi(c, s)$ projects c to a smaller set of contextual features by applying s. The contextual value f_i is included in the projection if $s_i = 1$. Two contextual profiles in two ratings, c and d, match subject to the contextual constraint s if $\pi(c, s) = \pi(d, s)$. A relaxation of s, s' is defined as any vector containing fewer values of 1. Contexts that match under the constraint s will also match under any relaxed version of s.

Let c be the context for which a recommendation is sought, and let C_1, C_2, C_3, and C_4 be relaxations of the full set of contextual variables with corresponding selection vectors s_1, s_2, s_3, and s_4.[1] The algorithm components are as follows:

Neighborhood Selection. The original neighborhood selection component of Equation 1 selects the k nearest neighbors for user a with a rating on i, subject to a minimum similarity threshold. In DCR, we instead select only neighbors as N_{C_1} who have issued their ratings for i in a context matching c under relaxation C_1.

Neighbor Contribution. The computation of $\bar{r}_u$ in the original equation is replaced by the one in which this average baseline rating for user u is computed using a filtered set of ratings by the constraint C_2. We will denote this filtered version of the average with the notation $\bar{r}_{u,C_2}$, and subtract it from the user's rating r_{u,i,C_2} to calculate the contribution of this neighbor towards the prediction.

User Baseline. The computation of $\bar{r}_a$ in the original equation we replace with the one using the filtered ratings of the user a as above: $\bar{r}_{a,C_3}$.

User Similarity. The computation of neighbor similarity $sim(a, u)$ involves identifying ratings $r_{u,i}$ and $r_{a,i}$ where the users have rated items in common. For context-aware recommendation, we have ratings $r_{u,i,d}$ and $r_{a,i,e}$ instead. We will consider

---

[1] Note that our previous work [29,30] used only three components and did not examine contextual effects in the user similarity calculation. Our experiments show introducing context relaxation to this additional component can help improve prediction accuracy and also save coverage, it is because it helps discover better neighbors in CF.

only ratings where $\pi(d, C_4) = \pi(e, C_4)$. In other words, when comparing two rating profiles, we require that the ratings be issued in matching contexts relative to C_4. Unlike the other components, we do not require that d and e match the context c in which recommendations are being made. We will indicate this version of similarity with the function $sim_c(a, u, C_4)$ which is measured by Pearson correlation coefficient in our experiments.

Thus the four-component DCR model is described in Equation 2:

$$P_{a,i,c} = \bar{r}_{a,C_3} + \frac{\sum\limits_{u \in N_{C_1}} (r_{u,i,C_2} - \bar{r}_{u,C_2}) \times sim_c(a, u, C_4)}{\sum\limits_{u \in N_{C_1}} sim_c(a, u, C_4)} \tag{2}$$

DCR tries to find an optimal context relaxation for each component in recommendation algorithm. In this process, it aims to achieve a balance of alleviating the problem of sparse contexts and maximizing the contextual effect of each component. This approach has several drawbacks:

– Context relaxation is still a strict action – the algorithm must choose to include or exclude each variable relative to each component. It works well for dataset with dense contextual ratings, but in datasets with less contextual information, sparsity remains a problem.
– Algorithm components can be dependent. For example, the neighbor contribution component is dependent on neighbor selection: it is not guaranteed that neighbor u has ratings under C_2, because u is selected by a different constraint C_1. In this case, the model rolls back to the original component representation in uCF.

These considerations give rise to the idea of differential context weighting (DCW).

4   Differential Context Weighting

Binary selection can be considered a special case of weighting where only 0 and 1 values are permitted. DCW exploits this idea, using, instead of a selection vector s, a vector of weights σ, real values between 0 and 1. The weights are used to control the contribution of each contextual feature to the recommendation algorithm components in a manner similar to DCR. Feature weighted collaborative filtering is not novel, e.g. Ujjin et al [26] applied feature weighting to neighborhood-based collaborative filtering. This prior work did not include contextual features, however, and did not apply them differentially compared with our work.

In DCW, we introduce the weighting vectors and the notion of similarity of contexts to realize "differential" and "weighting". We are no longer concerned with filtering out certain ratings, but rather with assigning a score to all ratings based on context. DCW assumes that the more similar the contexts of two ratings were given, the more valuable those ratings will be in making predictions. Given a target context c, we need to assess how much to weight a rating $r_{u,i,d}$ issued in some different context d, subject to a weighting vector σ. Our metric for the similarity of contexts is a simple one: the *weighted Jaccard* metric, J.

$$J(c, d, \sigma) = \frac{\sum_{f \in c \cap d} \sigma_f}{\sum_{f \in c \cup d} \sigma_f} \tag{3}$$

If we revisit the example shown in Table 1, we see that it is possible to use all three dimensions even if there are no users who have rated *Titanic* under the exact context {*weekday, home, sister*}. Because U3 rated *Titanic* under a partially-matching context {*weekday, theater, sister*}, it is possible to make use of this rating in making predictions for U1 based on the proposed Jaccard metric above – more similar the contexts of two ratings were given, these ratings are considered more reliable for further predictions. However, there is a limit to this effect: our experiments show that contexts with low similarity may add noise to the predictions. So, we use a set of similarity thresholds $\epsilon_1 ... \epsilon_4$ to filter ratings, for the each component. Context matches below the threshold are ignored. In addition, the weighting vectors assign different weights to each contextual dimension to indicate the power of influence instead of assuming all dimensions have equal effects.

As a result, DCW is supposed to be able to compensate the drawbacks of DCR – weighting is not as strict as relaxation because we can include more contextual ratings into calculations once it meets the minimal context similarity threshold, even if the algorithm components are dependent. With these preliminaries above, DCW is reformulated as Equation 4. The key parameters in this equation are the four σ vectors, one for each component, that weight the contribution of each contextual variable in that component, and the four ϵ values that set the threshold of context similarity in each component.

$$P_{a,i,\sigma} = \bar{\rho}(a, \sigma_3, \epsilon_3) + \frac{\sum_{u \in N_{a,\sigma_1,\epsilon_1}} (\rho(u, i, \sigma_2, \epsilon_2) - \bar{\rho}(u, \sigma_2, \epsilon_2)) \times sim_w(a, u, \sigma_4, \epsilon_4)}{\sum_{u \in N_{a,\sigma_1,\epsilon_1}} sim_w(a, u, \sigma_4, \epsilon_4)} \tag{4}$$

Neighborhood Selection. In DCR, we selected neighbors among those who had rated item i in a context matching the target context c. In the weighted version, we select neighbors by comparing their contexts for rating item i with the target context c and allowing them as neighbors if the context similarity is greater than a threshold ϵ_1. However, it is possible that a neighbor u has rated an item in multiple contexts, so we choose the maximally-similar context when applying the threshold. Alternatives are to choose minimally-similar context or averagely-similar context. In our experiments, we tried all three functions and the maximally-similar context is the best choice. We will denote this operation with N_{a,σ,ϵ_1} defined as follows, where c is the context of the current recommendation.

$$N_{a,\sigma,\epsilon_1} = \{u : \max_{r_{u,i,d}} (J(c, d, \sigma)) > \epsilon_1\}$$

Neighbor Contribution. In DCR, we chose a subset of the neighbor's ratings on which to compute that user's baseline and subtracted this average from the user's rating $r_{u,i,c}$. For DCW, it is possible that the user has multiple ratings for item i in different contexts that match the target context c to different degrees. These need to be combined via a weighted average and then from them subtracted an overall weighted average of all ratings issued in similar contexts. We will define our weighted average function for an item as follows:

$$\rho(u,i,\sigma,\epsilon_2) = \frac{\sum_{r_{u,i,d} \ni J(c,d,\sigma) > \epsilon_2} r_{u,i,d} \times J(c,d,\sigma)}{\sum_{r_{u,i,d} \ni J(c,d,\sigma) > \epsilon_2} J(c,d,\sigma)}$$

This function selects all ratings for i given by users u in contexts at least ϵ_2 similar to c, and applies a weighted average based on contextual similarity. Let I_u be the set of all items rated by user u. The overall average across all items rated in similar contexts is $\bar{\rho}$ defined here:

$$\bar{\rho}(u,\sigma,\epsilon_2) = \frac{\sum_{i \in I_u} \rho(u,i,\sigma,\epsilon_2)}{|I_u|}$$

User Baseline. The user baseline is the overall average of the target user's ratings of items in similar contexts, which is simply $\bar{\rho}(a,\sigma,\epsilon_3)$.

User Similarity. In DCR, we used Pearson correlation to compute the similarity between users, filtering out pairs of ratings with non-matching contexts. For sim_w, the weighted variant, we weight each comparison between ratings. We create the set T_{ϵ_4} by collecting all items i and pairs of contexts c and d for users a and u, respectively, such that each has rated i in that context and $J(c,d,\sigma) > \epsilon_4$.

$$T_{\epsilon_4} = \{\langle i,c,d \rangle \ni \exists r_{a,i,c}, r_{u,i,d} \wedge J(c,d,\sigma) > \epsilon_4\}$$

Once we have all of the relevant ratings and their contexts, we can compute a weighted version of the correlation function as shown in Equation 5.

$$sim_w(a,u,\sigma,\epsilon_4) = \frac{\sum_{\langle i,c,d \rangle \in T_{\epsilon_4}} (r_{a,i,c} - \bar{r}_a)(r_{u,i,d} - \bar{r}_u) J(c,d,\sigma)}{\sqrt{\sum (r_{a,i,c} - \bar{r}_a)^2 \sum (r_{u,i,c} - \bar{r}_u)^2 \sum_{\langle i,c,d \rangle \in T_{\epsilon_4}} J(c,d,\sigma)^2}} \tag{5}$$

5   Optimization

The remaining work for DCR and DCW is to find the optimal binary selection vectors or weighting vectors for algorithm components. In our DCR algorithm, we model relaxation as a process of binary selection – the vectors s_1, s_2, s_3 and s_4 are used to filter the contextual variables. In our prior work, the set of contextual variables was small and simple enough that we could use exhaustive search of all possible constraints [29]. However, this approach is not at all scalable. Moreover, the optimization space is highly non-linear and standard approaches such as gradient descent cannot be used. An efficient non-linear optimizer is required.

Particle swarm optimization (PSO) [17] is a form of swarm intelligence originally introduced by Eberhart and Kennedy in 1995. It is a population-based optimization approach inspired by social behaviors in swarming and flocking creatures like bees, birds or fish. It was introduced to the domain of information retrieval [12,11] and recommender systems [1,26,10] recently as a means of feature selection and feature weighting. Binary particle swarm optimization (BPSO) is a discrete binary version of the technique [18].

In PSO, optimization is produced by computations using a number of particles placed at different points in an optimization space. Each particle searches independently for the optimum, guided by the local value and the communication with the other particles. In our case, we use root mean square error (RMSE) as the value to be minimized and the position in the space corresponds to a set of weights for the σ vectors. If there are five contextual variables and four algorithm components, there will be a 20-dimensional search space.[2] Each particle records its personal best performance and corresponding best position. The algorithm also keeps track of the global best performance and corresponding position. These values are updated for the whole swarm in each iteration.

PSO and BPSO have been successfully demonstrated as efficient non-linear optimizers. They are to understand and implement, and there are several open source libraries online [3]. Our application of feature weighting for DCW is similar to the previous work by Ujjin et al. [26] on uCF, where they applied PSO and found it outperformed genetic algorithms. Furthermore, we realize DCR by feature selection and DCW by feature weighting – BPSO and PSO use binary vectors and real-value vectors as the position for particle respectively, a good match for the requirements for DCR and DCW.[4]

6   Experiment Setup

We evaluated our DCR and DCW models on four real-world datasets. For reasons of space, we discuss two of them in this paper.

Food Data is the "AIST context-aware food preference dataset" used and distributed by the author Hideki Asoh et al [24]. It is based on a survey of users' ratings on a menu under the context of different degrees of hunger: hungry/normal/full. The ratings were collected in two situations: real hunger is current degree of hunger, and virtual hunger is an imagined state of hunger. More information is shown in Table 2.

Movie Data is used by Adomavicius et al [3] and Karatzoglou et al [16], where the data was collected from a survey – subjects were requested to rate movies and report on the movie watching occasion. Three contextual variables were captured: Time (weekend, weekday), Companion (friends, parents, girlfriend or boyfriend, alone, siblings,etc) and Location (home, cinema). More information is shown in Table 2.

---

[2] It is 20-dimensional search space in DCR. Actually, there are additional dimensions due to the need for ϵ threshold values in DCW. In our experiments, we use the same threshold for all components in the algorithm and so only one additional dimension is needed in DCW.

[3] http://www.particleswarm.info/Programs.html

[4] As discussed in our prior work, we found that an improved version of BPSO [19] is was the best solution for feature selection in DCR [30]. For DCW, we use the variant constriction-factor PSO (CFPSO) [8], which promises quicker convergence than some other variants such as FIPSO [23] and CLPSO [21].

The rating scale for movie data is 1 to 13, and it is 1 to 5 for the food dataset. After filtering out subjects with less than 5 ratings and subjects with incomplete user profiles or item features, we got the final datasets shown in Table 2, where context-linked features [30] include both user profiles and item features. And the number of dimensions indicate the total amount of contexts and context-linked features.

Table 2. Description of Datasets

Dataset	# of users	# of items	# of ratings	# of dimensions	Density of Contexts
Food Data	212	20	6360	6	Dense
Movie Data	69	176	1010	5	Sparse

The predictive performance was measured by RMSE evaluated using 5-fold cross validation. We also measured coverage for each evaluation run, measured as the percentage of predictions for which we can find at least one neighbor. If we find no neighbors, the prediction is based on the user's baseline as shown in Equations 1, 2, and 4. We use a threshold to guarantee a minimum degree of coverage. The reason for this is to avoid a solution that works well in terms of RMSE but only fits a limited number of users. The reason why we do not evaluate models on precision or recall is that the datasets are relatively small and collected from surveys – it is possible users were required to rate all items. Previous research [24,3,16] on these two data sets used prediction errors, also.

The result below shows values from four algorithms. The first algorithm is uCF as described above, a context-free application of kNN collaborative filtering. We also implemented contextual prefiltering to provide a non-differential context-aware algorithm for comparison. This is just a variant of the DCR algorithm in which context is used only to pre-filter the neighbors.

We did a number of experiments using DCR on these datasets, the results of which are omitted for reasons of space. For the purposes of this paper, we compare against the top performer: DCR optimized using a 3-particle version of BPSO [5]. Finally, the fourth algorithm is DCW as described above.

There are several other DCW algorithm parameters worth mentioning. The minimal coverage thresholds are set as 0.7 for the food data and 0.5 for the movie data. These parameters were chosen based on performance on the standard collaborative recommendation algorithm and not changed for the context-aware algorithms. As mentioned above, we use the same ϵ threshold values for all components to reduce the number of dimensions in the optimization process. To reduce variability due to random particle positioning, we use the same initial particle positions for BPSO and PSO.

7   Experimental Results

We applied PSO to identify optimal weights for the DCW algorithm and compared the accuracy and coverage with those found with DCR. It is clear that feature weighting does offer improved accuracy over feature selection.

---

[5] We examined different numbers of particles for BPSO and PSO, where using 3 particles showed the best performances for these two datasets taking the running time into consideratoins. So we use 3-particle version of BPSO and PSO as comparisons.

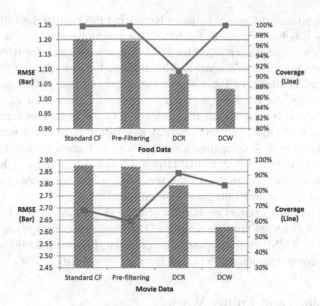

Fig. 1. Performance Comparisons

Consider the relative performance of the algorithms as shown in Figure 1. For food data and movie data, DCW shows strongly significant improvement comparing with standard CF, contextual pre-filtering and DCR. DCW outperforms DCR significantly in terms of RMSE, and it works well for the movie data where DCR does not offer significant improvements over the baselines [6].

DCW achieves higher coverage than DCR for food data. Surprisingly, in the movie data set, we see a small decline in coverage compared with DCR. We believe that the reason for this result is that the optimization criterion in PSO was RMSE, so the system may be minimizing RMSE at the expense of coverage in this dataset. One solution would be to optimize using a combination of RMSE and coverage. From other experimentation with this and other data sets, we believe that improvement over DCR in both coverage and RMSE is possible for DCW.

Table 3 provides running time for the algorithms, showing the number of iterations required to converge and the corresponding running time in seconds.

Table 3. Comparison of Running Performances Between BPSO and PSO

	Food Data		Movie Data	
	Iteration	Running Time	Iteration	Running Time
DCR via BPSO	11	66.9	18	4.9
DCW via PSO	13	248.4	66	23.2

---

[6] We use paired t-test to examine significance, where 0.05 is set as the threshold for p-value to evaluate the significance and p-value lower than 0.01 indicates strong significance.

The most significant difference between BPSO and PSO is that the value in the particle position – it is binary number for BPSO, switching between 0 and 1, and it is a decimal value ranging between [0, 1] for PSO. The search space for BPSO is limited because the combinations are countable. The unlimited search space of PSO results in much greater search times. In Table 3, it is not surprising that PSO required more iterations to converge and the average running time per iteration is increased due to the weighting process is more complex than selection. Our experiments find that the run time performance of DCW via PSO depends two factors: one is the number of contextual dimensions used – more dimensions, more parameters require to be learned; another one is the density of contextual ratings – more dense, the weighting calculations require more time. As shown by the food data which has more dimensions and more dense data, the running time goes up significantly.

We see that the finer-grained application of context in DCW is able to improve the predictions of DCR across multiple data sets. The results on coverage are inconsistent, due to the use of RMSE as the optimization criterion. Improved RMSE comes at the cost of greater computation time due to the learning complexity of PSO.

8   Conclusions and Future Work

This paper points out the drawbacks of DCR and introduces a generalization of DCR, differential context weighting (DCW), where contextual variables are weighted rather than selected, and it is demonstrated to compensate the drawbacks of DCR. DCW achieves better accuracy as compared to DCR with acceptable coverage and even better coverage than the baselines in our experiments. DCW also works when DCR does not work significantly. BPSO and PSO are shown as efficient optimizers for DCR and DCW respectively. However, DCW may require more costs due to the weighting process in DCW and learning complexity in PSO.

One direction in the future work is to explore other forms of similarity of contexts to DCW other than the simple Jaccard similarity, such as semantic similarities, which may help further ameliorate the sparsity problem. For example, in our Movie data set, the "companion" variable has values such as "friends", "family", "solo". It may make sense to treat "friends" and "family" as more similar than "friends" and "solo" because they are settings involving a group of individuals. Also, DCR and DCW are considered as general approaches to use context in recommendation and they can be integrated to other recommendation algorithms in the future. We have successfully applied them to item-based CF and slope one recommender, and we hope to further integrate them with latent factor models in the future, such as matrix factorization.

References

1. Abdelwahab, A., Sekiya, H., Matsuba, I., Horiuchi, Y., Kuroiwa, S.: Feature optimization approach for improving the collaborative filtering performance using particle swarm optimization. Journal of Computational Information Systems 8(1), 435–450 (2012)
2. Adomavicius, G., Mobasher, B., Ricci, F., Tuzhilin, A.: Context-aware recommender systems. AI Magazine 32(3), 67–80 (2011)

3. Adomavicius, G., Sankaranarayanan, R., Sen, S., Tuzhilin, A.: Incorporating contextual information in recommender systems using a multidimensional approach. ACM Transactions on Information Systems (TOIS) 23(1), 103–145 (2005)
4. Adomavicius, G., Tuzhilin, A.: Context-aware recommender systems. In: Recommender Systems Handbook, pp. 217–253 (2011)
5. Tasič, J.F., Košir, A., Odic, A., Tkalcic, M.: Relevant context in a movie recommender system: Users opinion vs. statistical detection. In: ACM RecSys 2012, Proceedings of the 4th International Workshop on Context-Aware Recommender Systems (CARS 2012). ACM (2012)
6. Baltrunas, L., Ludwig, B., Peer, S., Ricci, F.: Context relevance assessment and exploitation in mobile recommender systems. Personal and Ubiquitous Computing, 1–20 (2011)
7. Bourke, S., McCarthy, K., Smyth, B.: The social camera: a case-study in contextual image recommendation. In: Proceedings of the 16th International Conference on Intelligent User Interfaces, pp. 13–22. ACM (2011)
8. Clerc, M., Kennedy, J.: The particle swarm-explosion, stability, and convergence in a multidimensional complex space. IEEE Transactions on Evolutionary Computation 6(1), 58–73 (2002)
9. De Pessemier, T., Deryckere, T., Martens, L.: Extending the bayesian classifier to a context-aware recommender system for mobile devices. In: 2010 Fifth International Conference on Internet and Web Applications and Services (ICIW), pp. 242–247. IEEE (2010)
10. Diaz-Aviles, E., Georgescu, M., Nejdl, W.: Swarming to rank for recommender systems (2012)
11. Diaz-Aviles, E., Nejdl, W., Schmidt-Thieme, L.: Swarming to rank for information retrieval. In: Proceedings of the 11th Annual Conference on Genetic and Evolutionary Computation, pp. 9–16. ACM (2009)
12. Drias, H.: Web information retrieval using particle swarm optimization based approaches. In: 2011 IEEE/WIC/ACM International Conference on Web Intelligence and Intelligent Agent Technology (WI-IAT), vol. 1, pp. 36–39. IEEE (2011)
13. Gantner, Z., Rendle, S., Schmidt-Thieme, L.: Factorization models for context-/time-aware movie recommendations. In: Proceedings of the Workshop on Context-Aware Movie Recommendation, pp. 14–19. ACM (2010)
14. Hariri, N., Mobasher, B., Burke, R., Zheng, Y.: Context-aware recommendation based on review mining. In: Proceedings of the 9th Workshop on Intelligent Techniques for Web Personalization and Recommender Systems (ITWP 2011), p. 30 (2011)
15. Huang, Z., Lu, X., Duan, H.: Context-aware recommendation using rough set model and collaborative filtering. Artificial Intelligence Review, 1–15 (2011)
16. Karatzoglou, A., Amatriain, X., Baltrunas, L., Oliver, N.: Multiverse recommendation: n-dimensional tensor factorization for context-aware collaborative filtering. In: Proceedings of the Fourth ACM Conference on Recommender Systems, pp. 79–86. ACM (2010)
17. Kennedy, J., Eberhart, R.: Particle swarm optimization. In: Proceedings of IEEE International Conference on Neural Networks, vol. 4, pp. 1942–1948. IEEE (1995)
18. Kennedy, J., Eberhart, R.: A discrete binary version of the particle swarm algorithm. In: 1997 IEEE International Conference on Systems, Man, and Cybernetics. Computational Cybernetics and Simulation, vol. 5, pp. 4104–4108. IEEE (1997)
19. Khanesar, M., Teshnehlab, M., Shoorehdeli, M.: A novel binary particle swarm optimization. In: Mediterranean Conference on Control & Automation, MED 2007, pp. 1–6. IEEE (2007)
20. Lee, J.S., Lee, J.C.: Context awareness by case-based reasoning in a music recommendation system. In: Ichikawa, H., Cho, W.-D., Satoh, I., Youn, H.Y. (eds.) UCS 2007. LNCS, vol. 4836, pp. 45–58. Springer, Heidelberg (2007)
21. Liang, J., Qin, A., Suganthan, P., Baskar, S.: Comprehensive learning particle swarm optimizer for global optimization of multimodal functions. IEEE Transactions on Evolutionary Computation 10(3), 281–295 (2006)

22. Liu, L., Lecue, F., Mehandjiev, N., Xu, L.: Using context similarity for service recommendation. In: 2010 IEEE Fourth International Conference on Semantic Computing (ICSC), pp. 277–284. IEEE (2010)
23. Mendes, R., Kennedy, J., Neves, J.: The fully informed particle swarm: simpler, maybe better. IEEE Transactions on Evolutionary Computation 8(3), 204–210 (2004)
24. Ono, C., Takishima, Y., Motomura, Y., Asoh, H.: Context-aware preference model based on a study of difference between real and supposed situation data. In: Houben, G.-J., McCalla, G., Pianesi, F., Zancanaro, M. (eds.) UMAP 2009. LNCS, vol. 5535, pp. 102–113. Springer, Heidelberg (2009)
25. Park, H.-S., Yoo, J.-O., Cho, S.-B.: A context-aware music recommendation system using fuzzy bayesian networks with utility theory. In: Wang, L., Jiao, L., Shi, G., Li, X., Liu, J. (eds.) FSKD 2006. LNCS (LNAI), vol. 4223, pp. 970–979. Springer, Heidelberg (2006)
26. Ujjin, S., Bentley, P.: Particle swarm optimization recommender system. In: Proceedings of the 2003 IEEE Swarm Intelligence Symposium, SIS 2003, pp. 124–131. IEEE (2003)
27. Vargas-Govea, B., González-Serna, G., Ponce-Medellín, R.: Effects of relevant contextual features in the performance of a restaurant recommender system. In: ACM RecSys 2011, The 3rd Workshop on Context-Aware Recommender Systems, CARS-2011 (2011)
28. Woerndl, W., Huebner, J., Bader, R., Gallego-Vico, D.: A model for proactivity in mobile, context-aware recommender systems. In: Proceedings of the Fifth ACM Conference on Recommender Systems, pp. 273–276. ACM (2011)
29. Zheng, Y., Burke, R., Mobasher, B.: Differential context relaxation for context-aware travel recommendation. In: Huemer, C., Lops, P. (eds.) EC-Web 2012. LNBIP, vol. 123, pp. 88–99. Springer, Heidelberg (2012)
30. Zheng, Y., Burke, R., Mobasher, B.: Optimal feature selection for context-aware recommendation using differential relaxation. In: ACM RecSys 2012, Proceedings of the 4th International Workshop on Context-Aware Recommender Systems (CARS 2012). ACM (2012)

Exploiting the Semantic Similarity of Contextual Situations for Pre-filtering Recommendation

Victor Codina[1], Francesco Ricci[2], and Luigi Ceccaroni[3,1]

[1] Department of Software, Universitat Politècnica de Catalunya-BarcelonaTech (UPC)
Jordi Girona 1-3, K2M Building, Office 201, 08034 Barcelona, Spain
{vcodina,luigi}@lsi.upc.edu
[2] Faculty of Computer Science, Free University of Bozen-Bolzano,
Piazza Domenicani 3, 39100 Bolzano, Italy
fricci@unibz.it
[3] Barcelona Digital Technology Centre
Roc Boronat 117, 08018 Barcelona, Spain
lceccaroni@bdigital.org

Abstract. Context-aware recommender systems aim at outperforming traditional context-free recommenders by exploiting information about the context under
which the users' ratings are acquired. In this paper we present a novel contextual pre-filtering approach that takes advantage of the semantic similarities
between contextual situations. For assessing context similarity we rely only on
the available users' ratings and we deem as similar two contextual situations
that are influencing in a similar way the user's rating behavior. We present an
extensive comparative evaluation of the proposed approach using several contextually-tagged ratings data sets. We show that it outperforms state-of-the-art
context-aware recommendation techniques.

Keywords: Recommenders, Implicit Semantics, Collaborative Filtering, Matrix
Factorization.

1 Introduction

Context-Aware Recommender Systems (CARSs) differ from traditional recommenders because when they estimate the rating of a target user u for an item i they do not
only use a data set of ratings (of users for items), but they also exploit both the knowledge of the contextual conditions under which the ratings were acquired and the contextual situation of the target user asking for a recommendation [2]. We use the term
contextual factor referring to a specific *type* of contextual information (e.g. weather),
and *contextual condition* referring to a specific value for a contextual factor (e.g. sunny). The term *contextual situation* refers to a specific set of these contextual conditions that describe the context in which the user consumed and rated the item.

In the last years several CARS techniques have been proposed. We will illustrate
some of them in the next section. A common limitation of these solutions resides in
their requirement for a large data set of contextually tagged ratings, i.e., ratings for

S. Carberry et al. (Eds.): UMAP 2013, LNCS 7899, pp. 165–177, 2013.

items provided in all the various contextual situations that may be encountered by a user while experiencing an item.

A solution to this problem is, when making recommendations in a particular situation, to consider as relevant not only the ratings provided by the users in that situation but also to "reuse" ratings provided in similar situations. For instance, if we want to predict the rating for a place of interest, e.g., the South Tyrol Museum of Archaeology (in Bolzano, Italy), and the target contextual situation includes a condition such as, "group composition is two adults and two children", ratings acquired when the group composition was "two adults and three children" may still be used to generate an accurate predictive model in the target situation. But, what about ratings acquired while the weather was sunny? A sunny day and a family do not seem to be comparable contextual conditions.

Actually, we have developed an approach to estimate the similarity of apparently unrelated contextual conditions, by focusing on the effect of the contextual conditions on the ratings provided by the users in those cases. The similarity among contextual conditions is estimated by identifying the "meaning" of a condition by means of its implicit semantics: that is, the meaning of a concept (here, a contextual condition) is captured by the usage of the concept. Hence, contextual conditions are similar if they co-occur and produce a similar effect on the user's rating behavior. For example, in the recommendation of places of interest, weather conditions such as *cold* and *rainy* may have a positive effect on users' ratings for indoor places like museums, and a negative effect for outdoor places like castles. In this scenario, if *cold* and *rainy* are similarly influencing user's ratings on the same type of items, we consider them as semantically similar.

In a previous work it was shown that the accuracy of traditional recommenders can be improved by exploiting the implicit semantics of item attributes. For instance, Mobasher et al. [17] use Latent Semantic Analysis (LSA) [12] over the item-attribute matrix to calculate the semantic similarity between items, which then are used to boost an item-based Collaborative Filtering (CF) approach. Furthermore, in a more recent work [10], we show that the implicit semantic similarities between attributes captured in terms of how similarly users are interested in them (according to the user profiles previously learnt from user ratings), can be used to enhance a Content-Based (CB) prediction method [3]. Similarly, in this paper we show that the implicit semantics of contextual conditions can be exploited to implement an effective contextual pre-filtering approach that provides a better rating prediction accuracy compared with a standard two-dimensional (2D) Matrix Factorization (MF) method [15] and other state-of-the-art context-aware recommendation techniques.

The remainder of this paper is organized as follows. Section 2 positions our work with respect to the state of the art. Section 3 presents the method for acquiring the implicit semantics of contextual conditions. Section 4 describes the novel pre-filtering approach. Section 5 and 6 present the experimental evaluation of the proposed approach. Finally, section 7 draws the main conclusions and describes the future work.

2   Related Work

In [2], three different paradigms for incorporating contextual information into the recommendation process are presented (see Fig.1): (1) contextual pre-filtering, where context is used for selecting the relevant set of rating data before computing predictions; (2) contextual post-filtering, where context is used to adjust predictions generated by a context-free 2D prediction model; and (3) contextual modeling, in which contextual information is directly incorporated in the prediction model, usually by generalizing the 2D prediction model to an N-dimensional one.

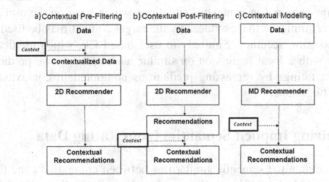

Fig. 1. Paradigms for incorporating context into the recommendation process

Among these paradigms, pre-filtering is especially appealing because it has a straightforward justification: when context matters, use in the recommendation process only the data acquired in the same contextual situation of the target user, because only this data is relevant for predicting user preferences. However, pre-filtering is not always the best option [18]. Its main limitation comes from the difficulty to obtain enough ratings in all the possible contextual situations in order to build a robust and largely applicable context-aware prediction model.

Adomavicius et al. [1] proposed a solution to this problem (also known as the *generalized* pre-filtering) that is based on the hierarchical structure of contextual information. In this approach more general contextual segments are used when there are not enough ratings in the specific target contextual situation. For instance, the *weekend* segment may be used when the target context is *Saturday* and not enough ratings have been acquired in that condition. As in the ontology-based approaches that exploit the explicit semantic relationships between item attributes to enhance the accuracy of CB recommendation [9][20], generalized pre-filtering strongly depends on the quality of the available domain-specific ontology, which is usually limited and only defines explicit relations between conditions of the same contextual factor. Moreover, it may produce a too coarse aggregation of contextual situations if the chosen contextual segments are too broad.

Another solution was proposed by Baltrunas and Ricci [8]. It is based on the idea of "item splitting" which consists of identifying in a selective way the relevant contextual conditions for the rating prediction of each single item. Hence, here ratings' filtering is selectively carried out item by item. Similarly, Baltrunas and Amatriain [4] proposed the idea of "user splitting" which splits the user profile into several sub-profiles, each representing the given user in a particular context. More recently, Zheng et al. [21] introduced a feature selection method that searches for the most relevant contextual factors, which are then applied to specific components of a user-based CF approach [14].

However, all previously mentioned solutions do not fully exploit the potential similarities between contextual situations. For instance, a *mild* temperature in a *cloudy* day may have, on the user evaluation of a place of interest, the same effect of a *cooler* but *sunny* day. In this paper we present a pre-filtering approach that is based on the intuition that ratings acquired in contextual situations which have on the user's rating behavior an *effect* similar to that produced by the target context may be used to improve the rating prediction accuracy. Similarly to user-based CF, which predicts the target user's ratings with a local regression on similar users' ratings, we predict here context-dependent ratings by regressing predictions computed in contextual situations similar to the target one.

3   Acquiring Implicit Semantics from Rating Data

In order to calculate the semantic similarities between contextual conditions we use the Vector Space Model (VSM), with an approach similar to that used in Information Retrieval to calculate similarities between two terms from a given corpus of documents [16]. It relies on the distributional hypothesis: terms repeatedly co-occurring in the same linguistic context (e.g. document, paragraph) tend to have similar meaning. Calculating semantic similarities between terms is divided in three steps: (1) term-document matrix (TDM) generation, where each entry stores the frequency, or a frequency-based weight (e.g. entropy), of a term in a document; (2) TDM transformation, which usually consists of reducing the matrix dimensionality, and (3) vector-matching calculation, where term vectors are compared using a vector-based similarity measure. A well-known example of this approach is LSA, where Singular Value Decomposition (SVD) is applied to the TDM for decomposing it, the term weights are computed with the entropy weighting function, and the cosine similarity is used to calculate vector similarity.

We have adapted these techniques to learn the semantic similarities of contextual conditions from contextually tagged rating data by considering two *contextual conditions as similar if they co-occur and influence the users' ratings in a similar way*. To accomplish this task, we have adapted the step of TDM generation proposing two different methods for measuring the influence of contextual conditions on the users' rating behavior: (1) an *item-based* method, in which a condition-item matrix is generated, terms (rows) correspond to contextual conditions, and documents (columns) to domain items, (2) a *user-based* method, in which a condition-user matrix is generated, and columns correspond to system's users. In both methods each element of the matrix stores a weight representing the general influence (positive, negative or neutral) of the condition; the methods differ in how this weight is computed. In the *item-based* method we measure the influence of conditions in an item-centered perspective, and the weight for a specific contextual condition c and item i (w_{ci}) is calculated as the average of the normalized ratings r_{uic} of the item i acquired in the contextual condition c. Denoting with R_{ic} this set of ratings, we have:

$$w_{ci} = \sum_{r_{uic} \in R_{ic}} (r_{uic} - b_{ui}) \frac{1}{|R_{ic}|} \tag{1}$$

where $b_{ui} = \mu + b_u + b_i$ is the baseline predictor [15] and is used to normalize the item ratings by subtracting the component of the rating prediction that does not take into account the contextual condition. Here μ is the overall rating average, b_u is the bias associated to the user u, and b_i the bias associated to the item i.

In the *user-based* method, the context influence is measured in a user-centered perspective, calculating the weight for a specific condition and user (w_{cu}) as the average of the normalized ratings r_{uic} given by the user u in that specific contextual condition c. If R_{uc} denotes this set of ratings, then we have:

$$w_{cu} = \sum_{r_{uic} \in R_{uc}} (r_{uic} - b_{ui}) \frac{1}{|R_{uc}|} \tag{2}$$

Once we have generated the condition-item or condition-user matrix M, we reduce its dimensionality using SVD. In a previous experimentation [11], we obtained the best results by setting the number of latent factors equal to the number of contextual conditions. Moreover, in the exceptional situation that the number of conditions is greater than the number of items or users, not transforming M yielded better results. We must note that in the considered data sets the number of conditions is small, and using an even smaller number of factors causes an information loss when computing the similarities between conditions.

Finally, we use the cosine measure to calculate the similarity between the semantic vectors of two contextual conditions. Table 1 shows, as an example, the top-5 similar conditions (and their corresponding similarity values) to the condition *cold* calculated by each method using the ratings of the tourism data set used for the experimentation (see Section 5.1 for more details on this data set).

Table 1. Top-5 similar conditions to the condition *cold* (in tourism data set)

Item-based	User-based
cloudy (0.84)	lazy (0.57)
working-day (0.81)	social-event (0.56)
rainy (0.79)	cloudy (0.49)
winter (0.75)	health-care (0.48)
night-time (0.71)	sad (0.47)

4   Exploiting the Implicit Semantics During Pre-filtering

The previously described semantic similarities between contextual conditions can be exploited to implement a novel pre-filtering approach that overcomes the stated limitation of the contextual pre-filtering paradigm, that is, the difficulty of producing predictions when rating data are missing in the target contextual situation. When the system is requested to compute recommendations in a target context we first identify the ratings that can be used to build a predictive model in that situation and then we compute a standard MF model based on the collected ratings.

Fig. 2 shows the algorithm used to perform the first step of the process described above, i.e., collecting the ratings relevant to a target situation. Here a contextual situation is modeled as a vector of k contextual factors, that is, $c = [c_1,..,c_k]$, where $c_j=0,1,..,z_j$ and $c_j=0$ means that the j-th factor value (condition) is unknown, while the other indexes refer to possible values of the factor. Given a training set of rating data provided by users for items in various contextual situations (Y), and given a target contextual situation (c*), all the available ratings are sequentially scanned and all the ratings acquired in a contextual situation equal or similar enough to the target one are added to the training set (X). A convenient threshold (t) defines the minimum similarity value for a contextual situation to be considered as usable in a target context.

```
Input
  Y: set of contextually tagged ratings
  c*: target context consisting of k contextual conditions
  t: similarity threshold
Output
  X: set of ratings relevant to the target context
for each (u,i) with ratings in Y do
  if (∃r_uic: c == c*) then
      add(X, r_uic);
  else
          # if r_uic* is missing in Y
          for each r_uic in Y do
            if (Sim(c, c*) >= t) then
                ratingSum += r_uic;
                nSimilars++;
            end if
          end for
          if (nSimilars > 0) then
            add(X, ratingSum / nSimilars); # Rating average
          else if (∃r_ui in Y) then
            add(X, r_ui); # Rating without specific context
          end if
      end if
end for
```

Fig. 2. Semantically-enhanced pre-filtering algorithm for rating collection

Note that when we identify ratings acquired in similar contextual situations, it is possible to identify, for a given user and item, more than one rating given by that user to that item in contextual situations similar to the target one. In this case, before adding them to X, we average these ratings, in order to generate a unique rating for a given user, item and target contextual situation triple. Finally, if we do not find any rating in conditions similar to the target one, we add to X the rating (if available) given by the user to that item not tagged with a specific context. In order to calculate the similarity between two contextual situations defined by multiple conditions, different *strategies* based on the *pairwise comparison* of the similarities of elementary contextual conditions can be used. We have evaluated two of them: (1)

best-pairs (summarized in Fig. 3), in which, for each contextual condition in the candidate rating situation, the best matching condition in the target situation is selected and then the similarities of these best pairs of conditions are averaged; and (2) *all-pairs* (defined in Fig. 4), where the similarities of all the pairs of conditions in the two contextual situations (target and candidate rating) are averaged. Note that the best-pairs similarity is asymmetric, that is $Sim(c,c^*)$!= $Sim(c^*,c)$, and the all-pairs similarity is symmetric.

```
Input
   c: candidate context
   c*: target context
Output
   s: similarity value (real)
for each (c_j in c AND c_j!=0) do
   c*_1 = getMostSimilarCondition(c*,c_j);
   s = s + getConditionSimilarity(c_j,c*_1);
   nMatchings++;
end for
return s / nMatchings; # Average value
```

Fig. 3. *Best-pairs* pairwise strategy method

```
Input
   c: candidate context
   c*: target context
Output
   s: similarity value (real)
for each (c_j in c AND c_j != 0) do
   for each (c*_i in c* AND c*_i != 0) do
      s = s + getConditionSimilarity(c_j,c*_i);
      nMatchings++;
   end for
end for
return s / nMatchings;
```

Fig. 3. All-pairs pairwise strategy method

5 Experimental Setup

5.1 The Data Sets

We have considered five real-world contextually tagged data sets. Table 2 shows their main characteristics. The Music and Tourism data sets contain multiple ratings for the same item and user, in contextual situations described by only one condition. The music data set contains eight contextual factors such as *driving style*, *mood* and *landscape*; the tourism one contains 14 factors such as *weather*, *companion* and *travel goal*. Each factor has multiple contextual conditions. For instance, *active*, *passive*, *happy* and *sad* are possible conditions of the *mood* factor. More details about these data sets can be found in [5] and [6].

"MovieAdom" is derived from the data set used by Adomavicius et al. [1]. The ratings were collected in a survey of college students who also provided information about the context of the movie-watching experience. In our experiments we used four contextual factors: *companion*, *day of the week*, *movie venue*, and if it was on the *opening weekend*. Differently from the previous data sets, in this case contextual situations are actually described by the conjunction of several contextual conditions.

The LibraryThing and MovieLens are data sets about books and movies, respectively, and ratings are augmented with user tags. They were extracted from their respective websites[1]. Here the contextual situation is given by the tags assigned by the users to the rated items: they provide a contextual clue of why the item is important for the user. Given the high number of distinct tags available and the inherent noise of tag information, we only used as contextual factors the 100 most popular tags, i.e., those with the largest number of users that used the tag at least once.

Table 2. Data sets' statistics

Data set	Users	Items	Factors	Ratings	Scale
Music	43	139	8	4013	1-5
Tourism	25	20	14	1679	1-5
MovieAdom	84	192	4	1464	1-13
MovieLens	849	2207	100	6784	1-10
LibraryThing	7112	37K	100	626K	1-10

5.2   The Evaluation Protocol

As suggested by Shani and Gunawardana [19], we measured the rating prediction accuracy of the considered models by conducting a per-user evaluation schema where, for each user, five ratings were randomly chosen as test set to compute the Root Mean Square Error (RMSE) and the Mean Absolute Error (MAE).

In order to avoid the new-user cold-start problem when evaluating the pre-filtering approaches, we selected as testing ratings those provided in contextual situations in which the user rated at least one additional item. As a result of this data partition, only some users could be finally considered for testing: 18 (42% of the users) in the music data set, 8 (32%) in the tourism one, 25 (30%) in MovieAdom, 71 (8%) in MovieLens and 2219 (31%) in LibraryThing. The remaining users and ratings were used to train the prediction models and to acquire the implicit semantics of contextual conditions. We also tried other variations for splitting the data but obtained quite similar results.

All the reported results are averages of per-user evaluations, and the statistical significance of the differences between the proposed methods and the baseline algorithms have been calculated by means of the paired Wilcoxon sign rank test.

5.3   Prediction Models

We have compared the performance of the proposed semantically enhanced, pre-filtering approach to four state-of-the-art context-aware CF models: a MF-based *exact* pre-filtering method, which generates rating predictions for a target contextual

---

[1] See [www.librarything.com] and [www.movielens.org], accessed January 6, 2013.

situation by considering only the ratings acquired in that situation; *CAMF-CC* and *CAMF-CI*, two model-based context-aware MF approaches proposed in [7]; and the N-dimensional Tensor Factorization (TF) model proposed in [13], which also follows the contextual modeling paradigm.

In particular, the pre-filtering approaches presented here generate rating predictions in a target contextual situation using the bias-based MF proposed in [15], but employing different methods for filtering the training ratings as explained above. In bias-based MF the rating estimation for the user u and item i is:

$$\hat{r}_{ui} = \mu + b_u + b_i + q_i^T p_u \tag{3}$$

where q_i is the factor vector of item i, and p_u is the factor vector of user u. To learn the model parameters we minimized the *regularized error* using stochastic gradient descent, which has been proved to be an effective approach [15]. We minimized the *absolute loss* function when using the MAE and the *squared loss* function for RMSE. When we applied bias-based MF, we always used a hyper-parameters' configuration [11] with which the models converged within 200 iterations in the music, tourism and MovieAdom data sets, 50 in MovieLens, and 25 in the LibraryThing data set. The pre-filtering models that we have compared are the following:

— *Exact-Prefiltering* is the *exact* pre-filtering method that trains the baseline MF in a target context using only the ratings whose context exactly matches the target one.
— *Semantic-Prefiltering-gt* and *Semantic-Prefiltering-dt* are two variants of the proposed pre-filtering approach that exploit the semantic similarities of contextual conditions (see Fig. 2 for more details). *gt* refers to the variant that uses a global similarity threshold for all targets' contextual situations, and *dt* corresponds to a variant that employs a different threshold per target context. In both variants, the optimal threshold values are learned in the training set by using the same per-user evaluation schema, but choosing three ratings for validation instead of five.
— *Semantic-Prefiltering-bp* and *Semantic-Prefiltering-ap* are the two further variants of *Semantic-Prefiltering-gt: bp* uses the *best-pairs* strategy (see Fig. 3) while *ap* uses the *all-pairs* strategy (see Fig. 4) for computing the similarity between contextual situations defined by multiple conditions. We chose *gt variant* for comparing the pairwise strategies to reduce the computational cost of the experiments.

The other rating prediction models included in the experimentation are:

— *User-Item-avg*, the non-personalized and not context-aware baseline prediction model defined by $\hat{r}_{ui} = \mu + b_u + b_i$;
— *MF*, the baseline 2D bias-based MF model whose estimation function is defined by Equation 3;
— *CAMF-CC* and *CAMF-CI*, the context-aware MF models proposed by Baltrunas et al. [7];
— *TF*, the N-dimensional Tensor Factorization model proposed by Karatzoglou et al. [13], which we used only for the MovieAdom data set due to the high computational cost of this approach when the number of contextual factors is greater than five (MovieAdom contains four factors).

6   Results and Discussion

Tables 3 and 4 show the main results of the prediction models evaluated. We note that in these experiments the semantically-enhanced variants use the *item-based* method for acquiring the context similarities, which produces better results compared to the *user-based* method.

The *Semantic-Prefiltering-gt* and *Semantic-Prefiltering-dt* algorithms can be used only when the contextual situation is defined by a single contextual condition, hence, only in the music and tourism data sets (see Table 3). The results show that *Semantic-Prefiltering-gt* is better than *Semantic-Prefiltering-dt*. *Semantic-Prefiltering-gt* reduces the MAE of *MF* by 16% (music data set) and 30% (tourism). We believe that the difference in the performance of these two variants can be related to the fact that learning optimal similarity thresholds for each target situation (a single condition in these data sets) can over-fit the small validation data set and therefore perform poorly on the testing data. *Semantic-Prefiltering-gt* also performs better than the other context-aware models.

Exact-Prefiltering reduces the MAE of MF by 12% and by 24% in the music and tourism data sets, respectively, while model-based approaches (*CAMF-CC*; *CAMF-CI*) only reduce the error of MF in the tourism data set. These results differ from the ones reported in [7] for the same data sets; we believe that these differences are due to the different evaluation protocols employed. An extended comparison of the models and the significance test results can be found in [11].

Table 3. Performance of evaluated models in the music and tourism data sets. Results in **bold** are statistically significant better (95% of confidence level) than the context-free models.

Prediction Model	Music		Tourism	
	RMSE	MAE	RMSE	MAE
User-Item-avg	1.186	.978	1.193	1.030
MF	.825	.573	1.124	.959
CAMF-CC	.858	.599	**.966**	**.775**
CAMF-CI	.912	.601	1.037	.779
Exact-Prefiltering	.769	.503	**.986**	**.729**
Semantic-Prefiltering-gt	.755	**.480**	**.944**	**.673**
Semantic-Prefiltering-dt	.791	**.483**	**.988**	**.715**

When considering the *Semantic-Prefiltering-bp* and *Semantic-Prefiltering-ap* variants we focus on their performance on the data sets where the rating context is defined by multiple conditions: the MovieAdom, the MovieLens and the LibraryThing data sets (see Table 4). The experimental results show that *Semantic-Prefiltering-ap* (*all-pairs* strategy) is more effective than *Semantic-Prefiltering-bp* (*best-pairs* strategy). We note that, in the MovieLens data set, the differences between the two variants are not significant. This is due to the fact that in this data set only a small percentage of the target contexts are defined by multiple conditions, hence it is not an unexpected result.

Table 4. Performance results in the data sets with multiple conditions per context. Results in **bold** are statistically significant better (95% of confidence level) than the context-free models. Results underlined are also significantly better than the other context-aware models.

Prediction Model	MovieAdom		MovieLens		LibraryThing	
	RMSE	MAE	RMSE	MAE	RMSE	MAE
User-Item-avg	2.459	1.990	1.583	1.332	1.432	1.213
MF	2.092	1.719	1.584	1.342	1.415	1.208
CAMF-CI	2.192	1.823	1.612	1.365	1.466	1.230
TF	2.292	1.928	-	-	-	-
Exact-Prefiltering	2.040	1.714	**1.426**	**1.191**	1.532	1.287
Semantic-Prefiltering-bp	2.210	1.825	**1.428**	**1.176**	1.415	**1.188**
Semantic-Prefiltering-ap	2.013	1.713	**1.427**	**1.175**	**1.405**	**1.179**

In this scenario only *Semantic-Prefiltering-ap* always improves the performance of *MF*: the most significant improvement is in the MovieLens data set, where we have obtained a 12% reduction of MAE. In contrast, *CAMF-CI* and *TF* do not improve the performance of *MF*. We believe these poor results may be due to the low relevance of contextual factors used in the data sets (above all the tag-based ones).

7   Conclusions and Future Work

We have presented a novel recommendation approach that overcomes the major limitation of contextual pre-filtering paradigm, i.e., using only user data acquired in the target context when the system is requested to make a recommendation in that target situation. Our solution relies on the identification and usage of ratings acquired in contextual situations that are semantically similar to the target one. We have introduced a novel notion of similarity among contextual situations that is based on how similarly two different situations are influencing the users' ratings. We have presented several variants of the proposed pre-filtering approach and experimentally compared their performance. The experimental results on several contextually tagged data sets show that our approach outperforms other state-of-the-art context-aware Matrix Factorization (MF) models.

As future work we plan to extend the performance comparison by investigating new variants of the pre-filtering approach presented here and by using larger real-world, contextually-tagged data sets. In addition, we will improve our experimentation on the tag-based data sets by filtering irrelevant tags, on the base of a statistical significance test such as the Pearson's chi-squared.

Acknowledgments. The research described in this paper is partly supported by the SuperHub and the Citclops European projects (FP7-ICT-2011-7, FP7-ENV-308469), and the Universitat Politècnica de Catalunya (UPC) under an FPI-UPC grant. The opinions expressed in this paper are those of the authors and are not necessarily those of SuperHub or Citclops projects' partners.

References

1. Adomavicius, G., Sankaranarayanan, R., Sen, S., Tuzhilin, A.: Incorporating contextual information in recommender systems using a multidimensional approach. ACM Transactions on Information Systems 23(1), 103–145 (2005)
2. Adomavicius, G., Tuzhilin, A.: Context-aware recommender systems. In: Ricci, F., Rokach, L., Shapira, B., Kantor, P.-B. (eds.) Recommender Systems Handbook, pp. 217–250. Springer (2011)
3. Ahn, J., Brusilovsky, P., Grady, J., He, D., Syn, S.: Open user profiles for adaptive news systems: help or harm? In: Proceedings of the 16th International Conference on World Wide Web, pp. 11–20 (2007)
4. Baltrunas, L., Amatriain, X.: Towards time-dependant recommendation based on implicit feedback. In: Workshop on Context-Aware Recommender Systems, CARS 2009 (2009)
5. Baltrunas, L., Kaminskas, M., Ludwig, B., Moling, O., Ricci, F., Aydin, A., Lüke, K.-H., Schwaiger, R.: InCarMusic: Context-Aware Music Recommendations in a Car. In: Huemer, C., Setzer, T. (eds.) EC-Web 2011. LNBIP, vol. 85, pp. 89–100. Springer, Heidelberg (2011)
6. Baltrunas, L., Ludwig, B., Peer, S., Ricci, F.: Context relevance assessment and exploitation in mobile recommender systems. Personal and Ubiquitous Computing 16(5), 507–526 (2012)
7. Baltrunas, L., Ludwig, B., Ricci, F.: Matrix factorization techniques for context aware recommendation. In: Proceedings of the 2011 ACM Conference on Recommender Systems, Chicago, pp. 301–304 (2011)
8. Baltrunas, L., Ricci, F.: Context-dependent items generation in collaborative filtering. In: Proceedings of the 2009 ACM Conference on Recommender Systems, New York, pp. 245–249 (2009)
9. Cantador, I., Castells, P., Bellogín, A.: An Enhanced Semantic Layer for Hybrid Recommender Systems: Application to News Recommendation. International Journal on Semantic Web and Information Systems 7(1), 44–77 (2011)
10. Codina, V., Ceccaroni, L.: Semantically-Enhanced Recommenders. In: Proceedings of the 15th International Conference of the Catalan Association for Artificial Intelligence, pp. 69–78. IOS Press (2012)
11. Codina, V., Ricci, F., Ceccaroni, L.: Semantically-Enhanced Pre-filtering for Context-Aware Recommender Systems. In: 3rd ACM Workshop on Context-Awareness in Retrieval and Recommendation, CaRR 2013, Rome, Italy, pp. 15–18 (2013)
12. Dumais, S.: LSA and information retrieval: Getting back to basics. In: Landauer, T.-K., McNamara, D.-S., Dennis, S., Kintsch, W. (eds.) LSA: A Road to Meaning, pp. 293–321. Lawrence Earlbaum (2006)
13. Karatzoglou, A., Amatriain, X., Baltrunas, L., Olivier, N.: Multiverse Recommendation: N-dimensional Tensor Factorization for Context-aware Collaborative Filtering. In: Proceedings of the 2010 ACM Conference on Recommender Systems, Barcelona, Spain, pp. 79–86 (2010)
14. Konstan, J., Miller, B., Maltz, D., Herlocker, J., Gordon, L., Riedl, J.: GroupLens: applying collaborative filtering to Usenet news. Communications of the ACM 40(3), 77–87 (1997)
15. Koren, Y., Bell, R.: Advances in Collaborative Filtering. In: Ricci, F., Rokach, L., Shapira, B., Kantor, P.-B. (eds.) Recommender Systems Handbook, pp. 145–186. Springer (2011)
16. Manning, C., Raghavan, P., Schütze, H.: Introduction to Information Retrieval. Cambridge University Press (2008)

17. Mobasher, B., Jin, X., Zhou, Y.: Semantically Enhanced Collaborative Filtering on the Web. In: Berendt, B., Hotho, A., Mladenič, D., van Someren, M., Spiliopoulou, M., Stumme, G. (eds.) EWMF 2003. LNCS (LNAI), vol. 3209, pp. 57–76. Springer, Heidelberg (2004)
18. Panniello, U., Tuzhilin, A., Gorgoglione, M., Palmisano, C., Pedone, A.: Experimental comparison of pre- vs. post-filtering approaches in context-aware recommender systems. In: Proceedings of the 2009 ACM Conference on Recommender Systems, New York, pp. 265–268 (2009)
19. Shani, G., Gunawardana, A.: Evaluating Recommendation Systems. In: Ricci, F., Rokach, L., Shapira, B., Kantor, P.-B. (eds.) Recommender Systems Handbook, pp. 257–297. Springer (2011)
20. Sieg, A., Mobasher, B., Burke, R.: Ontological User Profiles for Personalized Web Search. In: Proceedings of the AAAI 2007 Workshop on Intelligent Techniques for Web Personalization, pp. 84–91 (2007)
21. Zheng, Y., Burke, R., Mobasher, B.: Optimal feature selection for context-aware recommendation using differential relaxation. In: 4th ACM Workshop on Context-Aware Recommender Systems, CARS 2012 (2012)

Combining Collaborative Filtering and Text Similarity for Expert Profile Recommendations in Social Websites

Alexandre Spaeth and Michel C. Desmarais

École Polytechnique de Montréal,
C.P. 6079, succ. Centre-ville
Montréal (Québec) H3C 3A7, Canada
{alexandre.spaeth,michel.desmarais}@polymtl.ca

Abstract. People-to-people recommendation differ from item recommendations in a number of ways, one of which is that individuals add information to their profile which is often critical in determining a good match. The most critical information can be in the form of free text or personal tags. We explore text-mining techniques to improve classical collaborative filtering methods for a site aimed at matching people who are looking for expert advice on a specific topic. We compare results from a LSA-based text similarity analysis, a simple user-user collaborative filter, and a combination of both methods used to recommend people to meet for a knowledge-sharing website. Evaluations show that LSA similarity has a better precision at low recall rates, whereas collaborative filters have a better precision at higher recall rates. A combination of both can outperform the results of the simpler algorithms.

Keywords: Social Recommender Systems, Text Mining, People Recommendation, Content-based Recommender, Collaborative Filtering.

1 Introduction

Recommender systems try to predict, among many items, the ones that a particular user might like, according to the user's preferences [8]. Those preferences are usually based on explicit ratings (item votes) or implicit data (browsing behaviour or buying habits). Those systems are widely used in e-commerce and their applications greatly increase the chance for the user to like the proposed item, and therefore, the chances of the user to buy it. A great number of methods to compute the best recommendations have been proposed, including SVD decomposition [9], using tags [7], or including content-based information [15] for example.

The application of those techniques to people-to-people recommendation has become an important topic in the last few years [2,10,13,14]. The particularity of people-to-people recommendation is that the users and the items represent the same entity. Moreover, the sites that can generate people-to-people recommendations generally allow users to add free text and personal tags to describe

S. Carberry et al. (Eds.): UMAP 2013, LNCS 7899, pp. 178–189, 2013.

themselves, and to describe people they would like to meet or interact with. These particularities allow for the combination of techniques in a way that classical recommender systems cannot use [3].

The topic of expertise recommendation has been recently tackled. Often, the goal is to recommend experts to other experts, for example authors to co-authors [16], or teachers to teachers [1,4]. Sometimes, it's also used in a learning environment context to recommend more advanced peers to users [12].

In this paper, we use latent semantic analysis to compute similarity between users and combine this approach with collaborative filtering. The experiments, conducted with a knowledge-based meeting website, show an improvement in recall and precision for the prediction of who will meet whom.

The rest of the paper is organized as follows. Next section presents the data. Section 3 presents the different algorithms we used and combined. Section 4 presents the evaluation framework and the results.

2   Data Presentation

Social websites have plenty of data concerning the users. We used such data from an expertise requests and offers website [5]. The goal of this website is to facilitate the meeting between people, based on their respective expertise and needs. Users who are looking for help on a particular topic will post a query in the hope that someone with the expertise on this topic will answer the query. But the ultimate goal is that the two will actually meet face to face instead of posting answers or get involved in some other kind of electronic exchange.

The first step for a new user is to fill his profile. The member can then browse other profiles to find a matching expertise or use the search engine to look for interesting profiles. Figure 1 shows the browsing page. Finally, after completing his profile, he can also browse among our recommendations, as displayed in Figure 2.

Each user's profile is composed of a small essay, geographical information, and a list of expertise offers and demands. Each expertise has a short free text description and some custom tags attached. The distribution of the number of tags per expertise is shown in Figure 4. Each user is responsible for his own profile and for providing a correct description and tagging. It is possible to enter free tags but an auto-completion system provides suggestions and ensures that tags are correctly spelt.

Besides the data explicitly provided by the users, we also have access to the browsing behaviour of each user, including viewing events, messages and previous meetings. The Figure 3.

The statistics for the data are gathered in Table 1.

3   Recommendations

Users become member of the website and use it for two reasons: to fill a need for a specific expertise, or by curiosity. People who are on the website to fill a need

Fig. 1. Profile browsing page

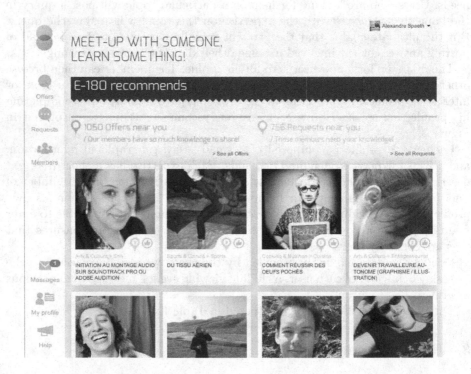

Fig. 2. Recommendations page

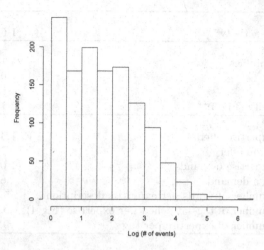

Fig. 3. Distribution of the number of events per user. Events include views, messages and meetings.

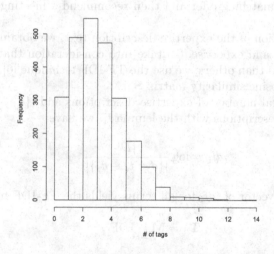

Fig. 4. Distribution of the number of tags per expertise description

will meet people with an offer matching their queries. We would expect that classical information retrieval techniques should yield appropriate suggestions to those users. But for people without queries or offers, and also to address the need of the mere curious, other strategies are required and collaborative filtering is a good candidate.

Table 1. Statistics about users' behaviour and expertise

Users	
Users with activity	1 655
Activities	
Browsing profiles	25 142
Messages	7 086
Meetings	557
Total activity (Fig 3)	32 785
Expertise	
Total of expertise offers	1 432
Users with an offer	793
Total of expertise demands	1 044
Users with a demand	651
Mean of number of words per expertise description	5.78
Mean of number of tags attached per expertise (Fig 4)	3.49
Mean of number of expertise per tag	9.85

3.1 Text Similarity

Expertise queries are much like information retrieval queries. It is possible to use them to find a matching offer and then recommend a meeting between the two users.

After lemmatization of the expertise description text, we obtain the $\mathbf{M}_d$ matrix between words and expertise. To take into consideration that some words are more meaningful than others, we use the TF-IDF technique [6] to obtain $\mathbf{T}_d$ and compute the cosine similarity matrix $\mathbf{S}_d$.

With $|D|$ the total number of expertise descriptions and $|\{d_j : t_i \in d_j\}|$ the number expertise descriptions with the lemma t_i, we have:

$$idf_i = \log \frac{|D|}{|\{d_j : t_i \in d_j\}|} \tag{1}$$

Taking IDF as the vector of idf_i for all terms yields the TF-IDF matrix:

$$\mathbf{T}_d = \mathbf{M}_d \cdot \text{IDF} \tag{2}$$

And finally, $\mathbf{S}_d$ is defined as:

$$\mathbf{S}_d = \frac{\mathbf{T}_d^{\mathrm{T}} \times \mathbf{T}_d}{||\mathbf{T}_d^{\mathrm{T}} \times \mathbf{T}_d||} \tag{3}$$

The score between two users is defined as the highest similarity between all the demands of one user and all the offers of the other one. Finally, for each user, we select the N best recommendations. We will refer to this technique as "text similarity".

3.2   Tag Similarity

The text similarity technique applied over free text descriptions has two weaknesses: the vocabulary can be large, resulting in a sparce matrix, and we run into the polysemy issue (people can use different words to mean the same thing). These weaknesses can be alleviated with tags because the auto-completion feature and the existing profiles tags provide suggestions that end up reducing the vocabulary space, and because users may have a natural tendency to avoid ambiguous terms for the choice of tags.

Using the same algorithm as described in 3.1, but using tags instead of lemmatized descriptions, we compute recommendations based solely on tag similarity. Starting from the knowledge-tags adjacency matrix $\mathbf{M}_t$, we compute the TF-IDF matrix $\mathbf{T}_t$ and then the similarity matrix $\mathbf{S}_t$. This technique is referred to as "tag similarity".

3.3   Combining Tags and Text Similarity with Latent Semantic Analysis

We combine the tags and text similarity measures into a single space and use Latent Semantic Analysis (LSA) in the hope of increasing the relevance of the similarity measure between the queries and the expertise offers.

Firstly, we build a new matrix $\mathbf{M}_c$ of tags and words combined in the column space and expertise profiles the row space. We use the TF-IDF technique to build the new weighted matrix $\mathbf{T}_c$ and compute the cosine similarity between expertise descriptions $\mathbf{S}_c$.

As described in [11], the latent semantic analysis can merge terms and tags together into concept dimensions and, using the singular value decomposition, it can thereby reduce the number of dimensions. In order to do this, the matrix $\mathbf{T}_c$ were decomposed using singular value decomposition: $\mathbf{T}_c = \mathbf{U}\mathbf{\Sigma}\mathbf{V}$. We reduced the number of dimensions by nullifing the smallest values of $\mathbf{\Sigma}$ and build a new $\mathbf{T}_{SVD}$ matrix and a new cosine similarity between expertise descriptions $\mathbf{S}_{SVD}$. We tried several dimensions and 50 latent factors seemed to give the best results. Future work should be done to validate and confirm this value.

3.4   Collaborative Filtering

The collaborative filtering approach uses browsing data along with two levels of interactions, messages and meetings. We create a vote matrix $\mathbf{M}_{CF}$ initialized to 0 and add the following values to the corresponding entry in the matrix:

Seen profile: 1 – the user (column) has seen the potential target's profile (row)
Message: 2 – the user (column) has sent a message to the potential target (row)
Meeting: 4 – the user (column) has met the target (row)

The choice of the values $1/2/4$ is based on the intuition of their respective importance, and no attempt to optimize it was made for this study. This will be done in a future work.

The values are additive. For example, if a user has seen a profile and sent a message, the resulting value will be 3. Although unlikely, it's possible for a user to meet someone else without viewing his profile: by answering directly to a meeting request without checking the profile of the requesting user.

The vote matrix $\mathbf{M}_{CF}$ can be considered a directed graph where weights are assigned to the edges. Figure 5 shows an example of such structure, with S and R representing users.

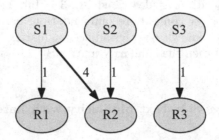

Fig. 5. Weighted graph of relationships

The first step towards a personalized recommendation is the similarity calculation: how to evaluate the proximity between two users? As usual in recommender systems, in order not to bias recommendations towards targets who are registered for a long time (and therefore with more votes), we rely on the cosine to measure similarity which eliminates such bias.

Considering the previously defined matrix $\mathbf{M}_{CF}$, the similarity is given by:

$$\mathbf{S}_{CF} = \frac{\mathbf{M}_{CF}^{T} \times \mathbf{M}_{CF}}{||\mathbf{M}_{CF}^{T} \times \mathbf{M}_{CF}||} \tag{4}$$

The process of finding a recommendation in a graph like the one represented Figure 5 is much like searching for $S_2 \to R_2 \leftarrow S_1 \to R_1$ links.

The cosine calculation between users helps to find all the $S_1 \leftrightarrow S_2$ links and the relevant links are calculated with: $\mathbf{R}_{CF} = \mathbf{S}_{CF} \times \mathbf{M}_{CF}^{T}$ or $\mathbf{M}_{CF} \times \mathbf{S}_{CF}$. The results obtained are the number of $S \to R \leftarrow S \to R$ links found, divided by the number of outgoing links, because we use the cosine similarity. Finally, we must remove the existing links to have a weighted list of recommendations.

3.5   Combining Tags and Text Similarity with Collaborative Filtering

The first technique, combining tags and description similarity, gives scores between expertise queries or expertise offers. The recommendation scores is given by the technique described in section 3.1 and is referred to as the $\mathbf{R}_{desc+tags}$ matrix between users.

The collaborative filtering technique gives recommendation scores between users directly, $\mathbf{R}_{CF}$.

We combine these scores by calculating a weighed geometrical mean between the two values. We tried several weights, as well as a weighted arithmetical mean and the best results were achieved with these values:

$$\mathbf{R}_{CF+tags+sem} = (\mathbf{R}_{CF} + 1)^{1/3} * (\mathbf{R}_{desc+tags} + 1)^{2/3} \tag{5}$$

Those scores should be validate in further experiments.

4 Experiments

4.1 Evaluation Framework

To assess the results of the different algorithms, we trained them with data from before October 1st and tested on data after October 1st 2012.

A recommendation is successful if the user viewed the profile and met the recommended profile. A recommendation is unsuccessful if the user viewed the profile and did not meet the recommended profile. In the test data set, we observe 452 meetings for $13,894$ view events, i.e. 3.25%. This value is our baseline and is the expected precision rate for a random recommender system. A gold standard based on manual recommendations is described below and will serve as an upper comparison point.

We calculated the recall-precision curve for each algorithm, varying the number of recommendations per user.

$$precision = \frac{\text{correctly recommended user}}{\text{number of recommendations}} \tag{6}$$

$$recall = \frac{\text{correctly recommended user}}{\text{number of good recommendations}} \tag{7}$$

It is important to note that even with a perfect recommender system, we cannot realistically expect to obtain a 100% precision rate. Indeed, the leap from browsing a profile to participating in a face to face meeting is large in terms of engagement, and many are not willing to make this leap. So far, there are only few people that are moving from browsing and messaging to actually meeting and our algorithm provides a signifcant improvement, compared to a random recommender.

To have a sense of the best result we could expect, we made 282 manual recommendations. For those recommendations, we sent an email to the users, explaining in sentences why they should meet. The precision-recall rates of these recommendations serve as our gold standard.

4.2 Results

First, we tried each of the three algorithms separately. The recall-precision curve are reported in Figure 6.

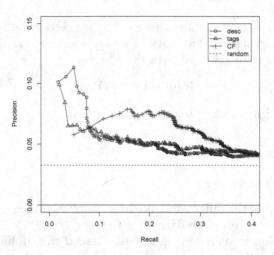

Fig. 6. Three basic algorithms

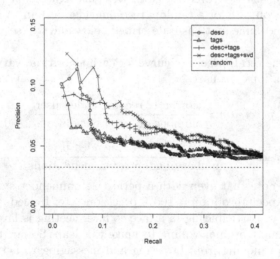

Fig. 7. Combination of text similarity and tags

Note that while tags and text similarity techniques have a better precision at smaller recall rates, the collaborative filter gives better precision at higher recall rates.

The combination between tags and text similarity is shown in Figure 7.

Globally, combining tags and text similarity data gives a better precision than the individual techniques, but only at recall rates between 0.05 and 0.4. Text similarity is slightly better between 0 and 0.05, i.e. with few recommendations.

Finally, the combination of the text similarity and tags recommendations algorithm with the classical collaborative filtering is shown in Figure 8. This figure also reports the results obtained with our gold standard, the manual recommendations.

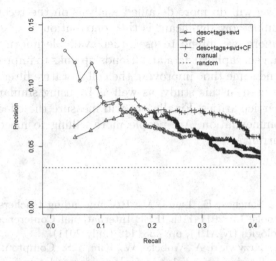

Fig. 8. Recall-precision for the combination

For fewer recommendations, i.e. at a smaller recall rate, the text similarity algorithm is still better, but if we want to do more recommendations, the combination approach performs better than any other algorithm. Furthermore, the precision obtained by our manual recommendations is slightly better than our algorithm, but this was expected because it is likely that human judgement will have a relatively high accuracy and, moreover, the personal email is an incentive to contact and meet the person that is not given in the other conditions and adds a positive bias. The fact that the best algorithm closely approaches this gold standard is encouraging.

5   Conclusions

People-to-people recommendations is a rapidly growing field that generates strong research interest. This study explores a particular and relatively new type of people-to-people recommendation, namely recommending people with sought expertise profiles. We investigate how text similarity and collaborative filtering techniques can be combined to outperform each individual technique.

Our results show that open text descriptions and tags can be combined in a single semantic space and that LSA can be applied to this space to further improve this technique. When performing only one recommendation per user, this approach of combining techniques is shown to almost match manual recommendations, which benefits from a positive bias provided by a personal email incentive. This is quite encouraging. The collaborative approach is shown to provide more accurate recommendations at higher recall rates, thereby providing an alternate source of recommendations under the condition where larger number of recommendations are required.

In future work, we will do more detailled analysis on the recommendations, especially to determine how significant is the contribution from each separated approach. Furthermore, we intend to use other available information, such as meeting evaluation, geographical data and friendship links to improve our results. We should also spend some time improving the collaborative filter, by validating different values we used in this study, as well as by using similarity and other people-to-people particularities. Finally, we will measure the effect of the third person in the recommendation. Are people more willing to meet someone if a third party is a warrant?

References

1. Bahritidinov, B., Sanchez, E., Lama, M.: Recommending teachers for collaborative authoring tools. In: 2011 11th IEEE International Conference on Advanced Learning Technologies (ICALT), pp. 438–442 (July 2011)
2. Cai, X., Bain, M., Krzywicki, A., Wobcke, W., Kim, Y.S., Compton, P., Mahidadia, A.: Collaborative filtering for people to people recommendation in social networks. In: Li, J. (ed.) AI 2010. LNCS, vol. 6464, pp. 476–485. Springer, Heidelberg (2010)
3. Cai, X., Bain, M., Krzywicki, A., Wobcke, W., Kim, Y.S., Compton, P., Mahidadia, A.: Learning to make social recommendations: A model-based approach. In: Tang, J., King, I., Chen, L., Wang, J. (eds.) ADMA 2011, Part II. LNCS, vol. 7121, pp. 124–137. Springer, Heidelberg (2011)
4. Fazeli, S., Brouns, F., Drachsler, H., Sloep, P.: Exploring social recommenders for teacher networks to address challenges of starting teachers (2012)
5. E-180 inc. E-180 platform (March 2013), http://www.e-180.com
6. Spärck Jones, K.: A statistical interpretation of term specificity and its application in retrieval. Journal of Documentation 28, 11–21 (1972)
7. Kim, H.-N., Ji, A.-T., Ha, I., Jo, G.-S.: Collaborative filtering based on collaborative tagging for enhancing the quality of recommendation. Electronic Commerce Research and Applications 9(1), 73–83 (2010)
8. Konstan, J.A., Miller, B.N., Maltz, D., Herlocker, J.L., Gordon, L.R., Riedl, J.: Grouplens: applying collaborative filtering to usenet news. Commun. ACM 40(3), 77–87 (1997)
9. Koren, Y., Bell, R., Volinsky, C.: Matrix factorization techniques for recommender systems. Computer 42(8), 30–37 (2009)
10. Kutty, S., Chen, L., Nayak, R.: A people-to-people recommendation system using tensor space models. In: Proceedings of the 27th Annual ACM Symposium on Applied Computing, SAC 2012, pp. 187–192. ACM, New York (2012)
11. Landauer, T.K., Foltz, P.W., Laham, D.: An Introduction to Latent Semantic Analysis. Discourse Processes 25(2-3), 259–284 (1998)
12. Modritscher, F., Krumay, B., Helou, S.E., Gillet, D., Govaerts, S., Duval, E., Nussbaumer, A., Albert, D., Dahn, I., Ullrich, C.: May i suggest? three ple recommender strategies in comparison (May 2011)

13. Pizzato, L., Rej, T., Chung, T., Koprinska, I., Kay, J.: RECON: a reciprocal recommender for online dating. In: Proceedings of the Fourth ACM Conference on Recommender Systems, RecSys 2010, pp. 207–214. ACM, New York (2010)
14. Pizzato, L.A., Rej, T., Yacef, K., Koprinska, I., Kay, J.: Finding someone you will like and who won't reject you. In: Konstan, J.A., Conejo, R., Marzo, J.L., Oliver, N. (eds.) UMAP 2011. LNCS, vol. 6787, pp. 269–280. Springer, Heidelberg (2011)
15. Salter, J., Antonopoulos, N.: CinemaScreen Recommender Agent: Combining Collaborative and Content-Based Filtering. IEEE Intelligent Systems 21(1), 35 (2006)
16. Sie, R.L.L., Drachsler, H., Bitter-Rijpkema, M., Sloep, P.: To whom and why should i connect? co-author recommendation based on powerful and similar peers. Int. J. Technol. Enhanc. Learn. 4(1/2), 121–137 (2012)

Adapting Recommendation Diversity to Openness to Experience: A Study of Human Behaviour*

Nava Tintarev, Matt Dennis, and Judith Masthoff

Department of Computing Science
University of Aberdeen
{n.tintarev,m.dennis,j.masthoff}@abdn.ac.uk

Abstract. This paper uses a *User-as-Wizard* approach to evaluate how people apply diversity to a set of recommendations. In particular, it considers how diversity is applied for a recipient with high or low Openness to Experience, a personality trait from the Five Factor Model. While there was no effect of the personality trait on the degree of diversity applied, there seems to be a trend in the way in which it was applied. Maximal categorical diversity (across genres) was more likely to be applied to those with high Openness to Experience, at the expense of maximal thematic diversity (within genres).

Keywords: Diversity, Serendipity, Personality, Recommender Systems.

1 Introduction

Recommender systems offer items for a user to try or buy based on what is known about their previous preferences or behaviours. Often these recommendations are presented as a list of items. Historically, the emphasis has been on ensuring that items are useful to the user. More recently, the need for diverse recommendations has been recognized by the recommender systems community [1–4].

There is some consensus that personality is a key aspect to consider when injecting novelty and diversity into recommendations, since attitudes towards new or diverse experiences vary considerably amongst users [5]. Such a recommender system would therefore require a model which accurately describes the personality of users. The trait model from Psychology is a fitting candidate for this. It describes a user's personality by scores on several dimensions, called traits, which are measured via validated self-report questionnaires. Among trait models, the Five Factor Model [6] (FFM, also known as the Big 5 model) has been shown to have excellent reliability in practice [7]. The model describes the personality of an individual by five traits: Extraversion (I), Agreeableness (II), Conscientiousness (III), Emotional Stability (IV), and Openness to Experience

---

* This research has been funded by the Engineering and Physical Sciences Research Council (EPSRC, UK), grant ref. EP/J012084/1.

S. Carberry et al. (Eds.): UMAP 2013, LNCS 7899, pp. 190–202, 2013.

(V). Of the five traits, Openness to Experience seems an ideal candidate for personalising the level of novelty and diversity in recommendations, as it describes qualities such as active imagination, aesthetic sensitivity, attentiveness to inner feelings, preference for variety, and intellectual curiosity [8]. It seems plausible that users who are less open to experience would prefer to receive recommendations that are similar to previously liked items, while those that are more open to experience would prefer to receive more novel recommendations. This paper will investigate this.

It can be claimed that one of the functions of recommender systems is to help users discover new unexpected items, or to support *serendipitious* discoveries [9]. It is still unclear how to apply diversity in a way that best supports these sort of discoveries, although some exciting attempts have recently been made in the area [10]. We approach this problem by studying how people make recommendations to others, based on the other person's preferences and openness to experience.

Section 2 outlines previous work in applying personality in recommender systems as well as recent developments in the application of diversity in sets of recommendations. Section 3 describes an experiment in which participants took the role of the system to investigate how they adapt a set of recommendations to a fictitious friend. Section 4 describes our results and Section 5 concludes with the implications of our findings.

2   Related Work

In relation to personalization and diversity this paper identifies two specific issues: 1) there may be a difference in preference for the degree of diversity in recommendations among users, and 2) the distinction between categorical (across categories) and thematic (within categories) diversity in recommendations has not received a great deal of weight in previous literature and would benefit from empirical testing with users.

Personality traits are "enduring patterns of perceiving, relating to, and thinking about the environment and oneself that are exhibited in a wide range of social and personal contexts" [11]. Generally it is assumed that: a) traits are relatively stable over time, b) traits differ among individuals (for instance, some people like to try new things while others prefer to stick to known options), and c) traits influence behaviour (e.g. ordering familiar food at a restaurant).

Given that traits influence behaviour, tailoring to traits may help improve the performance of a system. For example, a trait such as Openness to Experience is likely to affect a user's overall preference for more familiar or more novel items. This is not a new idea; personality-based recommender systems are a growing area of study [7, 12, 13], and some connections between personality and people's tastes and interests have already been found [7, 13].

The tailoring of recommender systems to personality has also been found to improve accuracy in two cold-start scenarios (sparse data sets and new users [14]), to help predict choices for presidential candidates [7], and to positively impact the acceptance of a system (such as the intent of users to return [15]). However, to our knowledge, the role of a specific trait on a specific behavior of a system, such as Openness to Experience on diversity, has not yet been investigated.

Although the connection between personality and diversity has not yet been established, there is a consensus that diversity should be considered to improve user satisfaction with sets of recommendations. Diversity in recommendation sets has been suggested as a heuristic [16], and has empirically been shown to increase user satisfaction with a list of recommendations [4], and help users to find target items faster [2]. In recent years, many researchers have focused on generating diverse recommendations; aiming to reach an optimal balance between diversity (between items) and similarity (to the user profile) [1–5, 17]. Recent approaches vary from graph theoretic approaches to reranking, fuzzy logic, and fusion (based on two or more seed items) [5].

In addition, if diversity is applied effectively, exposing users to a large range of items makes them more likely to be positively surprised. *Serendipity* has been defined as the extent to which recommended items are both useful and surprising to a user [9].

So, the question is: how can diversity be applied in a way that may improve serendipity? To start, the degree of serendipity is not merely based on the number of items the user is exposed to, for example as measured by catalogue coverage (defined in [9]). Nor is it the same as having maximally different or poor recommendations – while such recommendations may be surprising, they are less likely to be useful and more likely to damage accuracy metrics. Ziegler et al. (2005) proposed a topic diversification approach based on taxonomy-based dissimilarity [4]. As may be anticipated, this also impacted accuracy negatively. An alternate set of approaches which re-rank a list of top items was found to improve diversity without a great loss in accuracy [17]. A more user-centric clustering approach found that users preferred to be exposed to items in a diversified set of clusters, but with a less diversified set of items inside each cluster [1].

This latter result links tightly with the concept of balance, or the distribution of items within categories [18]. Balance, or *thematic diversity*, can be applied with or without any category coverage requirements, which makes it distinct from *categorical diversity*. The user-centric evaluation model for recommender systems (ResQue), on the other hand also distinguishes between diversity of recommendations and *perceived* categorical diversity [19]. Other work has modelled unexpectedness as the distance from expected items and used a weighted distance for the attributes of the item (e.g. language, genre, director, etc) [20].

This paper investigates how distance from known liked items is considered by humans when making recommendations for others. That is, not only *if* they apply a diversity-increasing measure when they know someone is open to experience, but also *how* they apply it. For example, a book may have the same author, but contain very different themes, or belong to a very different genre. It seems likely that variation on one dimension may affect similarity more than variations in other dimensions – for example: if two books have the same author and genre, but contain different themes, are they more similar than two books which have the same genre and themes, but different authors?

3   Experiment

The experiment was administered as an online questionnaire using Amazon's Mechanical Turk (MT) service [21], a popular crowdsourcing tool. Building on previous studies, which found that friends of a user consistently provided better recommendations than a recommender system [22], this experiment adopts the *User-as-Wizard* method [23, 24]. The participants took the role of the system in giving three recommendations (books) to a fictitious friend. The purpose is to investigate if they adapt their set of recommendations for this friend, given some information about their personality and preferences. More specifically, this experiment investigates how Openness to Experience may affect the diversity of the recommendations given by such a participant. It also studies how this adaptation, or application of diversity is applied.

3.1   Participants

On Amazon's Mechanical Turk (MT) participants (called *workers*) can complete small tasks (called *HITs*) made available by *requesters* and are paid a set sum (usually from $0.01 to $1 USD) for their time. If a worker fails to complete the HIT properly, their response can be rejected by the requester, and this will be reflected in the worker's acceptance rate. As most requesters require a high acceptance rate from workers, this can seriously affect a worker's ability to participate in future HITs. In our experience, this causes workers on MT take their acceptance rate very seriously and endeavour to complete HITs to the best of their ability. Nevertheless, our design was such that it would make any invalid responses easy to spot and remove, as described later in this section.

For our experiment (HIT), participants had to be based in the United States and have an acceptance rate of 90% (to ensure a good quality of responses) and were paid $0.50 (US). Prior to the main experiment, participants were asked to select their age from a range, their gender and how many books they read in a year (from a range). We then administered a very short Cloze Test [25] for English fluency due to the language based nature of the experiment. If participants did not pass the test, they were excluded from the rest of the experiment by the system, and instructed to return the HIT.

120 participants were used in analysis (after 128 participants, or 51.6%, were automatically excluded from the experiment due to failing the English fluency test) and were balanced between genders (57% female, 41% male, 2% undisclosed). The largest group of participants were 26-40 (46%), followed by the categories in the range of 16-25 (29%) and 41-65 (22.5%). All participants read at least one book a year - over 40% stated that they read over 20 books a year, 26% that they read up to 20, and 33% that they read up to 10 books a year. The average score for Openness to Experience[1] was 5.52 (StD=1.21) out of 7,

---

[1] This is the mean score based on two items, of which one is phrased positively and the other negatively [26].

and had a range from 2.5 to 7, which is normal for the general population[2]. The average time taken to complete the experiment was around 5 minutes (316 seconds), although we allowed up to 30 minutes.

3.2   Materials

This experiment uses short stories that have been previously validated for describing people who are low or high in Openness to Experience, but keep the levels of the other four traits within the normal range for the general population [28]. Originally the stories were adapted from the NEO-IPIP 20-item scales [29] by combining the phrases into sentences to form a short story, with the addition of a very common male name, Oliver. Table 1 shows the stories used.

Table 1. Stories used for two levels of openness to experience, high and low

openness_low	Oliver is not interested in abstract ideas, as he has difficulty understanding them. He does not like art, and dislikes going to art galleries. He avoids philosophical discussions. He tends to vote for conservative political candidates. He does not like poetry and rarely looks for a deeper meaning in things. He believes that too much tax money goes to supporting artists. He is not interested in theoretical discussions. Oliver is quite a nice person, and tends to enjoy talking with people.
openness_high	Oliver believes in the importance of art and has a vivid imagination. He tends to vote for liberal political candidates. He enjoys hearing new ideas and thinking about things. He enjoys wild flights of fantasy, getting excited by new ideas.

3.3   Experimental Design

A between subject design was used with participants randomly allocated to one of three conditions: baseline (no-story), openness_high and openness_low. Reasonably, if a person is required to make a recommendation for another they are likely to factor in attributes such as the taste and personality of the other person. Therefore participants were first introduced to Oliver, with the appropriate story (and none for the baseline) from Table 1 that gave the participants an idea of his personality. The interests for Oliver were given in the same way in all three conditions: *"Oliver just read a book called The Rose by the author John Smith, which he really liked."*.

Participants were instructed to recommend three books for Oliver to read next. For each recommendation, they were asked to specify how they varied the recommended book from *The Rose* (a fictional book created for this experiment),

---

[2] Values for openness to experience are typically high in the general population (m=5.38, StD=1.07) [27].

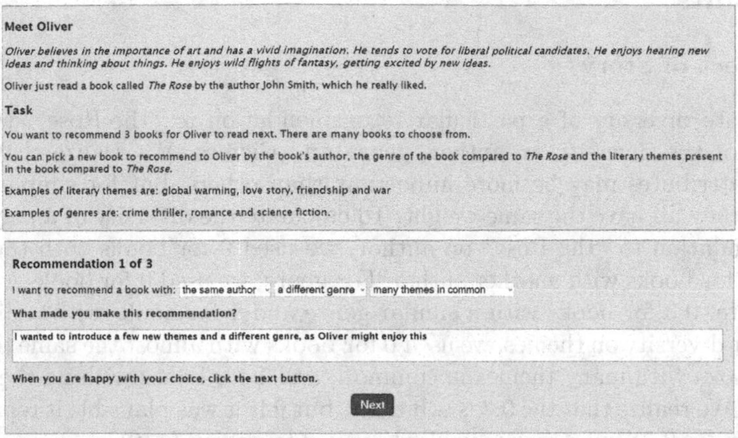

Fig. 1. A screenshot of the high openness variant of the questionnaire

which they already knew Oliver liked. They had to specify the degree of variation on *each* of the three dimensions: author (same or different), genre (same, similar or different) and themes (almost all themes in common, some themes in common, no themes in common). To make sure participants understood these types of dimensions, examples of both literary themes (global warming, love story, friendship and war), and genres were given (e.g. crime thriller, romance and science fiction). We did not specify the actual genre of, or themes present in, *the Rose*. Participants were then asked for a justification for their recommendation. Participants were only permitted to proceed to the next recommendation once they had specified all dimensions and provided justification for these, which among other things, ensured a large degree of qualitative feedback and helped to deter and remove spurious or malignant participants. Figure 1 shows the layout of the experiment and the story for high Openness to Experience.

An alternative design could have been to ask participants to select books from a list, where the books varied according to these properties. However, since we wanted participants to be able to specify three books that all differed (or did not) in the same way – which meant there should be 54 books (2*3*3*3) to scroll through – the more direct approach of asking them how they would vary the recommendation was chosen.

At the end of the questionnaire, participants were shown the three recommendations that they had made along with an optional comments box to allow them to comment on the list as a whole or any other aspect of the experiment.

Participants were then asked to complete a short TIPI personality test [26] to establish their own personality according to the Five Factor Model (which includes Openness to Experience), as this could have influenced their decisions.

Our main hypothesis is that the story with high Openness to Experience will lead to more diverse recommendations compared to the story with low Openness to Experience, as well as the baseline.

4   Results

4.1   Effect of Story

To calculate diversity of a particular recommendation to "the Rose", we took the sum of the diversity on author, genre and themes. We realize that some of these attributes may be more important than others, but for simplicity we assumed they all have the same weight. To calculate the diversity of a particular recommendation to "the Rose" on author, we used 0 for books with the same author, 1 for books with another author. For genre, we used 0 for books with the same genre, 0.3 for books with a similar genre and 1 for books with a different genre. For diversity on themes, we used 0 for books with almost the same themes, 0.3 for books with many themes in common, and 1 for books with no themes in common. We realize that the 0.3 is arbitrary, but felt it was plausible it represents a minority (< 0.5) but non-negligible degree of variation (> 0).

Table 2. How diverse the given recommendations were: the average and maximum diversity across the recommended set

Condition	DiversityAvg	DiversityMax
baseline	1.42 (0.31)	2.00 (0.42)
openness_low	1.41 (0.38)	2.08 (0.51)
openness_high	1.46 (0.30)	2.14 (0.44)
overall	1.44 (0.33)	2.08 (0.46)

We used two measures of diversity for the set of three recommendations: the average, and the maximum (of the diversity for each book, across the three books). Table 2 shows the diversity scores for the three conditions, and overall. While there is a trend for more diverse recommendations in the condition with the story for high Openness to Experience, this trend is not significant. However, we note that the diversity for all conditions is also very high. The average degree of diversity is around 1.5, which means that at least two dimensions were modified. The maximum diversity is over 2, which means either changing at least two dimensions to something completely different, and possibly changing all three dimensions. While this is not surprising for the condition with high openness to experience, it is more so for the condition with low openness to experience. Participant comments suggest that they would like to expose their friend to more diverse recommendations, even if it is only to decide they do not like certain types of books or to better understand their preferences: *"Oliver should read something completely different to find out whether or not he likes it"; "I would do this as a test to narrow Oliver's reading preferences the way English teacher make me narrow my essay thesis statement!"*

Given the similarity across conditions for the two diversity measures, we will only look at the average diversity (DiversityAvg), in the rest of the paper.

4.2 Diversity in a Sequence of Recommendations

Sets of recommendations differ from single recommendations in that diversity within the list is also an important factor. A less studied factor is how this diversity changes (or should change) across a sequence of recommendations. We investigated what happened with the diversity of the recommendations in the set, and found that it increases. Book2 is more different from the seed item than Book1, and Book3 is more different than Book2. These differences are significant at $p < 0.01$ (Bonferroni corrected). The values for diversity for the three books across conditions can be seen in Table 3.

Table 3. Change of diversity across the three recommended items

Condition	Book1	Book2	Book3
baseline	1.04 (0.58)	1.56 (0.49)	1.67 (0.67)
openness_low	1.18 (0.68)	1.35 (0.66)	1.72 (0.74)
openness_high	1.33 (0.63)	1.38 (0.61)	1.68 (0.72)
overall	1.18 (0.64)	1.43 (0.60)	1.69 (0.71)

It is worth noting that in the condition with the story for low openness, the diversity for Book3 is comparable to the other conditions, even if the diversity starts lower for the first two books. Participant comments give the impression that they are aiming to win the confidence of their friend by starting with familiar recommendations, but then making an effort to broaden their horizons: *Book1: "This is familiar ground for Oliver; he will probably like it just as well as the last book he read by this author. If not, however, he knows that he doesn't need to read any more of that author's books."; Book2: "This allows him to see someone else's take on the same genre and themes as the book he originally enjoyed. It helps him determine whether or not he would like to read more books of that genre in the future."; Book3: "This would be something just for variety, something to break him out of his usual pattern and maybe get him interested in something he perhaps wouldn't think he'd like. He may find something he really enjoys.".*

These findings bring into dispute previous results, which found that users thought that items recommended by friends mostly served as reminders of previously identified interests compared to those by online recommender systems which were "new" and "unexpected" [22]. However, participants made a clear effort to give familiar recommendations for the first item in particular, as was seen in the user comments: *"I think it'll be good for Oliver to broaden his horizons a little bit, but still be in his comfort zone. (low openness)"; "He liked the author so another one by him would be the next logical step. (high openness)"*

4.3 Effect of Participant Personality

In this experiment participants scored highly on Openness to Experience which is comparable to the norm for the general population. There was no correlation between the aggregated TIPI score on openness and the diversity of the recommendation set.

Also, when we controlled for effect of participant personality there was no significant correlation between the conditions and the diversity of the recommendations given. It seems like there was no significant influence of participant personality on the recommendations given.

4.4 What Is Diversified

We investigated if people applied diversity to the same extent to all three dimensions: author, theme and genre. Table 4 shows the average diversity of the three dimensions. While none of the differences are statistically significant, it is interesting that the trend for the low openness condition is the opposite as for the high openness condition. For low openness, participants varied themes more than genre, whilst for high openness they varied genre more than themes. If we survey the ranges for the conditions, all conditions cover the full range (0-3), except for high openness. For high openness, the range for genre only starts from 0.3 (i.e. no 0 diversity) and the range for themes is 0-2.3 (i.e. nobody applied maximum theme diversity for all three books). We can also see that the average genre diversity is largest for high openness. This is reflected in participant comments where genre diversity is often mentioned: *"Oliver has a vivid imagination; therefore, he would enjoy many different authors and genres of books. "; "This same author happens to have written another book, but it's in a completely different genre. Nevertheless, Oliver might like it given that it's the same writing style and has many themes in common with the book he liked.".* Similarly, the average theme diversity is lowest for the high openness condition. Again, participants' comments reflect that they are willing to consider recommendations with no common themes: *"Oliver may have enjoyed The Rose because of the author's writing style and would enjoy other books written by that same author, although with no similar themes in common."* Finally, there is also a difference in the range of diversity for authors across participants. In the low openness condition, participants occasionally did not introduce any variation in author for any of the three books (range=0-3), while at least one author (across the three books) was different in the other two conditions (range=1-3).

Table 4. Comparison of average diversity of the set along three dimensions: author, genre and theme. A comparison of the three levels of story and overall are given.

Condition	Author	Genre	Theme
baseline	1.92 (0.70)	1.22 (0.70)	1.12 (0.69)
openness_low	1.83 (0.71)	1.17 (0.63)	1.25 (0.78)
openness_high	1.88 (0.75)	1.45 (0.58)	1.06 (0.49)
overall	1.88 (0.72)	1.28 (0.64)	1.14 (0.66)

4.5   Same, Same but Different

One of our concerns was that participants should be able to pick several books with the same properties. So for example, if a participant wanted to recommended three very similar books this should be possible. There are instances in the data where two or even three books are selected with both a lot of variety (different, different, none) and very little variety (same, similar, many).

4.6   Discussion

Our results are in line with previous work which distinguishes between diversity across categories (implemented as genre in our experiment) and balance within each category (or thematic diversity in our experiment) [18]. A previous study found that a majority of users preferred recommendations based on an approach which exposed them to items in a diversified set of clusters, which could be analogous to categorical diversity, rather than within clusters (thematic diversity) [1]. The preference by a majority for categorical rather than thematic diversity in that study may reflect the fact that the general population normally scores relatively highly on Openness to Experience.

4.7   Implications for Recommender System Design

One potential implication is that if it is possible to detect the Openness to Experience of users the recommender system can apply more thematic variation for these users. An open question is whether this can be detected from the types of items users have already rated – those who are less open to experience are likely to have explored fewer different categories. For users that are new to the system, it may still be possible to ascertain if they are early adopters or use many different applications using a unified login (such as OpenID). An alternative would be to conduct a short personality test for all users, or to apply more categorical diversity by default (given the majority of people are more open to experience) and increase the degree of thematic diversity when users have low Openness to Experience (or if they rate many consecutive recommendations as poor). Despite the overlap with previous findings, these are speculative implications, since one limitation of our study is that we surveyed the behaviour of *Users-as-Wizards* rather than the behaviour of the recipient of such recommendations. Participants seemed to use a different strategy when recommending for a friend who has high compared to low Openness to Experience. While it is not certain if this is also an optimal way to adapt, it gives support to the theory that this is an adaption that is worthwhile to test with recipients as well. Secondly, distinguishing these two types of diversity (categorical and thematic) may have different roles on increasing serendipity for different types of users. We have not studied the effect of diversified lists on recipients, however creating a measure of diversity as is used by humans and that overlaps with current algorithms may be a first step towards tailoring for serendipity. Finally, for a set of recommendations, it seems like a good strategy to start with a familiar item and increasingly diversify as the set becomes larger. We caution however that further studies in other domains may be required to establish a more general theory for the application of diversity according to user personality. In future work we plan to investigate items that vary along the dimensions of degree of investment (e.g. movie vs holiday) and objectivity (e.g. movie vs camera) [30, 31].

5   Conclusion

This paper investigated the role of Openness to Experience on a set of recommended items. Participants acted as the system and gave recommendations for a fictitious friend for whom they knew an item they liked and were given a story about their personality. While we did not find a significant effect of story on the degree of diversity applied, there seemed to be a difference in how it was applied. Categorical (or genre) diversity was likely to be applied to greater extent to a friend who was open to experience, at the expense of thematic (or inter-genre) diversity. This is in line with recent findings in recommender systems which have found that users are more likely to prefer recommendations from different clusters rather than varied within a cluster. Despite the fact that users of recommender systems may be particularly high on the Openness to Experience personality trait, there may be room for tailoring. Participants who are low on the trait may benefit from more inter-theme (thematic) rather than inter-genre (categorical) variation. We also found that participants increased the diversity of their recommendations within the set of three items. While the sequence started with the most familiar items, in the low openness condition, the final item was highly diverse from the seed item (more so than in the high openness condition). This suggests that it would be good practice to start with familiar items to win the user's confidence, but to quickly diversify thereafter.

References

1. Abbassi, Z., Mirrokni, V.S., Thakur, M.: Diversity maximization under matroid constraints. Technical report, Department of Computer Science, Columbia University (2012)
2. Bridge, D., Kelly, J.P.: Ways of computing diverse collaborative recommendations. In: Wade, V.P., Ashman, H., Smyth, B. (eds.) AH 2006. LNCS, vol. 4018, pp. 41–50. Springer, Heidelberg (2006)
3. Smyth, B., McClave, P.: Similarity vs. Diversity. In: Aha, D.W., Watson, I. (eds.) ICCBR 2001. LNCS (LNAI), vol. 2080, pp. 347–361. Springer, Heidelberg (2001)
4. Ziegler, C.N., McNee, S.M., Konstan, J.A., Lausen, G.: Improving recommendation lists through topic diversification. In: WWW 2005, pp. 22–32 (2005)
5. Workshop on Novelty and Diversity in Recommender Systems, DiveRS 2011 (2011)

6. Goldberg, L.: The structure of phenotypic personality traits. American Psychologist 48, 26–34 (1993)
7. Nunes, M.A.S.N.: Recommender Systems based on Personality Traits. PhD thesis, Universite Montpellier 2 (2008)
8. Costa, P.T., McCrae, R.R.: NEO personality Inventory professional manual. Psychological Assessment Resources, Odessa (1992)
9. Herlocker, J.L., Konstan, J.A., Terveen, L., Riedl, J.T.: Evaluating collaborative filtering recommender systems. ACM Trans. Inf. Syst. 22(1), 5–53 (2004)
10. Said, A., Fields, B., Jain, B.J., Albayrak, S.: User-centric evaluation of a k-furthest neighbor collaborative filtering recommender algorithm. In: CSCW (2013)
11. APA: Diagnostic and Statistical Manual of Mental Disorders. 4th edn. American Psychiatric Association (2000)
12. Dunn, G., Wiersema, J., Ham, J., Aroyo, L.: Evaluating interface variants on personality acquisition for recommender systems. In: Houben, G.-J., McCalla, G., Pianesi, F., Zancanaro, M. (eds.) UMAP 2009. LNCS, vol. 5535, pp. 259–270. Springer, Heidelberg (2009)
13. Lin, C.H., Mcleod, D.: Exploiting and learning human temperaments for customized information recommendation. In: IMSA (2002)
14. Hu, R., Pu, P.: Enhancing collaborative filtering systems with personality information. In: Recsys (2011)
15. Hu, R., Pu, P.: Acceptance issues of personality-based recommender systems. In: Recsys (2009)
16. Pu, P., Chen, L., Hu, R.: Evaluating recommender systems from the users perspective: survey of the state of the art. UMUAI 22, 317–355 (2012)
17. Adomavicius, G., Kwon, Y.: Improving aggregate recommendation diversity using ranking-based techniques. IEEE Transactions on Knowledge and Data Engineering 24, 896–911 (2011)
18. Golbeck, J., Hansen, D.L.: A framework for recommending collections. In: Workshop on Novelty and Diversity in Recommender Systems in Conjuction with Recsys (2011)
19. Pu, P., Chen, L., Hu, R.: A user-centric evaluation framework for recommender systems. In: Recsys (2011)
20. Adamopoulos, P., Tuzhilin, A.: On unexpectedness in recommender systems: Or how to except the unexpected. In: Workshop on Novelty and Diversity in Recommender Systems in Conjuction with Recsys (2011)
21. MT: Amazon mechanical turk, http://www.mturk.com
22. Sinha, R., Swearingen, K.: Comparing recommendations made by online systems and friends. In: Proceedings of the DELOS-NSF Workshop on Personalization and Recommender Systems in Digital Libraries (2001)
23. Masthoff, J.: The user as wizard: A method for early involvement in the design and evaluation of adaptive systems. In: Fifth Workshop on User-Centred Design and Evaluation of Adaptive Systems, vol. 1, pp. 460–469 (2006)
24. Paramythis, A., Weibelzahl, S., Masthoff, J.: Layered evaluation of interactive adaptive systems: framework and formative methods. UMUAI 20, 383–453 (2010)
25. Taylor, W.L.: Cloze procedure: A new tool for measuring readability. Journalism Quarterly 30, 415–433 (1953)
26. Gosling, S.D., Rentfrow, P.J., Swann Jr., W.B.: A very brief measure of the big five personality domains. Journal of Research in Personality 37, 504–528 (2003)

27. Goz-lab: Tipi normal values, http://tiny.cc/9otwqw
28. Dennis, M., Masthoff, J., Mellish, C.: The quest for validated personality trait stories. In: IUI (2012)
29. Goldberg, L.R., Johnson, J.A., Eber, H.W., Hogan, R., Ashton, M.C., Cloninger, C.R., Gough, H.G.: The international personality item pool and the future of public-domain personality measures. Journal of Research in Personality 40(1), 84–96 (2006)
30. Tintarev, N., Masthoff, J.: Over- and underestimation in different product domains. In: Workshop on Recommender Systems in Conjunction with the European Conference on Artificial Intelligence, pp. 14–19 (2008)
31. Tintarev, N., Masthoff, J.: Designing and evaluating explanations for recommender systems. In: Kantor, P.B., Ricci, F., Rokach, L., Shapira, B. (eds.) Recommender Systems Handbook, Springer (2010)

Predicting Successful Inquiry Learning
in a Virtual Performance Assessment for Science

Ryan S.J.D. Baker[1] and Jody Clarke-Midura[2]

[1] Teachers College, Columbia University, New York, NY, USA
baker2@exchange.tc.columbia.edu
[2] Harvard Graduate School of Education, Cambridge, MA 02138
jody@post.harvard.edu

Abstract. In recent years, models of student inquiry skill have been developed for relatively tightly-scaffolded science simulations. However, there is an increased interest in researching how video games and virtual environments can be used for both learning and assessment of science inquiry skills and practices. Such environments allow students to explore scientific content in a more open-ended context that is designed around actions and choices. In such an environment, students move an avatar around a world, speak to in-game characters, obtain objects, and take those objects to laboratories to run specific tests. While these environments allow for more autonomy and choice, assessing skills in these environments is a more difficult challenge than in closed environments or simulations. In this paper, we present models that can infer two aspects of middle-school students' inquiry skill, from their interactive behaviors within an assessment in a virtual environment called a "virtual performance assessment" or VPA: 1) whether the student successfully demonstrates the skill of designing controlled experiments within the VPA, and 2) whether a middle-school student can successfully use their inquiry skill to determine the answer to a scientific question with a non-intuitive in-game answer.

Keywords: student modeling, skill modeling, inquiry learning, virtual performance assessment.

1   Introduction

Over the last decades, the field of user modeling and adaptive personalization, and related research communities, have worked to extend student modeling methods from more well-defined domains and learning systems to more ill-defined situations. Highly successful approaches for well-defined tutoring systems within domains such as mathematics and physics [6,8], have been followed with steps to extend student modeling to learning systems in more ill-defined domains and/or for more ill-defined competencies [cf. 3, 7, 10, 13, 15, 16].

Specifically, student modeling has been extended to the study of student inquiry skill within simulations and microworlds. For example, Sao Pedro and colleagues have developed machine-learned models that can infer whether a student has the skills

S. Carberry et al. (Eds.): UMAP 2013, LNCS 7899, pp. 203–214, 2013.

of designing controlled experiments and testing stated hypotheses, within scientific simulations that scaffold the process of selecting hypotheses, collecting data, and interpreting it to answer questions about the data [15,16]. In addition, Quellmalz and colleagues have developed knowledge-engineered models that infer student inquiry skill based upon well-scaffolded activities where students make observations, run experimental trials, and interpret data by answering questions about graphs and create concept maps [12].

Beyond these relatively structured scientific simulations, work has also extended modeling of students' scientific inquiry skills to less structured virtual environments, where avatars move around a large environment, acquiring objects of interest, interacting with non-player characters, and running experiments in a laboratory. Rowe and Lester used knowledge engineering to define the structure of a Dynamic Bayesian Network, which infers a learner's narrative knowledge, strategic knowledge, and content knowledge [13]. This DBN was shown to accurately predict student responses on content test questions, after use of the virtual environment. Sil and colleagues used machine learning to develop models which can replicate human judgments about the quality of an essay where the student justifies their hypotheses for why a phenomenon is occurring in a virtual environment [18]. Their models utilize information both from the linguistic features of the essay, and from features of the student's interaction with the virtual world.

In this paper, we present a model that can infer whether a student will successfully use their inquiry skill to 1) determine the answer to a scientific question with a non-intuitive in-game answer, and 2) successfully justify their claim based on causal evidence from within the game. We predict these aspects of inquiry skill using data from the student's interactions with an open-ended virtual environment, discussed in the following section, where students move around a virtual world, physically collecting data, talking to non-player characters, and running experiments in a laboratory. Only data from students' interactions with the virtual environment are included in the factors used to make predictions. As such, we both infer a key type of inquiry skill (whether the student can justify their claim) and whether the student has acquired content knowledge from their inquiry (whether the student produces the correct answer to the scientific question), doing so in the context of an open-ended virtual environment.

2   Virtual Performance Assessments

We conduct this research in the context of the Virtual Performance Assessment project at the Harvard Graduate School of Education. This project is developing and studying the feasibility of immersive virtual performance assessments to assess scientific inquiry of middle school students as a standardized component of an accountability program (see http://vpa.gse.harvard.edu). The goal is to provide states with reliable and valid technology-based performance assessments linked to state and national academic standards around science content and inquiry processes.

The virtual performance assessments are designed in the Unity game development engine [19]. The immersive nature of the three-dimensional (3D) environment allows for the creation and measurement of authentic, situated performances that are characteristic of how students conduct inquiry (see [11]). Students have the ability to walk around the environment, make observations, gather data, and solve a scientific problem in context. Further, these environments enable the automated, invisible, and non-intrusive collection of students' actions and behaviors during the assessment play.

Fig. 1. Screen shots of the Virtual Performance Assessments (VPA)

As seen in Figure 1, the assessment has the look and feel of a videogame, yet places students at the center of a scientific problem that they have to solve. Thus, the goal is to develop assessments that measure students' science learning *in situ*.

In the Virtual Performance Assessment studied within this paper, students must learn why the frogs at one farm have six legs, and can choose between a set of hypotheses, including parasites (the correct hypothesis), pollution, pesticides, genetic mutation, and space aliens. They can study frogs and water from different farms in order to collect evidence related to their hypotheses.

Students log into each assessment via a web browser. Once logged in, they work individually through the scientific problem. The assessments measure various aspects of students' inquiry skills, including:

- Student develops a causal explanation of what is happening in the virtual world that culminates in: 1) a claim about the phenomena, 2) the evidence (either empirical or observations), and 3) reasoning that links claims with evidence.
- Student gathers data that help explain or provide evidence to justify the claim being made.

As mentioned above, in the course of interacting with the VPA, students perform many actions that are recorded and stored as log data. This creates a large data set showing what students have viewed, collected and used in their experiments. Unlike traditional assessments, students are free to choose which tasks to do and in what order. This simulates a real world environment where there are choices, wrong paths and extraneous information.

3   Data Set

The data analyzed in this study were produced by 1,985 middle school students. These students were in grades 7-8, and were 12-14 years old. These students used the Virtual Performance Assessment within their science classes, spread across 40 teachers and 138 classrooms across the Northeastern and Midwestern US, and Western Canada.

The 1,985 students each used the Virtual Performance Assessment until they had completed analysis and produced a final answer, spending an average of 29 minutes and 29 seconds (SD = 14 minutes and 30 seconds) in the environment. As students used the VPA, their actions within the software were logged, including the type of action (for instance, moving between regions of the VPA, picking up and inspecting objects, running laboratory tests on objects, reading informational pages, and talking to non-player characters), the location of the action (in terms of a set of game regions), the object being manipulated (including specific game objects such as yellow frogs, specific informational pages, and non-player characters being interacted with), details of the interaction (such as which tests were run in the laboratory, or which topics were discussed with a non-player character), and the time stamp.

These log files were further distilled for analysis, producing a set of 48 semantically meaningful features that could be analyzed further. These features were of the following types:

- The number of times a student went to specific types of locations (e.g. farms to collect evidence, the laboratory to run tests) and the ratio between these values (e.g. how many farms did the student visit per trip to the laboratory)
- What percentage of time was spent in specific locations?
- How full the student's backpack became, both including repeats (e.g. picking up two green frogs counts as two objects), and not including repeats (e.g. two green frogs counts as one object) – both maximum fullness and average fullness over time were calculated
- How many times the student brought specific objects to the lab, including a count of how many distinct non-sick frogs were brought to the lab
- Number of tests run in the lab, both simultaneously, and separately, including and not including tests run multiple times
- Maximum degree of object coverage of a lab test across all tests so far (where full coverage would involve running a test on every object that test can be run on)
- How many tests were run on specific objects of interest (e.g. how many tests were run on the six-legged frog? How many tests were run on the frogs that were not ill?), both overall, and for specific tests
- How long did students pause (possibly to self-explain [cf. 17]) after running tests? (Average, Sum, and Standard Deviation)

- How many informational pages did student read, both overall and for specific pages of interest (e.g. the pages on the key hypotheses being investigated)? How many times did students read those pages?
- How long did students spend reading informational pages, both overall and for specific pages of interest? (Standard deviation was also computed for this metric, across all pages)

3.1 Dependent Measures

Two measures were predicted from students' behavior within the VPA: 1) the correctness of their final conclusion as to why the frogs had six legs and 2) their skill in designing causal explanations (DCE) for why that claim was correct.

The measure of the correctness of the student's final conclusion was based on whether the student's final conclusion was fully correct – e.g. did the student select at the end of the activity that the 6-legged frogs were caused by parasites, or did the student select one of the other potential hypotheses.

Designing causal explanation is defined as the student's ability to support their claim or conclusion with evidence. Most of the evidence in the VPA was consistent with parasites being the cause of the 6-legged frogs. Three of the four other claims had at least some evidence consistent with the claim: pollution, pesticides, and genetic mutation (there was no evidence in favor of space aliens), but there was other evidence against these claims. While even the non-causal data was strong enough to show that these claims were unlikely to be the cause, students were given partial credit if they provided supporting evidence for these claims. The students who are most successful at inquiry will be able to make a causal explanation and support it with causal inference; less successful students may fail at doing this, still demonstrating the ability to support a claim but not demonstrating an ability to fully distinguish causal and non-causal evidence.

The measure of students' ability to design a causal explanation (DCE) was operationalized through assigning points based on whether the evidence they provided supported the claim they made. Students were first asked to identify data that was evidence based on what they collected in their backpack and the tests they conducted. They were then allowed to choose from all possible data in the virtual environment, to give students who may not have collected all the necessary data a chance to support their claim with evidence. Then the student indicated for each piece of data whether or not it was evidence for their claim/conclusion, as well as identifying which farm was causing the problem. This evidence on DCE was aggregated across indicators into a single measure. The mean DCE was 50%, with a standard deviation of 23.33%.

4 Detector of Designing Causal Explanations

The detector of students' ability to design causal explanations was set up as a linear regression, as the metric for DCE was numerical. Linear regression was implemented using the M5' variable selection procedure [21] in RapidMiner 4.6 [9], using Leave

One Out Cross Validation (LOOCV), at the student level (which was the overall level of analysis). Linear regression was chosen as a relatively conservative algorithm, with a relatively low probability of over-fitting. Correlation was used as the goodness metric.

The final model achieved a cross-validation correlation of 0.531 to the student's success in designing causal explanations, comparable to the success of Bayesian Knowledge Tracing models attempting to predict post-test performance in more tightly-constrained intelligent tutoring systems domains such as genetics problem-solving [cf. 1].

When trained upon all data, the final model was as follows:

```
DCE =
- 0.165 * Maximum number of items in backpack (including repeats)
+ 0.322 * Maximum number of items in backpack (not including repeats)
- 0.656 * Average number of items in backpack (including repeats)
+ 0.651 * Average number of items in backpack (not including repeats)
+ 3.483 * Maximum degree of coverage for a lab test
- 5.120 * Percentage of time student spent at farms
- 0.644 * Ratio between trips to lab and trips to farms (lab trips
          divided by farm trips)
- 0.197 * Number of different (types of) non-sick frogs student took to
          the lab at the same time
+ 0.542 * Did the student ever run a blood test on the six-legged frog
          {0,1}?
+ 0.714 * Did the student ever run a blood test on a non-sick frog
          {0,1}?
- 0.657 * Did the student ever run a genetic test on a non-sick frog
          {0,1}?
- 0.834 * Did the student ever run a water test on farm water {0,1}?
- 1.137 * Did the student ever run a water test on lab water {0,1}?
+ 1.372 * Number of times student took lab water to the lab
+ 0.044 * How long, on average, did students spend reading information
          pages? (average per read)
- 0.025 * Standard deviation of time spent reading information pages
          (per read)
+ 0.004 * How long, in total, did student spend reading information page
          on pollution
+ 0.009 * How long, in total, did student spend reading information page
          on parasites
- 0.563 * Total number of times student accessed information page on
          space aliens
+ 0.799 * Total number of times student accessed information page on
          parasites
+ 9.153
```

The general complexity of this model indicates that many factors are associated with a student's success in designing causal explanations. It is worth noting that, due to the complexity of this model, some features may have negative coefficients when incorporated into the overall model, while having a positive correlation when taken in isolation (suggesting that they are only negative when other features are taken into account). In fact, all of the features with a negative coefficient in the model actually have a positive correlation to DCE when taken individually, with the single exception of the percentage of time the student spent at farms. However, no features with a positive coefficient in the model actually have a negative correlation to DCE when taken individually.

Taken individually, the feature most strongly correlated with DCE is the total number of times the student accessed the information page on parasites, which had a non-cross-validated correlation of 0.488 to DCE. Note that non-cross-validated correlations typically have substantially higher values than cross-validated correlations (in other words, it is not correct to assume that this single feature accounts for almost all of the total variance of the cross-validated model). This relationship indicates that student ability to design causal explanations is strongly connected with other information-seeking behaviors.

Other features particularly correlated with DCE when considered individually include: the maximum degree of coverage for a lab test (r=0.301), the percentage of time spent at farms (r= -0.265), whether the student conducted blood tests on 6-legged frogs (r=0.231) or other frogs (r=0.227), whether the student conducted water tests on lab water (r=0.233) or farm water (r=0.201), whether the student brought lab water into the lab (r=0.241), whether the student conducted a genetic test on non-sick frogs (r=0.209), and the maximum number of distinct non-sick frogs brought into the lab (r=0.216). The reasonably high correlation seen for a range of features, and the complexity of the eventual model, indicate that there are a number of indicators which have some degree of independent prediction of DCE.

5   Detector of Correct Final Conclusion

The detector of whether the student's final conclusion was correct was set up as a binary classification problem. A small number of algorithms were attempted that had been successful on similar problems: J48 Decision Trees, JRip Decision Rules, Step Regression, and K*. The most successful algorithm was JRip Decision Rules [2], a rule induction algorithm based on information gain. JRip was implemented in RapidMiner 4.6 [9], using Leave One Out Cross Validation (LOOCV), at the student level (which was the overall level of analysis). Kappa and A' were used as the goodness metrics. Kappa assesses the degree to which a detector is better than chance at identifying which clips involve the correct conclusion. A Kappa of 0 indicates that the detector performs at chance, and a Kappa of 1 indicates that the detector performs perfectly. For example, a Kappa of 0.31 would indicate that the detector is 31% better than chance. A' is the probability that the algorithm will correctly distinguish an example of a correct conclusion from an example of an incorrect conclusion.

A' closely approximates the area under the ROC curve in signal detection theory, also referred to as AUC ROC. A model with an A' of 0.5 performs at chance, and a model with an A' of 1.0 performs perfectly. The implementation of A' on our webpage (http://www.columbia.edu/~rsb2162/ edmtools.html) was used, as the implementation in RapidMiner 4.6 makes overly optimistic estimations in cases where several data points have the same confidence, a common case for JRip.

The final model achieved a cross-validated Kappa of 0.548 in predicting whether the student's final conclusion was correct, and an A' of 0.79 in doing so. This value for Kappa is comparable to detectors of science inquiry skill developed in much more constrained scientific simulation environments [e.g. 15, 16].

The final detector was as follows:

1. IF the student spent at least 66 seconds reading the parasite information page, THEN the student will obtain correct final conclusion (confidence = 81.5%)
2. IF the student spent at least 12 seconds reading the parasite information page AND the student read the parasite information page at least twice AND the student spent no more than 51 seconds reading the pesticides information   page, THEN the student will obtain correct final conclusion (confidence = 75.0%)
3. IF the student spent at least 44 seconds reading the parasite information page AND the student spent under 56 seconds reading the pollution information page, THEN the student will obtain correct final conclusion (confidence = 68.8%)
4. OTHERWISE the student will not obtain correct final conclusion (confidence = 89.0%)

It is worth noting that this detector relies solely upon students' time spent reading specific information pages. The most important thing (according to this model) is whether a student spent substantial time reading pages about the correct final conclusion, that parasites can cause frogs to have six legs. It can also be seen that spending too much time reading pages linked to incorrect hypotheses can be indicative that the student will eventually choose the wrong final claim.

5.1   Other Features Associated with Correct Final Conclusions

It is noteworthy that a student's behavior beyond reading informational pages – acquiring objects, experimenting in the lab, and talking to non-player characters – is not incorporated into the model given above. This finding indicates that the informational pages are highly important for learning about the domain; however, the finding does not necessarily indicate that the other activities are useless, but indicates that the other activities lead to correct understanding only if combined with time spent reading specific information pages. We can study whether the other features of student behavior in the virtual environment also matter, by re-running the model without using features regarding the student's use of the information pages.

When we do so, again using JRip, the final model achieves a cross-validated Kappa of 0.118 in predicting whether the student's final conclusion was correct, and an A' of 0.56 in doing so. These values are much worse than the goodness achieved when time spent reading specific information pages is taken into account – but these values are still above chance.

The resultant detector is as follows:

1. IF the student achieves coverage for a lab test of 80% or higher at least once, AND the student brings 3 or more types of non-sick frogs into the lab at least once, AND the students brings an average of 1.94 or more different types of non-sick frogs into the lab together across lab trips, THEN the student will obtain correct final conclusion (confidence = 69.0%)
2. IF the student achieves coverage for a lab test of 100% at least once, AND the student conducts no more than 8 total sets of lab tests, THEN the student will obtain correct final conclusion (confidence = 70.6%)
3. OTHERWISE the student will not obtain correct final conclusion (confidence = 79.2%)

As such, we can see that when time spent reading pages is no longer taken into consideration, the remaining features that are predictive of a correct final conclusion involve how dense the student's testing procedures are – e.g. how many tests the student ran at the same time, and how many total testing episodes there were. Tests run on non-sick frogs are particularly meaningful for this, suggesting that it is important for the student to see what features are common and different among frogs that are not sick. Simultaneous tests are apparently relatively more useful for enabling students to integrate different results, perhaps because of the difficulty of remembering and mentally comparing tests that are more spread out in time. However, the benefits of these behaviors are relatively minor for obtaining correct conclusions, compared to student time spent processing the information pages.

6   Discussion and Conclusions

In this paper, we have presented models that can infer students' ability to design causal explanations, and whether they will successfully conduct science inquiry to the degree that they obtain a correct final claim about the phenomenon being studied. Models of scientific inquiry have been developed for other domains and learning systems in recent years, but often in fairly well-scaffolded environments [e.g. 12, 15, 16]. In this paper, we extend these methods to model these constructs within a more open-ended inquiry game environment, where students physically collect data, talk to non-player characters, and run experiments in a laboratory. Rowe and Lester have successfully predicted student content knowledge from use of such an environment [13]; we extend this work to also infer students' ability to design causal explanations, and to infer student learning of the key question in the simulation. As such, this work brings together the goals of inferring content learning and inquiry skill with the goal of embedding student inquiry learning in a lightly-scaffolded game-like environment.

The detectors presented in this paper are fairly coarse-grained in nature. They assess the overall success of student inquiry across about a half hour of student behavior. As such, they assess inquiry at a larger time-scale than many past approaches [e.g. 12, 13, 15, 16]. One advantage to the finer-grained assessment used in other approaches is that it more directly affords real-time intervention (e.g. if you know that a student has failed to demonstrate inquiry skill in the last 3 actions, you can intervene right away).

However, it is challenging to assess at this time-scale in more open-ended virtual environments, particularly for the types of aggregate skills and learning studied here. The lack of a key action having occurred so far (such as the student reading the informational page on parasites) does not imply that the key action will never occur. Unless a student's behavior is clearly unrelated to the learning goals [e.g. 14, 22], a student may be on an appropriate path but exploring some aspect of the simulation relatively more thoroughly than other students. As shown in the models above, relatively brief actions can have a disproportionate impact on overall success, and these actions are not required to have occurred before a specific point.

However, the coarse-grained nature of these models does not preclude them models from being a useful tool for improving the VPA. In its current design, the VPA can infer key aspects of a student's inquiry skill after a half hour: whether the student was successful at obtaining the correct final conclusion and in designing casual explanations. The models presented in this paper can be used to assess a student's zone of proximal development as well: the difference between what the student can do without scaffolding, and what the student can do with help [e.g. 20]. For students who do not succeed at obtaining the correct final conclusion or in designing casual explanations, the model produced in this paper can be analyzed to select adaptive feedback. Each of the model features can be computed, and weighted as in the linear regression model above, in order to identify which feature(s) are most strongly associated with the student's inquiry failure. Then the student can be given feedback related to these model features – for instance, a non-player character could say "Hmm, I'm not sure your causal explanation was as good as it could have been. Did you ever run a water test on lab water?" As such, it would be possible to assess not just whether the student's initial inquiry is perfect, but how much feedback and help are needed to obtain fully correct answers. Approaches along these lines have increased the predictive power of assessment models in other domains [5]. The information from the model could also be used to help students reflect on their inquiry process after completing the VPA, to consider which of their decisions were effective and ineffective, towards promoting the student developing deeper meta-cognition about their inquiry skill.

The existing models could also be used to provide more in-the-moment feedback, by analyzing the internal features of the models. Within this environment, it is difficult to be certain that a desired action that has not yet occurred will never occur. But it is less difficult to identify specific actions as problematic based on the internal features of the models. For example, the more time a student spends reading information pages on space aliens, the less likely they are to successfully design causal explanations. A student who is spending considerable time on this page could be prompted by a non-player character to consider other pages, or to think about what evidence could support the claim that space aliens are causing farm frogs to have six legs. As such, it becomes possible to use these models – which are fairly coarse-grained in general – for adaptive personalization during learning.

In the long-term, developing student models for more loosely scaffolded learning environments will enable the methods and impacts of student modeling and adaptive personalization to apply to a wider range of learning situations. As this development occurs, the potential of individualized learning to improve student outcomes will expand to a greater range of interactive learning environments.

Acknowledgements. The research presented here was supported by the Bill and Melinda Gates Foundation. We also thank Chris Dede for his support and suggestions, and Michael Sao Pedro and one of the anonymous reviewers for their suggestions.

References

1. Baker, R.S.J.d., Gowda, S.M., Corbett, A.T.: Towards Predicting Future Transfer of Learning. In: Biswas, G., Bull, S., Kay, J., Mitrovic, A. (eds.) AIED 2011. LNCS, vol. 6738, pp. 23–30. Springer, Heidelberg (2011)
2. Cohen, W.: Fast Effective Rule Induction. In: Proceedings of the Twelfth International Conference on Machine Learning (1995)
3. Dragon, T., Woolf, B., Murray, T.: Intelligent Coaching for Collaboration in Ill-Defined Domains. In: Proceedings of the 14th International Conference on Artificial Intelligence in Education (AIED 2009), pp. 740–742 (2009)
4. Hanley, J., McNeil, B.: The Meaning and Use of the Area under a Receiver Operating Characteristic (ROC) Curve. Radiology 143, 29–36 (1982)
5. Feng, M., Heffernan, N.T., Koedinger, K.R.: Addressing the assessment challenge in an online system that tutors as it assesses. User Modeling and User-Adapted Interaction: The Journal of Personalization Research 19(3), 243–266 (2009)
6. Gertner, A.S., VanLehn, K.: Andes: A Coached Problem Solving Environment for Physics. In: Gauthier, G., VanLehn, K., Frasson, C. (eds.) ITS 2000. LNCS, vol. 1839, pp. 133–142. Springer, Heidelberg (2000)
7. Graesser, A.C., Chipman, P., Haynes, B.C., Olney, A.: AutoTutor: An intelligent tutoring system with mixed-initiative dialogue. IEEE Transactions on Education 48, 612–618 (2005)
8. Koedinger, K.R., Corbett, A.T.: Cognitive tutors: Technology bringing learning sciences to the classroom. In: Sawyer, R.K. (ed.) The Cambridge Handbook of the Learning Sciences. Cambridge University Press, New York (2006)
9. Mierswa, I., Wurst, M., Klinkenberg, R., Scholz, M., Euler, T.: YALE: Rapid Prototyping for Complex Data Mining Tasks. In: Proceedings of the 12th ACM SIGKDD International Conference on Knowledge Discovery and Data Mining (KDD 2006), pp. 935–940 (2006)
10. Mitrovic, A.: An Intelligent SQL Tutor on the Web. International Journal of Artificial Intelligence in Education 13(2-4), 173–197 (2003)
11. National Research Council: A Framework for K-12 Science Education: Practices, Crosscutting Concepts, and Core Ideas. National Academies Press, Washington, DC (2011)

12. Quellmalz, E.S., Timms, M.J., Silberglitt, M.D., Buckley, B.C.: Science Assessments for All: Integrating Science Simulations Into Balanced State Science Assessment Systems. Journal of Research in Science Teaching 49(3), 363–393 (2012)
13. Rowe, J., Lester, J.: Modeling User Knowledge with Dynamic Bayesian Networks in Interactive Narrative Environments. In: Proceedings of the Sixth Annual Artificial Intelligence and Interactive Digital Entertainment Conference (AIIDE-2010), Palo Alto, California, pp. 57–62 (2010)
14. Rowe, J., McQuiggan, S., Robison, J., Lester, J.: Off-Task Behavior in Narrative-Centered Learning Environments. In: Proceedings of the 14th International Conference on Artificial Intelligence in Education, pp. 99–106 (2009)
15. Sao Pedro, M., Baker, R., Gobert, J., Montalvo, O., Nakama, A.: Leveraging Machine-Learned Detectors of Systematic Inquiry Behavior to Estimate and Predict Transfer of Inquiry Skill. User Modeling and User-Adapted Interaction: The Journal of Personalization Research 23(1), 1–39 (2013)
16. Sao Pedro, M.A., Baker, R.S.J.: d., Montalvo, O., Nakama, A., Gobert, J.D.: Using Text Replay Tagging to Produce Detectors of Systematic Experimentation Behavior Patterns. In: Proceedings of the 3rd International Conference on Educational Data Mining, pp. 181–190 (2010)
17. Shih, B., Koedinger, K.R., Scheines, R.: A response time model for bottom-out hints as worked examples. In: Proceedings of the 1st International Conference on Educational Data Mining, pp. 117–126 (2008)
18. Sil, A., Shelton, A., Ketelhut, D.J., Yates, A.: Automatic Grading of Scientific Inquiry. In: Proceedings of the NAACL-HLT 7th Workshop on Innovative Use of NLP for Building Educational Applications (BEA-7), Montreal, Quebec, Canada (2012)
19. Unity Technologies. Unity Game Engine (2010)
20. Vygotsky, L.: Mind in Society. Harvard University Press, Cambridge (1978)
21. Wang, Y., Witten, I.H.: Induction of Model Trees for Predicting Continuous Classes. In: Proceedings of the European Conference on Machine Learning (1997)
22. Wixon, M., Baker, R.S.J.d., Gobert, J.D., Ocumpaugh, J., Bachmann, M.: WTF? Detecting Students who are Conducting Inquiry Without Thinking Fastidiously. In: Masthoff, J., Mobasher, B., Desmarais, M.C., Nkambou, R. (eds.) UMAP 2012. LNCS, vol. 7379, pp. 286–296. Springer, Heidelberg (2012)

Comparing and Combining Eye Gaze and Interface Actions for Determining User Learning with an Interactive Simulation

Samad Kardan and Cristina Conati

Department of Computer Science, University of British Columbia
2366 Main Mall, Vancouver, BC, V6T1Z4, Canada
{skardan,conati}@cs.ubc.ca

Abstract. This paper presents an experimental evaluation of eye gaze data as a source for modeling user's learning in Interactive Simulations (IS). We compare the performance of classifier user models trained only on gaze data vs. models trained only on interface actions vs. models trained on the combination of these two sources of user interaction data. Our long-term goal is to build user models that can trigger adaptive support for students who do not learn well with ISs, caused by the often unstructured and open-ended nature of these environments. The test-bed for our work is the CSP applet, an IS for Constraint Satisfaction Problems (CSP). Our findings show that including gaze data as an additional source of information to the CSP applet's user model significantly improves model accuracy compared to using interface actions or gaze data alone.

Keywords: Eye tacking, Eye Movement Data, Interface Actions, Interactive Simulations, User Classification, Clustering, Data Mining for User Modeling.

1 Introduction

With increasing interest in using Interactive Simulations (IS) for education and training, it has become evident that not all students learn well from the rather unstructured and open-ended form of interaction that these e-learning environments provide [1, 2]. The long-term goal of our research is to devise mechanisms to provide guidance during interaction with an IS, personalized to the needs of each individual student. Detecting these needs, however, is challenging because there is still limited knowledge of which behaviors are indicative of effective vs. non-effective interactions with an IS. Our general approach is to discover these behaviors from data, using (i) clustering to identify students who interact similarly with an IS, (ii) association rule mining to extract the relevant behaviors from each cluster, and (iii) finding ways to map these behaviors to learning performance. The resulting data is used to train a user model that recognizes the salient behaviors when a new user interacts with the system, and suggests interventions if those behaviors were labeled to be not conducive to learning. In previous work, we showed the effectiveness of this approach when only interface actions are used for clustering and classifying users [3]. We then started looking at the potential of gaze data as an additional source of

S. Carberry et al. (Eds.): UMAP 2013, LNCS 7899, pp. 215–227, 2013.

information for assessing how well a user learns with an IS [4]. The results in [4] were encouraging, because they showed that gaze data alone can help distinguish those users who learn from an IS and those who do not. The results, however, related to the performance of a classifier that predicts user learning after seeing gaze data from a complete interaction session. Thus, they do not tell us if and how soon during interaction, gaze data can be used to predict learning performance, which is crucial to provide adaptive support as students work with a simulation.

In this paper, we address this limitation by evaluating the over-time performance of classifiers that rely only on gaze data to determine learning, i.e. the performance of the classifier as a function of the gaze data available over time. We also thoroughly investigate the relative value of gaze data for user modeling in ISs by comparing the over-time performance of models trained on gaze data only vs. models trained on interface actions only vs. models trained on both data sources. While these comparisons are similar in nature to those described in [5, 6], the main difference is that this previous work focused on task-specific gaze patterns predefined a priori, while in our work we analyze gaze data in a much more general and automatic way, using task-independent gaze features and automatic clustering to discover the relevant patterns.

An additional contribution of this paper is an extension to the user modeling framework described in [3] to improve the effectiveness of behavior clustering. The extension is a mechanism known as the hybrid approach to clustering that extends the typical clustering used in [3]. When information on user learning performance is available for a given data set, the hybrid approach leverages this information to guide clustering so that users are grouped in terms of both their distinguishing behaviors and their learning performance. We show that on-line classifiers trained on the groupings generated by the hybrid approach are significantly more accurate than classifiers trained on groupings defined solely based on learning gain.

In the rest of the paper, we first discuss related work. Next, we briefly describe the CSP applet (the IS we have been using as a test-bed for our research). Then, we summarize our user modeling framework, followed by a description of the various dimensions of our evaluation (datasets, ways to generate the training sets, classifiers evaluated). Subsequently we report the results of the evaluation, and then present a second method for combining eye gaze and interface action data (using ensemble models) and its performance. Finally, we conclude with a discussion of future work.

2   Related Work

Eye tracking has long been used in psychology for understanding cognition and perception, but in recent years there has been increasing interest in leveraging eye-tracking data also in HCI and in user modeling. Most of the existing work still uses gaze data for off-line analysis of processes of interest, as it is traditionally done in psychology. For instance, gaze data has been used to assess word relevance in a reading task [7], to assess how well users process a given information visualization [8], to understand how users attend to adaptive hints in an educational game [9], to evaluate the impact of user differences on gaze patterns while processing a visualization [10], and to analyze attention to an open learner model [11].

Some researchers, on the other hand, started to investigate gaze data as a source for real-time modeling of users. Some examples of real-time use of gaze data include: assessing user motivation during interaction with an intelligent tutoring system (ITS) [12]; determining a variety of elements relevant to supporting users during visualization processing [13]; and detecting and reacting to disengagement in a gaze-reactive ITS [14]. Most closely related to our research on modeling users in ISs is the work by Conati and Merten [5] and Amershi and Conati [6]. They found that tracking a task-specific gaze pattern defined a priori helped modeling user learning with an IS for mathematical functions. We extend this work by looking at a much broader range of general eye tracking features that are either task independent or based solely on identifying the main interface components of the target IS. This is an important distinction, for two reasons: (i) pre-defining gaze patterns that indicate learning may not always be possible, due to the often unstructured and open-ended nature of ISs; (ii) task specific patterns likely do not transfer to a different IS. Additionally, while [6] only evaluates the performance of a model that leverages both interface actions and gaze data, our work specifically compares and combines eye gaze with interface actions to better evaluate the added value of gaze data for user modeling in ISs.

In the field of Educational Data Mining, clustering has been applied to different applications for discovering groups of similar users. Relevant to our work, in problem solving tasks, clustering has been used to find better parameter settings for models that assess student knowledge [15, 16]. Closer to our work, Shih and Koedinger employed clustering to discover student learning tactics and how these tactics relate to learning in a problem solving environment [17]. The clustering is done on sequences of student actions (namely, attempting to answer the problem and asking for help) using Expectation Maximization and Hidden Markov Models. Here, we are investigating student behaviors in ISs, where interactions tend to be open-ended and typically there are many valid actions available at each point which makes looking at sequences of user actions computationally expensive (see [3], for a detailed discussion). Thus, we calculate features that summarize the interactions of each user, and then cluster users based on these features to find users with similar behaviors. Then, we extract the salient behaviors of each cluster which is orthogonal to clustering similar sequences of actions from different users together as done in [17].

3   The AISpace CSP Applet

This section describes the Constraint Satisfaction Problem (CSP) applet, which is the IS we have been using as the test-bed for our research. The CSP applet, shown in Fig. 1, is one of a collection of interactive tools for learning artificial intelligence algorithms, called AIspace [18]. Algorithm dynamics are demonstrated via interactive visualizations on graphs by the use of color and highlighting, and graphical state changes are reinforced through textual messages.

A CSP consists of a set of variables, variable domains, and a set of constraints on legal variable-value assignments. Solving a CSP requires finding an assignment that satisfies all constraints. The CSP applet simulates application of the Arc Consistency

3 (AC-3) algorithm for solving CSPs represented as networks of variable nodes and constraint arcs. AC-3 iteratively makes individual arcs consistent by removing variable domain values inconsistent with a given constraint, until all arcs have been considered and the network is consistent. Then, if there remains a variable with more than one domain value, a procedure called domain splitting can be applied to that variable to split the CSP into disjoint cases so that AC-3 can recursively solve each case.

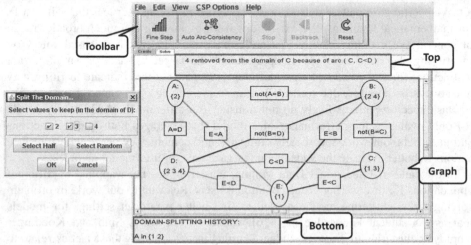

Fig. 1. CSP applet with an example CSP being solved

The CSP applet provides several mechanisms for the interactive execution of the AC-3 algorithm on a set of available CSPs. These mechanisms are accessible through the toolbar, or through direct manipulation of graph elements. The user can perform seven different actions: (i) use the Fine Step button to see how AC-3 goes through its three basic steps (selecting an arc, testing it for consistency, removing domain values to make the arc consistent); (ii) directly click on an arc to apply all these steps at once; (iii) automatically fine step on all arcs one by one (Auto Arc Consistency button); (iv) pause auto arc consistency (Stop button); (v) select a variable to split on, and specify a subset of its values for further application of AC-3 (see popup box in the left side of Fig. 1); (vi) recover alternative sub-networks during domain splitting (Backtrack button); (vii) return the graph to its initial status (Reset button). As a student steps through a problem, the message panel above the graph reports a description of each step. Another message panel situated below the graph reports the domain splits made by the user (i.e., the value-variable assignment selected at each splitting point).

4   User Modeling Framework

This section briefly summarizes our user modeling framework for providing support during interaction with an IS, personalized to each student's needs [3]. We will only focus on the components of the framework relevant to building the classifier user models evaluated later in the paper: Behavior Discovery (Fig. 2A) and User Classification (Fig. 2B) (see [3, 19] for more details on the complete framework).

In Behavior Discovery (Fig. 2A) user interaction data is first processed into feature vectors representing each user. Then, these vectors are clustered in order to (i) identify users with similar interaction behaviors, and (ii) determine which interaction behaviors are effective or ineffective for learning. The distinctive interaction behaviors in each cluster are identified via association rule mining [20]. This process extracts the common behavior patterns in terms of Class Association Rules (CAR) in the form of X→ c, where X is a set of feature-value pairs and c is the predicted class label for the data points where X applies. We use the Hotspot algorithm from the Weka datamining toolkit [21] for association rule mining, with an added initial parameter optimization step (see [3] for details). In order to associate behaviors to learning performance, it is first necessary to establish how the user groups generated by clustering relate to learning. This can be done in different ways, depending on whether information on the users' learning performance is available or not:

— If learning performance measures are not available, we face a problem of unsupervised learning. In this case, clustering is done using k-means with a modified initialization step (see [3] for more details on this technique and why it was selected). It is then left to the judgment of a human expert to evaluate how each cluster and associated behaviors may relate to learning. Since we have access to a learning performance measure, this case is not considered in this paper.
— If learning performance measures are available, one possible approach is to generate the clusters solely based on interaction data, and then assign a label for each cluster by comparing the average learning performance of the users in that cluster with the performance of the users in the other clusters. This is the approach we successfully adopted in [3] to support on-line classification of CSP applet users into high and low learners (called the *old approach* from now on). It is possible, however, that clustering solely based on behaviors do not generate groups with a clear (i.e., statistically significant) difference in learning performance, making it difficult to assign labels to the clusters automatically. To tackle this situation, we propose a solution that leverages user performance data to guide the clustering process, thus creating a *hybrid approach* (described in details in section 5.2).

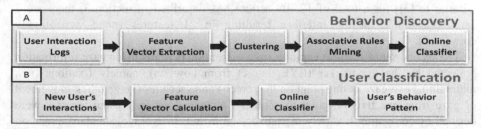

Fig. 2. Behavior Discovery and User Classification in the user modeling framework

In User Classification (Fig. 2B), the labeled clusters and the corresponding Class Association Rules extracted in Behavior Discovery are used as training data to build an on-line classifier student model (rule-based classifier from now on). As new users interact with the system, they are classified in real-time into one of the clusters generated by Behavior Discovery, based on a membership score that summarizes how well (i.e. higher is better) the user's behaviors match the discovered behavior patterns (i.e., association rules) for each cluster. This score is the normalized sum of weights of the satisfied rules over all the rules for each cluster as described in [3].

5   Evaluation Dimensions

The interaction data used as features by a classifier user model to perform on-line user classification can include a variety of sources. As we discussed in the introduction, in this paper we want to compare using features based on interface actions vs. eye gaze data vs. a combination of the two (see section 5.1). We also want to evaluate the effectiveness of each of the two major components of our classifier user model: (1) using the hybrid approach (described in section 5.2) to generate the training set for the classifiers (i.e. groups of users with labels that describe their learning performance) compared to a conventional approach; 2) using a rule-based classifier for learning vs. other available classifiers (see section 5.3). Thus, we have three dimensions in our evaluation: feature set, approach for training set generation, and type of classifier. In the rest of this section, we describe each of these three evaluation dimensions.

5.1   Different Feature Sets for Classification

We calculated three sets of features for each user. The data was collected from a user study with 45 computer science students. Each participant: (i) studied a textbook chapter on the AC-3 algorithm; (ii) wrote a pre-test on the concepts covered in the chapter; (iii) used the CSP applet to study two CSPs, while her gaze was tracked with a Tobii T120 eye-tracker; (iv) took a post-test analogous to the pre-test [4].

The first set of features consists of statistical measures that summarize a user's interface actions (ACTION dataset from now on). We calculated usage frequency for each action, as well as mean and standard deviation of time interval between actions (similar to [3]) for a total of 12,308 actions. As described in section 3, there are 7 actions available on the interface resulting in 21 features (none were highly correlated).

The second set of features captures user's attention patterns using gaze information collected by the eye-tracker (EYE dataset from now on), namely fixations (i.e., maintaining eye gaze at one point on the screen) and saccades (i.e., a quick movement of gaze from one fixation point to another). As was done in [4], the features were derived by computing a variety of statistics (sum (total), average, standard deviation and rate) as appropriate, for the measures shown in Table 1. These measures were taken both over the full CSP applet window as well as over four Areas of Interest (AOI) defining salient visual elements of the applet (Toolbar, Top, Graph and Bottom shown in Fig. 1). In addition to the features above, following [4], the proportion of transitions between different AOI pairs was also calculated. Unlike the ACTION dataset, of the initial 67 features in the EYE dataset, we found and removed 16 features that were highly correlated ($r > 0.7$), reducing the final number of eye-related features to 51.

Finally, the third set of features (ACTION+EYE dataset) is obtained by combining the two feature sets described above. For each user, the ACTION and EYE feature vectors are concatenated to form a new vector with 72 features. This process generated a dataset with 45 datapoints (participants) with 72 dimensions (features).

Given these three datasets, we want to test the following hypothesis:

H1: Combining both eye tracking and interface action data significantly enhances the performance of the resulting user model, as opposed to using either eye tracking or interface actions data alone.

Table 1. Description of basic eye tracking measures

Measure	Description
Fixation rate	Rate of eye fixations per milliseconds
Number of Fixations	Number of eye fixations detected during an interval of interest
Fixation Duration	Time duration of an individual fixation
Saccade Length	Distance between the two fixations delimiting the saccade
Relative Saccade Angles	The angle between the two consecutive saccades
Absolute Saccade Angles	The angle between a saccade and the horizontal axis
Transitions between AOIs	Transition of user's gaze between two Areas of Interest

5.2 Different Approaches for Training Set Generation

As mentioned earlier, the first step in our approach for building a classifier user model is to identify groups of users that interact similarly with the learning environment and then label these groups based on the learning performance of their members, in order to provide the training set for the classifier. As pointed out in section 4, our old approach for generating this training set relied on clustering users solely based on their interactions. However, without a clear (i.e., statistically significant) difference in average learning performance of different clusters, it is difficult to assign labels to the clusters found. We encountered this problem when using clustering on the EYE dataset. The only requirement for interpretability of the clusters in our approach is that there should be a significant difference between the average learning performances of members in different clusters, as measured by an appropriate statistical test. In other words, since we know the users in each cluster behave similarly, just knowing that the members of a cluster achieve significantly higher/lower average performance than other clusters, is enough to interpret salient behaviors observed in that cluster as effective/ineffective. Based on this requirement, we propose the hybrid approach first introduced in section 4. The hybrid approach finds the best cluster set (in terms of sum of within-cluster distances) with a significant difference in learning performance. The measure of learning performance used in this paper is Proportional Learning Gain (PLG), i.e., the ratio of the difference between post-test and pre-test, over the maximum possible gain; described in percentage ratio.

When determining the optimal number of clusters with the hybrid approach using the three different feature sets described in section 5.1 (ACTION, EYE and ACTION+EYE), we found that two clusters was always the optimal number of user groups, but with slightly different composition. We use Fleiss' kappa (a measure of agreement between more than two raters) for comparing the three different sets of user labels thus generated and found high agreement (kappa = 0.701). This kappa value shows that the two groups detected using each feature set share the same core of users (supporting the relevance of using clustering to detect these groups), with few users that are labeled differently when using different sources of data (showing that there are non-overlapping information captured by each source). For illustration, the size and performance measures associated with the two clusters generated by the hybrid approach applied to the ACTION+EYE dataset is shown in Table 2, where LLG stands for Low Learning Gain and HLG stands for High Learning Gain. The difference in PLG is significant ($p = 0.017 < 0.05$) with a medium effect size ($d = 0.625$).

When the performance measure of interest for classification is available (in our case, PLG), the conventional method for creating a training set of labeled classes is to divide the performance spectrum into different ranges and putting users within each range into one group. Thus, in our evaluation we want to compare our hybrid approach for generating the training set against the standard approach that relies solely on PLG[1]. We generate what we call the PLG-based training set by dividing users into two groups based on the median of the PLG measure (45.83). Table 2 reports the size and PLG measures for the corresponding groups.

Table 2. Descriptive statistics of the training sets generated via different methods

		Hybrid on ACTION+EYE	PLG-based
HLG	Number of users	19	22
	Average (std. dev.)	53.29 (SD = 22.79)	68.27 (SD = 12.39)
LLG	Number of users	26	23
	Average (std. dev.)	32.45 (SD = 39.33)	15.40 (SD = 30.29)

When grouping users together, the hybrid approach relies on both PLG as well as the similarity in user interaction data as opposed to only relying on PLG. Thus, we argue that it can generate better performing user models since the user models can only rely on user interaction data when classifying users. This is the second hypothesis we will test in our evaluation:

---

[1] Note that, the hybrid approach is an improvement over the old approach used in [3], to address cases when the latter approach fails to find clusters with significant learning difference (e.g., the EYE dataset). In other cases, e.g. the dataset used in [3], both approaches produce the same cluster set; therefore, a comparison between these two approaches is not necessary.

H2: The hybrid approach for training set generation outperforms the conventional PLG-based approach in terms of user model performance.

5.3   Different Types of Classifiers

Our goal is to evaluate the rule-based classifier generated by our user modeling framework. Thus, we compare its performance with a battery of ten different classifiers available in the Weka toolkit on the EYE, ACTION and ACTION+EYE datasets. These classifiers are C4.5, Support Vector Machine, Linear Ridge Regression, Binary Logistic Regression, Multilayer Perceptron, as well as Random Subspace and AdaBoost with different base classifiers. We tested the 10 Weka classifiers on each of the three datasets, and report the results for the classifier with the highest performance, which we will simply refer to as the Weka classifier. The third hypothesis tested in this study is the following:

H3: The rule-based classifier will have better performance compared to the best Weka classifier on each dataset.

6   Results and Discussion

In this section, we present the evaluation results across each of the three dimensions described in the previous section. We compare the performance of the rule-based and Weka classifiers described in the previous section in terms of their average over-time accuracy in classifying new users as high or low learners. This means that, over equal time intervals, the interaction features for a new user are calculated cumulatively from the start of the interaction, and the classifier is asked to provide a label for this. In [3], classifier accuracy was calculated after each user action, because only actions were used as data sources. Here, however, we have two different data sources, which provide information at different rates (typically length of a fixation is much shorter than the time between two interface actions). Thus, we compute current accuracy of the classifier at intervals of 30 seconds, i.e., long enough for observing at least one user action and a fair number of fixations. Then, to be able to combine accuracy data across users (with different interaction durations), we retrieve current accuracy after every one percent of user interaction, calculating 100 accuracy points for each user.

We use 9-fold cross validation for calculating the performance of the classifiers. Table 3 summarizes the average over-time accuracy of the two classifiers on the three feature sets (ACTION, EYE, ACTION+EYE) using both the hybrid and the PLG-based approach to generate the training set. We also report the average Cohen's kappa value for agreement between the actual labels and the labels predicted by the model. Cohen's kappa accounts for agreement by chance [23] and is useful here for comparing performance across different dimensions, because the size of the classes generated by the PLG-based approach and by the hybrid approach on each feature set are slightly different, changing the probability of agreement by chance in each case.

A 3 (feature set) by 2 (training set approach) by 2 (classifier type) ANOVA with kappa scores as dependent measure shows significant main effects for each factor ($F(1.43,198) = 294.27$ for feature set; $F(1,99) = 398.02$ for training set; $F(1,99) = 329.98$ for classifier type, with $p < 0.001$ for all factors).

Table 3. Average over-time performance results for different training sets, classifiers and feature sets. The best performance in each column is indicated in bold.

Training Set	Classifier	Measure	Feature Set		
			ACTION	EYE	ACTION+EYE
PLG-based	Weka	Accuracy	51.18	57.62	58.18
		Kappa	0.027	0.144	0.157
	Rule-based	Accuracy	57.24	64.29	62.2
		Kappa	0.134	0.283	0.245
Hybrid	Weka	Accuracy	79.87	71.49	77.24
		Kappa	0.359	0.384	0.522
	Rule-based	Accuracy	**84.04**	**81.76**	**84.51**
		Kappa	**0.471**	**0.614**	**0.675**

For post-hoc analysis we used pair-wise t-tests with Bonferroni adjustment using the estimated marginal means for each factor. Pair-wise comparisons over the feature set factor shows that the models trained on the EYE+ACTION dataset outperform the models trained either on EYE or ACTION feature sets ($p < 0.001$), thus supporting H1. Pair-wise comparisons over the training set factor shows that the hybrid approach outperforms the PLG-based approach ($p < 0.001$), thus supporting H2. Finally, pair-wise comparisons over the classifier type factor shows that the rule-based classifier significantly outperforms the Weka classifier ($p < 0.001$), thus supporting H3. The findings show that we were able to extend our user modeling framework with an effective training set generation approach (H2), and the updated framework is able to build models that employ interface actions and eye gaze data effectively (H3), reinforcing the validity of our findings regarding the added value of eye gaze data (H1).

7   Ensemble Model for Combining EYE and ACTION Features

The superior performance generated by the feature set that combines gaze and action information indicates that there is an advantage in leveraging both data sources. Thus, we decided to investigate whether we could further this advantage by using a more sophisticated approach to combine gaze and action information. In particular, for each combination of training set (hybrid and PLG-based) and classifier type (rule-based vs. Weka) we created an ensemble classifier [24] that classifies a new user by using majority voting among the three following classifiers on the ACTION+EYE dataset: one trained using only the action-based features subset, one trained using the eye-based features subset, and one trained over the complete ACTION + EYE feature set. This ensemble model benefits from the added information captured by the eye gaze data (if any) by being able to correctly classify the user in some of the cases where the classifier trained solely on the action-based features fails. Moreover, in some cases where combining the features in the way that it is done in previous section on the ACTION+EYE dataset, is introducing some noise in the dataset, thus diluting the information value gained, the classifiers trained on eye-based subset and action-based subset will not be affected and will be able to capture characteristics of each user as detected by each data source. Therefore, we hypothesize that:

H4: Each ensemble model outperforms the individual model equivalent to it (i.e., the model with the same classifier type and training set generation approach).

Table 4 shows the performance results for the ensemble models (measured by kappa scores). In order to evaluate the performance of the ensemble models vs. the individual models described in previous section, we performed a 2 (model type) by 2 (training set approach) by 2 (classifier type) ANOVA with kappa scores for the ACTION+EYE dataset as dependent measure. Here, we are only interested in testing to see whether there is a main effect for the model type factor (i.e., individual vs. ensemble). The analysis shows a significant main effect for the model type factor ($F(1,99) = 165.420$, with $p < 0.001$). Post-hoc analysis using pair-wise t-tests with Bonferroni adjustment shows that the ensemble models significantly ($p < 0.001$) outperform their individual model counterparts thus supporting H4. Particularly, we are interested in the best performing individual model (rule-based model trained using hybrid training set) and its ensemble equivalent, where in addition to improved average over-time performance (86.56% vs. 84.51%), the ensemble model exhibits a more balanced performance across the HLG and LLG classes as well (85.33% and 87.52% for the ensemble vs. 79% and 88.54% for the individual model respectively).

Table 4. Average over-time performance results for different training sets and classifiers for the ensemble models, in terms of kappa scores

Training Set	PLG-based		Hybrid	
Classifier	Weka	Rule-based	Weka	Rule-based
Kappa	0.194	0.315	0.585	0.725

Considering the ultimate goal of providing adaptive interventions to the users during their interaction, we are also interested to have a user model that can achieve an acceptable accuracy in early stages of the interaction. Thus, we plotted the over-time accuracy of the rule-based ensemble model trained using hybrid training set in Fig. 3. Performance of the majority class classifier is also plotted as the baseline. The model achieves 80% accuracy in both classes after observing 22 percent of the interaction (Fig. 3), which shows that this model is highly reliable for providing adaptive interventions during the user interaction.

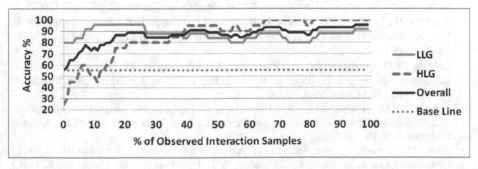

Fig. 3. Over-time performance of the rule-based ensemble model

8   Conclusion and Future Work

We presented an experimental evaluation of eye gaze as an additional source of user data for modeling user's learning in an IS for constraint satisfaction problems (the CSP applet). We also described a new approach for generating training sets from user data, called the hybrid approach. This mechanism extends our user modeling framework originally described in [3], to be able to effectively utilize eye gaze data when building classifier user models. Our main finding is that eye gaze data when used as an additional source of user data in combination with the interface actions significantly boosts the average over-time performance of the classifier user models trained to distinguish students who learned well from students who did not. We also demonstrated that using the hybrid approach leads to models with significantly higher performance compared to a conventional alternative.

One possible extension of this work is to combine the gaze data in finer grained setting by looking at the gaze patterns between consecutive interface actions. This enables the system to provide gaze based interventions in a more meaningful way. Another important aspect of future work is further evaluation of the hybrid approach for other interactive simulations and similar open-ended environments (generalizability). We are also working on evaluating the effectiveness of the rule-based user model in triggering adaptive interventions for the CSP applet [25].

References

1. Shute, V.J.: A comparison of learning environments: All that glitters. In: Computers as cognitive tools, pp. 47–73. Lawrence Erlbaum Associates, Inc., Hillsdale (1993)
2. Holzinger, A., Kickmeier-Rust, M.D., Wassertheurer, S., Hessinger, M.: Learning performance with interactive simulations in medical education: Lessons learned from results of learning complex physiological models with the HAEMOdynamics SIMulator. Computers & Education 52, 292–301 (2009)
3. Kardan, S., Conati, C.: A Framework for Capturing Distinguishing User Interaction Behaviours in Novel Interfaces. In: Proc. of the 4th Int. Conf. on Educational Data Mining, Eindhoven, The Netherlands, pp. 159–168 (2011)
4. Kardan, S., Conati, C.: Exploring Gaze Data for Determining User Learning with an Interactive Simulation. In: Masthoff, J., Mobasher, B., Desmarais, M.C., Nkambou, R. (eds.) UMAP 2012. LNCS, vol. 7379, pp. 126–138. Springer, Heidelberg (2012)
5. Conati, C., Merten, C.: Eye-tracking for user modeling in exploratory learning environments: An empirical evaluation. Knowledge-Based Systems 20, 557–574 (2007)
6. Amershi, S., Conati, C.: Combining Unsupervised and Supervised Classification to Build User Models for Exploratory Learning Environments. Journal of Educational Data Mining, 18–71 (2009)
7. Loboda, T.D., Brusilovsky, P., Brunstein, J.: Inferring word relevance from eye-movements of readers. In: Proc. of the 16th Int. Conf. on Intelligent User Interfaces, pp. 175–184. ACM, New York (2011)
8. Loboda, T.D., Brusilovsky, P.: User-adaptive explanatory program visualization: evaluation and insights from eye movements. User Modeling and User-Adapted Interaction 20, 191–226 (2010)
9. Muir, M., Conati, C.: An Analysis of Attention to Student – Adaptive Hints in an Educational Game. In: Cerri, S.A., Clancey, W.J., Papadourakis, G., Panourgia, K. (eds.) ITS 2012. LNCS, vol. 7315, pp. 112–122. Springer, Heidelberg (2012)

10. Toker, D., Conati, C., Steichen, B., Carenini, G.: Individual User Characteristics and Information Visualization: Connecting the Dots through Eye Tracking. In: Proc. of the ACM SIGCHI Conference on Human Factors in Computing Systems (CHI 2013), Paris, France (to appear, 2013)

11. Mathews, M., Mitrovic, A., Lin, B., Holland, J., Churcher, N.: Do Your Eyes Give It Away? Using Eye Tracking Data to Understand Students' Attitudes towards Open Student Model Representations. In: Cerri, S.A., Clancey, W.J., Papadourakis, G., Panourgia, K. (eds.) ITS 2012. LNCS, vol. 7315, pp. 422–427. Springer, Heidelberg (2012)

12. Qu, L., Johnson, W.L.: Detecting the Learner's Motivational States in An Interactive Learning Environment. In: Proceedings of the 2005 Conference on Artificial Intelligence in Education: Supporting Learning through Intelligent and Socially Informed Technology, pp. 547–554. IOS Press, Amsterdam (2005)

13. Steichen, B., Carenini, G., Conati, C.: User-Adaptive Information Visualization - Using eye gaze data to infer visualization tasks and user cognitive abilities. In: Proceedings of the International Conference on Intelligent User Interfaces, IUI 2013 (to appear, 2013)

14. D'Mello, S., Olney, A., Williams, C., Hays, P.: Gaze tutor: A gaze-reactive intelligent tutoring system. Int. J. Hum.-Comput. Stud. 70, 377–398 (2012)

15. Trivedi, S., Pardos, Z.A., Heffernan, N.T.: Clustering students to generate an ensemble to improve standard test score predictions. In: Biswas, G., Bull, S., Kay, J., Mitrovic, A. (eds.) AIED 2011. LNCS, vol. 6738, pp. 377–384. Springer, Heidelberg (2011)

16. Gong, Y., Beck, J.E., Ruiz, C.: Modeling Multiple Distributions of Student Performances to Improve Predictive Accuracy. In: Masthoff, J., Mobasher, B., Desmarais, M.C., Nkambou, R. (eds.) UMAP 2012. LNCS, vol. 7379, pp. 102–113. Springer, Heidelberg (2012)

17. Shih, B., Koedinger, K.R., Scheines, R.: Unsupervised Discovery of Student Strategies. In: Proceedings of the 3rd International Conference on Educational Data Mining, pp. 201–210 (2010)

18. Amershi, S., Carenini, G., Conati, C., Mackworth, A.K., Poole, D.: Pedagogy and usability in interactive algorithm visualizations: Designing and evaluating CIspace. Interacting with Computers 20, 64–96 (2008)

19. Kardan, S.: Data mining for adding adaptive interventions to exploratory and open-ended environments. In: Masthoff, J., Mobasher, B., Desmarais, M.C., Nkambou, R. (eds.) UMAP 2012. LNCS, vol. 7379, pp. 365–368. Springer, Heidelberg (2012)

20. Zhang, C., Zhang, S.: Association Rule Mining. LNCS (LNAI), vol. 2307. Springer, Heidelberg (2002)

21. Hall, M., Frank, E., Holmes, G., Pfahringer, B., Reutemann, P., Witten, I.H.: The WEKA data mining software: an update. ACM SIGKDD Explorations Newsletter 11, 10–18 (2009)

22. Thabtah, F.: A Review of Associative Classification Mining. The Knowledge Engineering Review 22, 37–65 (2007)

23. Ben-David, A.: About the relationship between ROC curves and Cohen's kappa. Eng. Appl. Artif. Intell. 21, 874–882 (2008)

24. Baker, R.S.J.d., Pardos, Z.A., Gowda, S.M., Nooraei, B.B., Heffernan, N.T.: Ensembling predictions of student knowledge within intelligent tutoring systems. In: Konstan, J.A., Conejo, R., Marzo, J.L., Oliver, N. (eds.) UMAP 2011. LNCS, vol. 6787, pp. 13–24. Springer, Heidelberg (2011)

25. Kardan, S., Conati, C.: Providing Adaptive Support in an Exploratory Learning Environment by Mining User Interaction Data. In: Proceedings of the 5th International Workshop on Intelligent Support for Exploratory Environments (ISEE 2012) (2012); In Conjunction with the 11th International Conference on Intelligent Tutoring Systems (ITS 2012), Chania, Greece (2012)

Utilizing Dynamic Bayes Nets to Improve Early Prediction Models of Self-regulated Learning

Jennifer Sabourin, Bradford Mott, and James Lester

North Carolina State University, Raleigh, North Carolina
{jlrobiso,bwmott,lester}@ncsu.edu

Abstract. Student engagement and motivation during learning activities is tied to better learning behaviors and outcomes and has prompted the development of learner-guided environments. These systems attempt to personalize learning by allowing students to select their own tasks and activities. However, recent evidence suggests that not all students are equally capable of guiding their own learning. Some students are highly self-regulated learners and are able to select learning goals, identify appropriate tasks and activities to achieve these goals and monitor their progress resulting in improved learning and motivational benefits over traditional learning tasks. Students who lack these skills are markedly less successful in self-guided learning environments and require additional scaffolding to be able to navigate them successfully. Prior work has examined these phenomena within the learner-guided environment, CRYSTAL ISLAND, and identified the need for early prediction of students' self-regulated learning abilities. This work builds upon these findings and presents a dynamic Bayesian approach that significantly improves the classification accuracy of student self-regulated learning skills.

Keywords: Student modeling, intelligent tutoring systems, self-regulated learning.

1 Introduction

The focus on encouraging student engagement and motivation has been growing rapidly in recent decades in both classroom-based and computer-based instruction. This attention is guided by the empirical findings that students' feelings of interest and motivation towards an activity, domain, or learning in general has a powerful influence on how long they will persist with a task and how willing they are to initiate an activity [1–4].

A common approach to encouraging engagement involves increasing student autonomy and allowing each individual student to guide his or her own learning [5–7]. The insight behind this approach is that students will be able to focus on tasks and topics that fit within their own learning goals and interests [8]. However, while this approach has gained popularity, there is increasing evidence that not all students are successful at guiding their own learning [5, 9, 10]. To be successful, students must be capable of setting meaningful learning objectives. They must then identify activities,

S. Carberry et al. (Eds.): UMAP 2013, LNCS 7899, pp. 228–241, 2013.
© Springer-Verlag Berlin Heidelberg 2013

behaviors, and strategies that may achieve these goals, monitor and evaluate their progress and alter their behavior and strategies accordingly. Unfortunately there is evidence that not all students are capable of guiding their own learning in this way [11] and may consequently experience limited success with systems that require these skills [5, 6, 12].

The ability to set learning goals, identify successful strategies and evaluate personal success is the hallmark of a self-regulated learner. Students who exhibit self-regulated learning (SRL) skills are able to drive their own learning and are often more successful in learning tasks and academic settings [13]. While SRL skills can be taught and often improve with practice [14], students who have not yet developed appropriate SRL strategies are more likely to flounder in self-guided learning systems. However, there is evidence that with appropriate scaffolding, these environments can be beneficial in improving learning and interest as well as aid in development of SRL skills [15, 16].

The issue of how to appropriately level and support SRL strategies in learning environments remains an important open question with a variety of conflicting evidence [17–21]. However, there is consensus that appropriate scaffolding involves a delicate balance of allowing autonomy but providing support when necessary [22]. To do this successfully, teachers and tutoring systems must be able to accurately identify a student's skill level and utilize this knowledge to deliver an appropriately leveled amount of support.

This paper describes an investigation of these issues within the self-guided game-based learning environment, CRYSTAL ISLAND. Prior work examining SRL behaviors in CRYSTAL ISLAND has indicated that students who are able to regulate their behaviors experience greater learning gains and report more interest and motivation, while students without these skills are significantly less successful [23]. These results have highlighted the need for targeted scaffolding based on early recognition of students' self-regulatory skills. This work uses Bayesian modeling techniques incorporating both empirical and theoretical knowledge to classify self-regulated learners early into their interaction with CRYSTAL ISLAND. Models learned from a corpus including data from 260 middle school students show significant promise in early prediction of self-regulated learning skills. The methodology, findings, and implications of this work are discussed.

2   Related Work

Identifying and scaffolding metacognitive behaviors such as self-regulated learning (SRL) has been a focus of much work in the intelligent tutoring systems community due to the strong influence of these behaviors on learning [5, 13, 24]. For example, in MetaTutor, a hypermedia environment for learning biology, think-aloud protocols have been used to examine which regulatory strategies students use, while analysis of students' navigation through the hypermedia environment helps to identify profiles of self-regulated learners [24, 25]. Similarly, researchers have identified patterns of behavior in the Betty's Brain system that are indicative of low and high levels of self-regulation [26] and utilized sequence mining techniques to further explore these patterns [27]. Aleven *et al.* [28] have hand-crafted a model of help-seeking behavior based on pedagogical theories of when students ought to seek help and the variety of help-seeking behaviors that are thought to be detrimental to learning.

While previous work has focused primarily on examining SRL in highly structured problem-solving and learning environments, there has also been work on identifying SRL behaviors in open-ended exploratory environments. For example, work by Shores *et al.* has examined early prediction of students' cognitive tool use in order to inform possible interventions and scaffolding [29]. Understanding and scaffolding students' SRL behaviors is especially important in open-ended learning environments where goals may be less clear and students do not necessarily have a clear indicator of their progress [30]. In order to be successful in this type of learning environment, students must actively identify and select their own goals and evaluate their progress accordingly. While the nature of the learning task may have implicit overarching goals such as 'completing the task' or 'learning a lot,' it is important for students to set more specific, concrete and measurable goals [31]. However, not all students are equally successful in regulating their learning in this way [5, 6, 9, 11].

This work represents an initial step in scaffolding such metacognitive behaviors by first predicting a student's skill level early into interaction with an open-ended self-guided learning environment so that future scaffolding can be targeted to a student's individual abilities. Prior work to predict self-regulated learning has demonstrated promise in being able to identify self-regulated learners early into their interaction with an open ended environment [23], though predictive accuracies were not believed to be sufficiently high for a functional runtime system. This work builds upon these findings by using Bayesian modeling techniques and incorporating theoretical and empirical knowledge to improve early prediction capabilities.

3   Method

The investigation of SRL behaviors was conducted with students from a local middle school interacting with CRYSTAL ISLAND, a self-guided game-based learning environment being developed for the domain of microbiology that follows the standard course of study for eighth grade science in North Carolina [32].

3.1   Crystal Island

CRYSTAL ISLAND (Figure 1) features a science mystery set on a recently discovered volcanic island. Students play the role of the protagonist, Alex, who is attempting to discover the identity and source of an unknown disease plaguing a newly established research station. The story opens by introducing the student to the island and the members of the research team for which her father serves as the lead scientist. As members of the research team fall ill, it is her task to discover the cause and the specific source of the outbreak. Typical game play involves navigating the island, manipulating objects, taking notes, viewing posters, operating lab equipment, and

Fig. 1. Crystal ISLAND learning environment   **Fig. 2.** Self-report device

talking with non-player characters to gather clues about the disease's source. To progress through the mystery, a student must explore the world and interact with other characters while forming questions, generating hypotheses, collecting data, and testing hypotheses.

3.2   Study Procedure

A study with 296 eighth grade students was conducted. After removing instances with incomplete data or logging errors, there were 260 students remaining. Among the remaining students, there were 129 male and 131 female participants varying in age and race. Participants interacted with CRYSTAL ISLAND in their school classroom, although the study was not directly integrated into their regular classroom activities. Pre-study materials were completed during the week prior to interacting with CRYSTAL ISLAND. The pre-study materials included a demographic survey, researcher-generated CRYSTAL ISLAND curriculum test, and several personality questionnaires. Personality was measured using the Big 5 Personality Questionnaire, which indexes student personality across five dimensions: openness, conscientiousness, extraversion, agreeableness and neuroticism [33]. Goal orientation was measured using a 2-dimensional taxonomy considering students' mastery or performance orientations along with their approach or avoidance tendencies [34]. Students' affect regulation tendencies were measured using the Cognitive Emotion Regulation Questionnaire which consists of nine subscales, each representing a different cognitive regulation strategy [35].

Immediately after solving the mystery, or after 55 minutes of interaction, students moved to a different room in order to complete several post-study questionnaires including the curriculum post-test. Students also completed two questionnaires aimed to measure students' interest and involvement with CRYSTAL ISLAND including the Intrinsic Motivation Inventory [36] and the Presence Questionnaire [37].

During the interaction students were prompted every seven minutes to self-report their current mood and status through an in-game smartphone device (Figure 2). Students selected one emotion from a set of seven options, which included the following: anxious, bored, confused, curious, excited, focused, and frustrated. After selecting an emotion, students were instructed to briefly type a few words about their current status in the game, similarly to how they might update their status in an online social network.

3.3   SRL Classification

The typed status reports were later tagged for SRL evidence using the following four ranked classifications: (1) specific reflection, (2) general reflection, (3) non-reflective statement, or (4) unrelated. (See [23] for more details). This ranking is motivated by the observation that setting and reflecting upon goals is strongly associated with self-regulatory behavior and that specific goals are more beneficial than those that are more general [9]. Students were then given an overall SRL score based on the average score of their statements. An even ternary split was then used to assign the students to a High, Medium, and Low SRL category.

From the 260 students, a total of 1836 statements were collected, resulting in an average of 7.2 statements per student. All statements were tagged by one member of the research team with a second member of the research team tagging a randomly selected subset (10%) of the statements to assess the validity of the protocol. Inter-rater reliability was measured at $\kappa = 0.77$, which is an acceptable level of agreement. General reflective statements were the most common (37.2%), followed by unrelated (35.6%), specific reflections (18.3%) and finally non-reflective statements (9.0%).

The ternary split of students into High, Medium, and Low SRL classes has yielded interesting findings in prior work [23]. One important finding is that High and Medium SRL students have both higher prior knowledge and higher learning gains than Low SRL students. This shows that Low SRL students start with some disadvantage and that the overall gap in knowledge is increased after interactions with CRYSTAL ISLAND. Though all groups have significant learning gains, Low SRL students are not receiving the same advantages of interaction with CRYSTAL ISLAND. Further analyses indicated that High SRL students reported experiencing significantly more interest, enjoyment, and attributed greater value and importance to the task than either Medium or Low SRL students.

Together these findings motivate the need for detection and scaffolding of SRL skill levels. Low-SRL students require more guided instruction and scaffolding to learn as effectively as their peers. Evidence suggests that Medium-SRL students may need slightly more scaffolding to have an optimal experience but overall are effectively learning on their own. Meanwhile, High-SRL students are experiencing the positive benefits expected from a self-guided learning experience and should not receive any intervention. The first step toward delivering targeted scaffolding based on SRL skill level is to first classify a student as a High, Medium, or Low SRL student early into their interaction with CRYSTAL ISLAND.

4   Early Prediction of SRL Behaviors

Initial classification of student SRL behaviors was conducted manually after the completed interaction with CRYSTAL ISLAND. In order to provide adaptive scaffolding, these classes must be recognized early into the interaction so that students do not spend too much time floundering with too little guidance. To this end, empirical models were learned from the corpus of student data and trained to classify SRL skill level early into the interaction.

4.1   Corpus

The comprehensive corpus for modeling SRL behavior originally included a total of 49 features. Of these, 26 features represented personal data collected prior to the student's interaction with CRYSTAL ISLAND. This included demographic information, pre-test score, and scores on the personality, goal orientation, and emotion regulation questionnaires. The remaining 23 features represented a summary of students' interactions in the environment. This included information on how students used each of the curricular resources, how many in-game goals they had completed, as well as evidence of off-task behavior (details on off-task behavior can be found in [38]). Additionally, data from the students' self-reports were included, such as the most recent emotion report and the character count of their "status."

    In order to examine early prediction of the students' SRL-use categories, these features were calculated at four different points in time resulting in four distinct datasets. The first of these (**Initial**) represented information available at the beginning of the student's interaction and consequently only contained the 26 personal attributes. Each of the remaining three datasets (**Report$_{1-3}$**) contained data representing the student's progress at each of the first three emotion self-report instances. These datasets contained the same 26 personal attributes, but the values of the remaining 23 in-game attributes differentially reflected the student's progress up until that point. The first self-report occurred approximately 4 minutes into game play with the second and third reports occurring at 11 minutes and 18 minutes, respectively. The third report occurs after approximately one-third of the total time allotted for interaction has been completed, so it is still fairly early into the interaction time.

4.2   Prior Work – Naïve Modeling Approaches

Prior work [23] has shown promise in being able to predict SRL class early into the interaction. This work compared the ability of naïve Bayes, neural network, logistic regression, support vector machine, and decision tree models to predict SRL class at different time intervals. Overall it was found that logistic regression and decision trees offered the best performance, correctly predicting 43% of students' classes before interaction begins and up to 57% of students' classes after one-third of their interaction with CRYSTAL ISLAND. Compared with a most-frequent-class baseline of 34%, this offers a significant improvement in the ability to recognize SRL skill.

However, while both logistic regression and decision tree models significantly outperformed baseline measures, the predictive accuracy did not seem to be sufficient for guiding adaptive scaffolding though they represented a positive indication that a more targeted approach to modeling had the potential to be successful.

4.3   Current Approach – Informed Bayesian Modeling

The promising results of the initial modeling approaches raised two questions: *1) What features are most beneficial for predicting students' SRL classifications?* and *2) How can knowledge of the learning environment and the processes associated with SRL be used to guide the development of models?* These two questions guided the development of a predictive model that is informed from empirical corpus data as well as a theoretical understanding of self-regulated processes. The objective of this line of investigation was to further improve predictive accuracy so that a runtime system could be used to reliably detect and scaffold SRL behaviors.

Feature Selection. The first step in developing an informed predictive model was to identify the features that were most beneficial in predicting students' SRL classifications. Stepwise logistic regression was selected as the approach to addressing this problem. Stepwise logistic regression involves iteratively adding and removing features to a predictive logistic regression model based on whether the inclusion of the feature significantly improves the model's predictive capabilities.

The stepwise logistic regression was run using the SAS® 9.3 statistical modeling package. A significance level of $\alpha < 0.05$ was required for a feature to remain in the selected model. In total, 15 features were identified as significant to the predictive process. These features included 9 static personal traits as well as the total pretest score. The 6 in-game features related to the students' statuses, use of the in-game tools and students' off-task behaviors.

Bayesian Modeling. The next step in model development was to select a modeling approach which could take advantage of both empirical and theoretical knowledge of SRL in CRYSTAL ISLAND. A Bayesian approach was selected for a variety of reasons. First, Bayesian methodologies have been used to represent a wide variety of phenomena in intelligent tutoring systems including models of learning [39, 40], affect [41, 42], and hinting [43]. More importantly for this application, Bayesian networks can accommodate both empirical and theoretical knowledge [41, 42]. Bayesian networks operate by representing the relationship between variables in terms of a probability distribution. Bayesian networks involve two main components, (1) a network structure, which describes which variables are related to others, and (2) a set of conditional dependencies which provide the exact specifications for these relationships. Both the structure and the conditional dependencies can be learned using a variety of possible algorithms [44] or specified by hand.

The proposed model includes a structure which has been hand-crafted to include the features indicated as beneficial for predicting SRL class. The relationship between these variables is determined by a theoretical grounding of SRL processes including the key behaviors of planning and monitoring [31]. The exact values of the conditional dependencies are then learned using an Expectation-Maximization (EM) algorithm [44]. In this way the model takes advantage of theoretical knowledge related of SRL processes as well as empirical evidence of how these phenomena occur in the CRYSTAL ISLAND environment.

5   Results

A Bayesian network structure was constructed using the 9 personal a 6 in-game attributes identified in the feature selection step. Three hidden states were also created based on understanding of the CRYSTAL ISLAND environment and SRL processes. These included:

- **Resource Use:** This variable aggregates information of a variety of in-game behaviors all related to the effective use of the in-game resources. This includes off-task behavior, diagnosis worksheet use and testing behaviors.
- **Planning:** This variable seeks to represent students' tendencies to engage in planning behaviors before beginning a task, a hallmark of SRL. Features that indicate planning include openness and agreeableness which reflect how students approach novel situations, as well as the planning subscale of cognitive-emotion regulation questionnaire.

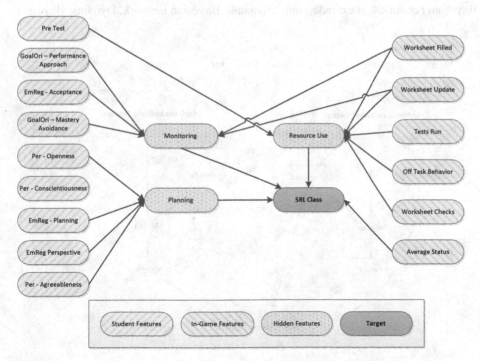

Fig. 3. Structure of Bayesian network for predicting SRL class

- **Monitoring:** This variable seeks to represent student behaviors and personal tendencies that lead to monitoring of learning activities, another hallmark of SRL. These include diagnose worksheet use, conscientiousness, and learning goals.

The structure was hand-crafted using the GeNIe modeling environment developed by the Decision Systems Laboratory of the University of Pittsburgh (http://dsl.sis.pitt.edu). This structure can be seen in Figure 3. Parameters were then learned using the EM algorithm provided by GeNIe using data from each of the four time-slices described in Section 4.1. However, since there is no in-game data available for the **Initial** dataset, this model included only the 9 personal attributes and 2 hidden attributes that do not involve in-game activities. Models were evaluated using 10-fold cross-validation.

Results indicated that the Bayesian network significantly outperformed both baseline measures and the naïve classifiers. At the **Initial** time slice, the handcrafted Bayesian network correctly predicted 64.8% of students' classifications and reached an accuracy of 68.5% by **Report₃**. This indicates that the model is twice as effective as the baseline measures. Examination of recall metrics indicate that the Bayesian model does not perform significantly better at recognizing any particular class.

While successful, the Bayesian model represents a static picture of SRL processes at a particular time. One of the key components of SRL is that a student's planning and monitoring activities impact future behaviors based on the success of adopted strategies. In order to account for the dynamic nature of SRL behaviors the static Bayesian network was extended into a dynamic Bayesian network. Dynamic Bayesian

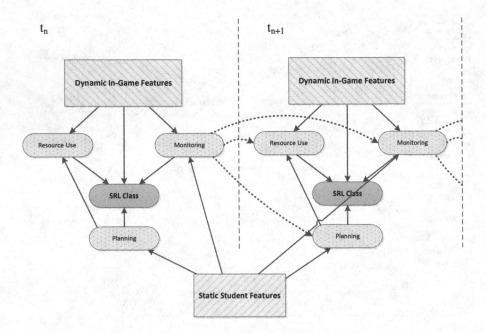

Fig. 4. Structure of dynamic Bayesian network for predicting SRL class

Table 1. Predictive accuracy for learned models

	Predictive Accuracy			
Model	Initial	Report$_1$	Report$_2$	Report$_3$
Top Prior Model	42.7	46.2	48.1	57.2
Bayesian Network	64.8	67.0	67.5	68.5
Dynamic Bayes Net	64.5	80.5	81.3	83.1

Table 2. Recall metrics for Bayesian models

	Bayesian Network				Dynamic Bayesian Network			
Class	Initial	Report$_1$	Report$_2$	Report$_3$	Initial	Report$_1$	Report$_2$	Report$_3$
Low	0.67	0.67	0.70	0.58	0.73	0.71	0.73	0.75
Medium	0.61	0.57	0.59	0.68	0.49	0.78	0.80	0.84
High	0.66	0.77	0.73	0.79	0.71	0.92	0.91	0.91

Networks (DBNs) are able to account for temporal relationships between variables, allowing observations at time t_n to inform observations at time t_{n+1}. Utilizing this framework, we extended the static Bayesian network to include temporal relationships between planning and monitoring across time. This extended dynamic Bayesian network is depicted in Figure 4. Again, the model was trained using GeNIe's EM algorithm and evaluated with 10-fold cross-validation.

Results indicated that for the **Initial** time slice the DBN achieved a predictive accuracy (64.5%) equivalent to that of the static Bayesian network. This finding is unsurprising as the model has no prior information to improve predictive accuracy. However, for each of the three time slices occurring during gameplay, the DBN is able to significantly outperform the static Bayesian network, reaching a predictive accuracy of 83.1% by **Report$_3$**. Further examination of recall metrics indicates that the model correctly recognizes approximately the same percentage of Low-SRL students regardless of how much time has passed. The increase in predictive accuracy over time appears to come from an increased ability to distinguish Medium and High-SRL students further into the interaction. Overall, the DBN matched or outperformed the static Bayesian model and achieved predictive accuracies that are believed to be sufficient for guiding future scaffolding approaches.

6   Conclusion

Learner-guided systems offer significant promise in fostering engagement and motivation by providing autonomy and allowing students to direct their own learning. However, evidence suggests that some students lack the self-regulatory skills to receive the maximum benefit these systems may offer. This was found to be the case with detailed analyses of the CRYSTAL ISLAND environment. Students with more developed SRL skills learn more and report higher levels of engagement and interest when interacting with CRYSTAL ISLAND than students lacking these skills, suggesting the need to provide adaptive scaffolding based on students SRL abilities.

Machine-learned models capable of early prediction of SRL classification show promise in being able to identify which students would benefit most from adaptive scaffolding. Specifically, Bayesian techniques using both empirical data and theoretical grounding were able to classify students into groups of High, Medium and Low SRL skills early into their interaction with CRYSTAL ISLAND. Dynamic Bayesian networks, which reflect the temporal dynamics of planning and monitoring behaviors offered significant improvements over static models which did not incorporate these features.

This work represents the first step in providing adaptive, appropriately leveled scaffolding of SRL behaviors in CRYSTAL ISLAND. Many areas remain for future work. First, it will be important to identify which specific behaviors should be supported or guided by the adaptive system. Recent work has shown that High, Medium, and Low-SRL students utilize the features of the CRYSTAL ISLAND environment differently. Further work should be undertaken to attempt to gain a more detailed understanding of these differences with modeling techniques such as pattern mining or Markovian approaches. Next, leveled scaffolding will be developed and evaluated to identify how much scaffolding is appropriate for each SRL skill level. This scaffolding will encourage goal setting and monitoring behaviors and guide students towards strategies identified by the analysis of real student behaviors. It will be important to measure outcomes in terms of both learning and engagement as it is expected that too much guidance or support may reduce interest and enjoyment. Furthermore, it will be important to investigate the relative cost of misclassification and incorrect delivery of scaffolding. An objective cost metric balancing engagement and learning can guide learned models towards policies that optimize a scaffolding strategy. Finally, the findings from each of these investigations will be incorporated into a comprehensive version of CRYSTAL ISLAND, capable of early detection and adaptive, leveled scaffolding of self-regulate learning.

Self-regulated learning is an important skill impacting the success of students on a variety of learning tasks. Students without these skills are unable to make the most of learner-guided environments that provide autonomy and self-guided learning in the hopes of increasing engagement and interest as well as learning outcomes. Scaffolding tailored specifically to the skill-level of the student is necessary to balance the engagement benefits of autonomy and the learning benefits of guided learning activities. The empirical models discussed in this work represent the first step in developing a system capable of early identification of SRL skills so that adaptation can be tailored directly based on students' specific needs.

Acknowledgements. The authors wish to thank members of the IntelliMedia Group for their assistance, Omer Sturlovich and Pavel Turzo for use of their 3D model libraries, and Valve Software for access to the SourceTM engine and SDK. This research was supported by the National Science Foundation under Grants REC-0632450, DRL-0822200, IIS-0812291, DRL-1114655, and CNS-0739216. This material is based upon work supported under a National Science Foundation Graduate Research Fellowship.

References

1. Baker, R.S., D'Mello, S., Rodrigo, S.K., Graesser, A.C.: Better to Be Frustrated than Bored: The Incidence, Persistence, and Impact of Learners' Cognitive-Affective States during Interactions with Three Different Computer-Based Learning Environments. International Journal of Human-Computer Studies 68, 223–241 (2010)
2. Kanfer, R., Ackerman, P.L.: Motivation and Cognitive Abilities: An Integrative/Aptitude-Treatment Interaction Approach to Skill Acquisition. Journal of Applied Psychology 74, 657–690 (1989)
3. Pekrun, R., Goetz, T., Titz, W., Perry, R.: Academic Emotions in Students' Self-Regulated Learning and Achievement: A Program of Qualitative and Quantitative Research. Educational Psychologist 37, 91–105 (2002)
4. Picard, R.W., et al.: Affective Learning — A Manifesto. BT Technology Journal 22, 253–269 (2004)
5. Young, J.D.: The Effect of Self-Regulated Learning Strategies on Performance in Learner Controlled Computer-Based Instruction. Educational Technology Research and Development 144, 17–27 (1996)
6. Easterday, M.W., Aleven, V., Scheines, R., Carver, S.M.: Using tutors to improve educational games. In: Biswas, G., Bull, S., Kay, J., Mitrovic, A. (eds.) AIED 2011. LNCS, vol. 6738, pp. 63–71. Springer, Heidelberg (2011)
7. Pintrich, P.R., Groot, E.D.: Motivational and self-regulated learning components of classroom academic performance. Journal of Educational Psychology 82, 33–40 (1990)
8. Pintrich, P.R.: A Conceptual Framework for Assessing Motivation and Self-Regulated Learning in College Students. Educational Psychology Review 16, 385–407 (2004)
9. Kirschner, P.A., Sweller, J., Clark, R.E.: Why Minimal Guidance during instruction does not work: An analysis of the Failure of Constructivist, Discovery, Problem-Based, Experiential, and Inquiry-Based Teaching. Educational Psychologist 41, 75–86 (2006)
10. Alfieri, L., Brooks, P., Aldrich, N., Tenenbaum, H.: Does Discovery-Based Instruction Enhance Learning. Journal of Education Psychology 103, 1–18 (2011)
11. Ellis, D., Zimmerman, B.J.: Enhancing self-monitoring during self-regulated learning of speech, pp. 205–228 (2001)
12. Azevedo, R., Moos, D.C., Greene, J.A., Winters, F.I., Cromley, J.G.: Why is externally-facilitated regulated learning more effective than self-regulated learning with hypermedia? Educational Technology Research and Development 56, 45–72 (2008)
13. Zimmerman, B.J.: Self-regulated learning and academic achievement: An overview. Educational Psychologist 25, 3–17 (1990)
14. Kostons, D., van Gog, T., Paas, F.: Training Self-Assessment and Task-Selection Skills: A Cognitive Approach to Improving Self-Regulated Learning. Learning and Instruction 22, 121–132 (2012)
15. Azevedo, R., Cromley, J.G., Winters, F.I., Moos, D.C., Greene, J.A.: Adaptive human scaffolding facilitates adolescents' self-regulated learning with hypermedia. Instructional Science 33, 381–412 (2005)
16. Aleven, V., McLaren, B.M., Roll, I., Koedinger, K.R.: Toward Meta-cognitive Tutoring: A Model of Help-Seeking with a Cognitive Tutor. International Journal of Artificial Intelligence in Education 16, 101–128 (2006)
17. Fiorella, L., Mayer, R.E.: Paper-based aids for learning with a computer-based game. Journal of Educational Psychology 104, 1074–1082 (2012)
18. Ifenthaler, D.: Determining the Effectiveness of Prompts for Self-Regulated Learning in Problem-Solving Scenarios. Educational Technology & Society 15, 38–52 (2012)

19. Kauffman, D.: Self-Regulated Learning in Web-Based Environments: Instructional Tools Designed to Facilitate Cognitive Strategy Use, Metacognitive Processing, and Motivational Beliefs. Journal of Educational Computing Research 30, 139–161 (2004)
20. White, B., Frederiksen, J.: Inquiry, Modeling, and Metacognition: Making Science Accessible to All Students. Cognition & Instruction 16, 3–118 (1998)
21. Davis, E.: Prompting Middle School Science Students for Productive Reflection: Generic and Directed Prompts. Journal of the Learning Sciences 12, 91–142 (2003)
22. Koedinger, K.R., Aleven, V.: Exploring the Assistance Dilemma in Experiments with Cognitive Tutors. Educational Psychology Review 19, 239–364 (2007)
23. Sabourin, J., Shores, L.R., Mott, B.W., Lester, J.C.: Predicting student self-regulation strategies in game-based learning environments. In: Cerri, S.A., Clancey, W.J., Papadourakis, G., Panourgia, K. (eds.) ITS 2012. LNCS, vol. 7315, pp. 141–150. Springer, Heidelberg (2012)
24. Azevedo, R., et al.: The effectiveness of pedagogical agents' prompting and feedback in facilitating co-adapted learning with metaTutor. In: Cerri, S.A., Clancey, W.J., Papadourakis, G., Panourgia, K. (eds.) ITS 2012. LNCS, vol. 7315, pp. 212–221. Springer, Heidelberg (2012)
25. Azevedo, R., Johnson, A., Chauncey, A., Burkett, C.: Self-Regulated Learning with MetaTutor: Advancing the Science of Learning with MetaCognitive Tools. In: New Science of Learning: Cognition, Computers and Collaboration in Education, pp. 225–248 (2010)
26. Biswas, G., Jeong, H., Roscoe, R.: Promoting Motivation and Self-Regulated Learning Skills through Social Interactions in Agent-Based Learning Environments. In: 2009 AAAI Fall Symposium on Cognitive and Metacognitive Educational Systems (2009)
27. Kinnebrew, J.S., Biswas, G.: Identifying Learning Behaviors by Contextualizing Differential Sequence Mining with Action Features and Performance Evolution. In: Proceedings of the 5th International Conference on Educational Data Mining (2012)
28. Aleven, V., Roll, I., McLaren, B.M., Koedinger, K.R.: Automated, Unobtrusive, Action-by-Action Assessment of Self-Regulation During Learning with an Intelligent Tutoring System. Educational Psychologist 45, 224–233 (2010)
29. Shores, L.R., Rowe, J.P., Lester, J.C.: Early prediction of cognitive tool use in narrative-centered learning environments. In: Biswas, G., Bull, S., Kay, J., Mitrovic, A. (eds.) AIED 2011. LNCS, vol. 6738, pp. 320–327. Springer, Heidelberg (2011)
30. Land, S.: Cognitive requirements for learning with open-ended learning environments. Educational Technology Research and Development 48, 61–78 (2000)
31. Zimmerman, B.: Goal Setting: A Key Proactive Source of Academic Self-Regulation. Motivation and Self-Regulated Learning: Theory, Research, and Applications, 267–286 (2008).
32. Rowe, J.P., Shores, L.R., Mott, B.W., Lester, J.C.: Integrating Learning, Problem Solving, and Engagement in Narrative-Centered Learning Environments. International Journal of Artificial Intelligence in Education, 166–177 (2011)
33. McCrae, R., Costa, P.: Personality in Adulthood: A Five-Factor Theory Perspective. Guilford Press, New York (1993)
34. Elliot, A.J., McGregor, H.A.: A 2 x 2 achievement goal framework. Journal of Personality and Social Psychology 80, 501–519 (2001)
35. Gernefski, N., Kraati, V.: Cognitive Emotion Regulation Questionnaire: Development of a Short 18-Item Version. Personality and Individual Differences 41, 1045–1053 (2006)

36. McAuley, E., Duncan, T., Tammen, V.: Psychometric properties of the Intrinsic Motivation Inventory in a competitive sport setting: A confirmatory factory analysis. Research Quarterly for Exercise and Sport 60, 48–58 (1989)
37. Witmer, B.G., Singer, M.J.: Measuring Presence in Virtual Environments: A Presence Questionnaire. Presence: Teleoperators and Virtual Environments 7, 225–240 (1998)
38. Sabourin, J., Rowe, J., Mott, B., Lester, J.C.: When Off-Task is On-Task: The Affective Role of Off-Task Behavior in Narrative-Centered Learning Environments. In: Proceedings of the 15th International Conference on Artificial Intelligence and Education, pp. 534–536 (2011)
39. Baker, R.S.J.d., Corbett, A.T., Aleven, V.: More accurate student modeling through contextual estimation of slip and guess probabilities in bayesian knowledge tracing. In: Woolf, B.P., Aïmeur, E., Nkambou, R., Lajoie, S. (eds.) ITS 2008. LNCS, vol. 5091, pp. 406–415. Springer, Heidelberg (2008)
40. Corbett, A.T., Anderson, J.R.: Knowledge Tracing: Modeling the Acquisition of Procedural Knowledge. User Modeling and User-Adapted Interaction 4, 253–278 (1994)
41. Conati, C., Maclaren, H.: Empirically building and evaluating a probabilistic model of user affect. User Modeling and User-Adapted Interaction 19, 267–303 (2009)
42. Sabourin, J.L., Mott, B.W., Lester, J.C.: Modeling Learner Affect with Theoretically Grounded Dynamic Bayesian Networks. In: Proceedings of the 4th International Conference on Affective Computing and Intelligent Interaction, pp. 286–295 (2011)
43. Gertner, A., Conati, C., VanLehn, K.: Procedural help in Andes: Generating hints using a Bayesian network student model. In: Proceedings of the 15th National Conference on Artificial Intelligence (1998)
44. Alpaydin, E.: Introduction to Machine Learning. MIT Press (2004)

Recommending Topics for Web Curation

Zurina Saaya, Markus Schaal, Rachael Rafter, and Barry Smyth

CLARITY: Centre for Sensor Web Technologies
School of Computer Science and Informatics
University College Dublin, Ireland
{zurina.saaya,markus.schaal,rachael.rafter,barry.smyth}@ucd.ie
http://www.clarity-centre.org

Abstract. A new generation of curation services provides users with a set of tools to manually curate and manage topical collections of content. However, given curation is ultimately a manual effort, it still requires significant effort on the part of the curator both in terms of collecting and managing content. We are interested in providing additional assistance to users in their curation tasks, in particular when it comes to efficiently adding content to their collection, and examine recommender systems in an effort to automate this task. We examine a number of recommendation strategies using live-user data from the popular Scoop.it curation service.

Keywords: curation, recommendation system, machine learning.

1 Introduction

The recent information sharing and discovery trend is exemplified by the new generation of curation services (e.g. delicious.com, storify.com, clipboard.com, pinterest.com, scoop.it etc.) which provide users with a set of tools to manually curate and manage topical collections of content. In one sense these services represent a new generation of online bookmarking sites but with an emphasis on providing a much richer curation context supporting a variety of content types and leveraging the power of the social web as a key distribution channel [10]. Interested parties can create content collections of topics of interest, share these collections with friends and followers, and support an active and collaborative model of curation to develop unique collections of topical content; for example, Pinterest and Clipboard allow users to create topical collections of web elements (text, images, etc.). Collections themselves become new types of media; for example Storify allows users to narratively knit together collections of links and content to form unique stories. The work by Duh et al. [4] suggests that there are various reasons for why curation services have become popular such as the ability of curated collections to capture conversational and collaborative endeavours.

Ultimately curation is a manual effort, distinguishing it from more automated content discovery approaches such as search and recommendation [17]. The job of the curator is to identify, organise and frame content that is relevant, interesting and useful. To assist in this effort many curation services provide a set of tools to

S. Carberry et al. (Eds.): UMAP 2013, LNCS 7899, pp. 242–253, 2013.

simplify the curation work-flow and to integrate curation features into a user's normal online activities; for example bookmarklets and browser plugins provide one-click curation by allowing a user to add a web page, image, or article directly to their collection as they browse. Nevertheless curation still requires significant effort by the curator and given that many curators will actively curate multiple collections deciding which collection to *assign* a new article to can introduce further friction to an otherwise streamlined workflow.

In this paper we are interested in providing additional support to curators and helping them to efficiently add content to their collections. To this end we propose to evaluate the use of recommender systems techniques in an effort to automate this assignment task. In short, our aim is to profile the evolving collections managed by a curator and to use these profiles as the basis for matching the target content at assignment time. In this way a curator can assign a new piece of content with a single-click, with the recommender system reliably choosing an appropriate collection without further intervention, or at the very least suggest a short-list of likely collections that the user can quickly chose from.

In what follows we will describe and evaluate a number of recommendation strategies for dealing with this assignment task. For the purpose of this study we will use live-user data collected from the popular *Scoop.it* curation service.

2   Web Curation Using Scoop.it

Scoop.it is a web-based curation tool that provides a platform for users to curate all of their favorite resources on a given topic for sharing with interested parties. Users can create their own collections (or *topics* in the Scoop.it parlance) and the service provides a range of tools to help users to identify and filter content for their collections. Creating a collection or topic is a simple matter of providing a name, a short description, and a set of suitable keywords.

A unique feature of Scoop.it is that it allows users to create a set of *trigger queries* and assign them to certain *sources* of content online with a view to periodically collecting results from these sources as candidate content for the curator to review. For instance, a curator may create a new *Web Dev* collection as a place to curate all things related to web development. They might set up trigger queries such as *'javascript news'* for Google and *'nodejs tutorials'* for SlideShare to access a daily stream of potential content that they can then filter and add to their collection. Creating a range of these trigger queries and using diverse sources such as Google, SlideShare, Twitter, YouTube at least simplifies the task of locating candidate content, although it does place a significant filtering burden on the curator. Scoop.it also provides more conventional curation tools in the form of a bookmarklet that curators can add to their browser. When browsing a page of interest the curator can select the bookmarklet to *rescoop* the page, and after assigning an appropriate collection the page is added.

For our research Scoop.it is a excellent opportunity to explore different ways to personalize, automate and otherwise support the curation process. It is a popular service attracting more than 1500 new curators every day and approximately 5 million visitors per month resulting in a growing collection of collections and content. Scoop.it has also released a comprehensive API making it possible to work with live data. In this work then we focus on the task of assigning a newly discovered page to a specific collection. For the curator, as mentioned above, this is an entirely manual task, and for curators with many collections it can be time consuming and error prone. Our approach is to treat this as a type of *page classification* task in which the job is to classify a given page (URL) as belonging to one of the curator's collections. And we will do this by capturing the essence of a collection (and a page) using a combination of content features extracted from pages (their URLs, titles, descriptions etc). Ideally, we would like to be able to classify a given page as belonging to a single collection and thus automatically assign the page to this collection. However, this is unlikely to be practical in the face of inevitable imperfections in the classifier models that we learn and so instead we propose to identify a short-list of k suitable collections, ranked by their relevance to the target page, and presented to the user for assignment. So, instead of an active curator having to chose from perhaps 10 or more possible collections she will instead be faced with a choice of only 2 or 3 collections.

3 Related Work

Novel technologies, algorithms, and functionalities for web curation services are demonstrated and explored by upcoming commercial applications such as Storify, Pinterest, or Scoop.it, to name a few. But up to now little has been published which is targeted specifically at the assistance of web curation.

Bookmarking can be seen as an early form of private content curation. Several researchers have examined ways to enhance the organization of one's bookmarks. For example Maarek and Israel [12] describe an automatic URL classification technique to organize documents based on their conceptual similarity. Staff and Bugeja [20] develop a browser extension to classify bookmarks based on the term overlap between the keywords of categories and incoming pages. Private bookmarking later gave way to social bookmarking, typified by sites like Delicious where users collect and share their bookmarks with others. Finally, HeyStaks [19] took the idea of sharing useful web resources even further and introduced the concept of collaborative search. Saaya et al. [16] have explored a solution similar to [20] for identifying the correct content collection for HeyStaks. This was later improved using a machine learning approach [15]. We extend this work in the domain of web curation, specifically for Scoop.it, where the personal topics of the users are presented it in a meaningful and organized way around a specific theme rather than general-purpose content collections.

Our work is also related to tag recommendation, because tags may relate to web pages in a similar way as topics. Various approaches have been proposed for tag recommendation, using methods such as content- and graph-based collaborative filtering and machine learning [11,8,14]. However, there are some differences between the tag assignment task and ours. For example, tags usually consist of single keywords, which are redundant and ambiguous and may make it difficult to describe the resources [13]. Opposite to this, topic titles and descriptions

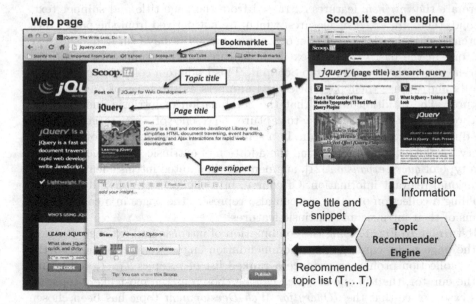

Fig. 1. Recommendation system overview

in Scoop.it, for example, provide more information, and therefore we consider the recommendation of the right topic for a web page as a crisp classification problem, while tagging is usually seen as a categorization process, see e.g. [6].

There are many web page features that can be exploited for classification. For example, Attardi et al. [1] use the page title and some content to suggest a target page's class. Alternatively Chakrabarti et al. [3] use the content of explicit links within the web page and Shen et al. [18] enhance this approach by combining explicit links found in the web page with implicit links gathered from the results of performing similar search queries. Finally, Baykan et al. [2] propose the URL as a main feature for topic classification. In our work, we use the title and snippet text as features of a page, and we experiment with combinations of intrinsic (found on page) and extrinsic (found on related pages) information.

4   Recommending Curated Collections

To begin we can consider a typical user U as being associated with a set of n collections or *topics* $T_U = T_1...T_n$; Scoop.it refers to its curated collections as *topics*, which we shall now adopt for clarity. The assignment task then is to suggest one or more of these topics as a suitable home for a given page or URL, by matching the page with a suitable topic.

This is reflected in the system overview presented in Fig. 1. In this case the curator is looking to add a page about *jQuery* to one of their collections. Two types of features are considered as the basis for recommending a topic. First, there are the *intrinsic* features extracted from the page title and snippet text. Second, there are *extrinsic* features, which are not derived from the page's own content but rather based on how other Scoop.it users have curated pages like this one in the past. Thus the extrinsic features are determined by using the current page title as a query into Scoop.it. This leads to a collection of Scoop.it results and we use their page titles and snippets as the basis of our extrinsic features. The intuition here is that the combination of intrinsic and extrinsic features will provide a useful way to capture the essence of a new target page for use during topic recommendation. In a sense, the intrinsic features form a basic query for the page in question and the addition of extrinsic feature corresponds to a type of *query expansion* [21], augmenting the limited intrinsic features with additional relevant information. Of course, in a similar way, when it comes to profiling a collection of pages, we can also represent the pages in a collection in terms of their intrinsic and extrinsic features.

Returning to Fig. 1, using the combination of intrinsic and extrinsic features of the page to be curated, the recommendation engine compares these to the topic/collection profiles to produce a ranked list of r topics $T_1...T_r$ for return to the curator, the top one of which can be chosen as the most likely topic; in this case we see that the *JQuery for Web Development* topic has been chosen as the default. Ultimately the question we wish to answer is to what extent these recommended topics might be considered useful recommendations. How often do they contain the correct topic, for example? In addition we will also explore the relative value of intrinsic and extrinsic features (both for the query and collection) in this recommendation task.

In what follows we will describe two complementary approaches to topic recommendation: (1) an information retrieval type approach based on the work of [16] such that each topic/collection is indexed by the pages it contains and at recommendation time the target page is used to retrieve a ranked list of relevant topics; and (2) a machine learning approach in which the target page is *classified* as belonging to one of the curator's collection based on a classification model of these collections.

4.1   An Information Retrieval Approach to Recommendation

Each collection or topic $T \in T_U$ (for User U) corresponds to a set of curated pages P_T and each page $p \in P_T$ can be associated with a set of intrinsic and extrinsic features, $p = \{t_1, ..t_x\}$. In this case, the features are simply terms extracted from the page titles and snippets after stop-word removal. So the intrinsic features of p_i are the words from its title and in its snippet text. And the extrinsic features of p_i are the words from the titles and snippets of the pages returned by Scoop.it's own search function for a query that corresponds to the target page's title. In this way we can produce a *topic summary index* (TSI) from the user's topics by indexing each topic by the combination of terms of its constituent pages. And to retrieve a set of relevant topics for a new page we use p_Q as a retrieval probe against the user's TSI, where p_Q is build from the intrinsic and/or extrinsic features of the new page. Specifically, we use Lucene [7] to do this probe which calculates a TF-IDF relevance score for each of the user's topics $(T \in T_U)$ according to Equation 2, in order to produce a ranked list of topics for recommendation to user U according to Equation 1.

$$TopicList(p_Q, T_U, TSI) = \frac{SortDesc(Score(p_Q, T, TSI))}{\forall T \in T_U} \tag{1}$$

$$Score(p_Q, T, TSI) = \sum_{t \in p_Q} tf(t, T) \times idf(t, TSI) \tag{2}$$

4.2   A Classification Based Approach to Recommendation

As an alternative to the term-based information retrieval approach to topic recommendation described above, we also consider the use of text classification techniques. In this case we use the terms of those URL's page titles and snippets that are already assigned to the topic to train the classifier that is capable of classifying future URLs. For a given user U who has a list of topics $T_U = \{T_1...T_n\}$ we train the n-class classifier based on the content of these topics. Each topic T_i contributes a set of training data in the form of $\langle p, T_i \rangle$ where $p = \{t_1, ..t_x\}$ is the set of intrinsic and/or extrinsic features for a single page p and T_i is the topic id (class). Note, whereas topic information is effectively compiled into a single document for the information retrieval approach described above, in this classification approach, individual pages are used as separate training instances.

To build our classifiers we consider the following two distinct machine learning techniques for the purpose of comparison; Naive Bayes Multinomial(NBM) [9] and Support Vector Machines (SVM). We use standard reference implementations for these classifiers from the Weka-library [5]. Once a topic classifier has been learned for a given user, it can be used as the basis for topic recommendation. A new page is transformed into a similar feature representation and classified by the user's topic classifier and a ranked list of topics is produced based on the classifier's class predictions and confidence scores.

Note that in the above each user is associated with their own individual topic indexes or classifiers, thus personalising the topic recommendation task with respect to an individual user. It is a matter for future work as to whether there are any meaningful benefits to be gained from a more centralised cross-user approach to recommendation. We have also assumed the availability and use of both intrinsic and extrinsic features when it comes to representing the page query and indexing or learning the topics. As mentioned previously we will go on to explore the relative benefit of using intrinsic and extrinsic information in this way and so it is equally possible to use different combinations of intrinsic and extrinsic features without loss of generality as we shall see.

5   Experiment

Ultimately the success of this work will depend critically on the ability to make accurate topic recommendations at curation time. If the correct topic is likely to be contained in the topic recommendations, then we can reduce the curation friction significantly by limiting the user's topic choice. To test this, and to also evaluate the relative benefits of using intrinsic and extrinsic data, we use a dataset collected from the Scoop.it API during October/November 2012.

5.1   Summary Dataset

In summary this Scoop.it dataset contains 3620 topics (collections) from 560 users. On average these users have 6.5 topics; 92% of users have between 5 and 10 topics, with the remaining users having between 11 and 29 topics. Each topic contains at least 5 pages and in total the 3620 topics contain a total of more than 550,000 pages. For the purpose of this experiment we split the data into training and test data for each topic. In other words, for each topic we identify a set of training URLs and a set of test URLs. In total there are 404,507 training URLs and 155,626 test URLs. The training URLs are used to build the topic indexes and classifier models for each of the users and the test URLs are used to evaluate the generated recommendations; for the test URLs we use the known topic assignment as the ground-truth. We do this by calculating a *accuracy* score as the percentage of times that the correct topic was included in recommendation lists ranging in size from 1 to 5 topics.

5.2   Test Conditions

As described previously we use 3 different recommendation techniques, information retrieval approach $TFIDF$, a multinomial naive bayes approach (NBM), and a support vector machine approach (SVM). In addition we also include two baseline recommendation strategies: (1) *Random* simply selects a topic at random from the user's topic-list; and (2) *Popularity* ranks the most popular topics (that is those topics with the most pages) for recommendation.

We also consider the performance of these 5 techniques under 4 different conditions based on the use of combinations of intrinsic and extrinsic features during training and testing.

- **I-I**: only intrinsic features are used during training and testing.
- **I-X**: intrinsic features are used during training while both intrinsic and extrinsic features are used for the test data.
- **X-I**: intrinsic and extrinsic features are used during training but only intrinsic features are used for the test data.
- **X-X**: intrinsic and extrinsic features are used during training and testing.

5.3   Results

The accuracy results are presented in Fig. 2(a-d) for the different combinations of intrinsic/extrinsic data during training and testing. In each graph we plot the average accuracy against the recommendation list size for each of the 5

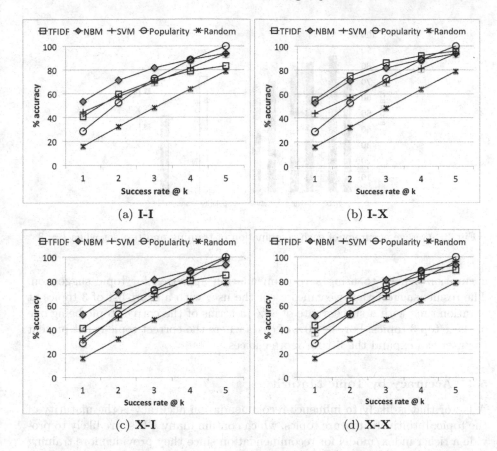

Fig. 2. Accuracy of topic recommendations for different feature conditions

recommendation techniques. Overall we can see that the baseline techniques of *Random* and *Popularity* perform poorly, especially for short recommendation lists. For example, they deliver sub-30% accuracy for Top-1 recommendation lists, although it is worth noting that *Popularity* tends to become competitive for recommendation lists of size 3 or more. *NBM* tends to win out overall, with accuracy rates ranging from 50-85% across all conditions.

To summarize these accuracy results and in an effort to better clarify the differences between the use of intrinsic and extrinsic features, Fig. 3 shows the average accuracy for recommendation lists of size 3 for each of the algorithms and test conditions. Overall we can see clearly that *NBM* performs consistently well across all feature conditions (with accuracy rates of circa 80%), and in fact there is little or no benefit to including extrinsic features when using this technique. *TFIDF* is less successful but does enjoy a significant benefit when extrinsic features are used for the page query. In this case it delivers an average accuracy of 86%; this is analogous to using a form of query elaboration at retrieval time. From a utility perspective the above results suggest that there is likely to be

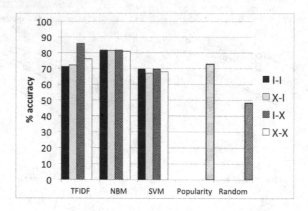

Fig. 3. Average accuracy of each combination of training and test set when $k = 3$

a curation benefit to using a recommendation approach for topic suggestion. The results suggest that we can present the user with a short-list of 3 topics at curation time with a success rate of 80% in terms of the correct topic being one of these top-3 topics. For the 20% of cases where the correct topic is not present the user can expand the list for more choices.

5.4   Accuracy by Topic Maturity

A factor that is likely to influence recommendation accuracy is the maturity of the topic. Intuitively, mature topics, which contain many URLs, are likely to provide a richer index/model for recommendation since they provide more training data. To test this we split the training data into topics of four different sizes to evaluate small topics (5-10 URLs), medium topics (11-30 URls), large topics (31-70 URLs) and very large topics (70+ URLs); see Fig. 4(a) for the relative number of topics of different sizes in the Scoop.it dataset. Next we replayed the above evaluation for the different feature conditions and recommendation strategies. Fig. 4(b-d) show the average accuracy results for recommendation lists of size 3.

Each graph focuses on a particular recommendation strategy and shows average accuracy bars for each of the 4 feature conditions across the 4 different topic sizes. We can see that in general there is a gradual increase in recommendation accuracy as topics increase in size. For example, NBM delivers accuracy rates of approximately 75% for small and medium topics but achieves accuracies of about 85% for the largest topics. Interestingly, we can see that once again a significant accuracy benefit accruing to $TFIDF$ when using extrinsic features for the page query. Even for small topics $TFIDF$ delivers accuracy rates in excess of 80% when extrinsic features are used for the page query. This is important for two reasons. First, it suggests that strong recommendation accuracy can be achieved even for small topics, which will be particularly important in a new-user context. In addition, the $TFIDF$ approach offers certain advantages when it comes to

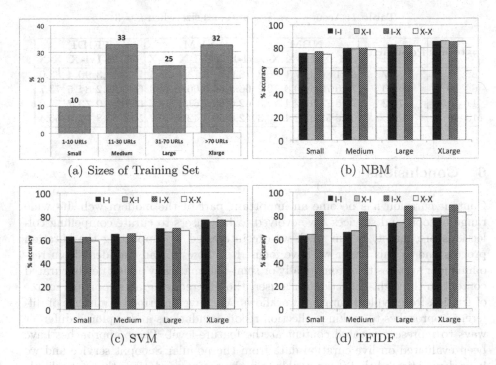

(a) Sizes of Training Set

(b) NBM

(c) SVM

(d) TFIDF

Fig. 4.

scaling. As topics grow and mature new pages can be incrementally added to the $TFIDF$ index compared to a more computationally expensive re-training that may be necessary when it comes to updating classification models.

5.5 Accuracy by Topic Count

As mentioned earlier, *Popularity* (and also *Random*) become competitive for recommendation lists of size 3 or more. This is not surprising since the average count of topics across all users is only 6.5 and so the task of selecting the right topic should be easier as we go towards this average with our recommendation list size. To investigate this, we computed recommendation accuracies across four different user groups. The results are presented in Table 1 for each of the 3 recommendation techniques (NBM, SVM and $TFIDF$) averaged across all feature conditions (**I-I**, **X-I**, **I-X**, and **X-X**). We can see that the performance of $TFIDF$ for the **I-X** feature condition is not only consistently better than all other techniques and conditions, but also that the relative benefit versus all other techniques increases with increasing topic count. For the situation of 15+ topics, $TFIDF$ in combination with the **I-X** feature condition is still well above 70% accuracy, while all other techniques and conditions are way below 60%.

Table 1. Accuracy vs. users' topics size when $k = 3$

#topics	Popularity	NBM				SVM				TFIDF			
		I-I	X-I	I-X	X-X	I-I	X-I	I-X	X-X	I-I	X-I	I-X	X-X
5	75.7	87.1	86.3	87.1	86.3	73.9	67.7	73.8	70.5	77.5	78.3	**90.4**	83.0
6 - 10	69.0	79.6	79.6	79.8	79.2	66.3	66.5	66.5	66.3	69.5	70.2	**84.5**	73.7
11 - 15	70.2	73.6	73.6	72.4	72.3	62.6	66.7	61.1	60.7	65.0	57.0	**73.7**	59.6
15+	60.0	54.6	53.2	52.4	50.3	42.6	50.0	42.8	40.7	53.4	53.8	**72.9**	56.4

6   Conclusions

Content curation has become an important part of the modern web. Its wide range of tools and services have evolved to help users to curate compelling collections of content. In our work we are interested in supporting the curation process and in this paper we have focused on how we can use ideas from recommender systems to automatically or semi-automatically assign newly curated content to the right collection for a user, thereby reducing an important source of friction from typical curation workflows. We have described a number of different approaches to making collection recommendations and explored different ways to represent curated content at the feature-level. These approaches have been evaluated on live curation data from the popular Scoop.it service and we have demonstrated that it is possible to make recommendations that are reliable enough to be useful in practice. In this paper we have focused on the assignment task in curation, which is of course just one place where improved support might be provided to users. In the future we will consider ways in which other curation tasks may be similarly enhanced including the recommendation of new topics to follow, recommending users to share collections or content with, recommending better tags for content or collections etc.

Acknowledgments. This work is supported by Science Foundation Ireland under grant 07/CE/I1147, Ministry of Higher Education Malaysia and Universiti Teknikal Malaysia Melaka.

References

1. Attardi, G., Gullì, A., Sebastiani, F.: Automatic web page categorization by link and context analysis. Proceedings of THAI 99, 105–119 (1999)
2. Baykan, E., Henzinger, M., Marian, L., Weber, I.: A comprehensive study of features and algorithms for url-based topic classification. ACM Transactions on the Web (TWEB) 5(3), 15 (2011)
3. Chakrabarti, S., Dom, B., Indyk, P.: Enhanced hypertext categorization using hyperlinks. ACM SIGMOD Record 27, 307–318 (1998)
4. Duh, K., Hirao, T., Kimura, A., Ishiguro, K., Iwata, T., Yeung, C.: Creating stories: Social curation of twitter messages. In: Sixth International AAAI Conference on Weblogs and Social Media (2012)

5. Hall, M., Frank, E., Holmes, G., Pfahringer, B., Reutemann, P., Witten, I.H.: The weka data mining software: an update. SIGKDD Explor. Newsl. 11(1), 10–18 (2009)
6. Halpin, H., Robu, V., Shepherd, H.: The complex dynamics of collaborative tagging. In: Proceedings of the 16th International Conference on World Wide Web, vol. 21, pp. 1–220. Citeseer (2007)
7. Hatcher, E., Gospodnetic, O.: Lucene in action. Manning Publications (2004)
8. Jäschke, R., Marinho, L., Hotho, A., Schmidt-Thieme, L., Stumme, G.: Tag recommendations in folksonomies. In: Kok, J.N., Koronacki, J., Lopez de Mantaras, R., Matwin, S., Mladenič, D., Skowron, A. (eds.) PKDD 2007. LNCS (LNAI), vol. 4702, pp. 506–514. Springer, Heidelberg (2007)
9. Kibriya, A.M., Frank, E., Pfahringer, B., Holmes, G.: Multinomial naive bayes for text categorization revisited. In: Webb, G.I., Yu, X. (eds.) AI 2004. LNCS (LNAI), vol. 3339, pp. 488–499. Springer, Heidelberg (2004)
10. Liu, S.B.: Trends in distributed curatorial technology to manage data deluge in a networked world. The European Journal for the Informatics Professional 11(4), 18–24 (2010)
11. Lu, Y.T., Yu, S.I., Chang, T.C., Hsu, J.Y.J.: A content-based method to enhance tag recommendation. In: Proceedings of the 21st International Jont Conference on Artifical Intelligence, pp. 2064–2069. Morgan Kaufmann Publishers Inc. (2009)
12. Maarek, Y., Ben Shaul, I.: Automatically organizing bookmarks per contents. Computer Networks and ISDN Systems 28(7), 1321–1333 (1996)
13. Milicevic, A.K., Nanopoulos, A., Ivanovic, M.: Social tagging in recommender systems: a survey of the state-of-the-art and possible extensions. The Artificial Intelligence Review 33(3), 187–209 (2010), http://search.proquest.com/docview/198036064?accountid=14507
14. Pujari, M., Kanawati, R.: Tag recommendation by link prediction based on supervised machine learning. In: Sixth International AAAI Conference on Weblogs and Social Media (2012)
15. Saaya, Z., Schaal, M., Coyle, M., Briggs, P., Smyth, B.: A comparison of machine learning techniques for recommending search experiences in social search. In: Research and Development in Intelligent Systems XXIX, p. 195 (2012)
16. Saaya, Z., Schaal, M., Coyle, M., Briggs, P., Smyth, B.: Exploiting extended search sessions for recommending search experiences in the social web. In: Agudo, B.D., Watson, I. (eds.) ICCBR 2012. LNCS, vol. 7466, pp. 369–383. Springer, Heidelberg (2012)
17. Scoble, R.: The seven needs of real time curators.e (2010), http://scobleizer.com/2010/03/27/the-seven-needs-ofreal-time-curators/ (accessed December 06, 2012)
18. Shen, D., Sun, J., Yang, Q., Chen, Z.: A comparison of implicit and explicit links for web page classification. In: Proceedings of the 15th international conference on World Wide Web. pp. 643–650. ACM (2006)
19. Smyth, B., Briggs, P., Coyle, M., O'Mahony, M.P.: Google shared. a case-study in social search. In: User Modeling, Adaptation and Personalization, pp. 283–294 (2009)
20. Staff, C., Bugeja, I.: Automatic classification of web pages into bookmark categories. In: Proceedings of the 30th annual international ACM SIGIR conference on Research and Development in Information Retrieval, pp. 731–732. ACM (2007)
21. Xu, J., Croft, W.B.: Query expansion using local and global document analysis. In: Proceedings of the 19th annual International ACM SIGIR Conference on Research and Development in Information Retrieval, SIGIR 1996, pp. 4–11. ACM, New York (1996)

Building Rich User Search Queries Profiles

Elif Aktolga[1], Alpa Jain[2], and Emre Velipasaoglu[3],[*]

[1] CIIR, UMass Amherst, Amherst MA 01003, USA
elif@cs.umass.edu
[2] Twitter, Inc., San Francisco, CA 94103, USA
alpajn@gmail.com
[3] Magnet Systems, Inc., Palo Alto, CA 94301, USA
emre.velipasaoglu@magnet.com

Abstract. It is well-known that for a variety of search tasks involving queries more relevant results can be presented if they are *personalized* according to a user's interests and search behavior. This can be achieved with user-dependent, rich web search queries profiles. These are typically built as part of a specific search personalization task so that it is unclear which characteristics of queries are most effective for modeling the user-query relationship *in general*. In this paper, we explore various approaches for explicitly modeling this user-query relationship independently of other search components. Our models employ generative models in layers in a prediction task. The results show that the best signals for modeling the user-query relationship come from the given query's terms and entities together with information from related entities and terms, yielding a relative improvement of up to 24.5% in MRR and Success over the baseline methods.

Keywords: User Profiles, Personalization, Named Entities.

1 Introduction

Commercial search engines answer millions of queries on a daily basis while serving a variety of user intents. To enable users to better formulate their search tasks, search engines offer query suggestion tools which auto-complete a user's partial query or suggest follow-up queries after the query is typed. A naive approach is to provide a static list of suggestions to *all* users for *all* search intents. This ignores information available from each user's unique search queries profile, which is required to achieve better personalization.

A critical challenge with building user profiles is testing their effectiveness. Typically, user profiles are employed as part of search personalization tasks such as search result reranking or query suggestion, and the effect of personalization is observed through the applied task. This way, it is not obvious which characteristics of queries are most effective for explicitly modeling the user-query relationship in general for any search personalization task. Therefore, in this

---

[*] All the authors were at Yahoo! Labs when this work was done.

S. Carberry et al. (Eds.): UMAP 2013, LNCS 7899, pp. 254–266, 2013.

paper we aim at *building rich user search queries profiles and measuring their quality in isolation of these other components.* This is framed by means of the following *prediction task*: given users' past queries, can we effectively predict the most likely user to have issued a given present/future query?

For this task we solely utilize users' queries obtained through historical query log data without soliciting any explicit input from users and without employing users' clicks on documents in search results.

Prior research has dealt with personalization for search results or building user profiles based on their search results interaction, i.e., clicked urls, content of the visited web pages [3], [4], [8], [13], [18]. These works primarily study users' intents over time for better *document ranking* [1], [4], [9], [11], [12], [15], [17], [19], [20] or they research query suggestion utilizing document click through [3], [8], [13], [16]. Building deep profiles from terse queries poses many interesting challenges: (1) we have a *cold-start problem* [17], [18], [20], i.e., information about the user needs to be gathered first before queries or results can be personalized; (2) a substantial fraction of queries does not yield to personalization (navigational queries like 'facebook', 'bank of america', etc.) or purely numeric queries; (3) search queries are terse and often ambiguous. Understanding how to effectively build user profiles from search queries can benefit many personalization tasks including query suggestion, search result reranking, and federation optimization.

Our proposed approach uses personalizable information from users' past queries. Our contribution consists of a generative model that employs related terms and entities to overcome the sparsity of queries in user profiles. We present an extensive evaluation suite to measure the personalization potential of our proposed algorithms over a large query log from a major search engine. Our experiments show that the best performing approach yields a relative improvement of up to 24.5% in MRR and Success over the baseline methods.

2 Related Work

Personalization is a well researched area that aims at better addressing search intents of users for tasks such as document (re)ranking or document retrieval [1], [4], [9], [11], [12], [15], [17], [19], [20]. The value of personalizing web search results has widely been studied [4], [12], [19]: Teevan et al. [19] analyze query intents of users and discover that there are noticeable variations in search intents for the same query and in the interpretation of these intents. Further, the difficulty of resolving abbreviated and ambiguous queries is identified. Teevan et al. show that by employing personalization, the results can be efficiently reranked to improve retrieval effectiveness. Mei and Church [12] study personalization through backoff, i.e., including information from similar users or from a user's group for estimating the likelihood of a document click for the given user. Morris et al., Teevan et al., and Xue et al. study several further techniques based on user groups [14], [21], [22]. Dou et al. [4] analyze when and how personalization is useful by using click-based and query-based personalization techniques. Luxenburger et al. study language modeling approaches for selectively personalizing queries only when it is required [10].

Some prior work has specifically focused on the personalization of query suggestions and query completion suggestions [3], [5], [8], [13]. All these techniques utilize click through data on documents for estimating user preferences instead of query history-based user profiles for personalization, whose construction we deal with in this paper.

There has also been a lot of prior work in applying user profiles for improved web search ranking: Sugiyama et al. employ two user profiles in combination for every user; one that represents the user's long term browsing history, and another one that represents her current browsing history [18]. Teevan et al. also study long-term and short-term interests of users in their profiles for better document ranking [20].

Unlike prior personalization related work, our paper studies user profiling for a more general situation: how can we build rich user profiles from queries as a basis for various personalization tasks? This is a substantial difference from prior personalization approaches that are geared towards optimizing a specific task such as document ranking only.

3   Modeling Search Behavior

In this section, we consider a variety of natural ways of designing user profiles for search queries. Specifically, we study *phrase-level* models that exploit the query terms and a *syntax-level* model that exploits the query syntax. We build these models in layers from users' queries so that gradually more evidence is included in the profiles. All the models estimate the likelihood of a given query to have been issued by a certain user.

3.1   Phrase-Level Models

These models include phrase-level information from a user's queries in the user profile. The simplest phrase-level model is **Query Terms (T)**, defined as follows:

$$P_T(u|q) = \sum_{t \in T(q)} P(u|t) \tag{1}$$

where $t \in T(q)$ denotes the set of unigram terms in q. The estimation of this probability is carried out as described in the generalized form in Section 3.3. The next model **Entities (E)** (referred to in the equations below as $P_E(u|q)$) includes tagged entity phrases as detected by our named entity recognizer. The model is mathematically the same as Equation 1; the only difference is that $t \in T(q)$ refers to the set of unigram terms *and* entity phrases (e,g,. 'pizza hut', 'toyota' etc.) in the query.

The following model **Entities and their categories (EC)** expands the **Entities** model further, by including the named entity categories that were located by our named entity recognizer:

$$P_{EC}(u|q) = \alpha \cdot \sum_{e \in E(q)} P(u|e) + (1 - \alpha) \cdot P_E(u|q) \tag{2}$$

where $e \in E(q)$ refers to the set of entity categories (such as 'person', 'product' etc.) in the query. Again, refer to Section 3.3 for the estimation of the probabilities. We interpolate α with Dirichlet smoothing by setting

$$\alpha = \frac{|E(q)|}{|E(q)| + \mu} \tag{3}$$

where μ is tuned by means of a parameter sweep on the training data. This means that the more entities are found in q, the heavier is the emphasis on the entity categories part, and otherwise the terms and entities will be weighted stronger in the model.

Our final phrase-level model is **Related Terms and Entities (RelTE)**, for which we first define how to estimate the likelihood of a certain user u to issue similar phrases:

$$P(u|\mathcal{S}) = \sum_{s \in Sim(t)} P(u|s) \cdot P(s|t) \tag{4}$$

where $\mathcal{S} = \{s|s \in Sim(t), t \in T(q)\}$ are similar phrases. Specifically, t are again terms and entities as in the **Entities** model above, and $Sim(t)$ are related terms and entities for t. To locate these, we use a term to term co-occurrence mined dictionary from a 1-year query log. On average, every term has 4-5 related terms and entities. Each entry $\langle s, t \rangle$ has an associated co-occurrence score $P(s|t) = \frac{tf(s,t)}{\sum tf(t)}$, describing the relatedness of the term or entity phrase s to t. $P(u|s)$ on the other hand denotes how likely user u is to use this related term or entity in his profile. We combine $P(u|\mathcal{S})$ together with **Entities and their categories** from Equation 2 into the following:

$$P_{RelTE}(u|q) = (1 - \gamma) \cdot P_{EC}(u|q) + \gamma \cdot P(u|\mathcal{S}) \tag{5}$$

where γ is again tuned similarly to α in Equation 3, depending on the availability of related terms and entities for q:

$$\gamma = \frac{|Sim(t)|}{|Sim(t)| + \kappa} \tag{6}$$

We tune κ with a parameter sweep on the training data.

3.2 Syntax-Level Model

The phrases for this model are derived by analyzing a user's queries with a dependency parser. For this, we observe dependency parse label sequences (DPLS), which allow us to extract phrases that are not necessarily sequential n-grams in the query. Figure 1 shows example parses for two queries. By observing 16 different DPLS, we can extract the following phrases from the query *chest x-ray showed evidence of peptic disease*:

- chest x-ray showed peptic disease (nn nsubj amod)
- chest x-ray showed evidence (nn nsubj dobj)
- x-ray showed peptic disease (nsubj amod)
- x-ray showed evidence (nsubj dobj)
- x-ray showed evidence disease (nsubj dobj prep)

Note that while extracting these phrases, we only consider nodes that are directly connected to the affected edge (see Figure 1). The resulting phrases generalize or specify the query in different ways. For comparison, our named entity tagger only recognized the phrase 'x-ray' in this query. From the other query *wood fired portable pizza oven* we can extract the following phrases:

- wood fired portable oven (nsubj amod)
- wood fired portable pizza oven (nsubj amod nn)
- wood fired oven (nsubj dobj)
- wood fired pizza oven (nsubj nn)

Again, the only named entity phrase that was detected is 'oven'. While in these examples the quality of the extracted sub phrases is good, this is not always the case for other queries. Therefore, we apply dependency parsing to queries having at least 3 terms to guarantee good sub phrase quality [7]. For queries with fewer than 3 terms, the approach defaults to one of the phrase-level models.

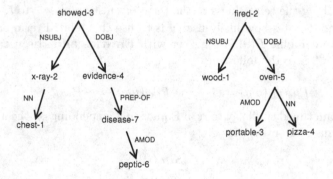

Fig. 1. Dependency parse trees for the two queries *chest x-ray showed evidence of peptic disease* (left) and *wood fired portable pizza oven* (right)

For this model – **Syntactic phrases (DP)** – we first estimate the likelihood of query q to have been issued by user u by means of the sub phrases $\mathcal{D}$ of q as follows:

$$P(u|\mathcal{D}) = \sum_{d \in Dep(q)} P(u|d) \cdot P(d|q) \qquad (7)$$

where $\mathcal{D} = \{d | d \in Dep(q)\}$ is the set of all sub phrases of q extracted through observing various DPLS in q. Each sub phrase d is extracted through exactly one dependency parse label sequence dp from the query q. The first factor $P(u|d)$ in

Equation 7 denotes the likelihood of user u issuing the given sub phrase d, which we calculate by observing the maximum likelihood of the DPLS $dp \in d$ in this user's profile. The estimation of these probabilities is carried out as described in the generalized form in Section 3.3. By utilizing DPLS here we avoid the problem of sub phrase sparsity in user profiles.

The second factor $P(d|q)$ in Equation 7 refers to the importance or quality of this extracted sub phrase d given the query q. This is estimated by observing the maximum likelihood of this sub phrase being generated as an exact match within all other sub phrases for q. Hence, sub phrases generated as exact matches within others through several DPLS have higher importance, whereas low-quality phrases occurring less frequently are demoted.

We then combine $P(u|\mathcal{D})$ together with the **Entities Model and their categories** from Equation 2 into **Syntactic phrases (DP)** as follows:

$$P_{DP}(u|q) = (1 - \delta) \cdot P_{EC}(u|q) + \delta \cdot P(u|\mathcal{D}) \tag{8}$$

where $P_{EC}(u|q)$ was defined in Equation 2. δ is again tuned similarly to α in Equation 3, depending on the number of sub phrases that were extracted for q:

$$\delta = \frac{|Dep(q)|}{|Dep(q)| + \tau} \tag{9}$$

Again, we tune τ with a parameter sweep on the training data.

3.3 Estimation and Smoothing

Model Estimation. All our models use conditional probabilities of the form $P(u|x)$. These are estimated as follows, using the Bayes' Rule:

$$P(u|x) = \frac{P(x|u) \cdot P(u)}{P(x)} \propto P(x|u) \cdot P(u) \tag{10}$$

where $P(x)$ is a constant denoting the prior likelihood of an item x, which is the same across all users and can therefore be safely omitted to yield rank-equivalent results. We obtain the probabilities $P(x|u)$ and $P(u)$ directly from the learned user profile of user u through maximum likelihood estimations.

Smoothing. We smooth the probabilities $P_{\text{MLE}}(x|u)$ for the models **Query Terms**, **Entities** and **Entities and their categories** for considering *missing items* in a user's profile. For simplicity, we apply Add-1 Smoothing [2] for this so that a *missing term* x is assumed to occur only once rather than not at all in the user's profile, and the probabilities for other items in the user profile are adjusted accordingly. This helps with the user profile sparsity problem.

4 Experimental Setup

4.1 Dataset and Statistics

We utilize queries that were collected in a query log of the Yahoo! search engine over a period of 2.5 months in 2011. Each query is associated with a user. We ran a series of filters to eliminate adult, robot, or garbled queries. Further, we prepared the data as follows:

1. **Filtering navigational queries:** Queries that have been identified as navigational are not suitable for personalization because the user's purpose is merely to reach a particular web page. We filter navigational queries by means of a dictionary with 1,000,000 entries.
2. **Which users to prefer for user profile learning and query prediction:** For our experiments we build user profiles and evaluate their quality by predicting the owners of unseen 'future' queries. We choose a qualitative set of users from the query log according to two criteria: (1) users with the highest number of unique queries; (2) users with the highest number of unique entity categories in their queries.
3. **Choosing users for user profile learning and query prediction:** From the two approaches to ranking users, we choose the top $k = 100$ users with their queries, yielding close to 37,000 queries for the experiments. The datasets are referred to as numQ (number of unique queries) and numE (number of unique entity categories).
4. **Train/test split:** In order to split the data into train and test we choose a *time-based split*: information from the first 2 months of the query log for the k users is used for model learning and construction, whereas the last 2 weeks are the basis for query prediction and testing. For model construction, we consider all the (unfiltered) queries of the k users.
5. **Prediction Queries:** For the experiments we use the test queries obtained from the time-based split of the query log described in step 4. We filter these queries to only retain those that have been issued by at least 2 unique users. This is to ensure an evaluation over a qualitative query set. The resulting queries are used for the prediction experiments.
6. **Experiments:** We do 5-fold cross-validation on this test query set by dividing it randomly into 5 roughly equal, non-overlapping splits. We report the average results over the 5 validation splits in the paper.

As named-entity tagger we use a production quality tagger at Yahoo! that identified 38 different named entity categories in the entire query log. Purely numeric queries such as phone or tracking numbers are filtered since they are unsuitable for personalization.

For the syntax-level models we utilize the Stanford Dependency Parser [6] for extracting sub phrases with 16 different dependency parse label sequences (DPLS). A quick analysis revealed that diverse DPLS are very well represented in users' profiles in the whole query log.

4.2   Evaluation Approach

Our objective in this paper is to model the user-query relationship independently of other search components: given users' past queries, can we effectively predict the most likely user to have issued a given present/future query? There can be several users that have actually issued a query. For each query we determine the set of correct users $C_q = \{c_1, \ldots, c_n\}$ as follows: each user c_i in the *test time split of the query log after time* $\mathcal{T}$ having issued the query q is regarded as a correct user for q. This guarantees that all correct users are unseen during the profile building or *training* stage, which uses the time split of the query log *before* time $\mathcal{T}$.

We want to evaluate whether at least one correct user was found until rank n. This can be measured with Success:

$$\text{Success@n} = I_{\text{correct}}(q, n) \tag{11}$$

where $I_{\text{correct}}(q, n)$ is an indicator random variable equaling 1 if at least one user $c_i \in C_q$ for q is present until rank n, and 0 otherwise. In our experiments, we report Average Success@n across all test queries. Then, we would like to know what the rank of the first correct user is, which can be addressed with (average) MRR:

$$\text{MRR@n} = \frac{1}{|Q|} \sum_{i=1}^{|Q|} \frac{1}{\text{rank}_{c_i}} \tag{12}$$

where rank_i is the rank of the first correct user c_i for q. Users are considered until rank n. Finally, we must evaluate how many of all correct users were found until rank n. We utilize Recall for this:

$$\text{Recall@n} = \frac{|\{\text{correct users until rank } n\}|}{|C_q|} \tag{13}$$

where the numerator denotes the number of correct users found for q until rank n, and the denominator refers to the total count of correct users $|C_q|$. Again, we report Average Recall@n over all test queries in our results.

5 Experimental Results

5.1 Effectiveness of Search Query Profiles

The following experiments have been performed by means of 5-fold-cross validation as explained in Section 4. In Table 1 we have the results for the prediction experiments for the numQ data set. In this data set the users have the highest number of unique queries in their user profiles. We compare all the methods that we introduced in Section 3 by observing MRR and Success at different ranks. In the MRR results, we can see significant incremental changes from **T** to **E** and to **EC** over all MRR ranks as more information from the user profiles is employed. It is not surprising that adding in entity phrases in addition to terms yields a larger gain ($\mathbf{T} \to \mathbf{E}$) than including named entity category information in addition to terms and entities ($\mathbf{E} \to \mathbf{EC}$). Related terms and entities (**RelTE**) result in another major boost over all ranks, yielding a maximum relative improvement of 24.5% over **T** at rank 1 for both measures (0.1868). This is statistically significant over all the other methods at the same ranks.

Table 1. Averaged cross-validation results on the numQ dataset for the baseline method (**T**), Entity Model (**E**), Entities and their categories Model (**EC**), Related Entities Model (**RelTE**), Syntactic Phrases Model (**DP**), and the Syntactic Phrases Model falling back to RelTE (**DP+RelTE**). Bold entries are statistically significant over all non-bold ones at same ranks with p-value < 0.03 using the paired two-sided t-test. Starred entries are statistically significant to immediately adjacent entries to the left.

MRR@rank	T	E	EC	RelTE	DP	DP+RelTE
1	0.1501	0.1715*	0.1771*	**0.1868***	0.1771	0.1779
5	0.2096	0.2254*	0.2389*	**0.2502***	0.2386	0.2403*
10	0.2231	0.2363*	0.2534*	**0.2642***	0.2532	0.2548*
20	0.2316	0.2424*	0.2617*	**0.2720***	0.2617	0.2632*
Success@rank	T	E	EC	RelTE	DP	DP+RelTE
1	0.1501	0.1715*	0.1771*	**0.1868***	0.1771	0.1779
5	0.3170	0.3166	0.3490*	**0.3658***	0.3473	0.3577*
10	0.4185	0.3978	0.4584*	**0.4706***	0.4575	0.4656*
20	0.5402	0.4891	0.5788*	0.5836	0.5815	0.5844

Table 2. Averaged cross-validation results on the numE dataset for the same methods as in Table 1. The same statistical significance test is performed with p-value < 0.05.

MRR@rank	T	E	EC	RelTE	DP	DP+RelTE
1	0.1440	0.1661*	0.1687	**0.1739***	0.1688	0.1718
5	0.1960	0.2151*	0.2245*	**0.2306***	0.2243	0.2274*
10	0.2083	0.2246*	0.2364*	**0.2423***	0.2360	0.2389*
20	0.2172	0.2318*	0.2452*	**0.2508***	0.2448	0.2476
Success@rank	T	E	EC	RelTE	DP	DP+RelTE
1	0.1440	0.1661*	0.1687	**0.1739***	0.1688	0.1718
5	0.2916	0.3034*	0.3217*	**0.3297***	0.3208	0.3250
10	0.3849	0.3753	0.4134*	**0.4196***	0.4103	0.4134
20	0.5145	0.4808	0.5439*	0.5443	0.5428	0.5407

However the **DP** and **DP+RelTE** models do not improve the rankings of the users further. In the Success results there is a similar trend as with MRR. **RelTE** remains the most successful model except for rank 20 at which we observe no significant difference between the models.

Table 2 shows the same results for the numE data set with slightly lower numbers over all. In this dataset the users have the highest number of unique entity categories in their profiles. This aspect makes the prediction task more difficult since some entity categories may be unseen in the user profile.

The next two Figures 2 and 3 show Recall at different ranks for all the methods. This allows us to understand how good the methods are at predicting *all* the correct users for a query. One observation in these results is that **E** gets worse in recall with higher ranks. We can clearly see the usefulness of including named entity category information here, which is stronger pronounced than in the MRR and Success results. **RelTE** has the highest Recall at all ranks except for rank 50: here **EC** dominates.

In order to see how the models perform on a user by user basis, we plotted the personalization potential in Figures 4 and 5 for the best performing three models. Using the same results as before, these graphs show for what fraction of

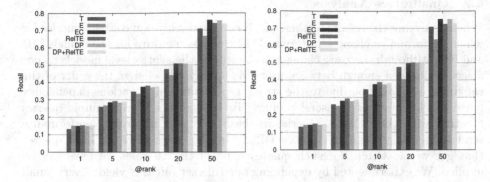

Fig. 2. Recall for all models on the data set numE at different ranks

Fig. 3. Recall for all models on the data set numQ at different ranks

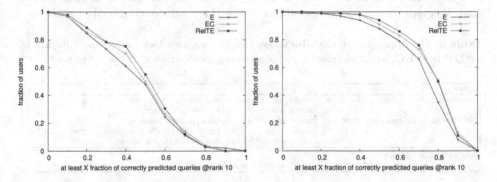

Fig. 4. Personalization Potential for data set numE displaying the fraction of users for which at least a certain fraction of queries were correctly predicted at rank 10

Fig. 5. Personalization Potential for data set numQ displaying the fraction of users for which at least a certain fraction of queries were correctly predicted at rank 10

the users at least a certain fraction of queries were predicted correctly at rank 10. A higher curve signifies that more queries were predicted correctly for more users. The graphs show that there is larger personalization potential with the numQ data set, which again confirms that the numE data set is more challenging. But in both graphs **RelTE** performs best, followed by **EC**, and then **E**. Only in the 0.8 - 1.0 range on the x axis in Figure 4 we can see a small inconsistency: it is harder for the better models to predict at least 80% of the queries correctly for a small fraction of users than it is for **E**. This is interesting and hints to entity phrases and terms being a reliable source of information when we want to achieve high recall for a single user – as opposed to achieving high recall for a query across several users (which is what the results in Figures 2 and 3 showed).

264   E. Aktolga, A. Jain, and E. Velipasaoglu

5.2   Qualitative Analysis

When analyzing the results further, we observe a roughly equal size of queries for which performance changes in terms of the Success measure for the models **DP** and **EC**. Although there are changes in the scores, the syntax level models do not discriminate well enough between users to significantly change the order of the rankings. This may be due to the strong representation of various dependency parse label sequences in users' profiles. Table 3 shows some example queries together with their DPLS. Queries in the upper part improving performance tend to be longer and have more DPLS. In the lower part we have queries that get worse. Often, for such queries none of the 16 rules we have can be applied. We experimented by expanding our rule set but this yielded very small performance gains. We conclude that for user profiling syntax level models may only be applicable to very long and well formed queries. In our current test data set fewer than 21% queries (for numQ; and 27% for numE) have at least 3 terms, so this candidate set is not ideal for testing syntax level models. DPLS are well-represented in user profiles, but the majority of the queries is short. This analysis gives us some intuition about where these approaches could be useful.

Table 3. The upper part of the table shows two queries for which performance improves for **DP** over **EC**, and two queries with decreasing performance in the lower part

Query	DPLS
consumer reports best coffee maker	nsubj nn: consumer reports coffee maker
	nsubj dobj: consumer reports maker
1980's south african president	nsubj nn: 1980 president african president
	nsubj amod nn: 1980 president south president african president
	nsubj amod: 1980 president south president
bristol motor speedway	—
it's a mad mad mad mad world	nsubj amod: it world mad world

6   Conclusions

User profiles are embedded in a variety of search personalization tasks in order to present more relevant results to users. To understand the user-query relationship, we study user search queries profiling models in isolation of other components. For this, we utilize named entities detected in the query, the corresponding entity categories, and related terms and entities in our models. Further, we analyze the syntactic structure of longer queries in syntax-level models. Our experimental results reveal that the best performing model employs related terms and entities in addition to the query's own terms and entities.

The next step is to utilize these findings for user modeling in search personalization tasks such as providing better query suggestions: given a user and a query, which query is most likely to be issued next? For this, we can modify our user profile learning model by just flipping the conditional probability around: instead of estimating the owner of a query, we would estimate the likelihood of a query for a given user. Of course, this model could be further extended to include other components like information from users' clicks on documents.

Acknowledgments. This work was supported in part by the Center for Intelligent Information Retrieval. Any opinions, findings and conclusions or recommendations expressed in this material are the authors' and do not necessarily reflect those of the sponsor.

References

1. Cao, B., Sun, J.-T., Xiang, E.W., Hu, D.H., Yang, Q., Chen, Z.: PQC: Personalized Query Classification. In: CIKM (2009)
2. Chen, S.F., Goodman, J.: An Empirical Study of Smoothing Techniques for Language Modeling. In: ACL (1996)
3. Chen, Y., Zhang, Y.-Q.: A Personalised Query Suggestion Agent based on Query-Concept Bipartite Graphs and Concept Relation Trees. Int. J. Adv. Intell. Paradigms 1, 398–417 (2009)
4. Dou, Z., Song, R., Wen, J.-R.: A Large-scale Evaluation and Analysis of Personalized Search Strategies. In: WWW (2007)
5. Kamvar, M., Baluja, S.: The Role of Context in Query Input: Using Contextual Signals to Complete Queries on Mobile Devices. In: MobileHCI (2007)
6. Klein, D., Manning, C.D.: Accurate Unlexicalized Parsing. In: ACL (2003)
7. Kumaran, G., Allan, J.: Effective and Efficient User Interaction for Long Queries. In: SIGIR (2008)
8. Leung, K.-T., Ng, W., Lee, D.L.: Personalized Concept-Based Clustering of Search Engine Queries. IEEE Transactions on Knowledge and Data Engineering 20(11), 1505–1518 (2008)
9. Lu, J., Callan, J.: User Modeling for Full-Text Federated Search in Peer-to-Peer Networks. In: SIGIR (2006)
10. Luxenburger, J., Elbassuoni, S., Weikum, G.: Matching Task Profiles and User Needs in Personalized Web Search. In: CIKM (2008)
11. Matthijs, N., Radlinski, F.: Personalizing Web Search using Long Term Browsing History. In: WSDM (2011)
12. Mei, Q., Church, K.: Entropy of Search Logs: How Hard is Search? With Personalization? With Backoff? In: WSDM (2008)
13. Mei, Q., Zhou, D., Church, K.: Query Suggestion Using Hitting Time. In: CIKM (2008)
14. Morris, M.R., Teevan, J., Bush, S.: Enhancing Collaborative Web Search with Personalization: Groupization, Smart Splitting, and Group Hit-Highlighting. In: CSCW (2008)
15. Shmueli-Scheuer, M., Roitman, H., Carmel, D., Mass, Y., Konopnicki, D.: Extracting User Profiles from Large Scale Data. In: MDAC (2010)
16. Sontag, D., Collins-Thompson, K., Bennett, P.N., White, R.W., Dumais, S., Billerbeck, B.: Probabilistic Models for Personalizing Web Search. In: WSDM (2012)
17. Stamou, S., Ntoulas, A.: Search Personalization through Query and Page Topical Analysis. User Modeling and User-Adapted Interaction (February 2009)
18. Sugiyama, K., Hatano, K., Yoshikawa, M.: Adaptive Web Search Based on User Profile Constructed without Any Effort from Users. In: WWW (2004)

19. Teevan, J., Dumais, S.T., Horvitz, E.: Beyond the Commons: Investigating the Value of Personalizing Web Search. In: Proc. Workshop on New Technologies for Personalized Information Access (2005)
20. Teevan, J., Dumais, S.T., Horvitz, E.: Personalizing Search via Automated Analysis of Interests and Activities. In: SIGIR (2005)
21. Teevan, J., Morris, M.R., Bush, S.: Discovering and Using Groups to Improve Personalized Search. In: WSDM (2009)
22. Xue, G.-R., Han, J., Yu, Y., Yang, Q.: User Language Model for Collaborative Personalized Search. ACM Trans. Inf. Syst. (March 2009)

Inform or Flood: Estimating When Retweets Duplicate

Amit Tiroshi[1], Tsvi Kuflik[1], and Shlomo Berkovsky[2]

[1] University of Haifa, Haifa, Israel
{atiroshi,tsvikak}@is.haifa.ac.il
[2] NICTA, Sydney, Australia
Shlomo.Berkovsky@nicta.com.au

Abstract. The social graphs of Twitter users often overlap, such that retweets may cause duplicate posts is a user's incoming stream of tweets. Hence, it is important for the retweets to strike the balance between sharing information and flooding the recipients with redundant tweets. In this work, we present an exploratory analysis that assesses the degree of duplication caused by a set of real retweets. The results of the analysis show that although the overall duplication is not severe, high degree of duplication is caused by tweets of users with a small number of followers, which are retweeted by users with a small number of followers. We discuss the limitations of this work and propose several enhancements that we intend to pursue in the future.

1   Introduction

The graphs of social network users represent the links established between the users. The entire graph can be decomposed into *ego-graphs* [9], representing the perspective of a single user on the network and containing only the links between the user and other users. In Twitter, user links are established through the 'Follow' feature, such that users have a set of users whom they follow (dubbed as *followees*) and a set of users who follow them (dubbed as *followers*). Previous works have shown that Twitter graph is a small-world network, i.e., most users can be reached within a small number of network hops [7]. As such, the degree of overlap between the ego-graphs of two users who established a link between them is high, and it increases over time, as users establish more links and their ego-graphs expand. This phenomenon is explained by the observed homophily of users: people often have mutual acquaintances and connect to like-minded people with similar interests [10].

Two popular ways of public communication in Twitter are to *tweet*, i.e., post new tweets to followers, and to *retweet*, i.e., re-post tweets from followees to followers. No official statistics of the number of followers of an average Twitter user are available. However, a 2009 data based on 56 million accounts, shows an average of 557 followers [1]. A 2012 dataset based on 80 million accounts that tweeted at least once, shows an average of 235 followers [2]. The expansion of the ego-graphs and the abundance of tweets/retweets may pose a significant information overload on the users. Furthermore, the high overlap between the ego-graphs of two linked users can potentially lead to a duplication of tweets reaching a user, as they may receive a tweet as

S. Carberry et al. (Eds.): UMAP 2013, LNCS 7899, pp. 267–273, 2013.

well as the retweets of the same tweet through a number of users. For example, consider three users – Alice, Bob, and Carol – such that Bob follows Alice, and Carol follows both Alice and Bob. In this setting, Alice's tweets will be duplicated in Carol's incoming stream, if retweeted by Bob. This may aggravate the information overload problem and make it even harder for users to identify tweets of interest and stay informed.

While the reasons for tweeting have been thoroughly studied [7,11], to the best of our knowledge the reasons for retweeting have received little attention so far. In [4], Boyd et al. survey the key motivating factors for retweeting, which can be split into three groups. The first includes *informative* factors, such as the desire to spread a tweet to followers because it matches their interests, will entertain them, or will make them aware of the tweet's topic. The second groups refers to *emotional* factors, such as endorsing the opinion expressed in the tweet, appealing to the user who posted the tweet, or trying to gain benefit from a tweet that might become popular. Finally, the last group includes *utility* factors, which virtually come to bookmark tweets of relevance. It should be noted that many emotional and utility factors can be fulfilled by other Twitter features, e.g., the 'Favorite' and the 'Reply' features.

As in many information sharing scenarios, retweets ought to strike the balance between the information need and the information overload (an example of how to aim for that balance in social news feeds is given at [3]). Although the value of the emotional and utility factors can hardly be quantified, the degree of duplication (as a proxy for information overload) caused by a retweet can be assessed and it can potentially affect the value of the informative motivating factor. For example, users may refrain from retweeting a tweet that has already been received by most of their followers or, conversely, be urged to retweet a tweet that a few followers have received so far. However, at the moment, Twitter users have no means for assessing the redundancy caused by their retweets.

Aiming to develop these means in the future, we present here an exploratory analysis of the degree of duplication created by more than 1000 real-life retweets. We computed the duplication caused by these tweets and found that, overall, 20% of Tweets caused duplicate posts for 20% or more of the recipients. The duplication depends on the number of followers of both the user who posted the original tweet and the user who retweeted it. We also discuss several interfaces that can communicate the duplication to users and potentially affect their retweeting decision.

2   Related Work

The problem of overlaps in social graphs and their effect on information propagation was examined by Boyd et al. [4], who focused on the retweeting phenomenon. It was noted that when Twitter users retweet posts, there may be an overlap between their followers and the followers of the user who posted the original tweet, but the retweeters are unlikely to be aware of this overlap. They also refer to a note made in [6] that in small-worlds, where people connect to each other seamlessly, the effort required for keeping tracks of who knows whom (or who follows whom) is immense.

Other works focused on various aspects of retweets, but provided possible explanations for the presence of overlaps in social graphs. For example, [10] evaluated several recency-, content-, and homophily-based computational models of retweeting. It was found that models that take user homophily into account, fit the observed retweeting behavior better than others. Besides being one of the key drivers for retweeting, homophily is also pivotal for establishing the follower/followee links [8,12]. In combination, these findings provide a strong evidence that user homophily may lead to a potential duplication of tweets. However, there is little evidence for the impact of the social graph overlaps on the duplication, which is the focus of this work.

3   Analysis of Overlapping Retweets

In this section we present an analysis of the overlap caused by post retweets on Twitter. Let us denote by O the user who posted the original tweet and by R the user who reposted the tweet. We consider the ego-graphs of Twitter users and denote by $fr(u)$ and $fe(u)$ the set of followers and followees of user u, respectively. Finally, we denote by $|s|$ the cardinality of a set s. Given this notation, we quantify the degree of duplication caused by R retweeting a tweet posted by O as:

$$OL(O,R) = \frac{|fr(O) \cap fr(R)|}{|fr(R)|}$$

Note that the intersection of the two sets of followers is divided by the cardinality of the set of followers of R, in order to stress the duplications caused by R's retweets.

In order to assess the overlap caused by retweets in the wild, we gathered in September 2012 a set of 1030 real-life retweets, as well as the ego-graphs of O and R for each. The data contains tweets posted by 1000 and retweeted by 1029 unique users. High-level statistics of the sets of followers[1] and their overlaps are shown in Table 1. Also, Figure 1-left shows the distribution of the $OL(O,R)$ values across the collected retweets. Although most retweets have a low overlap, it can be seen that for 20% of them (205 retweets) there is an overlap of 20% or more between the followers of O and R. The distribution of overlap frequencies fits the long tail distribution.

Table 1. Followers and overlap statistics

	$|fr(O)|$	$|fr(R)|$	$OL(O,R)$
Minimum	4	0	0%
25th percentile	378	90	1%
Median	2,346	201	6%
Mean	210,492	986	11%
75th percentile	52,902	489.75	16%
Maximum	9,175,388	206,535	100%

---

[1] The difference between the mean and median of $|fr(O)|$ is due to 60 retweets for posts of users who had more than a million followers each.

Since the number of followers distributes normally neither for O nor for R, we drill down to analyze how $OL(O,R)$ varies across different users. For this, we split all the collected retweets into two equal-size bins of 515 retweets each, according to $|fr(O)|$ and $|fr(R)|$. For the O-split we sort the collected retweets according to the number of O's followers, such that 515 retweets where $|fr(O)| \leq 2342$ are considered as tweets of users with a low number of followers and the other 515 retweets where $|fr(O)| > 2342$ are of users with a high number of followers. We repeat the same process for the R-split: 515 retweets where $|fr(R)| \leq 115$ are mapped to the bin of retweeters with a low number of followers and the other 515 to the bin with a high number of followers. Note that the cut-off point of the O-split is much greater than that of the R-split. This is due to the unbalanced distribution of retweets, which are often done to influential users and VIPs, and are less frequent for those using Twitter for everyday chat [4].

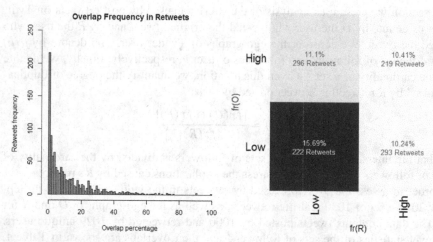

Fig. 1. Left – overall frequency of $OL(O,R)$ and right – heat map of $OL(O,R)$ for the combinations of O- and R-split

Figure 2 plots the cumulative distribution function (CDF) of $OL(O,R)$ obtained for the 'low' and 'high' bins for the O-split (left) and R-split (right). We observe that most retweets have a small number of users who receive duplicate tweets and only a small number of retweets causes duplication for a high portion of recipients. For the O-split, about 16% of retweets of users in the 'high' bin cause duplication for 20% of users of more, whereas in the 'low' bin this ratio stands at about 25%. This gap between the two CDFs functions is lower for the R-split; about 18% of retweets in the 'high' bin cause duplication for 20% of users of more, whereas in the 'low' bin this ratio is about 22%. However, in both splits we observe the same trend: the duplication caused by retweets in the 'Low' bin exceeds the one in the 'High' bin. That is, retweets of users having a small number of followers cause more duplication than retweets of users having a large number of followers. This finding can be explained by the higher homophily observed for small communities [10]. Indeed, the larger a community of users is, the harder it is to maintain a high degree of similarity of users across the community. In case of followers, one intuitive argument supporting this is that for

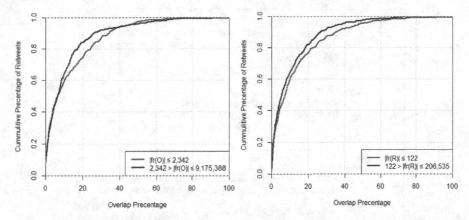

Fig. 2. CDF of $OL(O,R)$ for a low/high number of followers; left – O and right – R

users with a large number of followers, these followers would normally fragment into more topics of interests (or sub-groups); hence, the overlap will decrease.

To better understand the combined dependency between $|fr(O)|$, $|fr(R)|$, and $OL(O,R)$, Figure 1-right shows the heat map of overlaps obtained for the various combinations of the number of followers of O and R. Every segment of the heat map shows the number of retweets matching this combination and their average $OL(O,R)$, whereas the background color of the segment communicates the degree of overlapping and duplication. The highest $OL(O,R)$ is obtained for the segment with low $|fr(O)|$ and low $|fr(R)|$. That is, retweets of users with a small number of followers done for tweets or users with a small number of followers cause the highest duplication. A decrease in $OL(O,R)$ is observed when either $|fr(O)|$ or $|fr(R)|$ increases. The impact of the decrease in $|fr(R)|$ on $OL(O,R)$ is slightly higher than that of the decrease in $|fr(O)|$ and the observed overlap is lower.

4   Discussion

In this work we conducted an exploratory analysis of the information overload and duplication caused by retweets. We gathered a corpus of retweets and measured the degree of overlapping between the set of followers of a tweet originator and of the user who retweeted it. We discovered that the overlapping and duplication decrease as the number of followers in user ego-graphs increases. On the first look, the observed degree of duplication was not high: overall, around 20% of retweets caused duplicate posts for 20% or more of the recepients. While not looking severe, this rate may increase in small communities with dense graphs. For example, consider a group of followers of an academic conference Twitter account. Many users in this group may also follow each other, such that retweets of the conference announcements may be duplicated many times. Hence, the work into the discovery of these duplicate retweets is needed and timely.

We would like to highlight two limitations of this work. The first refers to the fact that our approximation of information overload through tweet duplication addresses only the informative factor of retweeting. Indeed, many users consider also the emotional and utility factors when retweeting, and may retweet despite the information

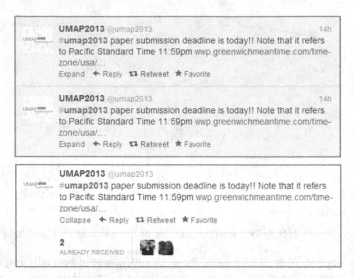

Fig. 3. Two mock-up interfaces to alert tweet duplication: top – traffic light rating; bottom – thumbnails of the recipients of duplicate tweets

overload they cause. Our overlapping computation cannot account for these factors and needs to incorporate techniques similar to the tie-strength model [5]. The second limitation refers to the small scale of the analysis. The size of the gathered data was constrained primarily by the REST API that prolongs the time needed to gather Twitter ego-graphs, especially when the set of followees and followers is large. There is no easy solution to this problem, but to substantially extend the duration of the data collection phase. As the density of the gathered ego-graphs resembles the density of those gathered in other works [1,2], we posit that our results reflect the results that could have been obtained in a larger-scale analysis.

Another issue that needs to be addressed is how to alert users to the potential overload of their retweets. We demonstrate two practical implementations. The first (see Figure 3–top) uses the traffic light rating system to color the 'Retweet' button according to the computed degree of duplication. This, however, is not a straightforward threshold-based coloring, but should rather consider the followers of the retweeters, the density of their ego-graph, and the nature of the followers (consider general interest users vs. professionals). Similarly, a different treatment should be given to different users. For example, a user may agree to cause duplicate tweets for some users and be reluctant to do this for others. Hence, we propose another implementation that shows the thumbnails of users, who will receive duplicate tweets due to the retweet (see Figure 3–bottom). The retweeter can then easily identify who will be affected by the retweet and take more informed retweeting decisions.

In the future we plan to conduct a user study with a cohort of users and a large corpus of tweets. We will expose the users to different alert visualizations and measure the persuasive impact of the alerts on their retweeting. In the study we will also be able to evaluate several personalized ways to compute the information overload, which will take into account the structure of the followers' ego-graphs as well as the strength of the links between the retweeters and their followers. This study is necessary to ascertain the uptake of the retweeting decision support tool by real users.

Acknowledgement. This work is supported by ISF grant 226/2010.

References

1. Bakshy, E., Hofman, J.M., Mason, W.A., Watts, D.J.: Everyone's an influencer: quantifying influence on twitter. In: Proceedings of the Fourth ACM International Conference on Web Search and Data Mining (WSDM 2011), pp. 65–74. ACM, New York (2011)
2. Basch, D.: Some Fresh Twitter Stats (as of July 2012, Dataset Included), http://diego-basch.com, http://diegobasch.com/some-fresh-twitter-stats-as-of-july-2012 (accessed July 31, 2012)
3. Berkovsky, S., Freyne, J., Kimani, S., Smith, G.: Selecting items of relevance in social network feeds. In: Konstan, J.A., Conejo, R., Marzo, J.L., Oliver, N. (eds.) UMAP 2011. LNCS, vol. 6787, pp. 329–334. Springer, Heidelberg (2011)
4. Boyd, D., Golder, S., Lotan, G.: Tweet, Tweet, Retweet: Conversational Aspects of Retweeting on Twitter. In: Proceedings of the 2010 43rd Hawaii International Conference on System Sciences (HICSS 2010), pp. 1–10. IEEE Computer Society, Washington, DC (2010)
5. Gilbert, E., Karahalios, K.: Predicting tie strength with social media. In: Proceedings of the SIGCHI Conference on Human Factors in Computing Systems (CHI 2009), pp. 211–220. ACM, New York (2009)
6. Granovetter, M.: Ignorance, knowledge, and outcomes in a small world. Science 301(5634), 773–774 (2003)
7. Java, A., Song, X., Finin, T., Tseng, B.: Why we twitter: understanding microb-logging usage and communities. In: Proceedings of the 9th WebKDD and 1st SNA-KDD 2007 Workshop on Web Mining and Social Network Analysis (WebKDD/SNA-KDD 2007), pp. 56–65. ACM, New York (2007)
8. Kwak, H., Lee, C., Park, H., Moon, S.: What is Twitter, a social network or a news media? In: Proceedings of the 19th International Conference on World Wide Web (WWW 2010), pp. 591–600. ACM, New York (2010)
9. Lacaze, A., Moscovitz, Y., DeClaris, N., Murphy, K.: Path planning for autonomous vehi-cles driving over rough terrain. In: Proceedings of Intelligent Control (ISIC), 1998. Held jointly with IEEE International Symposium on Computational Intelligence in Robotics and Automation (CIRA), Intelligent Systems and Semiotics (ISAS), September 14-17, pp. 50–55 (1998)
10. Macskassy, S., Michelson, M.: Why do People Retweet? Anti-Homophily Wins the Day! In: International AAAI Conference on Weblogs and Social Media, North America (July 2011)
11. Marwick, A., Boyd, D.: Tweet Honestly, I Tweet Passionately: Twitter Users, Context Collapse, and the Imagined Audience. New Media and Society 13, 96–113 (2011)
12. Weng, J., Lim, E.P., Jiang, J., He, Q.: TwitterRank: finding topic-sensitive influ-ential twitterers. In: Proceedings of the Third ACM International Conference on Web Search and Data Mining (WSDM 2010), pp. 261–270. ACM, New York (2010)
13. Wilson, C., Boe, B., Sala, A., Puttaswamy, K.P.N., Zhao, B.Y.: User interactions in social networks and their implications. In: Proceedings of the 4th ACM European Conference on Computer Systems (EuroSys 2009), pp. 205–218. ACM, New York (2009)

Predicting Users' Preference from Tag Relevance

Tien T. Nguyen and John Riedl

GroupLens Research, Computer Science and Engineering,
University of Minnesota, Minneapolis, MN 55455
nguy1749@umn.edu, riedl@cs.umn.edu
http://www.grouplens.org/

Abstract. Tagging has become a powerful means for users to find, organize, understand and express their ideas about online entities. However,
tags present great challenges when researchers try to incorporate them
into the *prediction task* of recommender systems. In this paper, we propose a novel approach to infer user preference from tag relevance, an
indication of how strong each tag applies to each item in recommender
systems. We also present a methodology to choose tags that tell most
about each user's preference. Our preliminary results show that at certain levels, some of our algorithms perform better than previous work.

Keywords: algorithms, recommender system, mutual information, tag
relevance.

1   Introduction

Tagging is, today, a popular means for users to organize, and express their opinions about any item of their interests. It also serves as a means to retrieve information. Originally, tags were used mainly in retrieval systems. Subsequently,
they are incorporated into other domains such as recommender systems, since
tags are considered as what users think about items [5]. Sen et al. propose that
tags are also bridges connecting users and items [3]. These bridges help users find
and make decision about items. Sen et al. credit Paul Lamere and his colleagues
with coining the term "tagomendations" to refer to any recommendation systems that incorporate tags into the *prediction task* (predicting users' preferences
for some items in the collections).

However, incorporating tags into the *prediction task* is challenging due to two
characteristics of the traditional tagging model. First, tags are **binary.** When a
user applies a tag to a item, he can only indicate a binary relationship between
the tag and the movie [7]. For example, a movie can be tagged as *romantic*,
but this tag alone cannot describe how romantic the movie is. Second, tags are
sparse. Not all users tag all the movies they watched [7]. Moreover, it is unlikely
that they apply the same sets of tags to the same set of movies.

To over come the two limitations, some researchers, such as Sen et al. [3], have
successfully inferred user preference from a tag via tag-clicks, or tag-search, and
then incorporate these preferences into the *prediction task*. Sen et al. introduce

S. Carberry et al. (Eds.): UMAP 2013, LNCS 7899, pp. 274–280, 2013.
© Springer-Verlag Berlin Heidelberg 2013

a tag-based recommender system that infers user preferences from tags. In order to capture these preference signals, they propose several algorithms, such as: 1) users have higher preference for tags if they themselves apply these tags (**tag-applied**) , or 2) if they themselves searched for these tags (**tag-searched**), or 3) if the tags are of high quality (**tag-quality**)[4]. Their analysis shows that prediction accuracy can be improved if these preference signals are taken into account. However, inferring user preference via users' actions on tags like Sen et al. [3] requires extra efforts such as tagging, searching, or clicking from users. Furthermore, Sen et al. [3] propose constant numbers of tags selected for their algorithms. Nevertheless, different users have different preference, leading to different numbers of tags required to express individual preference.

To avoid these troubles for users, we need to be able to asses user preference directly via the applied tags themselves. Vig et al.[7] define tag-genome for tag relevance, an information space that indicates how strong each tag applies to each item. To calculate the relevance for each pair of tag t and movie m, Vig et al.[7] use several techniques such as *Rating-sim* (the correlation between item preference and tag preference), and *Tag-lsi-sim* (which helps to capture missing signals when tags were not applied to movies even if they are relevant to these movies; where lsi stands for *latent semantic indexing*, a mathematical technique that expresses the relationships between tags and movies they are applied). We think that Vig et al.'s approach has great potentials for the inference of user preference directly from the applied tags. However, Vig et al. only use tag relevance to navigate through movie collections, not to predict user preference.

In this paper, we aim to overcome the issues with Sen et al.'s approach by incorporating tag relevance as proposed by Vig et al. into the *prediction task*. To the best of our knowledge, no recommender system has ever done this. Furthermore, we use the mutual information framework in information theory [6] to avoid the constant thresholds applied to all users as in Sen et al. Next, we present how we use this framework to choose tags for each user.

2   Selecting Tags for Each User Using Mutual Information

According to Information Theory [6], the *mutual information* of two random variables is the amount of information one variable can tell about the other. Given two random variables X and Y, their mutual information is defined as follow:

$$I(X;Y) = \sum_{x \in X} \sum_{y \in Y} P(x,y) \log_2 \frac{P(x,y)}{P(x)P(y)} \tag{1}$$

Our objective is to find a subset of quality tags $T' \subset T$ that can explain the most about users' preferences via their rating history and tag relevance. Hence, given user u and tag t, the two random variables are the user's rating history R_u and the relevances L_t of tag t to all movies s/he rated.

In our approach, dealing with continuous values of tag relevance is less desirable, since user rating behavior is discrete, i.e. users give either 1 star, or 2 star etc. for any given movie. We bucket the relevance of tag t to movie m into 8 buckets with the width of 0.2.

Deriving from equation 1, the mutual information of tag t and the preference of user u is defined as:

$$I_{u,t}(R_u; L_t) = \sum_{r \in R_u} \sum_{l \in L_t} P_{u,t}(r,l) \log_2 \frac{P_{u,t}(r,l)}{P_u(r) P_{u,t}(l)} \qquad (2)$$

where: $\forall$ rating $r \in R_u$, $P_u(r)$ is the probability that user u gave a rating r for all movies s/he rated; $\forall$ bucketed relevance $l \in L_t$, $P_{u,t}(l)$ is the probability that tag t has the bucketed relevance l for all movies that user u rated; $P_{u,t}(r,l)$ is the joint-probability of the two random variables, indicating the probability that user u gives a rating r for all movies that have tag t with bucketed relevance l.

The mutual information $I_{u,t}(R_u; L_t)$ ranges from 0 to the minimum of the expected values of the information contained in R_u and L_t. To select tags that have sufficient predictive power, we need to set a threshold, which is the minimum amount of information about the preference of user u (R_u) a tag can tell. Since user preference varies from user to user, the amount of information in their ratings also varies. Hence the threshold, if any, may be appropriate for one user, but not for another. To deal with this problem, we define *normalized mutual information*, $NI_{u,t}(R, L)$, the percentage of the information about user u's preference that tag t can tell:

$$NI_{u,t}(R, L) = \frac{I_{u,t}(R; L)}{H_u(R)} \times 100\% \qquad (3)$$

Therefore, we set a threshold α for a tag to be selected if it can tell at least a certain percentage of user preference. In this paper, we consider five α thresholds from 10% to 50% with 10% increment. For example: at $\alpha = 50\%$, a selected tag t must explain at least 50% of the information about the preference of user u.

3   Case Study: Predicting Ratings in MovieLens

To evaluate our approach, we use the MovieLens dataset[1], a tagging-supported movie recommender system. MovieLens has been in continuous use since 1997. As of 10/19/2012, there are 209,844 unique users who provide approximate 19 million movie ratings , and 28,421 tags for 19,515 movies. In this study, we calculate the relevances of 1,633 quality tags for 9,063 movies. We only consider users who rated more than 99 movies.

3.1   Tag-Based Recommender Algorithms

Since each user has a different number of selected tags, we prefer to use some machine-learning methods that are robust in making predictions for an individual. Among many available methods, we choose to use the followings:

---

[1] http://www.movielens.org

Linear Regression: The linear regression model expresses ratings as a linear combination of tag relevances. For each user u, and movie m associated with the selected set of quality tags T' by a vector of relevances L_m, his rating for movie m can be represented as: $r_{u,m} = Intercept_u + \beta_u L_m + \epsilon_{u,m}$, where β_u is the vector of coefficients learnt for user u, and $\epsilon_{u,m}$ is the residual error. We choose the linear approach for its simplicity. We build our linear regression model by using the lm command in R with 5 fold-cross-validation to learn the best β_u.

Support Vector Machine: We also study a non-linear approach to build our model. We choose support vector machine due to its robustness in gaining better generalization performance. We use Chang et al.'s svm library [2] with their suggested radial basis function kernel (RBF). We also optimize the SVM by using grid-search algorithm proposed by Chang et al [2] to find the best parameter for C and γ parameters of the kernel.

In order to evaluate our proposed algorithms, we compare our results with the results reported by Sen et al's [3] for their three algorithms *funk-svd*, *regress-tag* and *cosine-tag*. We choose these results for three reasons: 1) the *funk-svd* achieves the best results among tag-based as well as non-tag-based recommender systems, 2) the *regress-tag* achieves the best results, and 3) the *cosine-tag* achieves the worst results among the tag-based recommender systems. However, with the mutual information approach at high α thresholds mentioned above, we are required to have a large pool of users. Sen et al. study 1,315 users in their pruned set, which is not sufficient for our analysis. Therefore, we do not analyze on the same dataset as Sen et al. does. Furthermore, Sen et al. use different filtering methods to select tags and users. Hence, the comparisons we make in this paper are relative. To make our results comparable to that of Sen et al.'s work [3], we report the same metric they report: mean absolute error (MAE) and top-5. MAE is the average absolute difference between the predicted ratings and the observed ratings, reflecting the performance of an algorithm for the prediction task. Top-5 is the percentage of top predicted movies that users rate at certain stars or higher. Like Sen et al., we choose 4 stars as the cutoff point.

4   Results and Evaluation

Linear-regression algorithm with threshold $\alpha = k\%$ is denoted **k-LR**. SVM algorithm with threshold α is denoted **k-SVM**. Optimized SVM algorithm with the threshold $\alpha = k\%$ is denoted **opt-k-SVM**. Due to limited space, we only report results that are competitive to that of Sen et al.

Our Performance Compared to Sen et al. (2009) Results
Table 1 shows how our proposed algorithms performs against the results reported in Sen et al. [3]. In MAE term, our 50-LR algorithm achieves lower MAE (0.54) than all Sen et al.'s algorithms. Furthermore, the MAEs reported in Sen et al. (except that of *funk-svd*) are higher, and not in the 95% confidence interval of our 50-LR algorithm. The optimized SVM algorithms also achieve good performances (avg. MAE:0.64), approximately the same as *cosine-tag* algorithm

Table 1. The MAE and top-5 precision performances of our explicit algorithms. Lower MAE corresponds to better performance. Higher Top-5 precision corresponds to better performance. Sen et al.'s performances for Funk-svd: MAE=0.56, Top-5 precision=0.80; Regress-tag: MAE=0.58, Top-5 precision=0.83, Cosine-tag: MAE=0.64, Top-5 precision=0.62.[2]

Algorithm	MAE			Top-5 Precision		
	Avg.	95% CI	STD (σ)	Avg.	95% CI	STD (σ)
40-LR	0.79	[0.77,0.80]	0.93	0.70	[0.70,0.71]	0.25
50-LR	0.54	[0.53,0.56]	0.30	0.70	[0.69,0.70]	0.25
10-SVM	0.73	[0.72,0.73]	0.25	0.53	[0.53,0.53]	0.28
20-SVM	0.71	[0.70,0.71]	0.24	0.55	[0.54,0.55]	0.28
30-SVM	0.69	[0.68,0.69]	0.24	0.56	[0.55,0.56]	0.28
40-SVM	0.68	[0.67,0.68]	0.25	0.56	[0.56,0.56]	0.27
50-SVM	0.67	[0.66,0.67]	0.25	0.55	[0.55,0.56]	0.28
opt-30-SVM	0.64	[0.64,0.65]	0.21	0.61	[0.61,0.62]	0.27
opt-40-SVM	0.64	[0.64,0.65]	0.23	0.63	[0.62,0.63]	0.28
opt-50-SVM	0.63	[0.62,0.64]	0.25	0.61	[0.60,0.62]	0.28

(0.64). Some of our top-5-precision performances do not perform as good as Sen et al.'s algorithms do. We suspect that predicting a movie to be top-rated is harder than predicting across the rating-scale. We leave this for future work.

Mutual Information as a Way to Select Predictive Tags

As shown in table 1, although some of our algorithms do not achieve high performances, the others achieve very low MAEs, comparable to the results in Sen et al. This suggests that the mutual information approach is able to select the subsets of quality tags T' that have predictive power for each user. For example, at $\alpha = 30\%$, the top 10 tags that have predictive powers for at least 75% users are: {*masterpiece,good acting, great acting,imdb top 250, excellent script, interesting, great movie, drama, classic,oscar (best directing)* } respectively. On the other hand, the bottom 10 are {*tim robbins, united nations, vampire, william h. macy, matthew mcconaughey, jim carrey, michael keaton, jena malone,olympics,john turturro*}. The top-10 are tags that describe the quality of the movies. However, the bottom-10 are mostly only about the components of the movies. Furthermore, the number of selected tags is different for each user. For example, 230 users have 17 selected tags, but 400 users have only 8 selected tags. With the same number of selected tags, the tags are different, depending on the taste of each user. 5 tags {*weird, action packed, chase, fast paced, tense* }, which characterize action movies, are chosen for user 73782. The preference of user 129098 is described mostly by 5 tags {*chick flick, romantic, happy, ending, big budget, romance, girlie movie*}, which characterize emotional movies.

---

[2] The top-5 precision for cosine-tag was not reported in Sen et al.'s paper. We contacted the lead author to confirm our estimate from the reported figure.

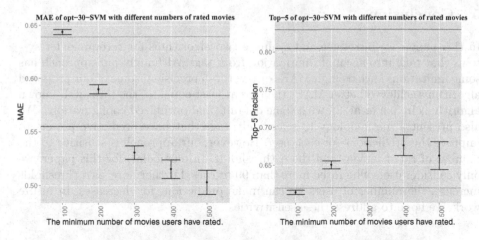

Fig. 1. Our performances compared to Sen et al.'s in term of MAE (left figure) and Top-5 precision (right figure) for the opt-30-SVM with the 95 % confidence intervals. Blue-line: Sen et al.'s MAE (0.56) and Top-5 precision (0.80) for Funk-svd. Red-line: Sen et al.'s MAE (0.58) and Top-5 precision (0.83) for Regress-tag. Green-line: Sen et al.'s MAE (0.64) and Top-5 precision(0.62) for Cosine-tag.

In addition, we observe that the higher the α threshold, the better the performance our SVM and linear regression (LR) can achieve. However, the higher α, the fewer users we can make predictions for. For example: with SVM algorithms, at $\alpha = 10\%$, we could make predictions for 48609 users. At $\alpha = 40\%$, only we could do it for 20705 users who rated at least 99 movies. As For 50-LR, due to the linear regression assumptions, we can only make prediction for 8400 users. Therefore, the higher the α, the wider the confident interval.

The Effect of the Number of Rated Movies on the Proposed Algorithms We also consider the number of movies a user has rated, because the probabilities in equation 2 vary with this number. We choose algorithm *opt-30-SVM* to analyze the effect due to two reasons. First, with this high α threshold, we still have a large pool of users (34309 users who rated at least 99 movies) to make our analysis reliable. Second, this threshold seems reasonable in real-life applications. As shown in figure 1 (right), as the minimum number of rated movies for our users increased, the MAEs *opt-30-SVM* decrease. For example, with the minimum of 100 movies, the achieved MAE is 0.64 (95% CI : [0.64,0.65]). With the minimum of 500 movies, the achieved MAE is 0.51 (95% CI of [0.49,0.51]). Nevertheless, like the α threshold, the higher the minimum number, the fewer users we can make predictions for.

5   Conclusion

In this paper, we introduce and evaluate two algorithms for recommender systems that take into account information from tags. Although, our approach has some limitations such as high MAEs or low top-5 precision, some of our proposed algorithms achieved better MAEs than, or at least equal to, the three well-known algorithms in Sen et al [3], with some default, and optimized configurations. We also present a methodology to select only tags that have predictive powers to improve the predictions for each user. However, our approach is sensitive to the number of rated movies and the α thresholds. In particular, for this paper, we only consider users who rated more than 99 movies. Furthermore, as α thresholds increase, the number of users we can make predictions for decreases. In future work, we hope to address these sensitivities.

Acknowledgement. This work has been supported by the National Science Foundation under grants IIS 08-08692, IIS 09-68483. The authors thank Daniel Kluver for information theory discussions. The authors also thank Duyen (Mary) Nguyen for proof-readings and suggestions.

References

1. Bell, R., Koren, Y.: Lessons from the Netflix prize challenge. ACM SIGKDD Explorations Newsletter Special issue on Visual Analytics, 75–79 (2007)
2. Chang, C., Lin, C.: LIBSVM: A library for support vector machines. ACM Transactions on Intelligent Systems and Technology 2(3), 27:1–27:27 (2011)
3. Sen, S., Vig, J., Riedl, J.: Tagommenders: connecting users to items through tags. In: ACM International Conference on World Wide Web, WWW, pp. 221–230 (2009)
4. Sen, S., Vig, J., Riedl, J.: Learning to recognize valuable tags. In: Proceedings of the 14th International Conference on Intelligent user Interfaces, IUI, pp. 87–96 (2009)
5. Shirky, C.: Ontology is overrated (2005),
   http://www.shirky.com/writings/ontology_overrated.html (retrieved on December 28, 2012)
6. Shannon, C.: A mathematical theory of communication. ACM SIGMOBILE Mobile Computing and Communications Review 5(1), 3–5 (2001)
7. Vig, J., Sen, S., Riedl, J.: Encoding Community Knowledge to Support Novel Interaction. ACM Transactions on Interactive Intelligent Systems, TiiS 2(3) (2012)

Recommendation for New Users with Partial Preferences by Integrating Product Reviews with Static Specifications

Feng Wang, Weike Pan, and Li Chen

Department of Computer Science, Hong Kong Baptist University
Hong Kong, China
{fwang,wkpan,lichen}@comp.hkbu.edu.hk

Abstract. Recommending products to new buyers is an important problem for online shopping services, since there are always new buyers joining a deployed system. In some recommender systems, a new buyer will be asked to indicate her/his preferences on some attributes of the product (like camera) in order to address the so called cold-start problem. Such collected preferences are usually not complete due to the user's cognitive limitation and/or unfamiliarity with the product domain, which are called *partial preferences*. The fundamental challenge of recommendation is thus that it may be difficult to accurately and reliably find some like-minded users via collaborative filtering techniques or match inherently preferred products with content-based methods. In this paper, we propose to leverage some auxiliary data of online reviewers' aspect-level opinions, so as to predict the buyer's missing preferences. The resulted user preferences are likely to be more accurate and complete. Experiment on a real user-study data and a crawled Amazon review data shows that our solution achieves better recommendation performance than several baseline methods.

Keywords: New users, partial preferences, product recommendation, consumer reviews, aspect-level opinion mining, static specifications.

1 Introduction

The importance of recommendation as an embedded component in various online shopping services has been well recognized [2]. Most recommendation algorithms are designed to make use of explicit or implicit feedbacks of experienced users. However, new buyers join a typical online service everyday, who usually have no explicit ratings and/or little implicit behaviors. Facing such a new-user recommendation problem, some deployed systems ask the buyer to indicate some preferences on certain attributes of the product [3,7], such as the camera's brand, price, resolution, etc. However, the limitation of such works is that the efforts required from the buyer would be inevitably high. Moreover, most buyers are in reality not able to state their full preferences (say over all attributes) due to their cognitive limitation and/or unfamiliarity with the product domain, even

S. Carberry et al. (Eds.): UMAP 2013, LNCS 7899, pp. 281–288, 2013.
© Springer-Verlag Berlin Heidelberg 2013

when they are involved in a conversational interaction with the system [6,18]. The challenging issue is then how to predict the buyer's missing preferences on un-stated attributes, which is actually for solving the *partial preferences* problem [10]. The weakness of classical model-based and memory-based algorithms in collaborative filtering is that they can not build collaborative relationships among users without users' feedbacks [11,16]. The content-based methods may also fail to accurately find matching products when users' preferences are only given on a subset of attributes [13,15]. In the traditional artificial intelligent systems, some logic-oriented approaches were proposed for representing and reasoning about user preferences [10,14]. For instance, [10] presents a hybrid of quantitative and qualitative approach grounded on multi-attribute utility theory (MAUT) to identify sup-optimal alternatives. However, the approach's practical performance in the online environment is limited due to its high time complexity.

Therefore, in this paper, we propose a novel preference enrichment framework, which aims to complete a new buyer's preferences by incorporating product reviewers' aspect-level opinions and attributes' static specifications. Specifically, by integrating with the fine-grained opinion mining results of textual reviews, we target to find like-minded reviewers for a target new buyer and hence enrich the buyer's preferences on all attributes. Indeed, the advantages of reviews are that: 1) product reviews are broadly accessible over the internet. Therefore, even for a new system, it can extract product reviews from similar sites (like from Amazon) to serve its buyers; 2) reviews to a product can truly reflect the reviewer's preferences on various aspects of the product, as they are based on her/his post-usage evaluation experiences. Thus, it is expected that the incorporation of product reviews can bring *true* user preferences so as to ideally augment the system's recommendation accuracy for the current new buyer. To the best of our knowledge, though recently there are increasing attentions placed to exploit the values of product reviews in recommender systems [12,21,22], the aspect-level opinions have been rarely investigated for addressing the *partial preferences* problem. In our previous work [20], we emphasized mining reviewers' similarity network by revealing their weights placed on different aspects, but did not map their opinions to the attributes' static specifications for identifying their value preferences. Therefore, in this paper, our main interest is in exploiting such information to particularly predict new buyers' missing preferences.

Our contributions can be summarized as follows: 1) we envision product reviews as valuable resource of other users' preference information to enrich the current buyer's preferences; 2) we study how to leverage reviewers' aspect-level opinions, by mapping them to the attributes' static specifications, for aiding the product recommendation; 3) we conduct an empirical test of the proposed approach on a real user-study data and a crawled Amazon review data, which shows the outperforming accuracy of our solution against several baseline methods in the real-world setting (i.e., digital camera recommendation).

Table 1. Some notations used in the paper

	Notation	Description
Product	$p = 1, 2, \ldots, m$	product, e.g., Casio EX-Z55 DC
	$a = 1, 2, \ldots, k$	product attribute, e.g., $weight = 129.9$
	$\mathbf{x}_p = [x_{pa}]_{k \times 1} \in \mathbb{R}^{k \times 1}$	product profile
Buyer	$u = 1, 2, \ldots, n$	user
	$\boldsymbol{\phi}_u = [\phi_{ua}]_{k \times 1}$	user's preference, e.g., $weight < 200$
	$\mathbf{y}_u = [y_{ua}]_{k \times 1} \in \{0, 1\}^{k \times 1}$	user preference indicator ($y_{ua} = 1$ if user u states preference on attribute a)
	$choice(u) \in \{1, 2, \ldots, m\}$	user's target choice (ground truth)
Reviewer	$\tilde{u} = 1, 2, \ldots, \tilde{n}$	reviewer
	$\tilde{\boldsymbol{\phi}}_{\tilde{u}} = [\tilde{\phi}_{\tilde{u}a}]_{k \times 1}$	reviewer's preferences on various attributes
	$\tilde{r}_{\tilde{u}p} \in \{1, 2, 3, 4, 5\}$	reviewer's rating to a product

2 Problem Definition and Methodology

We have n new buyers and m products, where each buyer indicates preferences on a subset of product attributes, e.g., $weight < 200g$, $price < \$300$. We also have some auxiliary data of online reviews on those m products. As mentioned before, our goal is to enrich the new buyer's preferences and then recommend a personalized ranking list of products to him/her. We list some notations used in the paper in Table 1.

Our proposed solution, called *preference completion and ranking* (henceforth called CompleteRank), mainly contains the following three steps.

Step 1: Aspect-Level Opinion Mining. The online product reviews written by the users who previously purchased products usually contain some positive and/or negative opinions on certain aspects of a product. Thus, it is straightforward to assume that these aspect-level opinions can reflect the inherent preferences of the author (i.e., the reviewer) on the product's attributes (note that *attributes* refer to the product's static specifications, while *aspects* are features discovered from reviews. The latter is mapped to the former through a predefined dictionary). Inspired from this observation, we emphasize the usage of aspect-level opinion mining outcomes for predicting a new user's missing preferences. Since reviews are written in natural language, we need to first extract the aspects and opinions from a large amount of reviews automatically. This issue was addressed in our prior work that is capable of identifying the aspect-level opinions from a review [19,20]. Basically, there are three sub-steps: (1) identify all (aspect, opinion) pairs in a review through the Part-of-Speech tagger[1] (which is for extracting frequent nouns and noun phrases as aspect candidates), syntactic dependency parser[2] (which is for identifying opinion words)

---

[1] http://nlp.stanford.edu/software/tagger.shtml
[2] http://nlp.stanford.edu/software/lex-parser.shtml

and WordNet [9] (for grouping synonymous aspects). (2) Quantify the opinion's sentiment strength (also called *polarity*) by applying SentiWordNet [8]. Formally, the aspect-level opinion is classified as negative (-1) or positive (1). (3) Map the opinion to the attribute's static specification in a structured form *(attribute, opinion, specification)*. For example, *("weight", 1, 200g)* indicates that the reviewer expresses *positive* opinion on the product's weight that is 200g, which can further imply that this reviewer's value preference on the attribute "weight" lies in a range that contains 200g.

Step 2: Preference Completion. For each new buyer u, we complete her/his preferences with the help of some like-minded reviewers' preferences,

$$\overrightarrow{\bar{\phi}_{ua}} = \begin{cases} (\overrightarrow{\phi_{ua}} + \sum_{\tilde{u} \in N_u} \bar{s}_{u\tilde{u}} \overrightarrow{\tilde{\phi}_{\tilde{u}a}})/2, & \text{if } \phi_{ua} \text{ is not missing} \\ \sum_{\tilde{u} \in N_u} \bar{s}_{u\tilde{u}} \overrightarrow{\tilde{\phi}_{\tilde{u}a}}, & \text{otherwise} \end{cases}, \tag{1}$$

where $\bar{s}_{u\tilde{u}} = \frac{s_{u\tilde{u}}}{\sum_{\tilde{u} \in N_u} s_{u\tilde{u}}}$ is the normalized similarity between buyer u and reviewer $\tilde{u}$. The similarity is calculated as $s_{u\tilde{u}} = \sum_{a=1}^{k} y_{ua} \times \cos(\overrightarrow{\phi_{ua}}, \overrightarrow{\tilde{\phi}_{\tilde{u}a}})$, where $\overrightarrow{\phi_{ua}}$ and $\overrightarrow{\tilde{\phi}_{\tilde{u}a}}$ are respectively the vector representations of the buyer u and reviewer $\tilde{u}$'s value preferences on the attribute a. For instance, suppose a is the camera's weight which is classified into 8 intervals: $[0, 200)$, $[200, 400)$, ..., and $[1200, 1400)$. If a reviewer's preference on "weight" is in the range $[200, 400)$, her/his corresponding vector representation $\overrightarrow{\tilde{\phi}_{\tilde{u}a}}$ is $[0, 1, 0, 0, 0, 0, 0, 0]$.

Thus, if the buyer's preference on an attribute a is not missing, similar reviewers' preferences regarding this attribute are used to adjust the buyer's preference on it, so as to fuse the reviewers' collective preferences. Otherwise, they are adopted to predict the buyer's preference on that attribute, i.e., which interval(s) her/his value preference lies in. We illustrate the preference completion procedure in Figure 1. Note that we use $|N_u| = 300$ for the size of group of like-minded reviewers in our experiment.

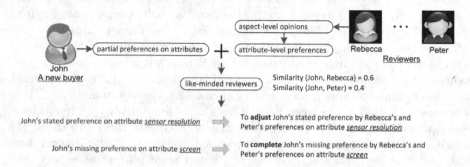

Fig. 1. Illustration of preference completion procedure with an example

Step 3: Ranking and Recommendation. With the enriched user preferences, we can then calculate the matching score between a buyer u and a product p,

$$M_{up} = \frac{1}{k} \sum_{a=1}^{k} match_w(\bar{\phi}_{ua}, x_{pa}) \tag{2}$$

where $match_w(\bar{\phi}_{ua}, x_{pa}) = \langle \overrightarrow{\bar{\phi}_{ua}}, \overrightarrow{x_{pa}} \rangle$ is the inner product of the expanded vectors w.r.t. attribute a. The obtained matching scores can then be used to rank products. The ones with highest scores are recommended to the target buyer.

3 Experimental Results

3.1 Data and Evaluation Metric

We have two data sets, one collected from a previous user study [4] and the other from Amazon review data. In our user study data, there are 57 users ($n = 57$), and 64 digital cameras ($m = 64$) where each product has 8 attributes ($k = 8$). Each user explicitly indicated her/his preferences on the product's attributes. Each user was also asked to check all products and carefully chose one product as her/his favorite product, denoted as $choice(u)$ (i.e., the user's target choice). For each product, we crawled the corresponding reviews from the Amazon website (http://www.amazon.com/). The total number of reviews is 4904 as from 4904 reviewers (since each reviewer posted only one review among those products). In our experiment, for each of these 57 users, we randomly select $2, 4,$ or 6 of her/his attribute preferences to represent the simulated buyer's *partial* preferences (e.g., 2 means that the buyer just stated preferences on 2 attributes).

For each user u, there is a target choice in the product set, i.e., $choice(u)$, which is taken as the ground truth in our evaluation. We use hit ratio of the recommended top-N products to evaluate the recommendation accuracy, $H@N = \frac{1}{n} \sum_{u=1}^{n} \delta(position(choice(u)) \leq N)$, where $choice(u)$ is the target choice of user u, $position(choice(u))$ denotes its ranking position, and n is the number of users. Note that $\delta(z) = 1$ if z is true and $\delta(z) = 0$ otherwise. In our experiment, we use $N = 10$, since a typical user only checks a few products which are placed in top positions [5].

3.2 Baselines

We compare our proposed solution with the following four baseline methods (most of which are from related literatures).

Random. We randomly rank the products for each target user. The result is calculated as $N/m = 10/64 = 0.1563$, denoting the probability that the user's target choice is ranked among top 10.

PopRank. We calculate the popularity of each product among the reviewers. A product is usually considered as *preferred* by a reviewer if the rating is larger

Table 2. The recommendation accuracy (hit ratio) of CompleteRank and other baselines. Note that for PartialRank, HybridRank and CompleteRank, we randomly took 2, 4, 6 attributes (each under five runs) to simulate *partial preferences*.

Method	Given 2	Give 4	Given 6	Given 8
Random	0.1563	0.1563	0.1563	0.1563
PopRank	0.2456	0.2456	0.2456	0.2456
PartialRank	$0.1825_{\pm 0.0457}$	$0.2211_{\pm 0.0342}$	$0.2772_{\pm 0.0288}$	0.3158
HybridRank	$0.2386_{\pm 0.0440}$	$0.2456_{\pm 0.0447}$	$0.2947_{\pm 0.0192}$	0.2982
CompleteRank	$\mathbf{0.2807}_{\pm 0.0372}$	$\mathbf{0.3088}_{\pm 0.0457}$	$\mathbf{0.3158}_{\pm 0.0277}$	**0.3333**

than 3 in 5-star numerical ratings [17]. The popularity of the product p among the reviewers can then be estimated as, $P_p = \frac{1}{\tilde{n}} \sum_{\tilde{u}=1}^{\tilde{n}} \delta(\tilde{r}_{\tilde{u}p} > 3)$. The obtained popularity scores $0 \leq P_p \leq 1$ are used to rank all products. Note that PopRank is not a personalized method since the popularity is user independent.

PartialRank. For each user u and product p, we calculate the matching score between the user's stated (partial) preferences and the product's profile, $M_{up} = \frac{1}{k} \sum_{a=1}^{k} y_{ua} \times match(\phi_{ua}, x_{pa})$, where $match(\phi_{ua}, x_{pa}) = 1$ if the attribute's static specification x_{pa} satisfies the user preference ϕ_{ua}, and $match(\phi_{ua}, x_{pa}) = 0$ otherwise. The obtained matching scores, $0 \leq M_{up} \leq 1$ with $p = 1, \ldots, m$, can then be used to rank the products for user u.

HybridRank. For each attribute a of product p, we can calculate the average opinion score from the reviewers, i.e. $opinion(p, a) \in [-1, 1]$, and the product p's overall opinion score via the method proposed in [1], $O_{up} = \frac{1}{k} \sum_{a=1}^{k} y_{ua} \times opinion(p, a)$. Then, with the preference matching score M_{up} (from PartialRank) and opinion score O_{up}, a hybrid score is produced for the product p, $H_{up} = \frac{1}{2}(M_{up} + O_{up})$. The obtained scores, $-1 \leq H_{up} \leq 1$ with $p = 1, \ldots, m$, are used to rank the products for user u.

3.3   Summary of Experimental Results

The results are shown in Table 2, from which we can have the following observations, (1) our proposed solution CompleteRank is much better than all baselines, which clearly shows the effectiveness of our preference enrichment idea, especially for the buyers with partial preferences; (2) PopRank is better than Random, which demonstrates the usefulness of incorporating online review data for augmenting new-user recommendation; (3) PartialRank performs worse than PopRank given 2 and 4 attribute preferences, but better than PopRank when given 6 and 8 attribute preferences, which shows the effect of taking into account the current user's preferences (especially when they are nearly complete) on increasing recommendation accuracy; and (4) HybridRank performs better than PartialRank in most cases, which shows the usefulness of combining the product's static specifications (by matching to users' preferences) and reviewers' opinions, though it is still worse than our solution.

4   Conclusions and Future Work

In this paper, we propose a preference enrichment approach, CompleteRank, via incorporating the mined reviewers' aspect-level opinions on products' static specifications. The completed preferences of a new user are then used to match the products' profiles, by which the products with highest matching scores are recommended to the target user. Experimental results show that our solution can provide more accurate personalized recommendation than several baseline methods. For future work, we plan to further integrate reviewers' weights (i.e., the importance degrees) placed on attributes (as learnt from our previous work [20]), so that a weighted value preference model might be built for each reviewer. The preference enrichment framework for new buyers could hence be additionally improved by leveraging these heterogeneous types of review data.

Acknowledgements. This research work was supported by Hong Kong Research Grants Council under project ECS/HKBU211912.

References

1. Aciar, S., Zhang, D., Simoff, S., Debenham, J.: Informed recommender: Basing recommendations on consumer product reviews. IEEE Intelligent Systems 22(3), 39–47 (2007)
2. Adomavicius, G., Tuzhilin, A.: Toward the next generation of recommender systems: A survey of the state-of-the-art and possible extensions. IEEE Trans. on Knowl. and Data Eng. 17(6), 734–749 (2005)
3. Butler, J.C., Dyer, J.S., Jia, J., Tomak, K.: Enabling e-transactions with multiattribute preference models. European Journal of Operational Research 186(2), 748–765 (2008)
4. Chen, L., Pu, P.: A cross-cultural user evaluation of product recommender interfaces. In: Proceedings of the 2008 ACM Conference on Recommender Systems, RecSys 2008, pp. 75–82. ACM, New York (2008)
5. Chen, L., Pu, P.: Users' eye gaze pattern in organization-based recommender interfaces. In: Proceedings of the 16th International Conference on Intelligent user Interfaces, IUI 2011, pp. 311–314. ACM, New York (2011)
6. Chen, L., Pu, P.: Critiquing-based recommenders: survey and emerging trends. User Modeling and User-Adapted Interaction 22(1-2), 125–150 (2012)
7. Edwards, W.: Social utilities. Engineering Economist 6, 119–129 (1971)
8. Esuli, A., Sebastiani, F.: Sentiwordnet: A publicly available lexical resource for opinion mining. In: Proceedings of the 5th Conference on Language Resources and Evaluation, LREC 2006, pp. 417–422 (2006)
9. Fellbaum, C.: WordNet: An Electronic Lexical Database. MIT Press, Cambridge (1998)
10. Ha, V., Haddawy, P.: A hybrid approach to reasoning with partially elicited preference models. In: Proceedings of the 15th Conference on Uncertainty in Artificial Intelligence, UAI 1999, pp. 263–270. Morgan Kaufmann Publishers Inc., San Francisco (1999)

11. Koren, Y.: Factorization meets the neighborhood: a multifaceted collaborative filtering model. In: Proceedings of the 14th ACM SIGKDD International Conference on Knowledge Discovery and Data Mining, KDD 2008, pp. 426–434. ACM, New York (2008)
12. Levi, A., Mokryn, O., Diot, C., Taft, N.: Finding a needle in a haystack of reviews: cold start context-based hotel recommender system. In: Proceedings of the 6th ACM Conference on Recommender Systems, RecSys 2012, New York, NY, USA, pp. 115–122 (2012)
13. Liu, Q., Chen, T., Cai, J., Yu, D.: Enlister: baidu's recommender system for the biggest chinese q/a website. In: Proceedings of the Sixth ACM Conference on Recommender Systems, RecSys 2012, pp. 285–288. ACM, New York (2012)
14. Nguyen, T.A., Do, M., Gerevini, A.E., Serina, I., Srivastava, B., Kambhampati, S.: Generating diverse plans to handle unknown and partially known user preferences. Artif. Intell. 190, 1–31 (2012)
15. Pazzani, M.J., Billsus, D.: Content-based recommendation systems. In: Brusilovsky, P., Kobsa, A., Nejdl, W. (eds.) Adaptive Web 2007. LNCS, vol. 4321, pp. 325–341. Springer, Heidelberg (2007)
16. Rendle, S.: Factorization machines with libfm. ACM Trans. Intell. Syst. Technol. 3(3), 57:1–57:22 (2012)
17. Sindhwani, V., Bucak, S.S., Hu, J., Mojsilovic, A.: A family of non-negative matrix factorizations for one-class collaborative filtering. In: The 1st International Workshop on Recommendation-based Industrial Applications held in the 3rd ACM Conference on Recommender Systems, RecSys: RIA 2009 (2009)
18. Viappiani, P., Faltings, B., Pu, P.: Preference-based search using example-critiquing with suggestions. J. Artif. Int. Res. 27(1), 465–503 (2006)
19. Wang, F., Chen, L.: Recommendation based on mining product reviews' preference similarity network. In: The 6th Workshop on Social Network Mining and Analysis, 2012 ACM SIGKDD Conference on Knowledge Discovery and Data Mining, SNA-KDD 2012 (2012)
20. Wang, F., Chen, L.: Recommending inexperienced products via learning from consumer reviews. In: Proceedings of the 2012 IEEE/WIC/ACM International Conferences on Web Intelligence, WI 2012, pp. 596–603. IEEE Computer Society, Washington, DC (2012)
21. Yates, A., Joseph, J., Popescu, A.-M., Cohn, A.D., Sillick, N.: Shopsmart: product recommendations through technical specifications and user reviews. In: Proceedings of the 17th ACM Conference on Information and Knowledge Management, CIKM 2008, pp. 1501–1502. ACM, New York (2008)
22. Zhang, W., Ding, G., Chen, L., Li, C., Zhang, C.: Generating virtual ratings from chinese reviews to augment online recommendations. ACM Trans. Intell. Syst. Technol. 4(1) (2013)

Cross-Domain Collaborative Recommendation in a Cold-Start Context: The Impact of User Profile Size on the Quality of Recommendation

Shaghayegh Sahebi and Peter Brusilovsky

Intelligent Systems Program
University of Pittsburgh
{shs106,peterb}@pitt.edu

Abstract. Most of the research studies on recommender systems are focused on single-domain recommendations. With the growth of multi-domain internet stores such as iTunes, Google Play, and Amazon.com, an opportunity to offer recommendations across different domains become more and more attractive. But there are few research studies on cross-domain recommender systems. In this paper, we study both the cold-start problem and the hypothesis that cross-domain recommendations provide more accuracy using a large volume of user data from a true multi-domain recommender service. Our results indicate that cross-domain collaborative filtering could significantly improve the quality of recommendation in cold start context and the auxiliary profile size plays an important role in it.

1 Introduction

For a new user who has not yet rated a sufficient number of items, collaborative filtering simply has too little information to reliably match him/her to the accumulated community wisdom and generate good recommendations (Cold-start problem [6]). This paper offers an extensive exploration of a specific approach to address a new-user problem: leveraging user rating data from a different domain (or cross-domain recommendation). We believe that the potential value of cross-domain recommendation is rapidly increasing in the modern social Web context. Nowadays the number and the diversity of web systems are increasing so rapidly that a typical internet user has ratings, votes, or bookmarks left in a number of different systems. In this context, cross-domain recommendation approaches could be very useful to offer a fast-start in a new domain by using the knowledge about user tastes and preferences accumulated in the other domains.

While the problem of cross-domain recommendation was discussed in a number of papers, very few papers reported empirical evaluation of reliable size. Worse, a good fraction of papers with empirical results was done in artificial context by subdividing a single-domain dataset and considering that as separate domains e.g. separating the movie domain based on their genres [1–3] or by using different user and items sets [4]. Consequently, there is still no extensive study

S. Carberry et al. (Eds.): UMAP 2013, LNCS 7899, pp. 289–295, 2013.

of cross-domain recommendation in a cold-start context [3]; there is even no reliable evidence that the cross-domain recommendation could fulfill its promise
as a cold-start helper in a real multi-domain context. The study presented in
this paper differs from the past studies in several ways: we use a large dataset
of user ratings in two different domains obtained from a real-world recommendation service; we do not consider any extra information such as content, tags,
or product features, which differ from case to case and might not be available;
and we explore the cross-domain recommendations in cold-start setting with two
different point of views in two studies.

In this paper we report the results of two experimental studies that explore the
value of cross-domain recommendation as a function of the user profile size within
and across the domains. The first study compares the accuracy of cross-domain
and traditional recommendation for the cold start situation of difference severity.
The second study explores whether the size of the user profile in *auxiliary* (old)
domain can also impact the quality of cross-domain recommendation in the *target*
(new) domain.

2   The Cold Start Studies

As explained in the introduction, the focus of this paper is an extensive study
of cross-domain recommendation in the cold-start context. The idea is simple:
if a user is new in a target domain (i.e., has few to none rated items), but
has a rating history in another (auxiliary) domain, we can use his/her auxiliary
domain profile to recommend relevant items, in the target domain. Our quality
study pursues two goals: examining the impact of the user profile size in the
target domain on the comparative quality of "cold-start" recommendation and
examining the impact of the user profile size in the *auxiliary* domain on the
quality of recommendations.

Previous studies of recommendation approaches in cold-start context demonstrated that the comparative quality of alternative approaches frequently depend
on the number of items in the user profile. I.e., a specific cold-start approach
could perform better when the number of items in the target domain user profile is very small, but after the profile grows over a threshold point (cold start
boundary), a regular approach surpasses it. Following that, our first goal is to
find the cold-start boundary for cross-domain recommendations. In other words,
expecting that at some point the quality of single-domain recommendations may
surpass the quality of the cross-domain recommendations. To determine that we
have to compare the quality of cross-domain and in-domain recommendations;
independently for each number of items rated in the target domain.

To achieve the first goal, as a baseline, we use a traditional collaborative filtering approach based on target-domain profiles. As a comparable cross-domain
approach, we use the most natural extension of the baseline approach to the
cross-domain context: collaborative filtering based on concatenated profiles in
auxiliary and target domains. We predict target user ratings on the target domain ratings by traditional collaborative filtering approach.

While the study introduced above represent a commonly accepted approach to study recommendation quality in a cold-start approach, it explores only one side of the phenomenon, i.e., the impact of the user profile size in the target domain on the quality of cross-domain recommendations. We believe, however, that the cold-start issue should be explored in respect to each of the domains. Given that the number of items rated in the target domain can impact the quality of recommendation, it is natural to expect that the number of items rated in the auxiliary domain have a similar impact. Thus, the second goal of our study is to discover the impact of the auxiliary-domain profile sized on the comparative recommendation quality of the cross-domain approach. To achieve this goal we run another study, which explores the quality of cross-domain recommendation as a function of cross-domain (auxiliary) profile size.

3   The Dataset and Experimental Setup

In this study we used an anonymized dataset obtained from an online Russian recommender service Imhonet (www.imhonet.com). Imhonet allows users to rate and review a range of items from books and movies to mobile phones and architectural monuments. For our study, we used an anonymized Imhonet dataset that includes two richest sets of ratings - on books and movies. Each rating record in the dataset includes a user ID, an item ID, and a rating value between 0 (not rated) and 10. In total, the dataset includes about 16 million movie rating records on about 50,000 movies and more than 11.5 million book ratings records on about 195,000 available books in the dataset.

If we look at the distribution of movie and book ratings in this dataset we can see that based on imhonet's request, many users rated at least 20 books and movies. The availability of many users who had at least 20 rated items in each of the used domain caused us to select this number as a basis of a smaller, but richer dataset that we used in our studies. To produce this dataset, we selected all ratings of users who had at least 20 ratings on books and 20 ratings on movies. The resulting dataset contains 2,363,394 movie ratings of 6,089 users on 12,621 movies and 1,138,401 book ratings of the same users on 17,907 books. For more detailed information about the dataset please refer to [5].

We pick 80% of the users randomly as training users and the rest as target users. We build 19 cold-start profiles for each target user in the movies domain: starting from having one movie in the profile to having 19 movies in the profile in a time-based order. In other words, the size-one cold-start profile of the target user has the first movie he/she has rated and the size-19 cold-start profile of this user has the first 19 movies he/she has rated. We run the CF algorithm 19 times on this data: once for each of the cold-start profiles.

To compare the results of single-domain recommendations with cross-domain recommendations, for each target user we combine all of his/her book ratings with the cold-start movie profiles and for each training user, we combine all of his/her books and movies as a whole profile. To see the effects of having movies on predicting books, we set up the same experiment having 19 cold-start profiles

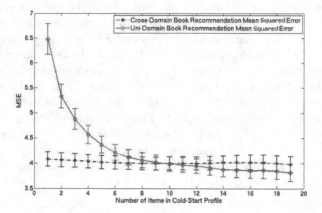

Fig. 1. MSE of Cross vs. Single -Domain Book Recommendations with 95% CI on Varying Cold-Start Profiles

for the book domain and the movie ratings as an auxiliary domain. We use k-NN algorithm with $K = 20$ for rating predictions in collaborative filtering.

4   Experimental Results

4.1   Study I: Impact of User Profile Size in Target Domain

Our first study was conducted to achieve the first goal described in section 2. The results for recommending books based on cold-start book ratings of users and cross-domain profiles of users are shown in Figure 1. This Figure shows Mean Squared Error (MSE) of recommendations including a 95% confidence interval. MSE is a measure that shows how much our predicted ratings for users are different from users' actual ratings. As we can see in this picture, while the user has five or fewer book ratings, the cross-domain recommendations achieve significantly smaller MSE than the single-domain recommendations. After adding the 6th book, the single-domain MSE decreases to the point when it becomes statistically comparable with cross-domain MSEs. This trend continues once more book ratings are being added to the cold-start book profile: the single-domain MSEs is gradually surpassing cross-domain MSEs, although not becoming better significantly within the explored window size. In other words, once the target profile becomes reasonably large (12 ratings or more) the cross-domain ratings introduces more noise than value from the prospect of rating prediction. Note it doesn't mean that the cross-domain approach becomes useless at that point. It has long been argued that even with the lower rating prediction quality, the cross-domain approach can offer other values such as novelty and diversity. Further studies are required to evaluate the comparative quality of two approaches from these prospects.

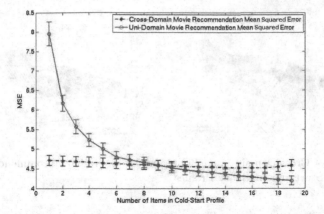

Fig. 2. MSE of Cross vs. Single -Domain Movie Recommendations with 95% CI on Varying Cold-Start Profiles

The result of a reverse study with movies as target (cold-start) domain and books as auxiliary domain are shown in Figure. 2. As the data shows, the overall trend is similar to book recommendations: for the users who have one to five books in the cold-start profile, cross-domain recommendations work better than cold-start recommendations. In this case, however, single-domain recommendations gets more advantage as the cold-start profile size increases. Starting from 16 movies in the cold-start profiles, these recommendations achieve reliably better MSE than cross-domain recommendations.

4.2   Study II: Impact of Auxiliary Domain Ratings' Volume

To explore the behavior of cross-domain recommendation in cold-start context more extensively and to achieve our second goal, we examined the effect of the auxiliary profile size on mean squared error of cold-start recommendations.

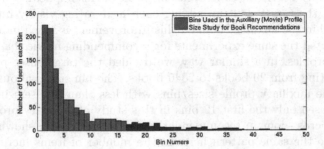

Fig. 3. Histogram of Number of Users in each Bin (Number of Movies in Auxiliary Profile) for Book Cross-Domain Recommendations

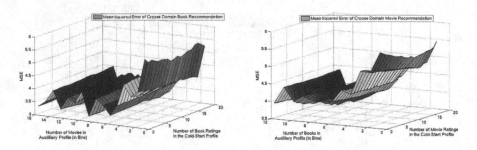

Fig. 4. MSE of Cross-Domain (left) Book and Movie (right) Recommendations with Varying Cold-Start and Auxiliary Profiles

To do that in book recommendations, we divided the target user profiles into 100 bins starting from having 20 movies in the auxiliary profile to about 3400 movies in the profile. Each bin has a gap of about 35 movies. Histogram of number of users in each bin is shown in Figure. 3. We do not display the bins with numbers over 50 to show a clearer picture. As we can see, the number of users decreases as the number of movies rated in the profile increases. To achieve more reliable results, we ignored the auxiliary profile sizes/bins with less than 30 users. The red bars in Figure. 3 indicate utilized bins. As a result, we used only the first 16 bins in study of auxiliary profile size on error rate of cross-domain recommendations. The results are shown in Figure 4. The results reveal that the number of ratings in the auxiliary profile has a strong impact on the accuracy of cross-domain recommendations. The accuracy is the lowest (MSE highest) for the users in the first bin with the number of ratings between 20 and 55. The accuracy improves considerably for the users in the second bin and then in the third bin. This tendency continues further although once the number of users in a bin falls below 100, the accuracy increase become less monotonic due to the small bin size. Overall, the data shows that the impact of the user profile size in the auxiliary domain is qualitatively similar to the impact of the profile size in the target domain: the more ratings are available in the auxiliary profile (i.e., the more information we have about user preferences), the better is the accuracy of recommendations. At the same time, the scale of this impact is very different. While within the target domain, adding each next rating visibly improves the accuracy, within the auxiliary domain this improvement is much more slow.

We conducted the same experiments for recommending movies based on auxiliary book profiles. In a similar way, we divided the target user profiles into 100 bins starting from 20 books to 2840 books. The bin size is about 23 books. We ignore the auxiliary profile sizes/bins with less than 30 users in them. As a result, we used only the first 12 bins in this study of auxiliary profile size on error rate of cross-domain recommendations. The results are shown in Figure 4. We can see the same pattern here: as the number of items increases in the auxiliary profile, accuracy of recommendation increases (MSE decreases).

5   Conclusion

In this paper we reported an extensive exploration of cross-domain recommendation in a cold start context with a relatively large number of movie and book ratings. Our studies demonstrated that even a simple cross-domain approach can increase the quality of recommendation when the number of in-domain rated items is small. Also, the added value of the cross-domain recommendation decreases quite rapidly. Finally, based on our study of impact of the auxiliary user profile size on the quality of recommendations, with the increase of the auxiliary profile size, cross-domain approach was able to produce better recommendations. This result indicates that the recommendation power of a cross-domain approach is not free: it is fueled by a considerable number of user ratings in a an auxiliary domain. For users with too few auxiliary domain ratings, cross-domain recommendation performs much worse than for the users with size-able profiles.

In future work, we plan to explore cross-domain recommendation for other domain pairs. In addition, the study part of this paper explored a relatively simple cross-domain approach and a traditional collaborative filtering approach. A smarter fusion of information from auxiliary and target domains could result in better cross-domain recommendations.

Acknowledgement. We thank imhonet.ru for providing us the dataset.

References

1. Berkovsky, S., Kuflik, T., Ricci, F.: Cross-domain mediation in collaborative filtering. In: Conati, C., McCoy, K., Paliouras, G. (eds.) UM 2007. LNCS (LNAI), vol. 4511, pp. 355–359. Springer, Heidelberg (2007)
2. Berkovsky, S., Kuflik, T., Ricci, F.: Mediation of user models for enhanced personalization in recommender systems. User Modeling and User-Adapted Interaction, UMUAI 2008 18(3) (August 2008)
3. Cremonesi, P., Tripodi, A., Turrin, R.: Cross-domain recommender systems. In: 2011 IEEE 11th International Conference on Data Mining Data Mining Workshops (ICDMW), pp. 496–503 (December 2011)
4. Pan, W., Xiang, E.W., Liu, N.N., Yang, Q.: Transfer learning in collaborative filtering for sparsity reduction. In: Artificial Intelligence, AAAI 2010 (2010)
5. Sahebi, S., Cohen, W.: Community-based recommendations: a solution to the cold start problem. In: RSWEB, in Conjunction with ACM RecSys 2011 (2011)
6. Schein, A.I., Popescul, A., Ungar, L.H., Pennock, D.M.: Methods and metrics for cold-start recommendations. In: Special Interest Group in Information Retrieval, SIGIR 2002, New York, NY, USA (2002)

Personalized Access to Scientific Publications: from Recommendation to Explanation

Dario De Nart, Felice Ferrara, and Carlo Tasso

Artificial Intelligence Lab
Department of Mathematics and Computer Science
University of Udine, Italy
{dario.denart,felice.ferrara,carlo.tasso}@uniud.it

Abstract. Several recommender systems have been proposed in the literature for adaptively suggesting useful references to researchers with different interests. However, in order to access the knowledge contained in the recommended papers, the users need to read the publications for identifying the potentially interesting concepts. In this work we propose to overcome this limitation by utilizing a more semantic approach where concepts are extracted from the papers for generating and explaining the recommendations. By showing the concepts used to find the recommended articles, users can have a preliminary idea about the filtered publications, can understand the reasons why the papers were suggested and they can also provide new feedback about the relevance of the concepts utilized for generating the recommendations.

1 Introduction

Reading scientific literature is a critical step for conceiving and developing scientific projects, but finding appropriate literature for scientific researches is still an expensive task. Recommender systems have been also utilized to support researchers since these tools can filter information according to the personal interests of the users. However, by just filtering a list of scientific papers, current systems provide only a basic support to the user (a list of potentially relevant papers), whereas it would be much more useful to highlight in the recommended paper concepts and knowledge relevant for the user. As a consequence, such approach still leaves a lot of work to the user who both (i) has to read the paper in order to identify the main concepts in the recommended paper and (ii) cannot understand why the paper is actually recommended to him. On the other hand, we claim that more semantic approaches can be integrated for overcoming these drawbacks and, in particular, in this paper we use keyphrases (KP) for: modeling the user interests, computing the utility of a resource for a user, explaining the recommendations, and collecting feedback from users in a quite unobtrusive way.

A keyphrase is a short phrase (typically constituted by one to three/four words) that indicates one of the main ideas/concepts included in a document. A keyphrase list is a short list of keyphrases that reflects the content of a single

S. Carberry et al. (Eds.): UMAP 2013, LNCS 7899, pp. 296–301, 2013.

document, capturing the main topics discussed and providing a brief summary of its content. In this work, a user profile is built by exploiting the keyphrase lists extracted from the papers which are relevant to a specific user. Then, in order to compute the relevance of a new article, the user profile is matched with the keyphrase list extracted from that article. More interestingly, the explicit representation of the scientific papers is used for explaining why the system recommended the documents by showing: (i) the keyphrases which are both in the user model and in the paper and (ii) other keyphrases found in the document which are not yet stored in the user model but can support the user in understanding/evaluating the new paper. The explanation of recommendations by means of keyphrases produces several benefits. First of all, the user satisfaction can be increased since explanations save his time: the user is not forced to read the entire document in order to catch the main contents of the paper. The trust of the users in the system can be increased as well since, by showing the recommended concepts, the user can better understand the criteria utilized by the system for computing the recommendations. Finally, by showing the concepts available in the user model as well as in the recommended papers we provide a simple way to the user for refining his interests: the user can decide to add a new concept to his profile or decrease (or even cancel) the relevance of a concept.

The paper is organized as follows: Section 2 reviews related work, the proposed approach is illustrated in Section 3, the evaluation performed so far is described in Section 4, and Section 5 concludes the paper.

2 Related Work

Several recent works focused on filtering relevant publications from huge collections of papers by exploiting both collaborative filtering approaches [3] and content-based mechanisms [4]. However, as shown in [1], improving the accuracy of the recommendation is not the only goal of researchers who work on scientific paper recommendation. In fact, the access to the knowledge stored in the recommended papers can be simplified by providing new services for accessing recommendations, new navigational interfaces, and new visualizations techniques. By following this research directions, in this paper, we propose a mechanism where the recommendations of scientific papers are explained to the users by showing the main concepts which are in the recommended publications. There is actually a growing interest on explanation of recommendations since, as showed by Zanker, explanations are essential to increase the users satisfaction [7]. The impact of explanations is also shown in [5], where the authors also provide a taxonomy of explanations by identifying three explanation styles: (i) the *human style* which provides explanations by showing similar users, (ii) the *item style* where similar items are reported as explanation (iii), and the *feature style* where the main features of the recommended items are shown. In our work, relevant concepts are extracted from scientific publications for both generating the recommendations and providing feature style explanations. The idea of representing the interests of researchers as concepts extracted from publications was also proposed in [2], where the authors train a vector space classifier in order to associate terms (i.e. unigrams) to the concepts of the ACM Computing Classification System (CCS). The hierarchical organization of the CCS is used to represent user interests and documents as trees of concepts which can be matched for producing recommendations. Our approach, on the other hand, does not need a training phase since we adopt more sophisticated NLP techniques for identifying relevant concepts (i.e. keyphrases constituted by n-grams) included in the papers. Since n-grams provide a more significant and detailed description of the ideas reported in publications, we use them in order to generate the explanation.

3   Recommendation and Explanation by Using Keyphrases

In order to support our claims we developed a recommender system, named *Recommender and Explanation System (RES)*, which is aimed at supporting researchers by adaptively filtering the scientific publications stored in a database called *SPC* (Scientific Paper Collection). Each paper uploaded in the SPC is processed by using the Dikpe KP extraction algorithm (described in [6]) in order to represent each paper as a set of KPs. Given a paper, Dikpe extracts from it a list of keyphrases where each KP has a weight (called *Keyphraseness*) that summarizes the several lexical and statistical indicators exploited in the extraction process. Higher is the Keyphraseness, more relevant is the KP.

Keyphrases are used to represent documents as well as to model user interests. More specifically, user models and documents are represented by a network structure called *Context Graph (CG)*. For each document stored in the SPC, a CG is built by processing its KP list. User profiles, on the other hand, are obtained by collapsing the CGs built for the documents marked as interesting by the user (as shown in Figure 1) and, possibly, enriched with other KPs gathered via relevance feedback.

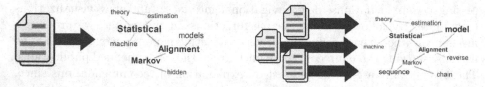

Fig. 1. Document content model and user profile construction

CGs are built by taking into account each single term belonging to each KP: each term is represented by a node of the graph and if two terms belong to the same KP their corresponding nodes are connected by an arc. Both nodes and arcs are assigned a weight which is the normalized sum of the Keyphraseness values associated to each KP containing the corresponding terms (such values are computed by the KP Extraction module). Heavy KPs will generate heavy nodes and arcs; term occurring in several KPs will generate heavy nodes and heavy arcs denoting frequent associations. Terms that never appear together in a KP won't have any direct link, but, if used together in the same context, may be connected indirectly, through other nodes, allowing the system to infer implicit KPs: for example the KPs "Markov alignment" and "hidden alignment" produce arcs that make possible the matching of the "hidden Markov alignment" KP. Finally, terms and phrases that are not used in the same context, won't be connected, creating isolated groups in the CG. Breaking KPs and then organizing terms in such a structure allows us to build, for each term, a meaningful context of interest, making it possible to disambiguate polysemic words in a better way than by matching phrases. Recommendations are provided to the users in three steps, as shown in Figure 2: Matching/Scoring, Ranking, and Presentation.

Fig. 2. The three steps of the recommendation process

In the first step every document in the SPC is matched against the user model by calculating the following parameters: *Coverage (C)*, *Relevance (R)* and *Similarity (S)*. C is the count of shared nodes between user and document CG, divided by the number of nodes in the document CG; by default, documents under a 10% coverage threshold are discarded, since the shared nodes are not enough for a meaningful ranking. R is the average TF-IDF measure of shared terms. S is the sum of the weights of shared arcs divided by the sum of the weights of all arcs occurring between shared nodes in the user CG. This last parameter is intended to assess the overlap between the two CGs and to measure how relevant are the shared arcs. In this way, each document is considered a point in a 3-dimensional space where each dimension corresponds to one of the three above parameters. In the Ranking phase, the 3-dimensional space is subdivided into several subspaces according to the value ranges of the three parameters, identifying in such a way different regions in terms of potential interest for the user. High values for all three parameters identify an excellent potential interest, while values lower than specific thresholds decrease the potential interest. Five subspaces are identified from *excellent* to *discarded* and each document is ranked according to where its three-dimensional representation is located. Being the system an experimental testbed, such threshold values have been manually tuned. Finally, in the Presentation step, documents are sorted by descending ranking order and the top ones are suggested to the user. Recommendations are presented as a ranked list of documents where the top items are those that better match the user profile. For each document two keyphrase (KP) lists are presented to the user: (i) KPs

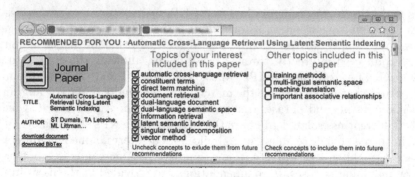

Fig. 3. Recommendation screenshot

appearing in both the user profile and in the document and (ii) relevant KPs present in the document but not in the user profile. This information, shown in Figure 3, serves two goals: it briefly explains why a document was recommended by highlighting its main concepts and, secondly, it offers the user a way to provide relevance feedback on the concepts extracted from each article.

4   Evaluation

In the first development stage of the system, we have performed a limited number of formative tests, mainly aimed at exploring different system tunings. A set of over 300 scientific papers dealing with Recommender Systems and Adaptive Personalization was collected and classified according to 16 topics. Later, 200 uncategorized documents dealing with several random ICT topics were added in order to create noise in the data and the whole set was processed, generating a test SPC. 250 user profiles were automatically generated for each one of the 16 topics using groups of 2, 4, 6, and 10 seed documents respectively; then, for each user profile, RES and a baseline reference system (ad-hoc developed) based upon the well-known and established TF-IDF metric, produced the 10 top-recommended items. For each recommendation, every recommended item dealing with the same topic as the seed document was considered a good recommendation. We have defined the *accuracy* as the number of good recommendations over the total recommended items, and averaging the accuracy values. Results gathered so far are very promising since RES outperformed the baseline mechanism when the user profile was built by using 2 seed documents (RES accuracy=0.57, baseline accuracy=0.42), 4 seed documents (RES accuracy=0.66, baseline accuracy=0.53), 6 seed documents (RES accuracy=0.70, baseline accuracy=0.55), and 10 seed documents (RES accuracy=0.72, baseline accuracy=0.60). Future evaluations will address the quality and the impact of the produced explanations.

5   Conclusion

By just filtering collection of papers, state-of-the-art recommender systems still leave a heavy work to researchers who have to spend efforts and time for accessing the knowledge contained in scientific publications. This issue is faced in this paper, where we propose a mechanism where concepts are automatically extracted from papers in order to generate and explain recommendations.

According to our first experiments the extraction of concepts can produce accurate recommendations and, at the moment, we are evaluating the effectiveness of the explanations in an on-line evaluation scenario, exploiting the system to filter CiteSeer query results. Future works will also use domain ontologies for identifying concepts/explanations by following the approach described in [6]. Finally, we will also address the possible advantages of utilizing our ideas in other scenarios such as news recommendations.

References

1. Sciencerec track at recsys challenge (2012),
   http://2012.recsyschallenge.com/tracks/sciencerec/
2. Chandrasekaran, K., Gauch, S., Lakkaraju, P., Luong, H.P.: Concept-based document recommendations for citeSeer authors. In: Nejdl, W., Kay, J., Pu, P., Herder, E. (eds.) AH 2008. LNCS, vol. 5149, pp. 83–92. Springer, Heidelberg (2008)
3. Ferrara, F., Tasso, C.: Extracting and exploiting topics of interests from social tagging systems. In: Bouchachia, A. (ed.) ICAIS 2011. LNCS, vol. 6943, pp. 285–296. Springer, Heidelberg (2011)
4. Govindaraju, V., Ramanathan, K.: Similar document search and recommendation. Journal of Emerging Technologies in Web Intelligence 4(1), 84–93 (2012)
5. Papadimitriou, A., Symeonidis, P., Manolopoulos, Y.: A generalized taxonomy of explanations styles for traditional and social recommender systems. Data Mining and Knowledge Discovery 24(3), 555–583 (2012)
6. Pudota, N., Dattolo, A., Baruzzo, A., Ferrara, F., Tasso, C.: Automatic keyphrase extraction and ontology mining for content-based tag recommendation. International Journal of Intelligent Systems, Special Issue: New Trends for Ontology-Based Knowledge Discovery 25, 1158–1186 (2010)
7. Zanker, M.: The influence of knowledgeable explanations on users' perception of a recommender system. In: Proceedings of the Sixth ACM Conference on Recommender Systems, pp. 269–272. ACM, New York (2012)

PoliSpell: An Adaptive Spellchecker and Predictor for People with Dyslexia

Alberto Quattrini Li, Licia Sbattella, and Roberto Tedesco

Dipartimento di Elettronica e Informazione,
Politecnico di Milano
{alberto.quattrini,licia.sbattella,roberto.tedesco}@polimi.it

Abstract. People with dyslexia often face huge writing difficulties. Spellcheckers/predictors can help, but the current systems are not appropriate for them, because of the assumptions behind the models and because of heavy-to-use interfaces. This paper presents a system for spellchecking/predicting words, which can adapt both its model and its interface according to the individual behavior. The model takes into account typical errors made by people with dyslexia, such as boundary errors, and the context for correcting real-word errors. The interface aims at reducing interaction with the user. The model and the interface are easily adaptable to general use.

Keywords: spellchecker, predictor, dyslexia, adaptive system.

1 Introduction

It is a well-known fact that spellcheckers/predictors can ease writing for people with dyslexia, thus improving their learning activities [1]. However, most of the spellcheckers assume that wrong words contain just few errors (the literature claims that 80% to 95% of spelling errors contain one error), in terms of the four classical edit operations (i.e., addition, deletion, transposition, substitution), and that errors are isolated (i.e., each error involves just one word) [2].

Such an assumption does not hold for people with dyslexia, however, as they tend to make many errors, often not isolated (for example, splitting or merging words). Authors of [3] quantify errors of English people with dyslexia, in Web-based applications, and they found that 39% of all the errors were multi-errors and 8% were word boundary errors.

Furthermore, the user interface of the common word processors and spellcheckers is not tailored to people with dyslexia. For example, usually, spellcheckers notify an error and show a possible list of corrections/predictions; this mode heavily interferes with the writing process of people with dyslexia, who have problem in reading such lists [4].

The impact of dyslexia on reading and writing skills greatly varies among individuals [5], showing considerable heterogeneity in errors they make and in reading/writing difficulties. Another factor affecting error frequency and the severity

S. Carberry et al. (Eds.): UMAP 2013, LNCS 7899, pp. 302–309, 2013.

of reading/writing difficulties is language [6,7]; for example, in Italian – a language with near-transparent grapheme-phoneme correspondence – people with dyslexia produce less errors than writing in opaque languages, like English [8].

Thus, a writer with dyslexia needs a spellchecker/predictor with a simple user interface, and able to adapt to her/his particular errors and difficulties. In literature, however, despite the fact that several works can be found about adaptive interfaces [9,10,11], none of them, to our knowledge, is related to dyslexia. Moreover, the interface and the model for correcting/predicting words are strictly related: if the spellchecker interface adapts to the user, but model does not, or vice versa, then all the benefits of having an adaptive system would be lost.

In this paper, we propose a spellchecker/predictor that adapts both corrections/predictions and interface to the specific user. The spellchecker/predictor is part of CATS [12], an ongoing research project aimed at designing and developing technological solutions for supporting students with special needs[1].

2   Related Work

Spellchecking involves: (a) non-word error detection, (b) isolated non-word error correction, and (c) context-dependent, real-word error correction [2]. For simple non-word detection, as in (a), a dictionary, which allows to check whether a word does exist or not, is enough. For non-word error correction, as in (b), it is crucial to have a list of (word, typo) pairs. Finally for correcting real-word errors, as in (c), a large corpus of error-free sentences is needed, because error correction depends on the context containing the wrong word. Models trained using such corpora are usually *static*: once trained, they do not change while the user uses the system. Example of such systems are [13], which builds a large list of so-called *confusion sets* (i.e., a list of confusable words) for spellchecking real-word errors, and [14], which collects data from the web to build a big corpus.

This approach cannot adapt the correction to the current user's error pattern (e.g., [15]). But, especially in the case of people with dyslexia, every person is different [5] and spellcheckers, to be really effective, should be able to adapt to their behavior. For example, suppose that a person makes several mistakes about the same word. Common spellcheckers propose a list of corrections; if that person always chooses the fourth choice, still the list of suggested words would not change. Similarly, prediction systems heavily rely on static models [16].

Only few works tried to model the user. The system proposed in [17] uses some weighted production rules, tailored to a specific user. The problem is that it cannot cope with unseen errors, as what dynamically change are the weights of the production rules; furthermore, the system does not consider the context. The system described in [18] adapts the errors on the basis of the context, but does not model the user and no adaptive user interface is available.

While most of the works concentrate on the model for correcting/predicting words, human-computer interaction received comparatively little attention.

---

[1] Campus Tools for Students (CATS) is funded by the Italian Ministry of Education, University and Research (MIUR).

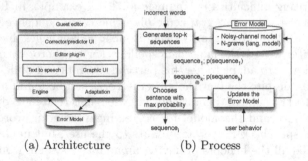

(a) Architecture   (b) Process

Fig. 1. PoliSpell: architecture and correction/prediction process

Several works researched on adaptive interfaces in different areas, e.g., information retrieval, recommender systems [9,10], ubiquitous web access [11], and in general focused on concepts, methods, and tools to cope with designing an interface that could be suitable for everybody [19]. However, to the best of our knowledge, nothing is available regarding adaptive interfaces for spellchecking/prediction. This aspect is considerably important for people with dyslexia, because they have difficulty in reading; thus, the interface should keep the interactions with the user at a minimum, avoiding to add further complexity to the writing process.

Most of the spellcheckers/predictors interfaces do not fulfill such a requirement. Indeed, common word processors have two modes of spellchecking: *automatic* and *manual*. The automatic mode is bothersome, because the user may not notice the correction, writing an unintended word; moreover, the user needs to explicitly undo undesired corrections. The manual mode is visually heavy, because the user has to select each wrong word and choose the correction from a list (or open a window and go through a specific error correction mode).

Common to such modes, there is no automatic mechanism that updates the list of suggested corrections (usually, it is possible to manually add some autocorrections, or non-existing words, to the dictionary). Authors of [20] found out that people with dyslexia were able to correct 83.5% of their errors, if the correct suggestion was the first one in the list, 71.5% if the correct word was not the first, and dropping to 24.7% when no choice was provided.

3   Adaptive System

Fig. 1(a) depicts the architecture of PoliSpell, the system we propose. Engine and Adaptation generate corrections and adjust the Error Model, respectively. The Corrector/predictor UI controls the text-to-speech (a common mean to improve reading comprehension of people with dyslexia [21]) and the Graphic UI modules, which allow users to interact with the corrector/predictor; the module is connected to the Guest editor, by means of the Editor plug-in module.

3.1   Correction/Prediction Engine

Fig. 1(b) shows how the process of correction/prediction evolves and how the model is updated. The model for correcting sentences and predicting words consists of a series of HMMs, whose probabilities derive from an *error model*, which contains a corpus-based language model, and a noisy-channel-inspired model. The language model has been trained on several error-free corpora. The noisy-channel model has been trained on corpora annotated with error corrections, from Facebook/Twitter posts; such model also incorporates typical errors types, whose information were gathered from experts in the field of dyslexia.

A correction/prediction w has a probability $P(x|w)P(w)$, where x is the input sequence, $P(x|w)$ is the noisy-channel, and $P(w)$ is the language model. Then, suggestions are ordered by descending probability and first n are shown.

When the system is deployed, there is a common model for every users; preliminary static experiments on texts written by persons with dyslexia show the good performance of such basic model. However, since each person makes different mistakes, the system collects the user behavior, by tracking the choices made over the corrections/predictions presented by our system. With such information, the system adapts corrections and predictions performing an online-learning procedure that updates the noisy-channel model (which accounts for the error patterns) and the language model (which regards the writing style).

3.2   Interface

There are several interface parameters that can be tuned, depending on the user behavior on the system. In particular, one of the key parameter for the spellchecker/predictor is the selection of the automatic/manual mode for correction and prediction. When the predictor is in *automatic* mode, the system uses text-to-speech to say the first word given by the model (see Fig. 2). The user can choose that word by pressing a particular key on the keyboard (the ACCEPT button). If the first suggestion is not correct, the user can open a list of suggestions, by means of the CORRECT button. Instead, when the predictor is in *manual* mode, the system shows a list of suggested predictions and the user can listen to the suggested words and choose the one that fits.

When in automatic mode, it is possible to switch to the manual mode: manually, by pressing the corresponding MANUAL button, or in an adaptive way if the first word is not selected for several times. Vice versa, when in manual mode, if the error rate drops, then the system switches back to automatic mode. The adaptation mechanism considers the number of not-accepted (i.e., ACCEPT button not pressed) or edited automatic predictions.

Considering the predictor in manual mode, the value that measures if a switch between the modes should happen, is the following:

$$H_{m_i} = \#\text{accepted\_first\_suggestion}/\#\text{predictions} \tag{1}$$

where #accepted_first_suggestion is the number of first-suggestions accepted by the user, while #predictions is the number of predictions made by the system

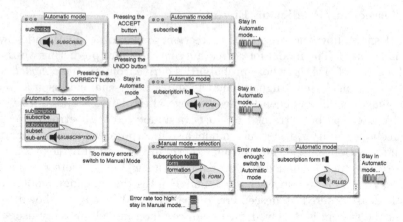

Fig. 2. Adaptation of predictor UI (MANUAL transitions not shown)

(both values calculated starting from the i-th entrance in the manual mode). H_{m_i} represents the current precision of the system during the i-th time interval in which the system is in manual mode. After each prediction, H_{m_i} is updated and the following rule is applied: if $H_{m_i} > H_{(m \to a)_i}$, where $H_{(m \to a)_i}$ is the threshold to switch from manual to automatic mode in the i-th time interval, then the system switches to automatic as the predictor is reliable enough.

Similarly, considering the system in automatic mode, that measure is:

$$H_{a_i} = 1 - \#\text{modified\_characters}/\#\text{first\_suggestion\_characters} \qquad (2)$$

where #modified_characters is the number of characters of the first suggestions generated by the system, that the user edited, while #first_suggestion_characters is the total number of characters of the first suggestions (both values calculated starting from the i-th entrance in the automatic mode). H_{a_i} represents the current precision of the system during the i-th time interval in which the system is in automatic mode. After each prediction, H_{a_i} is updated and the following rule is applied: if $H_{a_i} < H_{(a \to m)_i}$, where $H_{(a \to m)_i}$ is the threshold to switch from automatic to manual mode in the i-th time interval, then the system switches to manual mode as the predictor performed poorly.

Trying to maximize automatic mode time, such thresholds adapt according to the time spent (measured as number of characters typed) in a mode at time interval i, compared to the time spent in that mode at $i - 1$. If time spent in automatic mode decreases, the last $m \to a$ switch happened too early; $H_{(m \to a)_{i+1}}$ is incremented (i.e., next switch will require a higher precision):

$$H_{(m \to a)_{i+1}} = \begin{cases} s(H_{(m \to a)_i} + k_{(m \to a)}); & t_{a_i} < t_{a_{i-1}} \\ s(H_{(m \to a)_i} - k_{(m \to a)}); & \text{otherwise} \end{cases} \qquad (3)$$

where t_{a_i} and $t_{a_{i-1}}$ are, respectively, the times spent in automatic mode at time interval i and $i-1$, $k_{(m \to a)}$ is a predefined constant (which is static and represents

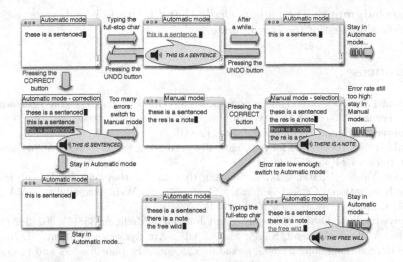

Fig. 3. Adaptation of correction UI (MANUAL transitions not shown)

the threshold adaptation rate), and the logistic function $s(x) = 1/(1 + exp(-x))$ ensures that $0 \leq H_{(m \to a)_{i+1}} \leq 1$; finally, $H_{(m \to a)_0}$ is initialized to $h_{(m \to a)_0}$, which is a predefined constant. Values $k_{(m \to a)}$ and $h_{(m \to a)_0}$ are optimally set by simulating errors and corrections given by our model.

If time spent in manual mode decreases, the last $a \to m$ switch happened too early; $H_{(a \to m)_{i+1}}$ is decremented (i.e., next switch will require a lower precision):

$$H_{(a \to m)_{i+1}} = \begin{cases} s(H_{(a \to m)_i} - k_{(a \to m)}); & t_{m_i} < t_{m_{i-1}} \\ s(H_{(a \to m)_i} + k_{(a \to m)}); & \text{otherwise} \end{cases} \quad (4)$$

where t_{m_i} and $t_{m_{i-1}}$ are the times spent in manual mode at time interval i and $i - 1$, respectively, and $H_{(a \to m)_0}$ is initialized to $h_{(a \to m)_0}$, which is a constant. The constants are computed in the same way as shown above.

The corrector works in a similar way, as shown in Fig. 3. Notice however that, unlike prediction, in automatic mode the correction does not require a confirmation (UNDO is available in both cases); we chose such approach because correction is not as error prone as prediction.

4 Conclusions

In this paper we have presented an adaptive spellchecking/predicting system, specifically tailored for people with dyslexia, which attempts to enhance their writing skills. Our approach allows the system to adapt to users' needs, according to her/his behavior, in terms of the model and as user interface. The next step of this work will be the evaluation of the system within a group of students with dyslexia. The system can be easily adapted to other contexts, training the model with a different document set.

Acknowledgment. The authors gladly thank Laura Loi for her contribution to the development of the user interface.

References

1. Rooms, M.: Information and communication technology and dyslexia. In: Townend, J., Turner, M. (eds.) Dyslexia in Practice: A Guide for Teachers, pp. 263–272. Kluwer Academic/Plenum Publishers (2000)
2. Kukich, K.: Techniques for automatically correcting words in text. ACM Computing Surveys 24(4), 377–439 (1992)
3. Baeza-Yates, R., Rello, L.: Estimating dyslexia in the web. In: Proceedings of the International Cross-Disciplinary Conference on Web Accessibility, W4A 2011, vol. 8, pp. 1–4. ACM, New York (2011)
4. Shaywitz, S.E.: Dyslexia. New England Journal of Medicine 338(5), 307–312 (1998)
5. Ellis, A.W., McDougall, S.J.P., Monk, A.F.: Are dyslexics different? II. Individual differences among dyslexics, reading age controls, poor readers and precocious readers. Dyslexia 2(1), 59–68 (1996)
6. Paulesu, E., Démonet, J.F., Fazio, F., McCrory, E., Chanoine, V., Brunswick, N., Cappa, S.F., Cossu, G., Habib, M., Frith, C.D., Frith, U.: Dyslexia: Cultural diversity and biological unity. Science 291(5511), 2165–2167 (2001)
7. Goulandris, N., Snowling, M.: Dyslexia in different languages: cross-linguistic comparisons. Dyslexia Series (Whurr) Series. Whurr Publishers (2003)
8. Zoccolotti, P., De Luca, M., Di Pace, E., Judica, A., Orlandi, M., Spinelli, D.: Markers of developmental surface dyslexia in a language (Italian) with high grapheme phoneme correspondence. Applied Psycholinguistics 20, 191–216
9. Brusilovsky, P.: Adaptive hypermedia. User Modeling and User-Adapted Interaction 11, 87–110 (2001)
10. Langley, P.: Machine learning for adaptive user interfaces. In: Brewka, G., Habel, C., Nebel, B. (eds.) KI 1997. LNCS, vol. 1303, pp. 53–62. Springer, Heidelberg (1997)
11. Billsus, D., Brunk, C., Evans, C., Gladish, B., Pazzani, M.J.: Adaptive interfaces for ubiquitous web access. Communications of the ACM 45(5), 34–38 (2002)
12. Sbattella, L., Tedesco, R., Quattrini Li, A., Genovese, E., Corradini, M., Guaraldi, G., Garbo, R., Mangiatordi, A., Negri, S.: The CATS project. In: Thaung, K.S. (ed.) Advanced Information Technology in Education. AISC, vol. 126, pp. 265–272. Springer, Heidelberg (2012)
13. Pedler, J., Mitton, R.: A large list of confusion sets for spellchecking assessed against a corpus of real-word errors. In: Calzolari, N.C., Choukri, K., Maegaard, B., Mariani, J., Odijk, J., Piperidis, S., Rosner, M., Tapias, D. (eds.) Proceedings of the Seventh International Conference on Language Resources and Evaluation (LREC 2010), European Language Resources Association (ELRA), Valletta (2010)
14. Ringlstetter, C., Schulz, K.U., Mihov, S.: Adaptive text correction with web-crawled domain-dependent dictionaries. ACM Transactions on Speech Language Processing 4(4) (October 2007)
15. Pedler, J.: Computer spellcheckers and dyslexicsa performance survey. British Journal of Educational Technology 32(1), 23–37 (2001)

16. Trnka, K., McCoy, K.F.: Corpus studies in word prediction. In: Proceedings of the 9th International ACM SIGACCESS Conference on Computers and Accessibility, Assets 2007, pp. 195–202. ACM, New York (2007)
17. Spooner, R.I.W., Edwards, A.D.N.: User modelling for error recovery: A spelling checker for dyslexic users. In: Jameson, A., Paris, C., Tasso, C. (eds.) Proceedings of the Sixth International Conference on User Modeling, UM 1997, pp. 147–157. Springer, Wien (1997)
18. Korhonen, T.: Adaptive spell checker for dyslexic writers. In: Miesenberger, K., Klaus, J., Zagler, W.L., Karshmer, A.I. (eds.) ICCHP 2008. LNCS, vol. 5105, pp. 733–741. Springer, Heidelberg (2008)
19. Stephanidis, C.: User Interface for All: Concepts, Methods, and Tools. Human Factors & Ergonomics. Taylor & Francis Group (2001)
20. MacArthur, C.A., Graham, S., Haynes, J.B., DeLaPaz, S.: Spelling checkers and students with learning disabilities: Performance comparisons and impact on spelling. The Journal of Special Education 30(1), 35–57 (1996)
21. Elkind, J., Cohen, K., Murray, C.: Using computer-based readers to improve reading comprehension of students with dyslexia. Annals of Dyslexia 43, 238–259 (1993)

A Framework for Privacy-Aware User Data Trading

Johnson Iyilade and Julita Vassileva

Computer Science Department, University of Saskatchewan, 110 Science Place
S7N 5C9 Saskatoon, Canada
{Johnson.Iyilade,Julita.Vassileva}@usask.ca

Abstract. Data about users is rapidly growing, collected by various online applications and databases. The ability to share user data across applications can offer benefits to user in terms of personalized services, but at the same time poses privacy risks of disclosure of personal information. Hence, there is a need to ensure protection of user privacy while enabling user data sharing for desired personalized services. We propose a policy framework for user data sharing based on the purpose of adaptation. The framework is based on the idea of a market, where applications can offer and negotiate user data sharing with other applications according to an explicit user-editable and negotiable privacy policy that defines the purpose, type of data, retention period and price.

Keywords: Privacy, Personalization, User Data Sharing, Policy, Incentives, Trust, Market, Framework.

1   Introduction

The ability to share user data across applications, services and devices has become crucial to personalization recently, with the emergence of cloud-based services and mobile app ecosystems, where many independent applications, services, or devices are interacting with and gathering information about the same user. In the last couple of years we have witnessed unprecedented numbers and dynamics of use of different applications by end users. Users constantly install, use and uninstall, on the fly, apps on their smart phones and tablets. When a user interacts with a new application, she should not have to re-enter the same information. Sharing the information that has already been collected by other installed applications would save the efforts and time of the user [1] and will address the cold-start problem in the personalization of the new application [2]. More information about the user would be available for user modeling (UM), covering more aspects in the aggregated model by both applications, which would allow higher quality personalization.

Sharing user data across applications raises several challenges: (i) the architecture of the user model – centralized (aiming to collect all user data at one place, in a consistent database), or decentralized (aiming to facilitate applications to share user data directly with each other on demand), (ii) ensuring user model (semantic) interoperability, and (iii) respecting user privacy and enabling user control over her data. There has been a lot of work in the field of user modeling that addresses the first

S. Carberry et al. (Eds.): UMAP 2013, LNCS 7899, pp. 310–317, 2013.

two challenges. The existing work on privacy however, is focused only on centralized architectures, where there is one user model maintained for each user on a UM server, using data from and for use of many applications. However, there is no work yet on privacy in decentralized architectures [3], where the user data sharing is taking place directly across applications, or is mediated for semantic interoperability [2].

Decentralized UM architectures can be viewed as marketplaces consisting of many interacting applications, which can be viewed as user data providers, user data consumers, and user data brokers (which facilitate the user data sharing by providing mediation services e.g. semantic mediation and lookup). The user can and should be an equal player in such a marketplace. She can trade her data, and gain benefits from sharing it. This short paper proposes a framework that can enable such a marketplace for sharing user data among applications. In our approach, the users have control on how their data is used by classifying their data based on its relevance to different purposes of use and sharing. We formulate a policy specification language through which user data providers can communicate the purpose and conditions of use under which user data that they have collected can be shared with user data consumers. The users provide their data after adapting and accepting the policy. Thus, the application has a contractual obligation to respect the policy and responsibility can be sought from applications that deviate. The framework ensures flexibility in the contracts through negotiation of some elements of the privacy policy such as *retention time, type of user data* that can be shared *and price*. The aim is to achieve a market, on which user data can be securely exchanged, traded and the user get properly compensated.

2   Related Work

There are several challenges involved in sharing user models gathered across applications. Existing solutions have focused on addressing different aspects of these problems. A key issue is whether the architecture of the system should be centralized or not. In centralized user modelling architectures, the user data is collected from various applications and stored in a database located on a server [4], many servers [5], or on a cloud [6]. According to principles governing databases, the information is kept consistent, secure and available. A centralized representation schema is used to store user data; semantic interoperability across the user data schemas of the feeding and consumer applications is ensured by the server. Therefore, as noted by [7], the system is logically centralized even when the data is stored in a physically distributed way. Most existing frameworks for reusing and sharing user models across applications follow the centralized architecture (e.g. IDIUMS [8], Personis Server [9], UMoWS [10]). Privacy in UM sharing has been addressed in the context of centralized UM server architectures. User data residing on servers can be more easily secured, but it also presents an attractive target of hackers. On a higher level, Wang and Kobsa [10] propose a framework for enforcing privacy in user modeling servers during data collection based on user preference settings and on a combination of the information privacy laws of country where the server is located and where the user resides. Other work addressing privacy in centralized UM servers, emphasizes user control over the accuracy of her data. The Personis Server [9] enables the user to view and control what is stored about them through a scrutable interface. However, the focus is on primary data collection, and the user is not provided means of controlling the secondary use and sharing of their data (it is assumed that secondary use is not happening). But, with the rise of social networks and Web 2.0 applications, where users voluntarily produce massive amounts of data, the challenge is how to protect user privacy not just in primary user data collection but also in secondary sharing and reuse of data. In addition, the dominant technology of centralized UM servers assumes a closed environment, where applications are trusted.

Another challenge is that of ensuring user model interoperability. A comprehensive review of current state-of-art in user model interoperability is provided in [3]. Generally, solutions to the challenge of interoperability have coalesced under two themes: standard-based (e.g. [12]) or mediation-based (e.g. [2]) approaches using frameworks, such as *Mypes* [13] for aggregating user information distributed across social networks, particularly, folksonomy systems. The main features of mediation-based approaches include user account mapping, linkage and aggregation of profiles. Mypes [13] focuses on aggregation of data from many sources and does not address privacy issues. Yet, sharing in decentralized architectures raises serious privacy concerns, related to which applications the data can be shared (trustworthiness), the purpose of the secondary use of data, how long it can be kept and who should be held responsible in case of violations of privacy. The user needs to have means to actively control not only what information is stored by applications about them (for primary use), but also the purpose and conditions of the use of data, the retention of the data, whether and with whom it can be shared. Also the user needs to be given an incentive for sharing data across applications, as currently, apart from personalized service there is no benefit directly for the user if she chooses to allow her data to be kept and shared.

3   Framework for Sharing User Data across Applications

As the ability to collect, share, and aggregate user data becomes crucial for personalized service delivery, we foresee the emergence of a user data sharing marketplace where user data will be securely collected, shared and exchanged in a mutually beneficial manner for all the players. The marketplace involves four active player types: *the users, data providers* (applications that have collected user data and can share it with other applications), *data consumers* (applications that need user data for their own personalization purposes), *data brokers* (applications that ensure semantic operability, monitor the trustworthiness of data providers and consumers, and carry out the negotiation process for each sharing according to policies for user data sharing). To enable interactions among the various players, we present a policy framework for user data sharing across applications, called *Purpose-to-Use (P2U)*. We further introduce a negotiation mechanism between the data consumers and data providers for P2U policy elements such as *data, retention time* and *price*. Finally, we discuss how users will be compensated for data sharing in the marketplace.

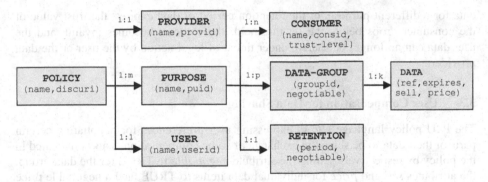

Fig. 1. Main elements of P2U Policy Specification Language

3.1   P2U Privacy Policy

The P2U privacy policy specification is inspired by the W3C's Platform for Privacy Preferences (P3P) [14] but does not follow its principles and syntax. While P3P is focused on limiting user data collection by websites, P2U is focused on enabling secondary information sharing and use. The P2U data sharing policy is based on a *purpose-relevance-sharing principle*. That is, only data relevant to the personalization purpose and context of use is shared. The main elements of P2U, their relationship and cardinality are illustrated in Figure 1. P2U defines eight policy specification elements each of which has some other attributes that further elaborate their usage. User privacy agreements should reflect the P2U privacy policy used by each application and they should be presented to the user allowing her to change the values of the attributes.

3.2   P2U Privacy Policy Negotiation

Policy Negotiation is done by the broker when a data consumer and data provider are ready to enter a contractual agreement for sharing user data. It may or may not require the participation of the user, depending on the degree of conflict in the request by the consumer and the parameters of data sharing set in the policy of the provider. The goal of the negotiation is to create a contract for data sharing that respects the P2U policies of the two applications and the user preferences. While it might be impractical to have negotiation over all the policy elements, some aspects of the privacy policy should be negotiable. For example, the provider, user and purpose for which data is shared may be non-negotiable. However, it should be possible for the data provider and consumer to negotiate the kinds of *data* in the data-group shared for that purpose, the *retention* period and the minimal *level of trust* that the consumer needs to maintain to be able to use the data [15,16]. After the negotiation is completed successfully, a contract between the data consumer and provider is made and the data will be shared according to the conditions of this contract. Compliance with the contract is enforced through a trust mechanism, which is part of the proposed user model sharing framework. Upon violation of any condition, e.g. the consumer uses data for a different purpose, or the retention period of data expires, the trust value of the consumer drops below the set threshold, the contract becomes invalid, and the user data can no longer be shared, under threat of legal action by the user or the data provider.

3.3   User Compensation for Data Sharing

The P2U policy language allows expressing user preferences for negotiating certain parts of their data to be shared in exchange of some compensation. This is indicated in the policy by respectively setting the attribute *negotiable* to TRUE for the data-group, the attributes *sell* and *price* for individual data items to TRUE, and a negotiable price value. The possibility of compensation for user data sharing was explored theoretically in [17] and has also been applied successfully in customer relationship management systems (loyalty reward programs) by credit cards, airlines and grocery stores. For example, the user can earn a certain percentage of the revenue made by the data provider from trading of his/her data, or earn points that are redeemable towards purchases or services.

4   Example Scenario

To illustrate how our data sharing framework might work in practice, we use a hypothetical scenario. Gena is a university graduate and a diabetic patient. She uses various web and mobile applications for her day-to-day activities such as a calendar, email, banking, shopping, photo-sharing, social networks apps. Recently, she installed some new apps on her smartphone: the FoodJournal app keeps a record of her daily food intake; the FitnessApp tracks her daily workout; and MedAdvice App provides her simple health advice; and a DietDataGatering Application by a researcher, who studies the correlation between food intake, exercise, and diseases such as diabetes.

While installing these apps, Gina recognizes that MedAdvice is asking her for the same information that she has already provided to other applications she uses, for example, the FitnessApp, the FoodJournal, the ShoppingApp and the Calendar. Gena does not want to re-enter the same information again and she knows generally, that sharing her data with the application will give her more personalized, and therefore, better services. So, she would like to grant access to the application to reuse the data she has already provided to the other applications. However, she is uncertain whether in this way she won't also grant access to other applications that she doesn't know of which may be harmful to her in some way. She wants to be able to control which applications have access to her data and to know for what purpose they use her data. She does not mind allowing third-party applications to use some of her data, if she is aware of the usage and can get some form of compensation, either monetary or in terms of improved services. However, she cannot trust the websites and applications she uses to protect her data from been generally released to other applications without her knowledge and consent.

Assuming that the P2U policy is adopted by a number of app service providers, Gena configures her data sharing preferences on all the websites and apps she uses. Through a uniform interface that indicates the possible purposes of use of user data, types of data, the duration of storing the data and negotiation preferences, she is able to control the usage and sharing of her data according to her privacy preferences. The information provided by her is converted into P2U policy files (in XML format), which are used by the data providers to control access requests to Gena's data by other applications (user data consumers) and to enter into negotiation on her behalf with them.

Table 1. FoodJournal Application User Model

Name	Zip code	Age	Nationality	Condition
Gena	S7N8C0	22	Canadian	Diabetic

Name	Date	Time	Food	Quantity	Hunger Scale (1-10)	Mood	Comment
Gena	13/01/2012	13:00	Chicken	100g	7	Motivated	None
Gena	13/01/2012	19:00	Pasta	200g	4	Tired	Sleepy
Gena	14/01/2012	07:00	Veggies	100g	8	Energetic	Woke up strong

```
Policy: FoodTrack
PURPOSE: To generate
health advice
RETENTION PERIOD:
unlimited
DATA TO SHARE (data,
sell, expires):
(food consumed,
false),
(quantity, false),
(hunger scale, false)
```
(a)

```
Policy: ShopRec
PURPOSE: To provide
shopping recommendations
RETENTION PERIOD:
unlimited
DATA TO SHARE (data,
sell, expires):
(food consumed, true,
180days),
(zip code, true, 180
days)
```
(b)

```
Policy: FoodRes
PURPOSE:     To   benefit
health research
RETENTION: 180 days
DATA TO SHARE    (data,
sell, expires):
(age, false),
(nationality, false),
(condition, false)
(food, false)
```
(c)

Fig. 2. Data sharing policies specified by Gena for three different purposes that can be used by (a) MedAdvice App, (b) Shopping App (c) DietDataGatering App

Assume the FoodJournal App user model contains two records, whose structure is depicted in Table 1 and Gena wants to allow the FoodJournal app to share the following information: with the MedAdviceApp → food consumed, quantity, and hunger scale; with the ShoppingApp → food consumed and zip code, with the DietDataGateringApp → age, nationality, condition and food consumed. Figure 2 shows three sample preference settings for sharing data that Gena has entered in the privacy settings of the FoodJJournal Application for three different purposes (the purposes are established by the developers of the FoodJournal App based on how they envisage user data collected by their application may be reused by other applications).

```
<POLICY discuri=http://mywebsiteonline.com/privacy.html name= "FoodTrack">
<PROVIDER name = "FoodJournalApp" provid="p1034m4" />
<USER name ="Gena" userid ="u1030050503050" />
<PURPOSE name="Get Health Advice" puid="102">
        <CONSUMER name="MedAdviceApp" consid="c10423" />
        <RETENTION period="unlimited" />
        <DATA-GROUP groupid="g090353" negotiable="false">
            <DATA ref="#dailyfoodintake.food" sell="FALSE" />
            <DATA ref="#dailyfoodintake.quantity" sell="FALSE" />
            <DATA ref="#dailyfoodintake.hungerscale" sell="FALSE" />
        </DATA-GROUP>
</PURPOSE>
</POLICY>
```

Fig. 3. Gena's *FoodTrack* policy translated to *FoodTrack* Contract

Each data consumer application can only access the data specified by Gena in the preference settings of the respective purpose for which it request the data. Figure 3 shows the contract established between MedAdvice App and FoodJournal App after the negotiation phase based on the *FoodTrack* policy.

5   Conclusion

Sharing user data for purposes other than the one for which the data was collected poses a threat of violating user privacy through secondary use. This paper proposes a decentralized framework for user data sharing based on purpose of adaptation, which allows for flexible negotiation of various policy elements such as *type of data, retention period, trust level of consumer,* and *price.* We present Purpose-to-Use (P2U) policy specification language which allows the creation of different purposes and specification of relevant data to the purposes. The framework addresses the important issue of providing incentives for users to participate in the specification of their privacy policies and to allow sharing of their data.

References

[1] Heckmann, D., Schwartz, T., Brandherm, B., Kröner, A.: Decentralized User Modeling with UserML and GUMO. In: Dolog, P., Vassileva, J. (eds.) Proceedings of the Workshop on Decentralized, Agent Based and Social Approaches to User Modeling, DASUM 2005, at UM 2005, Edinburgh, Scotland, pp. 61–66 (July 2005)

[2] Berkovsky, S., Kuflik, T., Ricci, F.: Mediation of User Models for Enhanced Personalization in Recommender Systems. User Modeling and User-Adapted Interaction 18(3), 245–286 (2007)

[3] Carmagnola, F., Cena, F., Gena, C.: User Model Interoperability: a Survey. User Model User-Adapted Interaction 21(3), 285–331 (2011)

[4] Kobsa, A.: Generic User Modeling Systems. User Modeling and User-Adapted Interaction 11, 49–63 (2001)

[5] Fink, J., Kobsa, A.: A Review and Analysis of Commercial User Modeling Servers for Personalization on the World Wide Web. User Modeling and User-Adapted Interaction 10, 209–249 (2000)

[6] Dolog, P., Kay, J., Kummerfeld, B.: Personal Lifelong User Model Clouds. In: Proceeding of the Lifelong User Modeling Workshop at UMAP 2009, Trento, Italy, pp. 1–8 (June 2009)

[7] Vassileva, J., McCalla, G., Greer, J.: Multi-Agent Multi-User Modeling. User Modeling and User-Adapted Interaction 13(1), 179–210 (2003)

[8] Prince, R., Davis, H.: IDIUMS: sharing user models through application attributes. Poster presentation. in Proc. User Modeling, Adaptation and Personalization, UMAP 2011, Girona, Spain, pp 40–42. Springer, Heidelberg (2011) ISBN: 978-3-642-22362-4

[9] Kay, J., Kummerfeld, B., Lauder, P.: Personis: A server for user models. In: De Bra, P., Brusilovsky, P., Conejo, R. (eds.) AH 2002. LNCS, vol. 2347, pp. 203–212. Springer, Heidelberg (2002)

[10] Bielikova, M., Kuruc, J.: Sharing User Models for Adaptive Hypermedia Applications. In: Proc. 5th Int. Conf. Intelligent Systems Design and Applications, Washington DC, USA, pp. 506–513 (2005)

[11] Wang, Y., Kobsa, A.: Respecting users' individual privacy constraints in web personalization. In: Conati, C., McCoy, K., Paliouras, G. (eds.) UM 2007. LNCS (LNAI), vol. 4511, pp. 157–166. Springer, Heidelberg (2007)

[12] Heckmann, D., Schwartz, T., Brandherm, B., Schmitz, M., von Wilamowitz-Moellendorff, M.: GUMO – The General User Model Ontology. In: Ardissono, L., Brna, P., Mitrović, A. (eds.) UM 2005. LNCS (LNAI), vol. 3538, pp. 428–432. Springer, Heidelberg (2005)

[13] Abel, F., Henze, N., Herder, E., Krause, D.: Linkage, Aggregation, Alignment and Enrichment of Public User Profiles with Mypes. In: Proc. 6th Int. Conf. Semantic Systems (I-SEMANTICS), Graz, Austria, Article No. 11 (September 2010) ISBN: 978-1-4503-0014-8

[14] W3C P3P Specification, http://www.w3.org/TR/P3P11/

[15] Buffett, S., Jia, K., Liu, S., Spencer, B., Wang, F.: Negotiating exchanges of P3P-Labeled information for compensation. Computational Intelligence 20(4), 663–677 (2004)

[16] Preibusch, S.: Privacy Negotiations with P3P. In: W3C Workshop on Languages for Privacy Policy Negotiation and Semantics-Driven Enforcement, October 17-18 (2006), Ispra, Italy (2006), http://www.w3.org/2006/07/privacy-ws/papers/24-preibusch-negotiation-p3p/ (last accessed: March 14th, 2013)

[17] Aperjis, C., Huberman, B.A.: A Market for Unbiased Private Data: Paying Individuals According to their Prvacy Attitudes (2012), http://www.hpl.hp.com/research/scl/papers/datamarket/datamarket.pdf (last accessed: January 10, 2013)

Understanding Email Writers: Personality Prediction from Email Messages

Jianqiang Shen, Oliver Brdiczka, and Juan Liu

Palo Alto Research Center, 3333 Coyote Hill Road, Palo Alto, CA 94304, USA
{jianqiang.shen,oliver.brdiczka,juan.liu}@parc.com

Abstract. Email is a ubiquitous communication tool and constitutes a significant portion of social interactions. In this paper, we attempt to infer the personality of users based on the content of their emails. Such inference can enable valuable applications such as better personalization, recommendation, and targeted advertising. Considering the private and sensitive nature of email content, we propose a privacy-preserving approach for collecting email and personality data. We then frame personality prediction based on the well-known Big Five personality model and train predictors based on extracted email features. We report prediction performance of 3 generative models with different assumptions. Our results show that personality prediction is feasible, and our email feature set can predict personality with reasonable accuracies.

Keywords: Personality, behavior analysis, email, text processing.

1 Introduction

Email is one of the most successful computer applications to date. Office workers around the world spend a significant amount of time writing and reading electronic messages - in fact, previous research even characterized email as the natural "habitat" of the modern office worker [7]. The growing importance of email as a communication medium has inspired many attempts to develop tools for presenting, organizing, classifying, and understanding emails (e.g., [2,5,6]). In this paper, we extend this line of research by focusing on an as-yet unexplored area: the inference of a user's personality based on emails.

Our work is inscribed in a broader research effort of enhancing user experience through user personalization and adaptation. Modeling user personality based on electronic communications could enable better personalization of user interfaces and content [8], more efficient collaboration (by forming groups of compatible individuals) [16], more precise targeted advertising, or improved learning efficiency by customizing teaching materials and styles [17], to name just a few possibilities. Personality modeling can also be important in the work place environment. Employers may prefer to match an employee's personality with suitable tasks to optimize performance. On the other hand, in high-stake work environments, a significant mismatch between personality and task requirement may impose risk. Our personality predictor is part of a larger system being developed to

S. Carberry et al. (Eds.): UMAP 2013, LNCS 7899, pp. 318–330, 2013.

detect such anomalies and prevent malicious behaviors in corporate networks. Personality profiling enables us to identify individuals having the motivation and capability to damage the work environment, harm co-workers, or commit suicide in the workplace.

Training reliable personality predictors is an unexplored territory in research and one major barrier is data collection. Although email is ubiquitous, public and realistic email corpora are rare due to privacy issues. Acquiring personality profiles can be even more challenging since personality is often considered private. To our knowledge, all public email sets including Enron [6] do not have personality information. We thus designed innovative strategies to retrieve predictive information while protecting privacy. Given a feature vector abstracted from one single email, our goal is to reliably predict the personality of this email's writer. In psychology, the Big Five model is one of the most widely-adopted standards [12]. Using this framework, each email message can be associated with a set of personality trait values. We explored 3 different generative models and as will become apparent, a method with label-independence assumption works best in our case, which suggests that in our data sets personality traits are relatively distinct and independent from each other.

The contribution of this paper is threefold. First, we show that it is possible to reliably infer an email writer's personality with the results from two large real-word email sets. To the best of our knowledge, this is the first attempt at inferring personality from emails using automatic content analysis. Second, we present our email features and their predictive power in detail to inform future work on personality. Third, we present a pilot exploration of different learning strategies for personality prediction, which could facilitate future studies.

2   Personality

Personality traits are consistent patterns of thoughts, feelings, or actions that distinguish people from one another [12]. A trait is an internal characteristic that corresponds to an extreme position on a behavioral dimension. Personality traits are basic tendencies that remain stable across the life span. Based on the Big 5 model, the following five factors, Neuroticism, Agreeableness, Conscientiousness, Extraversion and Openness have been shown to account for most individual differences in personality.

An individual's personality affects their behavior [12]. Scoring highly on a given trait means reacting consistently to the same situation over time. It is possible to estimate a stranger's personality based on their behaviors [13]. Our personality predictor is part of a larger system being developed to detect anomalies and prevent malicious behaviors in corporate networks. Corporations and government agencies are interested in predicting and protecting against insider attacks by trusted employees. We posit that some personalities are more likely to react with negative actions to job and life stress than others. Consequently, we introduce personality traits as static personal variables to consider when assessing an individual's relative interest in carrying out insider attacks.

Research shows that malicious intentions are more related to Extraversion, Agreeableness, Conscientiousness and Neuroticism, and less related to Openness [10]. Intuitively, the definition of each trait matches this finding well. Neuroticism concerns the extent to which individuals are anxious, irritable, depressed, moody and lacking self-confidence. Agreeableness concerns the extent to which individuals are trusting, non-hostile, compliant and caring – in particular, it is negatively correlated with antisocial personality disorder. Conscientiousness concerns the extent to which individuals are efficient, organized, dutiful, and self-disciplined. Extraversion is related to excitement-seeking that requires high levels of environmental stimulation to avoid boredom. By contrast, Openness includes facets of aesthetics and values but is less correlated with criminality. Therefore, we focus in this paper on predicting the values of Neuroticism, Agreeableness, Conscientiousness and Extraversion from the content of written emails.

3   Email Data Collection

Although email is ubiquitous, public and realistic email corpora are rare. The limited availability is largely due to privacy issues. Data collection is even more challenging for our problem, since we need two kinds of data from each user: the user's personality profile and their written emails. Both data are highly sensitive and need to be anonymized. Our logging tools take two measures to protect privacy: (1) participants are assigned a random unique ID, and only this ID is kept as identifier in the extracted data set; (2) only high-level aggregated features are extracted, while none of the raw email content is included in the feature set. By these steps, we ensure that it is impossible to reconstruct personal identifiable information and raw content from our feature data set.

We developed two email extraction tools: one is deployed as a software agent installed on participants' PCs to extract emails from Outlook, another is deployed as a web service to collect emails from a participant's Gmail account.

3.1   Email Anonymization

Email Preprocessing. We need to preserve the structure of email threads for constructing predictive features later. An email thread is a group of messages that are related by "reply/forward" links. By capturing email threads, we can further analyze the possible factors that lead to specific email responses. Those threading relationships can be reliably recovered by analyzing the subject lines and the RFC-822 header fields of email messages (e.g., *Message-ID*, *InReply-To*, *Reference*).

We also need to clean up emails before extraction to avoid being misled by irrelevant material. We detect and isolate *reply lines* and *signature blocks*. Many users tend to delete less important emails and there might be gap in the email thread. We thus rely on a hybrid content analysis approach for detection: each message is checked by both "false positive" regular expressions [15] and pre-trained automatic reply/signature detectors. When you reply to emails, popular systems such as Outlook and Gmail produce fixed patterns for the reply heads and lines. Signatures are typically at the end of the message and contain names and/or addresses. We designed specific regular expressions to capture such patterns. The pre-trained reply/signature detectors [4] utilize over 30 features (such as email patterns, name patterns, punctuations) and adopt Conditional Random Fields [14] for inference. To maximize the probability of thoroughly cleaning the email, we treat a line as a reply or signature if either of the approaches predicts so. In a small test set of 100 emails, our approach achieved over 95% accuracy.

Email Features. After performing the pre-processing steps outlined above, our data logger extracts the following high-level features from the raw written text.

Bag-of-word Features. The simplest and most prevalent approach to representation of a document is the bag-of-word space [11]. Instead of collecting every appearing word, we only build our features from words that are most commonly used in everyday life for three reasons. First, focusing on common words can protect an individual's privacy by avoiding collecting specific, unique and sensitive words. Second, research on sentiment analysis [18] shows that common words are most predictive to identify the viewpoints underlying a text span. Third, focusing on common words can also help to avoid associating specific, unique words to certain individuals in the training set and not to certain personalities. We started building the *common word list* with the top 20000 most common words from TV and movie scripts [26]. We then retrieved the top 1000 male first names, 2000 female first names and 5000 surnames based on the survey of U.S. Census Bureau for the year 2005. We removed those names from the word list. We further checked the list and removed any words related to addresses, names, research areas and job titles. This left us with a list of 16,623 common words. Each cleaned email was heuristically tokenized into a word list, and we counted the frequency for each word in the common word list.

Meta Features. From the email message, we calculated TO/CC/BCC counts, importance of the email, count of different punctuation symbols, count of words, count of characters, count of positive and negative numbers, count of paragraphs, count of attachments, month of the sent time, day of the month of the sent time, and day of the week of the sent time. We also recorded whether this is a reply/forward message. If it is, we then calculated the duration since he/she received the original email, and meta features in the original email.

Word Statistics. We applied *part-of-speech* (POS) tagging [22] to the cleaned email. Part-of-speech tagging is a process to read text and sequentially tag each token with syntactic labels, such as noun and verb, based on its definition as well as its context - i.e. its relationship with adjacent and related words in a phrase, sentence, and paragraph. We recorded the count of words for each POS tag.

We adopted *sentiment analysis* to generate features from the email content. Sentiment analysis is the task of identifying positive and negative opinions, emotions, and evaluations [27]. We used a sentiment polarity dictionary from UPitt [27] for this purpose. Compared with LIWC [19], this dictionary has a much higher coverage and contains detailed human-annotated polarity information on

8,221 distinct words. We scanned the email and counted the number of words in different sentiment categories, including positive/negative/neutral/both words, strongly/weakly subjective words. If it is a reply email, we also calculate the above features from the original email.

Studies have shown that the usage of *pronouns* and *negations* can be indicators of emotional states [21]. For example, the word "me" and "not" are related to anger and the word "I" is related to emotional vulnerability. We listed 76 pronouns and 36 negations to count the frequency of pronouns and negations.

We counted the number of words consisting of all low-case letters and words consisting of all up-case letters. We also wanted to get some sense of the *complexity* and *difficulty* of the words used by the writer. We attempted to achieve this using two calculations. First, we count the number of letters in each word and compute the histogram of those word lengths. Second, each word is assigned a difficulty level based on its ranking in the common word list. We then compute the average difficulty level for those words.

Writing Styles. Emails can have a conventional, structured format. Such a message is typically started with a greeting so as to help create a friendly tone. The choice of using the correspondent's name also depends on who is written to. Emails often end in a polite way with common endings such as "best regards". At the opposite end of the formality spectrum, email writers can also use smileys to convey emotional content such as sarcasm, laughter and other feelings, such as ":-)" or ":-p". Therefore, there are no mandatory formulas for writing emails. Not all social and business emails feature exactly one of the above formats, since emails strike a balance between the conventional format and the writer's own personal style. Their writing style can be very informative [1]. We tried to capture such difference in writing styles with:

1. *greeting patterns*: we collected 83 popular open greetings, e.g., "Hi", "Dear".
2. *closing patterns*: we collected 68 closing patterns, e.g., "kindly", "sincerely".
3. *wish patterns*: we collected 28 common wish patterns, such as "have a good day", "looking forward to seeing you".
4. *smileys words*: we collected 115 popular smileys, such as ":-)", "8-)".

Speech Act Scores. One important use of work-related email is negotiating and delegating shared tasks and subtasks [5,25]. To get a better understanding of the whole message, it is therefore desirable to detect its purpose. The Speech Act taxonomy is typically divided into verbs and nouns, and each email message is represented by one or more verb-noun pairs: for example, an email proposing a meeting would have the labels Propose, Meeting. We used a pre-trained Speech Predictor [5] to predict these Speech Acts from the email and adopted the prediction confidence of each act as a feature. This predictor averagely has nearly 70% F1 scores over all Speech Acts [5]. Although it is not extremely accurate, it nevertheless provides some additional information on the tone and purpose of the email, as shown in the experimental results.

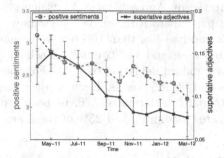

Fig. 1. Trend of average count of positive sentiment words and superlative adjective words per sent email, with 95% confidence levels

3.2   Email and Behavior: An Illustration

Before presenting our personality prediction models, we want to first use an example to illustrate how revealing email messages are regarding a person's personality and emotion states. We were fortunate to have access to the sent emails from an individual who left his job in March 2012 and kindly donated his email archive. He claimed that he started thinking about career change half a year beforehand, while none of his colleagues noticed. We therefore tried to see if his changing emotion could be reflected in the content of his messages prior to his eventual departure. As shown in Figure 1, the count of positive sentiment words this person used kept decreasing significantly, suggesting that he became disenchanted in his work. The count of superlative adjectives also decreased significantly, suggesting that he became less excited about work-related matters. In this particular case the email trends are quite revealing. It will be interesting to explore in general how email features are correlated with one's personality and emotion states, both in corporate email and in more causal settings.

3.3   Data Collection

We carried out two email data collections. One email set was collected in a research lab. Recruiting was done through email and door-to-door solicitations. We tried to recruit participants as diverse as possible. Our software agent was installed on participants' PCs to extract their sent emails in Outlook from the last 12 months. In another data collection, participants logged into our web service and let our servlet collect emails in their Gmail accounts from the last 12 months. We recruited participants from all over the U.S.. Although we were using emailing to colleagues and posting on Facebook for recruiting, most (> 90%) of our participants were not affiliated with our company or friends with any of the involved researchers.

Each participant first answered an online personality survey that was compiled by psychologists and consists of 112 questions. Based on the survey results, we calculated the ground-truth levels (low, medium, high) for each participant on the dimensions of Neuroticism, Agreeableness, Conscientiousness and Extraversion. We filtered out a participant if the survey answers were not consistent, or sent less than 5 emails and had less than 100 received emails. For the Outlook dataset, we have 28 valid users and 49,722 emails. Each subject sent an average of 1,776 emails, with a standard deviation of 1,596. For the Gmail dataset, this left us 458 valid users and 65,185 emails. Each subject had an average of 142 sent emails, with a standard deviation of 176. In both datasets, roughly 50% subjects' personalities are "medium", and 25% of them are "low" or "high".

4   Personality Prediction

Given a feature vector abstracted from one single email, our goal is to reliably predict the personality of this email's writer. We need to learn a function $f : \mathbf{X} \rightarrow \mathbf{Y}$ whose input $\mathbf{X}$ is the feature vector and output $\mathbf{Y} = \langle y_1, .., y_K \rangle$ is the personality trait value vector. Each element y_j of $\mathbf{Y}$ corresponds to a personality trait (e.g., Extraversion) and its value can be "low", "medium" or "high". Given an example $(\mathbf{X}, \mathbf{Y})$, the error of f is defined as $E(f, (\mathbf{X}, \mathbf{Y})) = \sum_{j=1}^{K} I(y_j \neq f(\mathbf{X})_j)$ where $I(\cdot)$ is indicator function. That is, E counts the cases where the predicted value of a trait is different from the real value. Appropriate f should have a low expected value of E.

Traditional *single-label* classification is concerned with learning from a set of examples that are associated with a single label y from a set of disjoint labels L. In this *multi-label* classification problem [23], the examples are associated with a set of labels $\mathbf{Y} = \langle y_1, .., y_K \rangle$. Given a message $\mathbf{X}_i$ and a set of personality values $\mathbf{Y}_i$, we imagine there could be the following models for generating feature x_{ij}:

- **Joint Model:** $\langle y_{i1}, .., y_{iK} \rangle$ work as a single entity and they jointly decide whether to select feature x_{ij}.
- **Sequential Model:** first select a label y_{ik} out of $y_{i1}, .., y_{iK}$, then y_{ik} decides whether to select feature x_{ij}.
- **Survival Model:** each label y_{ik} independently decides whether to select feature x_{ij}. If all labels decide to select x_{ij}, then finally x_{ij} gets selected.

Based on the above generative models, we derived different learning algorithms.

Joint Model. Joint Model assumes that each feature is jointly selected by all labels. It thus needs to consider each distinct combination of label values that exist in the training set as a different class value of a single-label classification task. In such cases, the number of classes may become very large and at the same time many classes are associated with very few training examples. To improve the computational efficiency and predictive accuracy, we adopt a simple yet effective ensemble learning method [24] for Joint Model. Our ensemble method initially selects m small labelsets $R_1, .., R_m$ from the powerset of label set L via random sampling without replacement. It then considers each labelset R_k as a different class value of a single-label classification task and learns m single-label classifiers $f_1, .., f_m$ independently. In this way, it aims to take into account label correlations using single-label classifiers that are applied on subtasks with manageable number of labels and adequate number of examples per label.

Sequential Model. Sequential Model assumes that first a label is selected from the label set and then this label selects a feature. Labeled Latent Dirichlet Allocation (LDA) [20] is an extension of Naive Bayes that exactly handles such situation. It constrains LDA [3] by defining a one-to-one correspondence between LDA's latent topics and user labels. This allows Labeled LDA to directly learn feature-label correspondences. If each document has only one label, the probability of each document under Labeled LDA is equal to the probability of the document under the Multinomial Naive Bayes event model. If documents have multiple labels, in a traditional one-versus-rest Multinomial Naive Bayes model, a separate classifier for each label would be trained on all documents with that label, so each feature can contribute a count of 1 to every observed label's feature distribution. By contrast, Labeled LDA assumes that each document is a mixture of underlying topics, so the count mass of single feature instance must instead be distributed over the document's observed labels.

Survival Model. Survival Model assumes that each label independently determines whether to use a feature. Only if all labels agree, this feature will get selected. Given a set of label values $\mathbf{Y}_i = \langle y_{i1}, .., y_{iK} \rangle$, the probability that x_{ij} gets selected is $P(x_{ij}|\mathbf{Y}_i){=}\prod_k P(x_{ij}|y_{ik})$. Given a set of D training instances $\{(\mathbf{X}_1,\mathbf{Y}_1),...,(\mathbf{X}_D,\mathbf{Y}_D)\}$, with naive Bayes assumption, we search for parameter to maximize the likelihood

$$\prod_i P(\mathbf{X}_i|\mathbf{Y}_i) = \prod_i \prod_j P(x_{ij}|\mathbf{Y}_i) = \prod_k (\prod_i \prod_j P(x_{ij}|y_{ik})) = \prod_k (\prod_i P(\mathbf{X}_i|y_{ik}))$$

This equals to independently searching for parameters to maximize the liklihood $\prod_i P(\mathbf{X}_i|y_{ik})$ for each label k. Given a test instance $\mathbf{x}$, we want to assign values to K personality traits to maximize the posterior probability $P(y_1,...,y_K|\mathbf{X})$. Using Bayes Formula and label independence, we get

$$P(\mathbf{Y}|\mathbf{X}) \propto P(y_1,..,y_K)P(\mathbf{X}|y_1,..,y_K) = \prod_k P(y_k) \prod_k P(\mathbf{X}|y_k) = \prod_k (P(y_k)P(\mathbf{X}|y_k)) \propto \prod_k P(y_k|\mathbf{X})$$

This equals to independently searching for optimal values for each label. We thus can consider each label as an independent classification problem. We transform this multi-label problem into one single-label problem for each label and independently train K classifiers $f_1,...,f_K$. Each classifier f_i is responsible for predicting the low/medium/high value for each corresponding personality trait.

Using Multiple Message for Prediction. In this paper, we focus on predicting the personality of the email writer based on one single email. Note that the accuracy of prediction could be improved if we can make inference based on multiple email messages. Assume we have n messages $\mathbf{X}_1,..,\mathbf{X}_n$. For each message $\mathbf{X}_i$, we can utilize the predictor to estimate P_{ik}, the probability that its writer has personality trait value y_k. We then use those estimated probabilities to "vote"

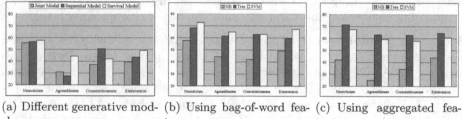

(a) Different generative models

(b) Using bag-of-word features

(c) Using aggregated features

Fig. 2. Accuracy of using different strategies, features, classifiers on Outlook dataset

for the final prediction: for personality trait value y_k, its overall score will be $\sum_i P_{ik}$. We rank trait values based on their overall scores and make predictions with those having highest scores.

5   Experimental Results

We evaluated the accuracy of the proposed algorithms with the collected Outlook and Gmail datasets. For the Outlook set, we hold one subject's data for test, use the rest subjects for training, and iterate over all subjects. For the Gmail set, all results are based on 10-fold cross validation [11] with the constraint that all emails from the same subject either go to the training set or the test set.

Effects of Generative Models. We first evaluated personality prediction using 3 generative models with the Outlook set. We used Naive Bayes as the underneath single-label classifier. We only used bag-of-word features of emails to simplify the comparison. The results are shown in Figure 2(a). It is clear that Joint Model performs badly. Its accuracies are worse than the simple Survival Model and the difference is significant for Agreeableness, Conscientiousness and Extraversion ($p<0.05$). Combining personality trait values together to train multiple classifiers decreases the accuracy. This suggests that personality traits are relatively distinct and independent characteristics in our dataset. Overall, Sequential Model does not perform well, either. Sequential Model assumes that the count mass of single word instance must be distributed over the document's observed labels, while Survival Model lets each word contribute a count of 1 to every observed label's word distribution. Such performance difference suggests that the choice of some specific words in the emails might be independently determined by multiple personality trait values. Considering its prediction accuracy and computation efficiency, we therefore adopted Survival Model.

Comparison of Single-Label Classifiers. Now that we saw that the learning strategy Survival Model performs best, we will evaluate it using different single-label classifiers and different feature sets. Naive Bayes, decision trees and support vector machines (SVM) are perhaps three of the most popular learning algorithms. We applied them as the single-label classifiers in the Survival Model

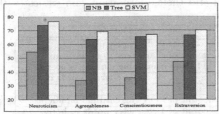
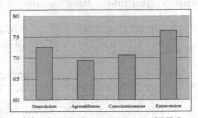

(a) Outlook dataset using different classifiers

(b) Gmail dataset using SVM

Fig. 3. Accuracy of using all features for Survival Model

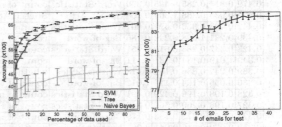

Predict / Real	low	medium	high
low	**5966**	2575	645
medium	1666	**25540**	2357
high	594	3855	**6524**

(a) Percentage of data used (b) # of emails for test

Fig. 4. Confusion matrix of Neuroticism for Outlook

Fig. 5. Accuracy sensitivity given different sizes of training/test data for the Gmail set

framework to the Outlook set. We used linear kernels for SVM since linear kernels work well for text-related data [11]. We are also interested in comparing bag-of-word features with other aggregated features (meta features, writing styles, etc). As shown in Figure 2(b) and 2(c), decision trees and SVM significantly outperform Naive Bayes ($p<0.05$). Decision trees show competitive accuracy, compared with SVM. Because decision trees are well suited to handle aggregated, heterogeneous data, they even outperform SVM when only using aggregated features. When using all available features, SVM achieved 69% overall accuracy on the Outlook set and 72% overall accuracy on the Gmail set, as shown in Figure 3. In both cases, it is more accurate when predicting Neuroticism and Extraversion. This is consistent with the previous findings that Neuroticism and Extraversion are more related to Internet usage [9].

Different prediction mistakes could have different costs. For example, if Neuroticism of a person is actually low, then it is worse to predict him as high than predict him as medium. The confusion matrix of predicting Neuroticism using SVM with all features for the Outlook set is shown in Table 4. It is less likely that a person with high Neuroticism will be predicted as low, vice versa.

Data Sensitivity. As we mentioned earlier, collecting realistic email and personality data can be challenging. Analyzing email content and abstracting features also takes considerable CPU time. Thus it is desirable to train an accurate predictor with limited data. We randomly sampled data from our email set and

Table 1. Top informative features in Gmail and their information gain values (x100)

Avg	N	A	C	E	Category	Feature
1.449	1.910	2.338	0.954	0.954	Word Statistics	count of POS Tag Symbols
1.278	1.084	0.855	1.466	1.706	Meta Features	count of characters after clean-up
1.206	0.281	0.242	1.781	0.878	Writing Styles	whether containing closing "sincerely"
1.056	1.046	0.544	0.705	0.838	Meta Features	count of all up-case-letter words in body
0.918	1.043	1.209	0.822	0.597	Speech Act	Speech Act score on "Data"
0.806	0.743	0.739	0.712	1.032	Word Statistics	count of POS Tag cardinal numbers
0.745	1.025	0.779	0.613	0.562	Word Statistics	count of 1-character words in body
0.730	0.065	0.393	1.488	0.975	Speech Act	Speech Act score on "Request"
0.656	0.222	0.567	1.225	0.612	Speech Act	Speech Act score on "Commit"
0.584	0.050	1.142	0.198	0.945	Writing Styles	count of wishes
0.580	0.431	0.591	0.826	0.473	Word Statistics	count of pronouns
0.569	0.260	1.144	0.135	0.738	Bag-of-word	count of word "college"
0.479	0.815	0.285	0.425	0.390	Word Statistics	count of negations
0.470	0.035	0.368	1.309	0.168	Speech Act	Speech Act score on "Deliver"
0.442	0.403	0.336	0.527	0.501	Word Statistics	count of strong subjective words
0.439	0.231	1.098	0.242	0.186	Bag-of-word	count of word "relation"
0.423	0.347	0.285	0.610	0.451	Word Statistics	count of positive sentiment words
0.349	1.019	0.134	0.131	0.111	Bag-of-word	count of word "music"
0.339	0.242	0.836	0.160	0.118	Writing Styles	whether containing any closing greeting
0.336	0.055	0.164	0.116	1.012	Bag-of-word	count of word "crazy"
0.328	0.198	0.196	0.429	0.491	Word Statistics	count of negative sentiment words
0.327	0.198	0.200	0.562	0.348	Word Statistics	count of POS Tag superlative adjectives
0.324	0.164	0.772	0.183	0.179	Bag-of-word	count of word "mr"
0.259	0.072	0.016	0.041	0.907	Writing Styles	whether containing any starting greeting

evaluated the accuracy given different sizes of datasets. The results for predicting Extraversion in the Gmail set from 20 trials are shown in Figure 5(a). Naive Bayes is very sensitive to the data and its accuracy has a high variance given different datasets of the same size. Decision trees and SVM are more stable and have a low variance. Once we utilized more than 50% of the data, the accuracy improvement becomes trivial. This suggests that collecting about 6 months of data from our participants might be sufficient for personality prediction.

So far we have focused on predicting the personality of the email writer based on one single email. The accuracy could be improved if we can make inference based on multiple email messages. Given n email messages, we could let SVM estimate the probability distribution of the personality trait values and then use those probabilities to vote for the final prediction. In the Gmail set, we randomly selected n messages for each user and predict this user's personality based on the voted probabilities of those messages. The results for predicting Extraversion from 200 trials are shown in Figure 5(b). We can more accurately predict the personality as we get access to more messages. The accuracy is more than 81% if we see more than 10 messages, and nearly 85% if we see more than 35 messages.

Informative Features. We are now interested in finding out which features are most predictive for specific personality traits. Information Gain (IG) [28] is a well-known criterion to measure a feature's power. It calculates the reduction of entropy in the predicted class distribution provided by knowing the value of a feature. We discretized our features by simple binning [11] and sorted features based on their average IGs of Neuroticism, Agreeableness, Conscientiousness and Extraversion. Some top features for the Gmail set are shown in Table 1. Some results fit our intuition well. For example, people with high Conscientiousness tend to write long emails and use more characters. People with high Agreeableness tend to use more "please" and good wishes in their emails. People with high Neuroticism could get nervous easily and use more negations.

6 Conclusions

Email is a ubiquitous office tool capturing a large share of a user's communication. We analyzed the email content from two large real-world email sets and predicted a writer's personality. To the best of our knowledge, this is the first attempt at inferring an email writer's personality through automatic content analysis. We show that it is possible to reliably infer personality. Such reliable personality inference based on written content could have important commercial and security applications. We described a privacy-preserving approach to collecting sensitive email and personality data. We presented the extracted email features and their predictive power. We then explored 3 learning strategies, showing that a method with label-independence assumption works best in our case.

Acknowledgment. The authors gratefully acknowledge support for this work from DARPA through the ADAMS (Anomaly Detection At Multiple Scales) program funded project GLAD-PC (Graph Learning for Anomaly Detection using Psychological Context). Any opinions, findings, and conclusions or recommendations in this material are those of the authors and do not necessarily reflect the views of the government funding agencies. The authors thank Nicolas Ducheneaut and Yiye Ruan for help and discussion, and anonymous reviewers for constructive comments.

References

1. Argamon, S., Whitelaw, C., Chase, P., Hota, S.R., Garg, N., Levitan, S.: Stylistic text classification using functional lexical features. Journal of the American Society for Information Science and Technology 58(6), 802–822 (2007)
2. Bellotti, V., Ducheneaut, N., Howard, M., Smith, I.: Taking email to task: the design and evaluation of a task management centered email tool. In: CHI 2003, pp. 345–352 (2003)
3. Blei, D., Ng, A., Jordan, M.: Latent dirichlet allocation. Journal of Machine Learning Research 3, 993–1022 (2003)
4. Carvalho, V.R., Cohen, W.W.: Learning to extract signature and reply lines from email. In: Proc. of CEAS 2004 (2004)
5. Cohen, W.W., Carvalho, V.R., Mitchell, T.M.: Learning to classify email into "speech acts". In: Proc. of EMNLP 2004, pp. 309–316 (2004)
6. Dredze, M., Brooks, T., Carroll, J., Magarick, J., Blitzer, J.: FernandoPereira: Intelligent email: reply and attachment prediction. In: Proc. of the 13th IUI, pp. 321–324 (2008)
7. Ducheneaut, N., Bellotti, V.: E-mail as habitat: an exploration of embedded personal information management. Interactions 8, 30–38 (2001)

8. Ehrenberg, A.L., Juckes, S.C., White, K.M., Walsh, S.P.: Personality and self-esteem as predictors of young people's technology use. Cyberpsychology & Behavior 11(6), 739–741 (2008)
9. Hamburger, Y., Ben-Artzi, E.: The relationship between extraversion and neuroticism and the different uses of the internet. Computers in Human Behavior 6(4) (July 2000)
10. Jakobwitz, S., Egan, V.: The dark 'triad' of psychopathy and normal personality traits. Personality and Individual Differences 40(0), 331–339 (2006)
11. Joachims, T.: Learning to Classify Text Using Support Vector Machines. Kluwer Academic Publishers (2001)
12. John, O.P., Robins, R.W., Pervin, L.A.: Handbook of Personality: Theory and Research. 3rd edn. The Guilford Press (2010)
13. Kenny, D.A., Horner, C., Kashy, D.A., Chu, L.C.: Consensus at zero acquaintance: Replication, behavioral cues, and stability. Journal of Personality and Social Psychology, 88–97 (1992)
14. Lafferty, J., McCallum, A., Pereira, F.: Conditional random fields: Probabilistic models for segmenting and labeling sequence data. In: Proc. of ICML 2001, pp. 282–289 (2001)
15. Lam, D., Rohall, S.L., Schmandt, C., Stern, M.K.: Exploiting e-mail structure to improve summarization. In: Proc. of CSCW 2002 (2002)
16. Lepri, B., Mana, N., Cappelletti, A., Pianesi, F., Zancanaro, M.: Modeling the personality of participants during group interactions. In: Houben, G.-J., McCalla, G., Pianesi, F., Zancanaro, M. (eds.) UMAP 2009. LNCS, vol. 5535, pp. 114–125. Springer, Heidelberg (2009)
17. Muldner, K., Burleson, W., VanLehn, K.: "Yes!": Using tutor and sensor data to predict moments of delight during instructional activities. In: De Bra, P., Kobsa, A., Chin, D. (eds.) UMAP 2010. LNCS, vol. 6075, pp. 159–170. Springer, Heidelberg (2010)
18. Pang, B., Lee, L.: Seeing stars: exploiting class relationships for sentiment categorization with respect to rating scales. In: Proc. of the 43rd ACL, pp. 115–124 (2005)
19. Pennebaker, J.W., Francis, M.E., Booth, R.J.: Linguistic Inquiry and Word Count (LIWC2001). Lawrence Erlbaum Associates, Mahwah (2001)
20. Ramage, D., Hall, D., Nallapati, R., Manning, C.: Labeled lda: a supervised topic model for credit attribution in multi-labeled corpora. In: Proc. of EMNLP 2009, pp. 248–256 (2009)
21. Shaw, E., Stroz, E.: Warmtouch: assessing the insider threat and relationship management. In: Parker, T., Devost, M., Sachs, M., Shaw, E., Stroz, E. (eds.) Cyber Adversary Characterization: Auditing the Hacker Mind, Syngress Publishing (2004)
22. Toutanova, K., Klein, D., Manning, C.D., Singer, Y.: Feature-rich part-of-speech tagging with a cyclic dependency network. In: Proc. of NAACL 2003, 173–180 (2003)
23. Tsoumakas, G., Katakis, I.: Multi label classification: An overview. International Journal of Data Warehousing and Mining 3(3), 1–13 (2005)
24. Tsoumakas, G., Katakis, I., Vlahavas, I.: Random k-labelsets for multilabel classification. IEEE Transactions on Knowledge and Data Engineering 23(7), 1079–1089 (2011)
25. Whittaker, S., Bellotti, V., Gwizdka, J.: Email in personal information management. Communications of the ACM 49(1), 68–73 (2006)
26. Wiktionary: a multilingual, web-based free dictionary (2013), http://www.wiktionary.org (retrieved)
27. Wilson, T., Wiebe, J., Hoffmann, P.: Recognizing contextual polarity in phrase-level sentiment analysis. In: Proceedings of HLT-EMNLP, pp. 347–354 (2005)
28. Yang, Y., Pedersen, J.O.: A comparative study on feature selection in text categorization. In: Proc. of ICML 1997, 412–420 (1997)

Modeling Emotions with Social Tags

Ignacio Fernández-Tobías, Iván Cantador, and Laura Plaza

Universidad Autónoma de Madrid, 28049 Madrid, Spain
{i.fernandez,ivan.cantador,laura.plaza}@uam.es

Abstract. We present an emotion model based on social tags, which is built upon an automatically generated lexicon that describes emotions by means of synonym and antonym terms. Using this model we develop a number of methods that transform social tag-based item profiles into emotion-oriented item profiles. We show that the model's representation of a number of basic emotions is in accordance with the well known psychological circumplex model of affect, and we report results from a user study that show a high precision of our methods to infer the emotions evoked by items in the movie and music domains.

Keywords: emotions, social tagging, folksonomies.

1   Introduction

Emotions are intense feelings that are directed at someone or something. In adaptive and personalized systems, emotions are usually considered as contextual signals that can lead to enhanced approaches in a wide array of applications, such as constructing user behavior models [2], tailoring search results [3], and recommending items [5], to name a few. Hence, modeling, capturing and exploiting emotions present challenging problems.

In this paper we focus on the emotion modeling task, and restrict our attention to situations where emotions are expressed in (and can be extracted from) text contents – such as reviews in blogs, and annotations in social tagging systems –, differently to e.g. situations where emotions are recognized in either the visual or auditory modalities.

2   An Emotion Lexicon

Among the existing dimensional models of emotion, the circumplex model [4] is a dominant one. It suggests that emotions are distributed in a two-dimensional circular space formed by two independent dimensions: *arousal* and *pleasure*. Figure 1a shows such distribution. Arousal represents the vertical axis and reflects the intensity of an emotion; and pleasure represents the horizontal axis and reflects whether an emotion is positive or negative. The center of the circle represents medium levels of arousal and pleasure. Any emotion can be represented at any level of arousal and pleasure, including a neutral level of one or both of such factors. The figure shows the distribution of 16 basic emotions. We also consider this set of emotions.

S. Carberry et al. (Eds.): UMAP 2013, LNCS 7899, pp. 331–334, 2013.

Our dimensional model is built upon an automatically generated lexicon $\mathcal{L} = \{t_1, ..., t_K\}$ composed of synonym and antonym terms t_k of the emotions' names – which are adjectives (e.g. *happy*, *sad*), as shown in Figure 1a. The synonym and antonym terms of each emotion's name are obtained from the online thesaurus provided by Dictionary.com (http://thesaurus.com).

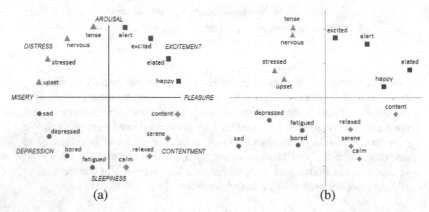

(a)   (b)

Fig. 1. Two-dimensional distributions of basic emotions established in the circumplex model (1a) and automatically obtained in our tag-based model (1b).

Once the lexicon $\mathcal{L}$ is generated, an emotion $e_i \in \mathcal{E}$ is represented as a vector $\mathbf{e}_i = (e_{i,1}, ..., e_{i,K}) \in \mathbb{R}^K$, in which the component $e_{i,k}$ corresponds to the term $t_k \in \mathcal{L}$, and is a numeric value defined as:

$$e_{i,k} = \begin{cases} tfidf(t_k, e_i) & \text{if } t_k \in synonyms(e_i) \\ -tfidf(t_k, e_i) & \text{if } t_k \in antonyms(e_i) \\ 0 & \text{otherwise} \end{cases} \qquad (1)$$

The component $e_{i,k}$ is greater than 0 if the term t_k is a synonym of the emotion e_i, lower than 0 if t_k is an antonym of e_i, and 0 otherwise. Its absolute value corresponds to the TF-IDF weight of t_k computed by considering the lexicon $\mathcal{L}$ as the *collection vocabulary*, and the set $\mathcal{E}$ of emotions (described as sets of synonym and antonym terms) as the *collection documents*. With the proposed vector representation, we can measure (dis)similarities between emotions. Specifically, we can use the well known cosine similarity $sim(e_i, e_j) = \cos(\mathbf{e}_i, \mathbf{e}_j)$.[1]

To validate the correspondences between our computational model and the theoretic circumplex model, Figure 1b shows the projections of the emotion vectors into a two-dimensional space by applying Principal Component Analysis. We can see that our model locates all the 16 basic emotions in their corresponding quadrants. More interestingly, in our model the axes defined by the two most informative components are related to the *arousal* and *pleasure* factors of the circumplex model.

3   Emotion-Oriented Tag-Based Profiles

The proposed representation of emotions lets transform social tag-based item profiles (i.e., the items' annotation sets) into emotion-oriented profiles. Formally, let an emotion

$e_i \in \mathcal{E}$ be defined as in formula (1). For an item (object) o_n, let $\mathbf{o}_n = (o_{n,1}, ..., o_{n,|\mathcal{T}|}) \in \mathbb{R}^{|\mathcal{T}|}$ be the item's *tag-based profile*, where $o_{n,i}$ corresponds to the tag $t_i \in \mathcal{T}$ of the item's folksonomy. Then, from such profile, we define the item's *emotion-oriented profile* as $\mathbf{q}_n = (q_{n,1}, ..., q_{n,|\mathcal{E}|}) \in [-1,1]^{|\mathcal{E}|}$, where the i-th component corresponds to the emotion $e_i^c \in \mathcal{E}$, and its weight is computed as $q_{n,i} = cos(\mathbf{o}_n, \mathbf{e}_i)$.

Moreover, for each emotion-oriented profile, we consider two alternatives for defining the emotion vectors $\mathbf{e}_i$: *basic vectors*, whose components correspond to terms of the lexicon, as defined in formula (1), and *extended_N* vectors, whose components correspond to the N folksonomy tags that cooccur most frequently (in the tag-based item profiles) with the terms of the basic vectors. These tags are not necessarily synonyms/ antonyms of the lexicon terms, and it is not clear whether they can be valuable.

4   Experiments

We conducted a user study in which participants, recruited via social networking sites, were presented with sets of movies or musicians (no combinations of both) from the HetRec'11 social tagging datasets [1]. They were requested to freely state which emotions they considered as relevant for each item (movie or musician), thus manually (and collectively) creating emotion-oriented item profiles, which we considered as ground truth. A total of 72 users participated, evaluating 178 movies and 132 musicians. They generated 713 evaluation cases, assigning an average of 3.30 and 4.18 emotions to items in the movies and music domains, respectively.[1]

To evaluate the quality of the emotion-oriented profiles generated by our methods with respect to the ground truth profiles, we compared them by means of the Precision at position k, P@k, which, for a particular item, is defined as the percentage of the top k emotions returned by a method that are relevant for the item, as stated by the users of our study. Table 1 shows average precision values of the different methods and a random emotion ranking method. The extended method was the best performing approach in both domains with P@1 values close to 70%, and was outperformed by the basic method in the music domain for P@2 and P@3. In general, the methods performed in the music domain better than in the movies domain.

Table 1. Average P@k values of the considered emotion-oriented profiles

Emotion vector model	movies				music			
	#evals	P@1	P@2	P@3	#evals	P@1	P@2	P@3
random	165	0.297	0.305	0.302	129	0.327	0.339	0.345
basic	107	0.598	0.528	0.514	109	0.606	**0.670**	**0.636**
extended_10	77	**0.675**	**0.643**	**0.589**	11	**0.636**	0.636	0.546

---

[1] The emotion lexicon, profiles, and evaluation tool are available at
http://ir.ii.uam.es/emotions

Acknowledgments. This work was supported by the Spanish Government (TIN2011-28538-C02) and the Regional Government of Madrid (S2009TIC-1542).

References

1. Cantador, I., Brusilovsky, P., Kuflik, T.: Second Workshop on Information Heterogeneity and Fusion in Recommender Systems. In: RecSys 2011, pp. 387–388 (2011)
2. Hastings, J., Ceusters, W., Smith, B., Mulligan, K.: The Emotion Ontology: Enabling Interdisciplinary Research in the Affective Sciences. In: Beigl, M., Christiansen, H., Roth-Berghofer, T.R., Kofod-Petersen, A., Coventry, K.R., Schmidtke, H.R. (eds.) CONTEXT 2011. LNCS, vol. 6967, pp. 119–123. Springer, Heidelberg (2011)
3. Meyers, O.C.: A Mood-based Music Classification and Exploration System. MSc Thesis. School of Architecture and Planning. MIT (2007)
4. Russell, J.A.: A Circumplex Model of Affect. Journal of Personality and Social Psychology 39(6), 1161–1178 (1980)
5. Winoto, P., Ya Tang, T.: The Role of User Mood in Movie Recommendations. Expert Systems with Applications 37(8), 6086–6092 (2010)

Unobtrusive Monitoring of Knowledge Workers
for Stress Self-regulation

Saskia Koldijk[1,2], Maya Sappelli[1,2], Mark Neerincx[1,3], and Wessel Kraaij[1,2]

[1] TNO, The Netherlands
{name.surname}@tno.nl
[2] Radboud University Nijmegen, The Netherlands
[3] Technical University Delft, The Netherlands

Abstract. In our connected workplaces it can be hard to work calm and focused. In a simulated work environment we manipulated the stressors time pressure and email interruptions. We found effects on subjective experience and working behavior. Initial results indicate that the sensor data that we collected is suitable for user state modeling in stress related terms.

Keywords: Experiment, stress, knowledge worker, user state modeling.

1 Introduction

In our connected environments, it can be hard to work in a calm and focused manner. Ruff (2002) speaks of 'plugged in compulsion' and 'hurry sickness', which easily cause interruptions and time pressure. Mark, Gudith and Klocke (2008) investigated the cost of interruptions and came to the conclusion that "after only 20 minutes of interrupted performance people reported significantly higher stress, frustration, workload, effort and pressure". Certainly, some amount of stress is not harmful and might even be beneficial to gain concentration and focus. However, extended periods of stress can be a danger to health. Bakker et al. (2012) explain that stress can either directly lead to illness through its physiological effects or indirectly, through maladaptive health behavior, like smoking, poor eating habits or lack of sleep.

In SWELL[1] we aim to improve well-being at work by supporting knowledge workers, who use and produce information as their main task, working on computers. We intend to use unobtrusive and easily available sensors to infer the user's state (Koldijk, Neerincx & Kraaij, 2012). This information will then be used to help knowledge workers maintain a healthy stress level. With the experiment and explorative analyses presented in this paper, we aim to gather insight in the concept of stress at work and ways in which it could be measured.

Stress is a broad concept referring to mental and physiological processes during emotional and cognitive demanding situations. We follow a pragmatic approach and hypothesize that *perceived stress* is a concept related to: (1) the *cognitive task load*,

---

[1] http://www.swell-project.net

S. Carberry et al. (Eds.): UMAP 2013, LNCS 7899, pp. 335–337, 2013.
© Springer-Verlag Berlin Heidelberg 2013

which poses demands on the worker, (2) the *mental effort*, which the worker needs to handle the task and (3) the *emotional response* that is raised, in terms of arousal and valence. In our experiment we manipulate the demands by providing external stressors in the form of email interruptions and time pressure. Given that the resources of the participants remain unchanged, we expect that the stressor conditions cause stress according to the resources-demands model of Karasek (1979). First, we investigate which effect our stressors have on subjective experience of task load, mental effort, emotions and perceived stress. Secondly, we investigate how we could measure stress and related aspects with unobtrusive sensors.

2   Experiment

We simulated a knowledge work scenario in which participants used a computer to write reports and make presentations on six specified topics (e.g. experience and opinion about healthy living). They were allowed to use the internet and a set of stored documents. While the participant worked, we collected data with several sensors: computer logging, cameras, Kinect 3D, heart rate and skin conductance sensors.

In a within-subject design each participant worked under the following conditions: 1) Neutral (pre-test without stressor), 2) Time pressure, in which they had less time to finish the tasks and 3) Interruptions, in which 8 emails were sent to the participant during the tasks (e.g. "When was Einstein born?" or "There is a meeting this afternoon."). The neutral condition was always presented first in order to get a natural, uninfluenced baseline for each participant. The order of the time pressure and interruption conditions was counterbalanced.

Before each condition, participants watched a nature film clip of 8 minutes to relax. After completion of a condition, they were asked to fill in a questionnaire and were allowed to take a short break. For measuring subjective experience we combined several validated questionnaires for assessing task load, mental effort and emotion (i.e. NASA-TLX, RSME and SAM). Perceived stress was measured with a Visual Analog Scale from 'not stressed' to 'very stressed'. This procedure of relaxation, tasks execution and questionnaire was then repeated for the two other conditions, yielding an experiment duration of about 3 hours. 25 students (8 female, average age = 25, stdv = 3.25) who are representative of knowledge workers participated.

3   Results and Conclusions

A statistical comparison (paired t-tests) of the time pressure and neutral condition showed that participants experienced significantly higher temporal demand (p =.033) and higher arousal (p =.001) under time pressure, which was in line with our expectations. The stressor email interruptions yielded reports of more mental effort (p = .011), but also more positive valence (p =.042) and dominance (p =.016), which we did not expect. Our emails might have caused a feeling of being connected and glad to help, but it is unclear whether this holds for office mail in general. Moreover, we found differences in computer-use behavior. Under time pressure we see significantly more key strokes (p =.005) than in the neutral condition, and under interruptions we see more application changes (p =.001) and left clicks (p =.014), so both stressors create typical behavioral patterns. Perceived stress did not differ significantly between the stressor and neutral conditions. Either our stressor conditions were not suitable to cause the typical feeling of stress, or the neutral condition was stressful, too, as it was always the first condition and many participants did not finish all required tasks.

The relation between different variables was analyzed by calculating Pearson correlations. We found that perceived stress is moderately related to task load in terms of mental demand (r =.464), temporal demand (r =.490) and frustration (r =.535). Moreover, stress is related to emotion in terms of valence (r = -.398) and arousal (r =.371, for all p < .001). Explorative correlation analysis of the sensor data thus far indicates that estimating 'perceived stress' from our sensors directly is probably difficult, due to weak correlations. However, moderate correlations (with p < .001) were found for mental effort with several facial features[2]. When working in a condition with higher mental effort, participants looked more disgusted (r =.505) and sad (r = .402) and they showed more activation in the facial action units LidTightener (r =.492), UpperLipRaiser (r =.462), BrowLowerer (r =.422) and CheekRaiser (r = .412).

As a conclusion, the experiment presented in this paper gave us insights in the effects of stressors at work and the relations among perceived stress and related concepts. Even though we used a simplified work scenario in a lab setting, the stressors changed aspects of subjective experience and behavior. Therefore, the collected sensor data can and will be used for user state modeling in stress related terms.

Acknowledgements. This publication was supported by the Dutch national program COMMIT (project P7 SWELL).

References

1. Ruff, J.: Information Overload: Causes, Symptoms and Solutions. Harvard Graduate School of Education, pp. 1–13 (2002)
2. Mark, G., Gudith, D., Klocke, U.: The cost of interrupted work: more speed and stress. In: Proceedings of the Twenty-Sixth Annual SIGCHI Conference on Human Factors in Computing Systems, pp. 107–110. ACM (2008)
3. Bakker, J., Holenderski, L., Kocielnik, R., Pechenizkiy, M., Sidorova, N.: Stess@ work: From measuring stress to its understanding, prediction and handling with personalized coaching. In: Proceedings of the 2nd ACM SIGHIT Symposium on International Health Informatics, pp. 673–678. ACM (2012)
4. Koldijk, S., Neerincx, M., Kraaij, W.: Unobtrusively measuring stress and workload of knowledge workers. In: Proceedings of Measuring Behavior (2012)
5. Karasek, R.A.: Job demands, job decision latitude, and mental strain: Implications for job redesign. In: Administrative Science Quarterly, pp. 285–308 (1979)

---

[2] From FaceReader, by Noldus Information Technology.

Topolor: A Social Personalized Adaptive E-Learning System

Lei Shi, Dana Al Qudah, Alaa Qaffas, and Alexandra I. Cristea

Department of Computer Science, University of Warwick
CV4 7AL, Coventry, United Kingdom
`{lei.shi,d.al-qudah,aqaffas,acristea}@dcs.warwick.ac.uk`

Abstract. This paper briefly introduces Topolor, a social personalized adaptive e-learning system, which aims at improving fine-grained social interaction in the learning process in addition to applying classical adaptation based on user modeling. Here, we present the main features of Topolor and its preliminary evaluation that showed high system usability from a student's perspective. The intention is to demonstrate Topolor hands-on at the conference.

1   Introduction

Topolor is a social adaptive personalized e-learning system built on Yii Framework[1] and Bootstrap[2], and hosted on Github[3] for open source sharing and version control. It has been used as an online learning environment for MSc level students in the Department of Computer Science, at the University of Warwick. It was designed based on the hypothesis that *extensive social features, personalized recommendations and Facebook[4]-like appearance of a system, would make the environment more familiar to the learners, so will subsequently increase the system usability*. This paper describes the system architecture and the primary evaluation on the system usability.

2   Main Features

As shown in Figure 1 a, Topolor has a Facebook-like appearance, i.e., the profile avatar and learner information, the fixed-position top menu and the left side bar for navigation, and the information flow wall for social interaction, etc. Topolor (Figure 1 b) supports learning content adaptation, learning path adaptation and peer adaptation, and provides a social e-learning environment, i.e., learners can comment on a topic, ask/answer a question about a topic, create and share notes related a topic, etc. This is a much broader range of adaptation than in regular adaptive hypermedia systems [1].

---

[1] `http://yiiframework.com`
[2] `http://twitter.github.com/bootstrap`
[3] `https://github.com/aslanshek/topolor`
[4] `https://www.facebook.com`

S. Carberry et al. (Eds.): UMAP 2013, LNCS 7899, pp. 338–340, 2013.

a. Topolor - Home   b. Module Center - Topic

Fig. 1. The Screenshot of Topolor

2.1   Learning Content Adaptation

Topolor provides various levels of granularity of learning content adaptation, such as the whole modules versus individual topics within a module, based on: a) the connection and distance among modules/topics, b) the number of same tags shared; c) the knowledge levels of related topics, d) the incorrectly answered questions related to learning topics, and so on.

2.2   Learning Path Adaptation

The learning path adaptation is based on the structure of online courses (e.g., the depth-first traversal in a tree structured module), so a learner can, for example, click on 'Previous' to review prerequisite topics. The learning path is dynamically changed when, e.g., the submitted quiz contains the precast maximum number of incorrectly answered questions related to a specific topic.

2.3   Learning Peer Recommendations

Different scenes of peer recommendations are provided, e.g., when a learner is in a module dashboard page, learning a topic, asking/answering questions or taking a quiz. The learning peer recommendation is based on learning history, previous performance and so on. For instance, for a topic page, peers are recommended based on their quiz score for that topic, ordered in a recommendation ranking list.

2.4   Social Interaction

Topolor provides a set of Web 2.0 tools that learners are familiar with. For instance, the system index (Topolor – Home, as shown in Figure 1 a) contains an information flow wall presenting social interaction events; navigation bar provides a messaging tool for synchronous and asynchronous communication. Learners can also comment on, share and 'favorite' a topic, a question, a status, a note and so on.

2.5   Adaptivity and Adaptability

Adaptivity is the ability to recommend automatically via pre-defined adaptation strategies, while adaptability is the ability to perform changes based on learner's direct intervention. Topolor provides both as main adaptation approaches.

3   Evaluation

Topolor was evaluated with the help of 21 students studying 'Dynamic Web-based Systems', a 4th year module at the department of Computer Science, University of Warwick. Before accessing the online course, a 'to-do list' was handed out to the students, to make sure they have a reminder of all actions at their disposal. The order of doing the actions, and if to repeat any actions was up to them. The system usability was tested using SUS [2]. SUS questions were answered on the Likert scale to provide a global view of subjective assessments of usability. The SUS assessment has a reliability value of 0.85 [3], and good systems should get a SUS score between 70-80 points. The SUS Score of Topolor is 75.75 (σ=12.36, median=76.25). Hence we claim that the usability of Topolor meets our initial expectation.

4   Summary and Future Work

In this paper, we have briefly introduced Topolor, a social adaptive personalized e-learning system, and showed results on usability from its preliminary evaluation. We plan to demo Topolor to researchers and practitioners and both showcase new adaptation features, as well as gather feedback on further development. Our results showed high system usability from a student's perspective. Additionally, during the online course session, a logging mechanism kept track of students' actions. Therefore for the future work, we intend to conduct an investigative study on learning behavior patterns by using data mining methods and visualization tools to analyze the extracted learning behavior data from the logging system, aiming at better understanding the learning process and thereby improve its adaptation and personalization mechanisms.

References

1. Brusilovsky, P.: Adaptive hypermedia. User Modeling and User-Adapted Interaction 11(1), 87–110 (2001)
2. Brooke, J.: SUS – A quick and dirty usability scale. Usability Evaluation in Industry. Taylor and Francis (1996)
3. Kirakowski, J.: The use of questionnaire methods for usability assessment (unpublished manuscript, 1994), http://sumi.ucc.ie/sumipapp.html (retreived)

RES: A Personalized Filtering Tool for CiteSeerX Queries Based on Keyphrase Extraction

Dario De Nart, Felice Ferrara, and Carlo Tasso

Artificial Intelligence Lab
Department of Mathematics and Computer Science
University of Udine, Italy
{dario.denart,felice.ferrara,carlo.tasso}@uniud.it

Abstract. Finding satisfactory scientific literature is still a very time-consuming task. In the last decade several tools have been proposed to approach this task, however only few of them actually analyse the whole document in order to select and present it to the user and even less tools offer any kind of explanation of why a given item was re-trieved/recommended. The main goal of this demonstration is to present the RES system, a tool intended to overcome the limitations of tra-ditional recommender and personalized information retrieval systems by exploiting a more semantic approach where concepts are extracted from the papers in order to generate and then explain the recommenda-tion. RES acts like a personalized interface for the well-known CiteSeerX system, filtering and presenting query results accordingly to individual user's interests.

1 Introduction

Reading scientific literature is a critical step for conceiving and developing sci-entific projects, however it still remains an expensive task. Actually, systems such as CiteSeerX, Google Scholar, and Mendeley allow researchers to discover new knowledge by querying and browsing millions of publications. Many systems have been developed to provide personalized access to such a huge amount of information, but all of them present their results as a bare list of items, occa-sionally displaying some lines extracted from the abstract, leaving to the user the burden of checking whether the recommendation is relevant or not by read-ing the paper. Moreover, most of those systems use collaborative mechanisms, meaning that the recommendation is driven by other users' behaviour, a princi-ple that may not work well for small research communities due to sparsisty and cold start issues [4]. We claim that a more semantic and content-based approach, assuring that the recommendation is driven by the actual content included in the paper, and a brief, yet detailed and informative, explanation of the recom-mendation could save much time and effort and could lead to a greater user satisfaction. In order to support our claim, we present RES, a Recommendation

S. Carberry et al. (Eds.): UMAP 2013, LNCS 7899, pp. 341–343, 2013.

and Explanation System using a completely content-based approach, based on the use of Keyphrases (KP), i.e. short phrases of up to three words. Using KPs instead of keywords allows to preserve information about the context in which terms are used and, moreover, KPs have a high cognitive plausibility. KPs are automatically extracted from texts by means of Dikpe, a Keyphrase Extraction tool previously developed in our laboratory [2].

2   Related Work

In [5] several collaborative techniques for recommending papers of CiteULike are presented and discussed. In [1], the relations involving users, publications, tags, and other metadata are used to produce a graph for computing personalized suggestions, without analysing the document content. Many other examples, here omitted due to shortage of space, feature other kinds of collaborative and/or metadata-based approaches. Content-based and hybrid approaches are used as well: in [3], the authors propose a filtering system based on keyphrase extraction for identifying potentially relevant documents, yet there is no explanation of the resulting recommendation. [4] points out how recommendation strategies based on explicit decision models are able to offer adequate explanations. Finally, [6] discusses the benefits of explanations on user satisfaction.

3   System Overview

The RES system includes a database called *SPC* (Scientific Paper Collection) and the following three main modules:

1) A *Web User Interface Module* devoted to: (i) let the user create and edit his profile, (ii) query CiteSeer, and (iii) access the recommended items. Recommendations are presented as a ranked list of documents where the top items are those that better match the user profile. For each document two lists are presented: KPs appearing in both the user profile and in the document and relevant KPs present in the document but not in the user profile.

2) A *KP Extraction Module*, devoted to: (i) gather CiteSeer results,(ii) extract KPs from each article, and (iii) store its representation in the SPC.

3) A *Recommendation Engine Module* devoted to: (i) build and maintain personalized user profiles representing specific interests of the user and (ii) matching user profiles against document representations stored in the SPC.

Our recommendation strategy is document-centric: in order to create a user profile the system requests the user to enter one or more sample articles or paragraphs that summarize his/her interests and then filters search results according to the similarity between them and the profile. Document contents are represented as lists of KPs, which are split into single terms in order to create a graph representation where terms are nodes and the arcs represent co-occurrence in the same KP. This modelling technique allows RES to build, for each term, a meaningful context of interest by simply checking its adjacency list. The same term used in the same context in different articles should reasonably refer to the same adjacent concepts, showing in such a way a certain degree of similarity: more shared concepts indicate higher similarity. The full recommending algorithm takes into account also the TF-IDF weights of shared terms in order to penalize trivial associations.

4 Evaluation and Conclusions

In the first development stage of the system, we have performed a limited number of formative tests, mainly aimed at experimenting different system parameterizations. A set of over 300 scientific papers dealing with Recommender Systems and Adaptive Personalization was stored in the SPC and manually classified according to 16 topics. Later, 200 uncategorized documents dealing with several random ICT topics were added in order to create noise in the data. 250 user profiles were automatically generated for each one of the 16 topics by means of groups of 2, 4, 6, and 10 seed documents; then, for each user profile, RES and a baseline reference system (TF-IDF based ad-hoc developed) were compared. For each recommendation, every recommended item dealing with the same topic as the seed document was considered as a good recommendation. We have defined the *accuracy* as the average percentage of good recommendations over the total recommended items. Results gathered so far are very promising since RES outperformed the baseline mechanism: accuracy of 57% vs baseline accuracy of 42% with 2 seed documents, up to accuracy of 72% vs baseline accuracy of 60% with 10 seed documents. Despite encouraging results, the improvement of RES is ongoing, focusing on: adapting it to other scientific collections, to reduce the time needed for content analysis, and to envisage more effective procedures for creating profiles. Evaluation is ongoing and in the future it will address the quality and the impact of the produced explanations.

References

1. Doerfel, S., Jäschke, R., Hotho, A., Stumme, G.: Leveraging publication metadata and social data into folkrank for scientific publication recommendation. In: Proceedings of the 4th ACM RecSys Workshop on Recommender Systems and the Social Web, pp. 9–16. ACM, New York (2012)
2. Ferrara, F., Pudota, N., Tasso, C.: A keyphrase-based paper recommender system. Digital Libraries and Archives, pp. 14–25 (2011)
3. Govindaraju, V., Ramanathan, K.: Similar document search and recommendation. Journal of Emerging Technologies in Web Intelligence 4(1), 84–93 (2012)
4. Jannach, D., Zanker, M., Felfernig, A., Friedrich, G.: Recommender systems: an introduction. Cambridge University Press (2010)
5. Parra, D., Brusilovsky, P.: Evaluation of collaborative filtering algorithms for recommending articles on citeulike. In: Proceedings of the Workshop on Web, vol. 3. Citeseer (2010)
6. Zanker, M.: The influence of knowledgeable explanations on users' perception of a recommender system. In: Proceedings of the Sixth ACM Conference on Recommender Systems, pp. 269–272. ACM, New York (2012)

Generating a Personalized UI for the Car:
A User-Adaptive Rendering Architecture

Michael Feld[1], Gerrit Meixner[2], Angela Mahr[1], Marc Seissler[3],
and Balaji Kalyanasundaram[1]

[1] German Research Center for Artificial Intelligence, Saarbrücken, Germany
[2] Heilbronn University, Faculty of Computer Science, Heilbronn, Germany
[3] German Research Center for Artificial Intelligence, Kaiserslautern, Germany

Abstract. Personalized systems are gaining popularity in various mobile scenarios. In this work, we take on the challenges associated with the
automotive domain and present a user-adaptive graphical renderer. By
supporting a strictly model-based development processes, we meet the
rigid requirements of the industry. The proposed architecture is based
on the UIML standard and a novel rule-based adaptation framework.

Keywords: Automotive, Personalization, User adaptation, UIML.

1 Introduction

User interfaces in the vehicle are in the middle of a major transition: from physical or "tangible" controls built into the consoles to visual controls rendered on
the screen. Being more flexible, the system can adjust the provided functions
(e.g. navigation, other assistance, infotainment) at any time, even pro-actively.
They can take into account who is using the system, in what state this person is, or any special characteristics of the situation. This ability that results
in a more personalized experience is well-known from mobile phones and home
computers [2], but it has not been adopted by the car industry yet. Among the
reasons are the absence of a rendering architecture that complies with the special
requirements imposed by the industry on HMI development processes.

In addition to the growing number of configurable systems in a modern car,
there is a need for shorter release cycles and lower costs for the development of
automotive UIs. One main source of problems is the communication overhead
caused by informal specifications [5]. This overhead is needed to reduce the
ambiguity and the incorrectness of the specification document. A more formal
approach can reduce this overhead dramatically, leading to shorter development
times, cost savings and fewer problems. (Semi-)Formal specification of UIs is
researched in the context of model-based user interface development (MBUID)
[8,6]. For a brief review of former and current MBUID approaches see [7].

A vast number of (XML-based) User Interface Description Languages (UIDLs)
exist already in the field of MBUID [3]. Some of the UIDLs are already standardized by e.g., *OASIS*, currently being standardized by e.g. W3C [1] and/or they

S. Carberry et al. (Eds.): UMAP 2013, LNCS 7899, pp. 344–346, 2013.

are subject of a continuous development process. The purpose of using a UIDL to develop a user interface (UI) is to systematize the UI development process [8]. UIDLs enable the developer to systematically break down a UI into different abstraction layers and to model these layers. Thus it is possible e.g. to describe the behavior, the structure and the layout of a UI independently of each other. Existing UIDLs differ in terms of supported platforms and modalities as well as in the amount of predefined interaction objects for describing UI elements.

2   Renderer Architecture

In our project we developed a design that combines the aspects of user modeling, rule-based adaptation, and rendering in a single architecture as outlined in Figure 1. The rendering pipeline consists of a three-layer process: There are two layers dealing with adaptation (layers 1 and 2) and one layer handling the actual rendering. These two aspects are generally independent, although they have been optimized for this scenario. The input to the renderer is a standards-compliant User Interface Markup Language (UIML) [4] document. The output is the rendering, which is directly displayed in a browser or stand-alone Flash application when the appropriate host Flash document is loaded. The coordination of the process is performed by the Adaptation Assistant component. The *UI Adaptation Layer* adapts the user interface elements of the original input UIML based on a user model and set of rules. The user model is obtained from a knowledge base component called *KAPcom* (Knowledge Management, Adaptation and Personalization Component). The adaptation rules are specified as an XML-based rule file. This file can contain multiple sets of tags to represent the rules. It provides a mapping between user model properties, UI elements, and the adaptation effects by indicating the properties depending on which the adaptation effect has to be applied. Examples of effects that can be performed are: adding/removing images, reordering UI items, changing fonts, changing the layout etc. For instance, there could be a rule that increases the margin around

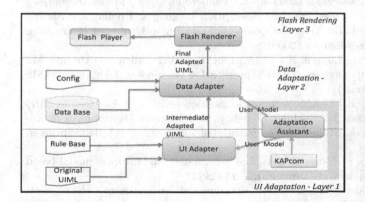

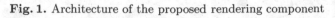

Fig. 1. Architecture of the proposed rendering component   **Fig. 2.** In-car HMI

buttons for elderly users or at high speed. The output of this layer is an adapted UIML file that may have some of the layout elements changed. This document is then processed by the *Data Adaptation Layer*. It performs adaptation based on the same user model, but it changes the content instead of the layout. This might affect for instance text labels. It is connected to a separate data store representing the current application data model (e.g. route information). This results in a further adapted version of the UIML code. The *Rendering Layer* finally takes the fully adapted UIML file and produces the Flash output. It consists of parser, layouting, and object generation modules that are implemented completely in *ActionScript*. The major work of this component consists of mapping the UIML elements to Flash widgets, thereby re-creating the original layout on the fly.

3 Conclusion and Outlook

We have leveraged existing standards to design a rendering architecture that combines two aspects: abstraction from a final user interface, so it can be integrated into an MBUID process that is part of modern automotive HMI design tool chains, and user-adaptive behavior. As part of our research, we have further created a personalized parking assistant application that utilizes the renderer, and which was designed completely in UIML (Figure 2). A small user study conducted with this application has confirmed that people were indeed seeing a benefit in the adaptive version, but also that the appropriateness depends largely on the use case. In the near future, we expect numerous personalized applications starting to appear in the vehicular context.

References

1. W3C Working Group Model-based User Interfaces,
   http://www.w3.org/2011/mbui/ (retrieved October 05, 2012)
2. Gajos, K., Weld, D.: SUPPLE: automatically generating user interfaces. In: Proc. of the 9th International Conference on Intelligent User Interfaces. ACM (2004)
3. Guerrero-Garcia, J., Gonzalez-Calleros, J., Vanderdonckt, J., Muoz-Arteaga, J.: A theoretical survey of user interface description languages: Preliminary results. In: Proc. of Joint 4th Latin American Conference on Human-Computer Interaction, pp. 36–43. IEEE, Los Alamitos (2009)
4. Helms, J., Schaefer, R., Luyten, K., Vanderdonckt, J., Vermeulen, J., Abrams, M.: User interface markup language (UIML) specification version 4.0. Tech. rep., OASIS Open, Inc. (2009) (draft)
5. Hübner, M., Grüll, I.: ICUC-XML format specification revision 14. Elektrobit (2007)
6. Hussmann, H., Meixner, G., Zuehlke, D. (eds.): Model-Driven Development of Advanced User Interfaces. Studies in Computational Intelligence, vol. 340. Springer, Heidelberg (2011)
7. Meixner, G., Paternò, F., Vanderdonckt, J.: Past, present, and future of model-based user interface development. i-Com 10(3), 2–11 (2011)
8. Puerta, A.: A model-based interface development environment. IEEE Software 14(4), 40–47 (1997)

Eliciting Affective Recommendations
to Support Distance Learning Students

Ángeles Manjarrés-Riesco, Olga C. Santos, and Jesus G. Boticario

aDeNu Research Group, Artificial Intelligence Dept. Computer Science School, UNED
C/Juan del Rosal, 16. Madrid 28040, Spain
{amanja,ocsantos,jgb}@dia.uned.es

Abstract. Affective support can be provided through personalized recommendations integrated within learning management systems (LMS). We have applied the TORMES user centered engineering approach to involve educators in a recommendation elicitation process in a distance learning (DL) context.

Keywords: Educational recommender systems (ERS), DL, affective computing.

1 Eliciting Affective Recommendations

Psychological research shows a strong relationship between learners' affective state and the cognitive process [1]. With this in mind, ERS can take into account user emotional information to recommend suitable learning resources [2]. In DL, both affective research and practice are rare: research mainly focuses on face to face interactions and practitioners do not have clear clues on how to deal with students' affective needs.

In order to identify recommendations dealing with affective issues in DL scenarios, we have applied the ISO 9241-210 TORMES methodology [3] to help educators identify when, who, what, how, where and why feedback needs to be provided to support learner's needs. In accordance with the methodology, 3 educators were asked to identify affective scenarios which present opportunities for recommendations based on character traits and emotions, customizable according to the learner profile. From the elicited knowledge, a focus group involving educators and researchers defined a taxonomy of affective scenarios (from a set of 47 identified) according to 2 independent classification criteria: (a) **Private** (see Table 1 for 2 of the 26 scenarios showing corresponding character independent recommendations, where identical situations may provoke different emotional responses which require recommendations differing either in tone or content) versus **Interpersonal** (see Table 3 for some situations plus emotional responses of the 21 scenarios: 11 student-student interactions and 10 student-tutor interactions); (b) **The main issue involved**: 15 concerning learning content and practice; 10 concerning learning assessment (6 self-assessment and 4 exam); and 13 concerning learning management (6 meta-learning, 7 course design, 2 assessment procedure and 7 LMS usability). Table 2 shows recommendations that depend on both emotion and character traits.

S. Carberry et al. (Eds.): UMAP 2013, LNCS 7899, pp. 347–349, 2013.
© Springer-Verlag Berlin Heidelberg 2013

Table 1. Some private scenarios and associated recommendations

Affective scenario	Recommendations
Main issue: Meta-learning *Situation*: Where to start? *Emotions*: (a) distraction/indolence/apathy (b) anxiety/confusion/frustration/helplessness	*Content*: Point to working plan, next learning objective & appropriate Learning Objects (LO) *Tone*: (a) kind but firm & slightly critical, (b) kind/reassuring/ suggestive
Main issue: Learning assessment *Situation:* Exam imminence. Going from one LO to another without focus on appropriate LO regarding exam/knowledge/competencies *Emotions*: (a) anxiety/depression, (b) distraction/detachment	*Content*: Point to appropriate LO focusing on gaps in knowledge & competencies, & exam objectives. Advise study plan review. Highlight (a) key learning objectives achieved (b) exam importance/imminence *Tone*: (a) empathetic/confident/convincing/ encouraging, (b) kind, firm & slightly critical

Table 2. Situation: The learner is having problems dealing with certain instructional material. She has successfully completed a significant part of the course.

Common content: Point to lack of knowledge & misunderstandings underlying the blockage		
Emotions: anxiety	*Traits:* nervous	*Rec tone*: empathetic/confident/convincing/encouraging
Content: Point to appropriate less difficult LO/review notes/ glossary. Post question for teachers/class mates. Advise changing activity. Point to relaxing/amusing LO (ed. games)		*Justification:* Should calm down practicing same competencies, and clarifying ideas to regain self-confidence
Emotions: boredom	*Traits: apathetic*	*Rec tone*: firm/animating
Content: - Point to a more suggestive and entertaining appropriate LO addressing the same objectives (i.e. interactive, amusing, interesting, stimulating, inspiring)		*Justification:* Only need stimulation to enhance motivation
Emotions: despair	*Traits:* pessimistic	*Rec. tone*: empathetic/understanding/cheering/affectionate
Content: Point to enjoyable appropriate LO of less difficulty addressing same objectives. Propose sharing worries with class mates		*Justification:* Should cheer up and adopt a more optimistic outlook practicing the same competencies with a simpler and more enjoyable LO.
Emotions: impatience	*Traits:* impatient/easily frustrated/narcissistic	*Rec. tome*: reassuring/critical
Content: - Point to more motivating, interesting and entertaining appropriate LO of less difficulty addressing the same objectives		*Justification:* Impatiently skipping study phases or theoretical explanations. Lack of key knowledge Show theoretical studies are not necessarily boring

Table 3. Interpersonal scenarios. Interaction identifiers: C student-student; T student-tutor. Issue identifiers: U usability; ML meta-learning; L learning; A, assessment; LM learning management; E, exams.

	Affective scenario description	
C_U	Angry with class mates due to forum misuse	
C_ML	Creating pleasant atmosphere in forums contributing positively to virtual social harmony	
C_L	Desolated, feeling ignorant & stupid compared to average level exhibited in forums	
C_A	After a bad mark in a team task, angry with team members missing their commitments	
T_LM	Critical of organization	(a) Aggressive/sarcastic/disrespectful; volatile personality
T_L	Critical of study materials	(b) Shy/self-incriminating/anxious; insecure personality
T_E	Critical of exam approach	(c) Discouraged; depressive personality

2   Conclusions and Ongoing Works

In DL, information on student affective states must be inferred from various sources (forums, emails, telephone calls, frequency of learners' communications/interactions in courses, etc.). The educators interviewed highlighted the difficulty in estimating the emotions, their intensity, permanency, etc. from these sources, given that they facilitate emotional dishonesty. The educators also pointed out that affective support is an essential but complex issue in DL. The affective experience issues in DL are distinctive and unique, being intricately linked to the experience of LMS-based interaction. This gives rise to particular scenarios and affective responses that require particular approaches to affective support. Adult students demand more participative teaching approaches, subtle and suggestive support, respect and appreciation of their experience, further reinforcement, friendliness and closeness. Therefore, to collect real-life practices of affective support and to evaluate them in real scenarios is a valuable activity for the implementation of affective ERS that hopefully will overcome the lack of teacher training in this area. The elicitation of expert educators knowledge demands a rigorous knowledge engineering approach, like TORMES, which is meant to support the elicitation process covering the main issues involved.

This research is part of the MAMIPEC project – funded by the Spanish Ministry of Economy and Competitivity–, in which we are developing an ERS that includes an Emotional Data Processor (which collects emotional data such as physiological data, physical interactions and learners' responses to specific questionnaires, and combines them to identify changes in the learner's affective state by applying data mining techniques [4]) and a Learner Profile (which models affective aspects). We are also designing a large-scale experiment involving learners and educators with different profiles to evaluate the benefits of the affective recommendations elicited. On the technological side, next we will study the viability of the recommendations being delivered by an ERS, and the formalization of the recommendation model obtained by translating the taxonomies and terminology of the participating educators to those of relevant standards (e.g. W3C EmotionML [5]).

References

1. Porayska-Pomsta, K., Mavrikis, M., Pain, H.: Diagnosing and acting on student affect: the tutor's perspective. User Model. User-Adapt. Interact. 18(1-2), 125–173 (2008)
2. Shen, L., Wang, M., Shen, R.: Affective e-Learning: Using "Emotional" Data to Improve Learning in Pervasive Learning Environment. Educational Technology & Society (ETS) 12(2), 176–189 (2009)
3. Santos, O.C., Boticario, J.G.: *TORMES methodology to elicit educational oriented recommendations* . In: Biswas, G., Bull, S., Kay, J., Mitrovic, A. (eds.) AIED 2011. LNCS, vol. 6738, pp. 541–543. Springer, Heidelberg (2011)
4. Santos, O.C., Salmeron-Majadas, S., Boticario, J.G.: Emotions detection from math exercises by combining several data sources. In: Proc. AIED. LNCS (in press, 2013)
5. Schröeder, M., Baggia, P., Burkhardt, F., Pelachaud, C., Peter, C., Zovato, E.: Emotion Markup Language (EmotionML) 1.0. W3C Candidate Recommendation 10 (May 2012)

Leveraging Encyclopedic Knowledge
for Transparent and Serendipitous User Profiles

Fedelucio Narducci[1], Cataldo Musto[2], Giovanni Semeraro[2],
Pasquale Lops[2], and Marco de Gemmis[2]

[1] University of Milano-Bicocca, Italy
narducci@disco.unimib.it
[2] University of Bari Aldo Moro, Italy
name.surname@uniba.it

Abstract. The main contribution of this work[1] is the comparison of different techniques for representing user preferences extracted by analyzing data gathered from social networks, with the aim of constructing more transparent (human-readable) and serendipitous user profiles. We compared two different user models representations: one based on keywords and one exploiting encyclopedic knowledge extracted from Wikipedia. A preliminary evaluation involving 51 Facebook and Twitter users has shown that the use of an encyclopedic-based representation better reflects user preferences, and helps to introduce new interesting topics.

1 Motivation and Research Problem

In this work we investigate whether a Wikipedia-based representation of user interests allows to produce more transparent and serendipitous user profiles. Transparency is related to the readability of profiles, while serendipity to the ability to suggest surprisingly interesting items that users might not have otherwise discovered. The main motivation for this reseach is that a system that adopts a more understandable representation can lead towards a more transparent personalization process. For example, a recommender system that uses a human-understandable profile could easily explain the reason for a suggestion. Furthermore, serendipitous profiles help to overcome the overspecialization problem, that leads to accurate but obvious (and so unuseful) suggestions. We address the following two research questions:

- Are Wikipedia concepts (i.e., titles of Wikipedia articles) more representative than keywords for modeling user interests?
- Is it possible to leverage encyclopedic knowledge to enrich user profiles with novel topics of interest?

[1] This work fullfils the research objectives of the projects PON 02_00563_3470993 VINCENTE (A Virtual collective INtelligenCe ENvironment to develop sustainable Technology Entrepreneurship ecosystems) and PON 01_00850 ASK-Health (Advanced system for the interpretations and sharing of knowledge in health care) funded by the Italian Ministry of University and Research (MIUR).

S. Carberry et al. (Eds.): UMAP 2013, LNCS 7899, pp. 350–352, 2013.

We indexed textual information extracted from Facebook and Twitter using different strategies, in order to obtain different user profiles whose effectiveness in terms of transparency and serendipity is evaluated in a user study.

2   User Profiling Strategies

For each Facebook user, we processed the title and description of liked groups and pages, attended events, personal status, title and summary of shared links, while for Twitter we used tweets of the user and her followings. We call *social items* the aforementioned pieces of information, that were indexed using three strategies and lead to the following representations of user profiles:

Social Profile: This is the simplest profile representation, based on keywords occurring in the social items collected for a user. The text of social items is tokenized and stopwords removed. Keywords are weighed using the TF-IDF score. This represents our baseline.

Tag.me Profile: This strategy exploits the *anchor disambiguation* algorithm implemented in TAG.ME [1] to identify Wikipedia concepts occurring in the text of social items. The titles of those concepts are included in the TAG.ME profile of the user, and weighed using TF-IDF.

Explicit Semantic Analysis (ESA) Profile: ESA represents a term or a text as a vector whose dimensions are Wikipedia pages. For example, the meaning of the term *Christmas* is described by a list of concepts it refers to (e.g. *Santa Claus, December 25*). Formally, given the space of Wikipedia concepts (articles) $C = \{c_1, c_2, ..., c_n\}$, a term t_i is represented by its *semantic interpretation vector* $v_i = < w_{i1}, w_{i2}, ..., w_{in} >$, where a weight w_{ij} represents the strength of the association between t_i and c_j, i.e. the TF-IDF of t_i in c_j [2]. The semantics of a text fragment f (i.e. a sentence, a tweet, a Facebook post) is the centroid of vectors associated with terms occurring in f. The ESA Profile of a user is built by including the 10 most relevant Wikipedia concepts in the semantic interpretation vector associated with her social items.

The difference between the last two approaches is that ESA implements a *feature generation* process, since it could generates *new* features related to the text to be indexed, while TAG.ME simply performs *feature selection*. As an example, let's consider the Facebook posts: *I'm in trepidation for my first riding lesson!, I'm anxious for the soccer match :(, I will flight by Ryanair to London!, Ryanair really cheapest company!, Ryanair lost my luggage :(, This summer holidays are amazing!, Relax during these holidays!*. Figure 1 depicts a sketch of the profiles produced by the different processing of social items. *Social* profile contains many non-relevant keywords, such as those referring to user moods (anxious, trepidation, etc.). The TAG.ME profile contains terms occurring in the *social* profile (soccer, London, etc.), whose weights are higher than those in social profile since the noise coming from non-relevant keyword has been filtered out. Finally, the ESA profile contains *new* topics somehow related to the other profiles (Vienna - which hosts a famous riding school, UK, low-cost), but not *explicitly* mentioned in the social profile.

Fig. 1. a) Social, b) Tag.me, c) ESA representations of user profiles shown as tag clouds

Table 1. Results of Transparency and Serendipity

Profile	Transparency				Serendipity			
	Avg. Rating	Min Rating	Max Rating	Std. dev.	Avg. Rating	Min Rating	Max Rating	Std. dev.
Social	1.33	0	3	0.65	0.42	0	2	0.57
Tag.me	**3.88**	2	5	0.82	0.54	0	2	0.61
ESA	1.16	0	4	1.00	**3.24**	0	5	1.24

3 Experimental Evaluation

The goal of the experiment was to identify which kind of user profile best represents user interests. For each kind of profile, we evaluated *transparency* as the overlap between actual user interests and keywords shown in the profile, and *serendipity* as the presence of *unexpected* and *interesting* features in the profile. 51 users were involved in the study, 36 of them gave us the consent to extract social items only from Facebook, 4 only from Twitter, 11 from both social networks. The experiment has been carried out for two weeks. For each user, the SOCIAL, ESA, and TAG.ME profiles were built and shown to her as tag clouds. The user provided feedback, on a 6-points discrete rating scale, on the extent to which 1) keywords in the profile reflect personal interests, and 2) the profile contains unexpected interesting topics. Results are reported in Table 1. Two main outcomes are observed: the best description of user interests is provided by the TAG.ME profile, while ESA shows the highest heterogeneity of results (highest standard deviation); highest serendipity is shown by ESA profiles ($p < 0.05$), since ESA is the only technique which enriches profiles with *new* features. In conclusion, we observe that a representation of user interests based on encyclopedic concepts might lead to more transparent and serendipitous profiles. As future work we will investigate possible ways to merge TAG.ME and ESA representations.

References

1. Ferragina, P., Scaiella, U.: Tagme: on-the-fly annotation of short text fragments (by wikipedia entities). In: Proc. of the 19th ACM Int. Conf. on Information and Knowledge Management, pp. 1625–1628. ACM, New York (2010)
2. Gabrilovich, E., Markovitch, S.: Wikipedia-based semantic interpretation for natural language processing. Journal Artif. Intell. Res (JAIR) 34, 443–498 (2009)

Modelling Users' Affect in Job Interviews: Technological Demo

Kaśka Porayska-Pomsta[1], Keith Anderson[2], Ionut Damian[3], Tobias Baur[3], Elisabeth André[3], Sara Bernardini[4], and Paola Rizzo[1]

[1] London Knowledge Lab, Institute of Education
23-29 Emerald Street, London WC1N 3QS, UK
{K.Porayska-Pomsta,P.Rizzo}@ioe.ac.uk
[2] Tandemis Limited
108 Blackheath Hill, London SE10 8AG, UK
keith@tandemis.co.uk
[3] Human Centered Multimedia, Augsburg University
Universitätsstr. 6a, 86159 Augsburg, Germany
{damian,baur,andre}@hcm-lab.de
[4] Department of Informatics, King's College London, UK, WC2R 2LS
sara.bernardini@kcl.ac.uk

Abstract. This demo presents an approach to recognising and interpreting social cues-based interactions in computer-enhanced job interview simulations. We show what social cues and complex mental states of the user are relevant in this interaction context, how they can be interpreted using static Bayesian Networks, and how they can be recognised automatically using state-of-the-art sensor technology in real-time.

Keywords: social signal processing, complex mental states modelling, job interviews, bayesian inference.

1 Introduction

A recruiter ascertains a job seeker's fit to a given job based largely on the social cues, i.e. the job seeker's conscious or unconscious behaviours. This demo shows an approach to recognising and interpreting relevant social cues of interviewees' that is based on a combination of social signal processing and Bayesian Networks (BNs). The work is conducted within the TARDIS project (http://tardis.lip6.fr/) – a scenario-based serious game where virtual agents act as recruiters.

2 Relevant Work

Recent work in the field of behavioural analysis has shown that social cues significantly influence the outcome of job interviews [1, 2]. Several computer-based environments for social skills acquisition have been proposed (e.g.[3], [4]).

In the field of signal processing, most research has focused on the recognition of emotions from speech [5] or facial expressions [6], with the analysis of postures

S. Carberry et al. (Eds.): UMAP 2013, LNCS 7899, pp. 353–355, 2013.

[7] and gestures [8] having received little attention, especially in the context of the interactive scenarios considered in TARDIS.

To help the target users acquire the relevant social skills, our system needs to recognise a comprehensive set of the users' social cues. Such cues provide the basis for inferring users' complex mental states and for selecting appropriate responses by virtual recruiters.

3 Analysis of Social Cues

We conducted a preliminary study with users, during which 10 real job seekers and 5 practitioners engaged in mock interviews. The data was video recorded and annotated manually. The analysis focused specifically on the frequency of social-cue occurrence across the different interactions.

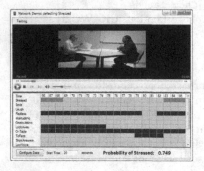

Fig. 1. Video playback facility, with the annotation data and Bayesian network output in the bottom-right corner of the screen

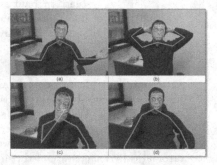

Fig. 2. Postures the system can recognize: (a) arms open, (b) hands behind head, (c) hand close to head, (d) leaning backwards

Episodes as in Fig. 1 were annotated for fine-grained behaviours, e.g. looking away, lack of direct eye contact, smiling, etc. The annotations were mapped onto seven complex mental states, identified by the practitioners during post-hoc walkthroughs and semi-structured interviews, as relevant to this context: *stressed, embarrassed, ill-at-ease, bored, focussed, hesitant, relieved.* The annotations were fed into a C# application which calculates the frequencies of the co-occurrences of groups of social cues with each mental state. This data is used to infer the BNs' probability tables, representing the complex mental states. Another C# application evaluates networks and consists of two components: (1) simultaneous playback of video, annotations used to the train the BNs, and BNs real-time output for a given mental state; (2) a facility that feeds the annotations through the network and produces statistics about the network's correct and incorrect classifications. A demonstration of these applications will be given.

4 Automatic Recognition of Social Cues

We investigated how the social cues identified during the user study can be recognised automatically, using a combination of sensors and software algorithms that yield best results in terms of accuracy, low intrusion, reliability, set-up time and cost. As a first step, we implemented the recognition of the following six social cues: *Hands to face; Looking away; Postures (arms open/ crossed and hands behind head); Leaning back/forward; Voice activity (interrupting the interviewer, short answers and long silence).* – see Fig. 2. These feed directly into the BNs.

We chose the Microsoft Kinect as the main sensor for social cue recognition because it is low-cost, it does not require any time-consuming configuration, it is relatively robust against lighting conditions, it incorporates a microphone and an RGB camera in addition to the depth camera, and it is minimally intrusive. For recording and pre-processing human behaviour data, our system relies on the SSI framework [9], the demonstration of which will be also provided.

Acknowledgements. This work was supported by European Commission (EC) through its funding for the TARDIS project FP7-ICT2011-7-288578.

References

1. Curhan, J., Pentland, A.: Thin slices of negotiation: predicting outcomes from conversational dynamics within the first 5 minutes (2007)
2. Arvey, R.D., Campion, J.E.: The employment interview: A summary and review of recent research. Personnel Psychology 35(2), 281–322 (1982)
3. Bernardini, S., Porayska-Pomsta, K., Smith, T.J., Avramides, K.: Building autonomous social partners for autistic children. In: Nakano, Y., Neff, M., Paiva, A., Walker, M. (eds.) IVA 2012. LNCS, vol. 7502, pp. 46–52. Springer, Heidelberg (2012)
4. Vala, M., Sequeira, P., Paiva, A., Aylett, R.: Fearnot! demo: a virtual environment with synthetic characters to help bullying. In: Proc. 6th Intl. Joint Conf. on Autonomous Agents and Multiagent Systems, AAMAS 2007, pp. 271:1–271:2. ACM, New York (2007)
5. Vogt, T., Andre, E.: Comparing feature sets for acted and spontaneous speech in view of automatic emotion recognition. In: IEEE Intl. Conf. on Multimedia and Expo, ICME 2005, pp. 474–477 (July 2005)
6. Zeng, Z., Pantic, M., Roisman, G.I., Huang, T.S.: A survey of affect recognition methods: Audio, visual, and spontaneous expressions. IEEE Transactions on Pattern Analysis and Machine Intelligence 31(1), 39–58 (2009)
7. Kapoor, A., Picard, R.W.: Multimodal affect recognition in learning environments. In: Proc. 13th Annual ACM Intl. Conf. on Multimedia, MULTIMEDIA 2005, pp. 677–682. ACM, New York (2005)
8. Kleinsmith, A., Bianchi-Berthouze, N.: Form as a cue in the automatic recognition of non-acted affective body expressions. In: D'Mello, S., Graesser, A., Schuller, B., Martin, J.-C. (eds.) ACII 2011, Part I. LNCS, vol. 6974, pp. 155–164. Springer, Heidelberg (2011)
9. Wagner, J., Lingenfelser, F., André, E.: The social signal interpretation framework (SSI) for real time signal processing and recognition. In: Proc. Interspeech 2011 (2011)

Multilingual vs. Monolingual User Models for Personalized Multilingual Information Retrieval

M. Rami Ghorab, Séamus Lawless, Alexander O'Connor, Dong Zhou,
and Vincent Wade

Centre for Next Generation Localisation, Knowledge & Data Engineering Group,
School of Computer Science & Statistics, Trinity College Dublin, Ireland
{ghorabm,seamus.lawless,alex.oconnor,vincent.wade}@css.tcd.ie,
dongzhou1979@hotmail.com

Abstract. This paper demonstrates that a user of multilingual search has different interests depending on the language used, and that the user model should reflect this. To demonstrate this phenomenon, the paper proposes and evaluates a set of result re-ranking algorithms based on various user model representations.

Keywords: User Modeling, Personalization, Multilingual Web Search.

1   Introduction

Today's Web is becoming increasingly multilingual, and users are increasingly faced with the challenge of finding documents which resolve their information needs in collections of different languages. Multilingual Information Retrieval (MIR) has been well studied [1], but many unexplored questions remain about modeling users interests for Personalized MIR (PMIR). User modeling for personalized search has been studied, but only on a monolingual level [2]. Taking multilinguality into consideration should change the way user information is modeled to improve PMIR.

This research argues that users' search behavior is influenced by language; this depends on the combination of their language capabilities, and the availability of content in various languages. For example, a user may use a certain language when searching for certain types of content (e.g. native language to search for news), yet use another language when searching for other types (e.g. English to search for technical content). Furthermore, a user may click on results of certain languages depending on the type of information sought. This behavior suggests that a user may have multiple personas (facets) in Web search. In support of this argument, this paper proposes and compares multilingual vs. monolingual approaches to adapt search results in PMIR. This involves evaluating a set of result re-ranking algorithms combined with various representations of the user's interests in both multilingual and monolingual form. The evaluation showed that maintaining user models that account for multilinguality, can achieve significant improvements in retrieval effectiveness.

S. Carberry et al. (Eds.): UMAP 2013, LNCS 7899, pp. 356–358, 2013.

2   Proposed Multilingual vs. Monolingual Approaches

In the experiments reported in this paper, three methods were used to maintain the terms (keywords) which represent the user's search interests:

1. *Multilingual User Model:* the model consists of multiple language groups, where each group holds clusters of interest terms that correspond to a language.
2. *Single-Language Fragment of Multilingual User Model:* this model comprises only one selected language group from the previous model (a pivot/preferred language that is specified by the user). The purpose of this is to indirectly examine whether there is a redundancy between the interests maintained in different languages.
3. *Monolingual User Model:* all interest terms from all the groups are translated to the user's preferred language and maintained together in one group.

In MIR, result lists are retrieved from multiple languages and then merged into a single list. The baseline system in this paper merged the lists using round robin. In order to evaluate and compare the contribution of the abovementioned user models to PMIR, they were used as the basis for the following re-ranking algorithms:

1. *Separate re-ranking based on multilingual user model:* each result list was separately re-ranked in its original language against the interests of the corresponding language group in the user model; the lists were then merged using round robin.
2. *Re-ranking based on similarity score with multilingual user model:* each result was given a score based on its textual similarity (cosine similarity) with the interest terms of the corresponding language group in the user model. All the results from all the lists were then put together and sorted based on their similarity score.
3. *Re-ranking based on similarity score with a single fragment of the user model:* all the results from all the lists were put together and translated to the user's preferred language, and then they were given scores based on their similarity with only the interest terms of the preferred-language-fragment of the multilingual user model.
4. *Re-ranking based on similarity score with the monolingual user model:* all the results from all the lists were put together and translated to the user's preferred language, and then they were given scores based on their similarity with the interest terms of the combined monolingual user model.

3   Evaluation

The experiment involved the participation of 26 users of different linguistic backgrounds and language capabilities. The multilingual Web search system provided results from 3 languages: English, French, and German. The experiment comprised 2 phases. In the first phase, each user was asked to choose a search topic (task). When a query was submitted, the baseline system returned a merged result list containing 30 results obtained from the 3 languages. The system logged user interactions. In the second phase, the last submitted query by the user was reserved for testing. The remaining queries, along with their associated clicked results, were used to construct the user models. Each test query was then automatically submitted to the search system multiple times so that a result list is generated for each of the aforementioned algorithms. Each user was presented with the last query they submitted in the task in the first phase along with the pool of generated results, and was asked to judge the relevance of each result on a 4-point scale. A total of 540 results were judged, corresponding to 18 test queries (in multiple languages). The precision of the result lists was evaluated using Normalized Discounted Cumulative Gain (NDCG). Table 1 reports the mean improvement percentages over the baseline, computed at different list positions (improvements highlighted in **bold are statistically significant** using T-test with $p=0.05$). The results show that the second algorithm achieved the highest improvements (up to 38%). Furthermore, the results show that the first and second algorithms, which were based on the multilingual user model representation, outperformed their monolingual; this supports the main argument presented in this paper. Although it may seem intuitive that an approach that handles all the user's interests together should be more representative of the user, the results suggest that this is not the case; this is perhaps due to translation in-accuracies introduced when combining the interest terms into a monolingual model. Based on the T-test, the results show that the third and fourth algorithms did not consistently achieve improvements. Finally, the difference between the results of the second and third algorithms suggests that the different fragments of the multilingual user model do not hold redundant information.

Table 1. Mean NDCG improvements at various ranks

List Position	1.Multi-UM: Separate Re-ranking	2.Multi-UM: Re-ranking on sim.	3.Single-Frag.-UM: Re-ranking on sim.	4.Mono-UM: Re-ranking on sim.
NDCG@3	**26.38%**	**38.41%**	33.7%	**28.36%**
NDCG@5	**22.8%**	**32.14%**	21.1%	17.91%
NDCG@7	**17.82%**	**28.6%**	15.36%	15.74%
NDCG@10	**13.42%**	**18.9%**	12.29%	13.18%

4   Conclusion

This paper has shown that users have language-dependent search interests in MIR and that user models should reflect this. To verify this, a set of re-ranking algorithms were evaluated based on various user model representations. The results support the argument that systems should maintain multilingual user models. The results also suggest that even if a user only speaks one language, a multilingual search system may exhibit different interests for them in different languages, based on browsed documents.

Acknowledgements. This research is supported by the Science Foundation Ireland (grant 07/CE/I1142) as part of the Centre for Next Generation Localisation (www.cngl.ie) at Trinity College, Dublin.

References

1. Oard, D.W.: Multilingual Information Access. Encyclopedia of Library and Information Sciences, 3rd edn., pp. 3682–3687 (2010)
2. Micarelli, A., Gasparetti, F., Sciarrone, F., Gauch, S.: Personalized Search on the World Wide Web. In: Brusilovsky, P., Kobsa, A., Nejdl, W. (eds.) Adaptive Web 2007. LNCS, vol. 4321, pp. 195–230. Springer, Heidelberg (2007)

A Prismatic Cognitive Layout for Adapting Ontologies

Francesco Osborne and Alice Ruggeri

Dept. of Computer Science, University of Torino, 10149 Torino, Italy
{osborne,ruggeri}@di.unito.it

Abstract. We propose a novel approach to personal ontologies, grounded on the concept of affordance and on the ontological theory of Von Uexküll, in which each concept can be viewed under different perspectives depending on the subjectivity of the user and thus can yield tailored semantic relationships or properties. We suggest a cognitive middle-layer interface between the user and the ontology, which is able on the run to modify and adapt the ontology to the user needs. The goal is to obtain an adapted version of the ontology that is tailored both to the context and to the user prospective and expertise, without the need of explicitly maintaining a high number of ontologies.

Keywords: Ontology-based Recommender Systems, Personal Ontology View, Ontology Learning, Affordance.

1   Introduction

In recent years ontologies proved to be very important tools for recommender systems, since they allow a formal representation of the concepts in a domain, thus being helpful for generating suggestions. However the use of a single ontology domain for all the users in a system is not always the best solution. In fact different users may have different needs and different prospective on a domain and would like to have items classified according their mental ontology. This is possible by using Personal Ontologies Views [1] (POV), which are ontologies tailored on the prospective and the specific domain view of a user. POVs have proven to be useful [2] for assisting the user in tasks as classification, navigation and search. However there are some issues with handling multiple POVs and their construction requires an abundance of evidence. Moreover the same user may have different prospective of the same ontology according to the social and geographical context and her/his expertise on certain topic. For example her/his view can change with time as she/he becomes more familiar with some parts of the domain. We thus need a tool more flexible then a POV and able to be adapted on the run on the basis of user needs.

2   The Prismatic Cognitive Layout

The ontologies are formal explicit specifications of a shared conceptualization [3]. They yield an objective meaning for each concept that does not change according to whom is using them. In this work we explore an alternative specification of

S. Carberry et al. (Eds.): UMAP 2013, LNCS 7899, pp. 359–362, 2013.

conceptualization, grounded on the concept of *affordance* introduced by Gibson [4]. According to his theory, an item meaning can change depending to the context. Gibson focused in particular on how different animals interact in different ways with their environment, but his idea can be extended to users and items in recommended systems. Moreover, it is demonstrated that cognitive processes are deeply rooted in the body's interaction with the world [5]. Von Uexküll et al [6] state that an entity acquires a meaning when it is used through an action. Thus the meaning is not objective, but is strongly linked to the interaction between an agent and an item. An entity can have a different meaning according to the user with whom it is interacting and to the action that it is used for. For example a concept like "alcoholic beverage" will have a different meaning for a sommelier and for a teenager. In the same way it will assume a different meaning, with different properties and relationships and thus a different ontological view, even for the same person when out for a romantic dinner or having lunch at work or in a pub with friends. This framework is particularly interesting for the user model community. In fact in this field it is often very helpful to be able to adapt the meaning of entity according to the user, the context and other external factors.

To implement this theoretical framework we need to transform a formal ontology in an adapting entity, which will present different classes, semantic relationship and properties to users with different prospective of the domain. We propose a **prismatic cognitive layout** (**PCL**), which is able to act as an ontology interface to this scope. We call it "prismatic" since this kind of ontology behaves as a prism, which shows different faces according to which one appears to be more tailored to the user.

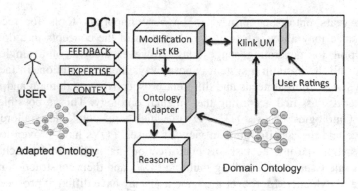

Fig. 1. The prismatic cognitive layout architecture

When a system needs to exploit the domain ontology (e.g. to facilitate user navigation or filter search results) it calls the PCL and feeds as arguments information about 1) the user expertise, 2) the context, 3) the user past feedback on the ontology elements she/he is most interested. Each of these three inputs is evaluated separately by the PCL to yield a list of suggested modifications on the main concepts of the domain ontology as "add property P" or "exclude relationship R between C1 and C2". As now, we solve the possible contradictions among the modification lists by assigning the following priorities: user feedback > expertise > context. We are however working on a more refined way to solve this issue.

The PCL is able to perform the following modifications on the ontology:

-Adding or removing a concept (e.g. "Sparkling Wine" or "Blue Mould Cheese")
-Adding or removing a semantic relationship between two concept (e.g. "skos:broaderGeneric")
-Adding or removing a property (e.g. Vintage or Alcoholic Content)

The user expertise is given a score from 1 to 3 according to the level of knowledge of the user on a concept. Every level is associated with a pre-compiled modification list designed to increase the ontology granularity with each level. Thus at level 1 only the more general concepts and their main properties are showed whereas at level 3 all available concepts and properties are used.

The context is defined as a label describing a situation as "romance_dinner", "food_fair" or "picnic". The modification list associated with each of them is computed semi automatically by exploiting Klink UM, a modified version of Klink [7], an algorithm which uses machine learning and statistical techniques to mine semantic relationships among keyword taking as input the co-occurrence graph. Klink UM goes further and exploits the patterns of user ratings on items associated with keywords to mine semantic relationships from those keywords. We run Klink UM on the ratings associated with each context to learn concepts and semantic relationships associated to that situation, which are then refined by ontology engineers and saved as a modification list in a knowledge base. Finally the user can also give direct feedbacks on concepts, semantic relationships and properties as in [2].

After the modifications are implemented, the ontology is checked for consistency with a reasoner as Pellet. If this control fails, the PCL excludes the modifications that give problems and tries all over again.

3   Conclusion

We presented PCL, a layer for ontologies grounded on the concept of affordance and on the ontological theory of Von Uexküll, which allows an ontology to be adapted in real time to a user and a context. As future work we plan to further develop Klink UM and its integration with the PCL. We are also working on a set of more complex heuristics to better integrate the modifications suggested by the tree inputs. A comprehensive evaluation on real users will be run to estimate the pragmatic advantage of using an adapted ontology.

References

1. Sosnovsky, S., Dicheva, D.: Ontological technologies for user modelling. International Journal of Metadata, Semantics and Ontologies 5(1), 32–71 (2010)
2. Sieg, A., Mobasher, B., Burke, R.: Web search personalization with ontological user profiles. In: Proceeding of the 16th ACM Conference on Information and Knowledge Management, CIKM 2007, pp. 525–534. ACM (2007)
3. Gruber, T.R.: A Translation Approach to Portable Ontology Specification. Knowledge Acquisition 5(2), 199–220 (1993)

4. Gibson, J.: The Theory of Affordances.In Perceiving, Acting, and Knowing: Toward an Ecological Psychology (1977)
5. Wilson, M.: Six view of embodied cognition. Psychonomic Bulletin and Review 9(4), 625–636 (2002)
6. Von Uexküll, J.: Umwelt und innenwelt der tiere. Springer, Berlin (1909)
7. Osborne, F., Motta, E.: Mining Semantic Relations between Research Areas. In: Cudré-Mauroux, P., Heflin, J., Sirin, E., Tudorache, T., Euzenat, J., Hauswirth, M., Parreira, J.X., Hendler, J., Schreiber, G., Bernstein, A., Blomqvist, E. (eds.) ISWC 2012, Part I. LNCS, vol. 7649, pp. 410–426. Springer, Heidelberg (2012)

Evaluation of Cross-Domain News Article Recommendations

Benjamin Kille

Technische Universität Berlin
benjamin.kille@tu-berlin.de

Abstract. This thesis will investigate methods to increase the utility of
news article recommendation services. Access to different news providers
allows us to consider cross-domain user preferences. We deal with recommender systems with continuously changing item collections. We will
be able to observe user feedback from a real-world recommendation system operating on different domains. We will evaluate how results from
existing data sets correspond to actual user reactions.

1 Introduction and Goals

Browsing the *world wide web*, users more and more face an overload of information. Their capacities do not suffice to deal with such an overwhelming extent of
information. Recommender systems (RS) tackle such issues by filtering all available information in a personalized fashion. In the thesis we aim to investigate
strategies to enhance news article recommender systems' utility. Subsequently,
we discuss the challenges we attempt to meet. We state research questions at
the end of each challenge emphasized with bold font.

Sparsity. RS require users to express their preferences towards items. Cremonesi
et. al. [8] discuss this requirement's inherent trade-off: on the one hand, RS demand sufficient data to provide adequate recommendations; on the other hand,
users try to avoid spending extensive time expressing their preferences. Such
avoidance tends to result in highly scarce data. The sparsity hampers the generation of adequate recommendations. Koren et. al. [13] show how matrix factorization techniques allow to leverage latent information thus overcoming sparsity
to a certain extent. Still, users need to provide their preferences to obtain recommendations. In addition, the recommendation quality depends on how well
the available data represents users' tastes. **How can other publishers' user
interactions contribute to decrease sparsity for the target publisher?**

Dynamic Item Collections. Generally, recommender systems assume item collections to be static. While new items as well as users may enter the system, the
item collection grows. Items remain in the system. Keeping the items appears
reasonable in domains such movies or music. Users may consume their favorite
songs or movies more than once. In contrast, news articles' relevance decays
rapidly. **What characteristics must recommender algorithms exhibit to
successfully cope with dynamically changing item collections?**

S. Carberry et al. (Eds.): UMAP 2013, LNCS 7899, pp. 363–366, 2013.

Evaluation. Herlocker et. al. [12] describe methods to assess a recommender system's utility. The evaluation method depends on how we choose to model the recommendation task. Hereby, we distinguish between the *rating prediction* scenario, and the *ranking* scenario. Recorded user interactions with recommender systems (usually in form of rating data sets such as *Movielens* or *Netflix*) allow to calculate a variety of metrics. Observations based on such data reflect historic utility (the tested recommendation algorithm *would* have predicted the ratings with error ϵ on average). Instead, we want to assess the actual utility to current users. We will have access to a multi-domain recommender system. We will generate actual recommendations. We will receive actual user feedback. We will implement a variety of recommendation algorithms. Those algorithms will subsequently interact with the system creating recorded user reaction. In addition, we will investigate further evaluation strategies suited to the given setting. **How to evaluate cross-domain recommender systems with dynamically changing item collections? How do standard evaluation metrics compare to the observed clicks?**

2   Related Work

Generally, recommender systems either utilize user preferences (collaborative filtering [1,5]) or additionally consider item features (content-based recommendations [16]). In addition, we may combine both techniques to a hybrid recommender system.

Cross-Domain Recommendations Fernández-Tobías et. al. [10] present a recent survey on cross-domain recommender systems. We adopt their definition of the term *domain* referring to a specific publisher. Winoto et. al. [21] conducted a user study to investigate how to leverage preferences of several domains to predict ratings more accurately. Li et. al. [14] define a codebook allowing them to transfer preferences from a relatively dense auxiliary domain to the target domain. Pan et. al. [17] elaborate on the codebook approach. They factorize rating matrices of both auxiliary and target domain obtaining latent factors. Subsequently, they transfer those factors to reduce the target domain's sparsity. Chen et. al. [7] consider the cross-domain setting as learning to rank task. They derive item features from the auxiliary and train a support vector classifier to rank items in the target domain. Cremonesi et. al. [9] introduce a framework for cross-domain recommendations. Their formalization of the cross-domain recommendation problem allows us to express our setting precisely. Tang et. al. [20] describe a method to recommend cooperation partners from different domains. Shi et. al. [19] utilize tags assigned to items in different domains to bridge recommendations. Their probabilistic graph model infers preferences for tags co-occurring in both domains. Berkovsky et. al. [3] consider cross-domain recommendations as mediating user models across various recommender systems.

Evaluation of RS with Continuously Changing Item Collections. Billsus and Pazzani [4] describe challenges for personalizing news services. Cantador et. al. [6]

introduce a news article recommender system using semantic relations to discover relevant news items. Golovin and Rahm [11] consider a reinforcement learning approach. Hereby, weighted rules combine several recommendation strategies. Shani et. al. [18] model the recommendation task as Markov Decision Process (MPD). Their method learns transitional probabilities to infer state changes. Li et. al. [15] introduce an evaluation strategy. The strategy entails replaying user interactions. The authors argue that their approach is unbiased in contrast to simulation strategies. Bar et. al. [2] investigate how ensembles encapsulating rather simple recommendation methods perform compared to complex yet individual models.

We can base our research on existing work with respect to cross-domain recommendations as well as evaluation of recommender systems whose item collections continuously change. To the best of our knowledge, there does not exist research on a combination of both settings. Fernández-Tobías et. al. [10] confirm this intuition. With this thesis, we attempt to close this gap.

3   Progress

We have access to data available through the *EPEN* project[1]. These data contain information on users (e. g., location, language, and operating system) as well as items (e. g., an news article's title, text, and meta-data). In addition, we can generate recommendations presented to actual users. Recommendations must be submitted in less than 200 ms in order to provide the user a adequate experience without delay. This requires us to select recommendation algorithms with low response times. Subsequently, we observe users' feedback in form of clicks. We access several data sources (publishers) generating ≈ 1 000 000 impressions on a daily basis. We do not observe data revealing users' identities. We receive session identifier which allow us to recognize re-appearing users on different publishers' platforms. Data analysis and recommendation algorithm implementation are ongoing. Additionally, we currently implement the replay evaluation from [15] in order to compare offline results with actual user feedback.

References

1. Adomavicius, G., Tuzhilin, A.: Toward the next generation of recommender systems: a survey of the state-of-the-art and possible extensions. IEEE Trans. on Knowl. and Data Eng. 17, 734–749 (2005)
2. Bar, A., Rokach, L., Shani, G., Shapira, B., Schclar, A.: Boosting simple collaborative filtering models using ensemble methods (2012)
3. Berkovsky, S., Kuflik, T., Ricci, F.: Cross-domain mediation in collaborative filtering. In: Conati, C., McCoy, K., Paliouras, G. (eds.) UM 2007. LNCS (LNAI), vol. 4511, pp. 355–359. Springer, Heidelberg (2007)

---

[1] http://www.dai-labor.de/en/irml/epen/

4. Billsus, D., Pazzani, M.J.: Adaptive news access. In: Brusilovsky, P., Kobsa, A., Nejdl, W. (eds.) Adaptive Web 2007. LNCS, vol. 4321, pp. 550–570. Springer, Heidelberg (2007)
5. Cacheda, F., Carneiro, V., Fernandez, D., Formoso, V.: Comparison of collaborative filtering algorithms: Limitations of current techniques and proposals for scalable, high-performance recommender systems. ACM TWEB 5, 1–33 (2011)
6. Cantador, I., Bellogín, A., Castells, P.: News@hand: A semantic web approach to recommending news. In: Nejdl, W., Kay, J., Pu, P., Herder, E. (eds.) AH 2008. LNCS, vol. 5149, pp. 279–283. Springer, Heidelberg (2008)
7. Chen, D., Xiong, Y., Yan, J., Xue, G.R., Wang, G., Chen, Z.: Knowledge transfer for cross domain learning to rank. Information Retrieval 13, 236–253 (2010)
8. Cremonesi, P., Garzottto, F., Turrin, R.: User effort vs. accuracy in rating-based elicitation. In: Proc. of the 6th ACM Conf. on Rec. Sys., pp. 27–34 (2012)
9. Cremonesi, P., Tripodi, A., Turrin, R.: Cross-domain recommender systems. In: IEEE International Conference on Data Mining Workshops, pp. 496–503 (2011)
10. Fernandez-Tobias, I., Cantador, I., Kaminskas, M., Ricci, F.: Cross-domain recommender systems: A survey of the state of the art. In: Proceedings of the 2nd Spanish Conference on Information Retrieval. CERI (2012)
11. Golovin, N., Rahm, E.: Reinforcement learning architectures for web recommendations. In: Proc. of the Int. Conf. on IT: Coding and Computing, pp. 398–402 (2004)
12. Herlocker, J.L., Konstan, J.A., Terveen, L.G., Riedl, J.T.: Evaluating collaborative filtering recommender systems. ACM Trans. Inf. Syst. 22(1), 5–53 (2004)
13. Koren, Y., Bell, R., Volinsky, C.: Matrix factorization techniques for recommender systems 42, 30–37
14. Li, B., Yang, Q., Xue, X.: Can movies and books collaborate?: cross-domain collaborative filtering for sparsity reduction. In: Proc. of the 21st Int. Joint Conf. on AI, pp. 2052–2057 (2009)
15. Li, L., Chu, W., Langford, J., Wang, X.: Unbiased offline evaluation of contextual-bandit-based news article recommendation algorithms. In: Proc. of the 4th ACM Int. Conf. on Web Search and Data Mining, pp. 297–306 (2011)
16. Lops, P., de Gemmis, M., Semerano, G.: Content-based Recommender Systems: State of the Art and Trends, ch. 3, pp. 73–105. Springer (2010)
17. Pan, W., Xiang, E.W., Liu, N.N., Yang, Q.: Transfer Learning in Collaborative Filtering for Sparsity Reduction. In: Proceedings of the 24th AAAI Conference on Artificial Intelligence, pp. 230–235 (2010)
18. Shani, G., Heckerman, D., Brafman, R.I.: An mdp-based recommender system. J. Mach. Learn. Res. 6, 1265–1295 (2005)
19. Shi, Y., Larson, M., Hanjalic, A.: Generalized tag-induced cross-domain collaborative filtering (2013)
20. Tang, J., Wu, S., Sun, J., Su, H.: Cross-domain collaboration recommendation. In: Proc. of the 18th ACM SIGKDD Int. Conf. on Knowledge Discovery and Data Mining, pp. 1285–1293 (2012)
21. Winoto, P., Lang, T.: If you like the devil wears prada the book, will you also enjoy the devil wears prada the movie? a study of cross-domain recommendations. New Generation Computing 26, 209–225 (2008)

Suggesting Query Revisions in Conversational Recommender Systems

Henry Blanco Lores

Free University of Bozen-Bolzano
Bolzano, Italy
hblancolores@stud-inf.unibz.it

1 Motivations

Recommender Systems (RS) are information tools designed to suggest items that suit users needs and preferences. They can also support users to browse a product catalogue and better understand and elicit their preferences. These activities are managed by Conversational RSs, which over a series of user-system interactions acquire and revise user preferences by observing the user reaction to proposed options.

In this research we focus on the suggestion of queries. We address the problem of helping a user to revise queries for searching in a product catalog with a conversational approach. We want to provide query suggestions that are likely to retrieve products with the largest utility increase, compared to the products retrieved in the previous interaction step. Suggesting query revision is a difficult task given that we do not know the user utility and we do not want to explicitly ask about it. Actually, by observing the query revision selected by the user we can infer some constraints on the user utility function and use this information in order to provide good query revisions. For example, suppose a user queries a product catalogue by issuing a query, such as "I want an hotel with AC and parking". The system, rather than recommending immediately the products that satisfy this query, assumes that the user may have also other needs and suggests some query revisions. A new query may add an additional feature to the current query, e.g., "are you interested also in sauna?". Products with more features, if available, will surely increase the user utility. But not all features are equally important for the user.

In this approach products are described by their features. The user utility function, also called as user profile, is modeled as a vector of weights which represents the importance the user assigns to each feature. The main challenge is to unveil the weights values which describe the user profile (i.e., the user preferences) by leveraging the information derived from knowing what revised query the user selects among those suggested by the system. This approach was introduced by [4] but it has some limitations that we want to address: 1) the high computational cost of computing the best query revisions; 2) the large number of suggestions at each interaction step; 3) it considers only Boolean features; 4) the imposibility to interact with users not having stable preferences.

S. Carberry et al. (Eds.): UMAP 2013, LNCS 7899, pp. 367–370, 2013.
© Springer-Verlag Berlin Heidelberg 2013

2 Approach

In our model a product p is represented as a Boolean vector $p = (p_1, \ldots, p_n)$. Note that using this boolean features we can model discrete attributes, but we do not discuss this for lack of space. $p_i = 1$ means that the i-th feature is present in the product, otherwise it is not. A catalogue is a set of products. Queries are represented as Boolean vectors as well: $q = (q_1, \ldots, q_n)$. $q_i = 1$ means that the user requests products that have the i-th feature, while $q_i = 0$ means the user has not yet declared her interest on it. A query is *satisfiable* if there exists a product in the catalogue such that all the features requested in the query are present in that product.

A user utility function (user profile) is defined as a vector of weights $w = (w_1, \ldots, w_n)$. $w_i \in [0, 1]$ models the importance that the user assigns to the i-th feature of a product. The user utility of product p is given by the formula: $U_w(p) = \sum_{i=1}^{n} w_i \times f_i(p)$, where $f_i(p)$ is the value function of the i-th feature of p. Moreover, the utility of a query q for a user with profile w, $U_w(q)$, is defined as the utility $U_w(p)$ of a product p with the same definition as q, i.e., $q = p$.

The general user-system interaction steps are performed as follows: 1) the user submit a query; 2) the system infers some constraints analyzing the query selected and submitted by the user; 3) new query revisions are generated (*Candidates* queries); 4) unsatisfiable queries are filtered out from the *Candidates* set; 5) dominated queries are computed and removed from the *Candidates* set; 6) the remaining query revisions are suggested to the user. This interaction is repeated while the user wants more advices and there are query revisions to suggest.

Step 2) is performed assuming that the user is rational and prefers products with larger utility. Therefore, the system can infer constraints on the user utility function by observing the user's selected query among those suggested. More precisely, if q_s is the selected query, then the system infers that $U_w(q_s) \geq U_w(q)$, for the suggested queries q.

In the step 3) we assume that the recommender system allows the user to revise the current query offering to the user a set of revised queries from which the user can select a new one. In fact, the system generates a set of next queries, the *Candidates* queries. These are queries that extend the current query in one or two features. The details about how to select these query revisions are described in [1].

Considering that the main goal is to suggest query revisions that are likely to increase the user utility, in the step 4) the system filters out from the *Candidates* queries those that do not retrieve any product from the catalog (unsatisfiable queries). Moreover, those queries that are proved to be inferior to other queries by considering the constraints on the user utility inferred so far are discarded and the final *AdviseSet* is produced (step 5). A query $q \in Candidates$ is considered by the system as *dominated* if there exists another query $q' \in Candidates$ such that for all the possible weight vectors w that satisfy the set of inferred constraints we have $U_w(q') > U_w(q)$.

3   Related Work

Critiquing, is a query revision technique similar to our proposal [5]. In critiquing the user is offered query revisions in the form of critiques to the current selected product (e.g., "I like this hotel but it is too expensive"). In our approach the user is offered query revisions of the current query that may add or remove constraints over the searched products (e.g., "in addition to the previous features I want also a hotel that is close to the center").

Multi-Attribute Utility Theory (MAUT) is an useful model to handle the tradeoffs among multiple conflicting objectives. In [7], similarly to our approach, the authors use MAUT to adapt the generation of critiques to user preferences. For each user an estimated preference profile (vector of weights) is adaptively maintained, and updated according to the critique selection made by the user. In our approach what we maintain for each user is a set of constraints on the user utility function, inferred by observing the user query revision. These constraints are used further to dicriminate among a set of predefined profiles (vectors of weights) which may represent the true user utility function and then compute the best suggestions considering our MAUT-based preference model.

Similarly to the *dominated query* concept considered in our work, in [6] the authors consider a user-motivated critiquing RS that suggests the top K options with the highest likelihood to be not dominated by others options according to Pareto optimality principle. The idea is to suggest not only options that best match the user's current preferences but to suggest options that will become optimal if the user adds new preferences. In our work, we use a MAUT-based approach to suggest the top K *not dominated* options (query revisions). We suggest queries that exhibit the largest utility increase for all the profiles satisfying the inferred user utility constraints. In [4] the problem of finding the *dominated* queries was approached using linear programming techniques, allowing an infinite number of profiles to be considered, implying a high computation cost.

4   Main Results and Future Work

Assuming that users can be modeled with a large but finite number of different utility functions we have overcome the computational issues mentioned above, and additionally we have achieved some important results listed as follows:

- The computation time of the best query suggestions for a user is reduced by two orders of magnitude, from minutes/seconds to tens of milliseconds, and the system performance is very close to the optimal values. In 18 different experiments where 100 user-system interactions were simulated, the system suggested a query which in 92% of the cases selected the optimal products among 4056 different options.
- In order to keep the number of query suggestions small we introduced a ranking method for selecting a reduced set of query revisions among those that are not dominated. This ranking method is based on the estimation of

the user utility considering the profiles that are compatible with the constraints so far acquired. The method generates the top K queries with the largest expected utility. The number of suggestions at each step was then dramatically reduced by a factor of 10 compared to [4].

– We have shown that this approach can be effectively implemented independently from the selected query editing operators that the system may use. Hence, our technique can be applicable in many scenarios, e.g., mobile, with a simplified set of query editing operators and in desktop-based applications with more complex user interfaces.
– We have extended the model considering discrete attributes, making possible to model the cost of a product. In this situation the system exhibits a good performance, i.e., the utility shortfall values are close to the optimal values.

The details of these results can be found in the workshop papers [2] [3] and the conference paper [1]. Future work efforts will be focused on 1) improving the set of predefined profiles by tailoring this set to the different types of users that interact with the system; 2) to further generalize the product model considering more general discrete features; 3) produce a robust preference inference method which considers users with no stable set of preferences during the interaction with the system and 4) fully evaluate the proposed approach through live user experiments using Web and mobile applications. This is very important to better understand user preferences and how the system performs when interacting with tens or hundreds of users concurrently. Moreover, these evaluations will provide more precise estimations on the quality of the system's query suggestions.

References

1. Blanco, H., Ricci, F.: Inferring user utility for query revision recommendation. In: Proceedings of the 28th Symposium on Applied Computing, vol. 1, pp. 245–252. ACM (2013)
2. Blanco, H., Ricci, F., Bridge, D.: Conversational query revision with a finite user profiles model. In: IIR 2012, Procs. of the 3rd Italian Information Retrieval Workshop, vol. 835, pp. 77–88. CEUR-WS (2012)
3. Blanco, H., Ricci, F., Bridge, D.: Recommending personalized query revisions. In: Decisions@Recsys 2012, Proceedings of the 2nd Workshop on Human Decision Making in Recommender Systems, vol. 893, pp. 19–26. CEUR-WS (2012)
4. Bridge, D., Ricci, F.: Supporting product selection with query editing recommendations. In: Proceedings of the 2007 ACM Conference on Recommender Systems, RecSys 2007, pp. 65–72. ACM (2007)
5. McGinty, L., Reilly, J.: On the evolution of critiquing recommenders. In: Ricci, F., Rokach, L., Shapira, B., Kantor, P.B. (eds.) Recommender Systems Handbook, pp. 419–453. Springer (2011)
6. Viappiani, P., Pu, P., Faltings, B.: Conversational recommenders with adaptive suggestions. In: Proceedings of the 2007 ACM Conference on Recommender Systems, pp. 89–96. ACM (2007)
7. Zhang, J., Pu, P.: A comparative study of compound critique generation in conversational recommender systems. In: Wade, V.P., Ashman, H., Smyth, B. (eds.) AH 2006. LNCS, vol. 4018, pp. 234–243. Springer, Heidelberg (2006)

Mining Semantic Data, User Generated Contents, and Contextual Information for Cross-Domain Recommendation

Ignacio Fernández-Tobías

Universidad Autónoma de Madrid, Madrid, Spain
i.fernandez@uam.es

Abstract. Cross-domain recommender systems suggest items in a target domain by exploiting user preferences and/or domain knowledge available in a source domain. In this thesis we aim to develop a framework for cross-domain recommendation capable of mining heterogeneous sources of information such as semantically annotated data, user generated contents, and contextual signals. For this purpose, we investigate a number of approaches to extract, process, and integrate knowledge for linking distinct domains, and various models that exploit such knowledge for making effective recommendations across domains.

Keywords: Cross-domain recommender systems, semantic networks, social tagging, context-aware recommendations.

1 Introduction

To cope with information overload recommender systems aim to find the items that best suit the user's tastes, interests and priorities, without requiring her to launch explicit search queries, as is usually done in information retrieval systems.

Most of current recommender systems target items in a single domain. For instance, Netflix makes personalized recommendations of movies and TV series, and Last.fm suggests music compositions and artists. E-commerce sites like Amazon, however, could take benefit from exploiting the user's preferences on diverse types of items to provide recommendations in different but somehow related domains. Recommendations across domains could mitigate the cold-start problem when little information about the user's preferences is available in a target domain, and are potentially more diverse and serendipitous than single-domain recommendations.

The goal of cross-domain recommender systems is to suggest items in a target domain by exploiting user preferences and/or domain knowledge available in a source domain. Hence, a major challenge for making cross-domain recommendations is how to transfer knowledge across different domains, i.e., how to build *bridges* between domains, in which usually there is little or no overlap between user preferences or item attributes. Motivated by this fact, in this thesis we aim to address the following research question: **How to effectively extract and exploit knowledge from a source domain to improve recommendations in a distinct, target domain?**

S. Carberry et al. (Eds.): UMAP 2013, LNCS 7899, pp. 371–375, 2013.

For such purpose, we shall investigate a number of methods that exploit different data sources to establish *links* between domains, and shall develop recommendation algorithms that make use of such links. We hypothesize these links will let improve recommendation approaches based only on user preference overlap between domains. Specifically, we propose to exploit semantically annotated data, user-generated contents (social tags, in particular), and contextual information.

In the so-called Semantic Web, and in its reference implementation Linked Data, there is a large number of inter-connected ontologies that describe and relate a wide array of domains. From these ontologies a system that identifies and extracts semantic concepts and properties (relations) belonging to particular domains of interest, could build and exploit semantic networks linking such domains. Similarly to ontologies, social tags assigned to items in folksonomies represent vocabularies describing distinct domains. A system able to somehow find related tags across folksonomies could establish similarities between social tag-based user and item profiles in source and target domains. Finally, contextual signals, such as time, location, mood, and social companion may be used by a system to establish domain-independent similarities between user preferences and item attributes in different domains.

2   Related Work

Cross-domain recommendation has been mostly addressed in the collaborative filtering setting, where there is some user preference (rating) overlap between domains, and where item attributes are not needed. In a seminal paper Winoto and Tang [10] identify three issues to investigate in cross-domain recommendation: the existence of global correlations between user preferences for items in different domains, the method to exploit data on a source domain for predicting preferences on a target domain, and the methodology and metrics to evaluate cross-domain recommendations. In [5] Li surveys works on cross-domain collaborative filtering. He classifies existing approaches according to the type of knowledge transferred: rating patterns, latent features, and user/item inter-domain correlations. Tiroshi and Kuflik [9] evaluate the influence of the involved domains in the recommendation using a kNN approach in which the neighborhood of a user in the target domain is selected among the most similar users from a source domain. To address the problem of little domain overlap, Cremonesi et al. [2] model user and item similarities through graphs, in which all possible paths linking two users or items are used to enhance user- and item-based neighborhood algorithms.

Besides collaborative filtering there have been some attempts to establish semantic relations between items of different domains. In [6] Loizou annotates and links items by means of concepts and relations extracted from Wikipedia. Then, using such relations, users and items are incorporated into a graph upon which a probabilistic recommendation model is built. Social tags have also been used to establish relations between items of different domains. In [4] Kaminskas and Ricci show that emotional tags can be used to effectively select music that fits places of interest. Shi et al. [8] utilize tags to build inter-domain user-to-user and item-to-item similarities. These similarities are proportional to the numbers of tags shared by profiles from different domains, and are incorporated as constraints into a probabilistic matrix factorization model for collaborative filtering. To the best of our knowledge, there is no work in the literature addressing the cross-domain recommendation task by means of contextual features. We believe that a recommender system could exploit relations established through contextual signals, such as the time (e.g. movies and music compositions usually consumed on Christmas), and the user's mood and emotions (e.g. movies and music compositions that usually yield nostalgic feelings).

3   Proposed Solution and Future Work

The main contribution we expect to achieve in this thesis is the development of a **framework for cross-domain recommendation capable of mining heterogeneous sources of information** such as semantic data, social annotations, and contextual features. For this purpose, we aim to investigate a number of approaches to extract, process, and integrate knowledge for linking domains, and various models that exploit such knowledge for making effective cross-domain recommendations.

3.1   Crossing Domains with Semantic Relations

In [1] and [3] we present an approach that exploits the multi-domain DBpedia ontology (http://dbpedia.org) to build semantic networks linking items from different domains. The approach consists of two main components: a class-level network of DBpedia classes and relations belonging to certain domains of interest, and instance-level networks that are automatically generated instantiations of the class-level network for particular input items, by extracting and filtering information from the above ontology. On the built instance-level networks, a graph-based spreading activation algorithm ranks items in the target domain according to their *semantic relatedness* with the input items.

We have evaluated our approach instantiating the framework for recommending musicians and music compositions semantically related to places of interest. Through two user studies we have shown our approach is able to effectively identify music items relevant for the users and suited to the target places. Current work is focused on using open information extraction tools like ReVerb (http://reverb.cs.washington.edu) to discover complex, arbitrary semantic relations across domains that are not available in DBpedia. Moreover, we shall evaluate the framework in other domains such as movies, music and books, and shall enhance it by incorporating user preferences as prior relevance values to compute personalized semantic similarities.

3.2   Crossing Domains with Social Tags

As shown in [4] and [8] tags can play the role of a common feature space for user/item profiles from distinct domains. In [4] Kaminskas and Ricci show that a limited set of emotional tags assigned to both music and places can reveal latent similarities between both types of items. In [8] Shi et al. use the tags common to two folksonomies for computing similarities between users/items in the folksonomies' domains.

We hypothesize that generic lexicons can be built with social tags, and that these lexicons can be used to generate profiles which would act as *bridges* to compute cross-domain user/item similarities. We have developed an approach that automatically builds a lexicon that describes core emotions (e.g. *happy, sad*), by mining synonyms and antonyms extracted from the online Dictionary.com thesaurus. We have proved that our emotion representation is in accordance with the well-known psychological circumplex model of affect [7]. Moreover, using tag co-occurrences, we have linked the lexicon with domain-specific emotion folksonomies extracted from social tagging systems, which let us transform domain-specific tag-based profiles into generic emotion-oriented profiles. For instance, in our approach, a movie annotated with tags associated to the emotional category *suspenseful* strongly overlaps with the *tense* and *nervous* core emotions of the circumplex model. We have conducted a user study showing our method accurately infers emotions evoked by items in the movie and music domains.

Our current work is aimed to exploit the emotion-oriented profiles for making personalized cross-domain recommendations sensible to the user's mood. We also intend to explore other sources of user generated contents such as textual reviews and comments to build generic lexicons suitable for opinion mining and sentiment analysis.

3.3   Crossing Domains with Contextual Information

Contextual information can be also valuable inter-domain features that characterize user preferences. Context features can be obtained through many signals such as the user's current time, location, and social companion. So far we have explored a context modeling approach, formulating the recommendation task as a classification problem, and investigating if using or not those features in addition to content attributes actually leads to better accuracy. Preliminary empirical results have indicated that time context has preference predictive power in the movies and music domains, and it is improved by including social context in the movies domain. Nonetheless, we still have to evaluate if users find common contexts meaningful enough for cross-domain recommendation. Future work in this direction begins with an analysis of correlations between context features and user preferences in different domains.

References

1. Fernández-Tobías, I., Kaminskas, M., Cantador, I., Ricci, F.: A Generic semantic-based framework for cross-domain recommendation. In: 2nd International Workshop on Information Heterogeneity and Fusion in Recommender Systems, pp. 25–32 (2011)
2. Cremonesi, P., Tripodi, A., Turrin, R.: Cross-domain recommender systems. In: 2011 IEEE 11th International Conference on Data Mining Workshops, pp. 496–503 (2011)

3. Kaminskas, M., Fernández-Tobías, I., Ricci, F., Cantador, I.: Ontology-based identification of music for places. In: 13th International Conference on Information and Communication Technologies in Tourism (to appear, 2013)
4. Kaminskas, M., Ricci, F.: Location-Adapted music recommendation using tags. In: 19th Intl. Conference on User Modeling, Adaptation, and Personalization, pp. 183–194 (2011)
5. Li, B.: Cross-domain collaborative filtering: A brief survey. In: 23rd International Conference on Tools with Artificial Intelligence, pp. 1085–1086 (2011)
6. Loizou, A.: How to recommend music to film buffs: enabling the provision of recommendations from multiple domains. PhD dissertation, Univ. of Southampton (2009)
7. Russell, J.A.: A circumplex model of affect. Journal of Personality and Social Psychology 39(6), 1161–1178 (1980)
8. Shi, Y., Larson, M., Hanjalic, A.: Tags as bridges between domains: Improving recommendation with tag-induced cross-domain collaborative filtering. In: 19th International Conference on User modeling, Adaption, and Personalization, pp. 305–316 (2011)
9. Tiroshi, A., Kuflik, T.: Domain ranking for cross domain collaborative filtering. In: 20th Intl. Conference on User Modeling, Adaptation, and Personalization, pp. 328–333 (2012)
10. Winoto, P., Ya Tang, T.: If you like The devil wears Prada the book, will you also enjoy The devil wears Prada the movie? A study of cross-domain recommendations. New Generation Computing 26(3), 209–225 (2008)

A POV-Based User Model: From Learning Preferences to Learning Personal Ontologies

Francesco Osborne

Dept. of Computer Science, University of Torino, 10149 Torino, Italy
osborne@di.unito.it

Abstract. In recent years a variety of ontology-based recommender systems, which make use of a domain ontology to characterize the user model, have shown to be very effective. There are however some open issues with this approach, such as: 1) the creation of an ontology is an expensive process; 2) the ontology seldom takes into account the perspectives of target user communities; 3) different groups of users may have different domain conceptualizations; 4) the ontology is usually static and not able to learn automatically new semantic relationships or properties. To address these points, I propose an approach to automatically build multiple personal ontology views (POVs) from user feedbacks, tailored to specific user groups and exploited for recommendation purpose via spreading activation techniques.

Keywords: Ontology-based User Modelling, Ontology-based Recommender Systems, Spreading Activation, Personal Ontology, Ontology Learning.

1   Introduction

In recent years a variety of ontology-based recommender systems, which make use of a domain ontology to characterize the user model, have proved to be very effective [1]. The usual implementation of ontology-based user modelling is as an overlay on a domain model represented as an ontology. For example Middleton et al [2] exploit the user feedback on research papers and use the relationships between classes to infer other topics of interest. Many of these works use spreading activation techniques [3] to propagate the interest on a certain item on to similar concepts in the ontology. These approaches are usually effective in alleviating the cold start problem, e.g. the situation at the beginning of an interaction with a user, when the system does not have enough data to provide an appropriate adaptation.

There are however some issues associated with most today ontology-based approaches. First of all, ontology crafting is often an expensive process that requires a variety of different expertise, and this is particularly true for very large ontologies. Ontologies are usually crafted by domain experts in cooperation with ontology engineers; however different experts may have different opinions on the conceptualization of a domain, and thus need to find some middle of the road compromise. More important, the expert's view of a domain can be different from the common user's view. Since the relationship between concepts is to be used to produce recommendations, the ontology should instead try to mirror as best as possible the personal view of a user. A personal ontology [4], also called Personal Ontology View [5] (**POV**), is an ontology that is

S. Carberry et al. (Eds.): UMAP 2013, LNCS 7899, pp. 376–379, 2013.

actually tailored on the prospective and the specific domain view of a user. POVs showed to be effective in assisting tasks like web navigation and search, allowing the user to classify items according to her/his own mental categories [6]. For example a group of users may have a personal ontology of the beverage domain that is structured according to the social context in which drinks are consumed, whereas another group may prefer a classification based on the alcoholic scale or sweetness.

Using spreading activation techniques on an ontology that is too different from the personal view of the user may mislead and fail to predict the right preferences: thus, the need for a spreading activation able to exploit the user own personal ontology, or a good enough approximation. A further problem is posed by the fact that a user may alternate her/his prospectives according to the social group she/he is in or the context. To find a way to integrate different perspectives by the same user instead than choosing only one is another interesting challenge.

2   Goals and Objectives

The ontology used in ontology-based user modelling is usually a static knowledge base that is exploited to support various techniques for learning user preferences associated to classes or instances, but which is not able to evolve by itself. A more appealing perspective might be to consider the ontology, and in particular the semantic relationships between concepts, as a dynamic structure that can be learned, adjusted and adapted to the needs of a user or group of users. The learning process may become bidirectional: ontologies help to handle user feedbacks by allowing to propagate interests to similar concepts and these information are returned to the learning module that supports the ontology evolution and adaptation.

Haase et al [6] propose an approach for suggesting to the users some adaptations to the domain ontology, mostly in terms of which topic is to be excluded from the personal view. The learning process can however go much further than accepting or rejecting topics or relationships in an existing ontology. A learning module should also be able to discover original concepts, relationships and properties by analysing patterns in the user behaviour. As an example, given an ontology that classifies cheese, we may discover that users who like the Italian cheese "Gorgonzola" tend to like also "Blue Danish" more often then one might expect on the basis of the semantic relationship expressed by the original ontology, in which they are two sibling classes with no apparent common property. Both of these two products are however blue mould cheeses; the original ontology should either include this characteristic or be adapted to accommodate the specific group of users who think that this relationship is significant. To this purpose either a common super-class "Blue Mould Cheese" or another property can be added.

The discussed issues suggest some interesting research questions:

Q1: How can the creation of ontologies for user modelling be made simpler and less expensive?

Q2: How can the user perspectives be integrated within the domain expert's opinions in the crafting process?

Q3: Is it possible to automatically learn the user POVs from the feedback?

Q4: What is the best way to handle different mental models of users that would call for different personal ontology views?

Q5: How can the spreading activation techniques be adapted to work in an environment with multiple POVs that can be updated on the run?

To investigate these research questions I propose a POV-based user model that should be able to:

1) Learn semantic relationships and relevant properties from user feedbacks and use them to craft, refine or adapt a domain ontology (**Q1, Q2, Q3**);
2) Cluster the users in terms of different mental models and assign to each group a POV derived from the main ontology (**Q4**);
3) Use a novel spreading activation technique that is able to propagate user feedback on multiple evolving personal ontologies (**Q5**).

The suggested POV-based user model is an overlay on the user specific POV that will keep being refined as the system learns more about the user and other users similar to her/him. The ability to learn semantic relationships and properties on the run makes this approach quite different from the state of the art POVs, which usually are obtained simply by selecting the slice of a human crafted domain ontology which appears to be more suitable to the user. It is also possible to theorize a POV-based user model that allows the user to belong to more than one group and is hence able to handle her/his multiple POVs. Of course, this requires a technique flexible enough to compromise among different views and/or to choose the one deemed most helpful for a given task or context.

3   Present Achievements And Future Directions

To address **Q1, Q2** and **Q3**, I am presently working on an algorithm called *Klink UM* (Klink for User Modelling). It is a modified version of *Klink* [7], an algorithm which uses a combination of statistical and machine-learning techniques to mine semantic relationships among research areas by exploiting the co-occurrences between keywords associated to scientific papers. Preliminary trials showed that such an approach could be adapted to take as input a set of user ratings on items associated with keywords/categories and use the rating patterns to infer semantic relationships among them. While the task of Klink is limited to building a complete ontology from scratch, Klink UM will also be able to receive as input an initial ontology and proceed to mould it according to the perspective inferred by user ratings. Thus Klink UM can be used both to semi-automatically craft a domain ontology (**Q1**) and to refine it by integrating the users point of view (**Q2**). If fed with the ratings of a specific group, it will yield a specific POV tailored to it (**Q3**).

The identification of groups of users with different mental models of the domain (**Q4**) will be based on a novel similarity distance that takes in consideration the closeness of the various perceptions of the relationships between the elements of the domain. So, a user who estimates a set of elements as conceptually very near when they are linked by semantic relationship R and instead very distant when they have different values for property P, would be clustered with users who share the same attitude and not with users who instead consider property P not very discriminant.

I plan to use this metric with a clusterization algorithm to find groups of users with a similar view of the domain and return their feedbacks to Klink UM for building their POV. I think that a clustering approach might be easier and more realistic than building a specific and probably redundant POV for every single user in the system. However a user may also adopt different mental models according to the context and the social group with which she/he is in a certain moment: thus my longer-term plan is to permit a user to be associated with more than one cluster with which she/he is compatible (non-exclusive clustering), e.g. to allow her/him to refer to different POVs. Finally, to address **Q5**, I am working on a spreading activation technique that takes in consideration 1) the nature of semantic relationships, 2) the properties and their values, and 3) the similarity of the classes according to user feedback. The stepping-stones have been two of my recent works, one on a propagation technique that uses the topic distance in a conceptual hierarchy [8] and the other on a conceptual similarity distance based on common or different properties of two classes [9].

I plan to evaluate the POV based User Model following two steps. First I will verify that the ontologies produced by the Klink UM algorithm are similar enough to the human crafted ones. To this scope, I will compare the semantic connections of the former ones with a set of gold standard ontologies representing the same domains and compute the recall and precision. The second step will be to show that a POV-based user model could give better recommendation then a standard ontology-based user model. To this end, I will apply different spreading activation techniques on the two kinds of user model and evaluate their performance in suggesting items with Pearson's correlation coefficient and mean absolute error.

The main challenge for the future will be to develop an original approach capable of maintaining a reliable and coherent user model even when using multiple POVs, with all of them able continuously enriched and refined by new evidence.

References

1. Sosnovsky, S., Dicheva, D.: Ontological technologies for user modelling. International Journal of Metadata, Semantics and Ontologies 5(1), 32–71 (2010)
2. Middleton, S.E., Shadbolt, N.R., DeRoure, D.C.: Ontological user profiling in recommender systems. ACM Transactions on Information Systems (2004)
3. Anderson, J.R.: A Spreading Activation Theory of Memory. Journal of Verbal Learning and Verbal Behavior 22, 261–295 (1983)
4. Chaffee, J., Gauch, S.: Personal ontologies for web navigation. In: Proceedings of the ninth International Conference on Information and Knowledge Management, CIKM 2000, pp. 227–234 (2000)
5. Kalfoglou, Y., Domingue, J., Motta, E., Vargas-Vera, M., Shum, S.B.: MyPlanet: an ontology-driven Web-based personalised news service. In: Proceedings of the Workshop on Ontologies and Information Sharing at IJCAI 2001 (2001)
6. Haase, P., Hotho, A., Schmidt-Thieme, L., Sure, Y.: Collaborative and usage-driven evolution of personal ontologies. In: Gómez-Pérez, A., Euzenat, J. (eds.) ESWC 2005. LNCS, vol. 3532, pp. 486–499. Springer, Heidelberg (2005)
7. Osborne, F., Motta, E.: Mining Semantic Relations between Research Areas. In: Proceedings of the 11th International Semantic Web Conference, Boston, USA (2012)
8. Cena, F., Likavec, S., Osborne, F.: Propagating user interests in ontology-based user model. In: Pirrone, R., Sorbello, F. (eds.) AI*IA 2011. LNCS, vol. 6934, pp. 299–311. Springer, Heidelberg (2011)
9. Cena, F., Likavec, S., Osborne, F.: Property-based interest propagation in ontology-based user model. In: Proceedings of the 20th Conference on User Modeling, Adaptation and Personalization, Montreal, Canada (2012)

Design and Evaluation of an Affective
BCI-Based Adaptive User Application:
A Preliminary Case Study

Giuseppe Rizzo

Dipartimento di Informatica,
Università degli Studi di Bari, Italy
giuseppe.rizzo@uniba.it

Abstract. The Brain-Computer interface (BCI) advancements made possible the use of techniques to recognize emotional aspects from the electroencephalographic signal (EEG). In this work I focus on the implementation of a BCI-based application, able to mine relevant information about user's emotion from his/her EEG signal and to adapt to it. To this aim a highly low cost and wearable device is employed, so as, a natural interaction is allowed.

Keywords: Adaptation, Affective Computing, BCI, User-Centred Evaluation.

1   Introduction

There is a consensus about the fact that using an interface that is based on extra-rational aspects (e.g. physiological aspects) to recognize emotions could improve the quality and effectiveness of human-computer interaction (HCI), by adapting properties' interfaces to the user, in real time. In this work I focus on the ability of automatic recognition of emotions and of translating the recognized emotions into user-oriented interaction rules, as it occurs in an adaptive application. A first kind of application I am interested to is in the field of serious games. In this context, I expect that a satisfying interaction will be based on the user emotional state monitoring and not only on the user directly controlling the game. An images viewer able to select contents on the base of the user's emotional state has been built as an example of "no Pain, no Gain" [1] application. The main goal of this kind of application is in the learning games. Here, to facilitate the learning process a right balance of positive and negative emotions should be induced in the user. Due to the weaknesses of traditional methods I employed a passive BCI[1] [2] to collect additional information on user's emotions. The same BCI has been employed in order to auto-induce (negative/positive) emotional states into the user himself. A set of preliminary usability experiments has been conducted for determining if the outcome of a low-cost BCI is suitable to carry out an emotionally-driven interaction's customization on each individual user, in the ad hoc "no Pain, no Gain" application.

---

[1] Passive BCIs consider brain activity as an additional source of information, to augment and adapt the interface instead of controlling it [2].

S. Carberry et al. (Eds.): UMAP 2013, LNCS 7899, pp. 380–383, 2013.

2   Objectives and Scientific Contribution

This work represents a first step in my Ph.D. project, in the field of Affective BCI (ABCI). The main goal of my Ph.D. project is to explore the neuro-physiological signals for the automatic recognition of affective states, in order to use this information in innovative applications (e.g. adaptive ones, as in the scope of this paper). The main challenge of my research concerns the employment of highly low cost and wearable devices, as requested in more natural and effective HCIs. To this aim, I focus on the following main hypotheses: (I) That the quality and effectiveness of an interaction are related to the ABCI believability, in that the ABCI-based application should convince the user that his mind reading really occurs; (II) That the ABCI believability could be accessed even if a restricted subset of the entire brain activity (EEG signal) is handled. My efforts are driven by applied and basic sciences such as affective computing and basic neuroscience advances. Until now I focused on the BCI implementation and evaluation in an adaptive ad-hoc application. To these main goals, my work spanned: Firstly, I implemented a BCI-based Experimenter which is able to record data and also to attempt an on-line analysis and classification of the input data stream. By using the Experimenter to read the brain activity of different subjects, I performed a set of formative evaluation tests in order to define requirements of a simple ad-hoc adaptive application, in which the user is called to exploit the built BCI in a passive way. Technical details and results about performed formative and summative tests are discussed in the following. The next 3 years of my Ph.D. project will be devoted to: The tuning of the ABCI in order to converge in a system able to be employed in several different application domains. In this context, I will perform new proper formative and summative usability tests based on the users' emotional level, which will become a User-Centred Evaluation activity. Finally, to overcome BCI limitations, I will explore the possibility of linking the implemented ABCI to a cognitive model of emotion in which emotions are recognized on the base of their appraisal mechanism too [1,3]. Details about applications and cognitive emotion modeling are out of the scope of this paper.

3   The BCI-Based Adaptive Application

This section describes the ad-hoc Adaptive Application: Once the application is activated, an emotional stimulus (e.g. an image from the International Affective Pictures System – IAPS [4]) is presented to the subject who is involved in the experiments. The EEG signal of the subject is recorded through electrodes, which are placed on his scalp. EEG signals are recorded by using Emotiv[TM] Epoc headset[2] and subsequently handled and classified by BCI2000 [5][3]. EEG signals are classified according to the valence/arousal space [3,4]. Based on the classification results, a new stimulus from IAPS is selected to be presented to the subject, so that the subsequent subject's felt

---

[2] http://www.emotiv.com.
[3] In this work AF3, AF4, F3, F4, FC5, FC6 channels have been investigated.

emotion is auto-induced[4]. More in depth, if the (i-1)-th image induced an emotional response in the subject and the Online Classifier recognized it as characterized by a specific combination of valence and arousal values, the Adaptive Application displays on the screen the i-th image that should induce an opposite emotion in terms of both valence and arousal (e.g. a positive/high valence/arousal state involves a stimulus labeled as negative/low is selected). I called this maximum contrast criterion. In the case of a neutral reaction (i.e. a combination of neutral/medium valence/arousal), the Adaptive Application will display on the screen a stimulus labeled as positive/high. According to formative evaluation tests (see section 4), the On-line Classifier uses the 10-Nearest Neighbors (10-NN) algorithm [6], as it shows the best trade-off between total response time and offline accuracy.

4   Requirements Gathering

By means of the Experimenter, I performed a set of architectural formative tests in order to choose the classification algorithm to be used in the BCI-based Adaptive Application, according to prediction accuracy. Due to the lack of standard datasets for the classification algorithms evaluation, I had to collect my own data by using IAPS images for elicitation activity. Images have been selected based on their valence-arousal values. Three subjects (25 years old) participated to the emotional stimulation. 4 series of stimuli, made up of 4 consecutive images with the same combination of valence and arousal values, has been displayed. Each image has been shown for 5 seconds and it has been followed by 6 seconds of black screen. At the end of each series of images the subject answered a few simple questions. I used the Short-Time Fast Fourier Transform (STFT) to extract the features from the EEG signal. In order to reduce data dimensionality, I employed correlation-feature selection [6]. Collected data have been labeled comparing valence and arousal values provided for each image in the IAPS database with the answers provided by the users with the self-assessment questionnaire. If an inconsistency was found between subjective and objective data, the data were discarded. Data collected from the beginning of the registration until the first displayed image were labeled as "Neutral", meaning that the subject start the experiment in his basic emotional state. In order to provide evidences in favor of the hypotheses related to my Ph.D research, I compared several widely employed classification algorithms[5]. I employed 10-fold cross validation. 10-NN [6] proved to be the best algorithm, approaching the 70% of prediction accuracy about valence. This result is mainly due to a better capability of negative-valence instances recognition. In the case of the arousal, even with respect to the original data, the algorithm is not able to recognize the instances of the "Medium"(i.e., the basic state in terms of arousal dimension) class, in contrast to the recognition of the instances of the "High" and "Low" classes. So the results are 10% lower at least.

---

[4]   In choosing the images I avoided the ones that could objectively induce psychological harm.

[5]   Naive Bayes, Bayesian Network k-Nearest Neighbors with (k=10), Sequential Minimal Optimization, Multi-level Perceptron and Random Forest algorithm [6].

5   Application and User Testing

The experiments involved 11 subjects, 21/26 years old. First, the consent form has been compiled by the subjects, then for each of them, 3 series of images (6 images for each one, selected from IAPS) have been displayed. A black screen has been displayed for 10 seconds. The first image followed for 6 seconds; 5 more self-induced images have been showed (each image for 6 seconds), broken up by a black screen for 25 seconds, to allow the subject to answer some simple questions about felt emotions. The 3 series have been showed at regular intervals of 5 minutes. As stated, each image has been selected according to the Online Classifier's output. At the end of the experiment, each participant answered a short questionnaire and has been interviewed to get an overall evaluation of the interactive experience. Then, I compared subjects' self-assessments with Experimenter's logs: From this, an alternation of images with positive and negative valence has been displayed. For all of the involved subjects, the system recognized emotions with high arousal and both negative and positive valence. On the other side, I noted a better classification performance in the first part of each interaction with the Adaptive Application, probably caused by the duration of experimentation rather than the inaccuracy of the classification. To the aim of this work, an adaptive application able to alternate passive interaction phases (BCI-based) and active ones (through a standard controller, in order to operate choices among alternatives) could prove to be useful to motivate the subject to longer focus himself.

References

1. Picard, R.: Affective Computing. MIT Press (1998)
2. Zander, O.T., Kothe, C., Jatzev, S., Gaertner, M.: Enhancing Human-Computer Interaction with Input from Active and Passive Brain-Computer Interfaces. In: Tan, D., Nijholt, A. (eds.) Brain-Computer Interfaces - Applying Our Minds to Human-Computer Interaction. Human-Computer Interaction Series. Springer, London (2010)
3. Russell, J.A.: Core affect and the psychological construction of emotion. Psychological Review 110, 145–172 (2003)
4. Schaaf, K.: EEG-based emotion recognition. Master's thesis, Univ. Karlsruhe (TH), Karlsruhe, Germany (2008)
5. Schalk, G., Mellinger, J.: Introduction to Brain-Computer Interfacing Using BCI2000: General-Purpose Software for Brain-Computer Interface Research, Data Acquisition, Stimulus Presentation, and Brain Monitoring. Human-Computer Interaction Series. Springer, London (2010)
6. Witten, I., Eibe, F., Hall, A.: Data Mining Practical Machine Learning Tools and Techniques, 3rd edn. Morgan Kaufmann Series in Data Management Systems. Morgan Kauffman (2011)

Inclusive Personalized e-Learning
Based on Affective Adaptive Support

Sergio Salmeron-Majadas, Olga C. Santos, and Jesus G. Boticario

aDeNu Research Group, Artificial Intelligence Dept., Computer Science School,
UNED, C/Juan del Rosal, 16, 28040 Madrid, Spain
ssalmeron@bec.uned.es, {ocsantos,jgb}@dia.uned.es

Abstract. Emotions and learning are closely related. In the PhD research presented in this paper, that relation has to be taken advantage of. With this aim, within the framework of affective computing, the main goal proposed is modeling learner's affective state in order to support adaptive features and provide an inclusive personalized e-learning experience. At the first stage of this research, emotion detection is the principal issue to cope with. A multimodal approach has been proposed, so gathering data from diverse sources to feed data mining systems able to supply emotional information is being the current ongoing work. On the next stages, the results of these data mining systems will be used to enhance learner models and based on these, offer a better e-learning experience to improve learner's results.

Keywords: Affective Computing, Emotions, User Modeling, Human-Computer Interaction, Data Mining, Artificial Intelligence, Multimodal Approach.

1   Theoretical Framework

Personalization in e-learning scenarios is known to result in benefits [1], but to obtain the best results from this personalization, an appropriate learner model is needed, and to build it, standards and specifications have to be followed [2]. As affective computing is a widely considered approach, complementing these models is an issue that is being commonly addressed in different domains [3].

In educational environments this approach has been extensively treated, but there is still a lot of work to due to the variety of open issues involved in affect recognition [4]. Learner's affective state detection has been contended from different points of view. As many researches have focused on emotion detection from a using a single data source, current researches are introducing a multimodal approach, basing their work on processing data given by different data sources in order to improve the detection affective states [5]. Many different data sources are currently being proposed, from the less intrusive solutions based on studying user's interactions with the system (such as keystrokes or mouse movements [6]) to other ones with different intrusion levels as a face tracking camera [5], some questionnaires or a wide range of physiological sensors (going from simple temperature-measuring probes or skin conductance sensors to electroencephalography or eye tracking systems). As this

S. Carberry et al. (Eds.): UMAP 2013, LNCS 7899, pp. 384–387, 2013.
© Springer-Verlag Berlin Heidelberg 2013

approach involves the use of many data sources and some of them (such as physiological sensors) offer a continuous data stream, big amounts of data have to be processed. To deal with this huge data processing requirement data mining techniques can be applied to obtain the needed information that ultimately will be integrated in the user model of the learner.

Once the first stage of affective detection [7] has been addressed, and the user model has been updated, the adaptation of the system response to the users' emotional state must be designed. To this, different feedback strategies may be followed, such as promoting positive emotions on the learner or avoiding those emotions that difficult the cognitive process. The feedback format may involve different approaches, such as customizing the content given to the learner to different ways and offering inclusive recommendations, which take into account users' functional diversity. Evaluation will be needed to check the impact of the recommendations on learner's performance [8].

2   The Research Approach

As previously remarked, the main goal of this research is to offer adaptive and personalized support in education by improving the learner model with affective information. To cope with interoperability issues, this improvement must be done taking the existing standards into account, and expanding these standards when necessary. Some of the standards to be used are IMS Learner Information to model users' learning features and Profile IMS Access For All to model users' interaction needs, the latter needed to cope with the use of assistive technology in inclusive learning scenarios. Interoperability will be taken into consideration also by easing the integration with existing e-learning platforms service-oriented open architectures. To attend the metacognitive issues involved in the learning process, the use of an open learner model strategy allowing learners to manipulate their own model is also considered. As for the adaptive feedback to be provided to the learner, the Semantic Affective Educational Recommender Systems (SAERS) approach will be used, which is based on delivering emotion-based recommendations, which are designed with TORMES user centered design methodology   [9]. The objective here is not only recommending passive actions (e.g. reading a given material) but also active actions (e.g. creating a new thread in a forum). All these issues are to be supported by a data-mining based multimodal approach to obtain emotional information [10]. To get there, a step-wise research methodology has been proposed in terms of the following steps:

1. Study the state of the art in emotion detection, specifically, multimodal approach on emotion detection in educational scenarios.
2. Carry out experiments in order to gather data from diverse sources to be used as training on our development.
3. Process the data obtained from the experiments according to the input source so that they can feed data mining algorithms. To this the different sources' information gain is to be evaluated.
4. Investigate different data mining algorithms to get the best results to be used in the user model.

5. Apply data mining on the obtained data, searching for the emotion detections based on the gathered data. This issue is closely related to the previous one.
6. Use the data generated by the data mining systems to feed the standardized user model (enhancing it if necessary).
7. Using the proposed model to offer adaptive support to learners via recommendations, which aims at helping them to achieve better results on their tasks.
8. Carry out experiments to evaluate achievements, i.e. the support given to learners in the previous task, taking into account a multi-layer evaluation approach to assess the quality of the proposed contributions (from input data acquisition to changes of system behavior and interactions through the inference and adaptations done).
9. Analyze results from the previous tasks in order to detect and apply improvements.

The main contributions expected from this work are: i) Offering a standards-based modeling approach to reflect learners' affective states based on a multimodal affect detection strategy, which combines different affective information sources, ii) A study of the information gain provided by each one of the data sources and techniques used in the multimodal approach searching the most efficient and less intrusive way to detect learner's emotions.. iii) The use of the proposed user model combined with a recommender system to provide affective based recommendations and its evaluation.

3   Progress to Date

Currently, the first three aforementioned steps are being addressed. While the study of the state of the art is still ongoing, in November 2012, in the context of the MAMIPEC [10] project, an experiment was designed and taken into the frame of Madrid Science Week. During that experiment nearly 100 participants came to our laboratory and solved a series of Math problems. Four different experiences were offered, three of them with the same structure and another one offering a collaborative activity instead the math problems. All the participants wore sensors and were monitored in order to get as much data as possible. The data gathered during those experiments consists of: i) heart rate measured with an electrocardiography system using three electrodes (two of them on the inner face o ankles and the last electrode over the chest); ii) breath frequency measured with a respiration belt used around the rib cage; iii) skin conductance measured with two sensors on their index and ring finger; iv) temperature measured with a probe in contact with the wrist.; v) facial expression captured with a Microsoft Kinect for Windows. As its SDK includes a face tracking system, the detected points were stored for being processed; vi) keystroke and mouse movement logs. A key-logger and a mouse-tracker were developed in order to get information from the learner's typing; vii) personality's main five structural dimensions with the Big Five Inventory (BFI) questionnaire; viii) self-beliefs to cope with a variety of difficult demands in life with the General Self-Efficacy Scale (GSE) questionnaire; ix) positive and negative affect schedule with the Positive and Negative Affect Schedule (PANAS) questionnaire.

With all that data collected, now data mining models are being built and tested in order to check the best results. To do this, different ways of using the information are being used as well as different supervised learning algorithms (e.g. naïve bayes or prediction trees) to get emotional data from them. In particular, we are trying to predict the tags given by the participants during the experiment by using a bidimensional system to tag valence and arousal dimensions of affective states. In parallel, experimentation goes on and some of the offered experiments during Madrid Science Week are being adapted and offered to people with disabilities in order to evaluate which adaptations are needed to perform the same experiments in an inclusive context. The same data is being gathered from the participants of the inclusive experiments. The next step will be the development of a user model based on the data collected and its evaluation to detect the points where the current approach should be improved.

Acknowledgments. Authors would like to thank experiments' participants, MAMIPEC project (TIN2011-29221-C03-01) colleagues and the Spanish Government for its funding.

References

1. Carro, R.M.: Applications of adaptive hypermedia in education. Computers and Education, 1–12 (2008)
2. Boticario, J.G., Santos, O.C.: An open IMS-based user modelling approach for developing adaptive learning management systems. Journal of Interactive Media in Education 2 (2007)
3. Tao, J., Tan, T.: Affective computing: A review. In: Tao, J., Tan, T., Picard, R.W. (eds.) ACII 2005. LNCS, vol. 3784, pp. 981–995. Springer, Heidelberg (2005)
4. Ritter, J.K.: On the Affective Challenges of Developing a Pedagogy of Teacher Education. Studying Teacher Education 7, 219–233 (2011)
5. Zeng, Z., Pantic, M., Roisman, G.I., Huang, T.S.: A Survey of Affect Recognition Methods: Audio, Visual, and Spontaneous Expressions. IEEE Transactions on Pattern Analysis and Machine Intelligence 31, 39–58 (January 2009)
6. Epp, C., Lippold, M., Mandryk, R.L.: Identifying emotional states using keystroke dynamics. In: Proceedings of the 2011 Annual Conference on Human Factors in Computing Systems, pp. 715–724 (2011)
7. Carberry, S., de Rosis, F.: Introduction to special Issue on "Affective modeling and adaptation". User Modeling and User-Adapted Interaction 18, 1–9 (2008)
8. Shen, L., Wang, M., Shen, R.: Affective e-learning: Using "emotional" data to improve learning in pervasive learning environment. Educational Technology & Society 12, 176–189 (2009)
9. Santos, O.C., Boticario, J.G.: Affective Issues in Semantic Educational Recommender Systems. In: CEUR workshop proceedings, vol. 896, pp. 71–82 (2012)
10. Santos, O.C., Salmeron-Majadas, S., Boticario, J.G.: Emotions detection from math exercises by combining several data sources. In: Proceedings of the 16th International Conference on Artificial Intelligence in Education (AIED 2013) (in press, 2013)

Tabbed Browsing Behavior as a Source for User Modeling

Martin Labaj and Mária Bieliková

Slovak University of Technology in Bratislava,
Faculty of Informatics and Information Technologies,
Ilkovičova, 842 16 Bratislava, Slovakia
{labaj,bielik}@fiit.stuba.sk

Abstract. In our research, we focus on improving the user model by using novel sources of user feedback – tabbed browsing behavior of the users (also called parallel browsing). The tabbing is nowadays established as the more accurate description of browsing activities than the previous linear representation. Users take advantage of multiple tabs in various scenarios, by which they express different relations and preferences to hypermedia being visited in such tabs. The aimed contribution is to include this behavior into the user model, so improving accuracy of modeled user's characteristics and thus improving personalization.

Keywords: user modeling, tabbed browsing, adaptive web-based systems.

1   Motivation

Nowadays, all major web browsers support visiting multiple pages at once using the mechanism of multiple tabs contained within one browser window. This behavior is called parallel browsing and in general, for the purposes of web usage mining, it is not discerned whether multiple tabs or browser windows are being used. For the purposes of this paper, we refer to such behavior simply as tabbing.

The tabbing has nowadays become accepted as a more accurate description of browsing activities than the previous linear models, in which a visit to one page was perceived as leaving the previous page. The acknowledgment of emergence of this behavior is found even in web standards, as the W3C specification of Page Visibility API (www.w3.org/TR/page-visibility/) was proposed in 2011 in order to enable web developers to determine visibility of pages and allow them to save on device and browser resources when the user is browsing in different tabs. The specification has only recently (Feb. 2013) entered the pre-final "Proposed Recommendation" stage. The fact that such measures are created for something as ample as processing power of current devices is a strong hint that the tabbing behavior is current issue.

Meanwhile, in the field of Adaptive Web-Based Systems, user model is the essential feature to facilitate the adaptation. It covers and represents user's interests, knowledge, goals, etc. Sourcing the indicators for such user features is the ongoing research issue. Our hypothesis is that using data on the tabbed browsing, observing which tabs the user is keeping opened, which tabs he opens and when, and how he opens the sites in existing or new tabs, has a potential to improve user models.

S. Carberry et al. (Eds.): UMAP 2013, LNCS 7899, pp. 388–391, 2013.

2   Related Work

Previous research has already shown that the tabbed browsing (also called tabbing or parallel browsing) is common amongst most users. This model better lines up with the real user behavior than earlier linear model where each visit to a web page replaces the previous page [1]. A study [2] was performed logging and then interviewing the users for *reasons* why they use tabs. The situations cited by users were: *reminders* (keeping opened tabs with things to do later), *opening links in background* (opening multiple links in multiple background tabs), *multitasking* (switching to a tab to perform a new task), *going "back and forth"* (switching between two or more pages), *frequently used pages* (keeping pages opened for later use), *short-term bookmarks*.

It was proposed that differences in tabbed browsing can indicate the type of search query [3], or differentiate sessions to improve recommendation algorithms [4]. When trying to observe the tabbed browsing, typical problems arise from its invisibility in the server logs (only pageloads). When basing the observation only on the server logs, the tabbing is only estimated within a large space of possibilities [1] or observed indirectly and partially, e.g. through the order of clicks and visits to a search results page [3]. When basing the observation on an augmented browser (plug-in or extension), the users and tabbing are observed precisely and sometimes at the scale [5], but we are then limited to participants with such modified browser.

It is worth noting that some approaches overlap with the notion of tabbed browsing even when they do not refer to tabbing explicitly. One example is the analysis of click streams. When the user follows a link from one page to another and then, later, from the same source page into different one, it can be inferred that the source page was still opened [3], representing branching in the tabbed model. Another example is the evaluation of time spent on a web page. When this measure is tracked in fragments (not only as a difference between two subsequent pageloads) and only time in focus is considered, this indicator partly represents switching between tabs in the tabbed model. However, neither current approach covers all aspects of tabbing from tab creation, through tab switching, to closing and a deeper exploitation of possible scenarios in which users browse in this way has not been researched.

3   Tabbed Browsing as a Source for User Modeling

Our aim is to propose a method for user modeling based on tabbed browsing. We create an overlay user model on top of open-corpus domain model, modeling *user interests*, *goals and tasks*, and *context of work* (device-centered, including user task), with possible inclusion of *individual traits*, specifically browsing style. Our proposed approach to user modeling consists of three steps: (i) Acquisition and modeling of the tabbed browsing actions, (ii) Recognizing the *scenarios of tab usage* being performed, (iii) Building or augmenting existing user model. Fig. 1 depicts an overview of our approach – user activities can be sourced either (i) from browsing agent (extension), covering only specific users, but all their activity, or (ii) from in-page scripts, covering all users, but only within given systems.

Reasons *for using tabs* [2] line up into the three categories of implicit feedback:

— *Examination behavior* (selection, duration, repetition, etc.). The multiple tabs can be used to examine multiple objects and selection and repetition are important aspects, as the user can revisit any opened page in a tab without loading it again.
— *Retention behavior* (save a reference, save an object, deletion, etc.). The user can keep important or interesting pages opened in the background tabs and retain them as a reminder or bookmark, closing them only when they are no longer needed.
— *Reference behavior* (object-object reference, object-portion reference, etc.). The user can open multiple links from a list of results, switch back and forth, etc.

These cited *reasons for using tabs* are however users' view – what should the user do in a given situation. For the reverse view, i.e. situation where we have observed an activity and we are interested in what could be the user trying to do, we propose the following *scenarios of tab usage*: *Retention of a tab* (*single future use, recurrent future use*), *Opening links in background and exploring them, Changing context* (switching to different task), *Comparing content*.

The proposed scenarios relate to both current and future activities and allow inference of several features of a user model, e.g. interest in pages in tabs kept for future use. Each tab can belong to multiple scenarios for various (possibly overlapping) time periods. Detected scenarios should be tracked for each tab together with information about group of other tabs in which was the scenario performed. This is the basis for user interests represented as weighted relations to domain terms of visited pages.

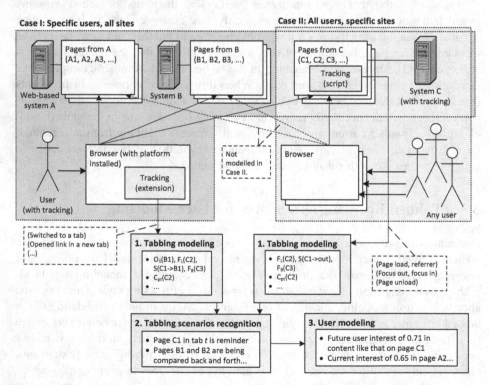

Fig. 1. Overview of our user modeling approach based on tabbed browsing

4   Current Work and Conclusions

We already proposed a model for user actions during tabbed browsing together with an algorithm for tabbed browsing reconstruction from events observed by script included in a page [6]. We evaluate our approach within an adaptive educational system ALEF [7]. We observed that the users (specifically students during a learning session) not only use tabbed browsing extensively, but relations which were not expressed explicitly in the domain model in ALEF were found, e.g. the students were commonly switching in tabs between given explanation-type learning objects. Browsing explanations concurrently with exercises was also common behavior. This suggests that even a relatively simple reasoning made directly from the tabbing model (the first phase of the proposed approach, see Fig. 1) can help also in domain modeling. Our experiments showed that tabbed browsing is valuable source for discovery of relations between objects being presented (e.g. learning objects in ALEF), which can serve for further improving of personalization.

Along with this line we explore the possibility of sourcing the user model from tabbed browsing more generally, i.e. considering browsing on the open Web. We have realized the tracking and tabbing modeling within BrUMo browser extension (brumo.fiit.stuba.sk). We currently collect dataset of user behavior.

Acknowledgements. This work was partially supported by the grants VG1/0675/11 and APVV-0233-10.

References

1. Viermetz, M., Stolz, C., Gedov, V., Skubacz, M.: Relevance and Impact of Tabbed Browsing Behavior on Web Usage Mining. In: 2006 IEEE/WIC/ACM Int. Conf. on Web Intelligence - WI 2006, pp. 262–269. IEEE (2006)
2. Dubroy, P., Balakrishnan, R.: A Study of Tabbed Browsing Among Mozilla Firefox Users. In: Proc. of the 28th Int. Conf. on Human Factors in Computing Systems - CHI 2010, pp. 673–682. ACM Press, New York (2010)
3. Huang, J., Lin, T., White, R.W.: No Search Result Left Behind: Branching Behavior with Browser Tabs. In: Proc. of the 5th ACM Int. Conf. on Web Search and Data Mining - WSDM 2012, pp. 203–212. ACM Press, New York (2012)
4. Bonnin, G., Brun, A., Boyer, A.: Towards Tabbing Aware Recommendations. In: Proceedings of the 1st Int. Conf. on Intelligent Interactive Technologies and Multimedia - IITM 2010, pp. 316–323. ACM Press, New York (2010)
5. Huang, J., White, R.W.: Parallel browsing behavior on the web. In: Proc. of the 21st Conf. on Hypertext and Hypermedia - HT 2010, pp. 13–17. ACM Press, New York (2010)
6. Labaj, M., Bieliková, M.: Modeling parallel web browsing behavior for web-based educational systems. In: Proc.of the 10th Int. Conf. on Emerging eLearning Technologies and Applications - ICETA 2012, pp. 229–234. IEEE (2012)
7. Šimko, M., Barla, M., Bieliková, M.: ALEF: A framework for adaptive web-based learning 2.0. In: Reynolds, N., Turcsányi-Szabó, M. (eds.) KCKS 2010. IFIP AICT, vol. 324, pp. 367–378. Springer, Heidelberg (2010)

Grasping the Long Tail: Personalized Search for Cultural Heritage Annotators

Chris Dijkshoorn

Department of Computer Science, VU University Amsterdam, The Netherlands
`c.r.dijkshoorn@vu.nl`

Abstract. Online collections of museums are often hard to access, because the artworks lack appropriate annotations. We develop a framework that supports niches of experts in the crowd in adding annotation of high quality. This thesis focuses on search strategies that match experts with artworks to annotate. Our approach uses explicit semantics for modeling the relations between the properties of the collection items, content-based filtering aimed at diversification, and trust-aware ranking of the results.

1 Introduction

Many cultural heritage organizations intend to provide online access to digital representations of their collection items. However, it is not enough to simply put the collection online, as it creates two problems. People are deprived from the narrative and context support provided by curators in special exhibitions. Also the well curated artifact descriptions in those exhibitions are missing online, as the majority of the collection items come straight from the content management system. Accordingly, these items are described with minimal information, typically in art-historian jargon and for the purposes of preservation [3]. As a result, despite the fact that numerous museums[1] have already provided their collections online, it is easy to get discouraged by the difficulties to explore them.

To increase the findability of collection objects, as well as to improve the experience of online visitors, cultural heritage institutions have started a number of initiatives to gather more annotations and to bridge the gap between the professionals and the general audience. However, the size of the collections, as well as the diversity of the topics covered, goes beyond any number that in-house annotators can handle in a feasible amount of time, and with the desired level of quality.

An opportunity to address this problem was presented by the increasing usage of human computation in various fields, including exact sciences [7]. Many museums embraced the crowd to gather the missing annotations and to bridge the gap between professional terms and user expressions [5,9,4]. This not only addressed the annotation problem, but also created new ways of engaging the audience online. The crowd proved to be a quick and inexpensive source for large

---

[1] `http://www.metmuseum.org/collections`
   `http://www.britishmuseum.org/collection`

S. Carberry et al. (Eds.): UMAP 2013, LNCS 7899, pp. 392–395, 2013.

quantities of user tags, but not enough mechanisms are in place to ensure the quality of tags, in terms of their specificity, presence in structured vocabularies, as well as their spread over the topics and the objects of the entire collection.

To address the aspects of tag quality, we propose an approach to identify and engage the *niche* within the *crowd*, i.e. the numerous knowledgable enthusiasts online [1]. This adds a number of challenges to the traditional crowdsourcing task:

- gather information about user's expertise
- match their expertise with the right objects from the collection
- assess their level of trust as contributors
- motivate them to become part of a community of annotators
- ensure an even spread of the user annotations across the entire collection
- deal with incomplete metadata, while the collection process is still running
- provide quality assessment while there is no gold standard available

This thesis aims at the design and development of personalization strategies to provide the online experts with the appropriate collection artifacts to annotate. Our approach uses *explicit semantics for modeling the links between collection items*, *content-based filtering aimed at diversification*, and *trust-aware ranking of search results*. More precisely, we focus our investigation on the automatic discovery and ranking of content patterns used in the diversification of recommendation results.

This research is performed in the larger context of the *Socially-Enriched Access to Linked Cultural Media* (SEALINCMedia) project, which aims at developing an online annotation system for the *the Rijksmuseum Amsterdam* (RMA) print collection (~600.000 prints). With this system we intend to leverage the niche knowledge within the crowd, and investigate novel ways for user profiling, tagging interfaces and trust assessment.

2   Research Questions

We guide our research through answering four research questions. The first research question is intended to help gather requirements, serving as input for the development of personalized semantic search strategies. For this we investigate how users interact with collections that are currently online:

   1. What are the information needs of novice and professional users for accessing online cultural heritage collections?

To enable access to all objects in a collection, we have to reach items in the long tail and recommend them for annotation. To accomplish this, we intend to leverage the notion that artworks are typically related to each other in various ways. These relations can be simple (e.g. *same artist* or *similar topic*), but they can also take the form of more complex content patterns (e.g. *created by an artist who is taught by an artist of interest*). We hypothesize that these patterns are present in existing datasets [2], and use the cultural heritage part of the linked data cloud for discovering new patterns. These available datasets are large and numerous potentially useful patterns can be extracted [6], making the manual assessment impossible. Our goal is therefore to provide a sustainable semi-automatic process for pattern discovery. We define two more research questions, one regards the discovery of patterns, the other the usefulness of patterns in grass-rooting the annotation process:

2. Can we automate the discovery of patterns within semantically-rich linked data?

3. Can we increase the number of distinct annotated objects in a collection by diversifying search results through the use of content patterns, without jeopardizing the quality of the annotations?

By using content patterns to recommend items we generate large result sets. When we present users with artworks to annotate or review, we have to prioritize between these obtained results in order to achieve maximum efficiency. For the ranking of results a context free feature is desirable, thus we hypothesize that trust values can be a suitable ranking indicator. Incorporating trust assessment in ranking is therefore subject of the final research question:

4. How can trust be incorporated in the ranking of search results?

3 Approach

For answering research question 1 we analyze the two methods of accessing the prints of the RMA: searching through the collection online or requesting the prints at the reading room. For the log analysis of the RMA website we classify the users search queries using the theory of Shetford [8]. This theory identifies abstract concepts (e.g. sky, romance), general concepts (e.g. woman, tree) or specific concepts (e.g. Rembrandt, Nachtwacht). We classify requests posed to the reading room by email in a similar way and compare them to the search queries. We hypothesize that these messages contain requests of mostly professional users, enabling a comparison between novices and professionals.

In order to answer research question 2, 3 and 4 we develop an online annotation tool: *Accurator*. Here we explore different search strategies for bootstrapping the annotation process. We aim at developing algorithms which take the characteristics of domain vocabularies in the Linked Open data cloud (AAT[2], Iconclass[3]) into account and construct new patterns based upon the findings. Agreeing on metrics to evaluate the success of these algorithms will be part of the research, in addition to finding an appropriate baseline. To evaluate the research question 3 we measure the effects of using content patterns for the retrieval of objects on the number of distinct annotated objects. For the fourth research question we will develop multiple ranking approaches which consider trust. A comparative study will be conducted, involving users who indicate which of the approaches performs best.

---

[2] http://www.getty.edu/research/tools/vocabularies/ulan
[3] http://www.iconclass.org

4   Achieved Results and Future Work

The PhD is in the beginning of its second year, with two and a half years still to go. Current work involves analyzing RMA user logs and results so far are:

– Design and development of demonstrator (Accurator alpha)
– User study setup with domain experts
– Design for a crowd-driven annotation workflow (workshop paper)
– Introducing the notion of nichesourcing (short paper)

Future work includes the publishing of the log and email correspondence analysis. For diversifying recommendation results we will analyze the linked data cloud for pattern discovery. In alignment with the requirements gained from the log and email analysis we will release version 1 of Accurator. Using this demonstrator we will collect the first usage data in order to determine trust values.

Acknowledgments. This work is supported by the Dutch national program COMMIT/ in the project SEALINCMedia.

References

1. de Boer, V., Hildebrand, M., Aroyo, L., De Leenheer, P., Dijkshoorn, C., Tesfa, B., Schreiber, G.: Nichesourcing: Harnessing the power of crowds of experts. In: ten Teije, A., Völker, J., Handschuh, S., Stuckenschmidt, H., d'Acquin, M., Nikolov, A., Aussenac-Gilles, N., Hernandez, N. (eds.) EKAW 2012. LNCS, vol. 7603, pp. 16–20. Springer, Heidelberg (2012)
2. Gangemi, A., Presutti, V.: Towards a pattern science for the Semantic Web. Semantic Web - Interoperability Usability Applicability 1(1), 61–68 (2010)
3. Gligorov, R., Hildebrand, M., van Ossenbruggen, J., Schreiber, G., Aroyo, L.: On the role of user-generated metadata in audio visual collections. In: Knowledge Capture, pp. 145–151. ACM Press, New York (2011)
4. Greg, A.: Your Paintings: Public access and public tagging. Journal of the Scottish Society for Art History 16, 48–52 (2012)
5. Oomen, J., Aroyo, L.: Crowdsourcing in the cultural heritage domain. In: Conference on Communities and Technologies, p. 138. ACM Press, New York (2011)
6. Presutti, V., Aroyo, L., Adamou, A., Gangemi, A., Schreiber, G.: Extracting core knowledge from Linked Data. In: Workshop on Consuming Linked Data (2011)
7. Quinn, A.J., Bederson, B.B.: Human computation: a survey and taxonomy of a growing field. In: Human Factors in Computing Systems, p. 1403. ACM Press, New York (2011)
8. Shetford, S.: Analyzing the subject of a picture: a theoretical approach. Cataloging and Classification Quarterly 6(3), 39–62 (1986)
9. Trant, J., Ave, L., Wyman, B.: Investigating social tagging and folksonomy in art museums with steve.museum. In: Collaborative Web Tagging Workshop, Edinburgh, Scotland, pp. 1–6 (2006)

Enforcing Privacy in Secondary
User Information Sharing and Usage

Johnson Iyilade

Computer Science Department, University of Saskatchewan,
110 Science Place S7N 5C9 Saskatoon, Canada
Johnson.Iyilade@usask.ca

Abstract. Secondary user information sharing and usage for purposes other than what it was primarily collected for has become an increasing trend, especially, as we witness a surge in the volume of data collected from and about users online. Although, allowing secondary sharing and usage of data in new and innovative ways is beneficial to the user and the society at large, it also poses the privacy risks of sharing and using personal information for unintended purposes. This paper discusses my PhD thesis towards creating a privacy framework for secondary user information sharing. The aim is to develop an infrastructure that enables sharing of user information across applications and services for beneficial purposes, while balancing it with protecting the user against the potential privacy risks. This paper discusses current work and open challenges.

Keywords: Privacy, Personalization, User Modeling, Secondary User Data Sharing, Policy.

1   Introduction and Motivation

Within the past decade, we have witnessed a surge in the amount of data collected from and about users. The data is gathered in various ways (e.g. volunteered by the user; from observation of user activities; or inferred from volunteered and observed data), and comes from various data sources (e.g. devices, sensors, applications, and services that interacts with the user). Unfortunately, most of these sources operate as "data silos" [1]. They store a lot of data about users but do not share it with other applications. Since both the user and the other applications may benefit from using the data in new and innovative ways, I believe that allowing secondary usage and sharing of user data for personalization purposes is advantageous. For the user, it will lead to better personalized services as there will be more information about him or her available, on which to make personalization decisions. The user is saved the time and effort required to duplicate the same information across applications and services [2]. For the society, secondary sharing of user data can yield significant economic and social impact in many areas such as health, agriculture, transportation, etc. [3]. In view of this, there have been various research efforts, particularly, within the user modeling community, to develop *data aggregators* and *brokers* that would facilitate

S. Carberry et al. (Eds.): UMAP 2013, LNCS 7899, pp. 396–400, 2013.

sharing and aggregation of disparate user information across applications and services [4]. While these efforts have led to a number of centralized user model architectures proposed [5] for life-long user modeling [6], and frameworks for distributed user modeling [7,8], the potential privacy risks that may result from sharing, aggregating, and analyzing user data for unknown purposes of use have been largely unaddressed. Several approaches [9] have addressed privacy in UM servers and life-long UM. However, they are based on traditional approaches and solutions to privacy, which had been successfully applied in a primary data collection context. These approaches are insufficient to address the threats to user privacy in the context of secondary user information sharing and usage for many reasons [3], including:

Changing User's Role: Many of the traditional privacy approach (particularly in websites) assume users as "data subjects" – a passive consumer of products and services, who give their data to the website in exchange for product and services. However, with the advent of social networks and web 2.0 technologies, the user's role has changed from being a passive consumer of information to active and massive producers of information about their day-to-day activities and events. The presumption is that user wants to share information.

Data Can be Used for Many Purposes after Collection: In many traditional privacy solutions and laws, organizations are required to disclose the purpose of use of data at the point of collection and the collected user data can only be used for this purpose. However, this approach fails to acknowledge the possibility of finding new and beneficial use of data for various secondary purposes that may not even be known when the data is collected.

Focus is on Protecting Usage of Data Rather than Limiting Disclosure: While various privacy-enhancing technologies, techniques and policies have been formulated (e.g. P3P, Do-Not-Track, etc.), most of them are focused on protecting the user and limiting disclosure of user information to websites. They do not address the challenges of secondary usage of data to privacy after the data is collected. In a secondary data sharing context, the concern is mainly on how the data is used later by the various consumer applications, and not on the initial collection.

In view of the limitations of existing privacy frameworks and solutions, this PhD research seeks to design a new flexible and adaptable privacy-aware framework for information sharing across various applications and services. Our aim is to develop an infrastructure that enables sharing of user information across applications for beneficial purposes, while balancing it with protecting the user against the potential privacy risks.

2   Approach

The main goal is to develop a privacy framework that allows user to be aware and control which part of their data is shared, for what purpose it is shared, with whom it is shared, and possibly get compensation. To achieve this, we are pursuing the following objectives:

1. Understanding the various factors that influence user privacy behavior particularly with respect to secondary information sharing.
2. Formulating privacy design guidelines and a framework for information sharing that are flexible and adaptable to various purposes of use of data and different user types and context.
3. To demonstrate and evaluate the applicability of the proposed framework in an appropriate test-bed.

2.1   Factors Influencing User's Behavior

In order to design a privacy framework that gives users choice and control over how their data is used and shared, it is important to understand the factors that influence user decisions with respect to information sharing and privacy protection. Previous studies have investigated the factors influencing user privacy behavior and have found factors such as *order and endowment effects* [10], presenting *justifications* [11], presence of *privacy indicator, statement or trust seal* [12], and *personality traits* [13] as influencing user behavior. However, most of these studies have investigated the factors in a primary data collection context, some other factors that can impact user's decision to allow sharing his/her data in a secondary usage context (e.g. *purpose of use, retention time, types of data, trust level of data consumer, compensation for data sharing*, etc.) have remain unexplored. We are conducting a user study that is designed to investigate which of these factors are important to user's secondary information sharing decision. The result of the study will guide towards choosing the main elements that user should be able to control in a privacy policy and it will also aid our understanding of how to adapt the privacy policy to various privacy personality types of users.

2.2   Policy Framework for User Information Sharing

We propose a privacy policy framework for user data sharing that balances the need for information flow with protection of user's privacy [14]. Our data sharing decision is based on the *purpose-relevance* principle: that is, *only data that is relevant to a defined purpose of adaptation is shared*. The framework for data sharing is based on the idea of a *data market*, where applications can offer and negotiate user data sharing with other applications according to an explicit user-editable and negotiable privacy policy that defines the purpose, type of data, retention period and price. We identified four main players in such a market: the user, the data consumers, the data providers and the data brokers. We then formulate a privacy policy specification language called *Purpose-to-use (P2U)* that allows the user, the data service providers and data service consumers to communicate and negotiate their privacy preferences and interests. I am addressing the issue of policy enforcement through a trusted framework that computes trust in applications providers and consumers of user data and allow the data-market community to police data usage itself and report potential violations to the framework management, and eventually to a government regulatory agency. If the consumer application's trust level drops below a defined threshold, the consumer will be unable to participate in the user data market.

2.3   Implementation and Evaluation

Finally, we intend to demonstrate the feasibility of the proposed policy framework through a prototype implementation in a real-life application test bed consisting of a number of mobile apps that share user data among each other and evaluate its effectiveness and usefulness in facilitating information sharing and influencing user's behavior.

3   Progress to Date and Challenges

We are currently running a user study to investigate the factors influencing user behavior with respect to secondary information sharing. We have also proposed a market framework for user information sharing and exchange [14]. We hope to get feedback on the choice of appropriate methods and platform for evaluating our privacy framework.

References

[1] Breslin, J.G., Passant, A., Decker, S.: The Social Semantic Web. Springer, Heidelberg (2009) ISBN: 3642011713, 9783642011719.

[2] Heckmann, D., Schwartz, T., Brandherm, B., Kröner, A.: Decentralized User Modeling with UserML and GUMO. In: Dolog, P., Vassileva, J. (eds.) Proceedings of the Workshop on Decentralized, Agent Based and Social Approaches to User Modeling, DASUM 2005, at UM 2005, Edinburgh, Scotland, pp. 61–66 (July 2005)

[3] World Economic Forum Report. Unlocking the Economic Value of Personal Data: Balancing Growth and Protection (October 2012),
http://www3.weforum.org/docs/WEF_IT_/UnlockingValueData_
BalancingGrowthProtection_SessionSummary.pdf

[4] Cena, F., Gena, C.: Designing and evaluating new generation user models (NewGUMs). Tutorial at UMAP (2012), Slides accessed,
http://umap2012.polymtl.ca/en/workshops-and-tutorials/
84-workshops-and-tutorials/104

[5] Kobsa, A.: Generic User Modeling Systems. User Modeling and User-Adapted Interaction 11, 49–63 (2001)

[6] Dolog, P., Kay, J., Kummerfeld, B.: Personal lifelong user model clouds. In: Proceeding of the Lifelong User Modelling Workshop at UMAP 2009 User Modeling Adaptation, and Personalization, pp. 1–8 (2009)

[7] Berkovsky, S., Kuflik, T., Ricci, F.: Mediation of User Models for Enhanced Personalization in Recommender Systems. User Modeling and User-Adapted Interaction 18(3), 245–286 (2007)

[8] Abel, F., Henze, N., Herder, E., Krause, D.: Linkage, Aggregation, Alignment and Enrichment of Public User Profiles with Mypes. In: Proc. 6th Int. Conf. Semantic Systems (I-SEMANTICS), Graz, Austria, Article No. 11 (September 2010) ISBN: 978-1-4503-0014-8

[9] Wang, Y., Kobsa, A.: Respecting users' individual privacy constraints in web personalization. In: Conati, C., McCoy, K., Paliouras, G. (eds.) UM 2007. LNCS (LNAI), vol. 4511, pp. 157–166. Springer, Heidelberg (2007)

[10] Acquisti, A., John, L., Loewenstein, G.: What is privacy worth? In: Twenty First Workshop on Information Systems and Economics (WISE) (2009)

[11] Knijnenburg, B.P., Kobsa, A.: Helping Users with Information Disclosure Decisions: Potential for Adaptation. In: Conference on Intelligent User Interfaces, IUI (2013), http://www.usabart.nl/portfolio/paper-iui2013.html

[12] Tsai, J.Y., Egelman, S., Cranor, L., Acquisti, A.: The Effect of Online Privacy Information on Purchasing Behavior: An Experimental Study. Journal of Information Systems Research 22(2), 254–291 (2011)

[13] Westin, A.: Harris Louis & Associates. Harris-Equifax Consumer Privacy Survey.Tech. rep, Conducted for Equifax Inc. 1,255 adults of the U.S. public (1991)

[14] Iyilade, J., Vassileva, J.: A Framework for Privacy-Aware User Data Trading. In: Carberry, S., Weibelzahl, S., Micarelli, A., Semeraro, G. (eds.) UMAP 2013. LNCS, vol. 7899, pp. 310–317. Springer, Heidelberg (2013)

Modeling Programming Skills of Students in an Educational Recommender System

Štefan Pero

Institute of Computer Science,
Pavol Jozef Šafárik University, Košice, Slovakia
stefan.pero@student.upjs.sk

Abstract. We present a so-called supervised educational recommendation framework in this paper aiming to recommend those programming tasks for a student which improve his skills and performance. The main issue of this approach is an appropriate student model w.r.t. his skills and other implicit factors. The student model can be derived from the solutions provided by the student and the teacher's (textual as well as numerical) evaluation of these solutions.

Keywords: educational recommendation, student model, personalization.

1 Introduction and Related Work

Education Data Mining (EDM) aims at improving student's learning and performance. EDM research area has emerged in recent years with related research issues as are described in [6], namely: *1) Analysis and visualization of data* to help educators to analyze students' behaviour and learning, *2) feedback for teachers*, to help teachers in decision making, *3) recommendations for students* the objective of what is to make pesonalized recommendations on learning materials, *4) predicting student performance*, to predict the likely performance of a student for given tasks [5], and, *5) student modeling* with the objective to develop cognitive models of a student, including skills and knowledges considering his characteristics (learning style, motivation, affective status and etc.).

The main objective of this research is to improve programming skills of students. This problem has its own specific characteristics. While the evaluation of a mathematical problem can be made on a specific scale (e.g. 1-5, or solved/failed), the analysis of a source code is more complicated. For example, we consider the task of *Multiplying two matrices*. In Math it is a direct task with a straightforward solution (except when the tasks is assigned in a tricky way checking if a student finds out the right approach). However, in case of Programming the solution is not so straightforward because it must meet some requirements such as time and memory complexity, programming conventions and style, etc. Thus, students need to posses some additional skills for solving the tasks they did not approached yet. How to identify the skills of a given student and how to utilize them in learning process and/or in educational recommendation is the subject of our research.

S. Carberry et al. (Eds.): UMAP 2013, LNCS 7899, pp. 401–404, 2013.

2   Problem Specification

We were motivated in this research by a real example from one course[1] at our university. We try to develop a student model and then to *recommend to student the tasks they will improve his skills and performance.* However, we have to consider two important issues in which this task of educational recommendation (ER) differs from the traditional case. Generally, in a traditional recommender system (RS), the user gives feedback on items according to his requirements and the RS recommends items which characteristics meet the requirements of the given user the most (see Figure 1).

The general principle of ER system (ERS) proposed by us is illustrated in Figure 2. First, it is important for recommendation to know/derive the skills of the student (user) instead of his requirements, and second, the feedback is not given by a student on tasks, but by the teacher on the student (through the evaluation of student's solution according to teacher's requirements).

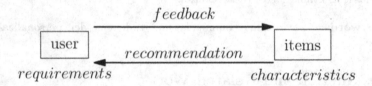

Fig. 1. General schema of a traditional RS

For solving this specific recommendation task, we need to derive student's skills by analyzing his solutions (i.e. source codes) and teacher's feedbacks (i.e. grades and/or textual comments). Instead of modeling students according to their explicit attributes (age, degree, etc.) we are developing a student model based on implicit factors such as skills, programming style, etc.

Skills. Pardos and Heffernan in [2] presented a very interesting method called "Knowledge tracing" and they used it to model students' knowledge and learning over the time assuming that all students share the same initial prior knowledge. To allow per student prior information to be incorporated, they introduced an elegant way within a Bayesian networks framework that fits for individualized as well as skill specific parameters [3]. They work is the basic motivation for our framework.

Programming Codes. As previously mentioned, programming tasks are usually different from mathematical tasks. In this part it is very important to provide an anlysis of source codes and programming styles. To say that the task is solved properly requires to verify, among others, that the complexity of code

---

[1] The "Programming, Algorithms and Complexity" lecture is provided by one lecturer and the tutorials are realized by five assistants each of them leading one group.

is sufficient, the code is in compliance with the programming language conventions, reusability of some parts of the source code, and, additional requirements of a teacher. In [1] is presented an approach for enabling programmers to find relevant functions to some query terms and their usages. The mentioned work contains many interesting ideas on how to represent a source code, however, we think that this could be extended and improved.

Teachers' Comments. Psychological aspects on the evaluation process are discussed in [7] where teacher's comments, i.e. textual evaluations, are considered as important and useful information besides the grades provided. Teacher's evaluation is a complex process depending on teacher's subjective criterias. We will use opinion and text mining as well as sentiment analysis techniques to analyze teachers' comments.

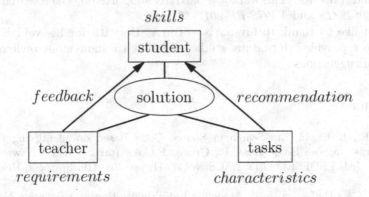

Fig. 2. General schema of our educational RS

Our ERS. We propose an educational RS enriched by the role of the teacher. The student provides a solution (source code) using his programming skills. The teacher verifies the fulfillment of his requirements on the solution and and provides a feedback on the student, i.e. a grading and/or a textual comment. The interpretation of this feedback is *how student's skills meet teacher's requirements.* Using this feedback, and analyzing the provided source code we derive student's skills and recommend those tasks to him which can more likely improve his skills. Our RS consists of three important components, the *student*, the *task* and the *teacher*, generally representing a *user*, a *item* and a *supervisor*, respectively. The general scheme of our framework we call **supervised recommendation** is introduced in Figure 2.

3   Conclusions

We have presented our framework of supervised recommendation which main part is student modeling according to skills and other implicit factors of a student. So far, we analyzed teachers' comments [4] and found out, that there is some inconsistency in teachers' evaluations and that the evaluation process depends not only on teachers' subjective requirements and criterias but also on the sample of provided solutions.

The proposed supervised RS can be utilized also in other application areas, for example recommending job applications[2], recommending conferences[3] to publish on, etc.

Our ongoing work is concerned with analyzing source codes and proposing their suitable representation for recommendation taking into account the results of [1]. In the future, we will focus on student modeling (inspired by [3]) as well as on the recommendation module. Further, we would like to try the proposed framework in different application domains such as the above mentioned job application and/or conference recommenders.

Acknowledgements. This work was partially supported by the research grants *VEGA 1/0832/12* and *VVGS-PF-2012-22*.

I would like to thank to my advisor Tomáš Horváth for his valuable help and support provided during my studies. Thanks to anonymous reviewers for interesting suggestions.

References

1. Kuric, E., Bieliková, M.: Search in Source Code Based on Identifying Popular Fragments. In: van Emde Boas, P., Groen, F.C.A., Italiano, G.F., Nawrocki, J., Sack, H. (eds.) SOFSEM 2013. LNCS, vol. 7741, pp. 408–419. Springer, Heidelberg (2013)
2. Pardos, Z.A., Heffernan, N.T.: Modeling Individualization in a Bayesian Networks Implementation of Knowledge Tracing. In: De Bra, P., Kobsa, A., Chin, D. (eds.) UMAP 2010. LNCS, vol. 6075, pp. 255–266. Springer, Heidelberg (2010)
3. Pardos, Z.A., Gowda, S.M., Baker, R.S.J.D., Heffernan, N.T.: The Sum is Greater than the Parts: Ensembling Models of Student Knowledge in Educational Software. ACM's Knowledge Discovery and Datamining (KDD) Explorations 13(2) (2012)
4. Pero, Š., Horváth, T.: Detection of Inconsistencies in Student Evaluations. Accepted to the 5th International Conference on Computer Supported Education (CSEDU 2013), Aachen, Germany (2013)
5. PSLCDataShop. Kdd cup 2010 educational data mining challenge (2010), https://pslcdatashop.web.cmu.edu/KDDCup
6. Romero, C., Ventura, S.: Educational Data Mining: A Review of the State of the Art. IEEE Transactions on Systems Man and Cybernetics Part C Applications and Reviews 40(6) (2010)
7. Suskie, L.: Assessing Student Learning: A common sense guide, 2nd edn. Malden: Jossey-Bass A Wiley Imprint, San Francisco (2009)

---

[2] Where student=job applicant, task=position, teacher=reviewer of the job application, solution=CV.

[3] With student=researcher, task=conference, teacher=reviewer(s), solution=paper sent to the conference.

Socially Adaptive Electronic Partners
for Socio-geographical Support*

Abdullah Kayal

Interactive Intelligence Group, Delft University of Technology
a.kayal@tudelft.nl

Abstract. Social software have been successful in gathering a large number of
users in the industrialized world. An opportunity exists in utilizing social software to enhance the quality of life of ourselves and those important to us. In our
research we focus on elementary school children as they begin to discover their
surrounding areas, and become more involved in interaction with their peers. We
explore the possibility of providing socio-geographical support by creating a system of electronic partners (or ePartners), which are intelligent agents that function
as teammates to their human users. Since social contexts and familial situations
can vary, it is crucial that ePartners are capable of providing personalized support.
We aim to achieve that by providing a rich specification language, allowing users
to enter their social requirements into the ePartner as norms.

1 Introduction

1.1 Aim and Motivation

With the advancement of the Internet, social environments are being built online and
constitute an important part of peoples' lives and organizational practices [11]. *Social
software* have been successful in gathering a large number of users in the industrialized
world, and while we witness the complexity and pace of our daily lives increasing,
we see an opportunity in utilizing social software into providing supportive services to
enhance the quality of life of ourselves and those important to us.

In our research we focus on elementary school children (between 6 and 12 years old)
and those of high influence and importance in their lives (parents, teachers, etc.). At this
age, children begin to discover their surrounding areas, and become more involved in
interaction with their peers. We envisage that our target group could benefit from such
social applications in various ways: For example, assisting a child in learning to explore
their surrounding areas (e.g. going to school, visiting friends), supporting the organization of events such as play dates and birthday parties, as well as increasing parents'
awareness of problematic situations (e.g. a child wandering in a risky environment).
Through this we help children form a better mental model of the socio-geographical
structure of the neighborhood in which they live, enabling them to increase their social
connectedness and awareness. We call that *socio-geographical support.*

---

* This publication was supported by the Dutch national program COMMIT.

S. Carberry et al. (Eds.): UMAP 2013, LNCS 7899, pp. 405–408, 2013.

1.2   Proposed Solution

We propose to explore the possibility of providing socio-geographical support by creating a system of so-called electronic partners (or *ePartners*), which are intelligent agents that function as teammates to their human users as they navigate through their environment. ePartners are said to follow a paradigm shift from automation extending human capabilities to automation partnering with a human, sharing tasks and developing a relationship [3], and have already been investigated in several contexts and platforms [14,1,10]. In this setting, ePartners may take the form of an application on a smart phone or a hand-held device.

For such ePartners it is crucial that they are able to provide *personalized* support to children and their parents, because different families have different values (and accompanying requirements) for the behavior of the ePartner: For example, the ePartner would need to behave differently in the case of child walking alone in the neighborhood. If a family is used to the child wandering around the area by themselves, an ePartner would only need to notify the parents in case the child has left the area considered familiar. If a family lives in a relatively unsafe area, an ePartner may promptly give a warning signal as soon as it detects that the child out of the sight of his parent(s). Moreover, ePartners should be able to *adapt* to the social context which their human users encounter (such as school, church, sports club, etc.). Examples on research done for making social applications adaptive and personalizable to better serve users' needs can be seen in[8,2].

As varying contexts result in varying requirements on how the ePartner should behave, we aim for a rich and flexible specification language, allowing users to enter the social requirements to which the ePartners should adhere (in a more advanced stage, norms can be learnt by the ePartner through user behavior as well). Therefore we propose to view ePartners to function in a *normative system*, where social requirements are expressed as norms [4,7].

1.3   Research Contribution

This research aims to discover (1) the important aspects of socio-geographical navigation for children within their various social settings in order to enhance the support they can receive from an ePartner, (2) how the norms that apply in a particular social context can be elicited from users, and (3) the requirements a normative framework will need to fulfill to adequately model these norms.

2   Approach

We aim to understand the social context in which ePartners will function, therefore we have opted to conduct user studies within the field. In the first year, we have collected data relevant to the social and family life in our target community through various methods such as focus groups [9], and cultural probes [5]. Collected data was used to create a conceptual model representing the relationship between the social context, values, and norms. The model (along with the collected data) will lead to the development of an ePartner prototype that can be used to conduct further user studies, where an evaluation of the prototype can be performed. This will take us back for another cycle of data collection and refinement (throughout the second year), in an iterative process that is a common practice in software engineering. In the third and fourth year, we will continue to iteratively expand the functionality of the ePartner, evaluating its performance through user testing and pinpointing the requirements that a normative framework will need to fulfill to permit a flexible, yet an extensive capability for inputting the various social requirements.

3 Current Status and Future Plans

3.1 Current Status

We have created a model which expresses how norms can be created to enhance the ePartner's supportive function through the qualitative analysis of data that we obtained through a series of user studies.

We have conducted three focus group sessions and one cultural probe study. The participants were six parents and six of their children (between 6 and 8 years of age) in a town of approximately 30.000 inhabitants in the south-west of the Netherlands. The first focus group session included the parents only, and resulted in a short discussion that was stimulated by our introduction of the project along with a number of pre-made usage scenarios. At the end of the session the parents were provided with cultural probing kits (each kit contains a map, an instant camera, post it notes, post cards, pens, and some glue) along with brief usage instructions. In the second (also parents only), they brought back the material they (along with their children) collected during that period, and then proceeded to describe the data (e.g., pictures, map highlights, etc.), stimulating a discussion for about 45 minutes in which many of their and their children's values were covered. The third session included the children only and was led by an experienced elementary school teacher, who asked the children a number of open ended questions related to their knowledge and usage of current technology, what activities they are allowed to do, how they connect with other children at school, sport clubs, and other places. All sessions were audio-taped.

To analyze this data we used a qualitative methodology that fits our goals in obtaining an understanding of the important themes in the social contexts in which the ePartner will function. This methodology is based on Grounded Theory, a bottom-up approach whereby theory is derived from data, as researchers do not begin the project with a preconceived theory in mind [12]. Analysis of the data resulted in a number of emergent themes (activities, concerns, limitations, etc.), which are linked together through values (activities are driven by values, concerns pose a threat to values, limitations obstruct the fulfillment of values). Values on the other hand are related to norms in the sense that norms can be created to support or demote specific values [13,6]. Therefore the result is a model which expresses what *agent-regulating* norms need to be created to enhance the ePartner's supportive function (namely to promote activities, alleviate concerns, and overcome limitations), through user values.

3.2   Future Plans

We are aiming to create an ePartner prototype with a small number of functionalities based on our model, accommodating user values we have obtained. We will test that prototype though another series of user studies, as data analysis and prototype evaluation will further clarify the requirements for a normative framework to elicit and support the values of our user group.

References

1. Arciszewski, H.F.R., de Greef, T.E., van Delft, J.H.: Adaptive automation in a naval combat management system. IEEE Transactions on Systems, Man and Cybernetics, Part A: Systems and Humans 39(6), 1188–1199 (2009)
2. Carmagnola, F., Cena, F., Console, L., Cortassa, O., Gena, C., Goy, A., Torre, I., Toso, A., Vernero, F.: Tag-based user modeling for social multi-device adaptive guides. User Modeling and User-Adapted Interaction 18(5), 497–538 (2008)
3. de Greef, T.E.: ePartners for dynamic task allocation and coordination. PhD thesis, Delft University of Technology (2012)
4. Dignum, V.: A model for organizational interaction: based on agents, founded in logic. PhD thesis, Universiteit Utrecht (2004)
5. Gaver, B., Dunne, T., Pacenti, E.: Design: Cultural probes. Interactions 6(1), 21–29 (1999)
6. Hansson, S.O.: Norms and values. Crítica 23(67), 3–13 (1991)
7. Hübner, J.F., Sichman, J.S., Boissier, O.: Developing organised multi-agent systems using the moise+ model: Programming issues at the system and agent levels. International Journal of Agent-Oriented Software Engineering (2007)
8. Loizou, S.K., Dimitrova, V.: Adaptive notifications to support knowledge sharing in close-knit virtual communities. User Modeling and User-Adapted Interaction 23, 287–343 (2013)
9. Kreuger, R.A., Casey, M.A.: Focus Groups: A Practical Guide for Applied Research, 4th edn. Pine Forge Pr. (2008)
10. Paping, C., Brinkman, W.P., van der Mast, C.: An Explorative Study into a Tele-delivered Multi-patient Virtual Reality Exposure Therapy System, pp. 203–219. IOS press, Amsterdam (2010)
11. Maloney-Krichmar, D., Abras, C., Preece, J.: History and emergence of online communities. Berkshire Publishing Group, Great Barrington (2003)
12. Strauss, A.L., Corbin, J.M.: Basics of Qualitative Research: Techniques and Procedures for developing Grounded Theory. Sage Publications Inc. (1998)
13. van de Poel, I.: Translating values into design requirements. Springer, Dordrecht (forthcoming)
14. van Diggelen, J., Neerincx, M.: Electronic partners that diagnose and guide and mediate space crew's social and cognitive and affective processes. In: Proceedings of Measuring Behaviour 2010, Wageningen, The Netherlands, pp. 73–76. Noldus InformationTechnology bv (2010)

An Adaptive Spellchecker and Predictor for People with Dyslexia

Alberto Quattrini Li

Dipartimento di Elettronica, Informazione e Bioingegneria,
Politecnico di Milano
Piazza Leonardo da Vinci 32, 20133, Milano, Italy
alberto.quattrini@polimi.it

Abstract. Spellcheckers/predictors can help people in writing more efficiently. It is a well-known fact, for example, that spellcheckers/predictors
can ease writing for people with dyslexia. However, most of the spellcheckers assume that wrong words contain just few errors (the literature claims
that 80% to 95% of spelling errors contain one error), in terms of the
four classical edit operation (i.e., addition, deletion, transposition, substitution), and that errors are isolated (i.e., each error involves just one
word). In addition, since standard spellcheckers do not use context, they
are not able to correct real-word errors. Finally, they usually are not predictors. This feature is very useful for people with dyslexia, as it allows
them to type less characters. The aim of my research is to address the
aspect of adaptation and personalization to the individual behavior for
the model and the user interface of spellchecker/predictor, considering
people with dyslexia. Specifically, we designed and trained a model that
takes into account the typical errors (even real-word errors) made by
people with dyslexia and the context for spellchecking and prediction,
and the experiments to carry out for evaluating its performance. In addition, we formalized the parameters for making the interface adaptive,
so that the user interaction with the system is light. In the next months,
we will finish the development of the adaptive user interface. Then we
will conduct experimental studies for testing the system. From a broader
perspective, we try to generalize the system to other user types.

Keywords: spellchecker, predictor, adaptive system, dyslexia.

1   Research Problem

Spellcheckers/predictors can help people in writing more efficiently. It is a well-
known fact, for example, that spellcheckers/predictors can ease writing for people with dyslexia. However, most of the spellcheckers assume that wrong words
contain just few errors (the literature claims that 80% to 95% of spelling errors contain one error), in terms of the four classical edit operation (i.e., addition, deletion, transposition, substitution), and that errors are isolated (i.e.,
each error involves just one word) [1]. These assumptions do not hold for people with dyslexia as they tend to make many errors, often not isolated (e.g.,

S. Carberry et al. (Eds.): UMAP 2013, LNCS 7899, pp. 409–413, 2013.
© Springer-Verlag Berlin Heidelberg 2013

splitting/merging words). Furthermore, the user interface of the common word processors and spellcheckers is not tailored to people with dyslexia, as they have problems in reading the list of suggestions spellcheckers usually show. Finally, the impact of dyslexia on reading and writing skills greatly varies among individuals [2], showing considerable heterogeneity in errors they make and in reading/writing difficulties.

This project, part of my PhD research and of CATS [3], an ongoing research project aimed at designing and developing technological solutions for supporting students with special needs[1], addresses the aspect of adaptation and personalization to the individual behavior for the model and the user interface of spellchecker/predictor, considering people with dyslexia. Specifically, on the one hand, the aim of my work is to design a model that takes into account the typical errors made by people with dyslexia and the context for spellchecking and prediction, and learns user's behavior. As a collateral effect, this work allows to gather data about errors made by people with dyslexia, so that it is easier to get quantitative data, besides errors types provided by experts in dyslexia. On the other hand, we will focus on the adaptive interface, which should keep the interactions with the user at a minimum, avoiding to add further complexity to the writing process. The model has been tailored to people with dyslexia, but it would be interesting to investigate whether it is adaptable to other user types.

2   Related Work

For correcting words, models are trained using corpora of texts and are usually *static*: once trained, they do not change while the user uses the system. Example of such systems are [4], which builds a large list of so-called *confusion sets* (i.e., a list of confusable words), and [5], which collects data from the web to build a big corpus. This approach cannot adapt the correction to the current user's error pattern (e.g., [6]), and does not satisfy needs of people with dyslexia. Similarly, prediction systems heavily rely on static models [7].

Only few works tried to model the user. The system proposed in [8] uses some weighted production rules, tailored to a specific user. The problem is that it cannot cope with unseen errors, as what dynamically change are the weights of the production rules; furthermore, the system does not consider the context. The system described in [9] adapts the errors on the basis of the context (n-grams trained with user's documents), but then does not adapt online. An interesting work [10] shows a prototype system to correct texts, written by deaf students, passed to the software, which models the user.

While most of the works concentrate on the model for correcting/predicting words (e.g., [8,9]), human-computer interaction received comparatively little attention. Several works researched on adaptive interfaces in different areas (e.g., recommender systems [11]), and in general focused on concepts, methods,

---

[1] Campus Tools for Students (CATS) is funded by the Italian Ministry of Education, University and Research (MIUR).

and tools to cope with designing an interface that could be suitable for everybody [12]. However, to the best of our knowledge, nothing is available regarding adaptive interfaces for spellchecking/prediction.

3   Proposed Solution

Fig. 1(a) depicts the architecture of the system we propose. Engine and Adaptation generate corrections and adjust the Error Model, respectively. The Corrector/predictor UI controls the text-to-speech (a common mean to improve reading comprehension of people with dyslexia) and the Graphic UI modules, which allow users to interact with the corrector/predictor; the module is connected to the Guest editor, by means of the Editor plug-in module (for more details, see [13]).

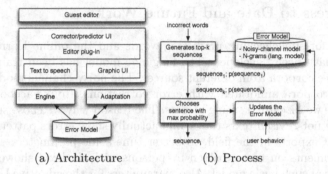

(a) Architecture   (b) Process

Fig. 1. Architecture and correction/prediction process

Fig. 1(b) shows how the process of correction/prediction evolves and how the model is updated. The generation of the different sequences is obtained by considering classic edit errors and boundaries errors (e.g., dyslexics tend to split a single word in two or more words, and merge two or more words in a single one). So, the model to correct sentences and predict words consists of a set of HMMs, whose probabilities derive from an *error model*, which contains a corpus-based language model, and a noisy-channel-inspired model. Corrections/predictions with higher probabilities are chosen. In this way, the spellchecker can correct wrong sentences (and not just word by word as it is in most of the state-of-the-art spellcheckers) and predict forthcoming words. Furthermore, the system is able to correct real-word errors on the basis of the context.

When the system is deployed, there is a common model for every users. However, this model can be adapted, by tracking the choices made over the suggestions presented by our system. With such an information, the system adapts corrections and predictions performing an online-learning procedure that updates the noisy-channel model (which accounts for the error patterns) and the language model (which regards the writing style).

About the adaptive UI, there are several parameters that can be tuned for minimizing the user/system interaction, depending on user's behavior. One of the key parameter for the spellchecker/predictor is the selection of the automatic/manual mode for correction and prediction. Specifically, when in automatic mode, basically, the system is confident on its first suggestion, and shows or immediately changes the corrected/predicted word. Obviously, the user has freedom on reverting the change or switch to manual mode, namely the system acts as common spellcheckers/predictors showing a list of suggestions, and the user chooses one of the list. The idea behind the adaptive UI is that, if the system is performing well – namely the user accepts the first suggestion made by the system – then the system should remain in automatic mode; otherwise, it should switch to the manual mode, so that the UI does not hassle the user with automatic changes and the system can learn from the user's behavior.

4   Progress to Date and Future Work

The engine for spellchecking/predicting words and the online learning part of the model have been developed. The language model has been trained on several error-free corpora from different sources. The noisy-channel model has been trained on corpora annotated with error corrections, from Facebook/Twitter posts, where we discarded "slang" terms. The reason why we chose such corpora is for having not-revised texts that could actually show errors patterns. In addition, we met experts in the field, to better tune some parameters. Preliminary static experiments on texts written by persons with dyslexia showed the good performance of such basic model. Also, parameters for the adaptive UI have been formally described, considering the user's behavior.

In addition, we designed experiments to test the system performance in closed environments: first, a test set taken by a small corpus containing wrong words (composed of texts written by dyslexics) was prepared for evaluating the precision and the accuracy of the system and comparing it with standard spellcheckers. Second, we collect data on real usage by dyslexics, divided into two groups: one, which uses standard spellcheckers, the other one, which uses our software.

Now, we are working on developing the UI for desktop environments. As soon as we finish it, we will conduct experimental studies. As broader future works, we could consider support in mobile environments and analyze whether the same type of adaptation could be used. We will also try to adapt the corrector/predictor to other types of users, e.g., to support non-native speakers of a language. Another interesting context is the correction of legal texts, because has a very limited scope, and training well our model on legal texts could lead to a good performance of the system. Furthermore, we will analyze how robust the model is with respect to the dataset used for training the error model, and if it is possible to enrich language models with other information (e.g., semantic [14]).

References

1. Kukich, K.: Techniques for automatically correcting words in text. ACM Comput Surv. 24(4), 377–439 (1992)
2. Ellis, A.W., McDougall, S.J.P., Monk, A.F.: Are dyslexics different? II. Individual differences among dyslexics, reading age controls, poor readers and precocious readers. DYSLEXIA 2(1), 59–68 (1996)
3. Sbattella, L., Tedesco, R., Quattrini Li, A., Genovese, E., Corradini, M., Guaraldi, G., Garbo, R., Mangiatordi, A., Negri, S.: The CATS project. In: Thaung, K.S. (ed.) Advanced Information Technology in Education. AISC, vol. 126, pp. 265–272. Springer, Heidelberg (2012)
4. Pedler, J., Mitton, R.: A large list of confusion sets for spellchecking assessed against a corpus of real-word errors. In: Proc. LREC (2010)
5. Ringlstetter, C., Schulz, K.U., Mihov, S.: Adaptive text correction with web-crawled domain-dependent dictionaries. ACM TSLP 4(4) (2007)
6. Pedler, J.: Computer spellcheckers and dyslexics–a performance survey. Brit. J. Educ. Technol. 32(1), 23–37 (2001)
7. Trnka, K., McCoy, K.F.: Corpus studies in word prediction. In: Proc. ASSETS., pp. 195–202 (2007)
8. Spooner, R.I.W., Edwards, A.D.N.: User modelling for error recovery: A spelling checker for dyslexic users. In: Proc. UM, pp. 147–157 (1997)
9. Korhonen, T.: Adaptive spell checker for dyslexic writers. In: Proc. ICCHP, pp. 733–741 (2008)
10. Michaud, L.N., McCoy, K.F.: Capturing the evolution of grammatical knowledge in a call system for deaf learners of english. Int. J. Artif. Int. Educ. 16(1), 65–97 (2006)
11. Brusilovsky, P.: Adaptive hypermedia. User Model. User-Adap. 11, 87–110 (2001)
12. Stephanidis, C.: User Interface for All: Concepts, Methods, and Tools. Taylor & Francis Group (2001)
13. Quattrini Li, A., Sbattella, L., Tedesco, R.: PoliSpell: an adaptive spellchecker and predictor for people with dyslexia. In: Carberry, S., Weibelzahl, S., Micarelli, A., Semeraro, G. (eds.) UMAP 2013. LNCS, vol. 7899, pp. 302–309. Springer, Heidelberg (2013)
14. Wandmacher, T., Antoine, J.Y.: Methods to integrate a language model with semantic information for a word prediction component. In: Proc. EMNLP-CoNLL, pp. 506–513 (2007)

Author Index